LIDC Contributions on Antitrust Law, Intellectual Property and Unfair Competition

More information about this series at
http://www.springer.com/series/11817

Pierre Kobel • Pranvera Këllezi •
Bruce Kilpatrick
Editors

Antitrust in the Groceries Sector & Liability Issues in Relation to Corporate Social Responsibility

Springer

Editors
Pierre Kobel
de Weck, Zoells & Kobel
Geneva
Switzerland

Pranvera Këllezi
Attorney-at-law
Geneva
Switzerland

Bruce Kilpatrick
Addleshaw Goddard LLP
London
United Kingdom

ISSN 2199-742X ISSN 2199-7438 (electronic)
LIDC Contributions on Antitrust Law, Intellectual Property and Unfair Competition
ISBN 978-3-662-45752-8 ISBN 978-3-662-45753-5 (eBook)
DOI 10.1007/978-3-662-45753-5

Library of Congress Control Number: 2015937966

Springer Heidelberg New York Dordrecht London

Printed on acid-free paper

Springer-Verlag GmbH Berlin Heidelberg is part of Springer Science+Business Media (www.springer.com)

Preface

The International League of Competition Law (LIDC) carries out a leading work every year in studying two topical questions selected among the fields of antitrust law, intellectual property or unfair competition. On each question, the key themes in the major jurisdictions are reflected in a series of national reports, whilst an international report identifies common features and trends from the national reports and draws conclusions on potential solutions or ideas to be explored in the future. The works of the LIDC have been a well of practical guidance for generations of lawyers, whether or not they are members of the LIDC, and for regulatory authorities.

LIDC has now decided to publish regularly the entire reports in the LIDC Contributions on Antitrust Law, Intellectual Property and Unfair Competition for the benefit of the legal practitioners, academics and authorities active in the field of antitrust, intellectual property and unfair competition. LIDC is therefore making full use of this opportunity to contribute in the development of these fascinating fields of law.

This publication provides a unique comparative analysis of two "hot topics" in the field of antitrust and unfair competition laws.

The first part of the book examines the grocery retail market and considers whether the antitrust rules in these jurisdictions are being applied in an efficient manner. There are 18 national reports, which analyse the most significant cases handled by the national competition authorities in the grocery retail sector and, in particular, how the antitrust rules have been applied to the relationships between suppliers and retailers in those jurisdictions, in the context of both antitrust cases and market inquiries. The book also contains a detailed international report, by Professor Frederic Jenny, which identifies general trends and highlights common themes that emerge from the national reports.

The second part of the book gathers contributions from various jurisdictions on the unfair competition question of the legal grounds on which commercial practices, i.e. manufacturing, marketing, distribution or advertisements of items produced or services rendered in violation of standards, statements or commitments voluntarily adopted by an undertaking as part of a corporate and social responsibility programme (CSR), could or should be sanctioned or prevented. These issues are explored in a series of national reports and the international report prepared by Guy Tritton, who is a barrister at Hogarth Chambers.

The editors would like to thank all the authors for their contributions and their patient collaboration during the editing of this book. They would like to express their sincere gratitude to the Members of the Bureau, of the Council and of the Scientific Committee for their kind support and encouragement during the preparation of this book.

Geneva, Switzerland — Pierre Kobel
Geneva, Switzerland — Pranvera Këllezi
London, UK — Bruce Kilpatrick

Abbreviations

AUD	Australian dollar
BGBl.	Bundesgesetzblatt (Germany)
BGH	Bundesgerichtshof (Germany)
BGN	Bulgarian lev
bn	Billion
BRL	Brazilian Real (reais)
B2B	Business to business
c./ca.	Circa
cf.	Compare
CFI	Court of First Instance of the ECJ (before 1 December 2009)
CFREU	The Charter of Fundamental Rights of the European Union, OJ 2010 C 83, p. 389
CHF	Swiss franc
CJEU	Court of Justice of the European Union (after 1 December 2009)
CR_n	Concentration Ratio measuring the percentage market share held by *n* largest undertakings
De minimis Notice	Commission Notice on agreements of minor importance which do not appreciably restrict competition under Article 81(1) of the Treaty establishing the European Community (de minimis), OJ 2001 C 368, p. 13
Directive 97/7	Directive 97/7/EC of the European Parliament and of the Council of 20 May 1997 on the protection of consumers in respect of distance contracts, OJ 1997 L 144, p. 19
Directive 2000/31	Directive 2000/31/EC of the European Parliament and of the Council of 8 June 2000 on certain legal aspects of information society services, in particular electronic commerce, in the Internal Market ('Directive on electronic commerce'), OJ 2000 L 178, p. 1

Directive 2011/7	Directive 2011/7/EU of the European Parliament and of the Council of 16 February 2011 on combating late payment in commercial transactions, OJ 2011 L 48, p. 1
DKK	Danish krone
DM	Deutsche mark
e.g. or eg	For example
EC	European Community
ECHR	Council of Europe, European Convention for Human Rights of 4 November 1950
ECJ	European Court of Justice (before 1 December 2009)
ECR	European Court Reports
EU	European Union
ff	And following
GBP	Pound sterling (UK)
GC	General Court of the CJEU (after 1 December 2009)
GDP	Gross Domestic Product
Guidelines on the effect on trade concept	Commission Notice—Guidelines on the effect on trade concept contained in Articles 81 and 82 of the Treaty, OJ 2004 C 101, p. 81
ha	Hectare
HMT	Hypothetical monopolist test
HRK	Croatian Kuna (*hrvatska kuna*)
HUF	Hungarian Forint (*Magyar forint*)
i.e.	id est (that is)
Id./Idem	The same as previously mentioned
IP	Intellectual property
kg	Kilogram
m	Million
m^2	Square metre
MFN	Most Favoured Nation
min	Minutes
NAAT-rule	The non-appreciable affectation of trade rule
Notice on the relevant market	Commission Notice on the definition of relevant market for the purposes of Community competition law, OJ 1997 C 372, p. 5
OECD	Organisation for Economic Co-operation and Development
OJ	Official Journal
p./pp.	Page(s)
para/paras	Paragraph(s)

Paris Convention	Paris Convention for the protection of industrial property of 20 March 1883
pt	Point
R&D	Research and development
Regulation 1/2003	Council Regulation No 1/2003 of 16 December 2002 on the implementation of the rules on competition laid down in Articles 81 and 82 of the Treaty, OJ 2003 L 1, p. 1
Regulation 139/2004	Council Regulation (EC) No 139/2004 of 20 January 2004 on the control of concentrations between undertakings, OJ 2004 L 24, p. 1
Regulation 330/2010	Commission Regulation (EU) 330/2010 of 20 April 2010 on the application of Article 101(3) of the Treaty on the Functioning of the European Union to categories of vertical agreements and concerted practices, OJ 2010, L 102, p. 1
RON	Romanian leu
SEK	Swedish Krona
SM	Significant market power
SMEs	Small and medium size enterprises
SSNIP	Small but Significant and Non-transitory Increase in Price
TEC	Treaty Establishing the European Community
TFEU	Treaty on the Functioning of the European Union
UAH	Ukrainian hryvnia
UK	United Kingdom
US/USA	United States of America
v	Versus

Contents

List of Contributors

Linda Arcelin Université de la Rochelle, la Rochelle, France

Susanne Augenhofer Humboldt-University, Berlin, Germany

Donald I. Baker Baker and Miller LLC, Washington, DC, USA

Bruno Bastos Becker Barbosa Müssnich & Aragão, São Paulo, Brazil

Sarah Beeston Van Doorne N.V., Amsterdam, The Netherlands

Howard Bergman Qian & Nemecek, Alexandria, VA, USA

Jan Blockx Hogan Lovells, Brussels, Belgium

Timur Bondaryev Arzinger Law Office, Kiev, Ukraine

Linda Brugioni Bird & Bird, Milan, Italy

Laurie Caucheteux Praetica, Brussels, Belgium

Julie Clarke TC Beirne School of Law, The University of Queensland, St Lucia, QLD, Australia

School of Law, Deakin University, Burwood, VIC, Australia

José Carlos da Matta Berardo Barbosa Müssnich & Aragão, São Paulo, Brazil

Gerhard Fussenegger bpv Hügel Rechtsanwälte OG, Brussels, Belgium

Marco Hartmann-Rüppel Taylor Wessing, Hamburg, Germany

Taylor Wessing, Brussels, Belgium

Lars Henriksson Center for Business Law, Stockholm School of Economics, Stockholm, Sweden

Mikko Huimala Castrén & Snellman Attorneys Ltd., Helsinki, Finland

Noriko Itai Aoki, Sekine & Tanaka, Tokyo, Japan

Barbora Jedličková TC Beirne School of Law, The University of Queensland, St Lucia, QLD, Australia

Frederic Jenny ESSEC Business School, Paris, France
University College, London, UK

Nizar Lajnef UGGC Avocats, Paris, France
SciencesPo., Paris, France

Suzan Lap Sonos, Hilversum, The Netherlands

Bernhard C. Lauterburg Prager Dreifuss Ltd., Berne, Switzerland

Sara Leone Rucellai & Raffaelli, Milano, Italy

Jessey Liauw-A-Joe Van Doorne N.V., Amsterdam, The Netherlands

Ádám Liber Bogsch, Budapest, Hungary

Katherine Mereand-Sinha District of Columbia Department of Consumer and Regulatory Affairs, Washington, DC, USA

Max W. Mosing Gassauer-Fleissner Rechtsanwälte, Vienna, Austria

Jonathan Moss Hogarth Chambers, London, UK

Anca Buta Muşat Muşat & Asociaţii Attorneys-at-Law, Bucharest, Romania

Paulo Parente Marques Mendes Di Blasi, Parente & Associados, Rio de Janeiro, Brasil

Anton Petrov Djingov, Gouginski, Kyutchukov & Velichkov, Sofia, Bulgaria

Daniel Piccinin Brick Court Chambers, London, UK

Alessandro Raffaelli Rucellai & Raffaelli, Milano, Italy

Michaëla Roegiers Praetica, Brussels, Belgium

Véronique Sélinsky Independent Practitioner, Paris, France

Suzanne Simon-Bellamy Castrén & Snellman Attorneys Ltd., Helsinki, Finland

Lana Sinichkina Arzinger Law Office, Kiev, Ukraine

Kenta Sugimoto Aoki, Sekine & Tanaka, Tokyo, Japan

Igor Svechkar Asters, Kyiv, Ukraine

Alexandr Svetlicinii Tallinn Law School, Tallinn University of Technology, Tallinn, Estonia

Shigeshi Tanaka Aoki, Sekine & Tanaka, Tokyo, Japan

Tihamer Toth Reczicza White & Case, Pazmany Peter Catholic University, Budapest, Hungary

Guy Tritton Hogarth Chambers, London, UK

Aleksandra Węrychowska-Karpińska Wierciński Kwieciński Baehr, Poznan, Poland

Agnieszka Wiercińska-Krużewska Wierciński Kwieciński Baehr, Warsaw, Poland

Part I

Antitrust in the Groceries Sector

International Report

1

Frederic Jenny

1.1 Introduction

This contribution synthesizes the eighteen national reports answering the questionnaire on the grocery retail sector.[1]

At the outset a caveat is necessary. A large proportion of respondents to this survey come from countries that are Member States of the European Union and share the same (European) legal system. At the same time, and even though non-European countries such as the United States, Japan or Australia responded to the questionnaire, some major countries with a long experience in competition law and competition policy are outside the scope of this report.[2] It should thus be clear that, to a certain extent, the observations and conclusions in this report are influenced by the particular set of countries that have responded to the LIDC questionnaire. We are, however, confident that the examination of the 18 countries that have contributed allows us to come to some robust conclusions.

Before starting our analysis with an examination of the structure of the grocery retail sector, five general observations are in order.

First, laws that apply to the grocery retail sector are to a large extent the same laws that apply to the retail sector in general. Those laws are partly laws that apply to all economic sectors (such as competition law), partly laws that are specific to the

[1] The eighteen reports surveyed are the reports from: Australia, Austria, Belgium, Brazil, Bulgaria, Czech Republic, Estonia, Finland, France, Germany, Hungary, Japan, Italy, Netherlands, Romania, Sweden, Switzerland, Ukraine, United Kingdom, United States of America.

[2] The reports are provided by national groups of the LIDC only.

F. Jenny (✉)
ESSEC Business School, Paris, France

University College, London, UK
e-mail: frederic.jenny@gmail.com

P. Kobel et al. (eds.), *Antitrust in the Groceries Sector & Liability Issues in Relation to Corporate Social Responsibility*, LIDC Contributions on Antitrust Law, Intellectual Property and Unfair Competition, DOI 10.1007/978-3-662-45753-5_1

retail sector (such as the laws establishing the conditions under which a large-scale retail store can be opened) and, more rarely, certain laws or regulations that are specific to the grocery retail sector (such as some consumer protection laws applying to the sale of fresh products). Whenever possible, we have tried to identify where laws are specific to the grocery retail sector or where general principles or laws applicable to the whole retail sector have been applied specifically in the grocery retail sector.

Second, while most countries that provided a report are countries that have a civil or continental system of law, this is not the case for Australia and the United Kingdom. As we shall see, the style of competition law enforcement for the grocery retail sector in those countries is markedly different from what it is in other countries (in particular, they rely more on self-regulation than the other countries in the sample).

Third, a study of competition issues in the grocery retail sector requires consideration of the relationship between retailers and their suppliers, whether they are manufacturers of prepared food or intermediaries trading in agricultural products. As we shall see, the relationship between the intermediaries and the suppliers is also of interest to understand their downward relationship with grocery retailers. Thus, most of the contributions extensively analyze the vertical chain that starts with farmers and ends with the retailers, and we will report on the sometimes complex relationships between the upstream level and the downstream level along the vertical chain to shape competition on the final market for grocery goods.

Fourth, the term "grocery" may be imprecise since, particularly in the modern retail sector, grocery stores have diversified their offerings and sell a wide variety of fresh or transformed products, some of which are food products and others are nonfood products. Most of the contributions focus on the offering of products derived from agriculture, whether transformed or not, in retail groceries. Indeed, it seems that it is in this part of the market that the competition problems are the most complex. This report also focuses on the foodstuff part of the grocery retail sector.

Fifth, the countries that are being investigated have different histories, different levels of economic developments, different cultures and different legal systems. A number of the observations that one can make when comparing the situation of competition and competition law enforcement in the grocery retail markets of these countries are grounded in those differences.

1.1.1 Economic Background

In our sample of countries, the concentration of the grocery retail sector varies widely from one country to the next. One can distinguish three groups of countries.

First are countries where the retail grocery sector is very highly concentrated: this group includes Australia ($CR_2 = 80\ \%$), the Netherlands ($CR_2 = 55\ \%$), Austria ($CR_3 = 87\ \%$), Finland ($CR_2 = 80\ \%$) and Belgium ($CR_3 = 75\ \%$). The Australian report suggests that large retailers have buying power over food processors but that their buying power over farmers is less certain because farmers have an alternative in export markets. Thus, it appears that the idea according to which more concentration usually means less intense competition may not always hold in the grocery retail sector.

A second group of countries exhibit medium to low concentration in the grocery retail sector. In this group, one finds Germany ($CR_4 = 85$ %), Sweden ($CR_4 = 80$ %), Estonia ($CR_3 = 60$ %), France ($CR_6 = 80$ %), the United Kingdom ($CR_8 = 85$ % and $CR_4 = 66$ %) and Italy, where the modern distribution model accounted for about 70–72 % of food product sales in recent years. In other words, the "natural" shift in food product sales from small traditional shops and other market entities to large-scale retail outlets seems to have stopped at the levels noted above. The Swedish report suggests that because food processors in Sweden are fairly concentrated, the buying power of retailers and the selling power of food processors are fairly balanced. Finally, the report concerning the United Kingdom suggests that farmers' unions are able to exert industrial and political pressure on processors and retailers (thus limiting their buying power).

In a third group of countries, concentration of the retail sector appears to be low or very low. This group includes the United States, where the top 20 retailers account for 63.7 % of the market and the top four retailers hold 37 % of the market. This group of countries with low concentration in the grocery retail sector also includes Hungary ($CR_3 = 40$ %), Bulgaria, Romania and Ukraine. In these countries, particularly in the latter three, the development of modern retail is relatively recent since this form of retail appeared only after the countries moved to a market economy in the 1990s and a strong attachment to traditional forms of small-scale retail still seems to exist in at least some of these countries. For example, in Romania, 60 % of Romanians prefer to buy their groceries from a traditional trade unit (corner or neighborhood shop) and in Bulgaria, in 2010, about 60–70 % of all grocery sales were channeled through traditional retail establishments.

It is more difficult to categorize intermediaries and food processors. Not only does the situation vary from one country to another, but also the situation varies from one grocery product to another within the same country. Furthermore, not all reports provide details about the intermediaries or the processors of food products.

If one moves now from processing to agricultural production, the situation can again be divided into three types of situations. In countries such as Bulgaria, Austria, Italy, Romania and Finland, the agricultural sector is extremely fragmented. It is interesting to note that two of these five countries—Austria and Finland—are countries where the level of grocery retail concentration is high. As we saw previously, there is some concentration at the food processing level in Finland and Italy, but this does not seem to be the case in Austria, where grocery retail chains are likely to have unchallenged buying power.

In countries such as the United Kingdom, the Netherlands or Sweden, even though agricultural production is atomistic, farmers sell through associations or cooperatives and thus have some market power. The United Kingdom report describes a situation where farmers are able to exert considerable political and business pressure on the downstream food processors, wholesalers and the retail sector.

Finally, the situation in Germany seems to be in a state of flux with a steady decline of the total number of agricultural production entities and a growing number of large entities in primary production.

The economic assessment of the structure of grocery retail, food processors and agricultural production suggests that different competition problems will be prevalent in different countries. In some countries, buyer power will be confronted with seller power and there will be a balanced confrontation between the two, sometimes in spite of a high level of grocery retail concentration (for example, in Sweden, the United Kingdom and Australia). In other countries (for example, Germany), buyer power will prevail and public policy will be focused on ensuring that this power is not used unfairly or anticompetitively. In a third type of country (such as Bulgaria, Romania and Ukraine), both retailers and suppliers will have an atomistic structure, at least at the general level, and the main issue will be the abuse of dominance of those few retailers having a large market share at the local level.

But in order to better understand the competition law issues in the grocery retail sector, one must have a close look at the legal and regulatory environments of retail grocery.

1.1.2 Legal Background

In many countries, a large number of laws and regulations apply to the retail sector. The goals of those laws are to promote competition or to ensure fairness in exchanges or to regulate certain aspects of the retail trade for sociopolitical reasons. Whereas those goals might seem at first sight to be complementary, they are often contradictory. The situation in the United States, however, is in sharp contrast with that of the other respondents. The United States has both less competition-specific regulation and less overall regulation when compared with many European countries.

1.1.2.1 Competition Law

In most countries, there is no specific competition regulation that applies to the grocery retail sector, which is subject to the general provisions of competition law. For example, in the United States, the grocery sector is covered by the Sherman Antitrust Act, the Federal Trade Commission Act and the Clayton Antitrust Act. The industry is also subject to the Robinson–Patman Act, which was an amendment to the Clayton Act, though federal enforcement under the act is largely dormant and private enforcement is dwindling. There are no sector-specific competition laws or exemptions for the grocery retail market in the United States.

In some countries,[3] national competition law includes not only a prohibition of anticompetitive practices or transactions, which might lead to the elimination,

[3] For example, Austria, Bulgaria, Estonia, Hungary and Ukraine.

prevention, limitation or restriction of competition, but also a ban on unfair competition.

In most other countries, national competition law and the law against unfair trade practices are separate laws that both apply to the grocery retail sector. This is, for example, the case in most Member States of the European Union where national competition laws are usually modeled on EU competition law and apply concurrently with it.

Typically, national competition laws will prohibit horizontal and vertical agreements and concerted practices that have as their object or effect the restriction of competition (such as cartels or exclusive dealing), the abuse of a dominant position or the misuse of market power (such as exclusionary practices whereby a firm with market power or a dominant situation eliminates competition) and anticompetitive mergers.

Several forms of conduct particularly relevant to the grocery sector such as cartels (price fixing, market and customer allocation), primary boycotts, third line forcing or minimum resale price maintenance are in certain countries subject to *per se* prohibitions.

In a few cases, the national competition law includes provisions that are specific to the retail sector. This is, for example, the case in Germany. The German Act against Restraints of Competition[4] explicitly prohibits undertakings with superior market power to abuse their market position by selling goods or services below cost price without an objective justification. However, the prohibition to sell below cost price is widely seen as of very limited scope.

Occasionally, competition laws have been amended to better deal with concerns raised primarily in the grocery sector. Thus, for example, in 2007 Australia introduced into its competition law a specific prohibition against predatory pricing, which applies when a company with substantial market share supplies, or offers to supply, goods or services for a sustained period at a below-cost price for a prohibited purpose. The adoption of this provision was driven largely by concerns about low-cost pricing in the grocery market destroying small business.

In some countries, even though there are no provisions specific to the retail sector in the competition law, the government is considering the introduction of such a provision. For example, in Finland, a recently adopted section of the Competition Act stipulates that an undertaking, whose market share is 30 % or more of the daily consumer goods retail market, is considered to hold a dominant market position. When calculating the market share of the grocery retailer, the total retail operations of all the undertakings belonging to a certain retailer group would be taken into account.

1.1.2.2 Exemptions from Competition Law Prohibitions

Different types of exemptions from competition laws can be found for the retail sector or some parts of the grocery business. First, in a number of countries

[4] Section 20 (4) of the German Act against Restraints of Competition.

(in particular, European countries and Australia), there is an exemption for anticompetitive practices—for example, anticompetitive agreements—that contribute to economic progress or have public benefits. Such exemptions are sparingly given, however. Second, in other countries where there are no formal exemption, groupings of small suppliers will get an exemption from competition law for otherwise prohibited practice on public interest grounds. Third, some countries (again, certain European countries) have a *de minimis* exemption either resulting from EU competition law or unrelated, in which case they only apply to domestic practices that have no effect on interstate trade. Fourth, a number of countries exempt, in part or in whole, agricultural producers' groupings from competition law (for example, cooperatives in Japan). Fifth, a smaller number of countries have (or had) block exemptions for voluntary chains of small retailers.

Exemptions from Competition Law for Agricultural Groupings

In several countries, specific anticompetitive practices may be exempted on the basis of their contribution to economic progress or on public interest grounds.[5]

Aside from the individual exemptions previously mentioned, farmers' groupings or associations are also frequently exempted from competition law either because the *de minimis* rules apply to them or because they benefit from a specific group exemption if they meet certain criteria.[6]

In France, there is no formal exemption from competition law for the agricultural sector. However, the French Competition Authority (hereafter "FCA") considers that groupings of producers of agricultural products can be exempted from competition rules because of their contribution to economic progress for the commercialization of products, provided that their practices remain proportionate to the objective. Furthermore, the French Rural Code[7] exempts from competition law agreements concluded within officially recognized interprofessional organizations aimed at (1) adapting supply to demand through a forecast of demand and a coordination or planning of production, (2) planning and restricting production to improve the quality of products, (3) limiting production capacity, (4) temporary restriction of the entry of new firms based on objective criteria and implemented in a nondiscriminatory manner or (5) fixing sales price by producers or the price at which they will buy back their production. No party to such an agreement should have a dominant position on the relevant product market, and those agreements have to be notified, after their conclusion and before they are enforced, to the Minister of Agriculture, to the Minister in charge of the Economy and to the FCA. In the dairy sector, the French Rural Code[8] allows interprofessional organizations to develop and issue information on product prices, without these practices being subject to the prohibition of anticompetitive practices.

[5] E.g., United States, Australia, or France.

[6] See, e.g., the reports of Austria, the Netherlands, Hungary, Finland, Romania and Germany.

[7] See Article L 632-2 II of the French Rural Code.

[8] See Article L 632-14 of the French Rural Code.

Exemptions from Competition Law for Groupings of Small Retailers
Just as farmers' groupings are exempted from competition law to allow them to withstand the pressure of large-scale retailers, small retailers in voluntary chains are also exempted from competition law in some countries to allow them to better compete with large-scale retailers.[9]

1.1.2.3 Laws Against Unfair Trade Practices

Unfairness Vis-à-Vis Other Firms
In most countries, the laws prohibiting unfair trade practices also apply to the retail sector and the grocery retail subsector. The content of laws against unfair trade practices varies from one country to the next but may prohibit a large number of practices. Some trade practices of large-scale retailers may be prohibited because they are considered to be unfair to suppliers (for example, suppliers of agricultural products); others may be prohibited because they are seen as unfair to competitors (for example, small grocery stores); finally, some practices are prohibited because they are considered to be unfair to final consumers.

When applied to the grocery retail sector, laws against unfair trade practices are often used to curb the negotiating power of large-scale retailers.

Some of those prohibitions tend to prevent retailers from abusing their buyer power by requesting or gaining "unjust economic benefits," "unjust price reduction," "unjust consignment sales contract" or "unjust assignment of work to employees of suppliers,"[10] "contributions from the suppliers related to the retailer's price reductions,"[11] "payment of fees or tariffs related to the expansion of the retailer's network, the development of its sale space or the operations and events for promoting the retailer's activity and brand image" or "payment for services that are not directly linked to the sale operation",[12] "retroactive benefit of rebates, discounts or commercial cooperation agreements".[13] In France, the submission of a partner to obviously abusive payment conditions[14] or to obligations creating a significant imbalance is also prohibited.[15] The retailers are prohibited from requesting payment for a supplier to be referenced before any order is made.[16]

The general prohibition against unjustified or abusive requests by retailers can lead to the prohibition of particular forms of business behavior of the retailers. The prohibited practices vary from country to country, reflecting the specificities of the tensions between retailers and their suppliers in each country.

---

[9] See, e.g., Sweden, the Netherlands and Ukraine.

[10] See Japan.

[11] See Hungary.

[12] See Romania.

[13] See Article L 442-6, II, a) of the French Commercial Code.

[14] Article L 442-6, I, 7° of the French Commercial Code.

[15] Article L 442-6, I, 2° of the French Commercial Code.

[16] See, e.g., France.

Some countries restrict the ability of retailers to delay payment of their suppliers in general or for specific products.[17]

In spite of the wide scope of laws against unfair trade practices, in a number of countries there is a debate as to whether general laws prohibiting unfair trade practices are sufficient to prevent the negotiating abuses of large retail chains vis-à-vis their suppliers. Although competition authorities have in several countries concluded that a specific legislation or regulation to curb the buying power excesses of large retail chains was unnecessary, a number of governments under pressure due to a large number of complaints by farmers or food processors have nevertheless adopted such laws or regulations.[18]

It is interesting to note that if slotting fees are considered to be unfair in some countries (such as in Italy), they are not necessarily always considered to be anticompetitive. In 2001 and 2003, the US Federal Trade Commission (the "FTC") published a staff report on slotting fees, also known as "pay-to-stay" fees paid by manufacturers. The reports resulted in theories for how such arrangements, where manufacturers pay retailers for premium shelf space, would be anticompetitive. However, the 2003 report was not able to find data and economic models that conclusively determined antitrust harm or injury resulting from slotting fees.

Unfairness Vis-à-Vis Consumers

In Australia, unfair terms in consumer contracts are also prohibited, and these prohibitions apply to the grocery sector. In Estonia, the Consumer Protection Act imposes certain information and transparency requirements on retailers and prohibits a range of unfair commercial practices. In the United Kingdom, the Consumer Protection from Unfair Trading Regulations 2008 sets out a broad prohibition on unfair commercial practices, which include both misleading actions and misleading omissions.

Enforcement of Unfair Trading Laws

While unfair trading laws are usually enforced through the courts rather than by competition authorities, there are some exceptions to this principle. For example, in Romania, the law on unfair competition[19] provides a general prohibition of unfair competition and applies to the grocery sector. This law was traditionally enforced by domestic courts, but the Romanian Competition Council took over the enforcement of this law and initiated a legislative process for the review of the law and the enactment of secondary legislation.

---

[17] See Hungary, Romania and France.

[18] See Bulgaria and Italy.

[19] Law no. 11/1991 on the fight against unfair competition.

1.1.2.4 Other Laws and Regulations Applying to the Retail and Grocery Sector

Besides competition law and laws against unfair trading practices, a number of other laws and regulations on retail distribution (such as zoning laws, laws on the opening hours of stores or price regulations, unit pricing laws) apply to the grocery retail sector or are sometimes specific to the grocery retail sector. A number of those laws and regulation have the object of protecting small retailers and the effect of restricting the strategic freedom of large-scale retailers, whether by making it difficult for them to open or enlarge their stores or by limiting the number of hours during which they can stay open.[20] In rare cases, some of those laws are designed to protect or promote competition in the grocery retail sector.

As a contrast to the situation in previously mentioned countries, in the United States, nonrestrictive local zoning and relatively little land use restrictions have allowed niche providers like green grocers, gourmet food stores and organic markets to enter urban and high-income areas in proliferation. At the same time, Wal-Mart has grown quickly in rural areas to openly compete with local and regional chains that previously faced little competition. Equally, while Sunday shopping laws that have a secular purpose are constitutional in the US, between 1966 and today many states and municipalities have repealed those laws or had them overturned for a variety of issues related to the Establishment Clause of the first Amendment to the US Constitution,[21] which prohibits any government interference with or support for any religion or creed, job creation, consumer preference, retail sales lobbying. Further, in 1964, the Supreme Court sustained, against an antitrust claim, a collective bargaining agreement that prevented a supermarket chain from selling meat on Sundays. Such clauses no longer exist in grocery market where unionized stores face vigorous competition from nonunionized ones.

1.1.2.5 Pricing Regulations

Pricing regulations in the grocery sector have a wide range of objectives. Some aim at eliminating predatory pricing[22] by large retailers[23]; others aim at allowing suppliers to impose a maximum resale price for grocery products or at controlling the resale price of goods sold through retailers.[24] Occasionally, such provisions

[20] See, e.g., in Japan, the Act on the Measures by Large-Scale Retail Stores for Preservation of Living Environment (Act No. 91 of June 3, 1998); in Belgium, the Act on the Authorization of trade Establishment of 2004; in Hungary, the Act No. LXXVIII of 1997 on the Formation and Protection of Built Environment; in Finland, the Land Use and Building Act 132/1999; in the Netherlands, the Opening Hours Act (Winkeltijdenwet) or the Commercial Code in France.

[21] See the U.S. Bill of Rights.

[22] Or reselling at a loss.

[23] See, e.g., Government Ordinance no. 99/2000 in Romania, the French Commercial Code or the Presidential Decree no. 218/2001 in Italy.

[24] See the Price Regulation Act (SFS 1989:978) in Sweden or Article 3 of the Law on State Support of the Agriculture in Ukraine.

impose a minimum resale price for products considered to be dangerous to the health of consumers.[25]

The United States has largely moved away from price controls and other efforts to ensure farm gate prices and has developed less anticompetitive means of supporting a critical sector of the economy—such as producer subsidies—rather than involving itself in the question of pricing or relative bargaining power throughout the supply chain. However, notable exceptions do exist. Domestic producers of some agricultural products—such as sugar—have been able by political means to obtain price controls or other barriers to lower-cost production from abroad, and the federal Robinson–Patman Act, dealing with price discrimination, was vigorously enforced by the Federal Trade Commission until the 1960s then was increasingly criticized by the DOJ, economists and others in the 1970s. Since the 1980s, the Robinson–Patman Act, while still on the books, has ceased to be enforced and therefore ceases to be a significant restraint on efficient markets in grocery products.

1.1.2.6 Laws Designed to Empower Consumers to Make Competition Work Better Among Retailers

Australia has adopted unit pricing laws specifically targeting supermarkets to promote competition in the grocery sector by ensuring that consumers are able to make informed choices. The unit pricing laws take the form of a mandatory industry code that applies to grocery retailers. This Code applies to grocery retailers with more than 1,000 m^2 of floor space and that sell a minimum range of food-based groceries. The Code also applies to online grocers. Once a retailer falls under the Code, all grocery items must have a unit price displayed unless the item is exempt (*e.g.*, bundled items). The unit price must be prominent, close to the selling price, legible and unambiguous and must be displayed in dollars and cents.

1.1.2.7 Laws Deregulating the Retail Sector

In all of the contributions except one, there is very little said about attempts to deregulate, partially or totally, the retail sector in general and the grocery sector in particular. Quite the contrary, as we just saw, there has been and there is still a tendency on the part of governments to constantly increase the regulatory burden in the grocery sector in an attempt to better monitor the tense relationships between large-scale retailers and other operators. One exception worth mentioning is Italy, where there has been a real effort at deregulation of the retail sector since the beginning of the 2000s.

The "Bersani Decree"[26] reformed the commercial sector and was a significant step towards the deregulation of the market and the simplification of bureaucratic and administrative procedures. The law establishes general principles and puts Regions in charge of planning commercial development and establishing urban

[25] See, e.g., the Alcohol Minimum Pricing Act 2012 of Scotland.

[26] Legislative Decree no. 114 of 31 March 1998.

planning measures. This Decree makes a distinction between "food" and "non-food" distribution, and this simple distinction replaces 14 goods categories previously used. It also distinguishes retail outlets in the following categories: neighborhood outlets, medium-sized sales structures, large sales structures and shopping centers. The law[27] implementing the EU directive on internal market services[28] provides that the access to and exercise of services may not be subject to unjustified or discriminatory limitations. A subsequent regulation[29] guarantees the principles of free enterprise and competition. Under this Decree, the provisions governing access to and exercise of economic activity must not contain restrictions unless in the public interest and must not discriminate, directly or indirectly, on the basis of the nationality and registered office of the enterprise.

Another piece of legislation[30] gave businesses the option of not complying with set opening and closing times, the obligation to close on Sundays and holidays and to close for a half-day during the week, on an experimental basis, and only for those businesses located in municipalities that are on regional tourist location lists or art cities. Subsequently, the "Save Italy Decree"[31] introduced further deregulations regarding both the management and opening of new sales outlets with the aim of relaunching the Italian economy. It extended the deregulation provisions to the opening days and times referred to under Law Decree no. 98/2011 to all commercial businesses and not just those located in tourist locations or cities of art. Starting from 1 January 2012, commercial enterprises[32] and businesses that provide food and drink in Italy can carry out their activities without any restrictions on opening times and without the obligation to close on Sundays or holidays.

1.1.3 Market Studies

As is clear from the developments above, the relationship between large-scale retailers, small-scale retailers and small-scale suppliers is a highly sensitive issue, and in most countries there is an elaborate, and sometimes quite complex, array of regulations to monitor the relationships between the various players.

The issues raised by the functioning of the grocery retail market are even more sensitive politically since, above and beyond the issues previously mentioned, the objective pursued by many governments is to keep the price of food as low as

[27] Legislative Decree no. 59 of 26 March 2010.

[28] Directive 2006/123 of the European Parliament and of the Council of 12 December 2006 on services in the internal market, OJ 2006, L 376, p. 36.

[29] Law Decree no. 138 of 13 August 2011, converted into Law no. 148 of 14 September 2011.

[30] Law Decree no. 98 of 6 July 2011, converted with amendments by Law no. 111 of 15 July 2011.

[31] Law Decree no. 20 of 16 December 2011 was enacted, converted with amendments by Law no. 214 of 22 December 2011.

[32] Pursuant to Legislative Decree 114/1998.

possible for consumers and the price of agricultural products sufficiently high for farmers to enable them to make a living.

The press is quick to suspect that lack of competition among intermediaries—such as wholesalers—or retailers is the source of the perceived high prices of food and that abuses of buying power is the source of the low level of prices paid to farmers for agricultural products.

With the exception of Estonia, where the competition authority has not done any market study on the grocery sector, the competition authorities of all the other countries that participated in the survey have undertaken one or several sector inquiries in the recent years. The scope and focus of those inquiries vary.

Some of these studies are general studies of the grocery retail sector either at the national level or in a given geographical area: the United States, Sweden (2002, 2004 and 2005), Nordic countries (2009 and 2011), Australia (1999), Austria (2007), the United Kingdom (2008), Romania (2009), food retail sector in France (2012) and Italy (2007, and a study started in 2010 and ended in 2013).

A second set of inquiries or market studies is focused on retail and/or supermarket prices and whether those prices are competitive: Australia (2008), Belgium (2012), Netherlands (2009) and Finland (2010).

A third set of market studies focused on the exploration of buyer power by retail chains and its implications for the upstream suppliers in general and the farmers: Netherlands (2004), Finland (2012), Japan (2011 and 2012) and Hungary (2007 and 2009).

A fourth set of market studies analyzed specific product markets of basic staples such as fish (Netherlands 2011), wheat, bread, dairy products, cooking oil (Bulgaria), milk (Germany 2012), eggs (Ukraine 2012), sugar, sunflower (Ukraine 2011) or dry pasta (Italy 2011).

Finally, a last set of market study analyzed specific issues related to the distribution of foodstuff such as the affiliation contracts of independent stores to retail chains and the conditions of purchasing commercial real estate in the food retail sector (France 2010) or category management agreements in the retail sector (France 2010).

As this list suggests, the grocery retail sector is probably one of the most frequently studied sectors.

1.1.3.1 Reasons for Conducting Market Studies

The reasons for undertaking those market studies are varied.

High Prices

A first set of market studies was undertaken to investigate high prices. In a substantial number of countries,[33] the concern that food prices are high or higher than in neighboring countries or rising rapidly has been one of the important reasons for which national competition authorities have undertaken a market

[33] Sweden, Belgium, Bulgaria, United Kingdom, Finland and Ukraine.

investigation of the grocery market. One can suspect that in some cases, public authorities or the media put pressure on the Competition Authority to do something about the high price of foodstuffs for consumers. If they lacked evidence of clear-cut anticompetitive practices to be investigated or sanctioned, the Competition Authority could respond to this pressure by launching a general investigation of price formation in the sector. The publication of reports following these market investigations could help the Competition Authority explain why it did not have any reason to use its sanctioning powers and simultaneously suggest to public authorities measures that could alleviate the perceived pricing problem.

For example, grocery market investigations were launched because of concerns that food prices were higher in Sweden in comparison to the EU average, because of concern in Belgium that grocery prices were higher and increasing more rapidly than in neighboring countries, because of concerns that there were sharp increases in retail prices of the most important staple foods (such as bread, milk, and cooking oil) in Bulgaria, because there were concern in the United Kingdom in the 1990s that prices and profits were high in the grocery sector as well as concerns that prices were higher there than in continental Europe, because of concerns about the difference in food product price trends in Finland and in other European countries, because there were concerns in some regions of France about the increase in price levels, because there were concerns about the price differential between different types of stores in Ukraine.

In Italy, a survey on agro-food distribution was carried out partly because of the widespread perception that fruit and vegetable prices increased with the changeover from the Italian lira to euro on January 2002. Another study on the "Price transmission mechanisms along the agro-food chain: an analysis of dry pasta supply chain" was carried out as part of a project by the Authority to monitor food product prices, with specific reference to the ways in which raw material fluctuations were transferred downstream by the operators at the various stages of the production and distribution chain.

High Concentration Levels

In some countries, the concerns that led to the launching of a market investigation were the high concentration level in the grocery retail sector (*e.g.*, Sweden) or the concentrated nature of the sector and the relatively homogenous nature of the products that created the risk of collusion (*e.g.*, Netherlands) or the fact that the emergence of large-scale retail chains led to a higher concentration of the food retail sector (*e.g.*, Hungary) or the perceived high level of market concentration at the retail level (*e.g.*, Austria or France).

Allegation of Abuse of Buyer Power

In a third set of cases, market investigations were launched because of allegations of abuse of buyer power by supermarkets (*e.g.*, Netherlands), because of concerns about the clauses of supplier contracts—applied by the retailers (*e.g.*, Hungary), because of complaints about buyer power and substantial pressure put on suppliers by large retailers (*e.g.*, Austria and Finland), because of persistent tensions between the retailers and suppliers (*e.g.*, Romania) or because of allegations of unfair trade practices by large-scale retailers to the detriment of suppliers (*e.g.*, Japan).

Low Purchase Prices, Anticompetitive Practices or Importance of the Sector for Consumers

In a fourth set of cases, market investigations were launched because of complaints about the low price paid by retail chains to producers of sour cherries, melons, apples or milk (*e.g.*, Hungary and Germany).

In a fifth set of cases, market investigations were launched because there was a suspicion of possible anticompetitive practices (*e.g.*, Germany and France).

In a last set of cases, market investigations in the food retail sector seem to have been launched because of the importance of the sector for consumers (*e.g.*, Netherlands and Ukraine).

1.1.3.2 Outcome of Market Studies

Turning now to the results of these market investigations of the grocery retail sector, three main observations can be made.

First, in most countries, competition authorities did not find that there was a major competition problem in the grocery retail sector even when concentration was high or increasing. Thus, most competition authorities responded to the concern about the high or rising prices of grocery retail products by saying that other factors besides the lack of competition were responsible for the high level of prices.

In contrast to previously mentioned studies, the French Competition Authority found that a lack of competition was an important cause of high prices in French overseas "departments" and made different proposals in order to revitalize competition on such local markets. First, it initiated investigations in order to sanction some of the anticompetitive practices that had been identified in the course of the market investigation (such as imposed sale prices, horizontal anticompetitive practices, or clientele exclusivity agreements and restrictions on parallel trade). Second, it proposed legislative modifications designed to eliminate unnecessary regulatory entry barriers and to improve consumer information. Third, it suggested that in each overseas territory, local and regional authorities and state authorities should set up study missions with the objective of defining the conditions under which procurement and storage centers could be created and operated. But the French Competition Authority took a strong stand against the temptation to reinstate price controls in the overseas territories in response to discontent about the high level of prices.

One should also mention that the Ukrainian market investigation resulted in a finding that prices were unjustifiably high for some grocery products (such as sugar or sunflower), and the competition authority took action on prices and to improve the retail market of some products and initiated proceedings against economic operators.

Second, for the most part, competition authorities recognized that there was an imbalance in the negotiating powers of retailers and their suppliers, particularly when suppliers were agricultural producers. But, in most cases, the competition authorities did not recommend the imposition of behavioral constraints on the negotiating practices of retailers. The dominant feeling expressed by competition authorities was that buying power was only occasionally a competition problem and that, when that occurred, competition law instruments were adequate to deal with the problem.

The Japanese competition authority was clearly more concerned about what it calls the abuses of superior bargaining power of large-scale retailers, and it requested that trade associations of wholesalers and larger retailers make their umbrella organizations thoroughly understand the contents of the "Guidelines Concerning Abuses of Superior Bargaining Position under the Antimonopoly Act" published by the JFTC. It also indicated that it would act against illegal abuses of superior bargaining position.

Third, several business practices by large-scale retailers were found to be problematic for competition.[34]

1.1.4 Codes of Conduct

In two of the countries surveyed, the United Kingdom and Australia, market investigations found that competition was working well in the grocery retail markets but that there were nevertheless problems between retailers and their suppliers. Neither recommended the adoption of new legislation to solve these problems—among other reasons because legislation could have unintended negative consequences—but suggested the adoption of codes of conduct. The experience of these two countries shows that such codes might be more appropriate ways to solve the problems raised by buyer power than legislation but that to be effective the codes need to be legally enforceable and to include a dispute resolution mechanism.

In the United Kingdom, in a report published in 2000, the Monopolies and Mergers Commission identified a number of competition concerns, falling into two broad categories: (1) concerns about grocery retailers' pricing strategies, in particular below-cost pricing and "price flexing," whereby higher prices were charged in some stores than others, and (2) concerns about grocery retailers' conduct towards their suppliers. It decided not to recommend any action in relation to the pricing concerns, however, because it considered that the potential remedies, such as a prohibition on below-cost selling or on price variations across stores, would either have too many unintended consequences—such as prohibiting desirable price cutting or differential pricing that reflects regional cost differences—or be too difficult to implement. In relation to concerns about supplier practices, the MMC recommended the adoption of a Supermarkets Code of Practice (the "SCOP") for all grocery retailers with a national market share in excess of 8 %.

[34] See, *e.g.*, in Finland, the Netherlands, Austria, the United Kingdom and France.

Such a code was drawn up and adopted by the four largest grocery retailers at the time.

On August 2005, the OFT (UK) concluded that the SCOP and competition in general were both working well. That decision, however, was challenged by the Association of Convenience Stores (the "ACS"), and in May 2006, its challenge led to a second reference of the grocery retail sector to the Competition Commission. Although the Competition Commission investigated a number of the concerns raised by the ACS, in each case the Competition Commission concluded that there was no restriction of competition. However, the Competition Commission recognized that the large retailers had buyer power and that some exercise of this buyer power could be problematic. In particular, the Competition Commission considered that the use of buyer power to "transfer excessive risks or unexpected costs to their suppliers through practices involving retrospective adjustments to supply agreements or giving rise to moral hazard on the part of the grocery retailer" "is likely to lessen suppliers' incentives to invest in new capacity, products and production processes . . . [and] will be detrimental to the interests of consumers." Particular examples of retrospective conduct that the Competition Commission identified included imposing price changes on suppliers after goods had been ordered or delivered or requiring them to contribute to the costs of promotions that had not been agreed in advance. Examples of excessive risk transfer giving rise to moral hazard included the practice of making suppliers liable for losses arising from goods being lost or stolen in store.

One of the remedies imposed by the Competition Commission in this second investigation was the establishment of the Groceries Supply Code of Practice ("GSCOP"), based on the existing SCOP, but amended to include a general requirement of fair dealing and specific prohibitions of the retrospective and excessive risk transferring forms of conduct considered above, together with a requirement that retailers should enter into binding arbitration to resolve any disputes arising under the GSCOP. Parliament then decided to legislate for a new role of Groceries Code Adjudicator to act as an enforcer for GSCOP.

In Australia, since December 2007, industry participants have had the option to follow a voluntary code of conduct, the Produce and Grocery Industry Code of Conduct, which was introduced in 2007 as part of the Australian Government's response to the Parliamentary report, Report of the Joint Select Committee on the Retailing Sector: Fair Market or Market Failure. This Code sets as its objectives "fair and equitable trading practices among industry participants" and "fair play and open communication between industry participants." Nevertheless, the Code failed to fulfill these objectives because of a lack of enforcement and "contractual obligation," which are key elements of a voluntary code of conduct. Furthermore, the provisions of the Code did not ensure well-balanced and fair negotiation of contracts and their subsequent application.

This code of conduct will be replaced by a new code of conduct. Although the government supports the adoption of a voluntary code of conduct, other parties involved in the negotiation prefer a mandatory code. The new code will be proposed by the competition authority (the ACCC) and a supermarket and grocery industry working group, including the major supermarket chains. It will set rules for conduct, such as unilateral changes of concluded supply agreements, payments and the determination of prices. This code will, for the first time, regulate delisting of products from supermarket shelves and will set arrangements for effective and accessible, low-cost dispute resolution. The new code of conduct may follow the UK trend of a mandatory code of conduct and could include a supermarket ombudsman.

The ACCC is in favor of a legally enforceable code of conduct as it recognizes that the existing code has failed to fulfill its objectives. In particular, it failed to ensure the enforcement of contracts and effective dispute resolution. Furthermore, the ACCC's inclination towards the enforceable code of conduct is based on its investigation of the industry, finding that the major supermarket chains do not always honor their contracts with suppliers. Often they demand additional payments and one-way penalties, which are not part of the original contract, as well as discriminating and failing to pay agreed prices. The suppliers comply with such practices, refusing to officially complain to the ACCC, for fear of the consequences on their supply to the supermarket chains.

If the code is legally enforceable, the ACCC will have the power to issue public notices, apply to the court to make orders to redress loss or damage suffered by other parties of a contract or arrangement in question and investigate its application and enforcement.

First, under s 51, the ACCC can advise the public by issuing a written notice if conduct by a corporation or a person contravenes the code of conduct. Second, under s 51 ADB, the ACCC may apply on behalf of a class of persons who suffered or could suffer loss or damage caused by a person contravening the code of conduct for orders to the court with jurisdiction in this matter. The court can make orders that will redress fully or partially the damage or loss suffered or prevent or reduce the loss or damages suffered. In particular, the court can make orders declaring the contract or arrangement in question (or its part) void or varying such a contract or arrangement, or it can enforce any of the provisions of the contract or arrangement in question. It can order the respondent to refund money or return property or provide parts, repair goods or supply specified services. Third, the ACCC has also investigation power under Division 5 of the CCA, meaning it can give written notice to a corporation asking for information or for a specific document.

Although the enforcement power of the ACCC can be assumed with certainty for the new code of conduct because it will be established under Part IV B of the CCA, the ACCC and/or other bodies could also be provided with additional powers under the code of conduct. For instance, it can be expected that the new code of conduct will include the institution of an ombudsman.

1.2 Competition Law Enforcement

As mentioned previously, some of the market investigations undertaken by competition authorities were based on suspicions of horizontal or vertical anticompetitive practices. Competition authorities have not limited themselves to market investigations and have, in a number of cases, used their enforcement powers against anticompetitive practices.

1.2.1 Competition Law Enforcement Against Anticompetitive Horizontal and Vertical Agreements

Several observations derived from national reports on horizontal and vertical anticompetitive practices and abuses of dominance in the grocery retail sector can be made.

First, the market for groceries can be affected by horizontal collusion either at the level of suppliers or at the level of retailers. However, the cases of collusion among suppliers of grocery products are much more frequent than the cases of collusion among retailers (even if collusion among retailers is not unknown).

1.2.1.1 Collusion Among Suppliers of Grocery Products

A large number of cases of supplier cartels in the grocery sector have been reported. Most of these cartels concern producers of agricultural products. But some of the collusion cases concern a combination of horizontal and vertical collusion between transformers or wholesalers of food products and retail distributors (of the "hub and spoke" variety). As farmers push for higher farm gate prices—sometimes through illegal collusion, sometimes through more violent expression of discontent—and put pressure on the downstream levels, there is a tendency for firms operating at the intermediate level, such as transformers or wholesalers, to push retailers to lower the intensity of competition among them through price monitoring so as to allow both the intermediaries and the retailers to absorb price increases called for by their supplies. For example, there have been cases in France of millers supporting, or even organizing, collusion among bakers so as to be able to increase the price of flour in response to demands by farmers for a higher price for wheat.

A number of country reports mention the existence of standard horizontal cartels among suppliers of foodstuffs that have the object or the effect of either increasing price or excluding competitors, *e.g.*, the United States, Austria (organic corn), the Netherlands (shrimp, silver skin onions, first-year onions, pork slaughterhouses, greenhouse grown vegetables), Hungary (bakery products, flour mill companies, eggs, Hungarian watermelons), Italy (Grana Padano cheese) or France (endives, flour, pork slaughterhouses).

If we now move to more complex hub and spoke agreements, several investigations of such agreements have been initiated in the United Kingdom, but the competition authority has not always been successful.

1.2.1.2 Collusion Among Grocery Retailers

As we saw in the previous section, in the hub and spoke type of collusion retailers and suppliers through a complex combination of vertical agreement and horizontal practices, try to reduce the intensity of price competition at the retail level. However, very few cases of pure horizontal collusion among retailers were reported.

On the contrary, in some countries such as the Netherlands, the competition authority considers that there is very active price competition among large-scale retailers and that consumers benefit from this active competition. The report concerning the United States similarly states that for at least 30 years, cartel enforcement in the domestic food sector has no longer been necessary as there do not seem to have been any prosecutions against groceries for cartel activity, since 1972, when the US DOJ prosecuted a group of small, independent grocers that organized to compete against larger chains.

One exception is Finland, where certain grocery retail operators belonging to the same retail group were sanctioned for prohibited horizontal price fixing. In France, the Paris Court of Appeals (CA Paris) has in two different instances sanctioned franchisors for anticompetitive horizontal clauses in franchise agreements that limited or made it impossible for a former franchisee of a retail chain to become a franchisee of a competing chain at the end of its first contract. In the US, in 1972, the Supreme Court struck down as *per se* illegal under Section 1 of the Sherman Act a territorial restriction in a joint venture agreement among small to medium-size supermarkets. The stores had created a national private label brand called "Topco" for use on standard grocery products, and each joint venture member was given an exclusive license to sell Topco-branded products in a defined service territory. At the time, decisions such as this one were important rules and occupied a significant amount of time and attention among grocery and other retailers and their counsel, as well as enforcement agencies. Today, they no longer matter in practical terms, which illustrates how United States antitrust law can evolve without old statutes being repealed or old court decisions being explicitly overruled by courts or repealed by Congress. In Bulgaria, a cartel among food suppliers seems to have resulted from a government initiative. Finally, in Ukraine, there were investigations on a number of cases in which increases in the price of food products within a retail chain or across retail chains were considered to be unjustified and potential violations of the competition law (*e.g.*, milk products, sour cream, butter and hard cheese, noodles, sunflower oil, cereals, meat and fish, garlic, poultry meat, lemon and onions).

1.2.1.3 Cooperation Within Franchise Networks

The horizontal relationship among members of a franchise network of agreements is sometimes examined to assess their compatibility with competition law provisions that prohibit horizontal restrictions to competition. In Estonia, the competition authority considered that cooperation among the members of a cooperative was not illegal because it allowed them to compete with major retail chains and therefore fostered competition on the retail grocery market. The competition authority considered the cooperative to be a single undertaking for the purposes of applying competition law but added that even if the members of the cooperative had been considered as separate undertakings, their cooperation practices would have been exempted under the national equivalent of Article 101(3) TFEU.

In Finland, prior to the abolishment of the possibility to apply for individual exemption in 2004, the competition authority granted an individual exemption to the S Group, concerning horizontal cooperation regarding pricing, procurement and marketing of daily consumer goods. The conditions imposed by the competition authority for the benefit of the exemption were that each grocery retailer within the group had to remain free to lower its prices from the agreed prices and had to advertise independently; that the commonly agreed prices concerning foodstuffs could only be in force for 3-month periods except for industrial foodstuffs, for which prices could be in force for 4 months; that the central organization could define at maximum 60 % of the individual retailers' product mix calculated on the basis of their sales value; and that the individual retailers had to remain free to procure products from sources other than the central purchasing organization.

Another network, the K Group, also benefited from an individual exemption from the resale price maintenance ban. The exemption concerned the imposition of maximum sales prices for 35 % of the products belonging to the mix of products that each K Group retailer had to stock, as well as the maximum pricing of the group's private label products.

The Finnish competition authority has also granted exemption decisions concerning the procurement cooperation between the procurement organizations of certain Finnish grocery retail groups.

1.2.1.4 Anticompetitive Horizontal Agreements Among Grocery Retailers at the Local Level

It is possible that some horizontal price fixing among retailers happens at the local level rather than at the national level since consumers are typically unable to move easily from one region to another and since it seems that retail chains adjust their prices to local conditions.

A number of countries are not well equipped to deal with such local horizontal anticompetitive practices either because they have *de minimis* rules that prevent them from intervening if the turnover of the firms investigated is below a threshold level or because the *de minimis* exemption is expressed in terms of a percentage of the national market. In addition, even when *de minimis* rules do not apply, competition authorities show a reluctance to pursue purely local practices because they are concerned with their own efficiency and prefer to focus on cases that they see as bringing the best impact/cost ratio. In such cases, competition enforcement is limited to civil actions.

For example, the Swedish report states that the companies with a turnover of less than SEK 30 million in the previous fiscal year can jointly hold a maximum market share of 15 % without being subject to the application of rules against anticompetitive agreements, but this rule does not apply to hard-core cartel violations. As in Sweden, in Finland, competition restrictions among competitors are considered to be of minor importance and are exempted from the prohibitions of the competition law if the market share of participants does not exceed 10 % on the relevant market; for vertical restrictions, a market share threshold of 15 % applies. However, hard-core competition restrictions such as price-fixing cartels, market sharing, resale price maintenance or granting of absolute territorial protection do not fall under the *de minimis* rule.

In the United States, the US DOJ and FTC rarely are involved in local antitrust enforcement outside of market remedies for larger mergers that affect small markets. Policing anticompetitive practices can happen through the State Attorneys General, through state or applied federal law or through private cases, though the latter are rare. Enforcement by the State Attorneys General varies greatly across the states.

As a contrast, in the Netherlands, the statutory *de minimis* exemption in the domestic competition law exempts even hard-core restrictions. Furthermore, the competition authority may decide not to investigate violations that have only a small economic effect, even if they do not fall within the scope of the *de minimis* exemption, because of its priority policy.

The legal situation in Hungary is similar to that in Sweden. Under the *de minimis* rule, agreements of minor importance are not subject to the general prohibition against anticompetitive practices. An agreement is of minor importance if the parties' joint market share does not exceed 10 % in the market concerned by the agreement. However, this exemption does not apply to agreements that are aimed at price fixing or market sharing so that local cartels can be pursued by the competition authority. Nevertheless, the Hungarian competition authority has not investigated such micro-violations in the food sector, possibly because of a lack of resources and the fact that it was not aware of possible local infringements because it has no local offices across the country.

In Austria, until 2012, even hard-core cartels were exempted from legal cartel prohibition if the members of the cartel had a joint market share of less than 5 % of the national market and less than 25 % of a regional market. However, in 2012, an amendment to the Austrian Cartel Act made the law consistent with the *de minimis* concept of the European Commission and hard-core infringements—irrespective of the market shares of the undertakings involved—are no longer exempted from the application of the cartel prohibition as stated in Section 1 Austrian Cartel Act.

In contrast to Austria, in Germany, anticompetitive practices at the local level are not exempted from the general cartel prohibition clause in the competition law. However, competition authorities are not subject to any obligation to take action against possible violations of the German antitrust regime. The decision of whether they start formal proceedings is subject to their own discretion.

In Bulgaria, the competition authority has not investigated any local anticompetitive behavior among retailers even though they have dealt with local anticompetitive agreements notably in the transportation sector (*e.g.*, buses and taxis).

In Estonia, the competition authority is unlikely to investigate local cases. However, due to the fact that horizontal hard-core cartels are criminal violations, the competition authority would be expected to investigate a local cartel if it becomes aware of the existence of such practices.

Unlike previously mentioned countries, Romania actively pursues antitrust violations at the local level.

In Italy, the competition authority deals with all "the understandings between companies that intend to or result in consistently preventing, restricting or distorting competition within the domestic market or a significant part thereof." The "significant part" of the domestic market referred to in the law must be considered in relation to the significance of the local market for the consumer and the reasonable alternatives available to the consumer. In 2008, the Italian competition authority found that the Bread-Making Association Union of Rome and the Province of Rome had violated the competition law, on September 2007, when it gave indications regarding the sales prices for the two main types of bread sold in the Province of Rome and "recommended" increases for all other types of bread. The Bread-Making Association was also considered to have violated the law by preparing and disseminating cost analyses of the main types of bread, aimed at calculating the relative end prices. The competition authority considered that by indicating minimum prices, the Bread-Making Association encouraged the bakers to align their prices at higher levels than the level that would have been reached in an ordinary competition environment.

The competition authority of Ukraine controls adherence to the competition law at both national and local levels. Local anticompetitive practices are handled by regional departments of the national competition authority of Ukraine and are authorized to impose fines for infringements in amounts not exceeding UAH 68,000 (approximately USD 8,500 or EUR 6,538). In 2011, the competition authority investigated abuse of the monopoly (dominant) position on the grocery market for bread and flour, eggs, milk and butter. Over 50 infringements were detected and sanctioned in a large number of cities.

In France, since 2008, the competition division of the Ministry of Foreign Affairs (and not the Competition Authority) has the power to make injunctions and to conclude financial transactions for local anticompetitive practices involving undertakings with limited turnovers. The anticompetitive practices at stake are those (1) that concern markets of local dimension, (2) that do not affect intracommunity trade and (3) that relate to undertakings whose individual turnover is below EUR 50 million and aggregated below EUR 100 million.

Finally, in the United Kingdom, the Competition Commission identified four features of the relevant markets that distort competition, three of which are relevant for local markets: (1) high levels of concentration in some local markets, (2) the planning system, (3) retailers' landholdings and (4) supply chain practices. In each case, the Competition Commission found that the features gave rise to detrimental effects on consumers, and accordingly the Competition Commission had a statutory duty to impose remedies.

1.2.1.5 Hub and Spoke Agreements

Second, if competition authorities have little evidence of horizontal cartels at the retail level, they are highly suspicious of the relationship between retailers and their suppliers or their service providers, and in the last 5 years competition authorities initiated a large number of investigations based on the idea that the close relationship between retailers and suppliers contributes to the increase in transparency at the horizontal retailer level and contributes to a weakening of competition among retailers.

For example, the competition authority of Belgium brought a case alleging an exchange of sensitive information among retailers through a supplier and coordinated price increases between retailers, but the case was dismissed on procedural grounds, the competition authority of Estonia is investigating two cases of interrelated vertical and horizontal collusive practices. In Bulgaria, the competition authority brought a case of price coordination against six modern retail chains. The competition authority alleged that the implementation of various clauses in supply agreements (such as most-favored-customer clauses, product promotion exclusivity clauses or clauses obliging suppliers to report to the retailer a lower net supply price granted to another retailer) led to a "network effect" that increased transparency on the supply market, thus allowing retailers to obtain current information about the supply costs and planned promotional activities of their competitors. In Germany, in 2010, the competition authority began an investigation into the vertical and horizontal relations between the agro-food industry and retailers, alleging price fixing of confectionery, coffee and pet food between the retailers and their suppliers. The competition authority of Austria also brought two "hub and spoke" cases respectively in the beer and dairy markets. In a case that involved the relationship between the retailers and a market research firm in Finland, the competition authority held that the information exchange between three major grocery retail groups through the research company AC Nielsen, which provided weekly detailed sales statistics to the participating grocery retail groups, had restricted competition contrary to the Finnish Competition Act and EU competition law.

1.2.1.6 Resale Price Maintenance and Recommended Resale Prices

Resale price maintenance is prohibited in most countries and is considered to be a hard-core violation in some countries, even though all competition authorities are not convinced of the fact that resale price maintenance should be considered a major competition law violation.

In most countries, it is possible for a supplier to recommend a sale price, provided that these recommendations are not combined with incentives for or pressure on retailers to apply the recommended prices. For example, the Italian report states: "The practice of recommending a resale price to a reseller or asking a reseller to abide by maximum resale prices may benefit from an exemption in accordance with the exemption rule by category when the market share of each of the parties to the agreement does not exceed a 30 % threshold on condition that this does not establish a minimum sales price or a price fixed in accordance with the pressure exercised or the incentives offered by any of the parties. The market position of the supplier is the most important factor in deciding whether there are any anti-competition effects due to the maximum prices or recommended prices. The stronger the market position of the supplier, the greater the risk that a maximum price or a recommended resale price will be applied as the resale price by most or all of the retailers."

Competition authorities have spent a lot of energy trying to distinguish between truly recommended prices and resale price maintenance masquerading as recommended pricing.

There are two ways in which resale price maintenance can be implemented. The first one is the diffusion of recommended prices combined with various incentives or threats to ensure that the retailers will effectively enforce the resale price. The second method is the hub and spoke method (a combination of vertical and horizontal collusion, which we commented on previously and which is not dealt with in this section).

In Japan, recommended resale prices in the retail grocery sector can be considered a violation of AMA under the condition that such recommended prices are binding the retailers.

In Sweden, Belgium, Estonia, the Netherlands, Finland and Romania, rules on resale price maintenance (RPMs) in vertical agreements are in essence the same as EU rules.

In Austria, recommended prices are treated as (bilateral) cartels if they have as their object or effect the restriction of competition, but they are exempted from the cartel prohibition if the nonbinding nature of the recommendation is "explicitly" mentioned and if there is no pressure to implement the price recommendation.

In Germany, according to the decision-making practice of the competition authority and the court, the pure dissemination of resale price recommendations does not violate German antitrust law even if the retailers follow these recommendations. But the competition authority and the court have adopted a restrictive interpretation of this exemption. If manufacturers do anything more than the pure dissemination of price lists with the aim to bring retailers to follow these recommendations (e.g., contacting the retailer to address the difference between the recommended resale price and the actual resale price), the competition authority and the courts consider this as a violation of the German cartel prohibition clause.

In Hungary, recommended resale prices are violations of the competition law if they are combined with means to make them mandatory or if there is a risk that they are a focal point for resellers and are followed by most or all of them or if they soften competition or facilitate collusion among suppliers. The 10 % *de minimis* exception applies to resale price maintenance.

In Bulgaria, setting minimum resale prices is considered a hard-core restriction that is *per se* illegal. The setting of maximum prices is not always regarded as anticompetitive and is subject to a case-by-case analysis. Price recommendations are permissible, as long as additional factors, such as penalties for noncompliance or incentives for compliance, do not alter their voluntary nature.

Under French law, distribution of recommended prices or the setting of a maximum price is lawful, provided that this does not dissimulate an imposed price. Recommended resale prices can be found illegal if three conditions are met: the recommended resale prices are known by the retailer, prices are monitored, and the prices chosen by the supplier are applied by a significant number of distributors.

In a number of countries,[35] there have not been any recent cases of resale price maintenance in the retail grocery sector. Several cases of alleged resale price maintenance are under investigation in Germany.

The competition authority of Bulgaria has dealt with several instances of resale price maintenance. In one instance, it considered that a yogurt manufacturer had abused its dominant position on the market of unflavored yoghurt for having entered into distribution agreements with its retailers that required them, inter alia, to resell the yoghurt at prices not higher than the retail prices it recommended and not to sell the yoghurt at prices lower than the prices indicated as list prices. An aggravating factor was the fact that the distribution agreements also included performance- and volume-based rebate incentive schemes. The competition authority of Bulgaria is also investigating allegations of resale price maintenance and territorial allocation against several manufacturers of sunflower oil and their distributors.

With respect to resale price maintenance, the situation in the United States has evolved recently. In 2005, the US Supreme Court repealed the 94-year-old *per se* prohibition on vertical pricing agreements. However, resale price maintenance was never an important factor in food distribution in the United States (unlike in distribution of pharmaceutical products), and the de facto absence of an RPM prohibition does not seem to be a significant barrier to consumers getting competitive prices in the retail grocery field. The US national reports state: "Part of the United States legacy may be that for many years the United States enforced RPM to protect smaller service-oriented retailers and image-creating manufacturers against free-riding services. Since RPM was never particularly important in grocery retailing, it is not clear whether removing effective RPM prohibitions has been pro-competitive or commercially irrelevant in this sector. Either way, there is little evidence that it has been anti-competitive in the main."

1.2.2 Abuse of Dominance

Except for the case of Ukraine and the United States, there are no reports of abusively high prices by the retailers of grocery products.

In the United States, abusively high consumer prices that could be linked to monopolization of a market would be evidence of monopoly under United States antitrust law. There are no major cases in the grocery retail market except the

[35] Japan, Belgium, Netherlands, Hungary, Austria, Romania or Estonia.

California ex. rel. Lockyer v. The Vons Companies case,[36] which involved retail grocery monopolization of a small California town. The plaintiff state, California, was able to demonstrate across-the-board price increases following monopoly control.

One reason might be that, in most countries, no grocery retailer has a market share sufficiently large to be recognized as having a dominant position on the relevant market.[37]

In other countries, provisions of the competition law define thresholds of dominance in the retail sector.[38]

One of the practices that is frequently mentioned as a possible abuse of dominant position by retailers in the grocery market is reselling below cost. In some countries, reselling below cost can be sanctioned only if it is considered to be predatory (Sweden, Belgium, Bulgaria, Finland and Germany). In other countries, reselling below cost is considered an abuse of dominance even if it is not predatory (for example, the Austrian competition law explicitly states that reselling of products (not services) below the purchase price is an abuse of dominance if not objectively justified). Finally, in a last group of countries, reselling below cost is *per se* prohibited irrespective of whether the retailer has a dominant position.[39]

There are relatively few cases of successful prosecution of resale below cost.

In Austria, a retailer with a market share of about 5 % failed to prove that Austria's biggest grocery retailer was abusing its dominance by reselling products below purchase price. The claim was rejected as the plaintiff could not even submit evidence with regard to its own purchase price (not to mention the purchase price of the dominant undertaking).

In Japan, three wholesalers of alcoholic liquors sold beer below cost to some retailers. It was considered that they were creating difficulties for the business activities of other retailers of alcoholic liquors, and the Japanese competition authority warned them to stop the practice.

In the Netherlands, a supplier of a well-known brand of gingerbread discontinued selling to a retail chain that sold its product below the purchase price. The discontinued retailer sued the supplier and argued that any attempt on the part of the supplier to force an increase in the resale price of the gingerbread would amount to resale price maintenance. The competition authority published a press release stating that resale price maintenance was prohibited but did not take any enforcement action.

---

[36] *California ex. rel. Lockyer v. The Vons Companies, Inc.* (C.D. Cal CV 05-8972 DSF January 03, 2006).

[37] See, for example, the United Kingdom and Estonia.

[38] E.g., Finland.

[39] For example, in Hungary, the Unfair Distributional Practices Act prohibits resale below cost, irrespective of the market power of the retailer, if the practice affects agricultural or food products; in Romania, reselling below costs is prohibited regardless of whether the company is dominant or not; in France, Article L 442-2 of the Commercial Code prohibits resale below purchase price.

However, in 2007, the German competition authority imposed a fine on the drugstore chain for having sold several products below cost. Indeed, in Germany, undertakings with a superior market position are prohibited from selling articles regularly below cost price without a reasonable justification. However, the decision of the competition authority was overturned on appeal.

Besides reselling below cost, there are also reports of other exclusionary practices by dominant firms. For example, in Italy, the competition authority dealt with a case where it found that a retail distributor, Coop Estense, systematically interfered with the attempts of the competitor to start up new food sales outlets, in potentially suitable areas and shopping centers and which were available to it, and also intervened in the administrative procedures that had been initiated by a competitor to obtain the necessary authorizations. The Italian competition authority stated that this strategy was carried out in a market environment that was already characterized by low availability of suitable areas and shopping centers and significant administrative barriers blocking entrance to the market. According to the ICA, this behavior allowed Coop Estense to maintain—and actually strengthen—its dominant position in the markets in question, gaining increasing market share over time. In addition, by blocking an "efficient" competitor from accessing the market, Coop Estense damaged consumers in terms of higher prices and/or lower choice.

1.2.3 Abuse of Buying Power

In most countries, abuse of buying power is considered to be a serious problem. In the group of surveyed countries, several questions arise: is such an abuse covered by the provision of a competition law prohibiting anticompetitive abuse of dominance? Or is there a specific provision in the competition law? How is dependency defined? What constitutes an abuse of dependency?

1.2.3.1 Legal Provisions Regarding Abuses of Buying Power

In a first group of countries,[40] abuse of buyer power or dependency is considered to be part of a wider category of abuses of dominant position. In these countries, the concept of dominance is applied both on the seller's side and on the buyer's side. Thus, to establish that a grocery retailer has buying power, it must account for a substantial part of the procurement of groceries or of a particular grocery product. This may in fact make it very difficult or impossible to bring abuse of buying power cases.

In a second group of countries,[41] it is easier to control the buying behavior of firms either because the concept of dominance is fairly wide or because the

[40] United Kingdom, Belgium, Sweden, Netherlands, Finland and Romania.

[41] Australia, Germany, Austria and Bulgaria.

competition law allows the control of the behavior of firms that have a strong (although not dominant) position.

In a final group of countries,[42] there are specific provisions concerning the abuse of buying power. In these countries, it is thus not necessary to show that a firm has a dominant position to be able to control its behavior on the buying side. As a result, the prohibition of buying power is different in nature from what it is in the previous groups of countries because it is clearly aimed at restoring fairness in vertical transactions rather than achieving competitive equilibrium of the market.

1.2.3.2 Definition of Buyer Power

Except for the Netherlands and Bulgaria, which define buying power as the ability of a firm to distort competition on the upstream market, buying power on the part of the seller is defined in most other countries as either a situation where the suppliers of the firm having buyer power have no economic alternative but to deal with the buyer or a situation where a buyer could disproportionately hurt its suppliers if it stopped dealing with them.

1.2.3.3 Is Abuse of Buyer Power a *Per Se* Offense?

In nearly all of the countries for which information has been gathered, irrespective of whether or not they have a specific provision regarding abuse of buying power, such abuses are not treated *per se* and the competition authority has to show that there was a restriction of competition on the market. There seem to be only two exceptions to this principle. In Romania, there is consensus between the competition authority and the courts that all abuses of dominance (including abuse of buying power) are *per se* violations of the national competition law. In Germany, abuses of a dominant market position, active and passive discrimination and unfair impediment of dependent undertakings are prohibited *per se*. Furthermore, there are two countries where it is unclear whether abuse of buying power is considered to be a *per se* violation of the competition law. In Estonia, the competition authority has traditionally considered the anticompetitive effects of abusive conduct, but the Supreme Court held in 2007 that the Competition Act does not require showing the anticompetitive effects in abuse of dominance cases. In Austria, the Austrian Cartel Courts focus on the "suitability" of the behavior of a dominant undertaking to create "negative effects concerning the market situation and the competitive relationship." Therefore, the approach in Austria concerning prohibited abuse seems to be between a *per se* prohibition and a factual restriction of competition.

1.2.3.4 What Constitutes an Abuse of Buyer Power?

In most countries, and in particular in EU Member States (such as Sweden or Belgium, Estonia, the Netherlands, Bulgaria, Austria, Romania) where abuse of buying power is a subset of abuse of dominance, there is no statutory definition of what constitutes an abuse of buying power.

---

[42] France and Japan.

This lack of statutory definition of what constitutes an abuse of buying power leaves competition authorities with the difficult task of finding a test. As the contribution from the Netherlands mentions, there is no clear distinction between fierce competition and abuse of buying power and the test applied by competition authorities can be rather vague.

The view expressed by the contribution of the Netherlands that it is difficult from a competition law standpoint to define an abuse of buying power is shared by the United Kingdom Competition Commission. The Competition Commission found that the largest retailers have buying power but that this is not in itself problematic from a competition perspective because the lower supply prices that their buyer power makes possible are passed on to consumers. In particular, the Competition Commission rejected the suggestion that retailers exercised their buyer power by withholding demand, which, if it had been established, would have had adverse effects on consumers. However, the Competition Commission drew a distinction between the normal exercise of buyer power to obtain better trading terms and the use of buyer power to "transfer excessive risks or unexpected costs to their suppliers through practices involving retrospective adjustments to supply agreements or giving rise to moral hazard on the part of the grocery retailer." According to the Competition Commission, such conduct "is likely to lessen suppliers' incentives to invest in new capacity, products and production processes ... [and] will be detrimental to the interests of consumers." Particular examples of retrospective conduct that the Competition Commission identified included imposing price changes on suppliers after goods had been ordered or delivered or requiring them to contribute to the costs of promotions that had not been agreed in advance. Examples of excessive risk transfer giving rise to moral hazard included the practice of making suppliers liable for losses arising from goods being lost or stolen in store.

The fact that it is difficult for competition authorities to define what could be an abuse of buying power is illustrated by Hungary, where the competition authority has stated in a decision that, in order to establish an abuse of buyer power under the Trade Act, it is necessary that the "supplier does not receive any benefit from the economic results of the large-scale selling." Such a criterion seems to be both vague and economically dubious.

In a few countries,[43] short of providing a test for the definition of an abuse of buying power, the competition law, or proposed amendments to the competition law, provides an exemplary list of such abuses.

1.2.3.5 Case Law on Abuse of Buying Power

The case law on abuse of buying power is relatively scarce, and very few cases involve the grocery retail market.

On this topic, we can identify three groups of countries.

First, in Austria, Sweden, Belgium, Finland, the Netherlands and Ukraine, there have been no cases (in the case of Estonia, no recent case) of abuses of buying

[43] See the Netherlands, Italy, Germany, Finland and Japan.

power examined by the competition authority during the past 5 years. In the case of France, the competition authority investigated cases but found that the practices did not amount to an abuse of buyer power.

Second, in four countries,[44] there is an abundant case law, and a wide array of practices of retailers that had buyer power were considered to be violations of the competition law because they were unfair or unjustified rather than because they restricted competition.

Third, in three countries,[45] the effect of the practices of grocery retailers on competition was examined in the course of an investigation into possible abuses of buying power, but no violations were found.

1.3 Merger Control

Competition authorities in most countries are in charge of merger control in the grocery retail sector at both the national level and the local levels. There are countries,[46] however, where the government can directly intervene to prevent a merger transaction.

In a large number of countries, there is a double threshold, one for the aggregate turnover of the parties to the merger and a second, which may be a threshold for the acquired firm or a threshold for at least two of the undertakings party to the merger. When one looks at the thresholds for merger control in the countries covered by this survey, one sees a striking difference between eastern European countries and the other countries. First, the thresholds for the aggregate turnover of the parties to the merger tend to be a great deal lower in a number of eastern European countries. For example, in Ukraine, the threshold for the aggregate turnover of the parties to the transaction is EUR 12 million worldwide, but there is also a domestic market share threshold of 35 %. In Romania, the threshold is EUR 10 million worldwide. In Bulgaria, the domestic threshold is EUR 12.78 million.

In comparison, aggregate thresholds tend to be much larger in other countries (EUR 115 million domestic in Sweden, EUR 100 million domestic in Belgium, EUR 113,450,000 worldwide in the Netherlands, EUR 350 million worldwide in Finland, EUR 482 million domestic in Italy, EUR 500 million worldwide in Germany). The same observation applies to the threshold for the turnover of two of the undertakings that are party to a merger transaction. This threshold is set at EUR 1 million worldwide in Ukraine, EUR 4 million domestic in Romania, EUR 1,530,000 domestic in Bulgaria, whereas the equivalent threshold is set at EUR 23 million domestic in Sweden, EUR 48 million domestic in Italy, EUR 40 million domestic in Belgium, EUR 30 million domestic in the Netherlands, EUR 20 million domestic in Finland, etc. Even though part of the difference in thresholds is justified

[44] See Japan, Germany, Hungary and Bulgaria.

[45] Australia, United States and France.

[46] See Romania, the United Kingdom and Germany.

by the difference in the size of the respective economies, it still seems that merger controls in Eastern Europe tend to be applied to many transactions that would not be controlled in developed economies.

In most jurisdictions, there are no special thresholds for the control of mergers in the grocery retail sector, and the general thresholds for merger control are applied. There is only one major exception and one minor exception.

In France, for retail trade, which includes retail grocery, the law of modernization of the Economy[47] has lowered the notification thresholds for mergers.[48] For overseas departments and territories, the Commercial Code sets even lower thresholds.[49]

In Germany, the thresholds that apply to merger control also apply to mergers in the retail (and thus the grocery retail) sector, but according to Section 38(2) ARC only three-quarters of the turnover generated through trade in goods (i.e., buying and reselling of goods) have to be taken into account, possibly to reflect the fact that the ratio of sales to value added is notoriously higher in the retail sector than in manufacturing, which means that turnover thresholds do not have the same meaning.

However, there may be occasional attempts by politicians to limit the concentration of large retailers in the grocery market. For example, in Australia, this has led some politicians to call for limits on the extent to which the major grocery chains should be permitted to merge, beyond the existing competition test in the CCA. To date, however, no such modifications to the merger laws have been made.

In most countries, there is a double threshold in turnover for the aggregate firm and the acquired company. In many cases, the acquisition by one retail chain of a retail outlet would not be caught by the merger regulation because the turnover of the acquired retail outlet would not reach the threshold for the acquired firm. However, in countries where merger notification thresholds are low or where there is no threshold on the turnover of the acquired company—mostly eastern European countries—even minor acquisitions of retail spaces have to be notified. This was the case in Bulgaria, where before 2008 every transaction involving change of control had to be notified if the joint turnover of the undertakings concerned exceeded BGN 15 million (EUR 7,670,000 million).

In the United States, the enforcement system makes it substantially less likely that the FTC, or the Justice Department, would seek to shape or prohibit a grocery merger than what seems to be true under the administrative enforcement systems that prevails in Europe. The numbers bear this out. Between 2004 and 2011, the NCAs conducted over 400 grocery retail merger inquiries, and 25 or so were required commitments from the parties. In that same period, the US FTC required divestment in only four mergers.

[47] LME no 2008-776 of 4 August 2008.

[48] See Article L 430-2 of the Commercial Code, paragraph 2.

[49] See Article L 430-2-III of the Commercial Code.

1.3.1 Market Definition in the Grocery Retail Sector

None of the countries under review has a statutory definition of relevant markets. Competition authorities define relevant products or service markets by examining substitutability for consumers (and using the SSNIP test) and occasionally by considering substitutability on the supply side. Most European countries follow closely the principles included in the European Commission notice on the definition of the relevant market. Australia also assesses the substitutability of product/services for consumers. But the entry of new actors such as Amazon in the grocery retail chain, in the United States, may lead to a profound change in the way the competition authorities of this country will define grocery markets.

Competition authorities in and outside of Europe claim to use the SSNIP test to try to assess the substitutability between products and services. However, due to the onerous data requirements required for the hypothetical monopoly test, some competition authorities take shortcuts. For example, the Australian competition authority notes that this test is "rarely strictly applied to factual circumstances" and that it generally takes "a qualitative approach to market definition," using the HMT as an "intellectual aid to focus the exercise."

In their decisions when competition authorities assess product market definition for retail groceries, they consider a number of features of retail stores, such as their size or their format or whether or not they belong to vertically integrated groups.

If we look first at the question of whether grocery retail stores of different sizes are on the same market, one gets not only results varying across countries (which may reflect different consumer habits across countries) but also different results within the same country (which may reflect a difference between competition authorities and the courts when it comes to employing the tools of economic analysis) and, sometimes, different results across time (which may reflect either increased knowledge of the grocery retail sector or an evolution in the buying habits of consumers). The overall picture, however, points to a certain level of *ad hoc* decisions and fuzziness in methodology used.

The formats of the stores are also often considered to assess whether they belong to the same markets. In many countries, stores of different formats are considered to belong to different markets. But there are exceptions. In Bulgaria, the competition authority has concluded that small-size convenience shops should be regarded as competitors to large supermarkets. Interestingly enough, the Bulgarian competition authority also considers that cash & carry stores are a type of "hypermarket" and included in the retail market. This is justified by the fact that although access to cash & carry outlets in Bulgaria requires registration, many final consumers acquire customer cards and purchase goods for personal consumption in cash & carry stores. The French competition authority takes into account the asymmetric substitutability among the different sizes of general food retailers. It considers that for some consumers, a hypermarket might be a local substitute for a supermarket, and so the former will be included in the relevant market of the latter. By contrast, it considers that the converse is rarely verified: supermarkets are not part of the relevant market of hypermarkets. Under the same logic, the competition authority stated that "small retail stores and supermarkets were competing with each other" and, following this, that "they both face competitive pressures of large supermarkets (sales space of over 1,000 m^2) and hypermarkets."[50] The competition authority also considers competitive pressures of discounters towards other general food retailers, leading to the conclusion that discounters should be included in the same relevant market. On the flip side, the French competition authority considers that the competitive pressure of specialist stores and street markets on other types of food retailers is too limited for them to be included in the relevant market of general food stores. Thus, it excludes specialist stores (such as bakeries, butcher shops, fishmongers, cheese boutiques, fruit and vegetable merchants) from the relevant market of general food stores. In one recent case in the United States, the market was defined as the market for a specific set of premium products sold in supermarkets. In the 2007 case, *FTC v. Whole Foods*, the US FTC considered that the merging parties, Whole Foods and Wild Oats, were "premium natural and organic supermarkets."[51] As the US FTC indicated, "The operation of premium and natural organic supermarkets is a distinct "line of commerce" within the meaning of Section 7 of the Clayton Act, 15 U.S.C. § 18." While ultimately the US FTC's theory that the market was distinct prevailed, the United States has not yet seen an attempt to use the inverse market definition of discount groceries used in an antitrust enforcement setting.

The fact that a retail chain may be vertically integrated is occasionally a source of difficulty in market definition of retail grocery. For example, the Australian report indicates that at times markets have been confined to a single functional level and at other times the court has taken a broader view and considered both wholesale and retail activity to be in the same market because of the extent to which one constrains the other where there is extensive vertical integration. The report observes that experts can themselves be divided on the issue of whether and when wholesale and retail groceries should be considered to belong to the same market.

To finish this review of grocery product market definitions, it is worth noting that the United States report commenting on the recent developments in grocery retail in this country suggests that the criteria traditionally used by competition authorities to define markets may be about to change due to the entry of new actors in the grocery retail chain and the profound transformation of the sector. The entrance of Amazon into grocery retailing is seen as completing the already underway international transformation of grocery retailing to general retailing. As a consequence, unnecessary middlemen like wholesalers, and possibly shipping companies, may exit entirely. The end result may be that the major market segmentation for retail will shift dramatically from the way that antitrust agencies in the United States typically see them (as product and geographic markets) to being primarily

[50] FCA, Opinion no 12-A-01 of 11 January 2012 relating to the competitive situation in the food distribution sector in Paris, paragraph 81.

[51] *FTC v. Whole Foods Market, Inc.* 548 F. 3d 1028 (D.C. Cir. 2008).

customer-segmented markets. While not having a completely settled doctrine for how to approach such dramatically new and shifting market definitions, United States antitrust regulators seem to have presaged this change with the 2007 Whole Foods merger case, in which the agency vigorously defended a market definition that was limited to a small, high-end customer profile.

When it comes to the geographical definition of markets, the practices of competition authorities in different jurisdictions seem to be fairly similar even though there may be minor differences. The catchment area for large store such as a hypermarket, a supermarket or a discount store is the area comprising places that can be reached from this store by car within 15–20 min in western European countries (or within a radius of 20–30 km) and within 20–30 min in eastern European countries such as Estonia, Bulgaria or Hungary (or within a radius of 30 km). In the United States, supermarkets are considered to draw their customers from within a radius of 3 or 4 miles. However, in the Whole Foods case, the US FTC considered that premium natural and organic supermarkets tend to draw their customers from within a radius of 5 or 6 miles.

The relevant geographic market for mid-size stores (when there is no hypermarket or one-stop shop in the vicinity) tends to be limited to the area that can be reached in 5–10 min from the store. Those figures are adjusted to take into consideration local circumstances (such as whether one is dealing with a rural or an urban area, what the local habits are in terms of shopping and road transport). What is noticeable, however, is that the figures chosen for the time of travel are rarely justified by a scientific assessment of the behavior of consumers and more by the intuitive appreciation of competition authorities.

1.3.2 Procurement Markets

Finally, a number of countries define procurement markets in the retail grocery sector. They tend to follow the EU approach and consider that such markets should be defined by 'product categories' as suppliers are not able to switch production to the relevant products and market them in the short term. Both in Belgium and in the Netherlands, procurement markets are considered to be national in scope. In Belgium, these markets include sales not only to grocery retailers but also to other distributors (such as hotels, restaurants or specialized distributors). In Austria, on the contrary, the procurement for food retailers/supermarkets is considered to be a separate procurement market from procurement markets for other distribution channels such as Cash & Carry, specialized outlets, gastronomy, petrol station shops, butchers and bakeries.

1.3.3 Merger Control and the Growth of Grocery Retail Networks

The growth of grocery retail networks (such as franchises and cooperatives) is considered to be problematic in some countries. This is the case in countries where the level of concentration in grocery retail is already high and where there is a perception that prices are higher than they are in benchmark countries.[52] In such circumstances, questions are raised about the adequacy of the merger control system to stem increases in concentration of the large network retail systems or the necessity to enact specific laws. However, in some countries where the concentration of grocery retail network is high but where the level of grocery prices is not considered to be high, or is considered to be decreasing, there is no particular concern about the concentration of grocery retail networks.

As a contrast to countries where the concentration of the networks of groceries are (or were) considered to be problematic, a number of countries have not been concerned with this issue, either because the level of retail concentration remained low or because it was considered that the competition authority had the adequate tools to fight any possible anticompetitive merger (even if it involved a small acquisition, such as a local store). This, for example, is the case of Australia, Sweden, Belgium, Estonia, Bulgaria (where small independent convenience stores remain predominant in retail sales of groceries), Romania (where, as of 2008, there were 52 retailers of grocery products) and Italy.

Finally, one should note that the way in which the franchisee members of a network are considered in the context of a merger control when a network acquires new franchisees varies from one country to another.

For example, in the Netherlands, the competition authority aggregates the turnovers of all the franchisees in the network on the relevant—national or local—market and the turnover of the new franchisee and computes the total share of the network after the acquisition of a new franchisee. If the market share of the network remains below 50 % of the relevant market, the competition authority will authorize the merger. If the aggregate market share of the relevant market exceeds 50 %, the parties have to bring forward mitigating circumstances, such as a high market share of competitor(s) on such a local market or evidence of customer movements that show that consumers do in fact visit supermarkets outside the town considered to constitute the relevant geographic market.

In contrast, so far the Hungarian competition authority considers that the individual members of a franchise network should be regarded as competitors since they are invested with independent decision-making competence, most importantly with respect to pricing methods and to determining the variety of goods they offer. Therefore, if new members join a franchise network, such a "change in membership" does not qualify as a concentration within the meaning of merger control law.

[52] See Finland, France and Germany.

1.3.4 Countervailing Buyer Power as a Mitigating Factor for the Concentration of Suppliers

In some countries, the concentration of the grocery retail sector has been offered as a motive for mergers among their suppliers, and this argument has been taken into consideration by the competition authority in a few cases.[53]

In two recent cases involving concentrations between Dutch suppliers of snacks, the suppliers put forward the existence of buyer power at the retail level as a justification for the large market shares that would be created as a result of the concentrations. However, in both cases, the competition authority rejected the argument and ruled that it was unlikely that retailers disposed of sufficient countervailing buyer power to justify the increase of market share of the producers on the production/sales markets.

The French competition authority has publicly stated that, in medium term, the weakening of the upstream sector through the market power close to an oligopsony in the downstream market is likely to drive a reduction of the supply or its diversity that might be detrimental to social welfare. It has called on the government to intervene. The competition authority looks at the countervailing power of large retailers when assessing mergers between suppliers but does not always consider this defense sufficient to allow anticompetitive mergers by suppliers.

1.3.5 Merger Remedies

When it comes to merger control among retail chains, competition authorities usually assess the extent to which competition is going to be restricted on local markets, and if local restrictions to competition are likely to result from the transaction, the competition authority accepts divestment commitments or impose divestiture of supermarkets, whether owned or franchised in the affected local markets.[54]

In a few cases, competition authorities have imposed behavioral commitments alongside divestiture requirements. For example, in the Netherlands, in two cases the purchaser agreed to refrain from (re)gaining economic influence on the divested supermarkets for a period of 10 years. In Austria, the competition authority cleared Pfeiffer's acquisition of three branches of Nussbaumer, on the condition that the parties guarantee that, first, prices in the respective location would be pegged to the prices in the competitive Vienna region and, second, that the parties would not acquire any other competitors in that region.

[53] See Sweden, Belgium, Finland, Italy, the United Kingdom and the United States.

[54] See, for example, Sweden, Finland, Germany, France and the United States.

1.4 Conclusion

From this review of the 18 national contributions, 3 conclusions can be drawn.

First, there are few "pure" competition law issues in the grocery retail market, and competition laws seem to be able to satisfactorily handle most of the competition problems raised. Merger control can be applied (and is applied) to the grocery retail sector and is quite extensive in some countries. The traditional abuses of dominant position provisions (such as provisions against abusively high prices or exclusionary practices such as predatory pricing) and the provisions prohibiting anticompetitive agreements can also be applied (and are applied) extensively to the grocery retail sector. Overall, competition in the grocery retail sector works well.

This is confirmed by the large number of reports that conclude that there is no need for legislative changes concerning the state of competition in their country.[55]

Further thinking should be, however, developed on the criteria to be used to decide whether or when individual members of a grocery retail network (for example, franchisees) should be treated as independent units or as part of aggregated undertakings, including the franchisor and the franchisees.

It would also be worth asking whether more enforcement of competition law in the grocery retail sector at the local level should be undertaken (and if so, by whom), given the limited size of the geographic retail markets for groceries.

However, there are serious difficulties in the use of competition law in the grocery retails sector due to conflicting public policy goals. Public policy goals are contradictory in the sense that public policy makers in many countries want to simultaneously achieve low and stable retail prices for food products (which leads them to promote competition and the emergence of modern forms of retailing, to prohibit resale price maintenance and sometimes to regulate the resale price of grocery products) while at the same time maintaining sufficiently remunerative prices for agricultural firms and suppliers of food products (which leads them to condone some blatantly anticompetitive agreements among farmers or intermediaries and to limit in many different ways the ability of large-scale retailers to make use of their buying power) and, in some countries, while also preserving small-scale retailers (which leads them to prevent large-scale retailers from engaging in some commercially aggressive tactics that would work to the detriment of their small-scale competitors).

The difficulties come from the fact that in order to achieve such contradictory goals a number of countries have included in their competition law or their law against unfair trade practices a large number of *per se* prohibitions against various business behaviors of either suppliers or large-scale retailers.

In this context, there is a serious risk that competition law is diverted from what its role should be, i.e. the protection of competition, to what its role should not be, i.e. the protection of competitors, whether small-scale retailers or small-scale agricultural firms. Furthermore, the inclusion of numerous *per se* prohibitions

[55] See Australia, Austria, Estonia, Germany, the United Kingdom and Sweden.

against the business strategies of economic operators in the grocery retail sector—whether in the competition law or in sector-specific laws—restricts competition beyond what would be strictly necessary to achieve the sociopolitical goals pursued by governments, and the enforcement of these prohibitions is ineffective to solve the tensions between large-scale retailers and other operators in the grocery retail sector.

Thus, several national reports call for a regulatory reform of the various provisions affecting competition in the grocery retail sector with the aim of either making the various applicable laws more consistent or streamlining the prohibitions to keep only those that are strictly necessary.[56] Several reports also call for a review of the restrictive rules that apply to commercial planning and of the role of local authorities who are in charge of granting authorizations for new stores.[57] From that last standpoint, it would be worth reflecting on the past experience of Italy.

In particular, the issue of abuses of buying power is worth revisiting. The questions raised by allegations of abuse of buying power are to a large extent related to the distribution of the surplus along the vertical chain in the food retail sector and not, contrary to what competition authorities occasionally pretend to believe, to issues of competition or efficiency.

It is doubtful whether any type of law against "abuses of dependency" or "abuse of superior market positions" could be fully effective, and it is clear that competition authorities, when they are assigned the task of enforcing the provisions against abuses of buying power, have some difficulty defining what buying power is and establishing a link between the alleged abuses of buying power and a restriction of competition. One of the alternatives to a full-fledged case-by-case analysis of the economic effects of alleged abuses of buying power is for the competition authority, or the law, to establish a list of all the "unfair" demands by buyers that are considered to be abuses of buying power. But even in countries where such a list exists, it is questionable whether the victims of abuses of economic dependency are in a position to make complaints about them.

In order to deal with the issues related to abuse of buying power, an alternative to the use of competition law or unfair trade law, which could both be more effective and entail fewer undesirable effects, could be the adoption of enforceable codes of conduct, including an effective dispute settlement mechanism.

While the report from Ukraine suggests that additional regulations should be adopted in order to solve some of the issues arising out of the imbalance in bargaining power between operators in the grocery retail sector, several country reports suggest that the adoption of mandatory codes of conducts and effective dispute settlement mechanisms is a more appropriate way forward.[58]

From that standpoint, the past experiences of the United Kingdom and Australia deserve to be studied carefully.

---

[56] See, for example, Hungary, Finland and Belgium.

[57] See, for example, France, Finland, Italy and Sweden.

[58] See Australia, the Netherlands, and the United Kingdom.

Australia

2

Barbora Jedličková and Julie Clarke

2.1 Economic Background

The Australian grocery retail market is concentrated, with two major competitors, Coles and Woolworths, holding a market share of approximately 80 %. In 2010, Coles had a market share of 37 % and Woolworths of 43 %. The third largest grocery stores in Australia, IGA and FoodWorks, unify independently owned supermarkets with a market share of 15 %. ALDI, the fourth largest grocery store, entered the Australian market in 2001 and currently has a market share of 3 %. The remaining 2 % of the market belongs to small local grocery stores and other supermarket chains, which have only entered the Australian market recently.[1] For instance, in 2008, Costco Wholesale Corporation entered the Australian market commencing sales in 2009 and targeting small food businesses and individuals.

The concentration of the two major competitors, Coles and Woolworths, significantly increased between 2007/2008 and 2010, accounting for approximately 50 %

The authors would like to thank Mr Alan Ducret and Ms Iolani Brady from the ACCC in Brisbane for their help with searching for the most recent information.

[1] Ferrier Hodgson, 'Ferriers Focus' (May 2011), available on www.ferrierhodgson.com; see also *Australian Competition and Consumer Commission v Metcash Trading Limited* [2011] FCAFC 151 (30 November 2011) at 278.

B. Jedličková
TC Beirne School of Law, The University of Queensland, St Lucia, QLD, Australia
e-mail: b.jedlickova@law.uq.edu.au

J. Clarke (✉)
TC Beirne School of Law, The University of Queensland, St Lucia, QLD, Australia

School of Law, Deakin University, Burwood, VIC, Australia
e-mail: julie.clarke@deakin.edu.au

P. Kobel et al. (eds.), *Antitrust in the Groceries Sector & Liability Issues in Relation to Corporate Social Responsibility*, LIDC Contributions on Antitrust Law, Intellectual Property and Unfair Competition, DOI 10.1007/978-3-662-45753-5_2

of fresh products such as meat, fruit and vegetables, and 70 % of packaged grocery sales in Australia in 2007 and 2008.[2] The number of supermarkets owned by the above-mentioned supermarket chains has been increasing every year.[3]

Coles, Woolworths, ALDI and Franklins are vertically integrated retailers operating at both the retail and the wholesale levels. While nearly all independent grocery stores are supplied by Metcash, the two major retail stores, Coles and Woolworths, purchase their fresh products directly from farmers and other producers.[4] Although the two retail chains concerned can have strong bargaining power in some cases, this power is lowered by producers' alternative selling means, such as exporting.[5] Indeed, agriculture is extremely important for Australian exports as roughly two-thirds of Australia's agricultural products are exported.[6]

Nevertheless, Coles, Woolworths and Metcash possess significant bargaining power in the packaged grocery market, leaving almost no option for suppliers to sell to anyone else.[7] Coles, Woolworths and Metcash also have options other than purchasing products from independent producers of packaged groceries, such as importing goods or selling their own label products, to negotiate the best conditions for themselves. These options increase their bargaining power and influence the first level of the vertical chain. The farmers and other primary producers producing products, such as sugar and wheat, make very low profits, as the price for their products is set by international demand and the low price of packaged products in general.[8] Furthermore, Coles' recent selling campaign, followed by Woolworths' campaign, initiated more intensive price competition that led to even lower retail prices, placing pressure on producers and suppliers to lower their prices.[9]

---

[2] Australian Competition and Consumer Commission, *Report of the ACCC inquiry into the competitiveness of retail prices for standard groceries* (July 2008, Commonwealth of Australia), xv; National Association of Retail Grocers of Australia Pty Ltd, 'Submission: Economic Structure and Performance of the Australian Retail Industry – A joint submission by the National Association of Retail Grocers of Australia and Master Grocers Australia to Productivity Commission in Canberra' (2 September 2011) available at www.pc.gov.au.

[3] Retail World, 46th Annual Report 'Supermarket Stores Numbers' (*Retailmedia Trade Magazine Publishing*, Vol. 65, No. 23, December, 2012) p. 31.

[4] Australian Competition and Consumer Commission, *Report of the ACCC inquiry into the competitiveness of retail prices for standard groceries* (July 2008, Commonwealth of Australia), xv, xx; see also *Australian Competition and Consumer Commission v Metcash Trading Limited* [2011] FCAFC 151 (30 November 2011).

[5] Australian Competition and Consumer Commission, *Report of the ACCC inquiry into the competitiveness of retail prices for standard groceries* (July 2008, Commonwealth of Australia), xx.

[6] Australian Government, Department of Agriculture, Fisheries and Forestry, 'Market Access Trade' (February 2013) available on www.daff.gov.au/market-access-trade.

[7] Australian Competition and Consumer Commission, *Report of the ACCC inquiry into the competitiveness of retail prices for standard groceries* (July 2008, Commonwealth of Australia), xx.

[8] Ibid.

[9] Ferrier Hodgson, 'Ferriers Focus' (May 2011), available on www.ferrierhodgson.com; see also ACCC, 'Additional Budget Estimates: ACCC Statement' (Parliament of Australia, Senate Committees, 13 February 2013, Tabled Document No. 6) available at http://www.aph.gov.au/Parliamentary_Business/Committees/Senate_Committees?url=economics_ctte/estimates/add_1213/index.htm.

2.2 Legal Background

2.2.1 Core Provisions

Australia's competition laws are contained in the *Competition and Consumer Act 2010* (Cth) (the 'CCA').[10] The Australian Competition and Consumer Commission (the 'ACCC') is entrusted with the task of enforcing the Act. It has significant investigatory powers and can itself institute proceedings in respect of conduct that, in its view, contravenes Part IV of the Act. It remains for the courts to determine whether there has been a contravention.

The core competition provisions are contained in Part IV of the CCA, and for constitutional reasons[11] there exists a 'schedule' version of this Part, enacted in consultation with Australia's states and territories, which ensures that Australia has a nationally consistent and broadly operating competition law. The competition provisions in the Act apply to the grocery sector in the same way they apply to other sectors.[12]

Several forms of conduct are expressly subject to *per se* prohibition:

- cartel conduct,[13]
- primary boycotts,[14]
- third line forcing (form of exclusive dealing),[15]

[10] The Act was originally enacted in the form of the *Trade Practices Act 1974* (Cth). Although the name of the Act changed in 2010, the substance of the competition law provisions did not.

[11] There are limits on the extent to which the federal government can legislate; the 'schedule' version of the Act, which for relevant purposes is on identical terms, effectively overcomes these limitations; in particular, it ensures that the conduct of non-corporate entities is captured by Australia's competition law.

[12] There is one key exception; Australia has recently introduced 'price signalling' laws, which currently apply only to the banking sector. However, where price signalling constitutes cartel conduct, it will be captured. The specific price signalling laws will not be discussed further as they currently have no application outside the banking sector. Outside the core competition provisions in Part IV, there are some competition provisions specific to certain industries, most notably the telecommunications industry.

[13] Part IV, Division 1 of the *Competition and Consumer Act 2010* (Cth). This incorporates price fixing, output restrictions, allocation of customers, suppliers or territories and bid rigging. This conduct is both a criminal offense and subject to civil penalties. Certain joint venture activity is excluded from the scope of the *per se* prohibition but remains subject to the general prohibition against anti-competitive agreements in s 45.

[14] In Australia, these are referred to as 'exclusionary provisions' and are *per se* prohibited where they involve an agreement between competitors having the purpose of preventing, restricting or limiting supply or acquisition to defined persons or classes of persons: sections 45 and 4D of the CCA. Joint ventures benefit from a limited competition defense: section 76C of the CCA.

[15] Sections 47(6) and 47(7) of the CCA prohibit third line forcing as a type of exclusive dealing. It occurs when supply is made on the condition that goods or services are purchased from an unrelated third party (or there is a refusal to supply because of failure to agree to such a condition). Unlike other forms of exclusive dealing, it is *per se* prohibited, but it is possible for the conduct to

– minimum resale price maintenance (including vertical price fixing).[16]

Since 2009, the cartel provisions of the Act have been subject to criminal penalties, including up to 10 years of imprisonment, as well as to civil penalties and sanctions. To date, there have been no criminal prosecutions in relation to cartel conduct. Although *per se* prohibited, all of these forms of conduct may be authorised, in advance,[17] if the parties can demonstrate that there are public benefits arising from the conduct that would outweigh the likely anti-competitive detriment. In practice, third line forcing conduct involving supermarkets regularly benefits from immunity on public benefit grounds,[18] and collective bargaining arrangements by small business groups in relation to their dealings with supermarkets, which would otherwise contravene the strict cartel laws, have benefitted from this immunity in a number of cases.[19]

In addition, various forms of conduct are prohibited where it can be demonstrated that they had either the purpose or likely effect of substantially lessening competition:

– anti-competitive agreements (this overlaps with cartel conduct),[20]
– exclusive dealing (for example, product bundling),[21]
– mergers.[22]

As with conduct that is prohibited *per se*, it is possible to seek authorisation, in advance, for all of these forms of conduct on public benefit grounds.[23]

be 'notified' and receive immunity on public benefit grounds. This immunity process has been widely utilised in the grocery industry and is discussed further below.

[16] Sections 4 and 48 and Part VIII of the CCA; see Sect. 2.6.

[17] It is not possible for conduct to be retrospectively authorised; approval must be provided in advance of the conduct occurring, or it will contravene the Act notwithstanding any demonstrated public benefits.

[18] This will be discussed further below.

[19] See, for example, Australian Dairy Farmers Ltd (A91263, 8 March 2011), in which Australian Dairy Farmers Ltd was granted authorisation by the ACCC to enable dairy farmers to collectively bargain terms and conditions of milk supply contracts with processors: http://transition.accc.gov.au/content/index.phtml/itemId/977053/fromItemId/401858.

[20] Section 45 of the CCA. There must be a 'contract, arrangement or understanding' between two or more parties. This largely excludes tacit collusion from the prohibition.

[21] Section 47 of the CCA.

[22] Section 50 of the CCA. Unlike anti-competitive agreements and exclusive dealing, it is not sufficient for merger to have the 'purpose' of substantially lessening competition—they must have this effect (or likely effect).

[23] Immunity on public benefit grounds is also possible through Australia 'notification' process for exclusive dealing and for small business collective bargaining.

Australia's competition laws also prohibit the misuse of market power. This now takes two forms.[24] The first is a general prohibition against a corporation with substantial market power taking advantage of that power for a prohibited purpose, including eliminating or substantially damaging a competitor, preventing entry or deterring or preventing a person from engaging in competitive conduct.[25] The second is a specific prohibition against predatory pricing. It applies where a company with substantial market share supplies, or offers to supply, goods or services for a sustained period at a below-cost price for a prohibited purpose.[26] The predatory pricing provision was introduced in 2007 and remains controversial. It was driven largely by concerns of low-cost pricing in the grocery market destroying small business.[27]

Australia has adopted unit pricing laws specifically targeting supermarkets.[28] This was introduced, in part, to promote competition between supermarkets by ensuring that consumers are able to make informed choices. The unit pricing laws take the form of a mandatory industry code under the CCA.[29] This Code applies to grocery retailers with more than 1,000 m^2 of floor space and that sell a minimum range of food based groceries. The Code also applies to online grocers. Once a retailer falls under the Code, all grocery items must have a unit price displayed unless the item is exempt (for example, bundled items). The unit price must be prominent, close to the selling price, legible and unambiguous and must be displayed in dollars and cents. The ACCC is responsible for providing guidance on the Code and taking enforcement action where appropriate.

In addition, a supermarket and grocery industry working group, which includes the major supermarket chains, the Australian Food and Grocery Council, National Farmers Federation and the ACCC, is in the process of negotiating an industry code that would be enforceable under the *Competition and Consumer Act*. On November

---

[24] Both of these forms of conduct are discussed in more detail below.

[25] Section 46(1) of the *Competition and Consumer Act 2010* (Cth).

[26] Section 46(1AA) of the *Competition and Consumer Act 2010* (Cth). The prohibited purposes are the same as for the more general prohibition.

[27] See, for example, second reading speech of Senator Barnaby Joyce, who was responsible for the introduction of the bill into Parliament and who said, in part, that 'A big liquor distributor attached to a big supermarket cannot drop the price of a case of beer to a level that puts out of business every bottle shop in town' (Senate Hansard, Trade Practices Legislation Amendment Bill (No 1) 2007, Second Reading Speech, Tuesday 11 September 2007, pp. 91–93, http://parlinfo.aph.gov.au/parlInfo/search/display/display.w3p;query=Id%3A%22chamber%2Fhansards%2F2007-09-11%2F0146%22).

[28] The Unit Pricing Laws were proposed as part of the Australian Competition and Consumer Commission's review of the Supermarket Industry: ACCC 'Report of the ACCC Inquiry into the Competitiveness of Retail Prices for Standard Groceries' (2008) at xxiii and from p. 445. See also the Hon Chris Bowen MP (2008), 'Rudd Government releases its preliminary action plan in response to the ACCC's Grocery inquiry', Media Release No 065, 5 August 2008 (http://www.treasurer.gov.au/DisplayDocs.aspx?doc=pressreleases/2008/065.htm&pageID=003&min=ceb&Year=&DocType=0).

[29] The code is contained in *Trade Practices (Industry Codes – Unit Pricing) Regulations 2009*.

2013, they drafted an industry code of conduct: the Food and Grocery Prescribed Industry Code of Conduct. Although this code may assist in improving relationships between the major retailers and their suppliers and provide a more effective dispute resolution forum, it would not involve additional competition law prohibitions.

There are no specific national laws aimed at controlling the structure of the grocery retail market outside competition laws. However, some state, territory and local planning and zoning laws may impact on local structures by restricting the ability of the major supermarkets to obtain leases or zoning approvals. Until May 2013, the Australian Capital Territory operated a *Supermarket Competition Policy*,[30] which aimed to achieve a competitive and diverse supermarket sector, principally through strict and selective application of zoning laws.[31] This policy has now been abandoned.

Following concerns identified by the ACCC in its 2008 Grocery Report about restrictive leasing provisions, the major supermarket chains voluntarily provided court enforceable undertakings to the ACCC to the effect that they and their subsidiaries will not give or threaten to give effect to a restrictive provision in an existing lease after a 5-year period from its commencement and that they will not enter into a future lease including one or more restrictive provisions.[32]

General consumer protection laws also apply to the grocery sector and prohibit, for example, unfair terms in consumer contracts, unconscionable dealing (including with other business), misleading conduct and false advertising.[33] These are based on principles of fair dealing and, to a degree, in correcting asymmetry of bargaining power. They are not designed to prevent inflationary pressure of grocery retail prices or other principles.

[30] This was introduced in 2008 and is directed primarily to planning and zoning issues that impact on the ability of supermarkets to establish new stores or lease in certain locations. It was reviewed in 2009 by John Martin (Martin, J., 2009, 'Review of ACT Supermarket Competition Policy', Martin Stone Pty Ltd for the ACT Government, Canberra, Australia). For criticism of the policy, see Tim Wilson, 'Forcing prices up: The impact of the ACT government's supermarkets policy and implementation' (Institute of Public Affairs, June 2010), who argues that the ACT's zoning laws effectively impost a 'market share cap by stealth' (p. 2).

[31] See, e.g., Productivity Commission, Economic Structure and Performance of the Australian Retail Industry (2011) p. 243 (http://www.pc.gov.au/__data/assets/pdf_file/0004/113773/11-retail-industry-chapter8.pdf).

[32] 'Undertaking to the Australian Competition and Consumer Commission given for the purposes of section 87B by Coles Group Limited' (17 September 2009; http://registers.accc.gov.au/content/index.phtml/itemId/893471) and 'Undertaking to the Australian Competition and Consumer Commission given for the purposes of section 87B by Woolworths Limited' (17 September 2009; http://registers.accc.gov.au/content/index.phtml/itemId/893470). See also ACCC, 'Supermarket agreement opens way for more competition' (18 September 2009; http://www.accc.gov.au/media-release/supermarket-agreement-opens-way-for-more-competition).

[33] These are contained in the Australian Consumer Law, which forms part of the CCA.

2.2.2 Exemptions

The retail sector is not exempted in part or in full from competition law. It is possible for the grocery sector (as with any sector) to seek approval to engage in activity that would otherwise contravene the competition provisions. Broadly, approval to engage in conduct may be granted by the ACCC[34] (or, in the case of merger, the Australian Competition Tribunal) where it can be demonstrated that there is a likely public benefit that will outweigh any likely anti-competitive detriment. For example, in some cases, supermarkets have been permitted to agree on fees to charge for plastic bags on the basis that there is a public benefit associated with reducing landfill waste.[35] These exemptions take one of two forms: an 'authorisation' or a 'notification' of the relevant conduct.

Authorisation provides a mechanism by which a party proposing to engage in conduct that will or may contravene the competition law provisions can receive immunity, on public benefit grounds, against action under the Act.[36] It is available only in relation to proposed conduct; there is no ability to authorise conduct that has already occurred.[37] It is also provided on a case-by-case basis; there is no facility for 'block' authorisation of certain forms of conduct. The precise public benefit test varies slightly depending on the conduct involved, but in practice the tests will be applied in a similar way.[38] For cartels, anti-competitive agreements and exclusive dealing (other than third line forcing), the test is whether the public benefit outweighs anti-competitive detriment associated with the conduct.[39] For all other forms of conduct (exclusionary provisions, third line forcing, resale price maintenance and mergers), the test is whether the proposed conduct would result in such a benefit to the public that it should be allowed to take place.[40]

The *notification* process is a faster, cheaper[41] and simpler way for obtaining immunity, which is available for a limited range of conduct. Until recently, only exclusive dealing conduct could be notified. It is now also possible for small

[34] Section 88 of the CCA.

[35] See, for example, ACCC Press Release MR227/08, 'ACCC issues final decision on plastic bag charge trial' (13 August 2008).

[36] Currently, there is a fee of AUD 7,500 attached to authorisation applications, but the ACCC has the discretion to waive, in whole or part, the lodgment fee in some cases. A streamlined process is available in some cases (ACCC), Streamlined collective bargaining for small business (2011). See https://www.accc.gov.au/publications/streamlined-collective-bargaining-for-small-business-2011.

[37] See, for example, comments of the Australian Competition Tribunal in *Re John Dee (Export) Pty Ltd* (1989), ATPR 40-938 at 50, 209.

[38] See, for example, *The Locksmiths Case* (1980) ATPR 40-176 at 42, 431.

[39] Section 90, subsections (5A), (5B), (6) and (7).

[40] Section 90(8) and section 95AZH.

[41] Fees vary depending on the conduct. For collective bargaining notification, the fee is currently AUD 1,000. For exclusive dealing conduct other than third line forcing, the fee is AUD 2,500. For third line forcing, the fee is AUD 100.

businesses to notify collective bargaining conduct.[42] Once notified, immunity will apply immediately in the case of exclusive dealing (other than third line forcing) or after 14 calendar days for third line forcing and collective bargaining notifications, unless the ACCC objects within that time.[43] The ACCC can only remove immunity if it is satisfied that the public benefit will not outweigh the potential detriment associated with the conduct.[44]

There are a large number of exclusive dealing notifications involving supermarkets, primarily relating to the offering of discounts conditional on purchases made elsewhere. For example, the ACCC has, in the past, permitted the major supermarkets to engage in exclusive dealing in the form of offering petrol discounts contingent on purchasing a certain amount of groceries from their supermarkets.[45] These are generally referred to as 'shopper docket' schemes. In a 2004 Report, the ACCC observed that it considered that there were significant benefits to consumers from shopper docket petrol discount schemes, in particular, lower petrol prices and increased non-price competition.[46] Subsequently, a 2007 Petrol Report[47] also found that the schemes benefited consumers and promoted competition, observing that there had been over 600 notifications received by the ACCC since 2004 (to 30 September 2007), although not all of these involve the major supermarkets. The 2007 Report acknowledged, however, that 'most industry participants consider that the introduction of shopper docket arrangements has made it harder for small independents with low volume sites to compete'.[48]

Coles and Woolworths combined now account for approximately 50 % of national petrol sales, and there has been a recent revival of concerns about the impact of shopper docket schemes involving fuel discounts and the major supermarket chains. The ACCC commenced an investigation 'into the effects of shopper docket discounting schemes on competition and long term consumer welfare' in the middle of 2012. This investigation culminated in both Coles and Woolworths providing the ACCC with enforceable undertakings pursuant to which they each agreed not to make fuel savings offers that were funded by any part of their business other than their fuel retailing business and to limit discounts linked to supermarket

[42] See Sect. 2.8.3.

[43] Section 93AD of the CCA.

[44] Section 93AC of the CCA.

[45] For example, in 2007, a notification by Caltex Roadhouse Manjimup to offer petrol and other fuel at discounted prices on the condition that the offeree had purchased products above a minimum value from Woolworths was allowed to stand (Notifications N92824 and N92825).

[46] 'Assessing shopper docket petrol discounts and acquisitions in the petrol and grocery sectors' (February 2004) p. 3 (https://www.accc.gov.au/system/files/Shopper%20Docket%20Petrol%20Discounts.pdf).

[47] ACCC, 'Petrol Prices and Australian Consumers: Report of the ACCC inquiry into the price of unleaded petrol' (December 2007).

[48] ACCC, 'Petrol Prices and Australian Consumers: Report of the ACCC inquiry into the price of unleaded petrol' (December 2007) p. 193.

purchases to a maximum of 4 cents per litre.[49] Despite these controversial undertakings,[50] concerns about the impact of shopper docket schemes continue.

2.3 Advocacy

The Commonwealth has undertaken investigations into the grocery retail market on a number of occasions, indicating that this market has raised a number of concerns,[51] with the most extensive report being published in 1999.[52] In 2008, the ACCC held a public enquiry 'into the competitiveness of retail prices for standard groceries' as required by the Minister for Competition Policy and Consumer Affairs under s 95H of Part VIIA of the CCA. This was followed by a report published by the ACCC on July 2008.[53] The main issue analysed and the primary reason for this enquiry was increased grocery prices and the extent to which a lack of competition had contributed to this phenomenon.[54]

The report analysed the grocery market, excluding products not essential for households such as liquor, stationary and cigarettes, and the causes for food price increases in the Australian grocery market at the time. It surveyed the competitive process, focusing on the bargaining power of the two main, vertically integrated retailers, Woolworths and Coles, and Metcash, the major wholesaler of the independent retailers.

The ACCC found that the grocery market was competitive; however, this competition was limited by high barriers to entry and a market structure where the two major retailers shared significant market power. Moreover, Coles,

[49] ACCC, 'Coles and Woolworths undertake to cease supermarket subsidised fuel discounts' (Press release, 6 December 2013, http://www.accc.gov.au/media-release/coles-and-woolworths-undertake-to-cease-supermarket-subsidised-fuel-discounts). See also ACCC, 'Monitoring of the Australian petroleum industry: Report of the ACCC into the prices, costs and profits of unleaded petrol in Australia' (December 2012) p. 34 and Blair Speedy, 'ACCC eyes clamp on shopper-docket petrol discounts' (The Australian, 18 July 2012), at http://www.theaustralian.com.au/business/accc-eyes-clamp-on-shopper-docket-petrol-discounts/story-e6frg8zx-1226428580787.

[50] See, for example, Rachel Trindade, Alexandra Merrett and Rhonda Smith, '2013: the year of waiting patiently' (*The State of Competition*, Issue 15 (Dec 2013), http://gallery.mailchimp.com/a19845714e72d615771c64903/files/TSoC_Issue_15_2013_Review_.pdf).

[51] See the discussion below; see, for instance, ACCC, 'Additional Budget Estimates: ACCC Statement' (Parliament of Australia, Senate Committees, 13 February 2013, Tabled Document No. 6), pp. 1–3, available at http://www.aph.gov.au/Parliamentary_Business/Committees/Senate_Committees?url=economics_ctte/estimates/add_1213/index.htm.

[52] The Parliament of the Commonwealth of Australia, 'Report of the Joint Select Committee on the Retailing Sector, Fair Market or Market Failure' (Commonwealth of Australia, August 1999, ISBN 0 642 71025 2).

[53] Australian Competition and Consumer Commission, *Report of the ACCC inquiry into the competitiveness of retail prices for standard groceries* (July 2008, Commonwealth of Australia).

[54] Ibid, xiii.

Woolworths and Metcash had significant buyer power in the packaged grocery market; however, its benefits were partially shared with consumers.[55]

The report concluded that, although the grocery market and its vertical chain included several factors limiting competition, these competitive imperfections played only a secondary role in the increased grocery prices. The increased consumer prices were significantly influenced by such factors as natural disasters and the increased cost of production reflecting an increased cost of inputs, including the price of petrol and fertilisers.[56] Furthermore, price competition had improved since ALDI entered the Australian market. The price competition among the two main retailers was at its most intense in the market with products that consumers determine as key products to assess values.[57]

The ACCC recommended, among other things, that the government carefully considers space for supermarkets in planning applications, where appropriate, to attract supermarket operators not currently trading in the relevant geographical markets.[58] It also recommended unit pricing (displaying the price by unit of measure) as a mandatory standard for the 'significant supermarket stores' in Australia.[59]

2.4 Merger Control and Grocery Retail Networks

2.4.1 Merger Control

Australia's competition laws contain a general prohibition on mergers that have the effect of substantially lessening competition.[60] It applies equally to all industries; there are currently no special thresholds for merger control in the retail sector. Australia operates a voluntary pre-merger notification system. Coles and Woolworths are, however, both signatories to the voluntary *Produce and Grocery Industry Code of Conduct*, which states that industry participants will notify the ACCC of acquisitions[61] and, in practice, they do so in the vast majority of cases.

[55] Ibid, xiv–xv, xvii, xx–xxi.

[56] Ibid, xiv–xvi, xiv.

[57] Ibid, xiv, xvi.

[58] Ibid, xix (see also Sect. 2.2.1).

[59] Ibid, xxiii–xxiv; this resulted in a code of conduct, Trade Practices (Industry Codes—Unit Pricing) Regulations 2009, Select Legislative Instrument 2009 No. 152, as discussed in Sects. 2.2.1 and 2.8.

[60] Section 50 of the CCA.

[61] Produce and Grocery Industry Code of Conduct (December 2007) clause 8 (www.produceandgrocerycode.com.au/). The parties typically abide by this undertaking, although the ACCC has observed a small number of cases in which notification has not occurred: ACCC, *Report of the ACCC inquiry into the competitiveness of retail prices for standard groceries* (July 2008) p. 427.

Concerns about the level of concentration in the grocery market have led some politicians to call for limits on the extent to which the major grocery chains should be permitted to merge, beyond the existing competition test in the CCA.[62] To date, however, no such modifications to the merger laws have been made.

2.4.2 Local Mergers and Market Definition

The ACCC is responsible for controlling mergers at both local and national levels. Until recently, there was some legislative uncertainty about the extent to which a market, for the purposes of merger analysis, could be defined as a local market. This was because legislation defined market, for purposes of the merger provision, as a 'substantial market' for goods or services in Australia or a state, territory or region of Australia. Although the ACCC had always taken the view that small geographic market could be a 'substantial market' for purposes of this definition,[63] concern that a court might, in future, interpret the word 'substantial' as excluding 'local' markets led to the passage of the *Competition and Consumer Legislation Amendment Act 2011* (Act 184 of 2011). This removed the word substantial with the result that 'market' is now defined in s 50(6), for purposes of the merger provision, as 'a market for goods or services in (a) Australia; or (b) a State; or (c) a Territory; or (d) a region of Australia'.[64] It was clear that Parliament was principally concerned about the ACCC's ability to assess local supermarket acquisitions when passing this legislation.

However, as the ACCC had already taken the view that it could capture these mergers, this change has brought some legislative clarity but otherwise has not altered existing practice.[65]

In addition to the market definition contained in s 50(6) of the CCA, s 4E of the CCA states:

> For the purposes of this Act, unless the contrary intention appears, ***market*** means a market in Australia and, when used in relation to any goods or services, includes a market for those goods or services and other goods or services that are substitutable for, or otherwise competitive with, the first-mentioned goods or services.

---

[62] See, for example, the private member's bill, *Trade Practices Amendment (Material Lessening of Competition – Richmond Amendment) Bill 2009*, which failed to pass through Parliament. See also Senate Standing Committee on Economics, Inquiry into Trade Practices Amendment (Material Lessening of Competition – Richmond Amendment) Bill 2009.

[63] ACCC, *Merger Guidelines* (2008), para's 4.29–4.30. See also ACCC, *Report of the ACCC inquiry into the competitiveness of retail prices for standard groceries* (July 2008) pp. 425–426 and ACCC, 'Statement of Issues—Woolworths Limited – proposed acquisition of the Karabar Supabarn supermarket' (4 June 2008), para 25.

[64] Section 50(6) of the CCA.

[65] See also Woolworths Limited – proposed acquisition of the Hawker Supa IGA (ACCC, Statement of Issues, 6 December 2012).

The clear focus has, therefore, been on substitutability for purposes of defining the scope of product and service markets. In applying this test, reference is frequently made to the Trade Practices Tribunal's decision in *Re Queensland Co-Op Milling Association Limited and Defiance Holdings Limited*,[66] in which the Tribunal defined market as 'the area of close competition between firms' or the 'field of rivalry between them', determined by reference to the substitution that occurs in response to changing prices, and further stated that the market 'is the field of actual and potential transactions between buyers and sellers amongst whom there can be strong substitution, at least in the long run, if given a sufficient price incentive . . .'.[67]

The current ACCC's 2008 *Merger Guidelines* reflect this view, noting that, in defining the market, the ACCC begins by 'selecting a product supplied by one or both of the merger parties in a particular geographic area and incrementally broadening the market to include the next closest substitute until all close substitutes . . . are included'.[68] When making this determination, the ACCC applies the hypothetical monopolist test (HMT) and assesses the exercise of market power by the hypothetical monopolist utilising the small but significant and non-transitory increase in price SSNIP test.[69] The ACCC's Merger Guidelines provide that an SSNIP 'usually consists of a price rise for the foreseeable future of at least 5 % above the price level that would prevail without the merger'.[70] Acknowledging the onerous data requirements required for the HMT, the ACCC notes that it is 'rarely strictly applied to factual circumstances',[71] with the ACCC generally taking a qualitative approach to market definition, using the HMT as an 'intellectual aid to focus the exercise'.[72]

The issue of market definition in the grocery sector has been a difficult one, particularly because of the level of vertical integration. At times markets have been confined to a single functional level, and at other times the Court has taken a broader view and considered both wholesale and retail activity to be in the same market because of the extent to which one constrains the other where there is extensive vertical integration.

For example, in *QIW Retailers Ltd v Davids Holdings*,[73] involving a proposed merger between two existing wholesalers of grocery products to independent retailers, the Court rejected the argument that there was no difference between the wholesale and retail *functional* level in this market, instead finding that the

---

[66] *Re Queensland Co-Op Milling Association Limited and Defiance Holdings Limited* (QCMA) (1976) 8 ALR 481.

[67] Ibid, p. 518.

[68] ACCC, *Merger Guidelines* (2008), para 4.12.

[69] Ibid, para 4.19.

[70] Ibid, para 4.21.

[71] Ibid, para 4.22.

[72] Ibid.

[73] *QIW Retailers Ltd v Davids Holdings* (1993) 42 FCR 255.

relevant market was the market 'for the supply of grocery products by independent wholesalers to independent retailers in Queensland and northern New South Wales'.[74] This approach was accepted on appeal to the Full Federal Court.[75] However, the difficult nature of market definition where key participants are vertically integrated was reflected in the economic evidence. Some of the experts argued that there should not be a distinction between wholesale and retail levels of distribution, while others considered they should be separate and, in this case, confined to wholesaling.[76]

More recently, the Federal Court in *Metcash*[77] rejected a narrow and functionally limited market definition. This case involved a proposed acquisition by Metcash Trading Limited (Metcash) of several Franklins stores. Metcash is Australia's largest wholesale supplier to independent retailers and also operates some stores at the retail level. Franklins operated a number of retail stores and also supplied wholesale groceries, both to its own retail stores and to Franklins franchise stores. The Court found, however, that it was 'essentially a supermarket retailing business'.[78]

The ACCC had argued that the relevant market for purposes of assessing the acquisition was the 'Independent Wholesale Grocery Market' in New South Wales and the Australian Capital Territory. This definition was rejected by the Court, which stated that in applying the HMT test 'it is unrealistic to speak in terms of an increase in the margin added on by wholesalers to their cost of acquiring goods from manufacturers and primary suppliers. It is meaningful ... only to speak in terms of an increase in the price charged by wholesalers to their customers, the retailers'.[79] Once that is accepted, it becomes clear that the position of the major supermarkets is such that they provide a 'very significant constraint on the capacity of independent retailers to increase price or decrease other services without the likely loss of business', which also 'constrains the capacity of the wholesaler to increase its prices to independent retailers'.[80]

In terms of store sizes, Justice Emmett in *Metcash* placed stores in three categories: supermarkets, with a floor space exceeding 1,200 m^2; 'top-up stores', which are smaller and have a less diverse product range; and 'convenience stores' of less than 350 m^2.[81] It was not necessary for the Court in Metcash to reach a concluded view about whether all three categories of store were in the same market, though it was clear that at least in some respects the smaller stores, including

[74] Ibid, per Justice Spender (para 292).

[75] *Davids Holdings v Attorney-General and QIW* (1994) 49 FCR 211.

[76] *Davids Holdings v Attorney-General and QIW* (1994) 49 FCR 211 paras 63–64.

[77] *ACCC v Metcash Trading Limited* [2011] FCA 967 and, on appeal in *ACCC v Metcash Trading* [2011] FCAFC 151.

[78] *ACCC v Metcash Trading Limited* [2011] FCA 967 per Justice Emmett at first instance.

[79] Ibid, [340] per Justice Emmett at first instance.

[80] Ibid.

[81] Ibid, para 9.

convenience stores, saw themselves in competition with the major supermarkets and looked for non-price mechanisms to remain competitive with them.[82] In a recent Statement of Issues for a proposed supermarket merger, the ACCC posited a local supermarket market as including smaller format independent supermarkets.[83] Regardless of whether smaller operators are included in the market definition, any competitive constraint they impose will be considered in the necessary competition analysis.[84]

Online grocery retail activity is subject to the same laws as brick and mortar food retail stores. However, the issue of whether online grocery sales fall share the same market as brick and mortar stores has not arisen as a decisive issue in Australia to date. This is largely because Australia has not embraced online grocery shopping to any significant extent so that it currently does not make up an important part of the retail grocery sector in Australia.[85] The issue has, however, been considered in the context of the liquor acquisitions involving supermarkets. In 2011, the ACCC announced that it would not oppose Woolworths' proposed acquisition of the Cellarmasters Group (Cellarmasters). Cellarmasters is a 'direct to home' wine retailer and provides contract bottling and wine making services. It sells online and via catalogues and has no bricks and mortar outlets. By contrast, until 2011, Woolworths sold liquor almost exclusively through bricks and mortar; on 8 March 2011, Dan Murphys, which is part of Woolworths' Liquor Group, began selling liquor online. As part of its assessment of the acquisition,[86] the ACCC considered whether bricks and mortar retailers and online/direct retailers were close substitutes. The ACCC observed that it received conflicting information on the issue[87] but concluded that while there was some substitution between them, 'bricks and mortar and online/direct retailers were not *close* substitutes'.[88]

2.4.3 Merger Remedies

The ACCC has the power to accept 'court enforceable undertakings' from parties proposing to merge that are designed to alleviate any competition concerns.[89] The

---

[82] *ACCC v Metcash Trading* [2011] FCAFC 151 para 350 per Justice Yates.

[83] Woolworths Limited – proposed acquisition of the Hawker Supa IGA (ACCC, Statement of Issues, 6 December 2012) para 41.

[84] Woolworths Limited – proposed acquisition of the Hawker Supa IGA (ACCC, Statement of Issues, 6 December 2012) para 45, observing that the target of the proposed Woolworths acquisition was the 'only full-line independent supermarket in the local market' as distinct from 'smaller format independent supermarkets'.

[85] See Sect. 2.8.2.

[86] Woolworths Limited – proposed acquisition of The Cellarmasters Group (ACCC, Public Competition Assessment, 27 May 2011).

[87] Ibid, para 23.

[88] Ibid, para 24. The ACCC did not, however, find it necessary to reach a concluded view on the issue, as the outcome would have been the same on either approach to market definition.

[89] Section 87B of the CCA.

ACCC does not have the power to 'impose' remedies on parties. Where competition issues arise, the ACCC has expressed a strong preference for structural remedies.[90] Mergers in the retail sector involving major supermarkets generally take the form of single acquisitions, and where opposed, they tend to be opposed outright, so the issue of remedies does not arise.[91]

The issue has, however, arisen in a limited number of cases where a significant number of stores have exited the relevant market at one time. For example, in 2001, Dairy Farm Management Services Limited, through its then subsidiary Franklins, proposed to undertake a managed exit from grocery retailing in Australia and to sell nearly 300 stores. It was proposed that some of these would be sold to Coles and Woolworths. The ACCC expressed concern that the acquisition of a substantial number of these stores by the major supermarkets, in cases where they might otherwise be acquired by independent operators, might substantially lessen competition in contravention of the CCA. To address these concerns, the sellers provided an enforceable undertaking to the ACCC not to sell Franklins stores to Woolworths or Coles other than those specifically identified in the undertaking or in cases where the ACCC provided prior consent.[92]

There have not been any instances of concluded mergers that have subsequently been challenged by the ACCC or of cases in which remedies have been imposed by the courts in the food sector in the last 5 years.

2.4.4 Grocery Retail Networks

Grocery retail networks have not been considered problematic in Australia. For instance, the Australian National Retailers Association (the 'ANRA'), which represents the country's leading retailers, has not been officially investigated in connection with anti-competitive practices. The two main retail corporations, Woolworths and Coles, have not established a formal network. Although IGA and FoodWorks form two networks of independently owned supermarkets, this is not recognised as problematic due to their low market share of 15 %. On the contrary, such cooperatives can enhance rather than restrict competition in the market as the networks of small independent retail stores are better placed to compete with the two major supermarket chains than conducting their business on their own.

Grocery retail networks, such as franchising and cooperatives, are not directly regulated in Australia. However, franchising systems, which could potentially

[90] ACCC, *Merger Guidelines* (2008) p. 63, para 11.

[91] See ACCC, *Report of the ACCC inquiry into the competitiveness of retail prices for standard groceries* (July 2008) Appendix F, p. 499.

[92] 'Undertakings to the Australian Competition and Consumer Commission pursuant to section 87B of the *Trade Practices Act 1974* by Dairy Farm Management Services Limited and Franklins Limited' (5 June 2001) (http://registers.accc.gov.au/content/index.phtml/itemId/331575).

include any grocery retail franchising, are regulated by a mandatory Code of Conduct under Part IVB of the CCA, giving the ACCC the power to investigate and observe their compliance.[93] The ACCC considers this Code to be effective, with its major strengths being the receipt of pertinent information prior to potential franchisees making decisions and requiring parties to undertake certain steps to resolve any potential disputes.[94]

2.5 Abuse of Power

2.5.1 Abuse of Buying Power, Abuse of Dependency

The Competition and Consumer Act 2010 (Cth) prohibits the misuse of market power in s 46.[95] The general clause on a misuse of market power, s 46(1), provides:

> A corporation that has a substantial degree of power in a market shall not take advantage of that power in that or any other market for the purpose of:
> (a) eliminating or substantially damaging a competitor of the corporation or of a body corporate that is related to the corporation in that or any other market;
> (b) preventing the entry of a person into that or any other market; or
> (c) deterring or preventing a person from engaging in competitive conduct in that or any other market.

It follows from this provision that three conditions must be satisfied to prove a misuse of market power. Firstly, the corporation must have substantial power, including both horizontal market power and buying power, as will be explained below. Secondly, the corporation in question must take advantage of this power. Lastly, it must take advantage of its power for one of three anti-competitive purposes, as stated in s 46(1)(a), (b) and (c).

Misuses of market power that occur on the vertical chain are included under s 46 (1)(b) and (c). Section 46 subsection(4)(c) expressly refers to buying and selling power as it provides that for the purposes of a misuse of market power under s 46, any reference to 'power' includes 'a reference to power, or to conduct, in that market either as a supplier or as an acquirer of goods or services in that market'. Furthermore, buying and selling power must be considered when determining the degree of power that the person concerned has, as stated in s 46(3)(b). Therefore, usage of the term 'power' for the purposes of misuse of market power also includes buying power, as stated above.

---

[93] *Trade Practices (Industry Codes—Franchising) Regulations 1998*, Statutory Rules 1998 No. 162 as amended made under the *Trade Practices Act 1974*.

[94] ACCC, Chairman, Graeme Samuel, 'Franchising' (excerpt from speech to Australia–Israel, Chamber of Commerce Brisbane, 24 February, 2005) p. 1 at http://www.accc.gov.au/system/files/20050224%20AICC%20Franchising%20insert.pdf.

[95] The CCA uses the term 'misuse' and not 'abuse' of market power. Therefore, this chapter uses 'misuse of market power', which has the same meaning as 'abuse of market power'.

The definition of 'buying power' is not provided in the CCA. Nevertheless, in the case of *Safeway*,[96] the Full Court of the Federal Court of Australia made reference to monopsony power and stated that buying power can be determined by a firm's ability to secure more favourable terms of purchase than competing buyers, including the best prices from its suppliers.[97] For s 46(1) to be contravened, a firm does not have to be absolute or almost monopsonist; it is enough for it to have a substantial degree of buying power. Therefore, it must be able to substantially control a market. To determine buying power and its significance, it must be shown whether, and to what extent, a firm is constrained by its competitors and potential competitors and by its suppliers and customers. Therefore, the number of competitors, their strength and size and the barriers to entry must be taken into account.[98]

Subsections 46(1) and 46(6A) explain what constitutes a misuse of power that includes buying power. This has three aspects, as follows from s 46(1) and as noted above. Firstly, a person[99] must have a substantial degree of power, which can be buying power, in a market. Secondly, it takes advantage of its buying power in that or any other market. Thirdly, the advantage is taken for at least one of three purposes where the second and the third purposes would apply to buying power or dependency. That is, the purpose of 'preventing the entry of a person into that or any other market; or deterring or preventing a person from engaging in competitive conduct in that or any other market'.[100]

Section 46(6A) provides a number of tests that courts can apply to assist in determining whether the person concerned took advantage of their power for one of the prescribed anti-competitive purposes.[101]Section 46(6A) was implemented in 2008.[102] Prior to the implementation of this provision, the courts had focused on the

[96] *ACCC v Australian Safeway Stores Pty Ltd* (2003) 129 FCR 339.

[97] Ibid, at [300].

[98] Ibid, at [301]–[302].

[99] This mainly applies to corporations.

[100] Section 46 subsections (1)(b) and (c).

[101] Under s 46(6A), the court may consider the following:

(a) Whether the conduct was materially facilitated by the corporation's substantial degree of power in the market;
(b) Whether the corporation engaged in the conduct relied on its substantial degree of power in the market;
(c) Whether it is likely that the corporation would have engaged in the conduct if it did not have a substantial degree of power in the market;
(d) Whether the conduct is otherwise related to the corporation's substantial degree of power in the market.

[102] See *Trade Practices Legislation Amendment Act 2008*.

counterfactual test, asking whether the corporation concerned would have acted in the same way if it operated in a more competitive environment.[103] Despite the introduction of s 46(6A), it is not anticipated that it will have any significant impact on the way the courts assess the 'take advantage' requirement in s 46.[104]

Cases based on claims of misuse of buying power are not common in Australia. Recently, on February 2013, the ACCC publicly expressed the view that the buying power held by the major supermarket chains is an important matter that has been investigated by the ACCC in connection with the misuse of this buying power.[105] Nevertheless, a case dealing with the major supermarket chains' misuse of buying power has not been officially lodged yet.

The Australian Federal Court has dealt with two cases where buyer power contributed or caused the misuse of market power. The older case, *Carlton United Breweries*,[106] dealt with the combination of the abuse of horizontal market power and buying power to stop competitor's activities. The case of *Safeway*[107] involved a claim of the misuse of buying power.

Safeway was the largest supermarket chain and the largest bread retailer in Victoria. The relevant market for *Safeway* was 'for the sale and acquisition of bread by wholesale in Victoria'.[108] Safeway's conduct, which was based on refusing to acquire bread from a supplier if the supplier was selling bread for less to another buyer, resulted in a misuse of buyer power. The Court explained that despite the fact that Safeway was not always successful in forcing the best price policy upon its suppliers, it had substantial market/buying power because it was able to reduce the quantity sold by the plant bakers concerned. Furthermore, the existence of a low level of brand loyalty between premium bread brands supported the argument of Safeway having a substantial degree of buying power. Thus, having substantial market/buying power, it could effectively increase the pressure on plant bakers to comply with Safeway's price condition. Plant bakers were not sufficiently able to replace their supply to Safeway with a supply to another retailer(s).[109]

Safeway's refusal to buy if the supplier in question was selling for less to another retailer constituted taking advantage of Safeway's substantial buying power with

---

[103] See, e.g., *Rural Press Ltd v ACCC* [2003] HCA 75, (2003) 216 CLR 53, 78 ALJR 274, 203 ALR 217, ATPR 41-965 at [51]; *Queensland Wire Industries v BHP* (1989) 167 CLR 177, 63 ALJR 181, 83 ALR 577, ATPR 40-925 at 585 (the first High Court's judgement on s 46).

[104] See, generally, Caroline Coops, 'A fly in the ointment for the ACCC? Implications of the *Cement Australia* decision for the interpretation of section 46' (Paper presented at the *Competition Law Conference*, 24 May 2014, Sydney).

[105] See ACCC, 'Additional Budget Estimates: ACCC Statement' (Parliament of Australia, Senate Committees, 13 February 2013, Tabled Document No. 6), available at http://www.aph.gov.au/Parliamentary_Business/Committees/Senate_Committees?url=economics_ctte/estimates/add_1213/index.htm.

[106] *TPC v Carlton United Breweries Ltd* (1990) 24 FCR 532.

[107] *ACCC v Australian Safeway Stores Pty Ltd* (2003) 129 FCR 339.

[108] Ibid, at [297].

[109] Ibid, at [314]–[315], [323].

the purpose to deter suppliers from selling bread to other retailers for less. This conduct satisfies the conditions of s 46(1)(c), which prohibits taking advantage of substantial power to deter or prevent a person (in this case, both the plant bakers and the independent retailers) from engaging in competitive conduct that had a form of discounting, in other words, negotiating different wholesale prices between plant bakers and their retailers.[110]

In the case of *Carlton United Breweries*, the corporation concerned had, according to the Federal Court and the Trade Practices Commission,[111] both horizontal market power and buying power. The Court stated that the corporation had 'a substantial degree of power in the market for beer in Australia and/or its market power as an acquirer of beverages cans in the beverage can market'.[112]

Carlton United Breweries was purchasing beer cans from the producer Gadsden, which had a market share of 30 % in the can market. Its competitor, Containers, had a market share of 70 %. Gadsden's supply of beverage cans to Carlton United Breweries represented 50 % of all cans sold and produced by Gadsden. Gadsden was also selling beer cans to Payless Superbarn, which sold beer for a substantially lower price than Carlton United Breweries. Carlton United Breweries tried to stop this sale and for this reason, among others, substantially reduced its purchase of cans from Gadsden. It also lobbied its competitor to stop selling beer to Payless Superbarn, which resulted in deterring Payless Superbarn from engaging in selling and supplying cheap Payless beer. Therefore, it contravened s 46(1)(c), the Court confirming that Carlton United Breweries misused not only its horizontal market power but also its buying power.[113]

2.5.2 Monopolistic Price

High prices set by monopolists are generally legal, and there is no recent case dealing with high prices in isolation. Nevertheless, such conduct can be found illegal as a form of misuse (abuse) of market power if the conditions of s 46(1) are fulfilled.[114] Although high prices may be unwelcome to consumers, they do not constitute a form of misuse of market power, as the third condition of s 46(1), the anti-competitive purpose(s) to eliminate or restrict competitiveness of others, is not satisfied in the case of mere monopolistic pricing. This has been confirmed by the Australian courts.[115]

[110] See ibid, at [335]–[346].

[111] The Trade Practices Commission is the former ACCC.

[112] *TPC v Carlton United Breweries Ltd* (1990) 24 FCR 532, at 533.

[113] Ibid, at 534–537.

[114] For further discussion on conditions provided in s 46(1), see Sect. 2.5.1.

[115] See, e.g., *ASX Operations Pty Ltd v Pont Data Australia Pty Ltd* (No 2) (1991) 27 FCR at 502; *Pont Data Australia Pty Ltd v. ASX Operations Pty Ltd v Pont data Australia Pty Ltd* (1990) 21 FCR 385 at 419.

However, monopoly pricing charged as part of other forms of misuses of power, such as price discrimination, price squeezing or leveraging, could fall within s 46 (1) and, thus, be found anti-competitive and illegal.[116] Furthermore, the CCA includes provisions that allow for enquiring, monitoring and even 'reducing' high monopolistic prices.[117] The (former) Minister for Competition Policy and Consumer Affairs formally required the ACCC to hold a public enquiry 'into the competitiveness of retail prices for standard groceries' as discussed above. However, the report subsequently produced by the Commission did not lead to any reduction of prices.

2.6 Resale Price Maintenance and Recommended Resale Price

Resale price maintenance ('RPM') is illegal in Australia; it is prohibited by the RPM-specific provisions in the CCA. Section 4, which defines terms used in the Act, simply refers to Part VIII rather than providing an exact definition. Section 48 (which appears in Part IV of the CCA) provides that RPM is *per se* illegal. Part VIII, sections 96 to 100, sets specific rules on RPM. Part VIII, s 96(3), establishes that the *per se* prohibition only applies to price fixing and minimum price fixing but not to maximum price fixing. Prohibited RPM is based on unilateral conduct rather than multilateral/bilateral conduct. Although, it also covers any agreements with buyers, the supplier is primarily liable and, hence, is considered to force, or in other ways influence, its buyers to maintain prices.[118] Indeed, s 96 includes situations where suppliers, and not their buyers, initiate and/or force their distributors to maintain minimum or fixed prices.

Therefore, the approach to RPM in the CCA is based on a presumption that suppliers and not their buyers initiate and are thus interested in RPM. Section 96 (3) specifies that such supplier's unilateral conduct can be in the form of influencing or forcing the buyer to maintain retail prices[119] or withholding supply based on the fact (or the presumption of the supplier) that the buyer did not maintain retail price.[120]Section 96(3) also includes situations where three persons of a vertical chain are involved in RPM. The supplier would contravene s 96(3) of the CCA if it forced or influenced its buyer to sell the product to the third person (the second

[116] See *Stevens v Kaibushiki Kaisha Sony Computer Entertainment* (2005) 224 CLR 193; *ASX Operations Pty Ltd v Pont Data Australia Pty Ltd* (No 2) (1991) 27 FCR; *Pont Data Australia Pty Ltd v. ASX Operations Pty Ltd v Pont data Australia Pty Ltd* (1990) 21 FCR 385.

[117] Divisions 3, 4 and 5 of Part VIIA of the CCA.

[118] See s 96(3)(c).

[119] Section 96 subsections (3)(a), (b), (c) and (f).

[120] Section 96(3)(d).

buyer on the vertical chain) only on the condition that the second buyer maintains and/or agrees to maintain its retail price.[121]

The CCA includes only one exemption when RPM imposed by the supplier is legal, the 'loss leader defence', as specified in s 98(2).[122] Furthermore, since 1995, suppliers have been able to apply for authorisation of RPM. This authorisation can be granted by the ACCC in situations where public benefits prevail over any public detriments caused by RPM, as provided in s 88(8A) of the CCA. However, this authorisation has never been used for RPM in practice.

Although s 96(3)(b) provides that resale price maintenance can take the form of 'the supplier inducing, or attempting to induce, a second person not to sell, at a price less than a price specified by the supplier', the Full Federal Court of Australia stated in a grocery case dealing with the supply of wine, *Penfolds Wines*,[123] that a supplier's attempts to persuade its buyer to increase price does not satisfy the requirements of s 96(3) if the minimum price is not specified in any way.[124] The statement about an actual price in dollars and cents is not necessary for the price to be specified.[125] The price or the minimum price is specified if the buyer/retailer can identify the price, for instance, when the supplier states that retailers should sell its products 'somewhere near the selling price' of a particular retailer.[126]

The ruling in *Penfolds Wines* was confirmed in the grocery case of *Safeway Stores*.[127] Based on the lack of specification of minimum prices, the Court held that s 96(3) had not been contravened. Other than those listed, Australia does not have RPM cases in the grocery retail market and there is no recent Australian case that discusses recommended prices in the retail grocery sector.

The use of genuine recommended resale prices is not prohibited by the Act. Section 97, in conjunction with ss 99 and 96(3)(b), specifies the forms of legal recommended price conduct. Firstly, the price is recommended, and thus legal, if the supplier makes only a statement of a price that is applied to the goods 'by being woven in, impressed on, worked into or annexed or affixed to the goods'[128] without doing anything else. Secondly, a price is recommended if the supplier's statement applies to 'a covering, label, reel or thing in or with which goods are supplied'[129] and includes the words 'recommended price'.[130] Thirdly, any notification to the

[121] Section 96(3)(e); see also s 96(3)(d)(ii).

[122] See also *TPC v Orlane Australia Pty Ltd* (1984) 1 FCR 157.

[123] *TPC v Penfolds Wines Pty Ltd* [1992] ATPR 41-163.

[124] Ibid, first point.

[125] *Heating Centre Pty Ltd v Trade Practices Commission* (1986) ATPR 40-674; 65 ALR 429, at 432.

[126] *TPC v Bata Shoe Co of Australia Pty Ltd* (1980) ATPR 40-161 at 42262, 42266-7.

[127] *ACCC v Australian Safeway Stores Pty Ltd*, [2001] FCA 1861, (2001) 119 FCR 1, [2002] ATPR (Digest) 46-215, [1003]–[1006].

[128] Section 99(1)(a); see also s 97(a).

[129] Section 99(1)(b).

[130] Sections 97(a) and 99(1)(b).

buyer stating price, which the supplier recommends, must explicitly or by implication clarify that '[t]he price set out or referred to herein is a recommended price only and there is no obligation to comply with the recommendation'.[131] However, a price is not recommended, even if it includes the word 'recommended', if it satisfies s 96(3) by further action(s) that indicate fixing prices, as specified in the case of *Mikasa*.[132] The Australian cases of *Prestige Motors*[133] and *Commodore Business Machines*[134] provide that the conditions of 97s are not satisfied and the retail price is fixed if the buyers concerned are not allowed to advertise below a certain price (or only at a certain price) even if they can sell below (and above) the 'recommended price'.

2.7 The Relevant Case Law

The ACCC is responsible for enforcing the competition laws, including cartel laws, at both the national and the local levels, although it does not have adjudicative powers in relation to the conduct of grocery retailers. The ACCC's enforcement responsibilities would include, for example, price fixing between the only two retail food stores in a small village. In this respect, there is no *de minimis* exemption from the competition law provisions. However, the size of the market and the nature of the conduct involved will influence whether the ACCC sought to pursue the matter with criminal sanctions or only seek civil penalties and will also influence the nature and extent of any penalties imposed. Relatively small cartel agreements have been pursued by the ACCC in other markets,[135] and there is every reason to believe they would be pursued vigorously should they arise in the grocery sector.

There has only been one competition law case involving grocery retailers before the courts in the past 5 years. That was the merger case involving Metcash, discussed above, in which the ACCC sought an injunction to prevent Metcash from acquiring Franklins stores. The ACCC argued for a narrow market definition, which was rejected by the trial judge and, on appeal, by the Full bench of the Federal Court of Australia. Once the ACCC's market definition was rejected, the case failed and a number of matters regarding merger analysis were left unresolved. Importantly, however, the Court did find that the major vertically integrated retailers operated as a constraint to Metcash's wholesale operations.[136]

[131] Section 97(b).

[132] *Mikasa (NSW) Pty Ltd v Festival Industries Pty Ltd* (1972) 127 CLR 617.

[133] *TPC v Prestige Motors Pty Ltd* (1994) ATPR 41-359.

[134] *TPC v Commodore Business Machines Pty Ltd* (1990) 92 ALR 563.

[135] See, e.g., *Australian Competition & Consumer Commission v Australian Abalone Pty Ltd* [2007] FCA 1834 (26 November 2007).

[136] *ACCC v Metcash Trading Limited* [2011] FCA 967 and, on appeal, in *ACCC v Metcash Trading* [2011] FCAFC 151.

There have been no cases in the past 5 years against grocery distributors where the 'waterbed effect' was a central issue. This has, however, been a matter for policy discussion. For example, the National Association of Retail Grocers of Australia[137] claimed that changes in milk pricing confirm that a 'waterbed effect' has developed since the dairy deregulation occurred in 2000.[138] The ACCC addressed this in its grocery report. It observed that the existence of a waterbed effect is not universally accepted[139] and that whether buyer power results in a waterbed effect must be determined based on 'an empirical judgement' utilising 'the evidence arising out of specific factual situation'.[140] The report concluded that the ACCC 'does not consider a waterbed effect to be a significant issue either in relation to groceries generally or milk in particular'.[141]

2.8 Regulations of the Grocery Retail Market: Code of Conducts

There are two codes of conduct that apply to the grocery retail industry: the Unit Pricing Code and the Produce and Grocery Industry Code of Conduct. The Unit Pricing Code[142] is a mandatory code established under Part IV B of the CCA. As discussed above, it provides that online retailers and supermarkets with more than 1,000 m^2 of floor space selling the minimum range of food-based grocery items must display unit prices, that is prices based on volume, weight and length, for food-based grocery items if not exempted.

From December 2007, industry participants had an option to follow a voluntary code of conduct, the Produce and Grocery Industry Code of Conduct.[143] The contents of this code are brief. It sets rather general principles in the areas of produce standards, specifications and labelling, packaging and preparation. It also sets rules for dispute resolution encouraging participants to resolve disputes effectively and, for that purpose, establishing an institute of the Produce and Grocery Industry Ombudsman.

---

[137] National Association of Retail Grocers of Australia, 'ACCC inquiry into the competitiveness of retail prices for standard groceries' (Public Submission, 13 March 2008, http://www.accc.gov.au/system/files/129%20%28late%2014%20Mar%29%20-%20National%20Association%20of%20Retail%20Grocers%20of%20Australia%20%28sub.2%29%20%2869%20pages%29.pdf).

[138] National Association of Retail Grocers of Australia, 'ACCC inquiry into the competitiveness of retail prices for standard groceries' (Public Submission, 13 March 2008) p. 11.

[139] ACCC, *Report of the ACCC inquiry into the competitiveness of retail prices for standard groceries* (July 2008) p. 321.

[140] Ibid, p. 324.

[141] Ibid, p. 354.

[142] Trade Practices (Industry Codes—Unit Pricing) Regulations 2009, Select Legislative Instrument 2009 No. 152.

[143] Available at http://www.produceandgrocerycode.com.au/.

The Code sets as its objectives in s 2 'fair and equitable trading practices among industry participants' and 'fair play and open communication between industry participants'. Nevertheless, it is reasonable to argue that the Code failed to fulfil these objectives based on a lack of enforcement and 'contractual obligation', which are key elements of a voluntary code of conduct. A voluntary form of code prevents further interpretation of these objectives by a court or the ACCC.

Furthermore, the provisions of the Code do not ensure well-balanced and fair negotiation of contracts and their subsequent application. On the contrary, the Code involves a limitation of suppliers, as it states in s 7 that retailers have the right to 'determine labelling, packaging and preparation requirements'. With the exception of s 7, it does not include further limitations of competition.

The Produce and Grocery Industry Code of Conduct will be replaced by a new code of conduct that will be enforceable under the CCA and will either have a mandatory form or be established as voluntary under Part IV B of the CCA.[144] Although the government supports the voluntary code of conduct,[145] other parties involved in the negotiation prefer a mandatory code.[146] The current drafted version is a voluntary code.

The proposed code of conduct, Food and Grocery Prescribed Industry Code of Conduct (the Australian Code), is jointly drafted by Coles, Woolworths and the Food and Grocery Council. It sets rules for conducts such as unilateral changes of concluded supply agreements, payments and the determination of prices. This code, if approved, will, for the first time, regulate de-listing of products from supermarket shelves and will set arrangements for effective and accessible, low-cost dispute resolution.[147] The drafted code of conduct follows

[144] See Stuart Rintoul, 'Coles, Woolies to face a watchdog' (*The Australian*, March 14, 2013), p. 1; Eli Greenbalt, 'Supermarkets close to code of conduct with suppliers' (*The Age BusinessDay*, April 10, 2013), available at http://www.theage.com.au/business/supermarkets-close-to-code-of-conduct-with-suppliers-20130410-2hktg.html#ixzz2RoRYwSCb; ACCC, 'Additional Budget Estimates: ACCC Statement' (Parliament of Australia, Senate Committees, 13 February 2013, Tabled Document No. 6), pp. 1–3, available at http://www.aph.gov.au/Parliamentary_Business/Committees/Senate_Committees?url=economics_ctte/estimates/add_1213/index.htm. A draft of the new code of conduct was not publically available at the stage of finalising this book chapter (May 2013). The mandatory code of conduct will bind all participants in the industry; a voluntary code of conduct under Part IV B of the CCA will bind only those participants that agree to be bound by the code, with the right to cease using the code.

[145] The Hon David Bradbury, Assistant Treasurer, Minister Assisting for Deregulation, 'Keynote Address to the International Bar Association: 9th Competition Mid-year Conference (Speech of 22/03/2013, No. 4, Sydney), available at http://ministers.treasury.gov.au/DisplayDocs.aspx?doc=speeches/2013/004.htm&pageID=005&min=djba&Year=&DocType=.

[146] Retail World, 'Farmers call for a mandatory code for supermarkets' (*Retailmedia Trade Magazine Publishing*, April 8, 2013) p. 20.

[147] The Hon David Bradbury, Assistant Treasurer, Minister Assisting for Deregulation, 'Keynote Address to the International Bar Association: 9th Competition Mid-year Conference (Speech of 22/03/2013, No. 4, Sydney), available at http://ministers.treasury.gov.au/DisplayDocs.aspx?doc=speeches/2013/004.htm&pageID=005&min=djba&Year=&DocType=.

to certain extent the UK trend of a mandatory code of conduct and includes a supermarket ombudsman.[148]

The ACCC is in favour of a legally enforceable code of conduct as it recognises that the existing code has failed to fulfil its objectives. In particular, it failed to ensure the enforcement of contracts and effective dispute resolution. Furthermore, the ACCC's inclination towards the enforceable code of conduct is based on its investigation of the industry, finding that the major supermarket chains do not always honour their contracts with suppliers. Often, they demand additional payments and one-way penalties, which are not part of the original contract, as well as discriminating and failing to pay agreed prices. The suppliers comply with such practices, refusing to officially complain to the ACCC, for fear of the consequences of their supply to the supermarket chains.[149]

The relationships between suppliers and major supermarket chains have been facing ongoing problems. The current Produce and Grocery Industry Code of Conduct was introduced in 2007 as part of the Australian Government's response to the Parliament's report, Report of the Joint Select Committee on the Retailing Sector: Fair Market or Market Failure.[150] The negotiation of this voluntary conduct began in 2000, when the Australian Government established the Retail Grocery Industry Code of Conduct Committee. This long process of negotiating the Code well illustrates the difficulties faced in the grocery retail market, primarily caused by different interests of the involved parties. Therefore, the involvement of an enforcing authority, in this case the ACCC, would be beneficial, and thus the mandatory code of conduct could be an appropriate step for a well-balanced vertical grocery market.

2.8.1 Enforcement of Codes of Conduct

The current Produce and Grocery Industry Code of Conduct is not enforceable; the new code of conduct will be established under Part IV B of the CCA and will thus be enforceable by the ACCC. The same provisions apply to the Unit Pricing Code, which was established under the CCA as a mandatory code of conduct. The CCA provides that the ACCC has the power to issue public notices, apply to the court to make orders to redress loss or damage suffered by other parties of a contract or arrangement in question and investigate its application and enforcement.

First, under s 51, the ACCC can advise the public by issuing a written notice if conduct by a corporation or a person contravenes the code of conduct. Second,

---

[148] Stuart Rintoul, 'Coles, Woolies to face a watchdog' (*The Australian*, March 14, 2013), p. 1;

[149] ACCC, 'Additional Budget Estimates: ACCC Statement' (Parliament of Australia, Senate Committees, 13 February 2013, Tabled Document No. 6), pp. 1–3, available at http://www.aph.gov.au/Parliamentary_Business/Committees/Senate_Committees?url=economics_ctte/estimates/add_1213/index.htm.

[150] The Parliament of the Commonwealth of Australia, 'Report of the Joint Select Committee on the Retailing Sector, Fair Market or Market Failure' (Commonwealth of Australia, August 1999, ISBN 0 642 71025 2).

under s 51 ADB, the ACCC may apply on behalf of a class of persons who suffered or could suffer loss or damage caused by a person contravening the code of conduct for orders to the court with jurisdiction in this matter. The court can make orders that will redress fully or partially the damage or loss suffered or prevent or reduce the loss or damages suffered. In particular, the court can make orders declaring the contract or arrangement in question (or its part) void or varying such a contract or arrangement, or it can enforce any of the provisions of the contract or arrangement in question. It can order the respondent to refund money or return property or to provide parts, repair goods or supply specified services. Finally, the ACCC also has investigation power under Division 5 of the CCA, meaning it can give written notice to a corporation asking for information or for a specific document.

This enforcement power of the ACCC will apply to any new code of conduct because it will be established under Part IV B of the CCA. In addition, the ACCC and/or other bodies could also be provided with additional powers. For example, it can be expected that the new code of conduct will include the institution of an ombudsman.[151]

2.8.2 Regulation of Online Shopping

Australia does not have specific regulations or a code of conduct that regulates internet retail stores and/or internet sales. The same rules applying to brick and mortar stores apply to online retailers. The only regulation that includes a direct reference to internet retail stores is the Unit Pricing Code, which, as discussed above, provides for online retailers selling the minimum range of food-based grocery items to display unit prices.

Generally, online grocery shopping is not a common way for Australian customers to purchase their groceries. The Australian Government's report from November 2011 states that online grocery shopping is low compared to developed countries such as the United Kingdom. Only around 2 % or less of the population in Australia purchased groceries online in 2009, 2010 or 2011, and the market share of online shopping is only at around 1 % of the total grocery shopping.[152] This market share reflects the retail grocery market in general, with Coles and Woolworths dominating the online grocery market.[153] Nevertheless, online shopping is a

[151] The Hon David Bradbury, Assistant Treasurer, Minister Assisting for Deregulation, 'Keynote Address to the International Bar Association: 9th Competition Mid-year Conference (Speech of 22/03/2013, No. 4, Sydney), available at http://ministers.treasury.gov.au/DisplayDocs.aspx?doc=speeches/2013/004.htm&pageID=005&min=djba&Year=&DocType=; Stuart Rintoul, 'Coles, Woolies to face a watchdog' (*The Australian*, March 14, 2013), p. 1.

[152] Australian Government, Productivity Commission, *Economic Structure and Performance of the Australian Retail Industry: Productivity Commission Inquiry Report* (Commonwealth of Australia, report no 56, 4 November 2011), 101–102.

[153] Retail World, 46th Annual Report 'Clicking with grocery shoppers online' (*Retailmedia Trade Magazine Publishing*, Vol. 65, No. 23, December, 2012) p. 27.

growing trend in Australia,[154] and it can be expected that online shopping will become a common way of purchasing groceries by Australian customers in the future.

2.8.3 Regulation of Relationships Between Large-Scale Retailers and Small Suppliers

Currently, relationships between large-scale food retailers and small suppliers or small-scale retailers are not directly regulated in Australia. The current voluntary code of conduct, the Produce and Grocery Industry Code of Conduct, includes few aspects regarding the relationship between suppliers and retailers (mostly large-scale food retailers and smaller suppliers). They include general principles and a few rules; however, they are not enforceable but are rather used as a guide, reflecting the voluntary basis of this code. Indeed, this code is generally seen as an unimportant instrument in the industry as it does not regulate the important issues such as unequal bargaining power and the consequences resulting from this phenomenon. As discussed above, the government and the ACCC have recognised competition imperfections and restrictions arising from relationships between large-scale food retailers and small suppliers. They are currently preparing, with the vertical, grocery-industry participants, a code of conduct under Part IV B of the CCA, which will be enforceable by the ACCC.

The CCA allows for smaller vertical participants with minimal bargaining power, such as a group of small suppliers, to negotiate their conditions collectively under Subdivision B of Division 2 of Part VII of the CCA. This bargaining can take place on the condition that the small businesses (suppliers) that take part in the collective bargaining notify the ACCC and that the ACCC does not object based on its findings that public detriment would prevail over any public benefit of the notified agreement. Furthermore, the small suppliers or small-scale retailers can apply at the ACCC for authorisation of their agreement to bargain collectively under general provisions of Division 1 of Part VII of the CCA.[155] Also, the parties can apply for a review of the ACCC's decision to the Australian Competition Tribunal.

For instance, in 2007, small-scale retailers of healthy food successfully applied for the authorisation of a collective price negotiating arrangement with health food suppliers. In 2008, the ACCC granted the authorisation for the period of 5 years. Several aspects, such as their low individual negotiating power towards the suppliers, the maintenance of non-price competition and retail price competition, played an important role in the ACCC decision. The authorisation allowed

[154] Ibid.

[155] For instance, small-scale retailers successfully applied for authorisations of recommended prices among small-scale retailers. Their size and the size of the major retailers were taken into consideration when granting the authorisations: A14165 (1979), A4006 (1979), A2239 (1978).

collective price negotiation without giving permission for collective boycotts.[156] Indeed, Australia has no case under current legislation, the CCA, in which small food retail stores would collectively boycott suppliers selling to discounters.

2.9 Recommendation

The legislative provisions of the CCA appropriately deal with significant anti-competitive practices. Nevertheless, in Australia, there are some specific issues in the grocery retail market arising from significant imbalances in negotiation power, primarily, between the major retailers and their suppliers. Serious consideration should be given to identifying ways of addressing the effects of these power imbalances without undermining the objectives of Australia's existing competition policy. There have been a number of reviews of supermarket conduct, and these are likely to continue. One suggestion currently being pursued is for the establishment of an enforceable code of conduct.

The current voluntary Produce and Grocery Industry Code of Conduct does not ensure acceptable conditions for sale between suppliers and retailers. It has failed to tackle important issues arising from a lack of balance in bargaining power and has failed in being applied and enforced by the industry. As a result of this experience, it is suggested that any future code of conduct be mandatory to improve the prospects of its success. An enforceable code of conduct, if appropriately constructed, could be more effective in ensuring fairness and transparency.

Although it is appropriate to highlight the prohibition of unfair unilateral conducts, such as changes of concluded supply agreements and payments, as well as other conduct identified by the industry and the ACCC, the most crucial aspect is the willingness of the parties concerned to complain and take dispute actions. This issue has two elements. First, mechanisms must be put in place to ensure that any complainant (usually a smaller supplier) be not 'penalised' (by a retailer) for making a complaint under the Code, for example, through cancellation of supply or imposition of new and onerous terms. Second, the dispute resolution must be affordable and reasonably quick and effective and the ACCC must be properly resourced to ensure it has the necessary capacity to enforce the code.

[156] Authorisation no. A91071, *ACT Health Food Co-operative Ltd* (6 February 2008, Public Register No. C2007/2195).

Austria

3

Gerhard Fussenegger

3.1 Economic Background

3.1.1 Agricultural Production

Based on figures from 2007,[1] there are approx. 190,000 agricultural and forestry operators/farmers in Austria. Due to the geographical scope of Austria, its structure is characterized by an above-average percentage of farmers who are (partly) foresters and mountain farmers. Structure-wise, the Austrian agricultural production is based on small farming. The average utilized agricultural area is 19 ha (compared, e.g., to EU's top, the Czech Republic with 152.4 ha and also Germany with 55.8 ha). Only 40 % of the farmers, who are active in Austria, are full-time farmers.[2]

Also within processing, the Austrian food market seems to be characterized by small and medium-sized undertakings. Within Austria's Top 100,[3] only two undertakings are (partly) active in the processing of food. The biggest one is Agrana Beteiligungs-AG-Gruppe (with a turnover of approx. EUR 2.5 billion, it is ranked as the 34th biggest undertaking in Austria), which is an Austrian processor of agricultural commodities active in the segments Sugar, Starch and Fruit.

[1] Bundesanstalt für Agrarwirtschaft (Publisher): "Grüner Bericht 2010," in particular Section 3. Agrarstrukturen und Beschäftigung, pp. 64–82; available at http://www.agraroekonomik.at/index.php?id=newsdetail&tx_ttnews%5Btt_news%5D=58&cHash=1f98a375c4.

[2] Grüner Bericht 2010, pp. 64–82.

[3] www.trendtop500.at, ranking based on turnover.

G. Fussenegger (✉)
bpv Hügel Rechtsanwälte OG, Brussels, Belgium
e-mail: Gerhard.Fussenegger@bpv-huegel.com

P. Kobel et al. (eds.), *Antitrust in the Groceries Sector & Liability Issues in Relation to Corporate Social Responsibility*, LIDC Contributions on Antitrust Law, Intellectual Property and Unfair Competition, DOI 10.1007/978-3-662-45753-5_3

3.1.2 Grocery Retail

In 2010, 5,726 grocery retailers in Austria achieved a turnover of approximately EUR 17.2 billion (the 628 discounters are included in the total amount of 5,736 retailers).[4]

Rewe Group (Billa, Merkur, Penny, Adeg) is the market leader in Austria with a market share of approx. 34.6 %, followed by the Spar Group (Spar, Eurospar, Interspar, Maximarkt) with a market share of 29.2 % and Hofer/Lidl (representing the segment "discount") with a common market share of 23.3 %.[5] Austria therefore is within the top five in Europe concerning the amount of concentration of the grocery retail market.[6]

3.2 Legal Background

Austrian competition law, which—in its entirety—has to be applied to the grocery sector, includes a prohibition of anticompetitive practices.[7] Only certain agreements and practices concerning the production, supply, storage and processing of agricultural products are excluded from the application of the Austrian Cartel Act if they do not include price fixing and if competition can be upheld.[8]

Besides general antitrust legislation, the Act on Local Supplies ("Nahversorgungsgesetz,"[9] "NahVersG") is a far-reaching national specific. In its Section 2, it is stated that suppliers, which offer different conditions to its resellers under the same conditions and without objective justifications, can be confronted with an injunctive relief claim of the discriminated reseller. Dominance of the supplier is not a precondition for submission of such a claim.

Additionally, Section 3 NahVersG prohibits any nondelivery as a retaliatory measure of undertakings based on injunctive relief claims of the discriminated resellers. Section 4 NahVersG obliges wholesalers to deliver to retailers if otherwise the local supply is threatened or if otherwise the competitiveness of the retailer would be essentially limited.

By introducing the NahVersG, the legislator especially focused on the food sector. However, the Austrian Cartel Supreme Court now clearly confirmed that

[4] "Handel in Österreich-Basisdaten 2009"/Konsumententrends 2009 (see Nielsen Jahrbuch 2009, LEH - die wichtigsten Handelsunternehmen, pp. 9–12).

[5] "Wo Österreich einkauft - LEH und DFH 2011": der aktuelle Überblick der Handelszeitung zum Download (österreichische "Handelszeitung," abgerufen am 31. August 2011).

[6] See BWB, Allgemeine Untersuchung des österreichischen Lebensmittelhandelsunter besonderer Berücksichtigung des Aspekts der Nachfragemacht, June 2007, p. 3.

[7] Cf. Sect. 1 Austrian Cartel Act (Kartellgesetz 2005, "Cartel Act").

[8] Section 2 Cartel Act.

[9] Bundesgesetz vom 29. Juni 1977 zur Verbesserung der Nahversorgung und der Wettbewerbsbedingungen, BGBl. Nr. 392/1977.

the term "resellers" includes not only the food sector but also all undertakings that are not end users but that resell their (also processed) goods.[10]

3.3 Market Studies

3.3.1 Factual Background

The retail grocery sector was examined in a sector inquiry of the Austrian Federal Competition Authority (*Bundeswettbewerbsbehörde*, the "BWB") in 2007 ("sector inquiry").[11]

The sector inquiry was based on complaints by suppliers, following which the two biggest Austrian grocery chains (Rewe and Spar) allegedly used their buyer and negotiation powers to put substantial pressure on their suppliers, e.g. by forcing suppliers to agree in adverse prices, conditions and rebates. In detail, the claimants mentioned, e.g., arbitrary delistings and substantial cash benefits without any substantial service in return (e.g., listing fees, "wedding boni" (i.e., suppliers were obliged to pay extra money after mergers of retailers) or advertisement subsidies).

In several decisions, the Cartel Court and the Cartel Supreme Court confirmed that due to the (current) market situation and the various complaints, the BWB was entitled to initiate its sector inquiry.[12]

3.3.2 Outcome of Market Study

Due to its focus on the retailer's buyer power, the inquiry exclusively concentrates on the retailer's procurement market, while the retail market with regard to end customers was not part of the inquiry.

In detail, the inquiry

1. defined the relevant product and geographical market[13];
2. outlined the term "buyer power";
3. illustrated effects that are based on buyer power (e.g., "spiral effect")
4. scrutinized in detail nine product categories/baskets, where the BWB saw indications that the respective segments were (specially) characterized by buyer power ("meat/sausages," "poultry/eggs," "bread (exclusively frozen

[10] Cf judgment of the Austrian Cartel Supreme Court of 23 June 2003, 16 Ok 8/03.

[11] See BWB, Allgemeine Untersuchung des österreichischen Lebensmittelhandels unter besonderer Berücksichtigung des Aspekts der Nachfragemacht, June 2007.

[12] See judgment of the Cartel Supreme Court of 15 July 2007, case number 16 Ok 06/09.

[13] Mainly following the European Commission's "product category," Commission Decision of 3 February 1999, M. 1221 - Rewe/Meinl, para 77.

products)," "dairy," "soft drinks," "hot beverages," "basic foods," "confectionary" and "beer");

5. examined retailer's behavior that can have adverse effects on the suppliers, such as listing fees, (retroactive) payments after new retail shops had been opened, advertisement subsidies, exclusive supply to retailers, or retroactive rebates.

The main conclusions drawn were as follows. The Austrian retail grocery sector is characterized by a high market concentration, high barriers to enter and (essential) buyer power. The market power varies among different product segments. In general, buyer power rises with the increase of the number of suppliers, the decrease of alternatives for the suppliers and the nonimportance of brands (e.g., in the meat sector).

Market power is not negative per se, especially if it results in efficiencies that are passed on to the end customer/consumer. However, buyer power can also result in a limitation of innovation and a variety of products. Additionally, the competitiveness of smaller retailers, who cannot rely on comparable economies of scales, decreases due to the buyer power of the main retailers. The BWB hereby explicitly mentions the "waterbed effect," following which smaller retailers are suffering from the economies of scale achieved by the dominant retailers on both markets, the procurement market and the retail market itself.

3.4 Code of Conduct

The BWB published *draft guidelines concerning resale price maintenance* ("RPM").[14] After a legal introduction, the BWB presents in its draft guidelines a detailed but nonexhaustive "code of conduct." It is hereby the intention of the BWB to provide some guidance for undertakings concerned, particularly for SMEs, in relation to RPM.

The draft guidelines are based on BWB's investigations in the grocery retail market but refer in general to vertical agreements. The guidelines are currently under revision.[15]

The list itself refers not only to direct *price fixing* (agreement, conduct), but also *rebates, trade margin neutrality* or *sanctions* based on violation of the resale price are considered as being illegal. Concerning *special offers/campaigns*, the BWB follows a strict approach and stresses that only the retailer itself may decide on the duration, the date and the respective price offers.

Moreover, the BWB also focuses on feared *horizontal effects*. For instance, following the guidelines, retailers in general are not allowed to support price

[14] The second draft is under consultation. For more information, see the press release of 17 June 2013, at http://www.en.bwb.gv.at/News/Seiten/FederalCompetitionAuthority(FCA)launchespublicconsultationonrulesofconductregardingverticalandtrilateralpricefixing.aspx.

[15] June 2014.

monitoring of suppliers (e.g., by reporting other retailers that offer products below the recommended price level). Also, the other way round, i.e. assistance of the supplier in the retailer's price monitoring (e.g., by sending receipts to the retailers), is considered of being anticompetitive. The supplier may also not inform other retailers of planned campaigns or increases of prices of other competitors. Moreover, retailers and suppliers may not agree on "most favoured nation clauses" or a certain retail price level practiced by other retailers.

Concerning *recommended* retail prices, the BWB also provides some "white clause" examples: for instance, the supplier is allowed to reason its recommended price level and to illustrate which strategy and marketing is intended, unless this supports directly or indirectly horizontal coordination of retailers.

3.5 Competition Law Enforcement

Austrian competition law in its entirety has to be applied to the grocery sector. Especially in the last years, the grocery sector had been in the focus of the Austrian competition authorities.

3.5.1 Collusion Among Suppliers/Collusion Among Retailers/ Horizontal Agreements

On the supplier's level, in 2010, the BWB has brought a case to the Cartel Court accusing two *sugar producers* of market allocation concerning the German and Austrian sugar markets. The undertakings involved allegedly agreed to respect each other's strongholds in the respective domestic markets. The case is still pending.

Furthermore, based on settlement negotiations between the undertakings concerned and the BWB, the Cartel Court imposed a legally binding decision of (in total) EUR 1.1 million against Austria's leading breweries, *Ottakringer*, *BrauUnion* and *Stiegl*,[16] in 2013. The fine was based on the brewer's refusal to supply draft beer to cash and carry markets based on "hygienic reasons." As a consequence, cash and carry operators were not to be able to enter the market for draught beer. Furthermore, the price for draft beer was far above the price for bottled beer.

With regard to horizontal aspects between grocery retailers, the Cartel Court imposed a fine of EUR 20.8 million on grocery retailer *Rewe*.[17] While the fine, which was based on a settlement, mainly focused on vertical aspects, also some horizontal elements (alleged "hub and spoke" agreements between retailers via its suppliers) were covered by the settlement/fine. Details were not disclosed.

[16] Judgment of the Cartel Court of 5 March 2012, case number not published.

[17] Judgment of the Cartel Court of 13 May 2013, case number and decision not published.

Similarly, in the current proceedings at the Cartel Court against SPAR, the proceedings are mainly based on alleged infringements of cartel law with regard to contracts of SPAR and its suppliers. However, the BWB also issued indirect horizontal coordination (i.e., coordination between retailers via their suppliers) in its request for fine.

In another recent decision, the Cartel Supreme Court came to the conclusion that the email correspondence between a producer and a retailer, on which the BWB based its request for an inspection, was sufficient to constitute a reasoned suspicion concerning vertical and horizontal competition infringements.[18] In substance, the argument of the producer that it was too small to enforce retail prices was rejected, as even (missing) economic significance of a participant cannot eliminate an existing suspicion concerning cartel agreements. The Courts therefore granted the request for an inspection.

3.5.2 Collusion Among Suppliers and Retailers/Vertical Agreements

Within the last 2 years, the BWB has been conducting extensive dawn raids in the main grocery chains in Austria. The inspections were mainly based on the suspicion of prohibited RPM coordination between suppliers and retailers.

Section 1 (4) Austrian Cartel Act states that the RPM is considered of being a bilateral cartel if these recommendations have as their object or effect the restriction of competition. However, the legal clause also states that recommendations are exempted from the cartel prohibition if the nonbinding nature of the recommendation is "explicitly" mentioned *and* if there is no pressure to implement the price recommendation.

The Cartel Supreme Court concluded that RPM infringes Art 101 (1) TFEU *per se*.[19] However, the Cartel Courts, under certain circumstances, seem to accept that RPM can be covered by an Art 101 (3) TFEU exemption from the general cartel prohibition in Art 101 (1) TFEU.[20]

Dawn raids were executed at the premises of *Rewe* (Billa, Merkur, Penny, Adeg), *Spar, Sutterlüty* (regional retailer in Vorarlberg) and *M-Preis* (regional retailer in Western Austria). The dawn raids concerning the two market leaders, Rewe[21] and Spar,[22] lasted eight business days respectively.

Furthermore, the business premises of numerous suppliers, especially beer and diary producers, have been searched. However, in one dissenting judgment, the

---

[18] Judgment of the Cartel Supreme Court of 11 October 2012, case number 16 Ok 5/12.

[19] Judgment of the Cartel Supreme Court of 1 December 2009, case number 16 Ok 10/09, "*Pressegrosso II*."

[20] Judgment of the Cartel Court, case number 26 Kt 17, 18, 27, 28/07.

[21] March 2012.

[22] January 2013.

Cartel Supreme Court in 2013 confirmed the decision of the Cartel Court, whereby a request of the BWB to conduct a dawn raid at the premises of a supplier to the Austrian Retail grocery market was rejected.[23] The Courts reasoned this rejection by referring to the fact that the documents provided by the BWB in order to prove that there was a vertical and horizontal ("hub and spoke") cartel failed. All documents provided clearly stated that the prices were "recommended" or "non-binding recommended." A price reduction of 1.5 %, which was offered in case the recommended price was in fact achieved, was considered to be too less essential to have as an object or effect a restriction in competition. Furthermore, the difference in size between a retailer and the respective supplier was considered to be too big to see the suspicion of a cartel established.

So far, with the exception of the ongoing SPAR proceedings (SPAR refused to settle), all investigations ended in a settlement between the BWB and the respective supplier. The Cartel Court, in its ruling, followed the factual coordination.

The biggest case with regard to the grocery sector is the *Rewe* case, where the Cartel Court imposed a fine of EUR 20.8 million.[24] Following the decision of the Austrian Cartel Court, Rewe agreed between 2007 and 2012 with its upstream suppliers on resale price maintenance. The respective dawn raid was based on the suspicion that Rewe agreed with its suppliers on RPM duration and date of campaigns, especially in the field of supply of beer and dairy products. The suspicion also included some horizontal elements ("hub and spoke" agreements between retailers via its suppliers). Following the BWB's press release, Rewe confessed the allegations already in front of the BWB before the Cartel Court opened its proceedings.

Rewe agreed in a special proceeding in front of the Cartel Court to accept "commitments," which will be in line with the BWB's mentioned RPM guidelines, of being legally binding.

At producer level, various undertakings got fined for vertical infringements. All proceedings were settled. For instance, concerning dairy products, the Cartel Court (on request of the BWB) imposed on January 2013 a fine of EUR 1.123 million on *Berglandmilch*, a leading Austrian producer of milk and dairy products.[25] Following the BWB's press release, Berglandmilch fixed retail prices with several undertakings active in the (retail) food sector between 2006 and 2012. The fine is legally binding, as Berglandmilch acknowledged the infringement and all parties waived their right to appeal the Cartel Court's decision. The decision was therefore based on the Austrian (informal) settlement procedure.

However, fines imposed were often substantially low. The proceedings also sometimes focused on anticompetitive behavior at *local level*. For instance, in *Vorarlberg Mühlen*, a regional mill was fined in the amount of EUR 58,000,[26]

---

[23] Judgment of the Cartel Supreme Court of 16 March 2013, case number 16 Ok 1/13.

[24] Judgment of the Cartel Court of 13 May 2013, case number and decision not published.

[25] Judgment of the Cartel Court of 23 January 2013, case number 29 Kt 77/12.

[26] Judgment of the Cartel Court of 3 October 2013, case number 29 Kt 80/13.

while the Cartel Court in *Rieder Bier* imposed a fine of EUR 52,000 on a regional brewery.[27]

3.5.3 Abuse of Dominance

3.5.3.1 Reselling Below Cost, Delisting of Suppliers, Abusively High Prices

Again, the general concept of Austrian competition law also with regard to abuse of dominance applies to the grocery sector. Therefore, once an undertaking or undertakings are (collective) dominant,[28] it must be proven by the authority that dominance has been abused.

In its Section 5 (1) 5 Austrian Cartel Act, the Austrian competition law explicitly states that *reselling of products* (not services) below the purchase price is an abuse of dominance (if not objectively justified). Concerning this special case (and contrary to the general concept of abuse of dominance), it is also legally stated in Section 5 (2) Austrian Cartel Act that the dominant undertaking must prove that there had been no reselling below the purchase price or that this behavior was objectively justified.

Furthermore, the behavior can be covered by the general predation/sale below costs concept, whereby the undertaking concerned must be (a) dominant and (b) abuse its dominance. The same applies to *de-listing of suppliers.*

Also, *abusively high prices* can under special circumstances be considered as an abuse of dominance, although decisions based on abuse of abusively high prices are rare. Generally speaking, the price of the dominant undertaking is compared with the price of comparable products in other periods of time. Usually, international case law is widely interpreted in the way that excessive pricing should be checked up on a two-stage test: (1) the cost side as well as (2) price comparison. Furthermore, the difference between prices and costs also has to be taken into consideration.

To the author's knowledge, with regard to grocery retail, there have not been any antitrust/abuse of dominance cases so far with regard to reselling below cost, delisting of suppliers or abusively high prices.

3.5.3.2 Buying Power

Definition

There is no Austrian statutory definition of buying power. In its inquiry, the BWB equates "buyer power" and "bargaining power." In this regard, the BWB refers to a definition of buying power that highlights the ability of favorable purchasing.

---

[27] Judgment of the Cartel Court of 25 October 2013, case number 26 Kt 104/13.

[28] The Cartel Act itself includes low market thresholds for a rebuttable assumption of dominance; see Section 4 (2) Cartel Act.

Another definition used by the BWB is based on a theory of negotiation focusing on low opportunity costs of the demander. As a consequence, it is far less to the disadvantage of the demander not to buy from the seller than the other way around. However, this theory is based on the buying power of the respective single demander, while the BWB favors a concept whereby the general power of negotiation on the whole relevant and geographical market is taken into account.

Buyer Power as a *Per Se* Offense?

Buyer power only infringes Austrian cartel law if it is considered as an abuse of dominance. In assessing whether a behavior of an undertaking qualifies as an abuse of a dominant market position, the Austrian Cartel Courts focus on the "suitability" of the behavior of a dominant undertaking to create "negative effects concerning the market situation and the competitive relationship."[29] Therefore, the approach in Austria concerning prohibited abuse seems to be between a "per se" prohibition and a factual restriction of competition.

Abuse of Buyer Power or Economic Dependency

To the author's knowledge, there has been no case law in Austria so far that is directly linked to an abuse of buyer power or economic dependency in the grocery retail segment.

Concerning general abuse of dominance cases, in *Red Bull*,[30] the claimant (retailer in Austria with a market share of approx. 5 %) could not prove that *Billa*, Austria's biggest grocery retailer, was abusing its dominance by reselling products (inter alia, Red Bull) below the purchase price. The claim was rejected as the plaintiff could not even submit evidence with regard to its own purchase price, not to mention the purchase price of the dominant undertaking.

Furthermore, the BWB investigated a case relating to the purchasing, storage and drying services of organic corn. The trading association *Österreichische Agentur für Biogetreide GmbH*, which had producers, processors and traders as members, was accused of foreclosure practices. It had entered into contracts with local storage and drying facilities for organic corn. These contracts were found to foreclose the purchasing of organic corn in certain regions in Austria. This case was closed with commitments.

---

[29] E.g., judgment of the Cartel Supreme Court of 16 July 2008, case number 16 Ok 6/08 with further references.

[30] Judgment of the Cartel Supreme Court of 16 December 2002, case number 16 Ok 11/02.

3.6 Merger Control

3.6.1 Thresholds for Merger Control

There are no special thresholds for merger control in the (grocery) retail sector. The BWB and the Federal Cartel Prosecutor (*Bundeskartellanwalt*, the "FCP") are the responsible authorities with regard to merger control in Austria. If none of these so-called Official Parties requests an in-depth investigation in front of the Cartel Court, notified transactions are legally deemed to be cleared after a 4-week waiting period.

In general, the Austrian competition authorities have jurisdiction over a transaction if

1. the undertakings concerned achieved a combined global turnover of more than EUR 300 million, as well as
2. a combined turnover of more than EUR 30 million in Austria, and if
3. at least two of the undertakings concerned each had a global turnover of more than EUR 5 million.[31]

3.6.2 Relevant Product (or Service) Markets Defined in the Grocery Retail Sector

The Cartel Courts, in general, refer in its market definition to the "demand" approach of Section 23 Cartel Act. Following this "concept of demand," the relevant market encompasses all products or services that, based on its criteria, differentiate from other products/services and that—from demand side—substitute each other. Following this concept of demand and referring to case law and legal literature, the BWB in its inquiry refers to "alternatives" of the demander/supplier.

The BWB, within the segment of food retail, therefore differentiates between the retail market as such (where the retailers compete against each other with regard to sale to end customers) and the procurement market.

Concerning the retail market, the BWB did not examine the respective segment; however, it can be assumed that the BWB will follow the European Commission's approach with regard to Austria.[32] Concerning the procurement market, the BWB considers, again in accordance with the European Commission's approach in *Rewe/Meinl*,[33] a market definition broken down by "product categories" as suppliers are

---

[31] If only one of the undertakings concerned had an Austrian turnover of more than EUR 5 million, and the combined worldwide turnover of the other undertakings concerned did not exceed EUR 30 million, the transaction will be exempt from the filing requirement (cf. Section 9 (2) Cartel Act).

[32] E.g., in Commission Decision of 2 June 2008, M. 5047, *Rewe/ADEG*, the European Commission defined the relevant product market as the "retail market for daily consumer through modern distribution channels," including hypermarkets, supermarkets and discounters.

[33] Commission Decision of 3 February 1999 relating to proceedings under Council Regulation (EEC) No 4064/89, Case No IV/M. 1221, *Rewe/Meinl*.

not able to switch production to the relevant products and market them in the short term. Following the BWB, the procurement for food retailers/supermarkets defines a separate market. Therefore, other distribution channels such as Cash & Carry, specialized outlets, gastronomy, petrol station shops, butchers and bakeries cannot be included in the relevant product market.

3.6.3 Relevant Geographical Markets Defined in the Grocery Retail Sector

The BWB follows the European Commission's approach concerning the definition of the relevant geographical market. Therefore, with regard to the procurement market for retail grocery, the BWB—again based on the European Commission's practice—defines a national geographical market. This definition is based on the size of producers (mainly small and medium-sized undertakings), preferences of consumers (especially concerning meat and dairy products), structure of distribution, different national legal requirements (e.g., concerning labeling and production) or different national range of products.

On retail level, the BWB established that the geographical market (1) for the pick-up cash and carry market was a maximum of 30 km from the business premises, and (2) for the delivery market it was 100 km from the business premises.[34]

3.6.4 Grocery Retail Networks and Countervailing Buyer Power

The market power of retailers is taken into account in assessing (planned) mergers at the suppliers' level. However, to the author's knowledge, so far, the Austrian competition authorities and courts did not publish that they had been dealing with grocery retail networks/countervailing buyer power. The reason might be that the Austrian retail segment is characterized by a high concentration of the market. Therefore, on the one hand, it seems to be unlikely that grocery retail networks, including the big market players, would be accepted by the authorities. On the other hand, networks of suppliers could be considered as strengthening the countervailing market power.

3.6.5 Merger Remedies

The essential mergers within retailers in Austria have been notified to the European Commission (*Rewe/Billa, Rewe/Meinl* and *REWE/ADEG*).[35]

---

[34] BWB/Z-1387, Pfeiffer/Nussbaumer.

[35] Cf Commission Decision of 27 August 1996, M. 803, *Rewe/Billa*; Commission Decision of 3 February 1999, M. 1221, *Rewe/Meinl*; Commission Decision of 2 June 2008, M. 5047, *Rewe/ADEG*.

Concerning remedies on a national basis, the BWB dealt, e.g., with a local merger in the cash and carry segment. *Pfeiffer* intended to take over the three branches of *Nussbaumer*.[36] Concerning one of the branches, the acquirer was the only competitor of the target. At the end, the BWB cleared the transaction on the condition that the parties guaranteed that, first, prices in the respective area were pegged to the prices in the competitive Vienna region and, second, that the parties did not to acquire any other competitors in that region.

With regard to the acquisition of *Römerquelle* by *Coca-Cola*,[37] the target was presumed to have a dominant position in the market for mineral waters characterized by long-term contracts and rigid structures. The BWB feared in particular that Coca-Cola would strengthen Römerquelle's position by virtue of its financial power and its know-how as a bottler and distributor. Another concern was that Coca-Cola would add a small but significant brand to Römerquelle's already very strong brand portfolio in the market for functional drinks. At the end, the transaction got clearance based on commitments offered by the parties. Remedies included (1) Römerquelle's halting of the production of the Coca-Cola functional drink brand, (2) the obligation to distribute competing mineral waters at nondiscriminatory prices, and (3) refraining from linking the delivery (including rebates and other contract conditions) of Coca-Cola products to those of Römerquelle in the distribution to the catering industry.

In 2011, dairy undertaking *Berglandmilch eGen*, after already acquiring two competitors in the past 2 years, agreed on commitments to get clearance for its acquisition of Stainzer Milch.[38] The acquirer agreed not only to buy raw milk (3.3 million kg) of third parties but also to sell raw milk to third dairies in an amount that was almost as high as the raw milk collected by the target. The commitments therefore were not only far-reaching; it was the first time ever that the Official Parties (besides the BWB, the Federal Competition Prosecutor) accepted commitments in Phase I. The BWB therefore also stressed that the authority in future will be open to accept such remedies already in Phase I to avoid often long-lasting Phase II proceedings in front of the Cartel Court.

3.7 Recommendations

As mentioned, the grocery retail sector was already examined in a detailed sector inquiry; the segment is in the current focus of the BWB, following which there had been numerous dawn raids and information requests in the sector.

Furthermore, due to high market concentration, the leading retailers are also legally considered of being collectively dominant. Therefore, in case of an allegation of abuse, the retailers must prove that they are not dominant.

[36] BWB/Z-1387.

[37] BWB/Z-726.

[38] BWB/Z-1511.

Hence, the Austrian competition authorities (BWB, FCP and Cartel Courts) are able to, and in fact, use all legal tools of competition law (i.e., prohibition of cartel, prohibition to abuse, merger control) to monitor and regulate the market and, if necessary, to impose fines. Additionally, there is the far-reaching NahVersG, which focuses on the grocery retail sector.

Last, with the 2012 amendment of the Austrian Cartel Act, the BWB's enforcement powers got essentially strengthened: the BWB now can enforce its own information requests; the BWB now has the power to seal premises and to ask any representative or employee for explanations on facts or documents relating to the subject matter of the dawn raid; additionally, the BWB now has the power to seize original documents.

Therefore, in the author's view, there is no current need for legislative changes with regard to Austrian competition law.

With regard to case law, special attention should be paid to the current proceedings at the Cartel Court against the grocery retailer SPAR. SPAR—contrary to Rewe—refused to settle. Therefore, it can be expected (and hoped from a practitioner's perspective) that the Cartel Court will rule on specific legal questions concerning vertical restraints in the grocery sector for the first time, which are at the moment still open.

Belgium

4

Jan Blockx

4.1 Introduction

This contribution provides an overview of the application of competition and related rules on the grocery retail market in Belgium.[1] Belgian competition law is modelled on European competition law, and some other rules that are applicable to the grocery retail sector are a reflection of European law as well. In the absence of specific Belgian case law, reference will therefore be made to European cases.

4.1.1 Economic Background

According to Eurostat data, more than half of Belgium's farms are specialised in livestock (meat and dairy).[2] Beef production is aimed specifically at consumption in Belgium, whereas pork meat is to a large extent subject to cross-border trade. Important crops include animal feed (corn), wheat, potatoes and sugar beet, as well as fruit and vegetables.

There are various intermediaries active in the delivery of agricultural produce to processors and consumers, including slaughterhouses and auction houses for fruit and vegetables. The processing of agriculture produce is to a large extent done by multinationals.

The supermarket sector is relatively concentrated in Belgium with three supermarket chains (Carrefour, Colruyt, Delhaize) of roughly equal size accounting for

[1] This contribution is updated until the end of May 2013.

[2] See http://epp.eurostat.ec.europa.eu/portal/page/portal/product_details/publication?p_product_code=KS-SF-09-099.

J. Blockx (✉)
Hogan Lovells, Brussels, Belgium
e-mail: jan.blockx@hoganlovells.com

P. Kobel et al. (eds.), *Antitrust in the Groceries Sector & Liability Issues in Relation to Corporate Social Responsibility*, LIDC Contributions on Antitrust Law, Intellectual Property and Unfair Competition, DOI 10.1007/978-3-662-45753-5_4

approximately 75 % of the market.[3] In recent years, discount retailers have gained significant market share.

The larger supermarket chains in Belgium also sell over the Internet (with the consumer either having to pick up the groceries at the store or having them delivered to his home), but Internet sales only make up a very small part of their total turnover.

4.1.2 Legal Background

4.1.2.1 Competition Law

As indicated above, Belgian competition law is modelled on European competition law. It prohibits agreements and concerted practices that have as their object or effect the restriction of competition as well as the abuse of a dominant position. Just like under European competition law, resale price maintenance is prohibited *per se*. There are no provisions in Belgian competition law that are specifically aimed at the retail market, and the retail sector is subject to the general competition law rules.

Note that the Belgian Competition Act of 2006[4] is currently being replaced by a new Code of Economic Law, the relevant parts of which were published in the Belgian Official Gazette on 26 April 2013.[5] The date of entry into force of most of the provisions of the new Code of Economic Law, which mainly introduces procedural changes, is still to be determined.[6]

4.1.2.2 Law Against Unfair Trade Practices

In addition to Belgian competition law, Article 95 of the Belgian Act on Market Practices and Consumer Protection of 2010[7] prohibits any action that is contrary to

[3] Their combined market share was 72.8 % in 2011, according to a study by Marketing Map as reported on http://www.retaildetail.be/nl/case-van-de-week/item/14349-%E2%80%98de-competitie-neemt-sterk-toe-op-de-belgische-voedingsdistributiemarkt%E2%80%99.

[4] Act on the Protection of Economic Competition coordinated on 15 September 2006, Belgian Official Gazette of 29 September 2006, p. 50613.

[5] Act Introducing Book IV "Protection of Competition" and Book V "Competition and Price Evolution" in the Code of Economic Law and Introducing the Definitions proper to Book IV and Book V and the Rules of Enforcement proper to Book IV and Book V, in Book I of the Code of Economic Law of 3 April 2013, Belgian Official Gazette of 26 April 2013, p. 25216 and Act Inserting the Provisions which concern Matters as referred to in Article 77 of the Constitution in Book IV "Protection of Competition" and Book V "Competition and Price Evolution" in the Code of Economic Law of 3 April 2013, Belgian Official Gazette of 26 April 2013, p. 25248.

[6] Certain provisions allowing for the appointment of officials of the new authority entered into force on 28 May 2013 as a result of the Royal Decree concerning the Entry into Force of Certain Provisions of the Act of 3 April 2013 Introducing Book IV "Protection of Competition" and Book V "Competition and Price Evolution" in the Code of Economic Law and Introducing the Definitions proper to Book IV and Book V and the Rules of Enforcement proper to Book IV and Book V, in Book I of the Code of Economic Law, Belgian Official Gazette of 27 May 2013, p. 33988.

[7] Act on Market Practices and Consumer Protection of 6 April 2010, Belgian Official Gazette of 12 April 2010, p. 20803.

fair market practices that harms the professional interests of one or more other undertakings. This covers not only anticompetitive practices under competition law but also certain other practices considered to be unfair against other undertakings (such as misleading advertising or inappropriate sale practices).

The Belgian Act on Market Practices and Consumer Protection of 2010 prohibits (re)sale at a loss, whereby sale at a loss is defined as any sale at a price that is not at least equal to the price at which the company has purchased the good or the price that the company would need to pay to restock the good. To determine the purchase price (or price for restocking), rebates that the company received or would receive can be deducted if these rebates are certain and relate to the procurement of the good in question. Rebates that the company received or would receive for other reasons than the procurement of the good in question cannot be taken into account to determine the purchase price of the good.

The Belgian legislation provides that the prohibition on resale at a loss does not apply in certain circumstances:

- in case of a liquidation or during the official sales periods;
- in case a good can no longer be preserved (goods that reach the end of their shell life);
- in case the product can no longer be sold at a price that is not at least equal to the purchase price, due to external circumstances; or
- in order to align the price to the price at which the same or a competing product is sold by competitors.

It is contested whether the prohibition on resale at a loss is compatible with the European Unfair Commercial Practices Directive.[8] In an order of 7 March 2013, which resulted from a request for preliminary ruling from the Commercial Court of Ghent, the Court of Justice of the European Union ruled that such a general prohibition of resale at a loss would be contrary to European law in case it pursues objectives relating to consumer protection.[9] It is clear from the legislative history of the prohibition on resale at a loss in Belgium that the provision at least also pursues other objectives than consumer protection. Whether in addition it also aims at consumer protection is debated.

Draft legislation to amend the rules on resale at a loss is currently being considered by the Belgian government.

[8] Directive 2005/29/EC of 11 May 2005 concerning Unfair Business-to-Consumer Commercial Practices in the Internal Market and amending Council Directive 84/450/EEC, Directives 97/7/EC, 98/27/EC and 2002/65/EC of the European Parliament and of the Council and Regulation (EC) No 2006/2004 of the European Parliament and of the Council, OJ 2005 L 149, p. 22.

[9] ECJ, case C-343/12,*Euronics Belgium CBVA v Kamera Express BV and Kamera Express Belgium BVBA*, ECR 2013 (not yet published).

4.1.2.3 Other Laws and Regulations Applying to the Retail and Grocery Sector

There is no specific legislation on the structure of the grocery retail market or the behaviour of large-scale grocery retailers, but certain legislation indirectly affects the ability of large-scale grocery retailers to develop and to take advantage of their size.

First of all, the Act on the Authorization of Trade Establishments of 2004[10] provides that new retail outlets of 400 m^2 (or the expansion of retail outlets to this size) require an authorisation from the municipality in which they will be located. In case the outlet exceeds 1,000 m^2, the National Socioeconomic Committee for Retail needs to issue an opinion on the request, taking into account the urban environment of the outlet and also consumer protection and employment. This legislation is sometimes perceived as protecting small and medium-sized retailers from the entry of large-scale (food or non-food) retail multinationals in their municipality.

According to the OECD and the European Commission, this legislation acts as a barrier to entry into local retail markets, but in its 2012 Report on the Price Level of Supermarkets (see below), the Belgian competition authority concludes that the effect of this legislation is limited.

Second, Belgium has relatively strict rules on trading hours, which are furthermore strengthened by agreements between labour unions and retailers (organisations). These rules are often seen as a protection for smaller retailers that do not have the means to offer as extensive opening hours as large retailers.

The Act Against Payment Delays in Commercial Transactions of 2002[11] provides that payment terms cannot be manifestly unfair, taking into account all relevant circumstances, good trading practices and the nature of the good or service. This rule can be enforced through actions before the courts, with a possibility for the president of the relevant court to grant an injunction following summary proceedings. Such cases are rare.

There are no specific rules on Internet retail stores, and, to the extent relevant, they are therefore subject to the same regulations as brick and mortar stores.

No price control of grocery products exists anymore since the abolition of the maximum price of bread on 1 July 2004. However, the new Code of Economic Law of 3 April 2013 introduces the possibility for the Belgian competition authority to impose temporary measures for a period of 6 months in case of 'a problem concerning prices or margins, an abnormal price evolution or a structural market problem'.[12] It remains to be seen how this will be applied.

[10] Act on the Authorization of Trade Establishments of 13 August 2004, Belgian Official Gazette of 5 October 2004, p. 70159.

[11] Act Against Payment Delays in Commercial Transactions of 2 August 2002, Belgian Official Gazette of 7 August 2002, p. 34281.

[12] Article V.3 and V.4 of the Code of Economic Law.

4.1.3 Market Studies

The Belgian competition authority in February 2012 published a Report on the Price Level of Supermarkets.[13]

This Report was commissioned by the Belgian minister of the economy on March 2011 after the Price Observatory, a body of the ministry of economy, had pointed out that consumer prices for groceries in Belgium were higher than in neighbouring countries (in particular, in the Netherlands and also, to a more limited extent, in France and Germany) and the European average. According to the Price Observatory, inflation for grocery prices was also higher in Belgium than in neighbouring countries.

The Report assessed the scale and the possible causes of the higher grocery prices in Belgium as compared to those in neighbouring countries and the European average. The characteristics of the Belgian supermarket sector were analysed, such as the size of supermarkets in Belgium, the concentration of the sector, its profitability and the ability to open new retail outlets. Also, the costs of the retail sector, in terms of personnel, procurement, tax, etc., were considered. The study also devoted attention to the impact of regulation: competition law, rules on establishment of new outlets, rules on sales at a loss, the regulation of opening hours, social regulation, etc.

The Report concluded that grocery prices were indeed higher in Belgium than in neighbouring countries (food was up to 12.5 % more expensive in Belgium than in the Netherlands).

The following factors were listed as explaining some of the price difference:

- VAT is slightly higher in Belgium than in neighbouring countries.
- Labour costs are slightly higher in Belgium than in neighbouring countries.
- Procurement costs are likely to be slightly higher in Belgium than in neighbouring countries.
- The characteristics of the retail market in Belgium with (1) the low profitability of one of the major retail chains (Carrefour), which prevents it from being aggressive on price, and (2) the "best price" policy of one of the other major retail chains (Colruyt), which reduces the incentive of other supermarkets to reduce prices.

The Report pointed out that the price difference between products in Belgium and the Netherlands was particularly noticeable in branded goods (as opposed to private label products). The Report indicated that suppliers of branded goods may also try to facilitate price discrimination between different countries.

The recommendations of the Report are as follows:

- Consumers should carefully choose between different retailers and between branded products and private labels to get the best deal.

[13] Available on http://economie.fgov.be/nl/binaries/studie_prijsniveau_supermarkten_tcm325-163021.pdf and http://economie.fgov.be/fr/binaries/etude_niveaux_prix_supermarches_tcm326-163021.pdf.

- Consumer organisations should facilitate the comparison between different types of products (in particular, as regards quality).
- Local authorities should facilitate the opening of additional retail outlets (in particular, discounters).
- Competition authorities should look for possible restrictive practices (in particular, so-called hub-and-spoke infringements and illicit provisions in franchise agreements).
- The statistical services should speed up their analysis of price evolutions (e.g., by using scanner data).
- Employers and employees in the sector should reduce barriers to exit, increase the flexibility in trading hours and revisit the indexation of wages.
- The Belgian legislator should revise the prohibition on sale at a loss, increase the flexibility in franchise agreements and facilitate price comparison by consumers.
- The European authorities should develop tools to compare prices for identical goods in the European Union.

4.2 Competition Law Enforcement

4.2.1 Competition Law Enforcement Against Anticompetitive Horizontal and Vertical Agreements

4.2.1.1 Collusion Among Grocery Retailers

The Belgian competition authority has decided only two cases in relation to the conduct of grocery retailers in the last 5 years.

In the beginning of 2008, the Belgian Competition Council imposed a fine of EUR 29,121 on the Flemish association of bakeries because it had developed and published a bread price index with the aim of influencing the price level of bread.[14] This fine has been annulled on procedural grounds by the Brussels Court of Appeal on 13 February 2013.[15]

On April 2011, the Belgian Competition Council decided on a report prepared by the Competition Prosecutors alleging that several Belgian supermarkets had coordinated price increases and exchanged sensitive information through the supplier Ferrero (so-called hub-and-spoke collusion). The Competition Council dismissed the case because it considered that the rights of defence of the companies involved had not been respected during the investigation.[16] Note that a number of cases of the

[14] Decision 2008-I/O-04 of 25 January 2008 in case MEDE-I/O-04/0045 Vlaamse Federatie van verenigingen van Brood- en Banketbakkers, Ijsbereiders en Chocoladebewerkers (VEBIC), available on http://economie.fgov.be/ccrm.jsp.

[15] Judgment of the Brussels Court of Appeal of 13 February 2013 in case VEBIC VZW, not yet published.

[16] Decision 2011-I/O-10 of 7 April 2011 in case CONC-I/O-08-0010B Hausses coordonnées chocolaterie, available on http://economie.fgov.be/ccrm.jsp.

Belgian competition authority have stranded in recent years because of procedural challenges.

In 2012, the Competition Prosecutors brought a new case for similar practices involving supermarkets and several suppliers of household, body care and hygiene products. The Prosecutors allege that, in the period between 2002 and 2007, 7 supermarket chains and 11 suppliers coordinated the resale price of some of the products concerned. This case is still pending.

4.2.1.2 Anticompetitive Horizontal Agreements Among Grocery Retailers at the Local Level

In terms of the geographic scope of anticompetitive practices, the Belgian Competition Act (and the new Code of Economic Law) provides that anticompetitive practices need to cover at least a substantial part of the Belgian market for such practices to be prohibited.[17] The Belgian Competition Council has in the past analysed a franchise agreement for one retail outlet,[18] which suggests that this criterion could be fulfilled even by practices at a local level. The Competition Council found in that case that there was no sufficient evidence of anticompetitive practices to grant the interim measures.

In its 2012 Report on the Price Level of Supermarkets, the Belgian competition authority pointed out that agreements to join a retail network often contain provisions preventing outlets from easily changing network and that the effects of these provisions would need to be analysed in further detail. No public information is available as to whether a more detailed analysis has taken place so far.

4.2.1.3 Resale Price Maintenance and Recommended Resale Prices

Since Belgian competition law needs to be interpreted in line with European competition law, the practice whereby a supplier recommends a resale price to a retailer is as such not prohibited. However, if recommended resale prices are combined with incentives for the retailer to apply the recommended price, this may be perceived as resale price maintenance and therefore prohibited.

The Belgian competition authority has not decided on cases concerning recommended resale prices by suppliers in the last 5 years.[19]

In case the company concerned is dominant, resale below cost and the de-listing of suppliers can constitute an abuse of dominant position under Belgian and European competition laws in the sense that they may constitute, respectively,

[17] Article 2 § 1 of the Act on the Protection of Economic Competition and Article IV.1 § 1 of the Code of Economic Law.

[18] Decision 2002-V/M-43 of 13 June 2002 in case CONC-V/M-02/2008 Interdamo S.A./ITM Belgium S.A. et Société Centrale d'Approvisionnement en Produits régionaux S.A., available on http://economie.fgov.be/ccrm.jsp.

[19] Note, however, the case of the recommended resale prices of the Flemish bakery association discussed above.

predatory pricing and a refusal to deal. In case the company concerned is not dominant, these practices are not prohibited by competition law.[20]

4.2.2 Abuse of Dominance

There are no recent cases on abuse of dominance in the grocery retail sector in Belgium. For the rules of abuse of dominance, Belgian competition law follows European competition law.

However, of note is the judgment of the Brussels Court of Appeal of 29 May 2012 ruling that press distributor AMP abused its dominant position by increasing a fee it charged to smaller press retailers because the increase was excessive as compared to the increase of AMP's costs.[21] Based on this judgment, a price increase can be excessive if it exceeds the cost increase of the supplier.

4.2.3 Abuse of Buying Power, Abuse of Dependency

Belgian competition law needs to be interpreted in line with European competition law and under European competition law the prohibition to abuse a dominant position also applies to undertakings whose possible dominant position is established in relation to their suppliers.[22] A dominant position can therefore also exist at the buyer's side.[23]

The Belgian Competition Act does not contain a statutory definition of buyer power nor of a dominant position. However, Article I.6 of the new Code of Economic Law introduces the definition of the European Court of Justice in its judgment in case 322/81 *Michelin v Commission*: an undertaking is dominant if it is able to hinder the maintenance of effective competition and can behave to an appreciable extent independently of its competitors and customers or suppliers.[24]

Just like European competition law, Belgian competition law does not contain a statutory definition of what constitutes an abuse of buying power or an abuse of dependency. However, Article 3 of the Belgian Competition Act (and Article IV.2

[20] See, however, the rules on resale at a loss in the Belgian Act on Market Practices and Consumer Protection of 2010 discussed above.

[21] Judgment of the Brussels Court of Appeal of 29 May 2012 in case Prodipress, Buurtsuper.be and VFP/AMP, not yet published.

[22] GC, case T-219/99,*British Airways v Commission,* ECR 2003 II-5917, pt 101.

[23] In fact, increased concerns of the European Commission on the existence of buyer power seem to have informed the inclusion of a market share threshold also at the buyer's level for agreements to benefit from the safe harbors of the Vertical Block Exemption Regulation. See Article 3(1) of Commission Regulation 330/2010 of 20 April 2010 on the application of Article 101(3) of the Treaty on the Functioning of the European Union to categories of vertical agreements and concerted practices, OJ L 102, 23 April 2010, p. 1.

[24] ECJ, case 322/81, *Michelin v Commission,* ECR 1983 3461, pt 30.

of the new Code of Economic Law), just like Article 102 TFEU, contains instances of abusive behaviour that can also be committed by dominant purchasers, e.g. applying dissimilar conditions to equivalent transactions with other trading parties, thereby placing them at a competitive disadvantage (discrimination).

The 2012 Report on the Price Level of Supermarkets did not identify any situations of abuse of buyer power, and the Belgian competition authority has so far not decided on cases concerning abuse of buyer power in Belgium. The director general of the Belgian competition authority stated in May 2013 that the authority is more concerned by the lack of buyer power than by too much buyer power.[25]

4.3 Merger Control

Changes of control over undertakings need to be notified to the Belgian competition authority if the parties to the concentration have combined turnover in Belgium exceeding EUR 100 million and if at least two parties to the concentration each have turnover in Belgium of at least EUR 40 million.[26] If a notification is made pursuant to the European merger regulation, no notification to the Belgian competition authority is required. There are no specific thresholds for merger control in the retail sector.

4.3.1 Market Definition in the Grocery Retail Sector

The Belgian competition authority systematically identifies the relevant market in grocery retail mergers as the market for the sale of daily consumer goods. Only outlets that sell a full range of daily consumer goods (food products, beverages, pet food, tobacco and domestic non-food goods) to the end consumer as their main activity are included in this market.

Until 2002/2003, the Belgian competition authority explicitly distinguished between retail outlets of different size (small retail outlets v supermarkets v hypermarkets). In more recent decisions, the authority seems to consider the entire grocery retail market as a whole, without distinction as to the format and the size of the outlet (presumably based on the wider geographic market definition discussed below).[27]

---

[25] Statement of Jacques Steenbergen, director general of the Belgian competition authority, at the GCR Live's 4th Annual Competition Law, Consumer Goods and Retail conference of 14 May 2013, as reported on http://globalcompetitionreview.com/news/article/33490/buyer-power-enforcers-concern.

[26] Article 7 § 1 of the Act on the Protection of Economic Competition. See also Article IV.7 § 1 of the Code of Economic Law.

[27] The reasoning is made explicit in decision 2002-C/C-67 of 11 September 2002 in case CONC-C/C-02/0041 SA Onveco et SA Ets Fr. Colruyt/SA Diswel, SA Disbo, SA Disroche et SA Boucherie Pasquasy, available on http://economie.fgov.be/ccrm.jsp.

There is no statutory definition of product markets or of the kind of test that needs to be used to define product markets.

The Belgian competition authority has pointed out that the retail market for daily consumer goods can be defined locally, according to the catchment areas of each store. Until 2002/2003, the authority also explicitly analysed competition at this local level. However, in more recent decisions, the authority always concluded that the relevant geographical market for grocery retail was national due to the overlaps between the catchment areas of different stores and because of the existence of national commercial policies at the main supermarket chains.[28]

There is no statutory definition of geographical markets or of the kind of test that needs to be used to define geographical markets.

4.3.2 Procurement Markets

In addition to the retail market, the authority in retail mergers also considers the procurement markets on which grocery retailers purchase their products. These procurement markets are defined from a supply-side perspective, such that, for example, beverages and fruit belong to different markets. These markets comprise sales not only to grocery retailers but also to other distributors (hotels, restaurants, specialised distributors, etc.).

The procurement markets for groceries have also been defined as national in scope.

4.3.3 Merger Control and the Growth of Grocery Retail Networks

The Belgian competition authority has so far not considered the concentration of grocery retail networks in Belgium to be problematic.

4.3.4 Countervailing Buyer Power as a Mitigating Factor for the Concentration of Suppliers

In one case, the Belgian competition authority has taken into account the buying power of grocery retail chains as a factor in a merger between suppliers. The parties to a 2012 merger between vegetable, fruit and flower auction houses argued that their transaction was partially motivated by the increased concentration of their customers (which include retail grocery stores and also specialised distributors and exporters). The Belgian Competition Council accepted the increased concentration

[28] *Ibid.*

on the demand side as one of the elements to conclude that the transaction would not result in any anticompetitive effects.[29]

4.3.5 Merger Remedies

In case it considers that a transaction would result in a significant impediment to effective competition on the Belgian market or a substantial part of it, in particular as a result of the creation or strengthening of a dominant position, the authority can make an approval decision subject to divestitures or behavioural remedies.

However, so far, the Belgian competition authority has not imposed any remedies in grocery retail sector concentrations.

4.4 Conclusion

Belgian competition law enforcement has been in a state of flux recently due to the procedural reforms that are being introduced by the new Code of Economic Law. Before introducing any further legislative changes in this field, it will be important to see how the new competition authority will take up its role.

However, it can be expected that the new system will place an additional burden on the Brussels Court of Appeal in terms of guaranteeing undertakings' rights of defence. The Brussels Court of Appeal is already short of adequate means today, and the reform risks increasing this bottleneck. This situation will need to be alleviated, through either budgetary or legislative means.

Outside of competition law, there are a number of regulations (e.g., on resale at a loss) that are not entirely in line with the spirit, if not the letter, of European law. It is recommended that these regulations are amended to ensure a uniform playing field across Europe.

[29] Decision 2012-C/C-30 of 30 November 2012 in case MEDE-C/C-12/0018 Mechelse Veilingen CVBA/Coöbra CVBA, available on http://economie.fgov.be/ccrm.jsp.

Brazil 5

José Carlos da Matta Berardo and Bruno Bastos Becker

5.1 Introduction

This article highlights the most relevant aspects of the enforcement of the competition law in the grocery retail market in Brazil as an introduction both to the general Brazilian rules on competition and the particularities of its application to the grocery retail sector.

Even though the authority has developed very sophisticated tools for reviewing mergers in the grocery retail sector over the years, no investigation of anticompetitive conduct in this sector has ever been pursued. Precedents and regulations lay the grounds for the prosecution of some types of behaviour of retailers and their suppliers, but so far enforcement has not been particularly active in this context. At the same time, no specific rules or exemptions apply to grocery retailers, regardless of the extension of their network or their relative size *vis-à-vis* competitors or suppliers.

The authors do not intend, because of the limited scope of this contribution, to address all the different details involving the retail sector but merely to provide an overview of the current understanding of this market by the local authority and the limits of the enforcement of competition law in this regard.

J.C. da Matta Berardo (✉) • B. Bastos Becker
Barbosa Müssnich & Aragão, São Paulo, Brazil
e-mail: jcm@bmalaw.com.br; bbr@bmalaw.com.br

P. Kobel et al. (eds.), *Antitrust in the Groceries Sector & Liability Issues in Relation to Corporate Social Responsibility*, LIDC Contributions on Antitrust Law, Intellectual Property and Unfair Competition, DOI 10.1007/978-3-662-45753-5_5

5.2 Economic Background

Brazil's grocery retail sector is generally thought to be moderately concentrated, following the trend of some major players (most of them international players such as Walmart, Carrefour, Casino/Pão de Açucar, Sonae and Cencosud). Those players have over the past decades, through organic growth and acquisition of key regional and niche players, such as cash and carry stores, tried to consolidate the industry. This is demonstrated by the number of merger cases reviewed by the authorities.

According to the Brazilian Association of Supermarkets, the country's largest 500 grocery retailers accounted for total revenues of approximately BRL 230 billion, while the top five chains account for approximately 60 % of those revenues and almost half of the number of stores.[1]

The industries in food processing and other suppliers, however, are generally more concentrated—some of the most high-profile mergers in Brazil involved food processors and grocery suppliers, such as Sadia/Perdigão, JBS/Bertin, Seara/Marfrig, Garoto/Nestle, Brahma/Antarctica, Kolynos/Colgate etc.—with some key large players representing a much larger share of the market, sometimes on the verge of dominance. Agriculture, on the other hand, is largely unconcentrated, as producers remain mainly local in scope (especially because of high transportation costs over the territory for low-value-added products).

For these reasons, and considering the continental dimensions of the Brazilian territory, analysts generally adopt the view that there is still room for consolidation among grocery retailers in the country, especially because of the scale gains that can result from the operation of a nationwide distribution systems and the yet low penetration of some types of stores in developing regions of the country.

5.3 Legal Background

5.3.1 Competition Law

The Brazilian competition law ("Competition Law"),[2] which replaced the former Brazilian competition law ("Former Competition Law")[3] on May 29, 2012, does not set forth any type of sector-specific exemptions or rules; the Brazilian IP Rights Law[4] prohibits unfair competition practices and is also general in scope, as per its article 195, without sector-specific rules. As a result, the general rules on the

[1] See, in Portuguese, http://www.abras.com.br/economia-e-pesquisa/ranking-abras/as-500-maiores/.

[2] Law no. 12,529/2011. An English version of this Law is available at http://www.cade.gov.br/upload/LAW%20N%C2%BA%2012529%202011%20%28English%20version%20from%2018%2005%202012%29.pdf.

[3] Law no. 8,884/1994.

[4] Law no. 9,279/1996.

prohibition of unfair competition and anticompetitive practices apply indistinctly to all market sectors, including the grocery retail.

The Brazilian competition law sets forth, in sum, that any practice can be considered anticompetitive if it has the restraint of competition as its object or potential effect (article 36 of the Competition Law). Practices deemed to be anticompetitive by their *object* (similarly to a *per se* prohibition) generally involve cartels and other agreements among competitors; unilateral pricing and non-pricing restraints (vertical conduct and abuses of dominant position in general) are usually assessed on the basis of their potential *effects* on competition (in a rule of reason fashion).

Enforcement of the competition law is still centred at the Federal Authority—Administrative Council for Economic Defense (hereafter "CADE", in its Portuguese acronym).[5] Nonetheless, individuals, public prosecutors and consumers' associations may challenge suspected anticompetitive behaviour directly in courts (article 47). Even if these cases are still rare, the CADE generally views this system of direct and actually decentralised recourse to court as the most efficient way to deal with local, "micro-violations" cases in a country that is as large and economically diverse as Brazil.

Pursuant to current competition law, a company deemed liable for a violation is subject to a fine ranging from 0.1 to 20 % of the gross turnover. This applies to the "company, group or conglomerate" in the "sector of activity" in which the violation occurred for the year prior to the formal initiation of the investigation. This fine cannot be lower than the gain obtained from the violation, if this is assessable (art. 37, I of Law no. 12,529), and it may be doubled in case of recidivism.

Companies may also be subject to ancillary penalties, such as (a) a publication of a summary of the decision in the newspapers; (b) a prohibition to enter into contracts with public banks; (c) a prohibition to take part in public bids or to enter into agreements with the government, for a minimum of 5 years; (d) the inclusion of the violator in a list of consumer offenders; (e) a recommendation for the compulsory licensing of patents held by the offender; (f) a recommendation to the public authorities not to grant, or to revoke if already granted, tax payment schedules, public subsidies or tax incentives; (g) a spin-off, transfer of control, sale of assets or any other measure necessary for the complete cessation of the illicit behaviour and its effects (art. 38 of the Competition Law).

Officers directly or indirectly responsible for the violation are subject to fines of 0.1–20 % of the fines applied to their respective entities if intent or fault is proven (art. 37, III of the Competition Law). Other individuals or entities that do not conduct corporate activities (trade associations, for instance) involved in violations are subject to fines that range from BRL 50 thousand to BRL 2 billion (art. 37, II of the Competition Law). Individuals may also be subject to a disbarment decision, with a prohibition on running a business under their own name or becoming legal

[5] *Conselho Administrativo de Defesa Econômica.*

representatives in corporations for a period of up to 5 years (art. 38, VI of the Competition Law).

Pursuant to the language of article 4 of the Brazilian Law for Economic Crimes,[6] which was revised by Law no. 12,529, hard-core cartels are considered criminal violations in Brazil. As criminal liability under Brazilian Law is generally only applicable to individuals (and not corporate entities or associations), individuals—regardless of their corporate ranking—found guilty of cartel crimes are subject to imprisonment, from 2 to 5 years, and to a criminal fine.

5.3.2 Other Laws and Regulations Applying to the Retail and Grocery Sector

Brazil does not have any laws aimed at controlling the structure of the grocery retail market or the commercial behaviour of grocery retailers. There are neither federal rules that differentiate large retailers from smaller shops, or brick and mortar stores from e-commerce, nor regulations of the relationship between suppliers and retailers, regardless of their sizes.

Regulations of pricing conduct also do not exist—at least directly through price controls, minimum or maximum prices—and they tend to be seen as a relic from the 1980s, when government officials would patrol supermarkets in order to avoid price increases in times of hyperinflation in the country. As a result, suppliers and retailers are free to determine their prices in view of the demand, and both adopt different strategies that they modify to meet demand needs. Retailers, more specifically, are also becoming more sophisticated in line with the mix of products sold in each store etc.

As a result, the retail market has generally been very open in Brazil (no restriction on foreign capital, no restrictions on size of entities, etc.) even before the transition to a market economy following the enactment of the 1988 Constitution of Brazil. No specific legislation is being actively pursued to change this situation in the near future.

As a clarification, health regulations, which mostly impact the retail business, apply indistinctly to all retailers, regardless of their size, and are generally set and enforced on a local (city) level; the same applies to consumer protection rules as to delivery and so on, which indistinctively apply to all retail segments, albeit these being federal in scope.

[6] Law no. 8,137/1990.

5.4 Anticompetitive Behaviour

There has been no finding of an infringement—either at the horizontal level or in unilateral, abuse of dominance cases—of the competition law in the grocery retail market either at the CADE or before national courts since, at least, the enactment of the modern generation of competition law in Brazil in 1994.

5.4.1 Horizontal Conduct

The CADE has wide powers to deal with this type of infringement, and it frequently does so in retail cases (see, for example, the abundant number of cartel violations found in relation to gas stations). In the grocery sector, however, there is no record of a decision or even an investigation for any type of horizontal conduct, such as collective boycotts or price-fixing practices.

No investigation of cases involving joint retaliation from suppliers, especially small-sized ones, has actually taken place, at least publicly. In this context, it is worth mentioning that Brazilian law does not prohibit the creation of association and cooperatives that allow small-sized producers to collectively sell their products. However, this does not except the application of the competition law in cartels inside associations or collective abuses, even if made in order to counter retailers' buying power.

5.4.2 Unilateral Conduct

An infringement involving unilateral conduct in Brazil will only be deemed to have taken place if it involves a dominant company. The CADE presumes (a rebuttable presumption) that a dominant position exists when a company is able to unilaterally alter market conditions or when its market shares exceed 20 % (article 36, § 2 of the Competition Law).

Holding a dominant position, however, is not unlawful[7] in itself, and the anticompetitive behaviour consists in the *abuse* of that power.[8] As it is the case with many civil law systems, the definition of an abuse is very controversial and is normally left to a case-by-case analysis. The CADE, however, tends to find an infringement (and thus, implicitly, an abuse) whenever it finds that a potential harm to competition can be associated to a certain practice by a company with a certain degree of market power or dominance. It remains to be seen how Brazilian courts

[7] Article 36, § 1 of the Competition law sets out that increased market presence that results naturally from the greater efficiency of the agent in comparison with its competitors is not unlawful.

[8] The Brazilian Constitution sets out that the law must repress the abuse of economic power that aims at dominating markets, eliminating competition or increasing profits arbitrarily (article 173, § 4).

will deal with this position, as up until now no decision on the merits from a Brazilian court has been delivered.

Article 36, § 3 of the Competition Law provides certain examples of anti-competitive practices that could result from unilateral conduct (abuse of dominance) carried out by dominant firms, among which are (item iv) "the creation of difficulties for the establishment, operation or development of a competitor company or supplier, acquirer or financier of goods or service"; (item ix) "the imposition, on the trade of goods or services, to distributors, retailers and representatives, resale prices, discounts, payment terms, minimum or maximum quantities, profit margin or any other market conditions related to their business with third parties"; and (item xv) "the sale of goods or services unreasonably below the cost price". These are only illustrative examples, and they do not restrict the CADE's ability to find infringements if it believes the conduct being investigated has the potential to lessen competition because of either its object or its effects.

5.4.2.1 Resale Price Maintenance and Recommended Resale Prices

There have been no precedents regarding recommended resale prices in the retail grocery sector.

The CADE, however, has recently condemned a company for resale price fixing.[9] In the decision, the CADE differentiated resale *price maintenance* from *price recommendation* (suggestion) and defined very strict criteria for the finding of an infringement in this type of case: the CADE, actually, set out that resale price maintenance cases entail an inversion in the burden of proof, by stating that they generally tend to lessen competition, and only cognisable efficiencies could justify the adoption of this type of practice. According to this same decision, resale price maintenance shall be deemed illegal if adopted by the supplier at the request of retailers.

5.4.2.2 Abusive Prices

There is no specific provision in article 36, § 3 of the Competition Law regarding exploitative or abusive prices. This was specifically mentioned in the Former Competition Law, excluded in the current legislation. However, despite not being specifically mentioned in the law as an example of an anticompetitive practice, abusive prices could theoretically be punished by the CADE under certain very strict conditions if they are capable of lessening competition in a vertically related market.

Nonetheless, according to the CADE's precedents,[10] it is very difficult to define standards of what should be considered abusive prices (margin, price or the

[9] See, for instance, Administrative Proceeding no. 08012.001271/2001-44(*SKF do Brasil Ltda.*), decided on January 30, 2013.

[10] See, for instance, Administrative Proceedings no. 08012.008708/2009-28 (*Comercial Amazônia de Petróleo Ltda. and Auto Posto Trevinho Ltda.*) decided on April 6, 2011; and 08012.000922/2000-27 (*Asta Médica Ltda.*), decided on June 4, 2008.

increase). Thus, they are considered only as evidence of abuse of dominant position or cartel, not being a *per se* conduct. It remains to be seen how the CADE will deal with this in the future.

5.4.2.3 Abuse of Buying Power

The Brazilian competition law does indeed prohibit the *abuse* of buying power if it has the potential to restrain competition, *i.e.*, vertical/unilateral practices involving companies with buying power are considered unlawful not on the basis of their object but instead because of their potential negative effects on competition. The CADE has never, however, found an infringement of the competition law on the basis of an abuse of buying power.

As there is no statutory (in hard or soft law) definition of buying power, the CADE will generally assess buying power using the same thresholds it uses for market power. For instance, the CADE presumes that a dominant position exists when a company is able to unilaterally alter market conditions or when its market shares exceed 20 %. The same rationale applies for buying power, *i.e.*, if a company buys 20 % of the market's total output, the CADE will presume it has buying power. As mentioned above, anticompetitive behaviour consists in the *abuse* of market or, in the case, buyer power.

In the past, several cases have dealt with dependency, but the CADE highlighted that dependency, *i.e.* one seller depending exclusively or almost exclusively on purchases made by one purchaser, does not in itself necessarily correspond to buying power, which obviously depends on aggregate market output and purchases.

Nonetheless, there is no precedent regarding infringements involving buying power or dependency. There have been a number of dependency cases in the early 2000s that superficially discuss the manufacturer–distributor relationship. These cases discuss the extent to which the private relation should be governed by competition law and state that if the plaintiff cannot show harm or potential harm to competition (as opposed to private harm to a single distributor), it should not be subject to the CADE's analysis. At the same time, there has been no case of "waterbed effect" related to retailers in Brazil.

5.5 Merger Control

5.5.1 Reportability Thresholds

There are no special thresholds for merger control in the retail sector, but the CADE may require the parties to submit transactions that have not met the notification threshold up to a year after a transaction has taken place (article 88, § 7 of the Competition Law).

As a background, in Brazil concentrations[11] are reportable, under a suspensive regime, if *i*) at least one of the groups involved registered an annual gross revenue (total turnover) or volume of business in Brazil, in the year before the transaction takes place, greater than BRL 750 million (~USD 400 million), and (*ii*) another group involved registered an annual gross revenue (total turnover) or volume of business in Brazil greater than BRL 75 million (~USD 40 million). The powers for merger control in Brazil are generally understood to be concentrated at the CADE. This means that there is no regional or local merger control.

In case the CADE has grounds to believe a concentration may lead to a substantial lessening of competition in Brazil, it can either impose remedies or outright prohibit a merger from taking place.

5.5.2 Market Definition

There is no statutory test for market definition in Brazil, but one of the competition authorities at the time issued, back in 2001, an ordinance that sets out horizontal merger guidelines, very similar in its structure to the US DOJ and FTC 1997 Horizontal Merger Guidelines. In the context of these guidelines, the CADE generally defined relevant markets on the basis of the hypothetical monopolist test (SSNIP). In more complex cases, the conclusions reached through this test are generally refined by additional quantitative techniques.

The CADE has a large number of precedents regarding supermarkets' mergers. In most of these precedents, the relevant market in the grocery sector is identified as comprising all *supermarkets*, *hypermarkets* and *self-service wholesale stores*. This contemplates, according to these precedents, the sale of durable and non-durable goods, separated by departments, in shelves and/or counters, allowing the consumers to pick up and acquire a large number of goods to be paid at checkouts. This refers to the self-service retail service offered in supermarkets and hypermarkets.[12]

For this purposes are defined as *supermarkets* any stores with groceries, bazaar and perishable goods sections; 3–40 checkouts; 1,500–5,000 items on display; and

[11] According to article 90 of Law no. 12,529, a concentration shall be deemed to occur when (i) two or more previously independent companies merge; (ii) one or more companies acquire, directly or directly, by any means control or parts of one or more other companies; or (iii) two or more companies enter into an association agreement or form a consortium or joint venture. A "partial acquisition of another company" is regulated by articles 9 through 10 of Resolution no. 2/2012, amended by Resolution no. 9/2014, and they include (a) the transaction results in the acquisition of sole or joint control over the target; (c) the transaction results in the acquisition of an interest higher than 20 %, if the acquirer (and its group) and the target company are not competitors nor active in vertically related markets; or (d) the transaction results in the acquisition of an interest higher than 5 %, if the acquirer (and its group) and the target company are either competitors or active in vertically related markets—any further 5 % acquisitions in this case are also notifiable.

[12] See, for instance, Merger Case no. 08012.006940/2007-60 (*Atacadão Distribuição, Comércio e Indústria Ltda. and Korcula Participações Ltda*), decided on December 17, 2008.

more than 300 m^2 of sales area. *Hypermarkets* have, additionally to the supermarket sections, also clothing and household appliance sections and have more than 40 checkouts, more than 5,000 items on display and a sales area larger than 5,000 m^2.

Bakeries, small grocery stores (any store with less than three checkouts), butchers, open markets and other small retail establishments are expressly excluded from the supermarket relevant market definition as they do not offer significant competitive pressure, according to the CADE, to the larger stores.[13] Internet retailers have never been considered in the context of mergers involving grocery stores, mostly because they are still an incipient distribution channel.

5.5.3 Geographical Market

As mentioned above, in Brazil, there is no statutory definition for the geographical relevant market for the retail sector. For its definition, the CADE's main precedents adopted an "area of influence" (or "catchment area") methodology,[14] which results in markets being defined from a local or "super-local" perspective, in view of the perceived notion that consumers are not willing to commute through long distances to do their grocery shopping.

According to this particular methodology, for cities with less than 200,000 inhabitants (which are considered small for Brazilian standards), areas of influence correspond to the whole area of the city, which leads to a single relevant market for each city. However, for cities with more than 200,000 inhabitants, geographic markets are delimited through the existence of the overlaps of the areas of influence of the different stores operated by the merging firms, in view of particular geographic features or traffic issues, in view of an average area of influence that varies according to population, density and size of the stores. As a result, a small store in a largely populated city will have a much smaller area of influence than a large store in a less-densely populated city. Table 5.1 shows the areas of influence generally adopted by the CADE.[15]

[13] See Merger Cases no. 08012.000787/1999-78 (*Peralta Comercial e Importadora Ltda and Companhia Brasileira de Distribuição*), decided on September 14, 2005; 08700.000435/2005-91 (*Petipreço Supermercados Ltda. and Bompreço Bahia S/A*), decided on August 31, 2005; and 08012.011699/2010-96 (*Serrana Empreendimentos e Participações Ltda. and GBarbosa Comercial Ltda*), decided on October 5, 2011.

[14] See Juracy Parente and Heitor Kato, "Área de influência: um estudo no varejo de supermercados", *Revista de Administração de Empresas* (RAE-FGV-SP), v. 41, n. 2, 2001. In this sense, see Merger Cases no. 08012.004897/2002-93 (*Jerónimo Martins, SPGS, S/A, Hermes – Sociedade de Investimentos Mobiliários e Imobiliários, Lda. and Companhia Brasileira de Distribuição*), decided on February 14, 2007, and 08012.009118/2008-31 (*Comercial Zimbreira Ltda. and Sonda Supermercados Exportação e Importação Ltda.*), decided on January 21, 2009.

[15] Translated from the Merger Case no. 08012.009959/2003-34 (*Companhia Brasileira de Distribuição and Sendas S/A*), decided on July 24, 2007, SEAE Technical Opinion, p. 15. Please note that 10,000 m^2 = 2.5 acres and 1 metre = 3.3 feet.

Table 5.1 Areas of influence generally adopted by the CADE

Area of influence of supermarkets and hypermarkets			
Number of checkouts	Population density	Range of population density (inhabitants/10,000 m^2)	Area of influence in metres (radius containing 60 % of customers)
3–5	Very low	Up to 50	1,000
3–5	Low	50–100	750
3–5	Medium	100–150	500
3–5	Medium–high	150–200	375
3–5	High	More than 200	250
6–9	Very low	Up to 50	1,500
6–9	Low	50–100	1,150
6–9	Medium	100–150	800
6–9	Medium–high	150–200	600
6–9	High	More than 200	450
10–14	Very low	Up to 50	2,200
10–14	Low	50–100	1,700
10–14	Medium	100–150	1,200
10–14	Medium–high	150–200	900
10–14	High	More than 200	650
15–19	Very low	Up to 50	2,700
15–19	Low	50–100	2,200
15–19	Medium	100–150	1,600
15–19	Medium–high	150–200	1,250
15–19	High	More than 200	950
20–29	Very low	Up to 50	3,200
20–29	Low	50–100	2,600
20–29	Medium	100–150	2,000
20–29	Medium–high	150–200	1,600
20–29	High	More than 200	1,200
30–39	Very low	Up to 50	3,800
30–39	Low	50–100	3,100
30–39	Medium	100–150	2,400
30–39	Medium–high	150–200	2,000
30–39	High	More than 200	1,600
40 or +	Very low	Up to 50	5,400
40 or +	Low	50–100	4,500
40 or +	Medium	100–150	3,600
40 or +	Medium–high	150–200	3,000
40 or +	High	More than 200	2,500

5.5.4 Concentration

Probably as a result of the CADE's approach to geographic market definition (which is always local in scope because of consumer preferences), concentration levels are assessed, naturally, on a local level. Generally, the CADE does not impose remedies or prohibit mergers when concentration levels are below 40 %, and in certain retail markets (durable goods) the CADE found concentrations of up to 60 % admissible whenever it could identify large rivals locally.

As a consequence, there has been no decision that considered concentration of the grocery retail chains on a national level as a problematic issue. On the contrary, a decision stated that in this market there are strong national competitors, which could contest any possible price increase.[16]

5.5.5 Countervailing Buying Power

The claim of creation of countervailing buying power was brought by merging parties in very specific cases in the retail sector, but as a mitigating factor and not as a rationale for the transaction. The CADE has not, however, considered grocery stores' bargaining power large enough to justify mergers that led to high concentration in upstream markets. For instance, in the *Sadia/Perdigão* case,[17] the CADE asserted that "the review does not allow one to infer that supermarkets and hypermarkets [...] hold enough buying power to, by itself, constraint the merging parties' market power".

As concentration in the retail sector increases, it is likely that the CADE will investigate this issue more closely.

5.5.6 Merger Remedies

There is no precedent of merger in the retail grocery sector during the last 5 years with the imposition of remedies—although in two transactions, during the early 2000s, the CADE required the divestiture of stores as a remedy. In a precedent involving a similar segment (retail hardline products),[18] the CADE required the significant divestitures of several stores throughout the territory.

[16] See Merger Case no. 08012.011699/2010-96 (*Serrana Empreendimentos e Participações Ltda. and GBarbosa Comercial Ltda*), decided on October 5, 2011.

[17] See Merger Case no. 08012.004423/2009-18 (*Perdigão S/A and Sadia S.A.*), decided on June 8, 2011.

[18] See Merger Cases no. 08012.004857/2009-18 (*Globex Utilidades S.A. and Companhia Brasileira de Distribuição*), decided on April 17, 2013 and 08012.010473/2009-34 (*Casa Bahia Comercial Ltda. and Companhia Brasileira de Distribuição*), decided on April 17, 2013.

These precedents indicate that the CADE is mainly concerned about assuring that consumers maintain a number of local choices, through the transfer of stores that allows newcomers to enter a certain region or competitors to expand their business (thus creating rivalry). This is probably the outcome of a relevant market definition that is focusing on consumers.

6 Bulgaria

Anton Petrov

6.1 Introduction

This contribution discusses the domestic competition law, policy, and practice towards the grocery retail sector in Bulgaria. The report reflects the law and enforcement practice in existence as of the end of May 2013.

6.1.1 Economic Background

6.1.1.1 Agricultural Production

The first level in the grocery supply chain in Bulgaria—agricultural production—is characterised by extreme fragmentation.[1] It is composed of a large number of farmers operating under various legal forms (cooperatives, sole proprietors, commercial companies), managing relatively small holdings.[2] According to Eurostat data for 2010, almost 80 % of the farms in Bulgaria have a size of less than 2 ha (see Table 6.1).

Low degree of concentration is present in all food product markets. Taking dairy production as an example, it can be stated that in comparison with other EU Member States (probably with the exception of Romania), Bulgaria has the most fragmented market for row cow milk—more than 95 % of local farms produce less than 100,000 kg of milk per year.[3]

[1] Commission on Protection of Competition (CPC) decision no. 1125/2012, page 122.

[2] A holding is defined as a techno-economic unit under a single management engaged in agricultural production (including the maintenance of land in good agricultural and environmental condition).

[3] CPC decision no. 1641/2010, page 15.

A. Petrov (✉)
Djingov, Gouginski, Kyutchukov & Velichkov, Sofia, Bulgaria
e-mail: anton.petrov@dgkv.com

P. Kobel et al. (eds.), *Antitrust in the Groceries Sector & Liability Issues in Relation to Corporate Social Responsibility*, LIDC Contributions on Antitrust Law, Intellectual Property and Unfair Competition, DOI 10.1007/978-3-662-45753-5_6

Table 6.1 Number of agricultural holdings by size, 2010 (1,000 holdings)

	0 ha	<2 ha	2–4.9 ha	5–9.9 ha	10–19.9 ha	20–29.9 ha	30–49.9 ha	50–99.9 ha	≥100 ha	Total
EU-27	258,100	5,608,460	2,407,420	1,303,040	900,530	377,580	395,210	391,350	324,840	11,966,440
% of EU-27	2	47	20	11	8	3	3	3	3	100
Bulgaria	13,150	294,960	30,390	10,730	6,820	2,950	3,060	2,930	5,490	370,490
% of Bulgaria	3.5	79.6	8.2	2.9	1.8	0.8	0.8	0.8	1.5	100

Source: Eurostat [Eurostat Pocketbooks 2012 edition: Agriculture, fishery and forestry statistics – Main results – 2010–11 (ISBN 978-92-79-25431-4)]

At the same time, the statistical data indicate comparatively diversified production, with a slight focus on animal breeding (see Table 6.2).

Lack of concentration on the principal production markets stimulates the existence of many go-between traders, which serve as intermediaries with the next level of the supply chain—food processing. The market is not very matured, and financial derivatives (such as futures contracts) are rarely used, resulting in low-risk management and high-price instability in long-term sales of agricultural products.[4] Lack of commodity exchanges, directly accessible to farmers, also leads to distortion of price information between the different levels of the supply chain.

6.1.1.2 Food Processing

Since the majority of farmers do not have adequate storage capacity, they are forced on selling their production as soon as possible—either directly to large consumers or (more often) to wholesalers. The Bulgarian national competition authority—the Commission on Protection of Competition (the "CPC")—has conducted several sector inquiries analysing the supply chain for various foods (bread, dairy, cooking oil), and the recurring results indicate that the food processing stage is less fragmented and better organised. Indeed, the majority of market players are SMEs, but there are also certain large companies—mostly local subsidiaries of international groups (such as Danone, Nestle, Coca-Cola) and also independent Bulgarian producers.

Since in general the number of food processing companies is much lower than the number of farmers, the former can negotiate with a large number of suppliers, which increases their bargaining power. Negotiating inequalities are reflected in dynamics of price changes along the supply chain leading to certain asymmetries.[5] Observations indicate that in the majority of cases, individual agreements with pricing and delivery terms are not signed in advance and supplies are negotiated on the spot (e.g., during the harvesting campaign for crops and horticulture). In fact, many transactions are based on oral agreements, which subsequently are confirmed by invoices.

Food processing companies are better organised, and there are many industry (branch) associations. Although there are no indications of trends for increased sector consolidation, in recent years discussions within industry associations may have led to partial and/or temporary coordination of behaviour in certain sectors.[6]

6.1.1.3 Retail Market

According to a recently published study,[7] the Bulgarian retail market [all fast-moving consumer goods (the "FMCG"), food included] has shrunk by EUR 1

[4] CPC decision no. 1125/2012, page 123.

[5] For example, in the second bread supply chain sector inquiry (CPC Decision no. 1125/2012), it was observed that reduction in prices of wheat is not promptly and equally reflected in the price of flour and bread.

[6] So far, the CPC has investigated, found, and penalised cartels in vegetable oils (CPC decision no. 1150/2007), poultry meat and eggs (CPC decision no. 170/2008), dairy products (CPC decision no. 650/2008), and bread & pastry (CPC decision no. 662/2008).

[7] http://gain.fas.usda.gov/Recent%20GAIN%20Publications/Retail%20Market%20Update_Sofia_1;Bulgaria_1-31-2012.pdf (last visited June 2014).

Table 6.2 Number of holdings by farm type, 2010 (1,000 holdings)

	Field crops	Horticulture	Permanent crops	Mixed cropping	Grazing livestock	Granivores	Mixed livestock	Mixed crop-livestock	Non-classifiable holdings	Total
EU-27	2,935.1	234.3	2,392.7	503.9	1,762.0	1,388.8	777.6	1,502.7	238.0	11,734.7
% of EU-27	25	2	20	4	15	12	7	13	2	100
Bulgaria	63.4	18.2	32.1	14.6	88.6	28.6	50.2	73.8	1.0	370.5
% of Bulgaria	17.1	4.9	8.7	3.9	23.9	7.7	13.5	19.9	0.3	100

Source: Eurostat [Eurostat Pocketbooks 2012 edition: Agriculture, fishery and forestry statistics – Main results – 2010–11 (ISBN 978-92-79-25431-4)]

Fig. 6.1 Evolution of shadow economy in Bulgaria as percentage of GDP. *Source*: AT Kearney, Bulgarian National Bank [see The Shadow Economy in Europe and Bulgaria, Study Results Presentation – a complete version available at http://www.bblf.bg/uploads/files/file_372.pdf (last visited June 2014).]

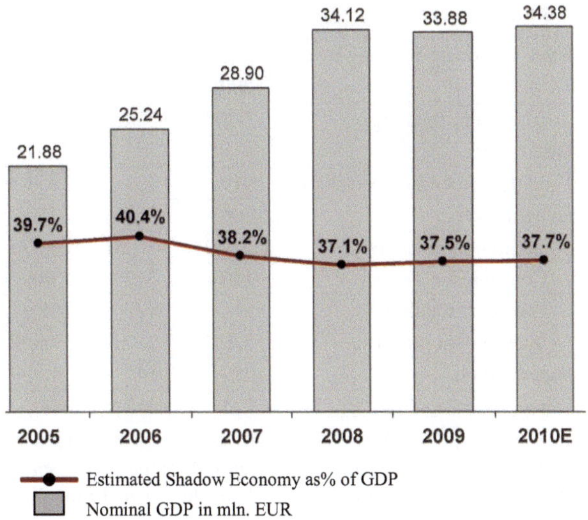

billion for the last 3 years due to declining consumption. While in 2008 the market was estimated at BGN 12 billion (EUR 6.6 billion), in 2010 it was estimated at BGN 10.7 billion (EUR 5.5 billion) and, respectively, BGN 10.5 billion (EUR 5.4 billion) in 2011. Grocery goods account for the majority of purchases, indicating constant increase in value in contrast to the general retail trend—BGN 6.2 billion in 2008, BGN 6.4 billion in 2009, and BGN 6.5 billion in 2010. However, there is also a significant portion of grey market transactions, which according to an AT KEARNEY estimation account for about a third of all deliveries (see Fig. 6.1).

With respect to the market structure, there is a visible trend in the increase of the share of commercial chains and the so-called modern trade, for the expense of traditional retail, represented by small grocery shops and minimarkets. Despite that, the Bulgarian retail market is still characterised by very low level of consolidation, and in 2010 about 60–70 % of all grocery sales in Bulgaria were channelled through traditional retail establishments (see Table 6.3).[8]

"Modern trade" outlets (hypermarkets and supermarkets above 300 m^2) have a low degree of penetration (customer access) in comparison with small supermarkets and "on-the-corner" type convenience shops. According to recently published GfK surveys,[9] while "modern trade" channels have become well developed in the capital and regional centres, they remain less prominent in smaller towns and villages across the country.

Proximity to home or workplace still determines the type of store where customers make the largest proportion of their purchases. The majority of Bulgarian consumers prefer to go to a nearby neighbourhood shop to buy their essentials on "as-the-need-arrive" basis, instead of going to a large hypermarket

[8] CPC decision no. 1199/2010, page 13.

[9] GfK Shopping Monitor 2010, Bulgaria – The expansion of modern trade.

Table 6.3 Grocery retail market

Sales in grocery retailing by category, value 2005–2010, million BGN						
	2005	2006	2007	2008	2009	2010
Total grocery retailing	5,109	5,506	5,777	6,227	6,443	6,526
Discounters	–	–	–	–	67.2	103.4
Food drink/tobacco specialists	919	935	953	1,085	1,120	1,147
Hypermarkets	206	352	459	644	756	839
Small grocery retailers	3,040	3,120	3,075	2,980	2,912	2,841
–Convenience stores	150	312	348	386	395	405
–Forecourt retailers	81	92	98	117	121	124
–Independent groceries	2,810	2,716	2,630	2,478	2,395	2,312
Supermarkets	689	847	1,039	1,265	1,330	1,335
Other grocery outlets	255	252	248	252	258	261

Source: Euromonitor International, 2010 [Extracted from GAIN Report no. 1203/31 January 2012, available at http://gain.fas.usda.gov/Recent%20GAIN%20Publications/Retail%20Market%20Update_Sofia_Bulgaria_1-31-2012.pdf (last visited June 2014)]

once or twice a month.[10] For many "daily necessities" (such as bread or meat), Bulgarian customers prefer to go to traditional specialised establishments. Finally, fruits and vegetables are also usually purchased from local specialised grocers.

As a result of this in recent years, most retail chains began to open new format of stores—smaller convenience-type outlets, closer to consumers, in downtown or in highly populated residential areas.[11] Until a few years ago, these locations belonged to independent groceries, while modern retailers grew in the outskirts. However, it turned out that the consumer shopping habits do not change quickly, and Bulgarians still prefer to shop more frequently in smaller volume. These stores have longer work hours adjusted to the usual work hours of costumers, and assortment is limited to staple products. Unlike in other foreign markets, in Bulgaria prices between such convenience stores and hypermarkets are not substantial because the market is highly fragmented. Convenience stores also bring benefits to traditional retailers. Most are not able to withstand the double pressure from the "modern" chains and from the economic crisis. Instead of going out of business, these players prefer to rebrand by franchising. Smaller outlets, especially in small towns, have the advantage to have loyal customers; often, shop owners and assistants know many consumers by name and try to cater to individual consumer needs. Finally, rebranding helps foreign retailers that sometimes face the resistance of local communities that feel that foreign investors may put local independent groceries out of business.

[10] In a GfK survey, made in 2011, consumers respond that they shop in convenience stores/minimarkets in neighbourhoods 18 times per month and at hypermarkets/discounters once per week. About 25 % of consumers do not shop at discounters—usually the youngest and the oldest consumers. Regular consumers of discounters are those at 20–49 years age, households with more than one member, and those with higher income. At the same time, often in smaller towns, groceries are also informal places for socialising (see GAIN Report no. 1203 of 31 January 2012).

[11] See GAIN Report no. 1203/31 January 2012.

6.1.2 Legal Background

Bulgaria introduced competition legislation in 1991 with the adoption of the first Protection of Competition Act[12] (the "PCA"). It was revised several times in line with developments in EU competition law doctrine and finally replaced by a new law in 1998.[13] Ten years later at the end of 2008, following Bulgaria's accession to the EU on 1 January 2007, a new PCA[14] came into force, which further harmonised Bulgaria's competition regime with EU law in line with the changes that were introduced by Regulation 1/2003 and Regulation 139/2004. The third version of the act was drafted with the assistance of the Italian competition authority[15] and EU financial support under the PHARE programme.

The PCA is the primary legislative act governing competition law in Bulgaria. It comprises the substantive rules on restrictive horizontal and vertical agreements, abuse of dominance and monopoly, merger control, sector inquiries, compliance review of legislation and administrative acts, and unfair trading practices. The PCA also constitutes the national competition authority—the Commission on Protection of Competition—and sets out the procedural rules for investigations, sector inquiries, enforcement, and imposition of penalties for breaches of competition regulations.

Pursuant to its Art. 2, the PCA applies to any relationship resulting from operations on the territory of the Republic of Bulgaria, or beyond it, as long as it does or may prevent, restrict or distort competition in Bulgaria. The act does not contain rules dedicated specifically to grocery retail or another business sector. There are also no sector-specific rules in other laws and regulations pertaining to grocery retail.

6.1.2.1 Unfair Trading Practices

Rules against unfair competition have existed in Bulgaria since the first enactment of a PCA in 1991, and they are regarded as a traditional element of the competition protection regime, together with antitrust enforcement and merger control. The original regulation of unfair trading practices was quite basic, and in 1998 the second PCA introduced a major upgrade by implementing in itsChapter VII detailed rules based on accumulated case practice. They were preserved in the third and currently effective statutory version with minor additions, the most notable being the introduction of specific prohibitions against misleading and comparative advertising.[16]

---

[12] Promulgated in State Gazette 39/17.05.1991, in force as of 20 May 1991.

[13] Promulgated in State Gazette 52/08.05.1998, in force as of 11 May 1998.

[14] Promulgated in State Gazette 102/28.11.2008, in force as of 2 December 2008, as subsequently amended and supplemented.

[15] Autorità Garante della Concorrenza e del Mercato, http://www.agcm.it/.

[16] Prior to 2008, advertising messages were regulated by the Consumer Protection Act, but the national legislator concluded that adverse effects of misleading advertising practices damage competitors as much as consumers and decided to implement Directive 2006/114 by consolidating its rules into the PCA's chapter on unfair competition (see Sec. 2 of the Supplementary Provisions of the PCA).

Pursuant to the statutory definition, "unfair competition" is any act or omission to act in the course of business activity that is inconsistent with fair business practices and harms or may harm the interests of competitors.[17]The PCA further defines and prohibits in its Chapter VII the following specific forms of unfair competition: (1) prejudicing of the trade reputation and good will of competitors; (2) misrepresentation with respect to goods or services; (3) misleading and prohibited comparative advertising; (4) imitations related to product appearance, trade names, trademarks or distinctive symbols, domain names or webpage design; (5) unfair solicitation of clients (e.g., promotional games with high rewards); and (6) use or disclosure of trade secrets in a way that is inconsistent with fair business practices.

Unfair competition is a form of tort, which is subject to the presence of the following prerequisites, applicable to all forms of unfair competition, envisaged in Chapter VII of the PCA:

- there is an act or omission to act within the course of business;
- the act or omission to act is inconsistent with fair business practices[18];
- the parties involved are competitors on the relevant market; and
- the act or omission to act has harmed or may harm the legitimate interests of competitors.

The general prohibition is regarded as subsidiary to the specific rules, but according to court interpretations, a violation of the latter must exhibit the general features of the former.[19] Thus, even if a particular case does not qualify under one of the specific forms of unfair competition (Arts. 30–37 PCA), it may still fall within the scope of the general unfair competition tort (Art. 29 PCA).

At first glance, unfair trading practices (the "UTPs") between undertakings operating on different levels of the supply chain seem to be left outside the scope of Chapter VII PCA. However, examples from case practice indicate that some types of unfair conduct between non-competitors (e.g., abuse of reputation and goodwill,[20] abuse of confidential information,[21] etc.) may also qualify as administrative violation under Art. 29 PCA. Moreover, the CPC has held explicitly that where proceedings are initiated without a petitioner (*sua sponte*), there is no need to analyse competitive relations in order to establish the existence of unfair competition.[22]

---

[17] Art. 29 PCA.

[18] According the statutory definition (Sec. 1, para. 2 of the Supplementary Provisions of the PCA), "fair business practices" means the rules regulating market behaviour, which originate from laws and common commercial usages and do not infringe the accepted principles of morality.

[19] Decision of the Supreme Administrative Court no. 7966/2006 on case no. 3345/2006, 2nd Grand Chamber.

[20] CPC decision no. 846/2009.

[21] Decision of the Supreme Administrative Court no. 8730/2008 on case no. 5489/2008, 2nd Grand Chamber.

[22] See, e.g., CPC decision no. 345/210 and CPC decision no. 375/2010.

Finally, it should be noted that the existing regulatory framework in Bulgaria is geared towards prevention of "unfair competition", which as a concept is somewhat different from UTPs as defined in the Green Paper on unfair trading practices in the business-to-business food and non-food supply chain in Europe.[23] Practices that indicate misuse of bargaining position to the detriment of the other contracting party seem to fall outside the PCA, as far as such unilateral conduct is not linked to a position of dominance.

6.1.2.2 Antitrust Enforcement

In its Chapter III devoted to illegal restrictions of competition, the PCA contains an open prohibition against all types of agreements between undertakings, decisions of associations of undertakings or concerted practices, which by object or result prevent, restrict or distort competition.[24] The general provision is supplemented by a non-exhaustive indicative list of anticompetitive practices.

Certain "hard-core" restrictions are regarded as *per se* anticompetitive due to their inherent ability to distort competition on the relevant market. Examples include price fixing, market and customer allocation, and output limitations. A mere plan or negotiation of hard-core restraints constitutes an infringement, even if no actual negative effect can be observed on the relevant market.[25]

6.1.2.3 Exemptions from Competition Law Prohibitions

The grocery sector is not exempted, and all restrictions of national and EU competition laws apply in full. Furthermore, no exemption exists for small farmers and suppliers, and SMEs in general are subject to the same competition law restrictions as large undertakings.

6.1.2.4 Contemplated Amendments to Competition Law

On September 2012, a draft bill for PCA amendment was submitted to the Parliament, with the stated purpose of countering unfair B2B practices in the retail supply chain. This draft was a product of long public discussions, spanning more than 2 years. Following the announcement of the European Commission's report on competition in the food supply chain, the Bulgarian Ministry of Finance asked the CPC whether in the light of the report specific national regulation was required. On May 2010, the CPC issued an official opinion stating that the existing rules for protection of competition are sufficient and any problems in the retail supply chain should be best handled by self-regulation within branch organisations.[26] Later the same year, however, in response to complaints from local suppliers alleging abusive practices in the distribution chain of consumer goods, the Ministry of

[23] See http://ec.europa.eu/internal_market/consultations/2013/unfair-trading-practices/index_en.htm (last visited June 2013).

[24] Art. 15(1) PCA.

[25] CPC decision no. 1150/2007.

[26] CPC decision no. 495/2010.

Economy and the Ministry of Finance created a Joint Task Group (the "JTG") to investigate further whether legislative intervention was necessary.

The JTG concluded that competition in the retail supply chain is distorted due to the existence of retailers with "significant market power" (the "SMP") that apply too much pressure on weak suppliers. The JTG dismissed without much discussion soft approaches (as industry self-regulation and special dispute settlement procedures) and started deliberating legislative intervention through an amendment to the PCA. Several proposals for PCA overhaul were circulated for public discussion, within which two principal approaches could be distinguished: (1) introduction of prohibitions against specific clauses within supply agreements (such as listing fees, deferred payment, labelling requirements, buy-back agreements, long-term resale below supply cost, etc.) and (2) adoption of a general prohibition against unfair business practices by SMP operators, following the approach for combating abuse of dominance. Within the second camp there was a debate on how to define SMP—whether to use strict criteria (such as annual turnover or number and size of outlets) or to implement an open definition, mirroring the respective rules on dominance.

Proponents of the second approach prevailed, and in the middle of June 2012 a draft bill was published on the Ministry of Economy's website, proposing a set of fresh rules on prohibited use of SMP to be integrated into the PCA chapter on abusive unilateral behaviour. By the end of the month, the CPC published its official opinion on the text, which though critical of the drafting quality was generally in support of the core ideas.[27] In September, a slightly revised version of this bill was submitted to Parliament, and it was sponsored by politicians from the four principal political parties—both majority and opposition.

The idea of the legislator was to introduce the concept of "significant market power" as a new category of market position (distinct from monopoly and dominance) that may support anticompetitive behaviour. According to the originally proposed definition, SMP is attributable to an undertaking having no dominant position, which nevertheless may distort competition on the relevant market due to the fact that its suppliers or customers depend on it. But despite the fact that SMP was differentiated from dominance, the draft did not envisage specific rules for it. The intention was to expand the scope of Art. 21 PCA, which contains an open prohibition and an exemplary list of abusive practices for dominant undertakings (similar to Art. 102 TFEU), to cover both abuse of dominance and abuse of SMP. In addition, it was proposed to add to the current list of potential abuses (price fixing, output limitation, tying, refusal to deal, etc.) "behaviour in violation of good faith commercial practices, which harms or may harm the interests of competitors". In short, the idea of the legislator was to impose on both dominant and SMP undertakings the obligation to refrain from UTPs.

The bill entered the agenda of the parliamentary committees, but the discussion progress was very slow. According to the publicly available information, until 15

[27] CPC decision no. 716/2012.

March 2013 (when the 41st National Assembly was officially dissolved) the internal review process was not completed in neither of the relevant committees. Following elections in May 2013, under its new composition the legislative body was striving to cover a lot of diverse hot topics and the PCA amendment was shelved until March 2014, when a new revised draft was presented, thus resuming discussions.

The new draft from 2014 contemplated introduction of three-tier control over grocery retail: first, it reinstated regulation on SMP; second, it provided for ex ante control of supply contracts and general terms of all large retailers, to be exercised by the CPC; and third, specific types of clauses were to be expressly prohibited. While SMP regulation was seen as universal, the two other sets of rules would be sector specific and would affect only food retailers with annual turnover of over BGN 50 million (approx. EUR 25 million). Such retailers would be obliged to send their contract templates to the CPC for review and approval, following which they were to be published on a website and made publicly available. Deviations from the authorised templates would not be permitted unless expressly authorised by the CPC. Last, but not least, the new draft also introduced the possibility for protection of the identity of complainants, if so requested.

As can be expected, the legislative proposal triggered strong opposition from modern trade, but retailers were supported by many other industries. It should be noted that the bill was marked by numerous drafting faults[28]—most of the texts were very ambiguous and allowed the implementing authorities considerable freedom to interpret the rules and expand their scope as seen fit. Therefore, many perceived the new regulation as another tool for exercising pressure on specific businesses.

The public campaign mounted by various business organisations was not sufficient to discourage the majority coalition from proceeding with the plan, though between first and second reading significant changes were introduced in the draft text. The final version, as adopted by the Parliament on 18 June 2014, contains the following three new types of rules: (1) prohibition against abuse of superior bargaining position, defined as a form of unfair competition; (2) administrative oversight over general terms of large retailers; and (3) specific requirements and limitations for contracts concluded by large retailers.

On 30 June 2014, the President imposed a partial veto, motivated by concerns that the contemplated regulation neglects consumer welfare for the benefit of selected businesses, while at the same time lack of precise legislative definitions

[28] For example, it was intended that the ex ante control over contract templates would follow the CPC procedure for "intercession for the benefit of competition". However, this procedure was originally intended to allow the NCA to adopt opinions on the compatibility of laws and decisions of other authorities with competition law. Since such opinions have purely advisory character, they are not subject to judicial control. But if the same procedure were to be applied to review and approval of contractual terms, the absence of possibility to appeal the CPC decision would amount to uncontrolled administrative intervention in violation of fundamental economic freedoms and due process rights.

providing broad authority for the CPC to issue implementing regulations was regarded as violation of the principle of separation of powers. The bill was discussed again in the Parliament on 11 July 2014, but sufficient majority was not present to overcome the presidential veto.[29] Thus, the legislative procedure was reinitiated once again, and a third reading is expected in the near future, but this time discussions will be limited to the texts covered by the presidential objections. Considering the political situation in the country and the fact that the government is expected to resign before the end of July, following which the 42nd National Assembly should be dissolved and new parliamentary elections should be held, it is quite likely that the discussion process over the bill will not be completed before the end of 2014.[30]

The principal features of the bill in its latest version can be summarised as follows:

New Regulation on Superior Bargaining Position

The original idea to regulate abuses of SMP as a form of antitrust violation was replaced by new rules on unfair competition, introducing the regulatory category of "superior bargaining position" (or "SBP"). According to the proposed definition for a new Art. 27a PCA, an undertaking would be deemed to have SBP where its commercial partners are dependent on it due to the characteristics of the relevant market, the specific relations between the undertakings concerned, the type of their activities, and the difference in their scale of business. The new regulation would prohibit any act or omission of a company with SBP that contradicts good faith commercial practices and harms or may harm the interests of the weaker contractual party. The criteria for SBP analysis and precision of the forms of abusive behaviour should be devised by the CPC in a special methodology. In case of violation, the CPC may impose on the undertaking concerned fines of at least BGN 10,000 (approx. EUR 5,000), up to 10 % of their aggregate annual sales in the affected product group for the preceding year (or up to BGN 50,000 in the absence of turnover).

It is clear that unfair trading practices are not a problem resulting from "market power" per se since in many cases abusive terms can be forced upon weaker contractual parties by companies commanding small market shares. Therefore, a regulation focusing on the specific contractual relationship indicating harmful effects seems more appropriate than antitrust rules, which only look at market structure. Still the statutory definition has many problems that open the room for discriminatory implementation. These flaws were among the principal reasons that prompted the President to refuse to promulgate the bill and return it for further deliberation.

---

[29] According to the Bulgarian Constitution, an absolute majority of all MPs is required to overcome a presidential veto.

[30] These observations are valid as of mid-July 2014.

First, elimination of bargaining power cannot be a goal by itself. It is completely possible that a behaviour that at first glance seems to exhibit the traits of an unfair practice is actually beneficial to consumers. For example, pressure for lowering procurement prices that is accompanied with a parallel decrease in retail prices is a gain for consumers. For this reason, SBP in itself and pressure on the weaker party should not be deemed to represent a violation of competition law, as far as there is no harm or threat for consumers.

The core objective of competition law is protection of consumer welfare, while promotion of economic efficiency is only the tool to reach that aim. The new statutory rules against abuse of SBP discuss only the interests of businesses and their inability to obtain better deals. Thus, the actual effects of bargaining power on consumer welfare are completely neglected. As a result, the contemplated regulation is not in compliance with the principle of consumer protection.[31]

Second, it was noted that delegation of competence to the CPC to devise all criteria for implementation of the new rules on SBP is not in line with the constitutional requirement that all material socio-economic relations are regulated by statutes. The contemplated legislative delegation would grant the CPC complete freedom to assess, in its discretion, which situations fall within the purview of the prohibition for abuse of SBP and which do not. Moreover, the possibility for frequent modification of the criteria would lead to lack of foreseeability with respect to the applicable requirements for exercise of economic activity and thus devaluate legal certainty and destabilise the very foundation of economic relations.

Administrative Oversight over General Terms of Large Retailers

The second regulatory line[32] introduced a general obligation for all food retailers with annual turnover exceeding BGN 50 million (approx. EUR 25 million) to submit their contracts and general terms used in food procurement transactions before the CPC for review. The templates must be published on the company websites and used in all relations with suppliers. The same notification procedure must be followed for all modifications. Clearly, the original idea for ex ante control was abandoned in favour of simple notification. However, the bill also states that the CPC must open proceedings on suspect abuse of SBP if it finds that some of the clauses in a template are not in compliance with the law. Moreover, deviations from the official templates are prohibited under the threat of severe sanctions that may reach 1 % of the average daily turnover calculated with respect to the preceding fiscal year.

The first problem identified in the presidential veto is the discriminatory scope of the new regulation: the rules impose obligations only on food retailers, disregarding the abusive potential of the behaviour of food manufacturers and traders. This is in sharp contrast with all market analyses, which indicate that unfair practices are

[31] Art 38 of the EU Charter of Fundamental Rights.

[32] The bill was designed as an amendment to the PCA, but it also supplements the Foods Act, where all new sector-specific rules would be introduced.

possible on all levels of the food supply, as indicated by the European Commission in its Green Book.[33]

In addition, the President supported the objections raised by businesses that the law would effectively limit the freedom of economic initiative in the food retail sector. The result would be super-regulation, which would affect only selected companies. The discriminatory approach finds no justification since the addressees are the largest companies, which are also the most transparent in their dealings, while the less law-abiding market players would not be affected. Thus, the contemplated regulation would in effect stimulate the grey economy.

In addition, it should be noted that the prohibition for deviation from the published templates is so broadly formulated that if interpreted literally could mean that the contract parties cannot negotiate any conditions that could take precedence over the general terms. Such a broad limitation of freedom of contract seems out of proportion with the declared legislative goals. The very requirement for uniform terms of dealing, with the additional obligation that such terms be announced publicly on a website, negates all freedom to rationalise economic behaviour in line with the market specifics. Moreover, this could lead to harmonisation of procurement terms of retailers, with an outcome that could hardly be expected to be pro-competitive.

Sector-Specific Contract Law Rules

The bill also introduced a new Art. 19a in the Foods Act, which regulates procurement agreements of large retailers by mandating written form and prohibiting the following type of clauses:

1. exclusivity arrangements, which ban or restrict the ability of a supplier to offer or purchase goods or services to or from third parties;
2. MFC clauses, which prohibit or restrict the ability of a supplier to provide the same or better commercial conditions to third parties;
3. sanctions for providing the same or better commercial conditions to third parties;
4. clauses for unilateral amendment of the contract;
5. fees or discounts related to services that are not actually rendered or with a value that does not correspond to the service actually rendered:
6. transfer of unreasonable or disproportionate commercial risk towards one of the parties;
7. payment terms, longer than 30 days as of the date of issuance of a supply invoice;
8. prohibition or restriction on a contracting party to transfer receivables to third parties;
9. clauses permitting the retailer to return to supplier goods with expired shelf life and/or to impose penalties on supplier for in-store shelf life expiry.

[33] Green paper on unfair trading practices in the business-to-business food and non-food supply chain in Europe (COM(2013) 37/2), pages 7–8.

The bill further requires that all grounds and procedures for unilateral termination shall be expressly set in the agreement. In case of unilateral termination without prior notification or in case of breach of the notification period, the aggrieved party shall be entitled to compensation for the damages caused by the termination.

All these rules have mandatory character, and any agreement in deviation shall be null and void. In addition, the food safety authorities are empowered to supervise compliance with the new contractual requirements and to impose fines in the range of BGN 2,000–3,000 (approx. EUR 1,000–1,500) for each case of established violation.

While some of the sector-specific rules seem straightforward, others are quite ambiguous, which was the reason for the presidential veto in this respect. It was noted that the prohibitions are too broadly formulated and may restrict perfectly legitimate practices. For example, the prohibition on unilateral modification of the agreement could prevent use of price update clauses in case of achieved turnover targets or pursuant to changes in official benchmarks. Similarly, the prohibition on return of goods with expired shelf life in effect prevents the use of consignment trading models. The rule concerning shifting of commercial risk is also ambiguous as there is no definition of what is "reasonable" and what is "proportionate".

More importantly, the authorities would be allowed to evaluate and balance counter-obligations of the parties and may declare that a specific fee is illegal (in whole or in part) because it is deemed disproportionate to the value obtained by the supplier. And while such an analysis could be theoretically possible with respect to services and the respective fees, it is not clear how anyone can measure the countervalue of a discount, which by its very essence means reduction of the price. It is also unclear what degree of discrepancy in the two values could lead to nullity of the specific arrangement—whether it should be significant or any (even formal) difference would suffice.

The President also asked the MPs to reconsider whether it is prudent to empower the food safety authorities to exercise control over the contents of commercial agreements. Considering that their primary competence is to supervise production and trade with foods with respect to hygienic and quality standards, it seems rather naïve to expect that the same officials could possess adequate knowledge to analyse the legal and economic effects of clauses in procurement contracts. At the very least, that would require building new administrative capacity, which in turn would have budgetary consequences that were discussed neither in the bill itself nor in the motives thereto.

New Approaches to Self-Regulation

In its final sections, the statutory amendment envisages the creation of a new National Consultative Council (the "NCC") on the better functioning of the food supply chain, comprising associations and professional organisation from the sectors of food production, processing, and retail. It should be supplemented by a conciliatory committee that would receive the task to resolve disputes between companies in the food supply sector through mediation.

The creation of a consultative body that would analyse the food retail sector and assist in the determination of best practices was supported by all principal stakeholders. This was clearly the preferred option for businesses, which vigorously opposed state intervention on the market. Still it must be noted that this last part of the bill is the least developed. Many essential issues with respect to the composition and functioning of the new bodies remain unsettled. Thus, the provisions are only declaratory in nature, and there are no clear solutions that could be effectively implemented.

Moreover, parallel introduction of the new administrative oversight with ambiguous self-regulatory mechanisms would undermine any possibility for development of the latter. The two types of regulation contradict with each other to a large extent, creating a risk from overlapping competences leading to over-regulation.

Short Comments

"Levelling the playing field" was among the principal reasons for the establishment of the JTG, which led to the conception of the first PCA amendment. The text of all drafts (including the latest regulation on abuse of SBP) also refers explicitly to "violation of good faith commercial practices". However, until the bill becomes an actual law, these phrases would not be scrutinised by the administrative or judicial authorities and their meanings will remain unclear.

There are significant fears that the latest legislative approach, introducing three separate new forms of state regulation, would result in duplication and even triplication of statutory restrictions, expanded to an unclear range of situations, falling within the scope of the ambiguous concept of "superior bargaining position". This would create double jeopardy risk of multiplied sanctions in clear violation with the principle of proportionality.[34]Over-regulation could limit competition instead of protecting it. The proposed amendments may result in deterioration of the business environment by increasing administrative burden and investment risks owing to the gross interference of the state into the freedom of contracting.

The stated purpose of the legislator is to combat unfair practices in the retail sector. However, the first group of rules, regulating abuse of SBP, is sufficiently broad to encompass any industry and every business in Bulgaria. If the PCA amendment is adopted by the Parliament (in this or in its next composition) and becomes the effective law of the land, the CPC would assume principal responsibility for the enforcement of the new rules against abuse of SBP. The latest bill leaves many issues open, which would need to be answered in implementing regulations adopted by the CPC. Due to the numerous imperfections of the draft statutory definitions, the NCA would have significant discretion to assess which situations fall within the purview of the prohibition for abuse of SBP and which do not. One may only wonder whether such broad delegation of competence is in line with the fundamental principles of separation of powers. Certainly, it would not enhance transparency of statutory requirements or foreseeability of administrative intervention.

[34] Arts 49 and 50 of the EU Charter of Fundamental Rights.

6.1.2.5 Other Laws and Regulations Applying to the Retail and Grocery Sector

Except for the contemplated new legislation discussed above, up until the present, in Bulgaria there were no special regulations governing the structure of grocery retail and behaviour of the market players. Indeed, there are many sanitary and quality regulations that require compliance with certain minimum production and distribution standards, and there are consumer protection regulations that govern advertising and marketing practices. All these regulations, however, do not limit the scope of competition among grocery retailers.

The only UTPs that are regulated by national commercial law are deferred payments between businesses. Following an amendment to the Commerce Act,[35] effective as of 3 March 2013, the new Art. 309a in its Sec. 3 prohibits limitation of liability for late payments where this would represent a clear abuse of creditor's interest or violate common morals. The rule is fairly new, and there is no published case law on its application.

Bulgarian law does not prescribe a specific legal form for retail operations. As indicated by the CPC in its merger control practice,[36] the Bulgarian retail market is characterised by significant fragmentation and great diversity of players organised in various legal forms—sole proprietors, partnerships, commercial companies, cooperatives—in fact, all legally permissible structures.

The activities of online merchants are governed by the same rules as brick-and-mortar shops. The only additional regulation comes from the E-Commerce Act[37] and Chapter III, Section II of the Consumer Protection Act,[38] which provide enhanced rights for consumers with respect to distance sales.

For the sake of completeness, it can be added that at the end of 2012, high-ranking officials from the Food Safety Agency made public comments that the government intends to restrict online sales of certain "homemade" foods. However, until the date of this report, no specific steps have been made in this respect or at least a draft bill has not been submitted to Parliament.

6.1.2.6 Pricing Regulations

Grocery products are not subject to price controls in Bulgaria, and all market participants along the entire grocery supply chain are free to determine unilaterally their prices and profit margins. There are no regulations that prevent or limit the ability of large-scale retailers from passing on discounts they obtain from suppliers.[39]

---

[35] Transposing into national law the rules of Directive 2011/7 on combating late payment in commercial transactions.

[36] See, e.g., CPC decision no. 284/2013.

[37] Transposing into national law the rules of Directive 2000/31 on electronic commerce.

[38] Transposing into national law the rules of Directive 97/7 on the protection of consumers in respect of distance contracts.

[39] In fact, the statement of objections in the Retail Cartel case (discussed in Sect. 6.2.1.2 below) highlighted the asymmetry in reductions in procurement prices with respect to retail prices as a principal anticompetitive effect of the alleged concerted practice.

The PCA, however, explicitly prohibits dumping sales, regarded as a form of unfair competition.[40] "Dumping" is deemed to exist where the following requirements are satisfied:

1. goods or services are offered at prices lower than prime cost—i.e., below production and marketing cost;
2. long-term sales—the duration of the campaign should not be insignificant; thus, long short-term promotions (for several weeks up to a couple of months) are in principle permissible;
3. significant quantities—according to CPC practice, the relative share of goods dumped on the relevant market must account for more than one-third of the overall turnover (if high-value goods—over 10 % may suffice);
4. for the purpose of unfair solicitation of customers.

On the objective side, sales below prime cost must be maintained for a significant period of time, and the overall quantities must be sufficient to "capture" customers. On the subjective side, the law requires that the seller acts with intention to drive competition out of the market. However, the violation does not require evidence of injury to competitors—i.e., the CPC does not investigate the result. It is deemed that maintaining unreasonably low prices, which do not cover the relevant production and marketing costs, is a form of bad faith behaviour in itself, unless an objective economic justification can be provided.

6.1.2.7 Laws Designed to Empower Consumers to Make Competition Work Better Among Retailers

No specific provisions in this respect exist in Bulgaria.

6.1.2.8 Laws Deregulating the Retail Sector

No specific provisions in this respect exist in Bulgaria. On the contrary, there is a trend in expanding administrative regulation over grocery retail.

6.1.3 Market Studies

So far, the CPC has completed four sector inquiries related to food supply and distribution, focusing on wheat and bread,[41] dairy products,[42] and cooking oil.[43]

[40] The PCA distinguishes between dumping as a form of unfair trade practice and predatory pricing as a form of abuse of monopoly or dominant position. Herein we only address dumping as a form of unfair trade practice.

[41] First in 2005 – CPC decision no. 50/2005, and again in 2012 – CPC decision no. 1125/2012.

[42] CPC decision no. 1641/2010.

[43] CPC decision no. 686/2012.

6.1.3.1 Reasons for Conducting Market Studies

All market surveys were triggered by sharp increases in retail prices of the respective products, and the declared aim was to establish whether this was a result of speculation or natural economic trends. It's worth noting that the focus of investigation in all cases was on the most important staple foods—bread, milk, and cooking oil. Upward price movements in these goods usually result in broad public outcry, especially in times of economic crisis. The former Bulgarian government was very sensitive to public pressure and hence proactive in all situations of adverse effects on poor members of the society. In most cases, there were public announcements from members of cabinet urging the CPC to start investigations in order to find "which cartel is behind the speculative price increase".

The First Bread Supply Chain Inquiry

In 2003, the CPC started its first sector inquiry in food supply, focusing on three interrelated products—wheat, flour, and bread. The analysis covered the period from 2001 to 2004. The CPC aimed to analyse the effect of the market structure on competitive environment in production of and trade with wheat, flour, and common bread, as well as vertical links between these three sectors. Five separate relevant markets were defined: (1) production of wheat, (2) storage of wheat, (3) trade with wheat, (4) production and distribution of flour, and (5) production and distribution of common bread.

Among the principal issues in wheat production, the CPC identified the high share of grey economy and bad organisation and procedures of the state intervention agency.[44] Lack of access to funding was noted as the primary reason for small farmers to sell their harvest on "green", leading to limitation of free sales, while lack of effective commodity exchanges was highlighted as one of the main reasons for farmers to resort to intermediary traders.[45] Although there was sufficient free grain storage capacity, access was artificially restricted since most of it is owned by grain merchants, which exercise pressure on farmers to sell, often without proper documents and in violation of tax regulations. Low contractual discipline was also observed—payments were often deferred, leading to constantly increasing intercompany debt.[46]

With respect to flour and bread production, it was noted that the principal problem is also grey transactions. Competition with respect to the end product—bread—was further distorted due to a number of unfair practices, related to violation of trademark rights and misleading marketing announcements.[47]

[44] CPC decision no. 50/2005, pp. 143–145.

[45] CPC decision no. 50/2005, pp. 35–38.

[46] CPC decision no. 50/2005, p. 41.

[47] CPC decision no. 50/2005, p. 151.

Milk Supply Chain Inquiry

In 2010, the CPC adopted a sector inquiry of the competitive environment in the production, purchasing, and processing of raw milk, as well as in wholesale and retail distribution of dairy products. The authority established a significant lack of balance between the degree of concentration on the market of raw milk production and concentration on the market of milk processing.[48] According to the CPC, this asymmetry provides milk processors with a stronger bargaining position, and they are able to impose on farmers lower purchase prices and other unfavourable trading conditions.

Cooking Oil Supply Chain Inquiry

This sector inquiry was triggered by sharp increase in prices of sunflower cooking oil during the second half of 2010. Its purpose was to analyse the market structure and conditions for production and trade with sunflower seed and the oil derived from it and to evaluate to what extent pricing trends were influenced by objective factors or whether there was artificial distortion due to anticompetitive practices.

Similar to preceding inquiries, the CPC established that the first level of the supply chain—the market for production of sunflower seed—is highly fragmented, comprising numerous small farms.[49] In fact, the 50 largest producers accounted for less than 10 % of the total harvest. At the same time, there were a total of 10 seed processing and oil producing companies. The market shares of the first five of them were in the range of 10–20 % each.[50] The HHI index for the oil production market in 2009 was 1,108, increasing to 1,293 in 2010. According to the CPC, these values indicated low degree of concentration and absence of a clear leader, which in itself should signify presence of effective competition.[51]

Nevertheless, a comparative analysis of benchmarking data indicated that prices in Bulgaria do not follow the same fluctuation trends as EU and world averages. It was established that during the period of investigation, national prices exhibited much broader margins of change than the other EU 27 countries. The CPC concluded that speculative transactions are common on both investigated markets, thus creating price instability and greater short-term volatility.[52] The anomalies were explained with lack of transparency and inequality between the undertakings occupying different levels in the supply chain—production, processing, and distribution.

---

48 CPC decision no. 1641/2010, p. 78.

49 CPC decision no. 686/2012, p. 10.

50 In fact, for the analysed period (2007–2010), none of them had reached a share in excess of 20 %.

51 CPC decision no. 686/2012, p. 18.

52 CPC decision no. 686/2012, p. 53.

Second Bread Supply Chain Inquiry

The fourth CPC inquiry in the food sector was triggered also by hysteric publications alleging asymmetric movement in prices of wheat and bread. This time the authority reviewed the composition and pricing trends in the three interrelated markets (for wheat, flour, and common bread) during the period 2008–2010.

The second analysis confirmed that the (wheat) farming level of production remains highly fragmented, trade is extremely unsophisticated, and there is no price transparency or stability.[53] Advanced risk management tools (such as futures and other financial derivatives) are rarely used. Absence of effective commodity exchanges also contributes to distortion of price information.

The number of market players is significantly reduced on the next level of the supply chain—wheat storage and trade. However, the majority of grain merchants are export oriented, and their operations do not have significant effect on the related national markets for flour and bread. In fact, the CPC concludes that there is no separate national market for grain storage since such services have become too expensive. Larger farming cooperatives use their own storage capacity, but small farmers (which account for the biggest part of all producers) are forced to sell shortly after harvest. Most milling and processing enterprises purchase directly from farmers, and the clear asymmetry in numbers between participants on the supply and demand sides of transactions[54] grants them a serious advantage with respect to bargaining position. In many cases, advance written contracts are not used and prices and quantities are negotiated "on the spot" during the harvesting campaign.

There is also a steady decrease in the number of bakeries, with only 824 registered in 2010, out of 2,500 in 2005.[55] There is a trend towards consolidation, but concentration ratios are still low.[56]

However, despite the evidence indicating comparatively healthy market structure on all levels of the supply chain, the CPC also observed the presence of asymmetries in dynamics of wholesale prices of wheat and flour. In particular, during the second half of 2010, the price of flour increased more sharply than the price of wheat. More importantly, the increase of flour prices occurred simultaneously with the increase of wheat prices—there was no time lag, which was considered common under normal market conditions. Suspecting prohibited coordination, the CPC opened parallel investigation against the Union of Bulgarian Millers and its members.[57]

---

[53] During the period of investigation, the 15 largest producers account for less than 5 % cultivated area and none of them has individual share exceeding 0.5 % (CPC decision no. 1125/2012, p. 19).

[54] In 2009 and 2010, the 12 largest milling companies processed more than 65 % of all grain sold on the national market. However, there is no actual concentration on this level either since only the three largest companies have shares in excess of 10 %, but the CR_3 index for 2009 was lower than 40. Indeed, in 2010, CR_3 exceeded 40, but the market could still qualify as relatively competitive (see CPC decision no. 1125/2012, pp. 49–50).

[55] CPC decision no. 1125/2012, p. 71.

[56] CR_4 for 2009 amounted to of 27 %.

[57] CPC decision no. 1125/2012, p. 124 and CPC decision no. 958/2012.

6.1.3.2 Outcome of the Market Studies

The First Bread Supply Chain Inquiry

The CPC found that the first-degree market (wheat production) is extremely fragmented and could only benefit from consolidation—either contractually based or corporate.[58] Regulatory intervention through simplified export rules and procedures was advised, but it was noted that the public authorities should put more effort in tax & financial controls rather than on pricing intrusion. Most importantly, stimulation of commodity exchanges was highlighted as a priority, as this was conceived as the best option for countering the excessive bargaining power of wheat merchants.[59]

Competition in the milling sector was considered sufficiently healthy since most operators were SMEs. It was noted that the state could contribute by introducing uniform technical and quality standards and stimulate their adoption by appropriate tax measures.[60]

In the end-product market, the CPC again noted that the presence of many competitors and lack of dominant undertakings signify healthy market structure. However, there were signs of emergence of anticompetitive agreements among market players, aiming to fix prices and restrict access of competitors to specific regions. It was advised that a standard for "common bread" is necessary in order to serve as a basis of comparison between products.[61]

Milk Supply Chain Inquiry

The CPC established that the sector of raw milk production is highly fragmented. Most of the animal farms are small or medium-sized enterprises. The majority had an average number of 40–50 cows. The fragmented nature of livestock breeding leads to a dependency of farmers on buyers and milk processors.[62]

According to the CPC, this asymmetry has the potential to lead to unfair distribution of value added along the entire supply chain, from milk producers to end users, as a result of which a significant part of the generated income stays on the level of dairy processing.[63] In view of the above, the CPC stated that it supports the recommendations and conclusions drawn by the European Commission—i.e., that no special legislation is required and such problems should be overcome by means of the mechanisms and measures existing in the framework of the rules on the Common Agricultural Policy and national and EU competition laws.

---

[58] CPC decision no. 50/2005, p. 53.

[59] CPC decision no. 50/2005, p. 54.

[60] CPC decision no. 50/2005, p. 109.

[61] CPC decision no. 50/2005, p. 149.

[62] In 2009, for example, there were about 2,500 milk-producing farms that supplied 20 milk processing companies (CPC decision no. 1641/2010, p. 78).

[63] CPC decision no. 1641/2010, p. 79.

Cooking Oil Supply Chain Inquiry

The CPC claimed that the lack of transparency and price instability are results of bargaining inequalities. Significant fragmentation in sunflower seed production places farmers at a disadvantage when negotiation with merchants and processing companies. Absence of commodity exchanges also contributes to distortion of price information along the supply chain. In order to remedy the situation, the authority proposed adoption of three priorities:

1. promotion of sustainable contractual relations based on free market prices,
2. enhancing of pricing transparency along the supply chain for the purpose of promoting competition and combating pricing instabilities,
3. promotion of consolidation among undertakings on national level (e.g., through cooperation on farming level).[64]

Second Bread Supply Chain Inquiry

The CPC noted that price instability problems are observed in recent years not only in the bread supply but also with respect to all farm products and foods. The authority urged the government to address the situation by introducing specific measures for the promotion of effective competition on all levels of the grocery supply chain, proposing focusing on

- the development of legitimate mechanisms for increasing price transparency, such as publicly accessible price-monitoring platform collecting and processing data on national historical aggregated prices;
- support for standard compliant products, especially for farmers (e.g. bio-farming subsidies);
- the promotion of written agreements with the aim to increase legal stability of commercial relations and limit grey sector supplies.[65]

As a remedy against future sharp variations, the CPC suggested improving the balance of bargaining power along the wheat-flour-bread supply chain by:

- stimulating SMEs by providing easier access to funding and reducing administrative burdens,
- stimulating production and supply of high-quality wheat,
- promoting adaptation of farmers to the changing market environment by stimulating consolidation through various cooperative forms and branch associations.[66]

[64] CPC decision no. 686/2012, p. 55.

[65] CPC decision no. 1125/2012, p. 124.

[66] CPC decision no. 1125/2012, p. 125.

6.2 Competition Law Enforcement

6.2.1 Competition Law Enforcement Against Anticompetitive Horizontal and Vertical Agreements

6.2.1.1 Collusion Among Suppliers of Grocery Products

Horizontal agreements between suppliers for the purposes of control over quantities have been penalised by the CPC on several occasions. The best example of such case is the *Poultry Cartel*[67] investigation, which started after a series of press publications on the "abrupt" increase of poultry meat prices in July–August of 2007. The CPC dawn raided the office of the Bulgarian Poultry Union and amassed sufficient documentary evidence to allege that its members have consorted for the purpose of limiting production and raising prices.

The authority established that on several Union meetings it was decided that egg producers should sell all excess supply (in compliance with a negotiated delivery schedule) to one designated processing factory, which should serve as a buffer by grinding surplus eggs into egg powder. On other sessions dedicated to poultry meat, the Union adopted several recommendations encouraging all members to reduce their production by 30–40 %, and a special committee was set up to "supervise market trends". In order for the "recommendations" to reach all market players, the Union regularly published them in its magazine "Poultry Breeding". Parallel to that, the Union disseminated letters directly to its members with information on the adopted recommendations.

The CPC held that the mechanisms of taking "surplus" quantities out of the market have maintained artificially prices at levels higher than the ones that would have resulted from standard market dynamics. Collection of periodic reports on individual output quantities and dissemination of that data to Union members in a non-aggregate form was also condemned as a prohibited exchange of sensitive information.

For the sake of completeness, it should be noted that the NCA has not reviewed any cases of small suppliers (such as farmers) jointly retaliating against large grocery food retailers to punish the latter for selling low-priced imported agricultural products cheaply. At the same time, there has been a lot of publicity around complaints from local farmers and food processing companies against low-price imports. However, any joint action of suppliers related to the adoption of uniform prices or other trading conditions towards one or more specific retailers would constitute a prohibited agreement that could be prosecuted and sanctioned in accordance with Art. 15 PCA.

6.2.1.2 Collusion Among Grocery Retailers

So far, there have been only two investigations where the CPC evaluated the conduct of retailers in Bulgaria from an antitrust perspective. Since the first case

[67] CPC decision no. 601/2008.

was related to alleged abusive unilateral conduct (see Sect. 6.2.2 below), only the so-called Retail Cartel[68] case is discussed hereinbelow.

In 2009, the NCA launched an investigation against several "modern trade" chains[69] in response to complaints by local suppliers of imposition of unfair terms in supply agreements and abusive practices. Following a preliminary investigation of more than a year, in February 2011, the CPC issued a statement of objections alleging coordination of marketing strategies and price fixing for products in promotion. The authority focused its analysis on the following types of provisions present in the supply agreements:

- most-favoured-customer (MFC) clauses, pursuant to which a supplier is obliged to extend to the retailer any reduction in the supply price that has been offered to another retailer;
- clauses obliging suppliers to report to the retailer a lower net supply price granted to another retailer;
- product promotion exclusivity (PPE) clauses, which prevent suppliers to launch simultaneous promotional price decreases of one and the same product with different retailers;
- clauses on access charges (and, in particular, on their amount), pursuant to which suppliers are obliged to make payments for product listing and shelf space.

Each of the defendants had some but not all of the above provisions in its supply agreements, and none of the above clauses were present in the supply agreements of all defendants. Nevertheless, the CPC formulated the following specific objections:

1. The application of PPE clauses allowed defendants to exchange (through suppliers) information about their future marketing and promotional plans leading to coordination of marketing policy.
2. The parallel existence of MFC and PPE clauses in the supply agreements resulted in horizontal coordination of prices of goods in promotion.
3. The combined application of MFC with clauses relating to calculation of supply prices, and in particular clauses regulating the level and amount of access fees, resulted in coordinated price fixing—pushing procurement prices down.

While some of the allegations may seem a variation of the "hub-and-spoke" theory, the CPC did not offer proof or allege any actual communication or exchange of information through suppliers. According to the authority, the "intentional" implementation of the suspect clauses in supply agreements had "network effects" that allegedly increased transparency on the supply market, thus allowing retailers

[68] CPC decision no. 833/2012 on case no. 404/2009.

[69] Defendants in the case were Metro Cash & Carry Bulgaria EOOD, Billa Bulgaria EOOD, Kaufland Bulgaria EOOD, Kaufland Bulgaria EOOD & Co KD, Piccadilly AD, Maxima Bulgaria EOOD, and Hit Hypermarket EOOD.

to obtain current information about the supply costs and planned promotional activities of competitors. Market data did not support the price fixing allegation either since procurement prices were not identical.

The theory applied by the CPC was vulnerable to criticism on many grounds, e.g., because some of the types of clauses were block exempt and their use as evidence of a horizontal cartel raises policy concerns about legal certainty in competition law enforcement. However, instead of dealing with those concerns under the framework of the applicable block exemption regulations (e.g., by withdrawing the benefit of the block exemption), the CPC brought cartel charges.

The case was closed without a final decision on the merits. Eventually, all six defendants offered to abolish[70] the suspect clauses from their supply agreements, which the CPC found sufficient to alleviate its concerns. It should be noted, however, that the PCA does not allow adoption of commitments in cases of "serious violations". In its own Guidelines on Commitment Decisions from 2010, the CPC had stated that it would treat all price-fixing cartels and other hard-core horizontal restraints as "serious". The authority did not provide any meaningful explanation to reconcile the apparent contradiction between the law and its acceptance of the proposed commitments. It merely stated that the alleged horizontal coordination did not constitute a hard-core violation of competition law and the adoption of commitments was fit to redress competition concerns. Thus, without any further elaboration on this point, the position of the CPC undermined its own cartel allegations.

The "Retail cartel" case of 2012 is the only example of investigation on collusion among retailers. In addition, it should be noted that in the summer of 2012 the Minister of Agriculture announced that he has secured the agreement of several commercial chains to "freeze" prices of certain staple foods. Indeed, most large retailers started to distribute leaflets and even run radio ads about "frozen" prices. The opposition challenged the campaign, arguing that the government is succumbing to populist demands and actually stimulating cartel practices. The CPC issued a press release that it intends to investigate the topic, suspecting potential price fixing collusion between the retailers. The government tried to defend its position, arguing that this is not a cartel but a promotion. There is no data of opening of official CPC proceedings, and the entire campaign died out completely by the middle of autumn 2013.

6.2.1.3 Anticompetitive Horizontal Agreements at the Local Level

So far, the CPC has not reviewed complaints of horizontal collusion between retailers in a small locality. Judging from case history related to other sectors of the economy (e.g., taxi services,[71] bakery,[72] bus transport[73]), the limited territorial

[70] Some of them had already done so in 2009; thus, the only commitments offered were "not to implement such clauses in the future".

[71] CPC decision no. 39/2012.

[72] CPC decision no. 622/2008.

[73] CPC decision no. 205/2005.

scope of a suspect infringement would not prevent an investigation or mitigate the risk of imposition of sanctions.

The internal governance of grocery franchises has not been subject to review by the NCA in Bulgaria.

6.2.1.4 Resale Price Maintenance and Recommended Resale Prices

Existing CPC case history indicates that any attempt of a supplier to influence the pricing behaviour of its clients would be regarded as a straightforward competition restraint.[74] Setting minimum prices is considered a hard-core restriction that is *per se* illegal. Maximum prices are not regarded as automatically anticompetitive, and their actual effect on the market should always be evaluated. Generally, price caps are considered restrictive if they distort or eliminate price competition on the relevant market.[75] However, effects on a neighbouring (upstream or downstream) market would also be considered in case of price correlation—e.g., because the analysed products (sunflower seed) serve as principal inputs for production on the downstream market (sunflower cooking oil).[76] Price recommendations are also in principle permissible, as long as additional factors (such as penalties for non-compliance or incentives for compliance) do not alter their voluntary nature.[77]

The best example so far where the CPC has reviewed the legality of price recommendations with respect to distribution of FMCG comes from the *Danone*[78] case decided under the old PCA 1998. The focus of that investigation was certain resale price maintenance practices in the distribution of dairy products manufactured by Danone-Serdika AD (Danone). During the first months of 2000, Danone released on the market yoghurt bearing a retail price tag. Danone also entered into agreements requiring its distributors, inter alia, (1) to sell Danone branded yoghurt at prices not higher than the retail prices recommended by Danone and (2) not to sell Danone branded yoghurt at prices lower than base procurement prices, as per the effective price list of Danone. The distribution agreements also established performance- and volume-based rebate incentive schemes. The CPC defined a relevant market of production and distribution of natural (non-flavoured) yoghurt. During the period under review, Danone was a dominant undertaking on that market with a market share of just over 35 %.

The CPC held that the agreements executed between Danone and its distributors contained minimum resale price-fixing arrangements in breach of Art. 9 PCA 1998 (the equivalent of the present Art. 15 PCA and Art. 101 TFEU). In its analysis of the

---

[74] CPC decision no. 1292/2012.

[75] CPC decision no. 576/2008.

[76] CPC decision no. 1150/2007.

[77] The best example where price recommendations were treated by the CPC as prohibited price fixing is provided by the 2010 investigation against the National Chamber of Construction Companies, which was penalised for publishing and maintaining price benchmarks that were considered anticompetitive because of the existence of disciplinary powers and mechanisms against noncompliant members (see CPC decision no. 496/2010).

[78] CPC decision no. 139/2000.

effect of RPM on competition, the CPC drew a distinction between (1) maximum price fixing and recommended prices, on one hand, and (2) the establishment of minimum or fixed prices, on the other hand. The CPC considered that the practice of establishing maximum resale price levels and/or provision of recommended prices would normally not raise competition concerns, *unless such practices disguise other forms of price fixing*. In contrast, the minimum and absolute price fixing was classified among the most serious restraints on trade with a number of anti-competitive effects.[79] In this respect, the CPC highlighted the inhibiting effect on intra-brand competition stemming from the inability of distributors to compete on price levels.

In this particular case, the CPC ruled that the resale price maintenance arrangement contained in Danone's distribution agreements could not possibly have any pro-competitive effects. This conclusion was based partially on the premise that the rebate incentive scheme applied by Danone (a dominant undertaking) was an aggravating factor inhibiting inter-brand competition.[80]

In addition, it should be noted that at the end of April 2013 the authority issued three separate statements of objections alleging prohibited vertical restraints in the form of RPM and territorial allocation against several manufacturers of sunflower oil and their distributors. According to the official press release,[81] during its sector inquiry on the vegetable oil supply chain (see Sects. 6.1.3.1 and 6.1.3.2 above), the CPC discovered price recommendation clauses in the distribution agreements applied by certain manufacturers, which were regarded as suspect. The available data indicate that originally the CPC intended to bring cartel charges for horizontal collusion, but since it was unable to find such evidence, proceedings were split in three and transformed into allegation of prohibited vertical restraints. Thus, without much evidence about additional incentives or monitoring mechanisms, relying only on the text of the respective clauses, the CPC brought formal charges against each group of supplier-distributors for direct or indirect fixing of resale prices and allocation of markets in the form of limitation of the territorial scope of operations of distributors. The case is currently pending at the stage of defence submission, and a decision may be expected early this summer.

---

[79] In *Danone*, the CPC fell short of establishing a per se rule with regard to minimum resale price maintenance. Rather, it suggested that there may be instances where setting minimum or fixed prices would be permissible, provided that such vertical restraints stimulated inter-brand competition. This proposition, however, does not seem to have been further developed in the practice of the CPC, which has since *Danone* applied a uniform per se rule with respect to price fixing (see CPC decision no. 1292/2012).

[80] In *Danone*, the CPC suggested that a more stringent test for review should be applied to price recommendations issued by a dominant undertaking. In its subsequent practice, the CPC has taken this proposition further to suggest that analysis under Art. 15 PCA would always require a higher level of scrutiny with regard to vertical agreements involving a dominant undertaking (see, in particular, CPC decision no. 174/2006).

[81] CPC press release from 24 April 2013, available at www.cpc.bg.

6.2.2 Abuses of Dominance

Article 21 PCA prohibits any abuse by one or more undertakings of a dominant position and provides an exemplary list of abusive practices. In its case law, the CPC has dealt, among others, with various types of abusive conduct, such as abusive or predatory pricing, margin squeeze, discriminatory treatment, refusal to deal, tying, and bundling.

With respect to exploitative abuses, the CPC has the burden to prove that prices imposed by the dominant undertaking are not cost oriented. However, if such prices are (1) determined without the application of clear and transparent cost-oriented criteria, (2) not subject to negotiation, and (3) forced upon customers because they do not have any alternative source of supply, an in-depth economic analysis would not be necessary and prices will be automatically deemed unjustified or excessive.[82] The burden of proof shifts to the dominant undertaking to justify the level of prices it charges and to prove that such prices are determined on the basis of the cost of the product or service or that such prices are comparable to the prices on neighbouring geographic or product markets.

Discriminatory pricing exists where a dominant undertaking applies dissimilar prices to similar transactions, and discriminatory application of trading conditions exists where a dominant undertaking treats differently its customers, as a result of which customers are placed at competitive disadvantage.[83] However, price differentiation among customers would not be regarded as discriminatory if it is based on objective criteria and such criteria are equally applied to all customers of the dominant undertaking. For example, in an investigation of the discount scheme applied by a dominant distributor of audio-musical products, the CPC held that transparent and uniformly applied volume rebates do not amount to price discrimination.[84]

6.2.2.1 Abuse of Dominance by Retailers

As noted in the introduction to this national report (see Sect. 6.1.1.3 above), the Bulgarian grocery retail market is characterised by low concentration, and none of the market players commands a share higher than 10 %. In these circumstances, unilateral conduct should not be a reason for concern. Nevertheless, there is one notable occasion in the past when the CPC tried to enforce the rules on dominance, arguing that nationwide "cash-and-carry" trade forms a special and independent market, on which one single undertaking—Metro Cash & Carry Bulgaria EOOD (Metro)—operates and enjoys the advantages of unrestricted market power.

[82] CPC decision no. 147/2004.

[83] CPC decision no. 628/2007.

[84] CPC decision no. 268/2008.

The investigation (*Vemira vs Metro*[85]) was initiated on complaint[86] from a small confectionary producer (a sole proprietor with five employees), claiming that the access fee collected by Metro is not objectively calculated since it does not take into consideration actual use of shelf space, as a result of which companies with identical shelf access pay different fees. Petitioner also complained that the fee was not refundable upon termination and demanded review of other clauses in the supply agreement, including the turnover bonus, advertising bonus (for posting of items in Metro post), price guarantee, and the most-favoured-client clause.

Petitioner entered into contractual relations with Metro in 1998 but commenced deliveries in 1999 when the first two Metro stores started operations. During the investigated period (1999–2002), the relative share of sales to Metro from all petitioner's sales indicated a declining trend—starting at 62 % in 1999 and dropping to just 15 % in 2001.

The disputing parties signed a supply agreement, which was subject to annual review and renewal. Before commencement of business operations, petitioner had to pay a one-time "access fee" of fixed value (BGN 3,500—approx. EUR 1,750). Payment of this fee allowed the supplier to deliver up to ten items to the two Metro stores. In 2002, following the opening of three new stores, Metro demanded payment of additional BGN 5,425 (approx. EUR 2,770). Petitioner did not want to pay any additional amounts but did not declare relations with Metro officially terminated. After petitioner's refusal to pay the new stores' access fee, Metro did not send any orders for its products.

First Case Ruling

In its legal analysis,[87] the CPC notes that "cash & carry" wholesale is a distinct form of distribution service compared to the one offered by large-scale retailers. The latter supply end customers and do not offer certain "comforts" for small retailers, associated with wholesale—e.g. bulk packages, greater assortment, tax invoices. It was also stressed that access to "cash & carry" stores is restricted to registered customers, and there are minimal purchase quantity requirements, which make them less suitable for end customers. Because of this, the CPC concludes that "cash & carry" wholesale distribution is a separate service market with national scope, on which Metro had dominant position (as the only other wholesaler operating under the same model had only one store in Sofia).

[85] CPC decision no. 187/2003 on case no. 26/2003; reversed on appeal – decision no. 6584/2004, Supreme Administrative Court, 5th Chamber; reversal confirmed on cassation – decision no. 6595/2005, Supreme Administrative Court, 2nd Grand Chamber; proceedings reopened on case no. 170/2005, ending with CPC decision no. 293/2005; reversed on appeal – decision no. 7404/2006, Supreme Administrative Court, 5th Chamber; reversal confirmed on cassation – decision no. 11909/2006, Supreme Administrative Court, 2nd Grand Chamber; proceedings reopened on case no. 309/2006 ending with CPC decision no. 257/2007, which was not appealed.

[86] Procedure was governed by PCA 1998, which did not provide for two stages separated by a statement of objections—this system was introduced in Bulgarian only in 2008 with the third PCA.

[87] In sharp contrast with its own practice on merger control cases in the retail sector.

With respect to the legality of the access fee, the CPC noted that it was clearly described in the supply agreement as a one-time "access" payment, associated with commencement of business operations, and not refundable upon termination. Because of this, the authority concluded that there was no unfair treatment on the part of Metro and the petitioner, being a merchant, should have been aware of the nature of the fee.

The CPC, however, found that the method for determination of the amount of the fee was not transparent. Metro claimed that the access fee was determined on account of various factors, including, in particular, estimated turnover, additional services used by the supplier, advertising budget, etc. The CPC dismissed Metro's explanations, noting that they sharply contradict the description of the fee as "remuneration for merchandising know-how". The authority stated that if the fee were based on the value of delivered intangible "property", it should have been the same for all suppliers, or at least variations should have been within a close range. However, in the investigated case, the fee varied from BGN 1,000 to BGN 10,000 (EUR 500–5,000). Because of this significant difference, the CPC concluded that Metro did not define clear criteria for the determination of the access fee amount and reserved itself considerable space for discretion. A consequence of the lack of transparency was the determination of unreasonably high access fees. Since Metro failed to provide conclusive evidence on the method of calculation, the CPC was not convinced that it was objectively justified and held that the amount was purely discretionary.

With respect to the price guarantee obligation, the CPC noted that observance of fixed prices for a short period of time is not tantamount to abuse of market power, as long as this could not affect adversely competition. In this case, it was important that Metro commended operations in 1999, and there were no sales history data. Thus, it was completely reasonable that the company would seek some levels of procurement prices to be guaranteed so that it could plan future orders and funding of operations. In addition, the CPC concluded that a price guarantee of 9 months, such as the one under the supply agreement, was acceptable in the circumstances. Although petitioner claimed that the clause was active for a longer period (up to conclusion of the agreement for 2001), there was no evidence induced that there was an actual request for increase in procurement prices. The supply agreement provided for a specific mechanism for price amendment, which required a written notification of a minimum term to be served to Metro before the contemplated effective date. In the absence of actual price increase notifications, the CPC dismissed all claims that Metro exercised pressure on petitioner to keep prices low.

With respect to the MFC clause, the CPC noted that although there is no explicit prohibition to sell products to third parties at better conditions, such an obligation would nevertheless result in restriction of the commercial freedom of petitioner. If the supplier was obliged to notify Metro about each transaction on more favourable terms (and further obliged to implement those terms immediately), that would represent an exploitative abuse because Metro would be using its market power to impose conditions and receive benefits that were not available in the case of effective competition.

For implementing prohibited clauses, the CPC imposed a fine on Metro in the amount of BGN 80,000 (approx. EUR 40,000). On appeal, the Supreme Administrative Court (SAC) quashed the administrative decision, noting that the relevant market was not correctly identified. The court advised that the CPC should have analysed the substitutability of all similar distribution services, offered by other merchants in the country, before assuming that "cash & carry" was a separate market. Cassation appeal confirmed this position, and the case was remanded to the CPC for de novo review.

Second Review (CPC Case No. 170/2005)

Trying to follow SAC's instructions, the CPC devoted a significant part of its analysis on interchangeability between retail and "cash & carry" distribution services. The authority again found that "cash & carry" wholesale is not substitutable with retail distribution. It was also stressed that Metro has started operations in Bulgaria in 1999 and just for a year managed to register a database of more than 600,000 clients. According to the CPC, this made the company a preferred partner for food manufacturers because it offers fast access to a large group of potential customers. For small manufacturers, in particular, which offer less advertised products, Metro provided an opportunity to participate in promotional campaigns in parallel with famous brands. Thus, according to the CPC, the "cash & carry" distribution concept, represented in Bulgaria solely by Metro, is very important for suppliers as it offered an unparalleled opportunity to enlarge their business.

Analysing the activities of confectionary producers and the various distribution channels available to them, the CPC concluded that the relevant market should be defined as the market for "cash & carry" distribution. Since Metro held a de facto monopoly position on that market (because there was no other national operator that offers the same service), its behaviour was abusive for reasons discussed in the first decision. Following this line of reasoning, the CPC re-imposed on Metro a fine of BGN 80,000 (EUR 40,000).

On appeal, the SAC again quashed the CPC decision, noting that the relevant market was not correctly identified. The court again advised the CPC that it should analyse substitutability of similar distribution services, but the focus should not be limited to differences between retail and "cash & carry", and the analysis should cover also all forms of wholesale operations. Cassation appeal confirmed this position, and the case was remanded again to the CPC for de novo review.

Third Review (CPC Case No. 309/2006)

In its third take on this case, the CPC defined the relevant market as "services for distribution of chocolate and sugar confectionery". The authority noted that the assortment structure of Metro's "Pastry and Sweets" department (comprising tea, coffee, cocoa, bread, pastry, etc.) indicates that chocolate sweets are not among its priorities. Accordingly, the share of sweets within the total turnover of Metro was less than 5 %. Thus, despite the lack of credible national statistics data, relying on information from major sweets producers (such as Kraft Foods, Nestle, and others) about the relative share of Metro sales from all their sales in Bulgaria, the CPC concluded that the actual market share of Metro on the relevant market during the period 1999–2002 should be less than 5 %.

Following this analysis, the CPC ruled that the position of Metro on the relevant market could not be defined as dominant. Accordingly, its behaviour was not subject to review since in the light of the insignificant market share in distribution, no practice could be deemed to have any negative effect.

6.2.2.2 Abuse of Dominance by Suppliers

Under the current PCA, reselling below cost and de-listing of suppliers could represent a violation only if the company is dominant. A good example where sales below cost for a significant period of time were condemned as a violation comes from the *Simid*[88] case, decided by the CPC in 2005.

The investigation on the pricing practices of Cooperative "Simid 1000" (Simid) was started pursuant to a complaint from one independent bakery, backed by the Bread and Pastry Producers Association, in 2004. It was alleged in particular that Simid sold bread at prices below production costs, thus aiming to drive its competitors out of the market.

At the time of the investigation, the cooperative owned two of the principal industrial scale bakeries in Sofia and was one of the strongest players on the markets for flour and bread in Bulgaria. Simid had established its own distribution network, which allowed for easy access to raw materials and retail channels. The cooperative owned or controlled a total of 22 vertically integrated companies, active on all stages of production on the supply chain wheat-flour-bread.

The CPC concluded that the economic characteristics of Simid, considered together with its market share in Sofia region of about 40 %, prove that it had a dominant position on the *regional market* for common bread.

Following a detailed analysis of price levels in the principal bakery and pastry classes and the associated production and distribution costs, the CPC established that during the period January–November 2003, Simid had applied unreasonably low prices. As a result of this, the cooperative had forced the other market players to sell below costs and suffer losses, or lose clients. This behaviour was also a clear signal to potential competitors not to enter the market.

The CPC noted that a distinction should be made between (1) sales below variable cost of production and (2) sales above variable cost but below total production cost. In the first case, the anticompetitive purpose of the practice could be presumed to exist since a sale below variable cost could not have any rational market explanation. In the second case, predatory pricing would be found to exist only if the pricing policy of the dominant undertaking was part of a plan to drive competitors out of the market. Most importantly, dumping pricing must be applied for such a period of time so that it has negative effect on competition.

[88] CPC decision no. 88/2005, reversed on appeal – decision no. 6894/2006, Supreme Administrative Court, 5th Chamber.

In applying the above rules, the CPC found that during a period of 11 months in 2003, Simid sold bread in Sofia at prices lower than its average variable cost. Although this alone would have been sufficient for the authority to find that the cooperative was abusing its dominant position, it was also noted that during the same period Simid was selling bread on other regional markets at higher average market price (transport costs accounted for). The CPC claimed that the malicious behaviour of Simid had specific anticompetitive results—its main competitor was forced to cease deliveries to several of the largest retail chains as a result of the low prices offered by the cooperative. Ruling that Simid's behaviour represented abuse of dominant position, the CPC imposed a fine of BGN 250,000 (the highest possible fine at that time was BGN 300,000).

On appeal, the Supreme Administrative Court quashed the CPC decision on the ground that the relevant product market *was national in scope* and Simid was not a dominant undertaking on such a broader market. The court did not address any of the substantive issues of the test for predatory pricing set by the CPC. A point that remained somewhat unclear was what duration of sales below prime cost would be sufficient evidence of abusive behaviour. From the *Simid* decision, it appears that the key issue with regard to the time of application of predatory prices is not the absolute duration of the dumping practice but rather whether such a period was sufficient to cause adverse effects on competition and competitors. In its dicta, however, the CPC noted that even a short period of time during which predatory prices were applied might suffice to establish abusive behaviour.

6.2.3 Abuse of Buying Power, Abuse of Dependency

6.2.3.1 Legal Provisions Regarding Abuses of Buying Power

The PCA in its current version does not prohibit abuse of dependency outside the scope of dominance. However, as explained in Sect. 6.1.2.4 above, since September 2012 several draft bills for PCA amendment were discussed by the Bulgarian legislators with the stated purpose of countering unfair B2B practices in the retail supply chain resulting from inequality of bargaining power.

6.2.3.2 Definition of Buyer Power

Neither the law nor the CPC case practice provides a specific definition for the term "buyer power". The latest bill for PCA amendment introduces the concept of "superior bargaining position" (SBP) as a new regulatory category, which shifts the focus of the analysis from the market structure to the specific contractual relationship. The definition states that an undertaking would be deemed to have SBP where its commercial partners are dependent on it due to the characteristics of the relevant market, the specific relations between the undertakings concerned, the type of their activities, and the difference in their scale of business.

6.2.3.3 Is Abuse of Buyer Power a *Per Se* Offence?

According to the rules regulating unilateral conduct by dominant undertakings, practices that may be deemed to restrict competition by object are prohibited *per se*, while in all other cases economic effect analysis is required.

Assuming that the PCA amendment is adopted in the present form, it would prohibit "any act or omission of undertaking with SBP, which contradicts good faith commercial practices and harms or may harm the interests of the weaker party by means of unreasonable refusal for supply or purchase of goods or services, implementation of unreasonable or discriminatory terms and conditions, or unreasonable termination of commercial relations". Considering that the exemplary enumeration at the end of the draft provision refers in all its items to "unreasonable" practices, it can be concluded that economic effect analysis would be required in all cases and only behaviour, which does not have objective justification, could be deemed abusive.

6.2.3.4 What Constitutes an Abuse of Buyer Power?

Under the present version of the PCA, abuse of "buyer power" may be found only on the part of dominant undertakings. The governing national rule (Art. 21 PCA) reproduces Art. 102 TFEU. Within the scope of the statutory prohibition would fall various practices related to imposition of exploitative prices, such as dumping prices pursuing predatory effects, discriminatory pricing and treatment in general, or bundling. However, a violation would exist only where such practices are implemented by a dominant company.[89]Non-dominant undertakings are not required to abide by the same increased standard of diligence, and application of unfair terms and practices on their part (as evidenced by the *Metro* case saga described in Sect. 6.2.2.1 above) would not constitute a violation.

As noted above, the draft PCA amendment introduces a new regulatory category, which expands the list of potential abuses to any behaviour in violation of good faith commercial practices, which does not have objective justification.

6.2.3.5 Case Law on Abuse of Buying Power

The CPC did not have many changes to review allegations of abuse on the part of dominant buyers. In its limited practice, the authority has ruled that arbitrary determination of access fees and the application of most-favoured-customer clauses constitute abuse on the part of a "dominant" distributor.[90] Furthermore, exercising pressure on suppliers to reduce procurement prices for the benefit of retailer's own margin of profit and without passing the benefit to consumers would also constitute an abuse.[91]

---

[89] Under Bulgarian law, "dominance" is defined as a position of market strength enjoyed by an undertaking, which with a view of its market share, financial resources, access to markets, level of technological development, and business relation to other undertakings is independent from its competitors, suppliers, and customers and may hinder competition on the relevant market (Art. 20 PCA).

[90] CPC decision no. 187/2003.

[91] CPC decision no. 833/2012.

6.3 Merger Control

There are no special thresholds for review of mergers in the grocery retail sector. Concentrations of commercial activities[92] in Bulgaria are subject to the mandatory prior control of the CPC. Under Bulgarian law, a notification must be filed where (1) the joint turnover of all undertakings concerned in Bulgaria for the year preceding the year of the concentration exceeds BGN 25 million (EUR 12.78 million) and (2) (a) the turnover of each one of at least two of the undertakings concerned in Bulgaria for the year preceding the year of the concentration exceeds BGN 3 million (EUR 1.53 million), or (b) the turnover of the target in Bulgaria for the year preceding the year of the concentration exceeds BGN 3 million (EUR 1.53 million).

It should be noted that the jurisdictional threshold under the preceding PCA 1998 was much lower, requiring notification and review of every transaction involving change of control as long as the *joint* turnover of the undertakings concerned exceeded BGN 15 million (EUR 7.67 million). Because of the over-simplified nature of the test, in many cases turnover of the acquirer was sufficient by itself to trigger a merger control review. In fact, large retailers had to notify the CPC and wait for clearance for each acquisition, no matter how minor.[93] With the entry into force of the PCA on December 2008, this practice was discontinued and now only acquisition of assets with attributable national turnover in excess of BGN 3 million (EUR 1.53 million) is subject to review.

For the purpose of turnover calculation, the CPC takes into account the entire turnover of the undertakings concerned in Bulgaria.[94] When an undertaking belongs to a group of companies, the Bulgarian turnover of the group as a whole must be taken into account. Turnover figures are calculated on the basis of revenues from sales of products and services generated during the financial year preceding the concentration. When the concentration involves acquisition of control over part of one or more undertakings, regardless of whether or not such part constitutes an independent legal entity, only the turnover of the respective part, which is subject to acquisition, is taken into account. In cases of vertical integration between a supplier and its distributor, the CPC takes into account both the turnover of the supplier from sales to the distributor and the turnover of the distributor from sales of the supplier's products to third parties.

[92] Defined in Art. 24 PCA as a lasting change of control over an undertaking as a result of (i) the merger of two or more independent undertakings or (ii) the acquisition of control over an undertaking by person(s) who already control one or more other undertakings or (iii) the creation of a full-function joint venture company.

[93] For example, in 2008, only Maxima was involved in 5 merger control proceedings, related to acquisition of assets of various size, ranging from part of the existing network of the "Evropa" retail chain to large buildings and even individual neighbourhood stores.

[94] Previously in its case law under the 1998 PCA, for undertakings domiciled in Bulgaria the CPC was using their aggregate turnover—both from national sources and sales abroad.

6.3.1 Market Definition in the Grocery Retail Sector

6.3.1.1 Relevant Product Market

Pursuant to the statutory definition, the product scope of the relevant market should be defined, taking into consideration all goods or services that are viewed by consumers as interchangeable with respect to their characteristics, intended use, and price.[95] The CPC practice on acquisitions at the retail level of the grocery sector in Bulgaria indicates a stable approach towards market definition. Since 2007, and the first major cases involving mergers between retail chains,[96] the authority has repeatedly defined a relatively broad relevant market encompassing "retail with fast-moving consumer goods in supermarkets, hypermarkets, and convenience shops selling food and non-food items".[97] In its analyses, the CPC has concluded that all types of mixed assortment shops, irrespective of size, are substitutable. Most importantly, small-size convenience shops are regarded as competitors of large supermarkets. This conclusion was challenged on a couple of occasions and reaffirmed most recently in 2010 when on the basis of GfK data[98] the CPC concluded that delimitation between various store formats would require a significant change in the habits of Bulgarian consumers. Although it is generally accepted that consumers visit "modern trade" outlets less frequently than small local shops (so-called traditional retail), marketing surveys for Bulgaria indicate similar intensity of visits for super/hypermarkets (44.8 average visits per month) and convenience stores (46.7). In addition, despite the different degree of penetration of "modern trade" outlets in the capital and big cities in comparison to small towns, the average monthly frequency of shopping for all residential areas in Bulgaria is quite similar—between 16.8 and 17.2 average visits per month. Moreover, there is clear evidence that retail chains are attempting to reach consumers by launching small store formats in towns and city districts. This, according to the CPC, indicates a policy driven by consumer preferences, who do not want to change their habits despite the conveniences offered by larger sales area, broad product assortment and ample parking space.

It is important to note that cash & carry stores are regarded as a type of "hypermarket" and included in the retail market.[99] Acknowledging that such establishments generally offer FMCG to the business (e.g., in larger packages—crates and cases), the CPC claims that Bulgarian operations deviate significantly from the classical model. The argument in support of this conclusion is the fact that

---

[95] Sec. 1, para. 15 (a) of the Supplementary provisions to the PCA.

[96] The acquisition of the local "Piccadilly" chain by the Serbian Delta Maxy group in 2007 (CPC decision no. 784/2007), the acquisition of the local "Evropa" chain by Maxima (CPC decision no. 1057/2008), the acquisition of the local Plus franchise by LIDL in 2010 (CPC decision no. 1199/2010), the acquisition of Delta Maxy by Delhaize in 2011 (CPC decision no. 456/2011).

[97] E.g., CPC decision no. 416/2007 and CPC decision no. 794/2007.

[98] See CPC decision no. 1199/2010, p. 17.

[99] See CPC decision no. 416/2007, footnote 7 at page 8, and CPC decision no. 794/2007, footnote 2 on p. 7.

although access to cash & carry outlets in Bulgaria requires registration, many individuals acquire customer cards and purchase goods for personal consumption. Package sizes are also not regarded as a serious distinguishing factor since most products are actually sold in consumer-friendly units.

So far, activities of Internet stores have not been subject to review by the CPC in a merger control context. Nevertheless, considering the broad definition for FMCG retail, it is quite possible that e-merchants will be regarded as competitors of brick-and-mortar shops. Moreover, some retailers already offer home deliveries and accept orders online, which indicates that Internet sales are just another means for reaching consumers.

6.3.1.2 Relevant Geographic Market

Pursuant to the statutory definition, the geographic scope of the relevant market should be defined with regard to a specific territory on which the corresponding interchangeable goods or services are offered and on which the conditions of competition are the same, while differing from those in neighbouring areas.[100] In its practice on mergers in the grocery retail sector, the CPC holds invariably that *the geographical scope* of the relevant market is limited to a specific territory where FMCG can be easily accessed by consumers (within approximately 20–30 minutes' drive from home). In other words, the market *is local or regional at most*.[101]

The NCA has noted that the retail of FMCG in Bulgaria indicates presence of a dynamic yet fragmented market, where "modern" retail chains compete with "traditional" small-scale merchants. The latter are much less organised[102] and still account for a larger share of the market, which makes it impossible to argue that all market players compete on a national scale. The CPC has concluded that even though large "modern trade" retailers have outlets in many regions (and some are fairly well nationally represented), in fact they compete with convenience and other shops on a local basis.[103]

[100] Sec. 1, para. 15 (b) of the Supplementary provisions to the PCA.

[101] See, e.g., CPC decision no. 794/2007 (referring to several relevant markets on "the territory of the cities of Sofia, Varna, Burgas, Veliko Tarnovo"), CPC decision no. 1244/2010 ("the territory of Sofia"); CPC decision no. 1545/2012 ("the territory of the city of Varna"); CPC decision no. 284/2013 ("the territory of the cities of Sofia and Varna").

[102] It should be noted that there is no representative association of small retailers on national level. The Bulgarian Retail Association is composed primarily of SMP retail merchants operating stores in malls and prime city locations. Some "traditional" retailers are members of the National Association of Small and Medium Businesses, which comprises primarily companies from the light industry sectors (food processing and textiles).

[103] CPC decision no. 284/2013, p. 11, referring to CPC decision no. 1244/2010 and CPC decision no. 1199/2010.

6.3.2 Merger Control and the Growth of Grocery Retail Networks

According to the most recent CPC merger control decisions,[104] there are numerous merchants in Bulgaria holding valid registrations for retail sale of foods and beverages. The majority is unspecialised grocery stores (some selling also alcohol and tobacco), and most are falling within the category of "convenience stores"—offering both food and non-food items. The constantly rising share of large chain stores indicates a trend towards consolidation and increasing role of super- and hypermarkets. However, the latter are located predominantly in the cities, and there is a significant regional disproportion in the development of their networks.

Differences in population density and revenues influence the asymmetry in penetration of "modern trade". Internal migration and natural increase of population in the cities are the principal reasons behind the expansion pattern followed by retail chains. Thus, most new super- and hypermarkets are opened in the capital and regional centres, where population density and purchasing power are higher. Competition is intensive and represented by many international players—Kaufland Bulgaria and Lidl (Schwarz Group), Billa Bulgaria and Peny (REWE Group), Piccadilly (Delhaize Group), Metro Cash & Carry Bulgaria (METRO Group), Carrefour Bulgaria (Carrefour Marinopoulos), Roda (Mercator Group), T-Market (Maxima Group)—as well as by local companies, such as Fantastico, Evropa, Coop, and CBA Bulgaria (some of them operating as cooperatives). A number of local companies also operate chains of convenience stores (under the brands "Pro Market", "Dar", "Verde", etc.), although they are concentrated mostly in the capital.

Despite the continuing penetration of "modern trade" outlets, traditional retail continues to play a leading role for Bulgarian consumers. The CPC notes that although the geographic scope of the retail market for FMCG is local, conditions of competition throughout the country are homogenous, and there are numerous different market players in each region. "Modern trade" still occupies a smaller share in comparison to traditional retail—the market has low concentration and fragmented structure. Because of this, none of the market players has sufficiently strong position, or market power, on any regional level in order to be deemed independent from their competitors, clients, and suppliers.[105]

6.3.3 Countervailing Buyer Power as a Mitigating Factor for the Concentration

As explained in Sect. 6.3.1 above, the grocery retail sector in Bulgaria has a low level of concentration. Mergers among suppliers are not very common, and considering the high fragmentation of most product markets there has not been a single

[104] See CPC decision no. 284/2013 and CPC decision no. 456/2011.

[105] CPC decision no. 284/2013, p. 18.

case where “mitigating” factors were needed in order to justify consolidation of businesses on the production or processing level of the grocery supply chain.

Likewise, since most supply markets in Bulgaria are extremely fragmented, countervailing buyer power argumentation cannot be used in defence of mergers in the retail sector.

6.3.4 Merger Remedies

So far, there are no cases where the combined market share of the merging retailers could raise suspicions of establishment of a dominant position. In fact, the most recent cases indicate that the retail market is still characterised by a low level of concentration.

6.4 Conclusion and Perspectives

According to recent surveys among national branch associations of suppliers, pressure exercised by the stronger party in a contractual relationship—reflected in unfair terms and practices—undoubtedly influences the redistribution of value added along the grocery supply chain. Most suppliers regard large retail chains with national coverage as parties with more bargaining power. Acknowledging the advantages of these chains as a distribution channel, they agree that retail merchants should receive a fair share in the revenues. However, all suppliers strongly believe that unreasonable and burdensome conditions, especially those related to transfer of commercial risk, should not be imposed on them without a proper justification.

On the other hand, “modern trade” representatives claim that the market structure in Bulgaria does not permit retailers to impose any unfair terms on suppliers. On the contrary, in many cases (especially the so-called must-have products), retailers are obliged to accept without negotiation supply conditions determined unilaterally by manufacturers.

In summary, while retailers resist introduction of new rules, there seems to be a general agreement between Bulgarian suppliers that “soft” approaches (i.e., internal institutional regulations and private enforcement mechanisms) are not efficient to counter abuse of bargaining power, while existing legislation, practices, and capacity of public authorities are not sufficient and do not result in the required level of prevention and control. The question, therefore, is whether the contemplated PCA amendment would provide the best possible remedy for the deficiencies present in the grocery retail supply chain.

Estonia

7

Alexandr Svetlicinii

7.1 Introduction

According to the classic categorization, the Estonian legal system belongs to the Continental (Civil Law) European legal tradition, Romano-Germanic family with strong historical links with the German legal system, especially in the field of civil/private law.[1] The Estonian legal system is formally norm based, i.e., statutory law is the primary source of law. It should be noted, however, that the influence of EU law on the development of the Estonian legal system strengthened the role of the precedents, particularly those of the Supreme Court, which is empowered to interpret legal rules, especially in cases of legal *lacunae*, and to carry out constitutional review of the legislation. These general features and historical background of the Estonian legal system has predetermined the emphasis on the public antitrust enforcement, while private enforcement of competition rules remains virtually nonexistent.[2]

As far as the substantive antitrust rules are concerned, Estonian competition law has been shaped under the influence of the EU rules and standards. According to the early comments on the harmonization of the Estonian competition rules with those of the EU, it was noted that "there is hardly anything in EU competition law that has

[1] See Miil K, Kuusik J and Ruttu M (2013) UPDATE: Guide to Estonian Legal System and Legal Research. http://www.nyulawglobal.org/globalex/estonia1.htm. Accessed 22 May 2014.

[2] See Sein K (2013) Private Enforcement of Competition Law – the Case of Estonia. *Yearbook of Antitrust and Regulatory Studies* 6(8):129–139.

A. Svetlicinii (✉)
University of Macau, Faculty of Law, Taipa, Macao SAR (China)
e-mail: AlexandrS@umac.mo

P. Kobel et al. (eds.), *Antitrust in the Groceries Sector & Liability Issues in Relation to Corporate Social Responsibility*, LIDC Contributions on Antitrust Law, Intellectual Property and Unfair Competition, DOI 10.1007/978-3-662-45753-5_7

not found its way into the Estonian Competition Act, often even word for word."[3] This early harmonization of the substantive competition rules has signaled the intention of the Estonian state to follow the EU model in the domestic competition enforcement.[4] At the same time, Estonian legislator has made a policy choice in favor of multilevel public enforcement, which led to the current situation when competition rules can be enforced under administrative, misdemeanour and criminal procedural rules. This diversity in procedural frameworks combined with the technical constrains of the national competition authority (limited human and financial resources), and a combination of the antitrust and regulatory functions under the responsibility of the same authority has shaped the Estonian antitrust enforcement.

As the following sections of the present report shall demonstrate, the Estonian legislator has not adopted any competition rules or exemptions that would be specific to the grocery retail sector. This reflects the general approach to adopt sector-specific legislation for the regulated sectors, while unregulated industries remain subject to the general competition rules. Another important aspect is the enforcement of the general competition rules in the grocery retail sector, and in this sense Estonia exhibits a relatively low record of antitrust enforcement. This outcome has resulted, *inter alia*, from the emphasis on public enforcement, multiple procedural frameworks for enforcement and the limits in technical capacity of the national competition authority. Another important factor is the current competitive conditions in the grocery retail and its links with the agricultural and processing industries. The following sections highlight the economic, legal and institutional factors that explain the current situation with antitrust enforcement in the Estonian grocery retail market.

7.2 Economic Background

According to the Estonian Ministry of Agriculture,[5] in 2013 there were 965,907 ha of usable agricultural land in Estonia, the biggest share of which remains under dairy farming.[6] The plant fields are primarily used for growing cereals, oil cultures, potatoes and vegetables. As many other EU Member States, Estonia experienced significant consolidation of agricultural holdings with their number steadily

[3] Thielert J and Schinkel M P (2003) Estonia's competition policy: a critical evaluation towards EU accession. *European Competition Law Review* 24(4): 175, available at http://arno.unimaas.nl/show.cgi?fid=463. Accessed 22 May 2014.

[4] See, generally, Clark J (1999) Competition Law and Policy in the Baltic Countries – A Progress Report. OECD, Paris. See also Vedder H (2004) Spontaneous Harmonisation of National (Competition) Laws in the Wake of the Modernisation of EC Competition Law. *Competition Law Review* 1(1):5–21.

[5] *Põllumajandusministeerium*, http://www.agri.ee/. Accessed 22 May 2014.

[6] Ministry of Agriculture (2014) Food, agriculture, rural life, fisheries in facts, http://www.agri.ee/sites/default/files/content/valjaanded/2014/trykis-2014-faktiraamat-eng.pdf. Accessed 22 May 2014.

decreasing, while the average used land per holding almost doubled during 2003–2007.[7] A large number of agricultural producers and processors of agricultural products are represented by the Estonian Chamber of Agriculture and Commerce.[8]

The food processing accounts for 17 % of the total output of the Estonian processing industry.[9] This sector has also experienced substantial consolidation during 1998–2002. Since 1993, the interests of the Estonian food producers have been represented by the Association of the Estonian Food Industry.[10] In the specific food sectors, the following industry associations exist: Estonian Association of Bakeries,[11] Estonian Breweries Association,[12] Estonian Association of Alcohol Producers, Estonian Association of Cheese Producers, etc.[13]

The grocery retail market is moderately concentrated with the three leading retailers (*ETK*, *Rimi*, *Selver*) accounting for about 60 % of the market.[14] Their interests are represented by the Estonian Traders Association.[15] According to the 2013 industry research, none of the retailers enjoys single dominance: *ETK* (19 %), *Rimi* (18 %), *Selver* (17 %), *Maxima* (15 %), etc.[16] Approximately 45 % of food retail is realized through department stores with retail space less than 100 m^2 (22 %) and supermarkets with retail space between 100 and 400 m^2, followed by large supermarkets with retail space of 1,000–2,500 m^2 (10 %).[17]

[7] The Ministry of Agriculture reported that the number of agricultural holdings decreased by 36.7 %; however, the average area of agricultural land of the holding increased 1.8 times (from 21.6 ha to 38.9 ha). See http://www.agri.ee/agriculture-and-food/. Accessed 22 May 2014.

[8] *Eesti Põllumajandus-Kaubanduskoda*, http://www.epkk.ee/. Accessed 22 May 2014.

[9] Almost a third from it is formed by dairy products; 18 % meat products; 15 % bread, bakery and other products; and 9.5 % fish products. See http://www.agri.ee/agriculture-and-food/. Accessed 22 May 2014.

[10] *Eesti Toiduainetööstuse Liit*, http://toiduliit.ee/. Accessed 22 May 2014.

[11] *Eesti Leivaliit*, http://www.leivaliit.ee/. Accessed 22 May 2014.

[12] *Eesti Õlletootjate Liit*, http://www.eestiolu.ee/. Accessed 22 May 2014. The Estonian Breweries Association brings together three major beer producers (*AS Saku Õlletehase*, *AS A.Le.Coq* and *AS Viru Õlu*). It has adopted its Code of Ethics with the aim to "facilitate, through the self-regulation of advertising communication, responsible actions of breweries by following common standards." See http://www.eestiolu.ee/code-of-ethics-in-english/. Accessed 22 May 2014.

[13] *Eesti Juustuliit*, http://www.juustuliit.ee/. Accessed 22 May 2014.

[14] Kusmin K (2010) Grocery retail in Estonia – does the competition work? 2010 Competition Day, available at http://www.konkurentsiamet.ee/?id=20076. Accessed 22 May 2014.

[15] *Kaupmeeste Liit*, http://www.kaupmeesteliit.ee/et/english-summary. Accessed 22 May 2014.

[16] See Country Report (2013) Grocery Retailers in Estonia. http://www.euromonitor.com/grocery-retailers-in-estonia/report. Accessed 22 May 2014.

[17] See Country Report (2013) Grocery Retailers in Estonia.

7.3 Legal Background

7.3.1 Competition Law

The Estonian Competition Act[18] applies to extraction of natural resources, manufacture of goods, provision of services and sale and purchase of products and services, as well as other economic activities, and therefore is equally applicable to the grocery sector.[19] Competition rules are applied to undertakings that are determined according to the functional approach related to the exercise of economic activity: "a company, sole proprietor, any other person engaged in economic or professional activities, an association which is not a legal person, or a person acting in the interests of an undertaking."[20] Following this approach, the state, local governments, legal persons in public law and other persons performing administrative duties can be treated as undertakings if they participate in a goods market.[21] The agricultural sector is subject to competition rules only to the extent determined on the basis provided for in Article 42 TFEU.[22] The Competition Act includes a ban on unfair competition[23] as well as prohibition of anticompetitive practices, which might lead to preclusion, elimination, prevention, limitation or restriction of competition.[24]

The national equivalents of Articles 101 and 102 TFEU have been incorporated in the Competition Act, which has been in force since 2001, with the most recent amendments taking place on July 2013.[25] Besides adding anticompetitive exchanges of information to the list of prohibited anticompetitive practices, the relevant provision of the Competition Act mirrors Article 101 TFEU.[26] The prohibition of abuse of dominant position in the Competition Act follows the structure of Article 102 TFEU, adding the following to the list of anticompetitive unilateral practices: (1) forcing an undertaking to concentrate, enter into an agreement that restricts competition, engage in concerted practices or adopt a decision together

[18] Competition Act, passed 6 May 2011, RT I 2001, 56, 332, entry into force 10 January 2011. See, generally, Thielert J and Schinkel M P (2003) Estonia's competition policy: a critical evaluation towards EU accession. *European Competition Law Review* 24(4):165–175.

[19] Competition Act, para 1(1).

[20] Competition Act, para 2(1). On the notion of undertaking in Estonian competition law, see Rüütel R, Konkurentsikeeld võib viia vangimajja [Definition of undertaking in competition law] Eversheds (2 May 2014), available at http://www.eversheds.com/global/en/what/articles/index.page?ArticleID=en/global/Estonia/en/definition-undertaking-competition-law. Accessed 22 May 2014.

[21] Competition Act, para 2(2).

[22] Competition Act, para 4(2).

[23] Competition Act, Chapter 7.

[24] Competition Act, Chapter 2.

[25] See European Competition Network Brief (2013) The Estonian Parliament amends its competition act, 15 July 2013, *e-Competitions Bulletin*, N° 58777.

[26] Competition Act, para 4(1)(4).

with the undertaking or another undertaking, and (2) unjustified refusal to sell or buy goods.[27]

The Competition Act does not contain any provisions that have been specifically aimed at the grocery retail market. However, certain forms of anticompetitive agreements and practices as well as abuses of dominant position might be especially relevant for the retail markets. For example, the Competition Act explicitly provides that a ban on fixing of prices or other trading conditions covers prices of goods, markups, discounts, rebates, basic fees and premiums, which is mostly aimed at the distribution (wholesale and retail) activities.[28] The provisions on the abuse of dominance explicitly mention unfair pricing, anticompetitive discrimination and refusal to deal.[29]

Estonia has pursued the criminalization of competition infringements,[30] and certain violations of competition rules are considered criminal offences under the Penal Code that should be prosecuted in criminal proceedings initiated by the Prosecutor's Office[31] upon request of the Estonian Competition Authority (the "ECA")[32]: repeated abuse of dominant position[33]; agreements, decisions and concerted practices restricting free competition[34]; repeated failure to perform obligations of undertakings in control of essential facilities.[35] Other infringements of competition rules are regarded as misdemeanors that should be prosecuted under the Code of Misdemeanour Procedure[36]: abuse of dominant position, implementation of concentration without permission, and the nonperformance of obligations by the undertakings in control of essential facility.[37]

The behavior of grocery retailers besides competition law is mostly regulated by the consumer protection legislation. For instance, Consumer Protection Act imposes on retailers certain information and transparency requirements and prohibits a range of unfair commercial practices.[38] The general conduct of the retail

[27] Competition Act, paras 16(5) and (6).

[28] Competition Act, para 4(1)(1).

[29] Competition Act, para 16.

[30] See, generally, Proos A (2006) Chapter 17: Competition Policy in Estonia. In Katalin J. Cseres, Maarten Pieter Schinkel and Floris O.W. Vogelaar (eds), *Criminalization of Competition Law Enforcement: Economic and Legal Implications for the EU Member States*, Edward Elgar.

[31] *Prokuratuur*, http://www.prokuratuur.ee/. Accessed 22 May 2014.

[32] *Konkurentsiamet*, http://www.konkurentsiamet.ee/. Accessed 22 May 2014.

[33] Penal Code, passed 6 June 2011, RT I 2001, 61, 364, entry into force 1 September 2002, para 399(1).

[34] Penal Code, para 400.

[35] Penal Code, para 402.

[36] Code of Misdemeanour Procedure, passed 22 May 2002, RT[1] I 2002, 50, 313, entry into force 1 September 2002.

[37] Competition Act, Chapter 9.

[38] Consumer Protection Act, passed 11 February 2004, RT I 2004, 13, 86, entry into force 15 April 2004.

trade is governed by the provisions of the Trading Act,[39] which lays down the registration and qualification requirements for traders and their personnel, conditions for labeling the products and displaying prices, etc. All of the above regulations are based on the principles of fairness and protection of weaker party. There are no specific rules on protecting a party with weaker bargaining power vis-à-vis large retailers in business-to-business transactions. These would be evaluated under the general principles of fairness and reasonableness embedded in the Law of Obligations Act.[40]

7.3.2 Exemptions from Competition Law Prohibitions

The Competition Act provides for various categories of exemptions from the application of the national equivalent of Article 101 TFEU: *de minimis* exemptions,[41] individual exemptions[42] in line with Article 101(3) TFEU and a set of block exemptions specified in the government's regulations on the proposal of the Minister of Economic Affairs and Communications.[43] At the same time, there are no regulations or bylaws that would provide further guidance on various aspects of antitrust enforcement carried out by the ECA. There are no specific exemptions from the application of Competition Act that would be applicable to the retail grocery sector. There is no automatic exemption for small-scale farmers or suppliers of food products from application of competition rules. Their agreements on joint selling and other forms of cooperation vis-à-vis large-scale distributors would have to be analyzed under the national equivalent of Article 101 TFEU[44] and can be exempted under the general *de minimis* rules,[45] under the equivalent of Article 101(3) TFEU[46] or under the block exemption regulations.[47]

[39] Trading Act, passed 11 February 2004, RT I 2004, 12, 78, entry into force 15 April 2004.

[40] Law of Obligations Act, passed 26 September 2001, RT I 2001, 81, 487, entry into force 1 July 2002.

[41] Competition Act, para 5.

[42] Competition Act, para 6.

[43] Government of Republic Regulation No. 197 of 30 December 2010 "Grant of Permission to Enter into Specialisation Agreements Which Restrict or May Restrict Free Competition (group exceptions)" (RT I, 04.01.2011,11); Government of Republic Regulation No. 60 of 27 May 2010 "Grant of Permission to Enter into Vertical Agreements Which Restrict or May Restrict Free Competition (group exceptions)" (RT I 2010, 23, 112); Government of the Republic Regulation No. 66 of 3 June 2010 "Grant of Permission to Enter into Motor Vehicle Distribution and Servicing Agreements Which Restrict or May Restrict Competition (Block exemption)" (RT I 2010, 28, 149).

[44] Competition Act, para 4.

[45] Competition Act, para 5.

[46] Competition Act, para 6.

[47] Competition Act, para 7. See, for example, Government of Republic Regulation No. 60 of 27 May 2010 "Grant of Permission to Enter into Vertical Agreements Which Restrict or May Restrict Free Competition (group exceptions)" (RT I 2010, 23, 112).

7.3.3 Other Laws and Regulations Applying to the Retail and Grocery Sector

The conduct of the grocery retailers is subject to a number of general and sector-specific regulations. Consumer protection legislation[48] regulates general marketing activities, determines the rights of consumers as purchasers of the products and provides for organization and supervision of consumer protection and liability of retailers. The Trading Act lays down mandatory conditions for the conduct of trading activities, including registration, qualification and information requirements. The Advertising Act[49] regulates advertising activities that may be employed by the grocery retailers. In particular, it prohibits misleading advertising[50] and restricts advertising directed at children[51] and advertising of alcoholic beverages.[52] In relation to the sale of alcohol products, sector-specific regulations impose numerous requirements and conditions on the way alcoholic beverages should be marketed by the retailers (retail locations, customers, labeling, displaying price, security measures, etc.), which significantly affects competition in relation to these products.[53]

The conduct of trading activities is generally regulated by the Trading Act, which is equally applicable to the traditional brick-and-mortar stores as well as to Internet retail stores, which have to comply with specific provisions relevant to e-trade—the offer for sale or sale of goods or services on the Internet without the parties being simultaneously physically present.[54] It provides, *inter alia*, that Internet retail stores have to comply with registration, information and transparency requirements of consumer protection legislation, as well as general contract rules and Information Society regulations.[55] Generally, Internet stores are not active in grocery retail sector in Estonia. One of the major retailers attempted to introduce Internet-based ordering system where the consumers were able to pick up the preordered goods at the store, but due to the lack of popularity this service was discontinued.

The ECA does not have specific competences in the adoption or enforcement of specific regulations in the food retail sector. The Competition Act provides that the ECA "may make recommendations to state agencies, local governments and natural and legal persons as to the improvement of the competitive situation."[56] The ECA

[48] Consumer Protection Act, passed 11 February 2004, RT I 2004, 13, 86, entry into force 15 April 2004.

[49] Advertising Act, passed 12 March 2008, RT I 2008, 15, 108, entry into force 1 November 2008.

[50] Advertising Act, para 4.

[51] Advertising Act, para 8.

[52] Advertising Act, para 28.

[53] Alcohol Act, passed 19 December 2001, RT I 2002, 3, 7, entry into force 1 September 2002.

[54] Trading Act, para 2(7).

[55] Trading Act, para 4(1)(11).

[56] Competition Act, para 61.

regularly reports on its enforcement activities and expresses its position vis-à-vis competition on various markets through annual reports[57] and official press releases.[58] There were no separate market inquiries conducted by the ECA in the retail grocery sector. Any market study activities were carried out in the course of regular antitrust investigations or merger control procedures.

The Competition Act prohibits only two types of unfair competition: (1) publication of misleading information, presentation or ordering of misleading information for publication or disparagement of competitor or goods of competitor,[59] and (2) misuse of confidential information or of employee or representative of another undertaking.[60] The existence of unfair competition prohibited by the Competition Act has to be established by the parties in a dispute held pursuant to the rules of civil procedure.[61] The unfair trading practices can be invalidated under the general contract rules concerning unfair standard terms and conditions.[62] However, the respective provisions are primarily aimed at protecting the consumers and do not contain any specific unfair trading practices that should be prohibited *per se* in business-to-business transactions.

7.4 Competition Law Enforcement

The 2010 amendments of the Penal Code have increased the sanctions imposed on a legal person for taking part in anticompetitive agreements up to 5 % of the annual turnover. In case of hard-core cartels, the fine could reach up to 10 % and cannot be less than 5 % of the annual turnover. Responsible natural persons for the involvement in a hard-core cartel will risk a pecuniary sanction or at least 1 year of imprisonment, which could be raised up to 3 years in case of hard-core cartels.[63]

In case of anticompetitive agreements, abuses of dominant position, violations of merger control rules or any procedural infringements under the Competition Act (such as failure to supply the ECA with requested information, interference with dawn raids or failure to appear when summoned), the ECA can issue a precept requiring the natural or legal person concerned to refrain from a prohibited act, terminate or suspend activities that restrict competition, restore the situation prior to the offence.[64] If a person fails to comply with the precept, the ECA may impose

[57] The ECA's annual reports are available at http://www.konkurentsiamet.ee/?id=23901. Accessed 22 May 2014.

[58] See http://www.konkurentsiamet.ee/?id=10461&op=archive. Accessed 22 May 2014.

[59] Competition Act, para 51.

[60] Competition Act, para 52.

[61] Competition Act, para 53.

[62] Law of Obligations Act, para 42.

[63] See European Competition Network Brief (2010) The Estonian Parliament adopts a new legislation on leniency and sanctions, 27 February 2010, *e-Competitions Bulletin*, N° 33407.

[64] Law Enforcement Act, passed 23 February 2011, RT I, 22.03.2011, 4, entry into force 1July 2014, paras 26-29., para 62(2).

penalty payments of up to EUR 6,400 on natural persons and up to EUR 9,600 on legal persons pursuant to the procedure regulated in the Substitutive Enforcement and Penalty Payment Act.[65]

In relation to violations of competition rules that are treated as misdemeanours, the ECA conducts the proceedings and imposes pecuniary penalties: refusals to submit information or submission of false information (up to 300 fine units[66] for natural person and up to EUR 3,200 for legal person), abuse of dominant position (up to 300 fine units for natural person and up to EUR 32,000 fine for legal persons), enforcement of concentration without permission to concentrate (up to 300 fine units for natural person and up to EUR 32,000 fine for legal persons), nonperformance of obligations by undertakings in control of essential facilities (up to 300 fine units for natural person and up to EUR 32,000 fine for legal persons), failure to comply with special requirement concerning accounting (up to 300 fine units for natural person and up to EUR 32,000 fine for legal persons).[67]

The ECA is unlikely to investigate cases of geographically isolated infringements. However, due to criminal prohibition of horizontal hard-core cartels, the ECA would be expected to investigate such cases if it becomes aware of such practices. In cases where harm to the general public interest could be subjectively assessed as insignificant, the relevant provisions of the Penal Code can be relied upon to impose symbolic fines on the convicted persons (both natural and legal) and leave them without criminal record. The decision to apply those provisions is with the prosecutors, and they have been applying those in cases of minor importance on many occasions.

In relation to leniency matters, the ECA has a very limited authority due to the fact that antitrust violations are criminalized and sanctioned in the criminal procedure before the court. Under the relevant provisions of the Competition Act, the ECA must confirm the receipt of leniency applications and forward them to the Prosecutor's Office that is heading the criminal prosecution.[68]

7.4.1 Competition Law Enforcement Against Anticompetitive Horizontal and Vertical Agreements

In 2010, the ECA commenced a cartel investigation concerning the retail of dairy products, involving both suppliers and retailers, where both horizontal and vertical concerns have been identified. Allegedly, one of the retailers complained to the

65 Competition Act, para 57^1.

66 A fine unit is a base amount of a fine and is equal to four euros. Penal Code, para 47(1).

67 Competition Act, paras 73^1, 73^5 - 73^8.

68 Competition Act, para 78^1. See also Paas-Mohando K and Käis L (2013) Current Developments in Member States: Estonia. *European Competition Journal* 9(3):779–784; Favart M (2010), The Estonian Parliament introduces new leniency programme and harsher sanctions, 20 January 2010, *e-Competitions Bulletin* January 2010, N° 41652.

ECA about the vertical agreements between a supplier of dairy products and another major retailer.[69] At the time of writing the case was still in the pretrial stage.

In 2012, a producer of alcoholic beverages and several retailers have been suspected of coordinating vodka prices. The producer was suspected of facilitating the coordination among the retailers.[70] As a result, the ECA's investigation could lead to establishing the existence of a vertical resale price maintenance arrangement or horizontal price coordination facilitated by the supplier. At the time of writing the case was still in the pretrial stage.

ETK is a cooperative of small and medium retailers that has operated continuously since 1919.[71] In 2002, the ECA received a complaint from a private person alleging, *inter alia*, that (1) *ETK* maintained uniform transportation prices, which allowed the remote cooperatives (on the islands or countryside) to minimize their costs at the expense of the more centrally located members; (2) *ETK* applied a recommended pricing policy, which is contrary to Competition Act; (3) *ETK* mandated its members to purchase the main assortment of goods from the centralized stock and excluded those members that did not comply with this purchase obligation. The ECA considered that such cooperation was not illegal because it allowed members of the cooperative to compete with the major retail chains and therefore fostered competition on the grocery retail market.[72] The competition authority considered *ETK* as a single undertaking for the purposes of applying competition law. The ECA was of the opinion that even if the members of *ETK* would be considered as separate undertakings, their cooperation practices would be exempted under the national equivalent of Article 101(3) TFEU.[73] According to the ECA, *ETK*'s recommended retail prices, common transportation and purchasing arrangements did not have anticompetitive effect, although formally they could not be exempted under the national *de minimis* rules[74] as *ETK*'s market share was around 20 %. The investigation was closed by a letter finding no violation of Competition Act.

As mentioned above, there are several ongoing investigations that concern large-scale retail grocery stores that, as reported by the media, have been allegedly involved in price coordination and limitation of competition among them. These

[69] According to the media reports, *Prisma* (retailer) complained about *Selver* (retailer) and *Tere* (dairy products supplier) practices. See http://arileht.delfi.ee/news/uudised/piima-kuriteo-kahtlus-lasub-kahel-eestimaisel-ettevottel.d?id=51283464, http://arileht.delfi.ee/news/uudised/prokuratuur-kaivitas-voimaliku-piimakartelli-uurimiseks-kriminaalmenetluse.d?id=33540637. All accessed 22 May 2014.

[70] See http://www.ohtuleht.ee/484324. Accessed 22 May 2014.

[71] *Eesti Tarbijateühistute Keskühistu*, http://www.etk.ee/. Accessed 22 May 2014.

[72] See http://www.ekspress.ee/news/paevauudised/majandus/etk-ulesehitus-meenutab-keelatud-kartelli.d?id=45762011, http://www.ekspress.ee/news/paevauudised/eestiuudised/konkurentsiamet-etk-ei-riku-seadust.d?id=46218769, http://www.delfi.ee/teemalehed/eesti-tarbijateuhistute-keskuhistu. All accessed 22 May 2014.

[73] Competition Act, para 6.

[74] Competition Act, para 5.

cases concern both retailers and suppliers with possible horizontal and vertical competition issues. At the time of writing none of these investigations have resulted in the finding of an infringement or prosecution of the undertakings involved.

7.4.2 Resale Price Maintenance and Recommended Resale Prices

The resale price maintenance (RPM) can be prohibited under the national equivalent of Article 101 TFEU,[75] as opposed to purely recommended prices, when it is enforced by certain means that include withdrawal of the supply, providing of incentives, establishing of the monitoring of competitors' prices on retail level and other measures facilitating price coordination. Another scenario that might be considered in relation to coordination of resale prices is a hub-and-spoke collusion with both horizontal and vertical dimensions where RPM can be effectively enforced. There are currently several cases being investigated by the ECA, the details of which are not public, that concern grocery retail sector and may include allegations of RPM. Some of them are likely to result in public court proceedings, which can shed light on their circumstances, as well as produce some court guidance on RPM, including how and when it can be considered an infringement of competition rules.

7.4.3 Abuses of Dominant Position

The Competition Act does not expressly prohibit abuse of buying power or abuse of economic dependency. There are no specific definitions of these concepts. Since the national equivalent of Article 102 TFEU[76] contains a nonexclusive list of actions of the dominant undertaking that can be qualified as abuse of dominance, the abuse of buying power or abuse of dependency is not therefore excluded.

The provisions of the Competition Act are not sufficiently clear in relation to the abuse of dominance test that should be applied to the conduct of the dominant undertaking. While the law does not explicitly prohibit the abuse of buying power or dependency, these abuses can take the form of imposition of unfair prices of other trading conditions, application of discriminatory practices or unjustified refusals to sell or buy goods and then can be caught by the prohibition provision.[77] Although in its enforcement practice the ECA has normally considered the anticompetitive effects of abusive conduct, the Supreme Court[78] has demonstrated acceptance of the *per se* approach as well. In 2007, the Supreme Court held that Competition Act does not require the showing of anticompetitive effects in abuse of

[75] Competition Act, para 4.

[76] Competition Act, paras 16(1)-(6).

[77] Competition Act, para 16.

[78] *Riigikohus*, http://www.riigikohus.ee/. Accessed 22 May 2014.

dominance cases.[79] The court reasoned that the existence of potential risk to competition is sufficient in itself, especially in relation to practices that have been characterized as *per se* abuses by the EU courts.[80]

The Competition Act expressly prohibits direct or indirect imposition of unfair purchase or selling prices as a form of abuse of dominant position.[81] The notion of unfair prices encompasses excessive or abusively high prices. The test for pricing abuses has been clarified by the Supreme Court in the *Eesti Telefon* case.[82] Referring to the EU jurisprudence,[83] the court confirmed that evaluation of the reasonableness of prices of the dominant undertaking is in line with EU competition law.[84] The reasonableness of the price is determined on the basis of a comparison between the established price and the economic value of the product or service. This is generally in line with the two-prong test established by the CJEU in the *United Brands* case.[85] The comparison can also be done between the profit margin obtained by the dominant undertaking and the profits made in other similar markets where competition is present.[86] The court also held that the price might be excessively high even in the absence of profit because it is not fair to expect the clients/consumers of the dominant undertaking to cover the costs resulting from the inefficient economic activities of the dominant undertaking.[87] Some commentators welcomed the ECA's assessment of prices in the industries where price competition is not possible due to the structure of the relevant markets.[88]

In 2011, the ECA investigated excessive pricing in the *Levira* case, which concerned the market for terrestrial broadcasting services.[89] In its assessment, the ECA followed the *United Brands* test and the Supreme Court's reasoning in *Eesti Telefon*. The ECA held that it should consider whether the pricing had a reasonable correlation with the economic value of the services provided. For that it was necessary to see whether the dominant undertaking had made profit that it could not have gained under ordinary and sufficiently competitive market conditions.

---

[79] Judgment *AS Eesti Post* No. 3-1-1-64-07 dated 5 December 2007, para 8.1.

[80] Judgment *AS Eesti Post*, para 4.1.

[81] Competition Act, para 16(1).

[82] Judgment *AS Eesti Telefon* No. 3-3-1-66-02 dated 18 December 2002.

[83] Case 26/75, *General Motors Continental N.V. v. Commission of the European Communities*, ECR 1975 I-1367.

[84] Judgment *AS Eesti Telefon* No. 3-3-1-66-02 dated 18 December 2002, para 15.

[85] Case 27/76, *United Brands Company and United Brands Continentaal B.V. v. Commission of the European Communities*, ECR 1978 I-207.

[86] Judgment *AS Eesti Telefon* No. 3-3-1-66-02 dated 18 December 2002, para 26.

[87] Judgment *AS Eesti Telefon*, para 26.

[88] See Tamm E (2007) Ebaõiglane hind. Turgu valitseva ettevõtja kohustuste analüüs konkurentsiseaduse rakenduspraktika alusel [Unfair Pricing. Analysis of the Obligations of an Undertaking in a Dominant Position, Based on the Implementation Experience of the Competition Act], *Juridica*, nr. 4, pp 263–273.

[89] ECA Decision No. 5.1-5/11-020 dated 16 September 2011, available at http://www.konkurentsiamet.ee/public/Otsused/2011/o2011_20.pdf. Accessed 22 May 2014.

According to the ECA's 2011 Annual Report, "the Competition Authority proceeded from the determination of whether the ratio of the profitability and the economic merit of the service provided by *Levira* were reasonable."[90] In its assessment, the ECA referred to the Supreme Court's determination that "the unfair pricing may also be asserted by the fact that the undertaking would not have the possibility to sell its products or services at given price if it would not have the dominant position."[91] The ECA considered *Levira*'s profitability to be too high, and the company decreased its profit margins in the course of the proceedings. In its *Levira* decision, the ECA also provided the elements of the predatory pricing test: (1) below-cost pricing, (2) exclusion of competitors, (3) possibility of recoupment for the dominant undertaking, (4) consumers obtaining short-term benefits in the form of lower prices but suffering from the elimination of competition in the long term.

7.5 Merger Control

There are no specific thresholds for retail or grocery retail sector. The ECA is in charge of evaluating the proposed mergers' effect on competition once the general notification thresholds are met.[92] The substantive test for assessment of concentration mirrors the SIEC test under the EC Merger Regulation[93]: "The Competition Authority shall prohibit a concentration if it is likely to significantly restrict competition in the goods market above all, by creating or strengthening a dominant position."[94]

7.5.1 Market Definition in the Grocery Retail Sector

The competition legislation provides little guidance on the definition of the relevant product market. The ECA's Guidelines for Submission of Notices of Concentration[95] merely provide that the parties should determine their product markets on the

[90] ECA 2011 Annual Report, p. 11, available at http://www.konkurentsiamet.ee/public/Aastaraamat/ANNUAL_REPORT_2011.pdf. Accessed 22 May 2014.

[91] Judgment *AS Eesti Telefon* No. 3-3-1-66-02 dated 18 December 2002, para 28.

[92] The general thresholds applied under the Estonian merger control regime are joint turnover of EUR 6,391,200 and individual turnover of EUR 1,917,350. Competition Act, para 21(1). See also Kalaus M (2002) Estonia: the new Competition Act introduces full merger control. *European Competition Law Review* 23(6):304–310.

[93] Council Regulation (EC) No 139/2004 on the control of concentrations between undertakings (the EC Merger Regulation) OJ L 24, 2004, 1–22, Article 2(2).

[94] Competition Act, para 22(3).

[95] Guidelines for Submission of Notices of Concentration, Regulation No. 69 of the Minister of Economic Affairs and Communications of 17 July 2006 (RTL 2006, 59, 1062), entry into force 29 July 2006, para 8(2).

basis of the definition of "goods market" as provided in the Competition Act: "goods which are regarded as interchangeable or substitutable (hereinafter *substitutable*) by the buyer by reason of price, quality, technical characteristics, conditions of sale or use, consumption or other characteristics."[96] The product market in the merger control proceedings is considered by the ECA in line with EU practices. Based on the commercial space of the retail locations, the following were distinguished: hypermarkets, supermarkets, discount stores. All of these have been recognized as competing retail locations, but even when a narrow product market was defined in merger assessments (including only certain category of retail locations), the competitive pressure was still substantial. For example, in 2006, the ECA approved in Phase I proceedings a merger of two food retailers, *OÜ VP Market* and *OÜ Soldino*.[97] In that case, the ECA, referring to the EU Commission's practice,[98] has defined the relevant product market as retail of food and groceries in nonspecialized stores. The practitioners have criticized the ECA for insufficient attention paid to the determination of the relevant market in its merger decisions, at least as far as nonhorizontal mergers are concerned.[99]

The competition legislation provides little guidance on the definition of the relevant geographic market. The ECA's Guidelines[100] merely provide that geographic market "shall include the area in which the parties to the concentration engage in the sale and purchase of goods." In the ECA's practice, the geographic markets are defined in line with EU practice: a 30-min drive from the place of residence to determine the geographic areas of competing retailers. In the above-mentioned *VP Market/Soldino* case, the ECA defined the relevant market as the city of Narva and its vicinity, while in another merger case Tallinn and its vicinity were used as a relevant geographic market.[101]

[96] Competition Act, para 3(1).

[97] Case 53-KO regarding concentration n° 29/2006, *OÜ VP Market/OÜ Soldino*, dated 1 December 2006. See Käis L (2006) The Estonian Competition Authority approves merger between two retailers on the basis of national merger regulation (VP Market and Soldino), 1 December 2006, *e-Competitions Bulletin*, N°21329.

[98] European Commission, 25 January 2000, Case COMP/M.1684, *Carrefour/Promodes* and 3 February 1999, Case COMP/M.1221, *Rewe/Meinl* and 15 November 2004, Case IV/M.3464, *Kesko/ICA/JV*.

[99] See Ginter C and Matjus M (2010) Assessment of nonhorizontal mergers in Estonia. *European Competition Law Review* 31(12):504–508. See also Kalmo H (2007) Definition of the Relevant Market in Merger Control: General Principles and Criticism of the Estonian Competition Board's Practice. *Juridica Abstract* 10:715–726.

[100] Guidelines for Submission of Notices of Concentration, Regulation No. 69 of the Minister of Economic Affairs and Communications of 17 July 2006 (RTL 2006, 59, 1062), entry into force 29 July 2006, para 8(2).

[101] Case 48-KO *Hansafood AS/AS Hüpermarket.*

7.5.2 Merger Control and the Growth of Grocery Retail Networks

The concentration of grocery retail networks has not been considered problematic in the notified merger cases as sufficient competition was preserved. At the same time, even in case of anticompetitive concentrations, the existing tools of merger control (prohibitions and remedies) could be used in order to contain the rising concentration levels. The ECA has somewhat limited but quite diverse experience with merger remedies accepting both structural divestitures and behavioral commitments aimed at remedying anticompetitive effects of a merger.[102] This experience could be of great assistance once the Estonian merger control encounters a concentration that would raise anticompetitive concerns in the retail grocery sector. Finally, the consolidation of market power in the retail grocery sector can be constrained by the ECA's power to prohibit anticompetitive mergers.[103] Already by its first prohibition decision issued in 2008, the ECA demonstrated that it is prepared to block concentrations that strengthen the dominant position even in case of minor acquisitions, which demonstrate a tendency of consolidation of market power through a series of acquisitions.[104] In that case, the ECA has prohibited a concentration in the pharmacy sector when pharmaceuticals wholesaler attempted to acquire a pharmacy that accounted for less than 1 % of the pharmaceuticals retail market. The ECA analyzed the acquisitions of the acquiring undertaking in the past 2 years and concluded that the notified concentration would not be the last but rather a part of the business strategy aimed at acquiring independent pharmacies, which might lead to significant reduction of competition in the long term. Although the ECA has been criticized for taking into account hypothetical future acquisitions in its merger assessment,[105] the above case demonstrated that the ECA is prepared to consider long-term market developments that can be influenced by applying merger control tools.

7.6 Conclusion

Despite the fact that Estonia is a small market, competition in the grocery retail sector remains intense with no single undertaking enjoying dominant position. Although the concentration levels on the national level are substantial, there is a significant number of rivals present in different geographic areas. As far as the bargaining power of the large-scale retailers vis-à-vis their suppliers is concerned,

[102] See Svetlicinii A and Lugenberg K (2012) Merger remedies in a small market economy: the Estonian experience. *European Competition Law Review* 33(10): 475–481. See also Paas K (2006) Non-structural Corrective Measures in Checking Concentrations. *Juridica Abstract* 5:340–349.

[103] Competition Act, para 22(3).

[104] Decision No. 3.1-8/08-020KO *Terve Pere Apteek OÜ/Saku Apteek OÜ* dated 8 May 2008.

[105] See Kalaus T (2008) The Estonian Competition Authority issues its first merger prohibition taking into account both previous acquisitions and potential future acquisitions in the pharmacy services sector (Terve Pere Apteek/Saku Apteek), 8 May 2008, *e-Competitions Bulletin*, N° 19964.

one should also acknowledge that both agricultural production and the food processing industry went through a process of consolidation, which has strengthened their bargaining position vis-à-vis grocery retailers. Due to the specifics of the market structures (including production, processing and retail), competition rules will remain an efficient tool of addressing increasing market concentration or possible anticompetitive practices in the grocery retail. Although the effectiveness of the criminal enforcement of competition rules carried out by the ECA and public prosecutors can be questioned, this would apply equally to all industry sectors where competition can be harmed by unilateral or collusive conduct of the undertakings.

Finland

8

Mikko Huimala and Suzanne Simon-Bellamy

8.1 Introduction

8.1.1 Economic Background

In the following, we discuss the Finnish food distribution market and introduce the relevant local legislation and case law, as well as examine what the main alleged competition concerns are in the market and whether they are effectively handled.

The most common topic for the public discussion on the grocery sector seems to be the increased concentration of grocery retail networks. Currently, two groups hold a combined market share of approximately 80 %, and there are only a few smaller chains in the market in addition to them. Another feature of the Finnish grocery retail market is that the prices of foodstuffs are relatively high in general. Among consumers and sometimes in public discussion, the blame for the price development is put on the concentration tendency. Market studies, explained in further detail below, have, however, shown that the price formation of groceries is not that straightforward, nor is the market structure, which is commonly simplified as a field of two major players. The market studies and a closer view on the market imply that the main reasons for the high prices are, in fact, found elsewhere, and on the other hand, the market is competitive even with an arguably small amount of operators.

The increasing level of concentration is, however, one factor that led to the Finnish parliament supplementing the Finnish Competition Act[1] with a new Section concerning a dominant position in the grocery retail market. The

[1] Competition Act (948/2011), effective date 1 November 2011.

M. Huimala (✉) • S. Simon-Bellamy
Castrén & Snellman Attorneys Ltd., Helsinki, Finland
e-mail: mikko.huimala@castren.fi; suzanne.simon-bellamy@castren.fi

P. Kobel et al. (eds.), *Antitrust in the Groceries Sector & Liability Issues in Relation to Corporate Social Responsibility*, LIDC Contributions on Antitrust Law, Intellectual Property and Unfair Competition, DOI 10.1007/978-3-662-45753-5_8

amendment of the Finnish Competition Act defining grocery chains with a market share of 30 % or more as dominant seeks to prevent, among other things, further concentration in the sector by attempting to prevent practices that would increase entry barriers. This amendment was, as expected, highly debated. It will be discussed in more detail in Sect. 8.1.2.2.

The value chain of the groceries consists of three vertical levels that are primary agricultural production, secondary production (processing) and grocery retail. In Finland, the primary agricultural production level is characterised by a large degree of domestic production. Most of the raw material used by the food processing industry is produced in Finland. Primary production is also characterised by fragmentation, as there are almost 60,000 farms in Finland. Individual farms are relatively small compared to several other European countries. Challenging climate conditions due to the northern location of Finland also weakens the competitiveness of Finnish agriculture.[2]

The food processing industry is the fourth largest industrial sector in Finland. Meat processing, dairy industry and beverage industry are the major branches. Certain food processing markets are relatively concentrated with only a few major players. The processing level also has experienced further concentration in the past years as a consequence of mergers. The main challenges for the food processing industry are expected to include increasing international competition, as well as the price development and the availability of raw materials.[3]

As regards the grocery retail sector, it has experienced further concentration during the preceding decade. Currently, the market can be characterised as concentrated with two major grocery chains, called S Group and K Group, which nationally have a combined market share of roughly 80 %, as mentioned above. Other players include another domestic grocery chain, Suomen Lähikauppa, as well as the international grocery retailer Lidl.[4]

8.1.2 Legal Background

8.1.2.1 The Finnish Competition Act

The Finnish Competition Act is a general law governing the protection of sound and effective economic competition. The act applies to all units that are engaged in economic activity, with the exception of agreements or arrangements concerning the labour market and certain agricultural activities. The Finnish Competition Act includes provisions almost identical to Articles 101 and 102 TFEU, as well as merger control provisions based on the Merger Regulation of the European Commission.[5] However, the national provisions apply regardless of whether the

[2] The Government Bill on the Amendment of the Finnish Competition Act, HE 197/2012, pp. 16–17.

[3] Ibid, p. 17.

[4] Ibid, p. 18.

[5] Regulation 139/2004.

restriction of competition may affect trade between EU Member States. Otherwise, the prohibitions set by the Finnish Competition Act are similar to the ones set by the Articles of TFEU, the prohibition of resale price maintenance and abuse of dominant market position as examples especially applicable to the grocery market.

8.1.2.2 Dominant Market Position in the Grocery Retail Market

Traditionally, the Finnish legislature has tended to avoid sector-specific competition law regulations. To the extent that sector-specific legislation has been enacted, they have been introduced in separate laws, for example, in the energy and telecommunications sectors. However, the development in the Finnish grocery retail market has resulted in the Finnish legislator considering it necessary to intervene in the situation by statutory means. Hence, in 2013, the Finnish parliament enacted an amendment to the Competition Act to tackle perceived issues relating to the high market power of the two major Finnish grocery retail chains.[6] The new provision in the Competition Act entered into force on 1 January 2014 and provides that a grocery retailer chain with a national market share of 30 % or more is considered to hold a dominant market position.[7]

When calculating the relevant market share, the total daily consumer goods sales of all the undertakings belonging to a certain retailer group are taken into account. The relevant geographic market of the grocery retail segment will be considered as national for the purposes of calculating the market share.[8] The more detailed definitions of the relevant product and geographic markets of the grocery retail sector in Finland are explained further in Sect. 8.3.2 below. The new amendment will apply to both the S and K Groups as both of them currently have a market share of above 30 %. The amendment was highly debated prior to its enactment, and there is still uncertainty as to the measures the Finnish Competition and Consumer Authority (the 'FCCA') is intending to take now that the amendment has entered into force.

The aim of this new provision is to increase competition in the Finnish grocery retail market. The amendment also seeks to ensure that the major retail chains treat suppliers and other operating parties in the grocery sector in a non-discriminatory manner. These goals are intended to be achieved by imposing the responsibilities of a company in a dominant market position on the two major grocery retail chains.[9]

Under the new law, there will, therefore, be no need to establish the existence of dominance in an individual case where either of the two major grocery retailers is

---

[6] The Government Bill on the Amendment of the Finnish Competition Act, HE 197/2012, p. 1; Finnish Competition and Consumer Authority (FCCA), Study on Trade in Groceries, 2012, p. 8.

[7] The entire Section 4a of the Competition Act reads as follows: 'A dominant position in the Finnish daily consumer goods market shall be deemed to be held by an undertaking or an association of undertakings, whose market share in the daily consumer goods retail market in Finland is at minimum 30 per cent. The daily consumer goods market includes both the retail market and the procurement market'.

[8] The Government Bill on the Amendment of the Finnish Competition Act, HE 197/2012, p. 8.

[9] Ibid, p. 20.

alleged to have abused their market power. The assessment of abusive behaviour is intended to remain equivalent to the assessment under Article 102 TFEU. The government bill expects that the new law is going to affect the operations of the two major grocery retailers in many ways, and careful observation will be required, for example, when deciding on pricing practices in order to avoid any conduct that could be deemed abuse of a dominant position.[10] However, the government bill and other preparatory material of the amendment do not include any precise examples of what kinds of past conduct of these two grocery retailers would be prohibited from engaging in under the new law.

8.1.2.3 Exemptions from Competition Law

In addition to the collective agreements in labour market, a specific exemption concerning the agricultural sector is included in the Finnish Competition Act. The prohibition of agreements restricting competition, i.e. the national equivalent of Article 101 TFEU, does not apply to certain agricultural activities. These are arrangements by agricultural producers, associations of agricultural producers, sector-specific associations and any associations formed by these sector-specific associations concerning the production or sale of agricultural products or the use of common storage, processing or refining facilities if the arrangement fulfils the substantive requirements of Section 42 TFEU, under which the rules on competition of Articles 101 and 102 of the said Treaty shall not apply.

The limitation in the scope of application regarding agricultural activities only includes cooperation arrangements between agricultural producers and associations of agricultural producers. Therefore, an agreement between, for example, a producers' cooperative and a slaughterhouse does not fall under the scope of the exemption. It must also be noted that the exemption does not cover the abuse of a dominant position.[11]

8.1.2.4 Laws Against Unfair Trade Practices

Legislation concerning unfair trade practices is distinct from competition law in Finland. The Unfair Business Practices Act[12] forbids unfair business practices such as the use of misleading marketing information and practices that may inappropriately harm the business of another undertaking. There are no *per se* prohibitions on such negotiation practices under unfair trade legislation in Finland. The Finnish unfair trade legislation concerns *per se* type prohibitions on certain forms of advertising, as well as the misuse of confidential information. The Market Court can issue a cease-and-desist order for practices prohibited by the unfair trade legislation. A criminal procedure is also applicable for certain wilful or grossly negligent violations of the unfair trade legislation.

---

[10] The Government Bill on the Amendment of the Finnish Competition Act, HE 197/2012, p. 23.

[11] The Government Bill on Competition Act, HE 88/2010, pp. 54–55.

[12] Unfair Business Practices Act (1067/1978), effective date 1 January 1979.

The Act on the Payment Terms in Commercial Agreements[13] was enacted in January 2013. The act regulates payments between companies as well as companies and public contracting entities. In accordance with the act, the term of payment may exceed 60 days between companies only if the parties specifically agree on a longer term. Under the act, any agreements that lead to the creditor waiving its rights for interest in delayed payments are null and void.

8.1.2.5 Other Regulations Applicable to the Grocery Retail Sector

Zoning regulations, for example in the Land Use and Building Act 132/1999, are often a publicly discussed factor that is considered to affect the structure of competition in grocery retail. The law has particular stipulations concerning zoning considerations for major retail stores, namely the size of 2,000 m^2 or more, such as accessibility by public transportation, minimisation of negative effects of traffic and viability of commercial operations in city centres. The grocery retail industry has also noted that, in addition to major retail stores, the current zoning legislation hinders the development of smaller convenience stores.

Other laws that have been considered to affect the grocery retail market structure are limitations on opening hours, namely small groceries are allowed lengthier opening hours than large ones. Another topic in active public discussion in Finland is the prohibition to sell over-the-counter medicines outside pharmacies. Smaller groceries could possibly be more viable if they could enlarge their product range to non-prescription medicines. Related to the discussion on the selling restrictions of over-the-counter medicines is the discussion on the prohibition of the retail sale of beverages with over 4.7 % alcohol outside the state monopoly liquor stores. In addition, one significant factor in the grocery retail market is the tax legislation, such as value-added taxation.

8.1.3 Market Studies

8.1.3.1 The Finnish Competition and Consumer Authority

The market situation in the grocery retail sector, as well as the value chain in general, has drawn the attention of other instances besides the legislator. The FCCA has published a study on buying power in the daily consumer goods trade, 'Study on Trade in Groceries' on 10 January 2012.[14] As a continuation of the study, the FCCA has published a study on the position of the primary producers in the food supply chain on 27 March 2013, 'Study on Primary Production'.[15]

---

[13] Act on the Payment Terms in Commercial Agreements (30/2013), effective date 16 March 2013.

[14] The study is available at http://www.kkv.fi/file/cd1a09b5-f5b7-4483-a18f-6673dead8182/FCA-Reports-1-2012-Study-on-Trade-in-Groceries.pdf.

[15] The study is available in Finnish at http://www.kkv.fi/globalassets/kkv-suomi/julkaisut/selvitykset/2013/kkv-selvityksia-2-2013.pdf.

The FCCA's Study on Trade in Groceries aimed at answering questions related to the application of competition law to the grocery retail sector. The study was undertaken as competition in the food supply chain had been under public discussion for several years. The grocery sector had faced criticism of industry concentration, the increases in the price levels of groceries and the differences in the price trends between Finland and other countries.[16] The main subject of the study by the FCCA was buyer power in grocery retail and whether it could potentially enable unfair practices in the food industry. Since there are two grocery retail chains with high market shares in Finland, it was considered possible that these retailers could use their buyer power in a way that could impede effective economic competition in the food supply chain. The other topics covered by the study were category management, private labels, slotting fees and transfer of risk between the actors.[17]

In its study on the Trade of Groceries, the FCCA concluded that private labels and category management in grocery retail may harm competition since private labels might not compete with branded products in a neutral manner. Furthermore, gratuitous marketing allowances and risk-transferring practices, by which risk is transferred from the retailer to the supplier, were found to be possibly harmful to effective competition. The main perceived competition problem arising from marketing allowances was that they increase entry barriers. According to the FCCA, the transfer of risk occurs mainly in the form of buy-back clauses that were seen to create uncertainty and pressure to raise prices. The FCCA concluded that further investigations into the grocery retail sector were necessary.[18]

In its study on primary producers, the FCCA examined whether other levels of the food supply chain hold buyer power towards the primary producer level and the possible consequences from the producers' point of view. The effects of regulation concerning primary production are also assessed in the report.[19] The main topic of the FCCA's study on primary production was the competition conditions under which primary producers operate. Sectors such as meat production, fish farming and open air and glasshouse cultivation were particular focus areas of the research.[20] In its study on primary production, the FCCA considered that certain contractual practices might be problematic for competition in primary production. The FCCA considered that the negotiating power of the producers was relatively weak compared to that of the players on the retail level. A possible solution for balancing the powers of different operators in the food supply chain would be further cooperation between primary producers. This is considered permissible under Finnish competition legislation provided that a fair share of the benefits resulting from the improved market performance is passed to the consumers.[21] The FCCA's study also pointed

[16] FCCA, Study on Trade in Groceries, 2012, p. 7.

[17] Ibid, pp. 7–8, 13, 36, 78 and 102.

[18] Ibid. pp. 119–120.

[19] FCCA, Study on Primary Production, 2013, p. 13.

[20] Ibid. pp. 23–17.

[21] FCCA, Study on Primary Production, p. 119.

out that strict regulation on primary production affects competitive neutrality. According to the producers interviewed for the study, some EU directives are applied both more rigidly and also ahead of time in Finland compared to other countries. In addition, taxation of producers differs, depending on the size of the company, which puts them in an unequal position. Compliance with various regulations also gives rise to administrative costs for the producers.[22]

In June 2013, the FCCA published a report focusing on regulation of store locations and its impact on competition in the retail sector. The FCCA's report "Regulation of store locations – Perspective of entry and competition" reveals that the present regulation system, which is seen as complicated, detailed, and open to interpretation, strengthens the position of the leading companies in the field. The report shows that due to strict interpretation of the Land use and Building Act large retail units are not able to be situated outside of urban centres. As the urban centres are in many cases densely built, the retail sector companies do not have many practicable options if they wish to enlarge their operations and build new large retail units. According to the report, the municipalities-owned plots are mainly sold by discretion or through negotiations which have caused difficulties particularly for smaller operators. Also the lack of transparency and openness in the plot sales process may hinder competition in the retail sector. As a result of the report, the FCCA published numerous recommendations including, for instance, amending the legislation of land use and building, as well as, increasing openness and transparency in all stages of land use planning and in plot policy.[23]

More recently, the FCCA has conducted a survey to investigate consumers' shopping behaviour in the grocery retail trade. The study, published in January 2015, considers that store location is explicitly the most important factor in the selection of the primary store. For customers, the other deciding factors on choosing the place for grocery shopping includes a product mix that meets the consumer's needs, the familiarity of the store, the reliable availability of goods and high quality of products. As regards the opening hours, the study revealed that it has a significant impact on customers' choices. However, factors related to loyalty programmes are of relatively small importance while this finding is dependent upon the different consumer groups.[24]

8.1.3.2 The Research Institute of the Finnish Economy

The Research Institute of the Finnish Economy (ETLA) has published a study on the price formation of the groceries and the functionality of the markets, 'Price Formation and Market Functionality of Foodstuffs', on 2 February 2010.[25] The

[22] Ibid, p. 120.

[23] The study is available in Finnish at http://www.kkv.fi/globalassets/kkv-suomi/julkaisut/selvitykset/2013/kkv-selvityksia-3-2013.pdf.

[24] The study is available in Finnish at http://www.kkv.fi/globalassets/kkv-suomi/julkaisut/selvitykset/2015/kkv-selvityksia-1-2015-kanta-asiakasjarjestelmat.pdf.

[25] The study is available in Finnish at http://www.etla.fi/wp-content/uploads/2012/09/dp1209.pdf.

study published by ETLA was commissioned by the Ministry of Employment and the Economy in order to investigate the factors having an impact on the price formation of groceries and the functionality of the markets.[26] More specifically, the study aimed at answering the question of why the prices of groceries are particularly high in Finland. In public discussion, the concentrated structure of the retail grocery sector has often been considered the reason for high prices. However, the study by ETLA showed that the reasons for the high price level may be found elsewhere, namely in high value-added taxation and weak competitiveness of the agricultural sector in Finland. According to ETLA, contrary to public opinion, competition is in fact effective in the retail grocery sector regardless of the small number of players.[27]

ETLA noted that the level of the VAT in Finland is one of the highest in the EU even after the decrease in the value-added tax rate on October 2009. After excluding the effects of the taxation, the price level of grocery consumption was estimated to be only 2 % higher in Finland than in the so-called old EU countries in 2005, which ETLA considered to clearly show the effects of taxation in Finnish grocery prices.[28]

ETLA also found that, despite the high concentration levels, the high price levels in Finland are not due to the lack of competition in the retail chain. Rather than the lack of competition, the lack of competitiveness due to high costs in the Finnish retail chain in comparison to new EU countries and the USA explains the high price levels. In comparison to the old EU countries, the problem in competitiveness was only observed in the agricultural sector. The low competitiveness of the Finnish agriculture is due to the challenging climate conditions that cause relatively low productivity.[29]

8.2 Competition Law Enforcement

8.2.1 Competition Law Enforcement Against Anticompetitive Horizontal and Vertical Agreements

Agreements restricting competition are prohibited in Section 5 of the Competition Act, which is a provision similar to Article 101 TFEU. For example, the exchange of competitively sensitive information and various price-fixing schemes, such as resale price maintenance, fall within the scope of the Section. The Finnish Competition Act does not have a particular provision concerning resale price maintenance in the grocery retail; neither does the act include any other specific provisions on anticompetitive horizontal and vertical agreements in this sector. Therefore, such

[26] ETLA, Price Formation and Market Functionality of Foodstuffs, 2010, pp. 1–2.

[27] Ibid, pp. 8–14.

[28] ETLA, Price Formation and Market Functionality of Foodstuffs, 2010, Conclusions.

[29] Ibid, Conclusions.

agreements and arrangements are analysed within the framework of the general prohibition on agreements restrictive of competition.

8.2.1.1 Exchange of Information in the Finnish Grocery Retail Sector

The FCCA considered that information exchange between three major grocery retail groups through the research company AC Nielsen had restricted competition contrary to the Finnish Competition Act and EU competition law. AC Nielsen provided weekly sales statistics to the participating grocery retail groups. The statistics included aggregated industry figures as well as grocery retail group specific figures on the basis of product groups, segments, producers, brands and product items on a nationwide basis. Statistics were also available on the basis of store size. Regional data was available as well but only to the extent that a particular chain, store or group did not have a share exceeding 40 % in the said region. Statistics of individual stores were not available to competitors. Suppliers were provided with more detailed statistics.

The FCCA decided not to propose to the Market Court the imposition of fines as the participants had terminated the information exchange scheme during the FCCA's investigation.[30]

8.2.1.2 Internal Governance of Grocery Retail Networks

The FCCA has examined the major grocery retail groups' internal governance both from horizontal and vertical restraint perspectives. However, these decisions date prior to 2004 when the system of individual exemptions was abolished in parallel to the entering into force of Regulation 1/2003.

Suomen Osuuskauppojen Keskuskunta (SOK), the central organisation of the S Group, was granted individual exemptions by the FCCA prior to the abolishment of the possibility to apply for individual exemption in 2004. As regards the S Group's grocery business, the FCCA had granted an individual exemption concerning horizontal cooperation regarding pricing, procurement and marketing of daily consumer goods. As a condition for exemption, the FCCA required, first, that each grocery retailer had to remain free to lower their prices from the agreed prices and advertise independently. Second, the FCCA stated that commonly agreed prices concerning foodstuffs could only be in force for periods up to 3 months, except for industrial foodstuffs, for which prices could be in force for 4 months. Other daily consumer good prices could also be in force for up to 4-month periods. As a third requirement, the central organisation could define at maximum 60 % of the individual retailers' product mix calculated on the basis of their sales value. And lastly, individual retailers had to remain free to procure products also from other sources than the central purchasing organisation.[31]

The K Group (Ruokakesko Oy) was also a recipient of a similar exemption decision prior to the abolishment of the system of individual exemptions.

[30] FCCA 154/61/2007, 19 June 2008.

[31] FCCA, 1095/67/2003, 16 April 2004.

Ruokakesko applied for the exemption from the ban on vertical price fixing as was set out in the former Act on Competition Restraints.[32] The exception concerned the imposition of maximum sales prices for products belonging to the mix of products that each K Group retailer had to stock, as well as the maximum pricing of the group's private label products. The mix of products that the retailers had to stock was announced to not exceed 80 % of the average annual sales of a retail store, and Ruokakesko would impose maximum prices on only up to 35 % of such products. Furthermore, an intra-group information exchange system received negative clearance (i.e., did not restrict competition at all, so the assessment of efficiencies was not required).[33]

The FCCA also granted exemption decisions concerning procurement cooperation between the procurement organisations of certain Finnish grocery retail groups.[34] The S Group had also been granted further exemptions concerning its hotel, agricultural product and fuel service station businesses.[35]

8.2.1.3 Horizontal and Vertical Price Fixing

The Market Court has imposed a total of EUR 110,000.00 in fines on certain grocery retail operators within the K Group for prohibited horizontal price fixing. The association of grocery retailers within the K Group had, on a horizontal level, discussed and proposed to the central organisation maximum prices for certain products. The infringement occurred before the Finnish Competition Act had been fully harmonised with Article 101 TFEU when also vertical maximum prices were considered prohibited under the applicable competition legislation. As the Market Court emphasises the fact that the setting of maximum prices was also a prohibited vertical restraint at that time, the case provides only limited insight as regards the assessment of the said restraints under the currently applicable legislation.[36]

There is no relevant case law on resale price maintenance in the grocery sector, but a noteworthy case can be found from late 2011. In the case, the Market Court imposed fines of EUR 3 million on Iittala Group Oy Ab, a Finnish glassware and ceramics manufacturing company. Iittala's products are commonly also sold in larger grocery retail stores. However, the FCCA did not propose the imposition of fines on the retailers. The Market Court considered that Iittala's objective was to raise the price level of its products at the retail level and to prohibit price competition between retailers.[37]

[32] Act on Competition Restraints 480/1992, effective date 1 September 1992, abolished on 1 November 2011.

[33] FCCA, 571/67/2003, 16 April 2004.

[34] FCCA 803/67/97, 3 April 2001; FCCA, 56/67/99, 3 April 2001.

[35] FCCA, 1173/67/2002, 2 February 2004; FCCA, 198/67/2003, 25 February 2004; FCCA, 1049/67/2002, 23 February 2004.

[36] Market Court, 132/05/KR, 21 December 2009.

[37] Market Court, 594/11, 20 December 2011.

8.2.2 Competition Law Enforcement Against Abuse of Dominant Market Position

Section 7 of the Finnish Competition Act prohibits the abuse of a dominant position by one or more undertakings or association of undertakings. As clarified above, this Section is equivalent to Article 102 TFEU. Due to the concentration of the market, the potential abuse of buying power has drawn a great deal of attention, at least in theoretical discussions. Also, practices such as reselling at loss, category management, upfront payments and slotting allowances are generally examined under the Competition Act in Finland, though only limited practice is available.

According to the Government Bill on the amendment of Competition Act, buying power of large grocery chains may be exercised in a manner that could constitute an abuse of a dominant position.[38] However, it should be noted that exercising buying power may not always be an impediment to competition. It has the potential to benefit the consumer provided that the economies of scale are also transferred to the consumers. The abuse of buying power should be considered prohibited in Finland only if it restricts competition. For example, negotiation strategies of powerful buyers should not be considered abuse *per se* but only insofar as they restrict competition to the detriment of the consumer.

There is no statutory general definition of buying power in Finland. In connection to grocery retail, buying power can be defined as a condition where a buyer purchases such a large share of the seller's production that the seller's possibility to use alternative distribution channels is limited and the loss caused by the buyer ceasing its purchases is relatively larger for the seller than for the buyer.[39] In general, abuse of dominance entails recourse to methods different from those that condition normal competition in products or services on the basis of the transactions of commercial operators and has the effect of hindering the maintenance of the degree of competition still existing in the market or the growth of that competition.[40]

The Government Bill on the amendment of the Finnish Competition Act provides some examples on how buying power could be abused in the grocery retail sector. According to the bill, buying power could be abused by means of price discrimination when the dominant undertaking applies different prices to equivalent products or similar prices to different products, thereby placing some trading partners at a competitive disadvantage. Also, predatory pricing, or rather predatory bidding, could be considered abusive when the dominant buyer pays to one supplier such high procurement prices that the competitors of the supplier are forced to exit the market. Also, price reductions may be abusive if they are used to drive

[38] The Government Bill on the Amendment of the Finnish Competition Act; HE 197/2012, p. 10.

[39] The Government Bill on the Amendment of the Finnish Competition Act; HE 197/2012, p. 10.

[40] ECJ, 85/76/1979, *Hoffmann-La Roche*, ECR 46.

competitors out of the market. This may occur, for example, by giving such discounts to the supplier that it cannot supply goods to other retailers. In addition, other forms of abuse of a dominant position, such as exclusive dealing, bundling and tying and unreasonable contract terms, may be considered as abuse of the buying power.[41] These examples of buyer power as an abuse of a dominant position have not been applied in practice in Finland.

8.2.3 Enforcement at the Local Level

In general, the market for grocery retail is considered to be national rather than local, even though a local point of view would sometimes be appropriate from the consumers' perspective. Local enforcement is not excluded, but local actions may fall under the limits of what is considered material enough to be intervened in. The FCCA applies the EU Commission's *De Minimis* Guidelines to clarify when a competition restriction does not appreciably restrict competition. Thus, competition restrictions between competitors are considered to be of minor importance if the market share of the participants does not exceed 10 % on the relevant market. For vertical restrictions, the market share threshold of 15 % applies. However, severe competition restrictions such as price-fixing cartels, market sharing, resale price maintenance or granting of absolute territorial protection do not fall under the *de minimis* rule. Therefore, the local nature of the practice, or a small village being its venue, does not, as such, prevent the FCCA from intervening in an infringement unless it would qualify as *de minimis*.[42] The Competition Act provides the authority with discretion as regards the alleged infringements that it investigates. For example, it may decide not to investigate a matter if competition is effective on the market as a whole.

As regards the recently enacted amendment of the Competition Act whereby grocery retail groups with a national market share of 30 % or more are considered dominant, the amendment will not affect the FCCA's assessment of micro-infringements. The provision concerning dominance only includes acts by the central organisation of the grocery retail chain and individual retailers only to the extent that they enforce decisions made by the central organisation. Regardless of the circumstances, only the central organisation is considered to hold a dominant market position under the new provision.[43]

[41] The Government Bill on the Amendment of the Finnish Competition Act, HE 197/2012, pp. 9–13.

[42] The FCCA; Commission Notice on agreements of minor importance, 2001/C 368/07.

[43] The Government Bill on the Amendment of the Finnish Competition Act, HE 197/2012, p. 23.

8.3 Merger Control

8.3.1 General Provisions

In Finland, the FCCA is the authority responsible for merger control as a first instance. The merger control provisions are included in the Competition Act.[44] All mergers that meet the jurisdictional thresholds shall be notified to it, unless notified to the European Commission under the Merger Regulation.[45] The substantive test is whether a concentration significantly impedes effective competition in the Finnish markets or a substantial part thereof, in particular as a result of the creation or strengthening of a dominant position.[46] The test applied in Finland therefore conforms to the one used by the Commission, namely the so-called SIEC test.[47] There are no sector-specific thresholds, but the same turnover limits are applied regardless of the sector concerned. The general jurisdictional thresholds constituting the notification obligation are that the combined turnover of the parties to the concentration exceeds EUR 350 million and the turnover of each of at least two parties exceeds EUR 20 million from Finland.

8.3.2 Market Definition in the Grocery Retail Sector

When defining the relevant markets, the FCCA takes demand and supply substitution as well as potential competition into consideration in line with the EU Commission's practice and guidelines. As regards the product dimension of the market, the FCCA has considered that, from a supply-side perspective, the relevant market is comprised of different kinds of daily consumer goods, namely of a 'shopping basket' of various kinds of daily consumer goods.[48]

The product group 'Daily consumer goods' consists of food, drinks, techno-chemical products such as detergents, domestic stationery, tobacco products, newspapers and daily cosmetics. In addition to the actual grocery stores, groceries are also sold in smaller shops such as kiosks and gas stations, which are not considered to compete with grocery stores, but to supplement them, due to the smaller product and service range that they provide. Competition takes place between suppliers that have a similar kind of product mix and that are substitutable from the viewpoint of the consumer. The FCCA has also examined the role of various sizes of grocery retail stores (smaller markets, supermarkets and

[44] The relevant Sections are Sections 21–30 placed in Chapter 4 in the Act. The Sections include, for example, the definition of a concentration, the proceedings for the notification of the concentration and for prohibiting a concentration and imposing conditions.

[45] Regulation 139/2004.

[46] Guidelines on merger control issued by The FCCA 2011, p. 58.

[47] Regulation 139/2004.

[48] FCCA, 657/81/2005, 4 January 2006.

hypermarkets) but does not consider them to belong to separate relevant product markets.[49]

In line with EU practice and guidelines, under Finnish competition law, the geographical market consists of the area in which the undertakings concerned are involved in the supply and demand of products or services, in which the conditions of competition are sufficiently homogeneous and which can be distinguished from neighbouring areas because the conditions of competition are appreciably different in those areas.

The Finnish grocery retail market may be analysed on both national and regional bases. From the individual consumer's point of view, the grocery retail markets are usually local. However, this observation is considered to be inadequate for the purposes of geographical market definition, as the Finnish grocery retail chains operate nationally. The stores of the retail chains are located all over Finland, and they all use similar competitive means, such as store disposition, procurement, marketing, selection planning and pricing, and this tends to unify the operations of the chains. In addition, from the consumer's perspective, the markets that are local as such may overlap with other local markets and thereby unify the markets with each other, which suggests a national market definition instead of local.[50]

A deviating approach towards market definition has been adopted earlier in a Finnish merger control case in which Suomen Osuuskauppojen Keskuskunta (SOK), the central organisation of the S Group, acquired the control over Suomen Spar Oyj, a competing grocery retail chain. In this case, SOK, as the notifying party, considered that the relevant geographical market is national. However, the FCCA assessed the effects of the merger on the national, regional and local levels, with particular emphasis on the local level. The FCCA considered that an analysis under the SSNIP framework points towards local markets. The need for a local level analysis was also supported by other factors, such as the sparse population of Finland and the fact that the centres of municipalities were located quite far from each other and most of the stores were located in these centres. Therefore, the FCCA considered that the catchment areas of grocery stores might not overlap to a sufficient extent for the geographical markets to be considered national. The FCCA approved the acquisition conditionally.[51]

8.3.3 Merger Control and the Growth of Grocery Retail Networks

The effect of the growth of the grocery retailers has been taken into consideration in the Finnish merger control proceedings. The buyer power of Finnish grocery retail chains has been assessed in the FCCA's merger control decision in case of a merger

[49] The Government Bill on the Amendment of the Finnish Competition Act, HE 197/2012, p. 7; FCCA, 657/81/2005, 4 January 2006.

[50] The Government Bill on the Amendment of the Finnish Competition Act, HE 197/2012, p. 8.

[51] FCCA, 657/81/2005, 4 January 2006.

between two ice cream suppliers, Unilever Finland Oy and Ingman Icecream Oy. Post-transaction, only two major branded ice cream suppliers remained on the market (Unilever and Nestlé). The FCCA placed emphasis on the fact that the ice cream suppliers in Finland are dependent on a small number of purchasers, and these purchasers also supply proprietary private label products. The purchasers could increase the supply of private label ice creams in case the merged entity would raise prices. In assessing the possibility of coordinated effects, the authority considered, among other things, that the strong buyers could alter their purchasing behaviour to counter any attempts at coordination between the remaining ice cream suppliers.[52]

The significance of private label products and the buyer power of major grocery chains have also been acknowledged in the FCCA's merger control case concerning two meat producers, HKScan Finland Oy and Järvi-Suomen Portti's business operations in Mikkeli.[53] The case was similar to an earlier merger between two meat producers. In approving this merger, the FCCA took the strong position of the grocery retailers into consideration, as well as the fact that the imports carried out by the retailers may limit the market power of the meat producers.[54]

8.3.4 Merger Remedies

In case a planned merger is considered to impede the effective competition in Finland, a primary alternative, rather than prohibiting the entire merger, is that the FCCA, the Market Court or, ultimately, the Supreme Administrative Court can impose conditions under which the merger is approved. Such conditions may be of a structural or behavioural nature. Divestitures are particularly common remedies.[55]

The merger of two grocery retail chains, Suomen Osuuskauppojen Keskuskunta (SOK) with Suomen Spar Oyj, received conditional approval from the FCCA. Initially, the FCCA considered that the merger would have created or strengthened S Group's dominance in certain geographical territories. In order to remove these concerns, the parties offered to divest the operations of certain stores to existing or potential competitors that were independent of the parties and that were approved by the FCCA.[56]

[52] FCCA, 801/14.00.10/2011, 11 November 2011.

[53] FCCA, 1102/14.00.10/2009, 6 October 2010.

[54] FCCA, 492/81/2007, 21 September 2007.

[55] The Government Bill on Competition Act, HE 88/2010, p. 9; Guidelines on merger control issued by the FCCA 2011, p. 98.

[56] FCCA, 657/81/2005, 4 January 2006.

8.4 Conclusion

The studies and discussions on the Finnish grocery retail sector draw different conclusions on the effects of the concentrated market structure. Some discussions suggest that the consequences are negative, but some market studies have shown that the competition in the market is relatively effective. Some problems have also been shown result from a number of different factors other than concentration. As for entering into the market, for example, zoning regulations and the questions related to demand play a significant role. Also, the price development contains many different features on all the levels of the value chain of food supplies that all have an effect on the final consumer price, for example, taxation and the competitiveness of agriculture. Also, the fact that practices related to the abuse of buying power have never been assessed by the authorities implies that the power is exercised in a manner compatible with effective competition.

An interesting theme in evaluating the future development in the branch is, of course, the recent amendment to the Competition Act setting the statutory limit for the dominant market position in the market. In practice, one complex question is whether the new law will, in fact, make appropriate competition authority intervention any easier, as practices engaged in by a dominant company should in general not be assessed separately from the level of market power held by the company. Indeed, a formal approach in prohibiting practices of a grocery retailer that has a dominant market position only due to a provision in law, but not due to real world economics, might lead to unwarranted intervention and deter the grocery retailers from engaging in consumer-welfare-enhancing practices.

In view of the lively public discussion concerning the competitive landscape in the grocery retail sector, it appears that a review of the competitive effects of some currently applicable legislation could allow for meaningful suggestions for improvements in the competitive conditions of the grocery retail industry. Those are zoning legislation, taxation—especially the value-added taxation of groceries—the prohibition of sales of medicines outside pharmacies and the prohibition on retail sale of most beverages outside state monopoly liquor stores.

France

9

Nizar Lajnef

9.1 Introduction

9.1.1 Economic Background

Grocery retail distribution in France is mainly performed by large distributors operating self-service supermarkets of different sizes (minimarket, supermarket, hypermarket).[1] The six major distributors account for almost 80 % of the market at the national level, making this sector a low concentrated market on the basis of the concentration threshold used by competition authorities or the Herfindahl–Hirschmann index. The market share of the biggest distributor does not exceed 20 %.

Upstream, purchasing offices negotiate with food industrialists and agricultural cooperatives. The negotiating process is quite tense as large retailers are charged of securing a too high profit margin and of dictating terms and conditions to

The following members of the working group contributed to this report: Mathilde Boudou, Sarah Darmon, Hervé Delannoy, Gildas de Muizon, Emmanuel Durand, Clément Hubert, Pauline Le More, Charles Saumon, Joffrey Sigrist and Anaïs Taviot.

[1] Between 60 % and 70 % of the sales in the food retail sector are made in the large-scale distribution stores; *see* no 11 of the publication "ECO" of the DGCCRF entitled "Grande distribution et croissance économique en France," December 2012; http://www.economie.gouv.fr/files/directions_services/dgccrf/documentation/dgccrf_eco/dgccrf_eco11.pdf (accessed 11 August 2014).

N. Lajnef (✉)
UGGC Avocats, Paris, France

SciencesPo., Paris, France
e-mail: n.lajnef@uggc.com

P. Kobel et al. (eds.), *Antitrust in the Groceries Sector & Liability Issues in Relation to Corporate Social Responsibility*, LIDC Contributions on Antitrust Law, Intellectual Property and Unfair Competition, DOI 10.1007/978-3-662-45753-5_9

agricultural producers whose precarious financial footing reduces their negotiating power. This situation gets even worse if there is a large increase of the prices of raw materials. Aware of this tight negotiation process, the French Government has reinforced the role of the Commission for prices and margins for agricultural products whose mission is "to enlighten economic actors and public authorities regarding pricing and margins within the supply chain for agricultural commodities." An annual report submitted to the Parliament traces the evolution of captured margins for each step on the vertical chain (agricultural production, transformation, distribution).

Downstream, retail price level borne by the consumers has always been a concern for public authorities. Many regulatory changes in the sector have occurred in the past years (Galland Act (1996),[2] Sarkozy agreements (2004),[3] Dutreil II Act (2005),[4] Chatel Act (2008)[5]). One meaningful impact of these regulatory changes was the gradual lowering of the threshold of resale at a loss, thanks to the integration of different rebates, refunds and back margins.

So far, paradoxically, large retailers are subject to a limited amount of litigation before the *French Competition Authority* (the "FCA"). Most of the concentrations filed relate to small operations at the local level. Cases of anticompetitive practices are not numerous: the FCA has been involved in the grocery retail distribution sector essentially through sector inquiries.

9.1.2 Legal Background

9.1.2.1 Competition Law

The grocery sector is subject to general French Competition Law, which applies to all the economic activities. Under French law, competition rules concern "all the production, distribution and service activities," whoever the actors might be.[6]

Competition law provisions, in their broadest sense, are comprised of (1) the prohibition of anticompetitive practices, including anticompetitive agreements,[7] abuses of a dominant position,[8] abuse of economic dependency[9] and abusively low pricing,[10] on the one hand, and (2) a merger control regime, including specific thresholds for the grocery sector (see Sect. 9.3 below), on the other hand.

---

[2] Act no 96-588 of 1 July 1996 on loyal and balanced commercial relations.

[3] "Commitment for a non-transitory decrease of price" of 17 June 2004.

[4] Act no 2005-882 of 2 August 2005 in favour of small and medium sized enterprises.

[5] Act no 2008-3 of 3 January 2008 for the development of competition for consumers.

[6] Art. L 410-1 of the Commercial Code.

[7] Art. L 420-1 of the Commercial Code.

[8] Art. L 420-2, para. 1, of the Commercial Code.

[9] Art. L 420-2, para. 2, of the Commercial Code.

[10] Art. L. 420-5 of the Commercial Code.

9.1.2.2 Exemptions from Competition Law Prohibitions

In general and not specifically applied to the grocery sector, law may, by exception, exempt in part or in full implementation of antitrust law. According to Art. L 420-4 of the Commercial Code, the prohibition of anticompetitive practices does not apply to (1) those that result from the implementation of legislation or a regulation adopted in application thereof, (2) those whose perpetrators can prove that they have the effect of ensuring economic progress, including by creating or maintaining jobs, and that they reserve for users a fair share in the resulting profit, without giving the undertakings involved the opportunity to eliminate competition for a substantial part of the products in question. Similarly, agreements or concerted practices are not subject to the provisions of Art. L 420-2-1 of the Commercial Code when their perpetrators can justify that such agreements are based on objective reasons with respect to economic efficiency and award consumers a fair share of the resulting profit.[11]

Finally, although it is not an exemption in the true sense, it is interesting to note that in the fight against high cost of consumer goods, Art. L 410-5 of the Commercial Code, as modified by Act no 2012-1270 of 20 November 2012, introduced a statutory exception to the principle of free price setting. This text provides for the intervention of the state in certain overseas territories to negotiate "each year with professional organizations in the retail sector and their suppliers, be they producers, wholesalers or importers, an agreement moderating the overall price of a comprehensive list of consumer products." Art. L 632-14 of the Rural Code also provides for such an exception in the dairy sector.

9.1.2.3 Laws Against Unfair Trade Practices

Title IV of Book IV of the Commercial Code lays down rules on transparency and forbids practices restrictive of competition (*pratiques restrictives de concurrence*).

Rules on Transparency

These rules, generally applicable to all traders, can be considered as regulating contractual relationships between large-scale food retailers and small suppliers or small-scale retailers. Their aim is to insure a better transparency of relationships between suppliers and retailers[12] by imposing a certain formalism regarding the contractual documentation governing these relationships.

Formal requirements apply to different levels of the contractual relations: (1) obligation for any producer, service provider, wholesaler or importer to issue General Terms and Conditions of Sale (the "GTCS")[13]; (2) obligation to respect maximum legal payment terms of 45 days from the end of the month or 60 days

---

[11] Art. L 420-4 of the Commercial Code.

[12] First Chapter of Title IV of Book IV of the Commercial Code, "Of Transparency" ("*De la transparence*"), include Art. L 441-1 to L 441-7 of the Commercial Code on the contractual documentation applicable to the relationship between suppliers and distributors.

[13] See Art. L 441-6 I of the Commercial Code. GTCS are the foundation stone of the commercial negotiation. They must mention certain information such as selling conditions, unit prices, price reductions and payment conditions.

from the date of the invoice[14]; (3) obligation to sign a single convention (convention unique) before 1 March of each year[15] indicating the obligations to which the parties are bound in order to determine the price following commercial negotiations[16]; (4) obligation for the seller to issue an invoice as soon as the sale is completed or the service performed[17]; (5) requirement of a written contract for any case where a retailer would like to benefit from rebates, discounts, refunds or remuneration of services performed for the resale of perishable agricultural products or with short production cycles, living animals, carcasses or for fishing or aquaculture products, as listed in a decree[18]; (6) requirement of a written commitment on a proportionate level of purchase to benefit from an advantage before any order.[19]

In addition, Art. 1 of the "Lefebvre" bill presented to the Parliament on behalf of the Government on 1 June 2011, "reinforcing the rights, protection and information of consumers," created the "single document," a kind of "convention unique"[20] applicable to the affiliation relationship between independent businesses and grocery mass retail distributors. The bill was later abandoned by the Government.

Practices Restrictive of Competition

Although applicable to any trader, the rules relating to Practices Restrictive of Competition are intended to deal with the obvious imbalance in favour of large-scale retailers in France[21] by prohibiting *per se* a large range of negotiating practices.

---

[14] See Art. L. 441-6 I of the Commercial Code. The parties can decide on a longer payment term, the maximum term being 45 days end of the month or 60 days after the date of issue of the invoice. However, professionals of a particular sector, clients and suppliers can jointly decide to reduce this maximal term. They can also propose to set the date of reception of goods or performance of the service as the starting point of this term. Agreements are concluded to do so by professional organizations. A decree can extend this negotiated payment term to all the operators of this sector or—if needed—validate the new kind of computation and extend it to such operators.

[15] Or within two months after the starting point of commercialization of products or services that would be subject to a particular commercialization cycle.

[16] See Art. L 441-7 of the Commercial Code. The law provides for the obligation, in certain cases, to conclude a written contract composed of an annual master agreement and implementation contracts. This contract aims at determining—among others—selling conditions as decided during the commercial negotiation and the conditions on how the retailer commits to provide any service to ease commercialization to the supplier that is not related to selling or purchasing obligations. This convention must mention the object, the date, the implementing modalities, the remuneration of the obligations and the products or services involved.

[17] See Art. L. 441-3 of the Commercial Code. The purchaser is under the obligation to require the invoice, which has to be drawn up in duplicate, and mention compulsory elements such as (beyond the names of the parties and their address) the date of the sale or the service provision; quantities; a precise designation; the unit price, excluding VAT; the date of payment; and the amount of the fixed allowances for the recovery fees owed to the creditor in case of a late payment.

[18] See Art. L 441-2-1 of the Commercial Code.

[19] See Art. L 442-6, I, 3° of the Commercial Code.

[20] See Art. L. 441-7 of the Commercial Code.

[21] As formulated in the Hagelsteen report, which initiated the recasting of these legal provisions applicable to structures or behaviors on the grocery retail market: "the underlying logic is quite

Art. L 442-1 et seq. of the Commercial Code provide a list of practices restrictive of competition that involve the civil or criminal responsibility of their authors or the nullity of the clauses, without proving any anticompetitive object or effect of these practices on the market. Some of these provisions relate, at least partly, to retail selling.

Art. L 442-1 takes over the rules set in the Consumer Code relating to sales or services with premiums, refusals to sell a product or to provide a service, and supplies, effected in batches or imposed quantities.

Art. L 442-2 of the Commercial Code forbids any merchant to resell at a loss except—in particular—for food products sold in a store with a selling area below 300 m^2 and nonfood products sold in a store with a selling area below 1,000 m^2 and which price is in line with those imposed by law for the same products sold in the same shopping area.

The actual purchasing price (*prix d'achat effectif*), under which resale is prohibited, has been decreased by "the amount of all other financial advantages granted by the seller," which includes every kind of rebates or discounts a supplier could grant to the distributor. Once a "financial advantage" is granted to a distributor, this advantage will be in principle passed on to the price under which the reseller will not be able to sell to final consumers.[22]

However, Art. L 441-2-2 of the Commercial Code forbids suppliers of fruits and fresh vegetables to grant rebates, discounts or refunds to their resellers. Art. L 446-2 of the Commercial Code provides restrictions on how suppliers shall grant rebates or discounts,[23] which can indirectly influence their passing on the final price.

Art. L 442-5 of the Commercial Code, on the other hand, forbids the imposition, directly or indirectly, of a minimum resale price of a product or good, of the price of a service or of a trading margin.

Art. L 442-6 I of the Commercial Code provides that any undertaking is liable and may be condemned to pay damages arising from (1) obtaining (or attempting to obtain) from its commercial partner any benefit with no relation to a commercial service actually performed or obviously disproportionate with its value and/or

simple: it is based on the observation that there is structurally – because of the introduction of an oligopolistic situation in favour of retailers - a balance of forces unfavourable to producers, and particularly to small and medium-sized firms." (See Marie-Dominique Hagelsteen, La négociabilité des tarifs et des conditions générales de vente, 12 February 2008, p. 7.)

[22] This specification has been added by the Act of 2 August 2005, as amended by the LME (2008). Under the Act "on loyal and balanced commercial relations" (the so-called *Loi Galland*, 1 July 1996), the "actual purchasing price" was "the unit price mentioned on the invoice, increased by taxes on turnover, specific taxes relative to this resale and transportation costs."

[23] According to Art. L 442-6, I, 8°) of the Commercial Code, a retailer is forbidden to deduce at his own initiative, from the invoice of the supplier, any penalty or rebate sanctioning a noncompliance with a delivery date or nonconformity of the delivered goods, when the debt is not certain, of a fixed amount and collectable, and when the supplier has not been able to control the veracity of the alleged claim. Moreover, Art. L 442-6 II forbids clauses (a) allowing to retroactively benefit from rebates, discounts or commercial cooperation agreements or (b) allowing to automatically benefit from the most favorable conditions granted to competitors by its contractual partner.

(2) submitting a commercial partner to obligations creating a significant imbalance in the parties' rights and obligations.

For instance, monthly installments required by a distributor who also imposed to his supplier to pay only by bank transfers, without any contractual clause allowing the modification of the installments of rebates, have been considered as a "serious risk" for the supplier and, as such, as creating a significant imbalance.[24]

On the contrary, mere differences of prices between two partners of a same supplier are not sufficient to prove that there is a "significant imbalance" in a distribution agreement.[25] The Commercial Practices Review Panel (the "CEPC")[26] brought some valuable guidance on this notion.[27]

The other practices restrictive of competition of Art. L 442-6 I of the Commercial Code that are sanctioned by civil liability include (1) obtaining (or attempting to obtain) a benefit, as a prior condition to an order, without a written commitment on a proportionate level of purchase and—if relevant—without a service requested by the supplier and formalized in a written agreement; (2) obtaining (or attempting to obtain), under the threat of a total or partial termination of commercial relationships, obviously abusive conditions regarding prices, payment terms, selling conditions or any services that are not linked to the selling or purchasing obligations; (3) immediate termination—even partial—of an established commercial relationship without any written notice that takes into account the duration of the commercial relationship and complying with the minimal notice period as set by commercial customs or interprofessional agreements; when the relationship involves own brands (*marques de distributeurs*, the "MDD's"), the minimal notice period is doubled; (4) submission of a partner to obviously abusive payment

[24] Commercial Court of Lille, 6 January 2010, Castorama, 09-05184. The Court acknowledged the significant feature of the imbalance stating that "CASTORAMA's practices of monthly instalments do not respect the spirit of the LME; they are not mutual; they are without any counterpart and distinctly unfavourable to suppliers; their extent is characterised; they are based on a dependence linked to the purchasing power of the distributor; they are abusive; the resulting imbalance is therefore significant."

[25] Court of Appeal of Versailles, 27 October 2011, No 10/06093, SAS Dexxon Data Media c/Fujifilm Recording Media GmbH. According to the Court, "the significant imbalance between the rights and obligations of the parties has to be appreciated in the formation and implementation of the commercial relations of the contractual parties (...) and not (...) in the comparison between the commercial conditions and pricing policies granted [to the distributor's competitors]."

[26] Commission d'examen des pratiques commerciales, http://www.economie.gouv.fr/cepc.

[27] See, in particular, CEPC, *Les abus dans la relation commerciale: sur la notion de déséquilibre significatif*, Questions-Réponses, 11 October 2011, available on: http://www.economie.gouv.fr/cepc/abus-dans-relation-commerciale-sur-notion-desequilibre-significatif#q4. For the CEPC, "the new notion of significant imbalance between the rights and obligations of the parties is dedicated to be applied to all kind of situations, even if the practice at stake can also be condemned by another subparagraph of Art. L 442-6 of the Commercial Code. It will be assessed in the light of the effects of the convention by the parties. Proving that a practice generates a significant imbalance to the detriment of a commercial partner does not imply to prove in advance that the author of the practice owns a purchasing or selling power."

conditions[28]; (5) refusal or return of goods or deduction of penalty or rebate sanctioning a noncompliance with the delivery date or nonconformity of the delivered goods, when the debt is not certain, of a fixed amount and collectable, and when the supplier has not been able to control the veracity of the alleged claim[29]; (6) refusal to mention the name and address of the manufacturer on the label[30]; (7) benefiting from rebates, discounts or refunds for the purchase of fruits and fresh vegetables.[31]

Art. L. 442-6 II of the Commercial Code states that are void the clauses or contracts that enable an undertaking to (1) retroactively benefit from rebates, discounts or commercial cooperation agreements; (2) obtain payment of a right to be referenced before any order is made[32]; (3) forbid its contractual partner to assign receivables he holds over him to third parties; (4) automatically benefit from the most favourable conditions granted to competitors by the contractual partner; (5) obtain from a reseller operating a retail selling area below 300 m^2 that he supplies but to whom he is not linked (directly or indirectly) by a trademark or know-how licensing agreement the following advantages: (a) acquire a preferential right on the divestiture or transfer of his business or a postcontractual noncompete obligation, (b) make his supply conditional to the commitment of the reseller to exclusively (or quasi-exclusively) buy his products or services for a duration above 2 years.

Regarding the practices prohibited by Art. L 442-6 of the Commercial Code (which is the main source of these *per se* prohibitions), proceedings are initiated before civil or commercial courts having jurisdiction by: (1) any person who has a legitimate interest, (2) the public prosecutor, (3) the Minister in charge of economy or (4) the President of the FCA, when he notices a practice covered by Art. L 442-6 of the Commercial Code when examining a case under his jurisdiction.[33]

Although some of these *per se* prohibitions give rise to numerous court decisions (payment terms, resale at a loss or significant imbalance),[34] even abundant case law (sudden termination of commercial relationships),[35] others have raised very few litigation, or even not at all (for instance, the fact of benefitting from rebates for the purchase of fruits or fresh vegetables).

Act No 2010-874 dated 27 July 2010 relative to the modernization of agriculture and fishing provides an obligation to formalize by contracts the relationships between producers and buyers of some agricultural products.

---

[28] Art. L 442-6, I, 7° of the Commercial Code.

[29] Art. L 442-6, I, 8° of the Commercial Code.

[30] Art. L 442-6, I, 10° of the Commercial Code.

[31] Art. L 442-6, I, 13° of the Commercial Code.

[32] Art. L 442-6, II, b) of the Commercial Code.

[33] Art. L 442-6 III) of the Commercial Code.

[34] Although this quite recent notion has not raised extensive case law so far.

[35] Beyond the negotiating practices of large-scale distributors, this provision applies in fact to all economic relationships, which explains why the case law is so abundant.

The enforcement of the rules relating to the threshold below which resellers cannot sell their products (*seuil de revente à perte*) can potentially lead to a limitation of competition. For instance, in a notable case of the early 2000, suppliers of calculators for educational use were condemned for having artificially established such thresholds by alleged conditional refunds (which were in fact guaranteed) in order to set up a system allowing the resellers to charge the same prices (which did not result from fair competition).[36]

It has also been considered that the obligation made by Art. L 441-6 of the Commercial Code to a producer or a service provider to issue his GTCSs to any professional purchaser could ease, in certain circumstances, an agreement between suppliers to fix higher prices.[37]

The prohibition of the immediate termination of established commercial relationships[38] can possibly rigidify the retail grocery market: the obligation to grant a notice period beyond the one contractually decided and the deterrence of important fines[39] can have a negative effect on the flexibility of relationships between suppliers and retailers and help less-efficient operators to remain.

9.1.2.4 Other Laws and Regulations Applying to the Retail and Grocery Sector

Commercial planning law experienced many reforms in France. After having tried to vainly protect small shops, which inspired the so-called Royer Act in 1973, the legislation has sought to remove the purely economic criteria in the Commercial Code in 2008.

French planning law requires an authorization for the opening of commercial sites with a sales area exceeding 1,000 m^2 or for the extension of a sales area that have already reached the threshold of 1,000 m^2 or that should reach this threshold by overtaking the project.[40]

Similarly, any sale area shall be authorized for any change in commercial sector of a business with an area exceeding 2,000 m^2, or 1,000 m^2 when the new activity of the store is predominantly food retail.

---

[36] FCA, Decision No 03-D-45 of 25 September 2003, Practices carried out in the sector of calculators for educational use.

[37] The explanation is that transparency makes easier the observation of competitors' prices by other suppliers. In the case of a collusive agreement (possibly implicit), a supplier could hide a departure from reference prices. Therefore, transparency can give credence to such agreements by limiting departures (Marie-Dominique Hagelsteen, *La négociabilité des tarifs et des conditions gé nérales de vente*, 12 February 2008, p. 15).

[38] Art. L 442-6 I 5° of the Commercial Code.

[39] If the notice taking into account the length of the commercial relationship is not respected, the reparable losses are calculated by the court by multiplying the gross margin made by the victim of termination by the number of months uncovered by the notice actually granted.

[40] Book VII, Title V of the Commercial Code, Art. L 750-1 et seq. of the Commercial Code.

Such provisions with respect to planning law initially aimed at protecting small shops. They tend now to reach territorially a balance between commercial development and complementarities of the commercial offering.

Act no 2009-974 of 10 August 2009 also interferes with the behavior of large retail distributors in the retail sector in the way that, while reaffirming the principle of Sunday rest, introduced many exceptions to this principle in public, touristic and thermal areas, as well as some large cities for volunteer employees. In addition, shall also open on Sunday stores within the perimeters of exceptional use of consumption in public or touristic areas or within the scope of exceptional derogations issued by the administrative authority (*préfet*).

9.1.3 Market Studies

During the last few years, the FCA has been one of the most active competition authorities in the world to render opinions in the retail sector. Since 2009, the FCA has rendered four opinions dealing directly with the retail grocery sector: (1) opinion 09-A-45 of 8 September 2009 relative to the maritime freight and mass retail distribution in the French overseas departments (*departments d'outre-mer* or *DOM*); (2) opinion 10-A-25 of 7 December 2010 relative to category management agreements in the food retail sector; (3) opinion 10-A-26 of 7 December 2010 relative to affiliation contracts of independent stores and of purchase modalities of commercial real estate in the food retail sector; (4) opinion 12-A-01 of 11 January 2012 relative to the competitive environment in the food retail sector in Paris.[41]

9.1.3.1 Reasons for Conducting Market Studies

The motivations supporting the aforementioned opinions of the FCA appear to be various.

Opinion 09-A-45 (French overseas departments) was rendered after a referral on 18 February 2009 from the Secretary of State for overseas, following several weeks of all-out strike in Guadeloupe and Martinique, protesting notably against the prices of essential products on these territories. The aim of the referral was clearly to examine whether the competitive environment in the food retail sectors in the overseas departments could partially explain the level of retail prices in these areas.

[41] The FCA has also made on 18 September 2012 an opinion (Opinion 12-A-20) closing a sector inquiry started on July 2011 relative to the competitive operation of e-commerce. Focusing on three particular sectors (electrical domestic appliances, cosmetic and personal care products and luxury perfume and beauty products), the conclusions of this opinion may therefore have an impact on the retail grocery sectors. In this opinion, the FCA wished that manufacturers and traditional retailers ensure that their marketing agreements (selective distribution, different purchase prices or shipping terms, etc.) do not curb the development of online sales and the resultant increase in competitive pressure. More specifically, the FCA considers that it is essential that manufactures do not obstruct the expansion of pure player retailers.

Opinion 10-A-25 (category management) was the conclusion of proceedings opened at the FCA's own initiative. The FCA noticed that the practices at stake, which have been previously only briefly examined by the European Commission, developed quickly in France, which led the FCA to make exhaustive investigations on such potentially problematic agreements.

Opinion 10-A-26 (affiliation contracts), which was also rendered at the FCA's own initiative, followed a contentious case opened by a professional organization representing franchisees and involving the large retailer Carrefour. In its Decision 10-D-08 of 3 March 2008, the FCA concluded that, in this particular case, the elements were not sufficient to fine Carrefour. One may, however, notice that the issues analyzed in this decision and the ones examined a few months later, on a wider basis, in opinion 10-A-26, are exactly the same. The link between these two cases seems to be quite obvious.

Opinion 12-A-01 (food retail sector in Paris) was rendered after a referral on 8 February 2011, in which the Paris municipality asked the FCA to look into the competitive environment in the food retail sector in the city. It should be noted that, in opinion 10-A-26, mentioned above, the FCA already referred to the particularly high levels of concentration in the food retail market within Paris.

9.1.3.2 Main Topics Covered by the Market Studies

Opinion 09-A-45 (French overseas departments) mainly tried to identify the reasons for the price discrepancies of consumer goods between mainland France and the DOM (French overseas departments). The FCA identified several particularities of the procurement circuits of the DOM markets that allow operators to partially avoid the effects of competition, including specific entry barriers (e.g., length of the logistics circuits towards the overseas territories, scarcity and high price of commercial real estate), high level of concentration, territorial exclusivity practices binding manufacturers and importers in each DOM, etc.

In opinion 10-A-25 (category management), the FCA identified numerous potential risks for competition linked to category management partnerships, particularly (1) risk of shelf space eviction for competitors (for example, advantage taken by the category captain from its privileged relationship with the retailer in order to influence the assortment and the merchandising to the detriment of its competitors or exclusive information exchanges giving the category captain a competitive advantage); (2) potential horizontal agreements between retailers: the FCA considered that in the case where a same supplier is simultaneously category captain with several retailers, there is a risk that it serves as cartel cornerstone by facilitating information exchange between retailers.

In opinion 10-A-26 (affiliation contracts), the FCA expressed its concerns regarding the concentration level of some customer catchment areas, particularly in the markets for large superstores (above 2,500 m^2) and for convenience stores (located in city centres). It noticed that the current competitive situation might be blocked because of various entry barriers and of obstacles to the mobility of independent stores across retail groups. According to the FCA, although independent in terms of pricing and buying decisions, affiliate stores are often captive from their retail group due to numerous clauses included in their agreements and status, which prevent them from moving to another retailing group (long duration of agreements, multiplicity of agreements with overlapping terms, entry rights with delayed payments, postagreement nonreaffiliation or noncompetition clauses). Finally, the FCA noted that priority rights included in the agreements may be activated by a distribution group when the independent shopkeeper tries to sell its store. They artificially restrict competition by limiting the competitors' ability to purchase independent stores and contribute to freezing the geographical establishment of distribution groups.

In opinion 12-A-01 (food retail sector in Paris), the FCA noted that the food retail sector is particularly concentrated in Paris, where the Casino group's stake in Monoprix has brought its market share to more than 60 % in terms of sales area, i.e., more than three times that of its main competitor. The FCA also noted that the arrival of competitors has had a negative impact on the net profits of Franprix outlets, which was probably due to a drop in customer numbers and to a rise in the costs associated with addressing increased competition in their neighbourhoods. Nevertheless, this new competition has not driven customer numbers down far enough for Franprix outlets to lower their prices significantly, despite the fact that net margins upstream (at central buying office level) and downstream (at retail outlet level) are such as would allow price cuts in the event of more intense competition.

9.1.3.3 Outcome of the Market Studies

In opinion 09-A-45 (French overseas departments), the FCA made different proposals in order to revitalize competition on the markets: (1) initiation of investigations in order to fine the anticompetitive practices identified during the examination of the request for opinion (imposed sale prices, horizontal anticompetitive practices, clientele exclusivity agreements, restrictions on parallel trade, etc.), (2) proposition to modify the law in order to facilitate competition by removing the regulatory entry barriers and by improving consumer information, (3) proposition that, in each DOM, the local and regional authorities and the state set up study missions with the objective of defining the provisions for the creation and operation of procurement and storage centres. The FCA expressly reiterated that, even in this case, price regulation may not be a solution.

In opinion 10-A-25 (category management), the FCA pointed out the lack of clarity within the current system and invited the sector operators and the *Commission d'examen des pratiques commerciales* (*commercial practices review panel*, CEPC) to publish a best practices code. It mainly underlined three points: (1) it wished that the appointment of a category captain is made public, for example, through a call for application proposition; (2) it called for more clarity and more formalization of this kind of partnerships; (3) it noted that the CEPC could play a very useful role in defining the best practices and monitoring the development of these collaborations at a time when the general framework lacks in clarity. To our best knowledge, such best practices code has not been established yet.

In opinion 10-A-26 (affiliation contracts), the FCA considered that, to revamp competition, behavioral barriers to entry, on the one hand (for example, practices aimed at freezing commercial estate), and obstacles to the mobility of independent stores across retail groups, on the other hand (in the form of agreements that are too long and too rigid), have to be removed. The FCA issued several recommendations. Among them are (1) removal of noncompetition clauses and of priority rights in the selling and purchasing commercial estate contracts, (2) limitation of the duration of affiliation contracts to a maximum of 5 years, (3) limitation of postagreement nonreaffiliation and noncompetition clauses, (4) prohibition of priority rights in the affiliation contracts.

In opinion 12-A-01 (food retail sector in Paris), the FCA made several recommendations in order to increase the market's fluidity and modify the structures. In particular, the FCA is in favour of abolishing the administrative authorization procedure for new outlets with floor space in excess of 1,000 m^2. It is also in favour of the Paris municipality ensuring that sufficiently large surface areas are provided for in commercial development zones to enable large supermarkets—or even hypermarkets—to be opened. Moreover, the FCA notes that, in its current form, the French legislation does not enable it to modify the structure of the market (i.e., to issue structural injunctions) in the absence of reiterated anticompetitive practices. In order to be able to modify the structure of the market, it therefore suggests the creation by the legislator of a new instrument—the structural injunction—the implementation conditions for which will need to be further defined. To our knowledge, such legislation is not under discussion yet.

9.2 Competition Law Enforcement

9.2.1 Case Law on the Conduct of Grocery Retailers in the Last 5 Years

Most of the relevant decisions in this sector have been made either by the FCA, but in opinions not in decisions with mandatory effects, or by courts, in disputes relating to the implementation of the rules set out in Title IV, Book IV of the Commercial Code (transparency and "restrictive practices," practices restricting competition). These decisions are very detailed and widely disseminated.

As for the decisions—in the strict sense—rendered by the FCA, setting aside merger control decisions, most of the decisions rendered in this sector relate to the behavior of suppliers. As far as we know, only three relevant decisions relating to the behavior of distributors in the sector of grocery retail have been rendered recently: (1) FCA, Decision No 11-D-03 of 15 February 2011 relating to practices carried out in the sector of wholesale distribution of fruits and vegetables and fresh products from the sea regarding postcontractual nonreaffiliation clause in the grocery retail distribution; (2) FCA, Decision No 11-D-04 of 23 February 2011 relating to practices carried out by Carrefour in the food retail sector regarding abuse of economic dependency, namely the hindrance to the exit of the network and to freedom of supply, the brutal imposition of new commercial conditions in the mass retail distribution; (3) FCA, Decision No. 11-D-20 of 16 December 2011 relating to practices implemented by Carrefour in the food retail sector regarding exclusionary practices, abuse of economic dependency in the mass retail distribution.[42]

9.2.1.1 Competition Law Enforcement Against Horizontal Anticompetitive Practices at Local Level

Since the adoption of the LME,[43] the DGCCRF,[44] and not the CFA, has the power to make injunctions and to conclude financial transactions for local anticompetitive practices involving undertakings with limited turnovers.[45] This statute allows fast treatment of these cases.

The anticompetitive practices at stake are those (1) that concern markets of local dimension, (2) that do not affect intracommunity trade and (3) that relate to undertakings whose individual turnover is below EUR 50 million and aggregated below EUR 100 million.[46]

9.2.1.2 Horizontal Agreements Between Grocery Suppliers to Withdraw Quantities in Order to Keep Prices Up

In Decision no 13-D-03 of 13 February 2013 relating to practices implemented in the pork pig sector, the FCA fined undertakings active in the sector of pork slaughter for a total amount of EUR 4.57 million.

The FCA noted that the pork slaughter undertakings had together decided to coordinately reduce their demand of pork towards breeders/producers during 2009, in order to influence the price of the pork in the Breton Pork Market, which serves as a reference on the national level. However, the practice at stake aimed at reducing the cost of pork paid to the slaughterers, not to maintain high prices towards grocery mass retail distributors.

As far as we know, the other decisions made relate to price-fixing practices, not quantities. In Decision no 11-D-17 of 8 December 2011 relating to practices implemented in the laundry detergent sector, the FCA imposed a total fine of EUR 367.9 million to the four principal detergent producers of the market for

[42] The Court of Appeal of Paris has recently rendered several decisions of interest in this sector: Court of Appeal of Paris, 6 March 2013, *Prodim and CSF Champion Supermarché France vs Société Etablissements Segurel*, RG 09/16817, regarding exclusionary and anticompetitive practice and postcontractual nonreaffiliation clause in franchise relationships; Court of Appeal of Paris, 3 April 2013, *Distribution Alimentaire Parisienne Diapar vs Carrefour Proximité France*, CSF Champion Supermarché France and M Christian Richard, RG 10/24013.

[43] The Act on the Modernisation of the Economy, no 2008-776 of 4 August 2008.

[44] Directorate General for Competition, Consumption and Fraud Repression, administrative body placed under the authority of the Ministry of Economy.

[45] The so-called micro PAC, Art. L. 464-9 of the Commercial Code.

[46] On this subject, see the interview of Nathalie Homobono, Le rôle de la DGCCRF en matière de concurrence, Concurrences No 3-2010.

taking part in a cartel which object was to jointly set the selling prices and the promotions towards grocery mass retail distributors.[47]

In Decision no 12-D-08 of 6 March 2012 relating to practices carried out in the endive growing and marketing sector, the FCA imposed fines to endives producers and several of their professional organizations for anticompetitive practices that led to maintain minimal prices of the products.

Among the practices at stake, the FCA noted that the undertakings concerned managed the volumes of endives sold by destructing merchandise when the endives price rate lowered under a certain level, in order to maintain the artificial price of the endive jointly decided.[48]

In Decision no 12-D-09 of 13 March 2012 relating to practices implemented in the packaged flour sector, the FCA imposed a total fine of EUR 242.4 million to undertakings that took part in (1) a French–German cartel aiming at limiting the imports of flour between France and Germany and (2) two anticompetitive practices on the national territory between French millers aiming at fixing prices, limiting production and sharing of the clients of packaged flour sold to grocery mass retail distributors, on the one hand, and to hard discount grocery retail distribution in France, on the other hand. The object of the anticompetitive practice between French and German millers was to manage the French–German exports of packaged flour by maintaining them to a level determined in advance (15,000 tons).[49]

Moreover, investigations are currently taking place in the yogurt[50] and in the poultry[51] sectors.

There is no clear information relating to the possible private actions undertaken in order to obtain damages for the loss suffered resulting from an anticompetitive practice.

9.2.1.3 Internal Governance of Grocery Retail Networks

In Decision no 11-D-20 of 16 December 2011 relating to practices implemented by Carrefour in the food retail sector, Carrefour was accused of imposing more restrictive conditions at the occasion of the switch from the "Champion" franchise agreements to the "Carrefour Market" franchise. Commitments have been taken by Carrefour as to the duration clauses, the nonreaffiliation clauses, the postcontractual noncompetition clauses in order to align the new Carrefour Market agreement with the previous Champion franchise agreement.

---

[47] This case is currently pending before the Court of Appeal of Paris.

[48] This case is currently pending before the Court of Appeal of Paris.

[49] This case is currently pending before the Court of Appeal of Paris.

[50] http://www.lefigaro.fr/societes/2012/03/22/20005-20120322ARTFIG00810-soupcons-d-entente-dans-le-yaourt.php.

[51] http://www.lefigaro.fr/conso/2008/03/13/05007-20080313ARTFIG00428-soupcons-d-ententechez-les-geants-du-poulet-.php.

9.2.1.4 Recommended Resale Prices

There are no specific rules applicable to the sector of grocery retail distribution as to diffusion of recommended resale prices. One has to refer to the decisions made by the FCA and court decisions, which are anterior to 2008, in order to assess the validity of these practices under competition law.

Under French law, distribution of recommended prices or the setting of a maximum price is lawful,[52] provided that this does not dissimulate an imposed price.

Proving the existence of the vertical anticompetitive practice requires the following "beam of serious, precise and concurring indicia" (*faisceau d'indices graves, précis, et concordants*): (1) the retail selling price wished by the supplier is known by the distributor, (2) prices are monitored and (3) the prices wished by the supplier are significantly applied by the distributors.[53]

In its Decision no 07-D-50 of 20 December 2007 relating to practices carried out in the sector of toys distribution, the Competition Council (now FCA) imposed a total of EUR 37 million fine to five suppliers and three distributors for setting the price of sale of toys. These vertical anticompetitive practices were accompanied by actions aiming at monitoring the prices applied by the deviating distributors in order to obtain a prompt realignment of the prices of the toys.[54]

In some cases, anticompetitive practices relating to prices can also be prosecuted on the ground of restrictive practices.[55] In the toys distribution case cited above, for example, not only have the suppliers and distributors been condemned for their anticompetitive collusion on prices, but the President of the Competition Council also referred the matter to the courts on the ground of Art. L 442-6 III of the Commercial Code.

9.2.1.5 Resale Below Cost, Delisting of Suppliers, Resale Price Maintenance

Resale below prices can fall under the scope of the prohibition of the provisions relating to abusively low prices,[56] resale at a loss[57] and predatory prices, which can

[52] FCA, Decision 94-D-60, 13 December 1994, laundry detergent sector.

[53] FCA, Decision no 06-D-04 of 13 March 2006 relating to practices observed in the luxury perfume sector. This decision has been appealed and referred to different courts several times. This case is currently pending before the Supreme Court (*Cour de cassation*).

[54] See also, in this case, Court of Appeal of Paris, 28 January 2009, RG 2008/00255, and Supreme Court, Commercial section, 7 April 2010, 09-11936.

[55] "Practices restricting competition," Title IV of Book IV of the Commercial Code.

[56] See Art. L 420-5 of the Commercial Code.

[57] See Art. L 442-2 of the Commercial Code.

constitute an anticompetitive agreement or an abuse of a dominant position,[58] according to the same criteria as under EU competition law.[59,60]

Delisting of suppliers is governed by Art. L 442-6, I, 5° of the Commercial Code, and resale price fixing is prohibited under the conditions described above.

A retailer is prohibited from obtaining obviously abusive conditions regarding prices, payment terms, selling conditions or any services that are not linked to selling or purchasing obligations under the threat of a (total or partial) delisting of his supplier, and "imposing, directly or indirectly, a minimum resale price regarding a product or a good, a service or a commercial margin is punished by a € 15,000 fine."[61]

9.2.1.6 Small Suppliers Retaliating Against Large Grocery Food Retailers for Selling Low Priced Imported Agricultural Products

In the agricultural branch, spontaneous demonstrations by producers (fruit, vegetables, dairy) generally endorsing political opinions undeniably exist, even if they do not lead to any anticompetitive behavior. Nevertheless, the FCA is said to have opened an inquiry aiming at a number of undertakings in the diary industry intervening in retail brands, suspecting them to have agreed not to answer to bids of large/medium-sized stores because of too low prices.[62] The inquiry is said to be ongoing.

These situations mainly reflect the difficulty to take into consideration the high price volatility of agricultural row materials in respect to commercial transactions in the whole agrifood branch,[63] both for the retail brands (annual contracts concluded at fixed prices) and for producers' brands (*marques de fabricants*–the "MDF"), without any possible price review.

These aspects falling within the scope of contractual agreements, in 2011 and 2012, the CEPC attempted to deal with the issue of the absence of price review clauses or the refusal to integrate one, which can lead to a situation of "significant

---

[58] See Art. L 420-1 or L 420-2 of the Commercial Code.

[59] French competition authorities apply the principles developed by the Court of Justice of the European Union in the decisions Akzo Chemie (ECJ, 3 July 1991, case C 62/86) and Tetra Pak (ECJ, 14 November 1996, case C-333/94).

[60] For illustrations under French law, see FCA, Decision no 07-D-09 of 14 March 2007 relating to practices implemented by GlaxoSmithKline France laboratory; Court of Appeal of Paris, 8 April 2008, RG no 2007/07008 and Supreme Court, Commercial Section, 17 March 2009, 08-14503; FCA, Decision no 07-D-39 of 23 November 2007 relating to practices implemented in the sector of railway passenger transport of on the Paris-London line.

[61] See Art. L 442-5 of the Commercial Code.

[62] "*Yaourts: huit entreprises de l'industrie laitière soupçonnés d'entente sur les prix?*" Les Echos, 21 March 2012.

[63] Price increase on "raw" products: eggs in 2012, price tensions on salmon in 2013 or ingredients used for industrial products (*pork, wheat flour, milk...*) DGCIS study: "*Enjeux et perspectives des industries agroalimentaires face à la volatilité des prix des matières premières,*" October 2012.

imbalance."[64] In 2012, CEPC advised regarding a fixed price contract (procurement/public bids) to introduce a "useful" price review clause allowing the contract to be implemented, "even if these measures results in a review of the initial agreement."[65]

Such opinions are a first step in the battle against raw material price increases in a context of growing tensions in the food sector. In the same vein, a recent bill that suggests that contracts should contain clauses that allow price reviews following raw material price fluctuations (increase or decrease), has been proposed regarding agreements lasting longer than 3 months and targeting certain agricultural products.[66] This clause will refer to "one or more public indexes related to agricultural or food products defined by the parties to the agreement and aiming at allocating in an equitable manner between the parties the increase or decrease of the costs of production resulting from these fluctuations."

Actions are undertaken by producers—in particular in the fruits and vegetable sector—against large-scale food retailers, as demonstrations, destruction of extra stock on car parks or in front of grocery shops or distribution of free products. Usually, all brands are concerned. Actions carried out by distributors are brought before criminal or civil courts (which can enjoin the people prosecuted to put an end to their actions and/or to pay damages to the victims). Such actions hardly ever fall within the scope of competition law.

However, Decision no 12-D-09 of 13 March 2012 concerning practices on the wheat flour market can be cited on this topic. The FCA condemned the practices consisting in counterpromotions on pork meat organized twice a year by large-scale food retailers. National Syndicate for the Pork Trade invited pork slaughters to refuse selling pork meat to large-scale food retailers lower than a certain reference price (fixed by the Syndicate). Similarly, two pig slaughters have been fined in this case for having agreed on a minimum price of certain pieces of pork meat towards a large-scale food retailer and on the price of pork meat intended to national promotions of this brand.

9.2.2 Abuse of Buying Power, Abuse of Dependency

9.2.2.1 Definition

Art. L 420-2, para. 2 of the Commercial Code prohibits "when it is likely to affect the functioning or the structure of competition, abusive exploitation by an undertaking or a group of undertakings of the state of economic dependency in which is a client or supplier undertaking."

[64] CEPC, Opinion 11-06.

[65] CEPC, Opinion 12-07, Opinion of a professional federation operating in the electronic devices sector (about scarce components in fluorescent lamps).

[66] New Art. L 442-8 of the Commercial Code in the draft Act in favour of consumption, presented on 2 May 2012 to the Council of Ministers.

According to the FCA, in order to characterize the existence of a situation of economic dependency, one should take into account "the notoriety of the supplier's brand, the importance of the supplier's market share, the importance of the share of the supplier in the turnover of the reseller, and finally, the difficulty for the distributor to obtain equivalent products from other suppliers."[67]

For the Court of Appeal of Paris, "the state of economic dependency is defined as a situation of a firm which does not have the possibility to substitute to its supplier (s) one or several suppliers that can satisfy its demand for supplies under similar technical and economic conditions; it follows that the only circumstance that a distributor realises a substantial or exclusive share of its supply with a single supplier is not sufficient to characterize its state of economic dependency under Art. L 420-2 of the Commercial Code."[68]

9.2.2.2 The Prohibition of Abuses of Buying Power or Dependency

The demonstration of an abusive exploitation of a state of economic dependency is not enough to impose sanctions to the undertaking concerned on the basis of that provision. Those practices also need to hinder competition, at least potentially. The FCA verifies if the challenged practices had "an anticompetitive object or anticompetitive effects," or had "*the object or effect to limit supply capacities or to reduce competition on the marke*t."[69]

The FCA tends to consider that this condition is satisfied when this abuse is implemented by a dominant firm on the relevant market. It even occurred that certain practices were described both as an abuse of a dominant position and as an abuse of economic dependency.[70] However, in practice, the demonstration of a notable change in the organization of competition is hard to prove, which often dissuades to take this action.

Also, the LME repealed the former Art. L 442-6 I 2° b) of the Commercial Code, which punished the abuse of a relation of dependency and buying or selling power. The sanction of such practice involved the characterization in advance of the buying (or selling) power of the author of the suspicious practice on the market. The LME liberalized the negotiations between suppliers and distributors. As a consideration to this greater freedom left up to operators, the LME introduced a new "practice restrictive of competition": the "significant imbalance in the parties' rights and obligations."[71]

---

[67] FCA, Decision no 04-D-26 of 30 June 2004 relating to a referral by SARL Reims Bio against practices implemented by the public interest group Champagne Ardenne, para. 55.

[68] Court of Appeal of Paris, Judgment of 15 October 2008, SCEA Vergers de la Motte.

[69] See Art. L 420-2 of the Commercial Code.

[70] FCA, Decision no 04-D-44 of 15 September 2004 relating to a referral by movie theater du Lamentin in the distribution and exploitation of movie sector; Court of Appeal of Paris, 29 March 2005.

[71] See the new Art. L 442-6 I 2° b) of the Commercial Code.

In practice, certain distributors appear to be inspired by the 22 % threshold observed in the European Commission's practice,[72] fixing for the supplier the portion of total turnover "from which it starts to be difficult to find any other sales potential." Reaching this "threshold of threat" generally includes various requirements (in particular, providing worthy information about the firm) to avoid the possibility of a dependency.

The FCA and French courts have not condemned any abuse of economic dependency in the food distribution sector since 2007.

In its Decision no 10-D-08 of 3 March 2010 relating to practices implemented by Carrefour in the local food and groceries retailing sector, the FCA stated that the alleged practices (obstruction to the exit of the network, disproportionate infringement to the freedom of procurement and to the commercial freedom of franchisees, in particular to the freedom of price) did not characterize, in this case, an abuse of economic dependency.

Similarly, in its Decision no 11-D-04 of 23 February 2011 relating to practices implemented by Carrefour in the food distribution sector, the FCA stated that the decision not to renew a commercial lease for the space where a supermarket was operating did not characterize an abuse of economic dependency, as the lessor simply used the right of each party to terminate the lease contract at the end of its term.[73]

9.3 Merger Control

Since 2009, the FCA has been in charge of monitoring mergers, including local operations if the notification thresholds are reached.[74]

For retail trade (which food distribution is part of), the LME has lowered the notification thresholds for mergers.[75] For overseas departments and territories, Art. L 430-2-III of the Commercial Code sets even lower thresholds.

[72] European Commission, COMP M.1221, *Rewe/Meinl*, 3 February 1999; European Commission, COMP M1684, *Promodes/Carrefour*, 25 January 2000.

[73] FCA, Decision no 11-D-04 of 23 February 2011 relating to practices implemented by Carrefour in the food distribution sector, paras 58 to 60. See also Decision no 11-D-20 of 16 December 2011 relating to practices implemented by Carrefour in the food distribution sector, para. 58.

[74] The three following conditions must be met: (i) the total worldwide turnover, taxes excluded, of all the undertakings or group of natural persons or undertakings involved is above EUR 150 million; (ii) the total turnover, taxes excluded, realized in France by at least two of the undertakings or group of natural persons or undertakings involved is above EUR 50 million; (iii) the transaction does not fall within the scope of Council Regulation (EC) no 139/2004 of 20 January 2004 on the control of concentrations between undertakings (Art. L 430-2, I of the Commercial Code).

[75] The three following conditions must be met: (i) the total worldwide turnover, taxes excluded, of all the undertakings or group of natural persons or undertakings involved is above EUR 75 million; (ii) the total turnover, taxes excluded, realized in France in the retail trade sector by at least two of the undertakings or group of natural persons or undertakings involved is above EUR 15 million; (iii) the transaction does not fall within the scope of Council Regulation (EC) no 139/2004 of 20 January 2004 on the control of concentrations between undertakings (Art. L 430-2, II of the Commercial Code).

9.3.1 Market Definition

9.3.1.1 Product Market

The FCA's practice differentiates between several categories of food stores on the basis of their size, selling technique, accessibility, the nature of the service provided or the magnitude of their product portfolios. There are, namely, hypermarkets (mainly selling food products with a sales space over 2,500 m^2), supermarkets (sales space between 400 and 2,500 m^2), specialist stores (bakery, butchery, etc.), small retail stores (including small supermarkets with a sales space of less than 400 m^2), discounters and online sales companies (for instance, online supermarkets).

The FCA takes into account the asymmetric substitutability among the different sizes of general food retailers. It considers that for some consumers a hypermarket might be a local substitute for a supermarket, and so the former will be included in the relevant market of the latter. By contrast, it considers that the converse is rarely verified: supermarkets are not part of the relevant market of hypermarkets. Under the same logic, the FCA stated[76] that "small retail stores and supermarkets were competing between each other and, following this, that they both face competitive pressures of large supermarkets (sales space of over 1000 m^2) and hypermarkets." The FCA also considers competitive pressures of discounters towards other general food retailers, leading to the conclusion that discounters should be included in the same relevant market.

On the flip side, the FCA considers that the competitive pressure vested by specialist stores and street markets is too limited to be included in the relevant market of general food stores. Thus, it excludes specialist stores (bakeries, butcheries, fishmongers, cheese boutiques or fruit and vegetable merchants) from the relevant market of general food stores.

9.3.1.2 Geographic Market

The geographical delineation of markets in the grocery sector is defined by the FCA as being the trade zone surrounding a targeted store. More precisely, it looks at local competition conditions according to the size of the concerned stores for two different areas: (1) a market where consumers' demand and supermarkets' offer or equivalent businesses' are situated less than a 15-min car ride; those forms of business can include, besides supermarkets, hypermarkets situated nearby consumers and discounter stores; (2) a second market where consumers' demand of an area meets the offer of hypermarkets to which they have access in less than a 30-min car ride and that are, from their perspective, substitutable. Other criteria can be taken into consideration to evaluate the impact of a merger on the competitive environment of the retail grocery sector. Those criteria might help fine-tune the

[76] FCA, Opinion no 12-A-01 of 11 January 2012 relating to the competitive situation in the food distribution sector in Paris, para. 81.

usual demarcations presented above. For example, the FCA held that a trade zone of a range between 2 and 4 km corresponds to a 5-min car ride.[77]

9.3.2 The Countervailing Force of Retailers

In 2008, the FCA, while noting the imbalance between upstream and downstream, held that "In itself, the (first) issue a priori does not originate from competition policy, whose main objective is not to intervene in the surplus sharing between operators. Nevertheless, in medium term, the weakening of the upstream sector through the market power close to an oligopsony in the downstream market is likely to drive a reduction of the supply or its diversity which might be detrimental to social welfare."[78] It is thus the role of the Legislator to intervene to compensate and to correct the sectorial imbalance towards distribution, which has been made in the particularly atomized primary production of agricultural products.[79]

As far as this imbalance is concerned, the FCA can also take into account "the role of counter-power of large-scale distributors in the case of mergers between producers" that would raise a competition issue. Many criteria are taken into account to illustrate the counterpower or the mitigating factors of an anticompetitive impact of a proposed concentration, including (1) the buying or the bargaining power of the partners "deriving from, in particular, to their size, the size of the supplier, the possibility to resort to other suppliers and the power to de-list certain products"[80]; (2) distributors' freedom of choice towards suppliers' brands, in particular with the possibility to diversify sources of supply, given the reinforcement of a supplier's market shares or the role played by retailer's brands, thus creating direct competition with suppliers' brands in the absence of a notorious trademark.[81]

[77] FCA, Decision no 10-DCC-25, para. 20.

[78] Similarly, see FCA, Opinion no 11-A-04 relating to a draft decree specifying the content of the agreements on margin reductions in the distribution sector as stated by Art. L 611-4-1 of Rural and Fisheries Code for the fruit and vegetable sector.

[79] Act on the modernization of agriculture and fisheries no 210-874 of 27 July 2010, in particular through the reinforcement of the powers of producers and organizations operating a transfer of ownership of the products. Since 2004 and in this regard, see the "Canivet" report (2004), "*Restaurer la concurrence par les prix. Les produits de grande consommation et les relations entre industrie et commerce,*" Paris, La Documentation française, 2004.

[80] FCA, Opinion no 98-A-09 of 29 July 1998 relating to the proposed acquisition of Pernod Ricard assets by the Coca-Cola Company relating to the branded soft drink "Orangina," p. 10.

[81] FCA, Decision no 12-DCC-92 of 2 July 2012 relating to the acquisition of six companies owned by Patriarche group by the SAS Castel Frères, para. 136; FCA, Decision no 10-DCC-48, LDC Traiteur/Marie surgelé; FCA, Decision no 10-DCC-110 relating to the acquisition of sole control of the cooperative group Entremont by Sodiaal group.

As far as *retailer's own brands* (*marques de distributeurs—MDDs*) are concerned, and for some products, the FCA acknowledges that "MDDs exercise a strong anticompetitive pressure on the suppliers' brands," leading to substitutability between MDDs and suppliers' brands.[82] Market tests have tended to demonstrate that the price and product quality criteria overcome the brand criterion (for instance, that is the case for packaged salad "4th range salads"): (1) monoproduct/multiproduct supplier capable of implementing much more complex bargaining strategies[83]; (2) absence of constrained demand by the final purchaser (in particular, in the absence of a strong brand backed by an advertising campaign); (3) precarious trading relationship: limited duration and annual trade agreements, selection through a tendering process, denunciation at all time with a notice; (4) allocation and variety of the sources of supply[84]; (5) size and degree of integration of the distributor in the production chain[85]; (6) excess of production capacities.[86]

The compensating effect of the retailers' bargaining power is limited when retailers do not retain the "real possibility of alternative supplies" (production capacity of others suppliers, essential product).[87]

9.3.3 Merger Remedies

The FCA having been in charge of the merger control only since 2009, the statistics are only available for 4 years, between 2009 and 2012. Over this period, 212 proposed concentrations have been examined in the food distribution sector (roughly 30 % of overall proposed concentrations, taking all sectors into consideration; see Fig. 9.1).

The vast majority of proposed concentrations have been authorized without conditions. Only six proposed concentrations have been authorized subject to remedies, which represent less than 3 % of the overall proposed concentrations (see Table 9.1).

[82] FCA, Decision no 13-DCC-23 of 28 February 2013 relating to the acquisition of sole control of many companies owned by Bakkavör group by cooperative group Agrial, para. 43.

[83] FCA, Decision no 12-DCC-84, Holding Saint Amand Cristaline brand, para. 48.

[84] FCA, Decision no 09-DCC-67, LDC Volailles/Arrivé. For instance, for the opening to other products' origins.

[85] FCA, Decision no 12-DCC-84, Holding Saint Amand, exploiting its own sources and bottling capacity.

[86] FCA, Decision no 10-DCC-60, Soparo/R&R Ice cream.

[87] FCA, Decision no 11-DCC-150 of 10 October 2011 relating to the acquisition of the sole control of the cooperative Elle-et-Vire by the cooperative group Agrial.

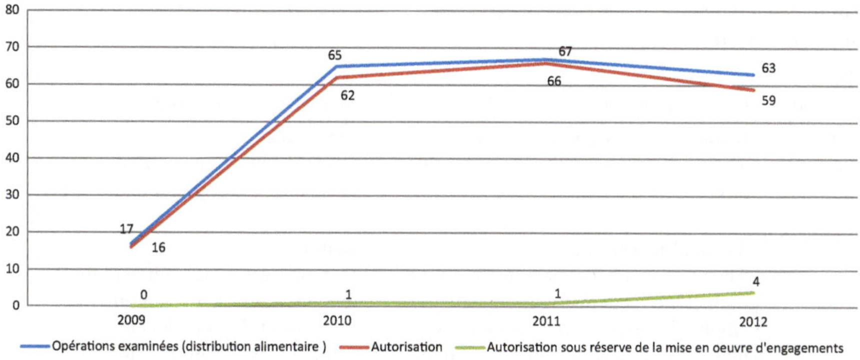

Fig. 9.1 Statistics on mergers. *Source*: FCA website, the number of proposed concentrations may slightly differ from the number of authorizations due to some cases of control unenforceability

Each time the competitive issue identified was of horizontal nature (market share additions, creation of a dominant position or duopoly), the proposed commitments were structural. They generally consisted into divesting stores to avoid overlapping in the same area or to limit the market share addition effect. In one case, the chosen remedy consisted in reducing the sales space of the store. By doing so, the store switched from hypermarket category to the supermarket category. The only behavioral remedy responded to a risk of vertical anticompetitive foreclosure effect linked to vertical integration of the new merged entity at the retail distribution level, and also upstream at the supply level.

In March 2013, the FCA decided to open an in-depth investigation phase on the acquisition of sole control of Monoprix by Casino Group, considering that "the proposed concentration raises serious doubts about harm to competition." It is the first "phase II merger case" in the food distribution sector in France.

Internet stores. Up to now, online sales carried out by supermarkets have not been taken into account in the analysis of proposed concentrations of brick-and-mortar retail stores. The FCA considers e-commerce for food products, leading to home delivery or "drive" store delivery, as not substitutable to predominantly food retail stores. The main argument finds its roots in the fact that at this time online sales only account for a small share of the total food expenditures of households (less than 1.1 % for the people living in Paris, for example).[88]

[88] FCA, Opinion no 12-A-01 of 11 January 2012 relating to the competitive situation in the food distribution sector in Paris, para. 89.

Table 9.1 Synthesis of the commitments concerning concentrations between grocery retail distribution stores

FCA decision	Competition issue	Remedies/commitments
10-DCC-25	**Dominant position on a local area** The market share of the entity would have reached 77 %.	**Structural** Suppression of any overlap in the concerned area by selling the target store
11-DCC-134	**Vertical foreclosure** The new vertically integrated entity, both at the retail distribution and wholesale supply levels, would have closed the access of competing large-scale retail distributors to the supply of grocery products and nonfood products that it distributes at the wholesale level.	**Behavioral** During 3 years, commitment to renounce any clause limiting the freedom of the suppliers to commercialize their products to competitors, transparency of the allocation of commercial cooperation budgets, nontransmission of information
12-DCC-48	**Dominant position on four local areas** Market shares would have reached, respectively, 50–60, 80–90 and 100 %. **Creation of a duopoly on a local area** The new entity would have held 40–50 % behind the leader, holding 50–60 %.	**Structural** Suppression of any overlap on the five concerned areas by selling target stores
12-DCC-57	**Dominant position on two local areas** Market share of the new entity would have reached 60–70 and 50–60 %.	**Structural** Selling of a store allowing to lower the market share of the new entity to 40–50 and 30–40 %
12-DCC-58	**Dominant position on a local area** Market share of the new entity would have reached 50–60 %.	**Structural** Selling of a store allowing to lower the market share of the new entity to 40–50 %
12-DCC-59	**Dominant position on a local area** Market share of the new entity would have reached 40–50 %.	**Structural** Reduction of the selling space of a hypermarket, turning it into a supermarket and allowing to reduce the market share of the new entity to 40–50 %

9.4 Other Related Issues

9.4.1 Price Control of Grocery Products

Although prices of grocery products are in principle freely determined by competition, Art. L 410-2, para. 2 of the Commercial Code provides that a State Council decree (*décret en Conseil d'État*) can rule on prices (following an advice of the FCA) in sectors or areas where price competition is limited because of (1) monopolistic situations or lasting supply difficulties or (2) statutes or regulations.

In addition, in order to cope with excessive price increases or decreases, the French Government can adopt a State Council decree providing temporary measures justified by a situation of crisis, exceptional circumstances, a public disaster or an obviously abnormal situation of the market in a specific sector. The decree can only be issued after having consulted the National Council of Consumers (*Conseil national de la consommation*). The decree specifies its period of validity, which cannot exceed 6 months.[89]

In the dairy sector,[90] since 2009, Art. L 632-14 of the Rural Code has enabled interprofessional bodies of this sector to develop and disseminate "trend indicia, including forecast expectations, of the milk markets, and any information enable to enlighten the actors of the dairy industry" and even "values which are a component of the sale price between collectors and processors." The text explicitly specifies that these practices are not subject to the prohibition of anticompetitive agreements or abuse of dominance. The operators of the dairy sector can thus refer to such indicatives and values in their contractual relationships.

In Opinion No 09-A-48 dated 2 October 2009 on the functioning of the dairy sector, the FCA had advocated a greater formalization of the relationship between producers and processors by concluding written contracts.

Moreover, on 18 March 2010, the European Commission has involved the national competition authorities, including the FCA, in the preparation of guides that present the solutions that competition law can provide so as to strengthen the negotiating power of producers towards processors.[91]

9.4.2 Role of the FCA in the Adoption and Enforcement of Regulations of Large-Scale Food Retailing and Vertical Relationships Between Suppliers and Retailers

Art. L 462-2 of the Commercial Code provides a mandatory consultation of the FCA by the Government for any draft regulation creating a new regime implying (1) to submit the access to a profession or to a market to quantitative restrictions, (2) to establish exclusive rights in certain areas or (3) to impose uniform practices regarding prices or selling conditions.

[89] Art. L 410-2, para. 3, of the Commercial Code.

[90] Particular attention has been paid to this sector by EU and French competition authorities. Dairy farmers as sellers are often in a weaker negotiation position vis-à-vis their stronger counterparts, the dairy companies and large-scale distributors. In many respects, dairy farmers also face more difficulties than other farmers. While both need to adjust their production to respond to changes in often volatile markets, dairy farmers have high stranded investment costs in installations and production animals, and milk production is constant and cannot be reduced in the short term. In addition, milk is a highly standardized product, and there is fierce competition on the international milk product markets.

[91] The press release of the FCA on these guides is available at the following address: www.autoritedelaconcurrence.fr/user/standard.php?id_rub=367&id_Art.=1374.

Otherwise, the FCA can be consulted on an optional basis by the Government or parliamentary commissions on any question relating to competition,[92] in particular when adopting a regulation on vertical relationships between suppliers and distributors. For example, the Opinion of the FCA of 13 December 2010, on two draft decrees imposing a formalization by contract in the agricultural sector, was issued on this legal basis. Moreover, the FCA must give its assent before any decree exempting categories of agreements or certain agreements aiming at improving the management of small and medium-size enterprises.[93] Finally, the FCA must be consulted for any State Council decree aiming at ruling prices in areas where price competition is limited.[94]

9.4.3 Small-Scale Farmers and Suppliers of Food Products

The agricultural sector remains subject to the prohibition of anticompetitive practices.[95] However, inspired by EU Regulation no 1182/2007, France has wished to facilitate the joining by small producers of more structured organizations of producers (either through organizations of producers acting as representatives without any transfer of property of products or through the PO governance associations). The FCA acknowledged that these kinds of structures could be exempted from competition rules because of their contribution to economic progress for the commercialization of products, provided that the practice remains proportionate to the objective.[96]

Nevertheless, food industrialists, who are not included in the primary agricultural sector, are subject to competition law without any restriction.

More generally, Art. L 420-4 II of the Commercial Code provides that categories of agreements can be exempted from competition law, after a decree issued after the consent of the FCA, in particular when they aim at improving the management of the small and medium-size firms. To our knowledge, this provision has never been applied to date.

More precisely, Art. L 632-2 II of the Rural Code provides that agreements concluded within one of the interprofessional organizations recognized to be specific to a product under official identification label, and aiming at adapting supply to demand, are allowed to bring limitations to competition rising from (1) a forecast and coordinate planning of production based on the outlet, (2) a planning aiming at improving the quality of products having as a direct

[92] See Art. L 462-1 of the Commercial Code.

[93] See Art. L 420-4, II of the Commercial Code.

[94] See Art. L 420-2, para. 2 of the Commercial Code.

[95] See for instance, regarding resale price maintenance, FCA, Decision no 12-D-08, 6 March 2012, cited above.

[96] FCA, Opinion no 08-A-07, 7 May 2008, relative to the economic organization of the fruits and vegetables sector.

consequence the limitation of the production volume, (3) a limitation of production capacity, (4) a temporary restriction of the access of new operators based on objective criteria and implemented in a nondiscriminatory manner or (5) price fixing by producers or recovery of raw material price fixing.

Beyond the fact that no party to the agreement has to hold a dominant position on the relevant product market, such agreements have to be notified, after their conclusion and before they are enforced, to the Minister of Agriculture, to the Minister of the Economy and to the FCA.

In the dairy sector, Art. L 632-14 of the Rural Code allows interprofessional organizations to develop and issue information on product prices, without these practices being subject to the prohibition of anticompetitive practices.

9.5 Recommendations to Improve the Competitive Landscape in the Grocery Retail Sector in France

The rules applicable to commercial town planning (urbanism) seem to constitute some kind of barrier to entry to the grocery retail distribution market in France: they hinder the entry of new operators on the market, such as the American wholesaler/retailer Costco. A reform of these rules could be contemplated.

In view of the recent opinions and decisions made by the FCA, postcontractual nonreaffiliation clauses can appear as a hindrance to the change of store chain, thereby affecting competition. Rules limiting its duration could be usefully introduced.

This being said, the solution consisting in retaining a fixed duration does not appear to be satisfactory since *in concreto* assessment of the contractual situation between the operators involved is required, as is done by the FCA and the courts in their recent decisions.

Germany

10

Marco Hartmann-Rüppel

10.1 Economic Background

Consolidation, market saturation, strong price competition and low prices are key characteristics of the German food retail market. The sector is dominated by four large retail groups. According to the Federal Cartel Office (the "FCO"), the combined market share of these undertakings amounts to roughly 85 % of the food retail market. The major chains face low margins due to fierce price competition in the sector. Specific to the German market is the success of discounters with an overall market share of approx. 40 %. In recent years, there has been a trend in consumer preference towards smaller grocery formats, including convenience stores, small grocery retailers and independents. A further feature of Germany's food-retailing industry is the relative absence of foreign retail groups.

On the supply side, a number of big multinational groups with branded products are active on the German market, most of them with relatively high market shares. However, most grocery products come from a range of small and medium-sized suppliers with a narrower national or even regional focus and often only minor market relevance. Most of demand is met with domestic products, but Germany remains a net importer of food products. In recent years, there has been a strong trend towards concentration along the supply chain. The broader trend also affects primary agricultural production in Germany. There, the major structural trend in recent years has been the steady decline of the total number of agricultural businesses, while the number of large entities in primary production is growing strongly.

M. Hartmann-Rüppel (✉)
Taylor Wessing, Hamburg, Germany

Taylor Wessing, Brussels, Belgium
e-mail: mhr@taylorwessing.com; m.hartmann-rueppel@taylorwessing.com

P. Kobel et al. (eds.), *Antitrust in the Groceries Sector & Liability Issues in Relation to Corporate Social Responsibility*, LIDC Contributions on Antitrust Law, Intellectual Property and Unfair Competition, DOI 10.1007/978-3-662-45753-5_10

Internet shopping in the food sector has not yet been embraced by consumers in Germany, and none of the four big retail groups offers a nationwide or supra-regional online supply with food and beverages. A market survey conducted by the Gesellschaft für Konsumforschung (the "GfK") in 2012 found that only 10 % of German consumers had ever shopped online for groceries, beverages or drugstore articles.

The few existing online activities in the grocery sector are mainly operated by small and medium-sized food retailers and have not yet raised relevant competition concerns in relation with their existence. Some of the big retail groups have started limited online activities in select metropolitan areas.

10.2 Legal Background

10.2.1 Competition Law

The German Act against Restraints of Competition (the "ARC") does contain only a few specific provisions aimed at the retail market. Alongside EU competition law, the grocery sector is subject to the general rules of the ARC. In recent years, the relevant cartel provisions in the ARC have been aligned with Art. 101 TFEU. Section 1 ARC prohibits all agreements, concerted practices or decisions by associations that have as their object or effect a restriction of competition. This applies in particular to hard-core restrictions of competition such as price fixing, sharing of customers and markets, allocation of production, market share quotas or bid rigging. In recent years, the FCO has imposed fines for information exchanges between competitors.

Substantive differences exist between German and EU antitrust rules in the area of dominance. According to German law, hindrance and discrimination are also prohibited to undertakings with a relatively strong market position (*marktstarke Stellung*), i.e. small or medium-sized enterprises, as suppliers or purchasers of certain kinds of goods or commercial services depend on them in such a way that sufficient and reasonable possibilities of resorting to other undertakings do not exist. However, Sections 19 and 20 ARC deal with anticompetitive behaviour only in terms of prohibiting abusive conduct by an undertaking with a dominant or relatively high market position. Section 20(3) ARC explicitly prohibits undertakings with superior market power (*überlegene Marktmacht*) to abuse their market position towards small and medium-sized enterprises by selling goods or services below cost price without an objective justification.

According to German law, resale price maintenance (the "RPM") is considered a restriction of competition by object. In a recommendation paper, the FCO has provided some guidance on RPM and a number of other competition law aspects of vertical distribution agreements between manufacturers and retailers. According to the FCO, RPM may under certain circumstances lead to efficiencies, which may result in an exemption under Art. 101(3) TFEU. It is, however, on the parties to demonstrate such efficiencies.

According to German law, there are no specific provisions beyond the ARC aimed particularly at controlling the structure of the retail sector. The general provisions of the German merger control regime apply.

10.2.2 Exemption from Competition Law

In principle, in Germany, the retail sector is neither fully nor partly exempted from competition law.

However, a sector exemption for certain agreements between producers of agricultural products is contained in Section 28 ARC. The aim of the German Market Structure Act (the "MStG"), which has implemented this provision, is to improve the market position of farms. It enables producer collectives to be set up and permits what is termed "dual membership", i.e., membership of a cooperative and of a producers' union.

Furthermore, Section 3 ARC contains a specific provision for small and medium-sized enterprises with requirements that, if they are fulfilled, justify an exemption from the cartel prohibition. Systematically, this provision constitutes a legal fiction with the content that the general exemption requirements of Section 2 (1) ARC in general are fulfilled if the requirements of Section 3 ARC are fulfilled. However, this provision regulates only cases without any interstate effect and applies to all sectors.

In addition, German law permits certain forms of cooperation of small and medium enterprises. The FCO has published guidelines on the criteria for agreements that are *de minimis* and thus fall outside the scope of the prohibition to restrict competition in Section 1 ARC. The scope of the exemption is limited as the FCO has to apply Art. 101 TFEU in cases where an agreement affects trade between member states.

10.2.3 Other Regulations

In Germany, there exists also no specific regulation applying to retail grocery market structures or behaviours beyond the general rules of the ARC that have any appreciable effect on competition.

The ARC deals with the accumulation and abuse of market power and the anticompetitive coordination of business decisions of companies. However, it does not stipulate a general ban on unfair competition. Whether commercial practices by dominant or non-dominant undertakings against competitors, consumers or other market participants are improper is determined by the Act against Unfair Competition (the "AUC"), which applies to the grocery retail sector in the same way as to other sectors. The anticompetitive effect of the AUC is quite low because it restricts the retailers only regarding a number of unfair and abusive practices.

Also beyond the AUC, in Germany there is no sector-specific regulation that, for example, provides an administrative price control, the prohibiting of the passing on of discounts or rebates to consumers or special provisions regarding internet retail stores.

10.3 Sector Enquiries in the Grocery Sector

On February 2011, the FCO has initiated a sector enquiry into the food retail sector. The investigation is focused on the competitive conditions in the markets for the procurement of food and beverages by food retailers. The authority has sent questionnaires to 21 food retailers and 200 manufacturers of food and beverage products on September 2011. The enquiry into the food retail market is still ongoing. [Addendum: The FCO has finished its sector enquiry and published the results in September 2014.]

On January 2012, the FCO completed a sector enquiry on market power in the milk industry. The enquiry was already launched in 2008, and an interim report was published in 2010.

10.3.1 Reasons for the Sector Enquiries

The sector enquiry into the food retail sector has been initiated against the backdrop of the high level of concentration in the retail market and frequent contacts between suppliers and retailers. The FCO saw a necessity to get a better overall picture of the market situation in retailing and the relations between retailers and manufacturers. According to the public statements, the FCO has received several complaints by food suppliers in recent years. Moreover, several high-profile horizontal cases among suppliers highlighted competition concerns in the food sector.

To clarify allegations of abusive behaviour, the authority has also started investigations concerning the procurement practices of two leading retailers. Moreover, in a prominent case opened in 2010, the FCO is investigating the vertical relations between the agro-food industry and the retailers. On January 2010, the authority raided the premises of 11 retailers and 4 manufacturers of branded consumer goods based on allegations of price fixing between retailers and suppliers. The ongoing cartel investigation has been focused at the beginning on the product categories "confectionery", "coffee" and "pet food" but has ultimately been extended to the product groups "body care", "baby food" and "beer".

The sector enquiry on market power in the milk sector was triggered by complaints the FCO received from various market participants. According to the authority, the complaints covered a wide range of allegations, including price fixing and sales below cost price in the retail sector, difficulties in switching to competing dairies and abusive long-term supply contracts with dairies.

At the same time, allegations of an unfair calculation model for and the low level of milk prices, which allegedly threatened the very existence of small milk producers, were widely discussed in the German public after farmers had organised a fully fledged boycott of milk deliveries to dairies on May 2008. The FCO later found that with its call for a boycott, the milk farmers association violated competition law.

10.3.2 Outcome of the Sector Enquiries

With its sector enquiry on the food retail sector, the FCO is currently analysing the effects of the concentration among retailers for smaller competitors and suppliers. The aim is to determine whether and, if so, to what extent the leading food retailers enjoy purchasing advantages over their smaller competitors. Furthermore, the investigation will address the effects of purchasing advantages in procurement markets on competition in the sales markets. In this regard, the development of buying alliances as a specific form of cooperation among retailers in procurement markets seems to be of particular importance. According to the FCO, the scope of the enquiry is limited to the clarification of specific questions and certain product groups.

The authority announced to investigate the structure of the procurement markets in the food sector in a first step before turning its attention to the procurement practices of the large retailers. According to the FCO, the procurement shares of the retailers will be investigated both with regard to larger product categories and, in a sample survey, with regard to nine product markets (tinned vegetables, milk, butter, cold coffee beverages (with milk), ketchup, frozen pizza, roasted coffee, sparkling wine and jam).

To date, no conclusions or recommendations on the investigation of the food retail sector investigation have been published. [Addendum: The FCO has published the results of its sector enquiry in September 2014; they are available for download at: http://www.bundeskartellamt.de/Sektoruntersuchung_LEH.html?nn=4592442]

Generally, the milk sector enquiry encompassed the market levels of the milk producers, the dairies and the food retail sector and focused on the downstream (dairy/retail relationships) and upstream (producer/dairy relationships) markets for milk. While the main focus of the enquiry in the milk sector was on the examination of market power on various levels of the supply chain, a major part of the investigation concerned the retail level. In particular, the FCO was concerned that the market power of retailers vis-à-vis the more fragmented dairy cooperatives would give them an overly strong negotiating position on the procurement market.

In its final report on the structure of the milk sector, the FCO concluded that power imbalances between dairies and the food retail sector exist but have to be addressed individually. According to the authority, the market position of dairies depends strongly on the share of sales to retailers, the product portfolio and distribution alternatives. Evidence for anticompetitive behaviour from retailers was not found in the investigation.

In addition, the FCO announced to further examine the payment terms that retailers requested from dairies. The FCO recommended action to avoid further market transparency, in particular with regard to market information systems that publish current and dairy-specific data on the price of raw milk. The exchange of such data permits competing dairies to align prices for milk and further strengthens the bargaining position of retailers.

10.4 Competition Law Enforcement Regarding Anticompetitive Horizontal and Vertical Agreements

10.4.1 General Provisions and Responsibilities

Section 1 ARC prohibits all agreements, concerted practices or decisions by associations that have as their object or effect a restriction of competition and is therefore consistent with Article 101 TFEU. It applies to all anticompetitive horizontal and vertical agreements. Even anticompetitive practices at the local level are generally not exempted from the cartel prohibition clause in Section 1 ARC.

However, the German competition authorities are not subject to any obligation to take action against possible violations of the German antitrust regime. The question whether they start formal proceedings is subject to their own discretion. The FCO has published general guidelines regarding its policy on how to apply this discretion. According to these guidelines, the FCO in general will not start any proceedings under Section 1 ARC if the combined market share of the undertakings is below 10 % (horizontal agreements) or 15 % (vertical agreements) and if the agreement does not contain any hard-core restrictions (such as price fixing, geographic market sharing or customer sharing). In all other cases, the FCO exercises its discretion in each particular case. This is also true for the competition authorities of the federal states that are responsible for infringements with only local or regional effects. However, according to the previous decision-making practice, the competition authorities focus their resources on cases with certain significance.

10.4.2 Enforcement of Anticompetitive Agreements

As far as it is possible to analyse the published decision-making practice of the FCO and the courts, no grocery retailer has been sanctioned for a horizontal agreement, in particular to limit competition on prices.

Furthermore, neither the FCO nor the courts have so far dealt with the internal governance of grocery retail networks from the point of view of competition law or at least published a respective decision. In Germany, the question of the legality of anticompetitive agreements between members of retail networks (such as franchises or cooperatives) is covered by the general cartel prohibition clause of Section 1 ARC. With regard to such networks, it has to be noted that Section 1 ARC only applies to agreements between commercially independent undertakings. Companies that are part of a retail network are considered by the authorities to be independent if they bear the entrepreneurial risk of their business.

With regard to vertical agreements, in the grocery retail sector the enforcement focuses on two case groups.

10.4.2.1 Hub-&-Spoke Agreements

In 2010, the FCO started an investigation into the vertical relations between the agro-food industry and the retailers. On January 2010, the authority raided the premises of 11 retailers and 4 manufacturers of branded consumer goods based on allegations of price fixing between retailers and suppliers (hub & spoke). The ongoing cartel investigation has focused primarily on the product categories "confectionery", "coffee" and "pet food" but has been extended to other product groups, i.e., "body care", "baby food" and "beer". The retailers include leading grocery retailers as well as smaller retail companies, a drugstore chain and a pet food retailer, while on the suppliers' side there are involved several producers for all kinds of these products. The proceedings have not yet been concluded.

10.4.2.2 Retail Price Maintenance and Resale Price Recommendations

With the exception of books, magazines and drugs, which are regulated by specific price regulations, resale price maintenance in general violates German antitrust law.

According to the decision-making practice of the FCO and the FCJ, the pure sending of resale price recommendations, however, does not infringe German antitrust law even if the retailers follow these recommendations. It has to be noted that the FCO as well as the FCJ have adopted a restrictive interpretation of this exemption. In cases where manufacturers do anything more than the pure sending of price lists with the aim of bringing the retailers to follow these recommendations (such as contacting the retailer to address the difference between the recommended resale price and the actual resale price), the FCO and the FCJ consider this as a violation of the German cartel prohibition clause.

Actually, several cartel proceedings are in progress with regard to resale price recommendations in the retail grocery sector but not yet decided. However, besides the retail sector, the FCO and the FCJ have decided several cases in the last 5 years relating to resale price recommendations.

For example, in 2012, the FCJ held in a civil law case that a manufacturer who contacted a retailer and questioned why the retailer defined his resale prices below the recommended prices violated German antitrust law.[1] Also in 2012, the FCO imposed a fine of EUR 8.2 million on a German tool manufacturer who financially penalised retailers who did not follow his price recommendations.[2]

---

[1] FCJ (BGH), judgment of 06 November 2012, KZR 13/12, available at http://juris.bundesgerichtshof.de/cgi-bin/rechtsprechung/document.py?Gericht=bgh&Art=en&sid=a64ed0b973af83b49a783150f16d33f7&nr=62438&pos=0&anz=1.

[2] FCO, decision of 20 August 2012, case B 5-20/10, available at http://www.bundeskartellamt.de/SharedDocs/Entscheidung/DE/Fallberichte/Kartellverbot/2012/B5-20-10.html.

According to publicly available resources, neither the FCO nor the courts have dealt with the issue of punishments of grocery food retailers by several suppliers, for example by withdrawing quantities. Such retaliatory measures may infringe either the cartel prohibition clause or (if their combined market power leads to a dominant market position of this association) the prohibition of the abuse of a dominant position if the suppliers use their combined market power to influence the resale prices or the procurement policy of the retailers. Furthermore, such retaliations might violate Sections 3, 4 no. 1 AUC.

As far as the case law is published, there has also never been a case in which the FCO or a German court dealt with suppliers who punished food retailers for selling low-priced imported agricultural products cheaply. The only known retaliation measure by small suppliers was an agreement of dairy farmers in 2008 to boycott all creameries that pay less than the price demanded by the farmers.

10.5 Abuse of Buying Power, Abuse of Dependency

The German competition law does not provide a definition of "buying power". It has a general approach prohibiting, according to Section 19 ARC, abuse of a dominant market position on the one hand and, according to Section 20 ARC, active and passive discrimination and unfair impediment of dependent undertakings on the other hand, both aiming at, *inter alia*, the control of buying power.

10.5.1 Dominant Undertakings and Undertakings with Strong or Superior Market Power

10.5.1.1 Market Dominant Undertakings

As regards the definition of a dominant market position, the German competition law distinguishes between single and collective dominance.

A single undertaking being a buyer (or supplier) of specific products or services has a dominant market position insofar as it does not have any competitors at all, is not exposed to considerable competition or has an outstanding market position compared to other competitors. In this regard, the German competition law provides for an (rebuttable) assumption stating that an undertaking is dominant if it has a market share of at least 40 %.

In principle, the aforementioned definition applies also to two or more undertakings. Additionally, it is required that there is no considerable competition between those (two or more) undertakings. The statutory (rebuttable) assumption defines that a number of undertakings is dominant if it is comprised of 3 or less undertakings having a combined market share of at least 50 % or if it is comprised of 5 or less undertakings having a combined market share of at least two-thirds.

Notwithstanding the fact that the above-mentioned statutory assumptions state clear and simple rules to determine the market position of an undertaking or of a few undertakings, in practice these assumptions are rebutted very often. Therefore, the test applied by the German competition authorities in order to find a single or collective dominance is an overall consideration of all relevant market structure factors and competition conditions, such as market share, financial power, access to buying and sales market, integration with other undertakings, market access barriers for other undertakings, factual or potential competition of undertakings outside Germany, ability to switch its offer or demand on other products or services as well as the possibility of the market opposition to switch to other undertakings.

A dominant position is assumed if the competition authority comes to the conclusion that it is in a position in which it does not have to expect considerable control of the market opposition and thus may act independently as regards its pricing policy, amount and selection of production, quality of products or innovation efforts (which is quite similar to the ECJ's approach). With regard to the grocery retail sector, this question arises because of the concentration in this sector.

10.5.1.2 Relatively Strong or Superior Market Position

As mentioned before, according to German competition law, not only undertakings with a dominant market position but also undertakings with a relatively strong market position (*marktstarke Stellung*) are subject to legal control of conduct. An undertaking has such a relatively high market position if small or medium-sized enterprises depend on it for certain kinds of input or output.[3]

Furthermore, undertakings having a superior market power (*überragende Marktmacht*) towards small and medium-sized enterprises may not sell food below costs.

In cases of active discrimination and unfair impediment, there is a specific statutory rebuttable assumption stipulating that a supplier of specific products is dependent on a buyer if this buyer regularly receives benefits from the supplier in addition to usual rewards and that are not granted to similar buyers. When assessing the dependency of undertakings in cases of passive discrimination, competition authorities are allowed to act on presumptions based on (buying share) thresholds, taking into account the entire grocery sector. However, the buyer concerned may refute such presumption if it demonstrates that the specific competition situation on the specific product market is different or if due to the importance of a specific product the buyer may not abstain from it.

[3] M. Dreher and J. Körner, Germany. In: P. Këllezi, B. Kilpatrick, P. Kobel (eds), Antitrust for Small and Middle Size Undertakings and Image Protection from Non-Competitors, LIDC Contributions on Antitrust Law, Intellectual Property and Unfair Competition, Springer 2014, p. 134 ff.

10.5.2 Abusive Behaviour

Abuses of a dominant market position, e.g. active and passive discrimination and unfair impediment of dependent undertakings, are prohibited *per se* because they imply a competition restriction for the undertaking concerned. A detection of a competition restriction referring to the entire relevant market is not required.

The German competition law provides for an exemplary list of market behaviours constituting abuses of a dominant market position. The most important abusive market behaviours that may become relevant in the retail grocery market are the following:

firstly, the request of rewards or other business conditions diverging from those that most likely would result from an effective competition (the so-called exploitation abuse);

secondly, the request of rewards or business conditions that are unfavourable in comparison to those that the dominant undertaking requests from comparable purchasers on comparable markets, if the difference is not justified objectively (the so-called abuse by discrimination in price);

thirdly, the discrimination or impediment of other (dependent) undertakings; in this respect, the German competition law provides for statements of rather general nature, stating only that dominant undertakings or undertakings with a dominant or a relatively high market position are not allowed to:

1. unfairly impede other undertakings in the course of business that usually is accessible to similar types of undertakings;
2. unfairly impede small and medium-sized competitors, in particular, by selling goods or services permanently below cost price;
3. treat undertakings of similar type differently without objectively justified grounds, i.e., so-called active discrimination; and
4. prompt undertakings to grant them financial benefits without objectively justified grounds, i.e., so-called passive discrimination. In this regard, it is commonly understood that addressees of this provision are buyers only.

In all these cases, the detection of an unfair impediment or discrimination is made on the basis of a weighting of interests of all undertakings concerned. In case of the aforementioned passive discrimination, the decisive question is whether the buyer is requesting for benefits that gear into existing agreements and thus have no equivalent.

For example, a dominant buyer fulfils a passive discrimination if it requests from its suppliers retroactive bill reductions in order to “ensure collective growth”.

Price marking performed by suppliers may constitute an example for an unjustified request for benefits only if it is done free of charge and thus not part of the overall conditions agreed between the buyer and its supplier.

10.5.3 Case Law on Abuse of a Dominant or Superior Market Position

In 2007, the FCO accused the drugstore chain *Rossmann* for selling several products below cost price and imposed a fine on *Rossmann* of EUR 300,000. According to Section 20(3) ARC, undertakings with a superior market position are prohibited to sell articles regularly below cost price without a reasonable justification. However, as a result of the subsequent court proceedings in 2009, the Higher Regional Court of Düsseldorf acquitted the defendant and reversed the fine by rejecting the approach of the FCO to calculate the cost price.[4] In light of this decision, the prohibition to sell below cost price is widely seen as of very limited scope. According to informal statements from the FCO, further enforcement action in this area is unlikely as it is deemed too complex to prove a sale below cost price, given the extensive number of discounts and conditions agreed upon between retailers and suppliers.

The most prominent example considered an abuse of buying power is the request for so-called *Hochzeitsrabatte* (wedding rebates) as defined by the FCO: a buyer that purchased a competing company and thus gained insight into its price conditions bargained with its suppliers is not allowed to request from those suppliers retroactively the same price conditions. In 2013, the FCO issued a statement of objections against *EDEKA* after its takeover of the retailer shops *PLUS* as the FCO considers EDEKA's demands on suppliers abusive.[5] It has to be seen whether the FCO will take a formal decision in this case.

10.6 Merger Control

In Germany, the general merger control regime applies also to transactions in the (grocery) retail sector. There exist no special thresholds.

10.6.1 The Merger Control Thresholds

In general, a merger has to be notified to the FCO if in the last business year the combined aggregate worldwide turnover of all undertakings concerned exceeded EUR 500 million and the domestic turnover of at least one undertaking concerned exceeded EUR 25 million and that of another undertaking concerned exceeded EUR 5 million (Section 35(1) ARC). These thresholds also apply to mergers in the

[4] OLG Düsseldorf, judgment of 12 November 2009, case VI-2 Kart 9/08 OWi, 2 Kart 9/08 OWi, http://www.justiz.nrw.de/nrwe/olgs/duesseldorf/j2009/VI_2_Kart_9_08_OWiurteil20091112.html.

[5] FCO, press release of 24 July 2013, http://www.bundeskartellamt.de/SharedDocs/Meldung/EN/Pressemitteilungen/2013/24_07_2013_Edeka.html?nn=3591568.

retail (and thus the grocery retail) sector, but according to Section 38(2) ARC only three-quarters of the turnover generated through trade in goods (i.e., buying and reselling of goods) have to be taken into account.

As opposed to other areas of competition law, e.g. cartels or abuse of dominance, the FCO has exclusive jurisdiction to decide merger control cases where the German merger control thresholds are exceeded (unless the case falls within the jurisdiction of the European Commission). Therefore, the FCO is also in charge of assessing mergers at a purely local level if the turnover thresholds are exceeded.

10.6.2 The Definition of Relevant Markets

The ARC does not contain a legal test to define the relevant markets, but such a definition has been established by long-standing case law of the FCO and the Federal Court of Justice (the "FCJ" or Bundesgerichtshof, the "BGH"). According to the FCJ,[6] the product market has primarily to be defined according to the demand-side oriented market concept. Pursuant to this case law, all products belong to one market, which are substitutable from the view of the consumers, taking into account the product characteristics, the purpose of use and the price.

The German FCO has a well-established practice relating to mergers and market definitions in the grocery sector, reaching back as far as the early 1980s. According to the FCO,[7] the product market in the grocery sector is subdivided into a market for general grocery retailers (such as supermarkets or discount stores) and markets for the different types of specialised food stores (such as bakeries, butcheries or street market traders) and the cash and carry market. In the view of the FCO, the overall market for general grocery retailers cannot be further subdivided into separate markets for the different distribution channels, e.g., full-range supermarkets, discount stores and self-service department stores.

The FCO emphasises that this market definition corresponds with the view of most of the consumers who would expect their nearby grocery retailers to offer a full range of food and so-called near-food products for everyday consumption. For that reason, general grocery retailers would not compete with specialised food stores that offer a restricted range of food. On the other hand, the FCO states that most consumers would regard the different types of general grocery retailers (supermarkets, discounters. . .) as substitutable; hence, they form a uniform market.

Both the FCO as well as the German courts have decided that the market for general grocery retailers consists of regional markets.[8] In its decision-making

[6] BGH, judgment of 25 June 1985, WuW/E BGH, 2150, 2153 "*Edelstahlbestecke*".

[7] FCO, decision of 30 June 2008, B2-333/07, http://www.bundeskartellamt.de/wDeutsch/download/pdf/Fusion/Fusion08/B2-333-07_Internet.pdf "*EDEKA/Tengelmann*".

[8] FCO, decision of 30 June 2008, B2-333/07, http://www.bundeskartellamt.de/wDeutsch/download/pdf/Fusion/Fusion08/B2-333-07_Internet.pdf, "*EDEKA/Tengelmann*", p. 32 seq.; OLG Düsseldorf, judgment of 19 December 2001, WuW/E DE-R 781, 786 "*Wal-Mart*"; FCJ, judgment of 12 November 2002, WuW/E DE-R 1042, 1043 "*Wal-Mart*".

practice, the FCO has used radii of 20 km or 20 driving minutes around the regional centres in which the grocery stores are situated to define the regional markets.[9] However, this radius might be adjusted in individual cases if the economic geography of the region concerned necessitates it.

On this basis, the FCO has identified 345 geographic markets for the retail grocery sector in Germany. The FCO links these markets to postal area codes and has published a list of these postal codes, as well as a map showing all identified geographic markets as annexes 1 and 2, respectively, to its *EDEKA/Tengelmann* decision.[10]

Furthermore, it is also an established practice of the FCO in the retail grocery sector not to make an isolated assessment of the conditions in a regional market and to also take into account the market conditions on neighbouring regional markets when assessing the conditions on a regional market (so-called cluster assessment).

10.6.3 Concentration of Grocery Retail Networks

In Germany, the grocery retail sector has been characterised by a high degree of concentration for several decades now. The FCO has assessed that the four largest retail companies (EDEKA, Schwarz-Group, REWE, ALDI) have a combined market share of roughly 85 % of the food retail market.[11] From the point of view of the FCO, these high market shares cause problematic market imbalances between grocery retailers and food manufacturers. For this reason, the FCO has initiated a sector enquiry into the grocery sector to analyse the competitive conditions in this sector, especially with regard to the relations between retailers and manufacturers. On the purchasing side of the market, however, the FCO recognises a high level of competitive pressure between these four grocery retailers, resulting in very low prices for end consumers.

The only legal instrument in Germany to control the concentration of the grocery sector is the merger control regime. There exist no further instruments like divestiture proceedings or similar structural controlling instruments.

On the other hand, and as far as it is possible to analyse the sparsely published merger decision practice of the FCO, the high degree of concentration of the retail grocery sector has so far not been used as an argument to clear a (problematic) merger on the supply side among grocery suppliers.

---

[9] FCO, decision of 30 June 2008, B2-333/07, http://www.bundeskartellamt.de/wDeutsch/download/pdf/Fusion/Fusion08/B2-333-07_Internet.pdf "*EDEKA/Tengelmann*".

[10] FCO, decision of 30 June 2008, B2-333/07, http://www.bundeskartellamt.de/wDeutsch/download/pdf/Fusion/Fusion08/B2-333-07_Internet.pdf "*EDEKA/Tengelmann*".

[11] FCO, Practice Report 2009/2010, 69, http://www.bundeskartellamt.de/wDeutsch/download/pdf/Taetigkeitsbericht/TB_2009_2010.pdf.

10.6.4 Remedies in Merger Control Cases

If a notified concentration significantly impedes effective competition, especially by creating or strengthening a dominant position, the FCO has to prohibit it. If the parties nonetheless proceed to implement the concentration (or should have failed to notify such an inadmissible merger in the first place), the FCO will order the divestiture of the merged undertaking.

To avoid a prohibition decision, the parties to the transaction and the FCO can agree on conditions and obligations to a clearance decision. In practice, the FCO expects the parties to submit adequate commitments. In the published decision practice of the FCO, there have been two decisions over the last 5 years where the FCO issued a conditioned clearance decision for a concentration in the food retail sector.[12] In both cases, with the leading German grocery retailer *EDEKA* being involved in each of them, the parties were obliged to sell a considerable number of stores and to make certain behavioural commitments for the time after this sale. In another case, *EDEKA* withdrew a notification after having been confronted with the FCO's concerns on some regions and successfully re-notified a modified transaction excluding the stores in the problematic regions. Similarly, in another case, *EDEKA* excluded one market from the transaction to avoid a phase 2 investigation.

10.7 Conclusion

From our point of view, legislative changes in Germany are not necessary with regard to the grocery retail sector. However, the FCO and the national courts are invited to consider the economic and commercial needs and requirements of the stakeholders in the grocery retail sector by applying the existing competition law.

[12] FCO, decision of 30 June 2008, B2-333/07, http://www.bundeskartellamt.de/wDeutsch/download/pdf/Fusion/Fusion08/B2-333-07_Internet.pdf "*EDEKA/Tengelmann*", and FCO, decision of 28 October 2010, B2-52/10, http://www.bundeskartellamt.de/wDeutsch/download/pdf/Fusion/Fusion10/B02-052-10.pdf, "*Edeka/Trinkgut*".

Hungary

11

Tihamer Toth

11.1 Economic Background

In 2011, agricultural production contributed to the Hungarian GDP with 4.6 %. Agriculture employed 4.9 % of all employees, and its share in investments was 5.6 %.[1] According to preliminary data, the contribution of the agricultural sector to the GDP decreased in 2012, but at the same time its share in the overall employment increased slightly.[2] In Hungary, the agricultural sector is highly deconcentrated. More than 432,000 undertakings are active in agriculture, of which only about 3 % are companies, while the rest are individual farmers. Agricultural producers must register with the Hungarian Chamber of Agriculture from this year.

The share of food and agricultural product processing in the overall consumption was almost 30 % in 2011. The processing industry in general is also fairly deconcentrated, although market structures may vary significantly in different subsectors. For example, the production of vegetable oil or sugar is highly

The author would like to thank Tunde Gonczol and Eszter Takacsi-Nagy (Réczicza White & Case), Julianna Baki and Zoltán Hegymegi-Barakonyi (Baker & McKenzie), Zoltán Marosi and Gábor Fejes (Oppenheim) and Márton Kocsis and Márk Pánczél (Hungarian Competition Authority) for their valuable inputs. The content of this report does not represent the official position of the Hungarian Competition Authority.

[1] Central Statistical Office, Mezőgazdaság 2011, 2012, available at http://www.ksh.hu/docs/hun/xftp/idoszaki/mezo/mezo11.pdf (accessed 27 August 2014).

[2] Central Statistical Office, A kedvezőtlen időjárás ellenére is szinten maradt a mezőgazdasági kibocsátás értéke, 2012, available at http://www.ksh.hu/docs/hun/xftp/gyor/msz/msz212.pdf (accessed 27 August 2014).

T. Toth (✉)
Reczicza White & Case, Pazmany Peter Catholic University, Budapest, Hungary
e-mail: tihtoth@whitecase.com

P. Kobel et al. (eds.), *Antitrust in the Groceries Sector & Liability Issues in Relation to Corporate Social Responsibility*, LIDC Contributions on Antitrust Law, Intellectual Property and Unfair Competition, DOI 10.1007/978-3-662-45753-5_11

Table 11.1 Size and market share of stores

Type of stores (segmented by size)	Market share in %
Above 2,500 m^2	30
401–2,500 m^2	35
201–400 m^2	8
51–200 m^2	18
50 m^2 and below	9

Source: Nielsen data (2012), available at http://hu.nielsen.com/site/20120110.shtml (accessed 27 August 2014)

concentrated in Hungary; the mill and the bakery or milk sectors are less concentrated. Processing companies established their industry association, the Federation of Hungarian Food Industries, which has various subsector associations among its members.[3]

The share of food retail in the overall retail sector amounted to almost 50 % on December 2012.[4] The grocery retail sector includes hypermarkets, supermarkets, discounts and smaller traditional stores, as well as cash-and-carry outlets. Shares of the different types of stores in September 2012 are shown in Table 11.1.

Among the retail chains,[5] the largest market player is Tesco, but the second and third place is taken by Hungarian franchise chains Coop and CBA (franchise cooperations of large number of smaller stores). The first three players have more than 40 % market share. Other significant players are the Spar group, hypermarket chain Auchan, discount chains Lidl, Penny and Aldi, and Hungarian franchise alliance Reál. As shown in the table, smaller stores have not more than 10 % market share.[6]

Retail chains, and in particular multinational chains, purchase products usually through their centralized acquisition system, but local units may have some independence to purchase from local producers. Hungarian franchise chains have both a centralized system and regional centres and also allow their members to purchase from local producers individually.

---

[3] Such as the Hungarian Meat Industry Federation, the Hungarian Baker Association, the Sugar Industry Association, the Association of Hungarian Confectionary Manufacturers, the Association of Hungarian Producers of Frozen and canned Products, the Association of Manufactures of Soft and Fruit Drinks and Mineral Water, the Hungarian Mineral Water Association, the Association of Hungarian Grape and Wine Producers, the Association of Hungarian Alcohol Producers and the Association of Hungarian Beer Producers.

[4] Central Statistical Office, Decemberben 2,1 %-kal csökkent a kiskereskedelmi forgalom volumene, 2013, available at http://www.ksh.hu/docs/hun/xftp/gyor/kis/kis21212.pdf (accessed 27 August 2014).

[5] Hypermarkets selling daily consumer goods, discounts and supermarket chains focusing on food products.

[6] This summary is based on data of market research companies Nielsen and GfK (for the latter, see http://www.gfk.com/hu/news-and-events/press-room/press-releases/Lapok/GfK-j%C3%B3l-alakulhat-az-%C3%A9v-v%C3%A9ge-a-napi-%C3%A9s-tart%C3%B3s-fogyaszt%C3%A1si-cikkek-kereskedelme-sz%C3%A1m%C3%A1ra.aspx – accessed 27 August 2014).

11.2 Legal Background

11.2.1 The Competition Act

Act No. LVII of 1996 on the Prohibition of Unfair Market Practices and the Restriction of Competition (the "Competition Act") contains no specific rules with regard to the grocery sector. As a general rule, the Competition Act provisions are applicable to all companies carrying out economic activities in Hungary, unless otherwise specified by a relevant act. Thus, as a general rule, the behaviour of companies active in grocery sector is governed by the Competition Act.

The Competition Act includes rules on unfair competition, certain types of misleading advertising between business players and anticompetitive practices (agreements, abuse of a dominant position and merger control).

There are no specific thresholds for the grocery sector. According to the general rules, a merger shall be notified if the combined turnover of the parties in Hungary exceeds HUF 15 billion (approx. EUR 48 million)[7] and each of at least two of the undertakings concerned has total net sales revenue in Hungary in the preceding year of the merger in excess of HUF 500 million (approx. EUR 1.6 million).

11.2.2 Other Regulations

Besides the Competition Act, there are other laws that specifically govern activities carried out in the retail market. Act No. CLXIV of 2005 on Trade (the "Trade Act"), for example, sets out provisions applicable to traders having significant market power.

Further, Act No. XCV of 2009 on the Prohibition of Unfair Distributional Practices Applied Towards Suppliers with regard to Agricultural and Food Products (the "Unfair Distributional Practices Act") contains agricultural and food-industry-specific provisions prohibiting unfair distribution practices applied by traders towards suppliers.

Relevant provisions of the Trade Act and the Unfair Distributional Practices Act will be elaborated on in more detail below.

There are several pieces of legislation relevant from the perspective of the retail market, but those legislation are outside the scope of competition law. The Trade Act and the Unfair Distributional Practices Act, for example, contain specific provisions concerning the retail sector.

The Trade Act's provisions regarding the prohibition of abuse of significant market power is applicable to all traders having significant market power, whereas the Unfair Distributional Practices Act's provisions are only applicable to traders active in the agricultural and food industry, however, regardless of the market

[7] Calculated with 313 HUF = 1 EUR (exchange rate on 26 August 2014).

power of an undertaking. If an unfair business conduct falls under the Unfair Distributional Practices Act, the Trade Act shall not be applied.

There are no specific laws primarily aimed at controlling the present structure of the grocery retail market (general merger rules shall apply) or the behaviour of existing large-scale grocery retailers, except for the Trade Act mentioned above.

There are legal provisions, however, that may affect the foundation of new large grocery retailers. Relevant provisions of Act No. LXXVIII of 1997 on the Formation and Protection of Built Environment (the "Built Environment Act") are aimed at minimizing the number of newly created large retail stores and shopping malls (retail stores and shopping malls are collectively referred to as "Commercial Buildings"). The Built Environment Act prohibits (1) the establishment of Commercial Buildings the floor area of which exceed 300 m^2 and (2) the enlargement of existing Commercial Buildings as a result of which their floor area exceeds 300 m^2. Such large Commercial Buildings cannot be created, unless the relevant minister provides for its approval.

As a general rule, retail grocery sector is not exempted from competition law. However, there are sector-specific regulations, which provide exemptions under certain circumstances.

The recently adopted amendment to Act No. CXXVIII of 2012 regulating the Conduct of Interbranch Organizations in the Agricultural Sector (the "Interbranch Organizations Act") introduced new rules that aim to create better market circumstances for farmers by taking into account special features of the agricultural sector and introduce an exemption from the prohibition of anticompetitive agreements and concerted practices in the field of agricultural products. Since the scope of the Interbranch Organization also covers the processing stage of the product chain, even wholesalers, multinational retail chains and food processors may benefit from the exemption.

11.3 Advocacy

The Hungarian Competition Authority (Gazdasági Versenyhivatal, the "GVH") continuously monitors different sectors; therefore, it carried out and ordered several market studies in the grocery retail sector some years ago.

In 2007, the GVH ordered a market study on the relationship between large retail chains and their suppliers (hereby referred to as "the 2007 Study"),[8] as a preparatory step for conducting a broader market study. On September 2009, the GVH published its market study (hereby referred to as "the 2009 Study") in which

[8] See http://www.gvh.hu//data/cms1024199/elemzesek_gvhtanulmanyok_beszallitok_2007.pdf (in Hungarian).

it analyzed the buying processes of agricultural products in 2008, a year that was very turbulent for various reasons in the sectors concerned.[9]

The emergence of big retail chains led to higher concentration in the vertical chain of the retail sector, altering the bargaining positions of different market players in the vertical chain. To address the issues caused by these changes, the Hungarian legislator introduced the Trade Act, which aimed to protect suppliers from several conducts of large retail chains. The GVH conducted the 2007 Study to assess the effects of the Trade Act on the food retail sector and the concept of buyer power.

On September 2008, the Agricultural Committee of the Hungarian Parliament called upon the GVH to analyze the buying process of agricultural products in 2008. The GVH was asked to do so because in 2008 it focused its attention on the buying process of four agricultural markets. The low price paid by retail chains to producers of sour cherry, melon and apple caused serious tensions, and the European milk market crisis also hit the Hungarian market players. These events were followed by the GVH with increased attention in the course of its competition supervision activity. However, no proceedings under the Competition Act were initiated by the GVH since it could not have been presumed that buyers or merchants formed a cartel or abused their market dominance.[10]

The 2007 Study focused on the relationship between large retail chains and their suppliers. The study aimed at discovering the important features, market position of the suppliers. Also, the study examined the effects of the Trade Act (suppliers' awareness of the new law, application of the law in the business, etc.). The 2007 Study showed the vulnerability of suppliers *vis-à-vis* large retail chains having and sometimes abusing significant market power. Abusive conducts may be the following: various fees and conditions that serve as a "tax" that suppliers have to pay to the buyers in order to access the market, breach of contractual terms (such as deadlines for payment), threat of termination of contracts, etc.

The 2007 Study concluded that the larger a retail chain became, the more of its conducts resembled the above-mentioned patterns. The study also found that bigger suppliers were more likely to suffer from these practices than smaller competitors, resulting from the fact that they needed access to the market in order to grow. Many companies did not respond to the questionnaires. It is very likely that the most vulnerable companies were afraid to provide data for the study.

The 2007 Study also found that the high standards applied by the retail chains affect the competitiveness of the suppliers positively: in order to comply with those standards, the suppliers have to improve and invest in their activities.

---

[9] See http://www.gvh.hu/gvh/elemzesek/gvh_tanulmanyok/6026_hu_elemzes_a_2008_evi_mezo gazdasagi_termenyfelvasarlasi_folyamatokrol.html (in Hungarian).

[10] In 2008, however, the GVH conducted five investigations against retailer chains. In these cases, the GVH investigated the clauses of supplier contracts—applied by the retailers—under the Trade Act.

The 2009 Study concluded that legislative actions altering the legal environment of the activities of the market players cannot solve those deep-rooted problems that producers face (such as asymmetry in the level of concentration in the vertical chain or low efficiency). Competition law and the specific rules cannot deal with issues that arise from the illegal market (the so-called black market) activities such as breaches of tax obligations. In addition, SMEs shall become more "market-oriented," i.e., more adaptive to the changing economic environment and competitive challenges. Different legislative and enforcement activities shall be systematic in order to initiate substantial changes in the sectors concerned. The GVH concluded that it would be neither desirable nor legally defendable to exempt the agricultural sector from competition law because it would lead to poor competitiveness of the producers.[11]

11.4 Market Definition in the Grocery Sector

11.4.1 Product Markets

There is no special statutory definition for relevant markets in the grocery retail sector. According to the practice of the GVH, the relevant product market extends to the retail sale of daily consumer goods, which embraces the retail sale of food, soft drinks and alcoholic drinks, domestic chemical products, cosmetic goods and other daily necessaries.[12] In its earlier case law, the GVH also highlighted that a unified market definition has to be applied covering smaller stores, supermarkets and hypermarkets.[13]

In its recent decisions, the GVH considered the complexity of the question as to whether substitutability exists between the hypermarkets and smaller store formats.[14] Although the definition of the product market remained unified, the GVH articulated in numerous decisions that it could not be entirely ruled out that the hypermarkets could be regarded as a separate product market within the grocery retail market due to their specificities compared with smaller shops (such as their wide range of goods, lower price level, longer opening hours and suburban location). For the time being, however, the GVH has been reluctant to declare hypermarkets to be active on a separate market within the grocery retail sector. In its recent decisions, the GVH underlined that even if a hypermarket could not be

[11] The agricultural cartel exemption introduced in 2012 by the Parliament may be the sign of another approach.

[12] GVH, decision of 5 December 2012, case Vj-95/2012.

[13] GVH, decision of 14 December 2009, cases Vj-125/2009 and GVH, decision of 12 October 2010, case Vj-67/2010.

[14] GVH, decision of 5 December 2012, case Vj-95/2012 and decision of 18 December 2012, case Vj-59/2012.

substituted by smaller stores, a hypermarket could mean an alternative for smaller stores; thus, at least a partial substitutability exists in this respect.[15]

To sum up, the GVH believes that different store formats, as a general rule, can be considered to be substitutes of each other, and thus they were regarded to be in the same product market. However, the GVH was eager to note that it could not be entirely ruled out that under special circumstances hypermarkets may constitute a separate product market.

11.4.2 Geographic Markets

Similarly to the product market dimension of the retail grocery market, there is no statutory definition for the geographical dimension of this market either. However, some guiding principles can be deduced from the GVH's enforcement record in this respect as well.

Following the practice of the European Commission, the GVH took the view that the market for grocery products is local in scope.[16] These local markets, in general, extend to the territory of one or more municipalities; however, in some cases, the GVH found that either a narrower or a wider market definition has to be applied.[17] In order to determine the proper extent of these local markets, the GVH applies the "substitution chain test" in line with the Notice on the relevant market issued by the European Commission.

In some cases, the GVH defined the territory of neighbouring municipalities (local district) as the relevant market for grocery products.[18] This territory is often called a "local district," which is originally a unit of public administration, comprising several communes in an area of approx. 30 km in diameter. However, the territories of those neighbouring municipalities are only regarded to be the relevant geographic market if they are situated close enough to each other so that the stores located there, in fact, compete with each other.[19]

In some recent cases, the GVH also stated that in case of larger cities, a narrower market definition (i.e., a geographical market covering some districts of the city

[15] GVH, decision of 5 December 2012, case Vj-95/2012.

[16] GVH, decision of 12 October 2010, case Vj-67/2010 and GVH, decision of 11 July 2011, case Vj-92/2012.

[17] GVH, decision of 5 December 2012, case Vj-95/2012 GVH, decision of 31 January 2013, case Vj-53/2012.

[18] GVH, decision of 20 March 2013, cases Vj-8/2013 and GVH, decision of 13 March 2013, case Vj-106/2012.

[19] Nevertheless, the GVH stressed that even if a "local district" is examined it does not entail that the whole territory of this local district is concerned automatically. See GVH, decision of 5 December 2012, case Vj-95/2012 and decision of 18 December 2012, case Vj-59/2012.

instead of covering the entire area of the city) may be possible, but the GVH found it unnecessary to address this issue since none of the mergers raised any competition concerns.[20]

11.5 Abuse of Buying Power

11.5.1 Legislative Background

The Competition Act does not define buying power or dependency. Interestingly, the merger notification form[21] refers to "buyer power" as a factor, which may offset the possible anticompetitive effects of a merger; however, it does not contain any definition. As buying power is not defined by the Competition Act, abuse of buying power is not per se prohibited by the Competition Act, whereas abuse of dominant position (including dominant buying power) is prohibited in general.

Buying power is defined by the Trade Act as "significant market power."

According to the Trade Act, "the term 'significant market power' refers to a market situation as a consequence of which the dealer becomes or has become a contracting partner for the supplier which the latter is unable to reasonably evade at forwarding its goods and services to the customers and which is able, due to the size of its share in the turnover, to influence regionally or all over the country market access of a product or a group of products."

According to the Trade Act, significant buyer power *vis-à-vis* suppliers exists where the consolidated net turnover derived from commercial activities of the group of undertakings in question, including all the parent companies and subsidiaries under Act C of 2000 on Accounting or, for the case of joint purchasing, all the undertakings establishing the purchasing association in the previous year was higher than HUF 100 billion (approx. EUR 343 million). Further, significant market power of the dealer also exists where the commercial undertaking or the group of undertakings or the purchasing association is in, or acquires, based on the structure of the market, the existence of entry barriers, the market share and the financial strength of the undertaking and its other resources, the size of its trading network, the size and location of its outlets and all of its trading and other activities, a one-sidedly favourable bargaining position vis-à-vis its suppliers.

Should the statutory turnover threshold not be met, the GVH may still find the existence of significant market power if, for certain goods, a significant part of the market transactions is conducted through large-size stores.[22]

[20] GVH, decision of 5 December 2012, case Vj-95/2012, GVH, decision of 12 February 2013, case Vj-100/2012, GVH decision of 22 March 2013, case Vj-13/2013 and GVH decision of 19 April 2013, case Vj-14/2013.

[21] Available at http://www.gvh.hu/gvh/alpha?do=2&st=2&pg=145&m5_doc=4257&m170_act=1.

[22] GVH, decision of 28 July 2008, case Vj-149/2007.

In respect of the Trade Act, there is no need to show restriction of competition to label a practice abusive. The Trade Act contains a detailed indicative list of abuses:

(a) unjustifiably discriminating against suppliers,
(b) unjustifiably restricting suppliers' access to sales opportunities,
(c) imposing unfair conditions on suppliers, which result in a distribution of risks one-sidedly benefiting the dealer, in particular disproportionately shifting costs which are incurred also in the business interests of the dealer, as costs of storage, advertising, marketing etc., on the suppliers,
(d) unjustifiably altering contract terms, to the detriment of the suppliers, after concluding the contract or reserving this option for the dealer,
(e) subjecting future business relations of the dealer with the suppliers to conditions, in particular stipulating or retrospectively enforcing the application of a most-favourable-conditions clause or obliging the suppliers to give discounts, in respect of certain products and for a specified period of time, exclusively to the dealer in question or obliging the suppliers to produce, in order to get any of their products to be distributed, products sold under the trade mark or brand of the dealer,
(f) charging fees one-sidedly to suppliers for, in particular, putting them on the dealer's suppliers-list or allowing their goods to become part of the dealer's product range or in consideration of services not demanded by the suppliers,
(g) threatening with termination of the agreement (delisting) with the intention to enforce one-sidedly beneficial contractual terms,
(h) unjustifiably forcing suppliers to avail themselves of third persons as suppliers or of an own service provider of the dealer,
(i) applying sales prices, in cases in which the dealer is not the owner of the goods, which are lower than the invoice prices determined in its contracts, save for prices applied in the sales of substandard goods or in clearance sales within a seven-day period before the expiry of the quality preservation term or introduction prices applied no longer than 15 days or prices applied in end-of-season clearance sales or in cases where the types of products dealt with or the field of activities are changed or in clearance sales of stocks of outlets which will be closed down.[23]

11.5.2 Law Enforcement

The Trade Act is applicable to all traders, irrespective of the products distributed by the trader having significant market power. With one exception, the GVH carried out formal inspections exclusively against large retailers of daily consumer goods.

[23] GVH, decision of 28 July 2008, case Vj-149/2007. According to the GVH's termination decision in the OBI case, in order to establish abuse under the Trade Act, it is necessary that the supplier does not receive any benefit from the economic results of the large-scale selling.

11.5.2.1 Infringement Decisions

There has been only one case[24] so far where the GVH concluded that the retailer abused its significant market power by a unilateral and unjustified application of turnover-based bonus. The GVH acknowledged that retailers have the right to ask for a bonus from the supplier if it is based on actual and significant sales results, i.e., no bonus can be requested for the use of the facilities of the retailer. In the case at hand, the GVH found that the bonus system of retailer was abusive as the so-called fix part of the bonus system was simply a fee to be paid for the use of the facilities of the retailer. Further, the GVH found that the so-called moving (dynamic) part of the bonus was also abusive, given that the dynamic bonus had to be paid to the retailer if the retailer did not achieve the target or even when the retailer sold a single unit of the goods in question. Finally, the GVH also found that the application of the bonus system was obligatory for the suppliers; therefore, in practice, it worked like a listing fee and thus constituted an abuse.

Several other cases were investigated by the GVH, but most of them ended with commitments.

11.5.2.2 Commitments

Section 75 of the Competition Act contains provisions on the commitment procedure, which also applies in cases under the Trade Act.[25]

Practices involving the passing on of retailer's costs to suppliers were eliminated as the result of the commitments undertaken by the retailers. In one case, costs of coordinating the activities of shelf filling service providers were passed on to suppliers.[26] In another case, the retailer passed the costs of changing suppliers on to suppliers.[27]

The nontransparency of the selection of third-party service providers was also challenged. In one case, the retailer decided to limit the number of shelf filling service providers. In the course of the procedure started by the GVH following complaints, the retailer undertook to choose the service providers in a transparent tender procedure by taking into account the preferences of the suppliers and the suppliers' previous experience in connection with the applicants. Further, the retailer also promised that the maximum price applicable by the service providers would be an important factor in the tender process.[28]

---

[24] GVH, decision of 28 June 2012, case Vj-47/2010. The infringement decision has been challenged by the retailer; the case is still pending before the court.

[25] It must be noted that in such decisions, the GVH does not establish the infringement of the law.

[26] GVH, decision of 2 September 2007, case Vj-92/2006.

[27] GVH, decision of 2 February 2009, case Vj-94/2008.

[28] GVH, decision of 2 September 2007, case Vj-92/2006.

Charging unjustified fees is also not allowed. One of the retailers charged a fee for the quality examination of the goods, irrespective of the result of the examination. According to the commitments, fees like that can only be charged to the supplier if the goods were found to be defective.[29]

Advance billing of retailer services may also constitute an infringement. In a case, the retailer issued invoice on services before the services were actually delivered.[30] The procedure was closed following a cease-and-desist kind of commitment.

There were a couple of cases where the supplier contracts contained a clause according to which the retailers had unlimited right to return goods. Under the commitments made by the retailers, the ratio of goods return was limited to a fair share.[31]

Exclusive discounting requirement in supplier contracts was also criticized by the GVH.[32]

As a result of the objection of the GVH in a case, the retailer offered commitments to provide up-to-date information to suppliers about the circulation of their products upon request.[33]

In two other cases, the GVH objected to the small letter size of the supplier contracts. The retailers offered commitments to change the size of the letters (see Table 11.2).[34]

11.6 Anticompetitive Agreements Affecting the Grocery Sector

11.6.1 Practices at Local Level

The Competition Act prohibits anticompetitive agreements in general (both horizontal and vertical). However, under the so-called *de minimis* rule, agreements of minor importance are not subject to this general prohibition. An agreement is of minor importance if the parties' joint market share does not exceed 10 % in the market concerned by the agreement. When calculating such market share, the share of the companies not independent from the parties to the agreement shall also be taken into account. This exception cannot be applied to agreements that are aimed at the fixing of purchase or selling prices between competitors or the dividing of the market among competitors.

Based on the above, cartels aimed at fixing prices, even indirectly such as through unlawful information exchange, or dividing markets are also challenged

[29] GVH, decision of 3 November 2008, case Vj-23/2008.

[30] GVH, decision of 3 November 2008, case Vj-23/2008.

[31] GVH, decision of 2 February 2009, case Vj-94/2008.

[32] GVH, decision of 2 February 2009, case Vj-94/2008.

[33] GVH, decision of 2 February 2009, case Vj-93/2008.

[34] GVH, decision of 2 February 2009, case Vj-91/2008.

Table 11.2 GVH actions against grocery retailers under the Trade Act over the past 5 years

No. of case	Parties concerned	Type of conduct	Grocery format	Comment
Vj-23/2008	TESCO-GLOBAL	Abuse of significant market power	Hypermarket	Commitment decision (Tesco was fined for not complying with commitments)
Vj-91/2008	Cora/Match/Profi (as Provera)	Abuse of significant market power	Hypermarket/supermarket/discount	Commitment decision (commitments were fulfilled—Provera avoided to apply clauses in its contract that required exclusivity of promotions)
Vj-92/2008	Spar	Abuse of significant market power	Hypermarket/supermarket	Termination decision (the proceeding was launched due to the application of allegedly unfair contractual clauses, but Spar changed its contract already during the proceeding, so the GVH closed its investigation as the public interest did not require to continue it)
Vj-93/2008	Auchan	Abuse of significant market power	Hypermarket	Commitment decision (Auchan was fined because of nonfulfillment of commitments to cooperate fully with suppliers to minimize suppliers' risks in case of goods return by giving up-to-date information to the suppliers on the circulation of their products)
Vj-94/2008	Metro	Abuse of significant market power	Cash & carry	Commitment decision (Metro was fined because of only partial fulfillment of commitments – not to require exclusivity of promotions, not to apply unlimited goods return right, not to require compensation for the loss of discounts in case of change of supplier or change in the program of the supplier)
Vj-90/2009	Auchan	Abuse of significant market power	Hypermarket	Termination decision (Auchan did not abuse its market power when applied a system whereby the negative effects of the increase of VAT rate were taken both by the retailer and its suppliers)
Vj-47/2010	Spar	Abuse of significant market power	Hypermarket/supermarket	Infringement decision (the GVH fined Spar because of applying unfair bonus schemes)

at the local level, while other practices that are less restrictive may fall under the *de minimis* exception and may not be sanctioned at all.

Despite of this clear regulatory background, the GVH has not investigated such microviolations in the food sector. One reason for that can be the lack of resources; the GVH has no local offices in the country. It can also be assumed that there were no signals from the markets that such an infringement happened; therefore, the GVH did not investigate such cases.

11.6.2 Recent Cartel Cases

11.6.2.1 Baker Cartel

The GVH sanctioned the Baker Association and several producers of bakery products (members of the Baker Association) for various anticompetitive conducts. According to the decision of the GVH (upheld by the courts), the Baker Association determined minimum prices for bread and excluded repurchase of products and marketing promotions, as well as called its members several times to raise prices of bread or to agree on price increases, also communicated recommended retail prices, and organized unlawful information exchange between bakers.[35]

The producers of bakery products exchanged sensitive information on planned price increases and regarding the reactions of retail grocery chains to such price increases. When imposing a fine on the companies concerned, the GVH took into account the limited market impact of the cartel.

11.6.2.2 The Mill Cartel

The GVH sanctioned the majority of mill companies active in Hungary for a single and continuous infringement of antitrust rules between 2005 and 2008 with regard to the prices of flour and meal and for dividing the Hungarian flour market.[36] The concerted practices included an exchange of sensitive information with regard to discounts required by retail grocery chains. The GVH imposed significant amounts of fine on the mills. The GVH's decision is still under court review.[37]

11.6.2.3 The Sugar Cartel

The GVH investigated large sugar companies suspecting that such companies continuously (from 2003 to 2009) concerted their market practice in order to determine the price level of certain product groups, to freeze the market shares of the companies involved in such concerted practice, and in some cases also agreed

[35] GVH, decision of 31 July 2009, case Vj-57/2007.

[36] GVH, decision of 29 March 2011, case Vj-69/2008.

[37] The second instance review court annulled the decision, taking into account the new legislative development described later at the section on Interbranch Organizations that effectively authorized certain cartels in the agricultural sector. This judgment is final but is subject to an extraordinary review by the supreme court, the Curia.

on the prices of certain products and on the delivery quantities sold to certain purchasers (including retail grocery chains).[38]

The GVH terminated this case due to insufficient evidence and regarding the fact that a new exemption was introduced under the amendment of the Act on Interbranch Organizations.

11.6.2.4 The Melon Cartel

The GVH investigated an agreement on the minimum price of Hungarian watermelon sold in large retail grocery chains and on the potential hindering of import by agreeing on not selling imported melons at a lower price.[39] The agreement was supported and even facilitated by the Ministry of Agriculture and Rural Development, and the Association of Melon Farmers was also party to the agreement.

The GVH launched an investigation into an alleged cartel between the large retail supermarkets and the Associations of Melon Farmers on August 2012. The much-publicized collaboration among retail chains and the association of melon producers maintaining the symbolic HUF 99/kg (approx. EUR 0.3/kg) minimum price for Hungarian-grown watermelons was intended to guarantee a safe income for farmers. The agreement was organized and publicly acknowledged by the agricultural ministry.

The GVH has adopted its termination order in the melon cartel case on the 10th of April.[40] The order is fairly detailed on the facts side, suggesting that there are good reasons to believe that there was a minimum price cartel and that foreign products were discriminated against. One of the Hungarian-owned retail franchises, CBA, even placed tables in its shops informing customers that following consultations with the ministry they will offer high-quality Hungarian water melon at a price of HUF 99/kg instead of HUF 69/kg as advertised before.[41]

Although the GVH had the option to further investigate the case based on EU competition rules, it nevertheless decided to terminate the lengthy investigation. The reason behind this was that the new agricultural exemption law hindered the imposition of fines even in cases brought under EU competition law.[42] The GVH stressed that for public interest reasons it would be needless to adopt a decision simply noting that there was a cartel (there was no need for a termination order since the cartel does not exist anymore). Nonetheless, the GVH also pointed out that it believes that the provisions of the Interbranch Organizations Act hindering the

[38] GVH, decision of 7 January 2013, case Vj-50/2009.

[39] GVH, decision of 12 April 2013, case Vj-62/2012. See also T. Toth, The fall of agricultural cartel enforcement in Hungary, ECLR 2013 34:(7) pp. 359–366.

[40] This "last minute" decision is not final yet; it can be challenged before the Competition Council.

[41] This notice may have been warranted to avoid sanctions by the GVH due to misleading advertising.

[42] Interestingly, the EU Commission did not start a cartel investigation of its own. Rather, it challenged the Hungarian legislation in an infringement procedure.

GVH to effectively sanction anticompetitive conducts falling under Article 101 TFEU are not in compliance with the provisions of Regulation 1/2003/EC.

11.6.2.5 The Egg Cartel

This case can also be described as small suppliers acting jointly against large grocery food retailers because of selling low-priced imported agricultural products.[43] The GVH imposed fines on several egg producers and their association for operating an information sharing system and establishing a joint venture to collectively increase the egg prices. The companies argued that their action was motivated by the misuse of purchasing power by some retail chains that were prepared to sell large quantities of imported products. The JV established by a couple of producers was regarded as a vehicle for the price cartel rather than an efficiency enhancing cooperation deserving an exemption from the prohibition. The GVH's approach was upheld by the courts.

11.6.3 Internal Governance of Grocery Retail Networks

The internal governance of retail networks was widely discussed in cases where franchise systems were allegedly engaged in unfair commercial practices. At the outset, it should already be noted that the attitude of GVH has changed substantially in this respect. Back in 2005, the GVH was of the view that the franchisees themselves are to be held liable for the unfair commercial practices if they failed to comply with the conditions of countrywide rebates that were initiated and announced by the franchisor and introduced on a group level. However, in 2011, the GVH imposed a fine on the same franchisor due to its unfair commercial practice during a similar group level rebate on the basis of the fact that the franchisees did not keep enough quantity on stock of the discounted product that would satisfy the consumers' needs and failed to apply the discounted price announced by the franchisor. The 2011 decision thus suggests that the franchisor might be held liable even for those unfair commercial practices that were carried out by its franchisees through noncompliance with the rebate conditions that were introduced by the franchisor.

The investigation of 2005 concerned unfair commercial practices allegedly committed by CBA Kereskedelmi Kft., a franchisor of a grocery retail system.[44] During the investigation, the internal governance of the franchise was examined in connection with the central system run by the franchisor to coordinate countrywide, group level rebates. The GVH found that the franchisor set up an appropriate

[43] GVH, decision of 29 January 2007, case Vj-199/2005. There were occasions when farmers demonstrated loudly against the "unfairly" low prices of retail chains applied for milk products and various types of fruits. These attracted some media attention, but no lawsuits or formal investigations have been initiated.

[44] GVH, decision of 14 July 2005, case Vj-58/2005.

system for coordinating and monitoring the rebates, which enables it to effectively control the franchisees' conduct with respect to the group level discounts. The GVH emphasized that it examined the franchisor's system in general and not a concrete failure in the operation of the system. The GVH argued that the responsibility for any failure in complying with the franchisor's system should be borne by the franchisees. Therefore, this decision suggests that even though the announcement of the conditions of the group level rebates falls within the exclusive competence of the franchisor, the individual franchisees would be held responsible for the failure to meet the conditions of group level rebates. Finally, the investigation was terminated without condemning the franchisor for the franchisees' behaviour.

In a more recent decision, however, the GVH came to a different outcome.[45] The competition authority investigated the rebate system of CBA Kereskedelmi Kft. once again. The reason for the investigation was a countrywide rebate during which several franchisees ran short of the discounted goods and some of them offered the goods for a higher price than it was indicated in the advertisements. The GVH found that the franchisor omitted to run a system by which it could have controlled the stocks held by the franchisees in order to satisfy the needs of the consumers. The franchisor argued that it did not have the capacity to control the stock of every member of the franchise throughout the whole duration of the nationwide rebate. It was further stated that although the framework agreements on the supplies of the rebated products were concluded between the franchisor and the supplier, the franchisees had the capacity to determine the exact amounts of the orders that were not disclosed to the franchisor. This approach was refused by the GVH, and it argued instead that a detailed controlling system is expected from the franchisor and in the present case the franchisor was invested with all legal means to set up an effective monitoring system to ensure that the franchisees could comply with the conditions of the rebate. Finding that the franchisor failed to set up a system required, the GVH imposed a HUF 30 million (approx. EUR 95,000) fine on the franchisor due to unfair commercial practices.

11.6.4 Recommended Resale Prices in the Retail Grocery Sector

According to the practice of the GVH, unlike fixed or minimum retail prices, recommended resale prices can be considered anticompetitive only if:

1. additional circumstances, i.e. indirect means or supportive measures, make recommended prices work as resale price maintenance; or
2. there is a risk that recommended prices will be a focal point for the resellers and are followed by most or all of them; or
3. recommended prices soften competition or facilitate collusion between suppliers.

[45] GVH, decision of 7 January 2013, case Vj-26/2011.

The market position of the supplier is an important factor for assessing anti-competitive effects of recommended resale prices. The market position of the supplier may make recommended resale prices work as a uniform price level applied by the retailers. If only Hungarian law is to be applied, the 10 % *de minimis* exception applies to RPM as well.

There have been no cases concerning RPM problems in the grocery sector in Hungary so far.

11.7 Abuse of Dominance in the Form of High Prices

The Competition Act forbids dominant companies to charge unfair prices. The practice of the GVH interpreted this provision as referring to unfairly high prices.

There have been no related investigations in the grocery sector since the GVH could not have established the dominant position of any of the market players.

The test would be to compare the costs related to the product or service investigated with the price charged. Investigations used to be frequent in the cable TV sector when this was still considered as a monopoly. The GVH managed to prove unfairly high prices only in relation to small local service providers where the cost calculation was feasible. Increase in prices was compared to the level of inflation, and the level of profit rates were also taken into account (in comparison to actual rates of loans and level of risk premiums).

In some cases, the GVH refrained from detailed cost analysis and preferred other alternative methods to establish whether a price is unfairly charged. One such method is the comparison of regulated prices and free market prices of the same product. Since regulated fees are set based on the costs of the undertakings concerned, it is presumed that the regulated price could serve as a reference to assess the fee charged in the free market to nonregulated consumers.

11.8 Obligations Imposed by Laws Other than the Competition Act

11.8.1 The Trade Act

The Trade Act contains provisions aimed at prohibiting unfair and abusive behaviour of traders enjoying significant market power towards their suppliers. The preamble of the Trade Act refers to "the survival and development of micro, small and medium-sized enterprises" and "fair market practices."[46]

Significant market power may be established if the concerned company group's net revenue generated in the preceding business year exceeds HUF 100 billion (approx. EUR 320 million). Further, significant market power may also be

[46] There is no statutory or judicial interpretation of such concepts.

established if the concerned company, company group or purchasing association enjoys or is likely to enjoy a one-sided bargaining power towards its suppliers due to the existing market structure, entry barriers to the market, the company's market shares, financial strength, other resources, the extent of the company's commercial network, the size and location of its retail stores, commercial and any other activities.

The Trade Act sets out that companies falling under the Trade Act shall not abuse such significant market power towards their suppliers. The Trade Act provides for a nonexhaustive list of unfair business conducts, which amount to an abuse of significant market power. Under the Trade Act, abusive conducts include unfair discrimination against suppliers, unfair risk sharing, unjustified amendment of contractual conditions to the detriment of suppliers or below-cost reselling.

Provisions prohibiting abuse of significant market power are not applicable if the given conduct falls under the Unfair Distributional Practices Act.

11.8.2 Unfair Distribution Practices Act

The Unfair Distribution Practices Act is applicable if unfair distribution practices of traders involve agricultural and food products. The preamble of the Unfair Distributional Practices Act explicitly refers to the need for "balanced bargaining position" of the parties and to "ethical business behaviour."

Contrary to the Trade Act's provisions prohibiting significant market power, the prohibition of unfair distribution practices established by the Unfair Distributional Practices Act applies to all traders and suppliers in the agricultural and food industry independent of their revenues or bargaining powers. However, such rules are only applicable to unfair distribution practices involving agricultural and food products.

The Unfair Distributional Practices Act aims to ensure that traders of agricultural and food products carry out fair business conduct towards their suppliers by listing prohibited unfair distribution practices.

Under the Unfair Distributional Practices Act, unfair distribution practices include—among others—one-sided risk sharing at the detriment of suppliers; the application of contractual provisions setting out repurchase obligation for suppliers; cost externalization towards suppliers; application of shelf prices, listing charges; extra charges for services not rendered; provisions containing payment deadlines exceeding 30 days; exclusion of late payment interest or penalty payment; requirement regarding exclusive supply of suppliers without proportionate payment; unjustified unilateral contract amendment by the trader; below-cost pricing by the trader; application of discriminative customer prices with regard to equivalent products, depending on the country of origin.

The Unfair Distributional Practices Act stipulates additional requirements applying to traders, which annual net sales revenue exceeded HUF 20 billion (approx. EUR 64 million) in the preceding business year. Such larger traders are obliged to prepare and publish their business rules and submit such business rules to the National Food Chain Safety Office[47] Such business rules shall include the services offered by such larger trader, the terms and conditions of providing such services, the maximum price that may be charged for such services, the calculation method of such prices and the conditions of inclusion in and the exclusion from the trader's suppliers list.

NÉBIH is the relevant authority in charge of enforcing unfair distribution practices, which may initiate proceedings at request or *ex officio*. In case the GVH initiated competition proceedings against a company on the grounds of abuse of dominance (based on the provisions of the Competition Act and not that of the Trade Act), the proceedings before the NÉBIH must be suspended for the term of such competition proceedings. In case the GVH has established that the given company abused its dominant position, or the competition proceedings closed due to commitments undertaken by the relevant company, the NÉBIH cannot initiate proceedings, any possible ongoing proceedings must be closed and any imposed sanctions must be withdrawn.

11.8.3 The Interbranch Organizations Act

Small-scale farmers or suppliers of food products are not expressly exempted from competition law so that they should be able to sell their products collectively to counterbalance the buying power of large-scale distributors.

The Interbranch Organizations Act was created to be the special Hungarian version of Council Regulation 1234/2007 (Single CMO Regulation). The Interbranch Organizations Act contains some narrow exemptions from competition law. These rules provide exemption for the Interbranch Organizations; therefore, they are not specifically aimed at SMEs. The Act states that agreements of Interbranch Organizations caught by the general prohibition of anticompetitive agreements of the Competition Act shall not be prohibited when they carry out the activities listed in Article 123 paragraph (3) point c) and paragraph (4) point c) of the Single CMO Regulation if they

[47] In Hungarian: Nemzeti Élelmiszerlánc-Biztonsági Hivatal; hereinafter referred to as the "NÉBIH."

a) do not affect the organization of the market harmfully,
b) do not lead to—by any means—the sharing of Hungarian markets,
c) do not lead to restriction of competition that exceeds the extent necessary to attain the goals of the interbranch organization,
d) do not lead to price fixing of any form, and
e) do not lead to discrimination and the complete elimination of competition in respect of a substantial part of the products concerned.

Interbranch Organizations have to notify these agreements to the agricultural minister. The exemption is only available if—within 2 months from the notification—the minister and the GVH both approve the agreement concerned.

Pursuant to the Interbranch Organizations Act, interbranch organizations representing suppliers of big retails chains can coordinate the conduct of their members if the economic and social benefits from such cooperation exceed the disadvantages from the restriction of competition.

Act No. CLXXVI of 2012 adopted on November 19, 2012, amended the Interbranch Organizations Act. The aim of the legislator was to relax the rigor of competition rules, taking into account the special characteristics of the agricultural sector, including security and seasonality of supply, unpredictable weather changes, and mainly to guarantee a fair income for farmers.

The new Article 18/A paragraph (1) provides that "The infringement of Article 11 of the Competition Act cannot be established in case of agricultural products if the distortion, restriction or prevention of competition resulting from an agreement according to Article 11 of the Competition Act does not exceed what is necessary for an economically justified, fair income, provided that the actors of the market affected by the agreement are not debarred from benefiting from such income and that Article 101 TFEU was not applied." According to paragraph (2), the fulfillment of the conditions of exemption provided for in paragraph (1) shall be established by the agricultural minister. Paragraph (3) provides that the GVH shall obtain and adhere to the resolution of the minister if it conducts an investigation into agricultural products based on Article 11 of the Competition Act. The GVH suspends its procedure while awaiting the minister's resolution, which is expected to be made within 60 days of receipt of the request by the GVH.

Paragraph (4) obliges the Competition Council [the decision-making body of the GVH] to suspend the imposition of fines if an agreement according to Article 11 of the Competition Act or an agreement or concerted practice between competitors according to Article 101 (1) TFEU relates to agricultural products. Instead, the Competition Council shall set a time limit for the parties involved in the agreement or for concerted practice to reconcile their behaviour with the provisions of the acts. Should the parties fail to comply with this, the Competition Council must impose fines.

Since the scope of the act also covers the processing stage of the product chain, even wholesalers, multinational retail chains and food processors may benefit from the exemption.

11.8.4 Role of the Competition Authority in the Enforcement of Such Regulations

The GVH was not playing a proactive role during the adoption of these regulations. However, since there is a statutory obligation to ask for the GVH's opinion on legislative proposals that could affect the tasks of the GVH, the GVH tried to fully exercise its advocacy powers during the drafting procedure and provided several studies, papers, opinions, etc., to the legislator. The objectives of the GVH were clearly to promote fair competition in the sector and to underline to the legislator that unnecessary exemptions from competition rules do not help suppliers to achieve higher efficiency, thus increase their success on the market.

Between 2005 and 2009, there was only one regulation, the Trade Act. According to the Trade Act, the GVH is vested with the competence to conduct proceedings against retailers with significant market power for any case of abuse defined in the Trade Act.

Since 2010, the Unfair Distributional Practices Act has been enforced by the NÉBIH. Prior to the 1st of August 2012, the NÉBIH had to suspend its proceedings when the GVH was conducting an investigation related to the same subject matter on the basis of Article 7 of the Trade Act or the abuse of dominance provision of the Competition Act. From 1st of August 2012, the GVH only has competence to conduct investigations based on Article 7 of the Trade Act related to "non-food" products and the NÉBIH enforces the Unfair Distributional Practices Act related to food and agricultural products. If the GVH conducts investigations applying the abuse of dominance provision of the Competition Act, the NÉBIH still has to suspend its proceedings related to the same conduct.

As for the case law of the NÉBIH, first of all, we must state that it is not connected closely to competition law. Second, the NÉBIH is a quite new governmental body, while it only exists from 2012 and only applies the Unfair Distributional Practices Act exclusively from 1st of August 2012. Therefore, case law is quite limited.

11.9 Prospective

With regard to the legal background of grocery retail market in general, the consolidation of the overlapping and very similar provisions of the Trade Act and that of the Unfair Distributional Practices Act should help make the legal environment more transparent and coherent.

Furthermore, some of the Unfair Distributional Practices Act's provisions seem to overregulate the relationship between suppliers and traders (such as deadlines with regard to payment obligations, which in practice have proven to be unnecessary even from the perspective of suppliers).

With regard to the recently adopted provisions of the Interbranch Organization Act, I am convinced that such provisions offer an excessively broad exemption from the prohibition of anticompetitive agreements and concerted practices in the field of agricultural products by practically allowing wholesalers, multinational retail chains, etc., to take advantage from such exemption. These provisions should be amended in a way to exclude market players other than farmers from taking advantage of such exemption.

With regard to merger rules, the grocery retail market's unique features may justify a specific merger regime by introducing higher grocery sector-specific merger thresholds. According to the GVH's information notice on mergers in the grocery retail sector dated March 22, 2013 (the "Information Notice"), 13 merger filings were submitted from June 2012 to February 2013 to the GVH, which amounted to two-thirds of the total merger filings submitted during such time period. According to the Information Notice, the grocery retail market is a highly competitive market, where the concerned companies' both individual and post-merger market shares do not exceed 10 %. On the basis of the above, we are of the view that more flexible merger rules would be beneficial for merging companies and ease the administrative burden of the grocery-retail-market-related transactions when the given transaction does not have a material impact on competition in the relevant market.

On the other hand, the creation of monopolized local markets can be an issue. However, if entry barriers are low, then the availability of competitive retail units within even the narrowest geographical markets is able to restrict the negative effects on consumers of more concentrated local markets.

Italy

12

Alessandro Raffaelli and Sara Leone

12.1 Introduction

This contribution contains a description of grocery retail market in Italy and the more significant cases handled by the Italian Competition Authority (the "ICA")[1] in this sector.

Firstly, it has to be underlined that the structure of the three levels of the agro-food supply chains varies considerably according to the stage considered, especially with respect to its specific structural characteristics and the main corresponding strategies used by the companies that operate within it.

With reference to the national market structure at the main vertical levels, the agro-food production sector still suffers from considerable market fragmentation with numerous operators often working in conditions of competitive unfairness while being financially dependent on parties operating at the lower levels of the supply chain. Products may even be of high quality, but since they do not have the essential elements to differentiate them from lower quality products in terms of image and service, the relationship with the downstream stages becomes difficult due to the high degree of substitution between the producers.

No generalisation can be made about industrial production: on the one hand, some sectors and areas have suffered a reduction, but on the other hand others have undergone an ever-increasing concentration in recent years. We believe that the two strategic variables that can account for the existence of these sectors and the areas are the following: the importance of the static type economies of scale and the

[1] Italian Competition Authority – *Autorità Garante della Concorrenza e del Mercato*, http://www.agcm.it/.

A. Raffaelli (✉) • S. Leone
Rucellai & Raffaelli, Milano, Italy
e-mail: a.raffaelli@rucellaieraffaelli.it; s.leone@rucellaieraffaelli.it

P. Kobel et al. (eds.), *Antitrust in the Groceries Sector & Liability Issues in Relation to Corporate Social Responsibility*, LIDC Contributions on Antitrust Law, Intellectual Property and Unfair Competition, DOI 10.1007/978-3-662-45753-5_12

degree of differentiation of offerings. By combining these two variables, much more fragmented structures, or more consolidated production structures, can emerge. The gradual consolidation process may constitute a general tendency; however, the intensity and speed of this process vary according to the specific importance of the two critical variables considered above.

With respect to commercial distribution, Italy still suffers from clear structural delays since its efforts to modernise the distribution system have been slower and it started later than the other countries. As we know, this modernisation mainly comprises the introduction and progressive acceptance of modern off-the-shelf type areas.

However, modern distribution, with its off-the-shelf stores, has accounted for over 70 % of food product sales (fresh and packaged) in Italy for several years. In 1996, the modern distribution model accounted for about 50 %, rose to approximately two-thirds in 2000 and stabilised at about 70–72 % of food product sales in recent years. In other words, the "natural" shift in food product sales from small traditional shops and other market entities to large-scale retail outlets seems to have stopped at the levels noted above.

This analysis makes specific reference to the level of concentration recorded in the retail sales market. The picture changes if we examine the consolidation levels attained by modern distribution at the purchasing stage, in its negotiation relationships with the other parties on the supply chain. In this case, the actual consolidation level is higher because of the widespread nature of what are known as large-scale purchasing centres, which include almost all the large-scale retail operators purchasing packaged industrial products on a group basis.

In general, it seems that the most important phases of the agro-food chain are progressively moving downstream. First, there was a shift from the merely agricultural stage to the commercial stage, when the sale of unprocessed, raw agricultural materials was the main source of goods, followed by a shift towards primary transformation when the first food factories were established and, more recently, to the commercial management of the product as well as the focus on distribution, with large-scale retail groups originating and strengthening further.

12.2 Law and Regulations

12.2.1 Italian Competition Law

Italian competition is governed by Italian Law no. 287 of 10 October 1990[2] ("Italian Law"), and the ICA is in charge of its application.

With respect to the food sector, the overall aim of the Italian Law is to ensure that competition is fair, for example, by encouraging restraint in price increases,

[2] "*Norme per la tutela della concorrenza e del mercato*" (Regulations to protect competition and the market, also known as Law 287/90).

more competition on the markets or the access of new players. The objective of the ICA in the food sector is to remove critical competition situations that can occur at both horizontal and vertical levels. With reference to the horizontal levels, it focuses, for example, on preventing what are known as "purchasing centres"[3] from implementing more extensive, well-organised coordination forms that could jeopardise competition between the member companies and therefore go beyond joint purchasing. As a result, the bargaining power of large-scale retailers towards small and medium-sized producers would increase. With respect to the vertical levels, for example, the imposition of retail prices or any exclusion caused by the sale of own-brand products (or private label products), which leads to large-scale retailers increasingly acting as direct competitors to their own suppliers, creates competition effects. Therefore, a careful assessment is needed to ensure that it does not prejudice consumers.

In addition to the provisions of the antitrust Italian Law,[4] in Italy there are specific laws aimed at controlling the structure of the grocery retail market and the behaviour of large grocery retailers. In particular, such rules were issued with the aim of monitoring the structure of retail sale food market, as well as the actions of large-scale food distributors. Among them, mention should be made of Art. 62 of Law no. 27 of 24 March 2012[5] containing urgent provisions on competition, infrastructure development and competitiveness. It represents the legislative response to the growing tensions in Italy between primary agricultural producers and the food processing sector, on the one hand, and commercial distribution sector, on the other, with respect to how the purchasing terms are negotiated for products meant for distribution.[6] This provision, conferring the ICA with the institutional

[3] "A purchasing centre (in some cases also referred to as "super-centres") is an association that companies or medium-sized and big distribution consortiums belong to, with the aim of increasing their bargaining power with respect to the producers; however, the companies belonging to a purchasing centre may be in competition against one another on the end market. The aggregation of a number of entities in a centre therefore aims to obtain discounts on the sales prices of the producers. Contracts refer to prices and some national advertising activities, generally without any restrictions on the quantities purchased. Agreements usually last for a year, with limited options to review the contracts at interim periods. The contracts agreed by the purchasing centre are a type of "framework agreement" that applies to all members of the centre. After entering into the agreement, the obligations under the contract (including the terms and conditions of payment) must be met by the individual distributors that form part of the purchasing centre". See Bank of Italy, Questioni di Economia e Finanza – La grande distribuzione organizzata e l'industria alimentare in Italia [Large scale retailing and the food sector in Italy], Number 119, March 2012.

[4] Law no. 287 of 10 October 1990, "Norme per la tutela della concorrenza e del mercato".

[5] Conversion into law, with amendments, of Law Decree no. 1 of 24 January 2012.

[6] Senate of the Republic, XVII LEGISLATURE – *Relazione sull'attività svolta dall'Autorita Garante della Concorrenza e del Mercato* (year 2012) [Report on the activities of the Italian Competition Authority] and C. Rabitti Bedogni, Conclusioni al X Convegno Antitrust tra diritto nazionale e diritto dell'Unione Europea, [Conclusions of the X Antitrust Conference between National law and EU law] (Session "Pratiche antitrust nella grande distribuzione"), Treviso 17–18 May 2012.

responsibilities and power to monitor its application,[7] introduced certain restrictions to ensure greater transparency and balance in the relationships between the various agro-food supply chain operators. It has thus put an end to unjustified contractual imbalances between the parties, which damaged the weaker one. More specifically, Art. 62, para. 1, established the obligation to put these types of agreement in writing, indicating their essential elements, such as duration, quantity, price, characteristics of the product, delivery terms and payment, under penalty of voidance. This provision states that such contracts must be "conform to the principles of transparency, fairness, proportionality and reciprocal performance with reference to the goods provided". It identifies a series of legally prohibited actions, as regards both the enforcement of contracts involving the sale of agricultural and food products and, more generally, the "commercial relations between entities operating in the sector".

According to this law, payment of the remuneration must be made within the maximum time limit of 30 days for perishable goods and 60 days for all other goods. In both cases, the term starts from the last day of the month in which the invoice was received, and interest will automatically accrue from the day after the term expires. The interest rate is increased by a further two percentage points in these cases and is non-negotiable.

In addition to the aforementioned Art. 62, further provisions were introduced to regulate this sector. These include the *Bersani Decree*,[8] which reformed the commercial sector, thus marking a significant step towards deregulating the market and simplifying bureaucratic and administrative procedures. The law establishes general principles, and Regions are in charge of planning commercial development and establishing urban planning measures. This reform modernised the sector by bringing regulations more in line with most European countries and, more specifically, providing for the introduction of two goods areas—"food" and "non-food"—replacing the previous 14 tables or goods categories and also separating sales outlets into the following types: neighbourhood outlets, medium-sized sales structures, large sales structures and shopping centres.

Another substantial deregulation measure was Law no. 248 of 4 August 2006, which provided—among other things—for specific subjective requirements, both professional and moral, that were needed to carry out trading activities in the food sector. Municipalities are in charge of checking that these requirements are met and valid in order to start up a business providing food and drink.

In addition, Legislative Decree no. 59 of 26 March 2010[9] regulated the requirements necessary for access to and exercise of commercial activities. More specifically, this decree provided that the access to and exercise of services express

[7] In accordance with Article 62, the ICA is in charge of monitoring the application of the provisions of the law and the imposition of any sanctions. It can act in its official capacity if given notice by interested parties.

[8] Legislative Decree no. 114 of 31 March 1998.

[9] Implementing Directive 2006/123/EC of the European Parliament and of the Council of 12 December 2006 on services in the internal market, OJ 2006 L 376, p. 36.

the freedom to exercise economic activities and may not therefore be subject to unjustified or discriminatory limitations. However, this prohibition on limitations does not apply if the service involves general economic interest for which there are no exclusive regimes in place, to the extent that this is not an obstacle to the specific idea of the interest of the public.

Law Decree no. 98 of 6 July 2011, converted with amendments by Law no. 111 of 15 July 2011, gave businesses the option of not complying with set opening and closing times, the obligation to close on Sundays and holidays and to close for half a day during the week, on an experimental basis and only for those businesses located in municipalities that are on regional tourist location lists or art cities.

The subsequent law decree[10] revived and guaranteed the principles of free enterprise and competition. Under the decree, the provisions governing access to and exercise of economic activity must not contain restrictions unless in the public interest and must not discriminate, directly or indirectly, on the basis of the nationality and registered office of the enterprise.

Finally, the "Save Italy Decree"[11] introduced further deregulations regarding both the management and opening of new sales outlets with the aim of relaunching the Italian economy. More specifically, it extended the deregulation provisions to the opening days and times referred to under Law Decree no. 98/2011 to all commercial businesses and not just those located in tourist locations or cities of art. Starting from 1 January 2012, commercial enterprises pursuant to Legislative Decree 114/1998 and businesses that provide food and drink in Italy can carry out their activities without any restrictions on opening times and without the obligation to close on Sundays or holidays.

12.2.2 Advocacy

Recently, the ICA completed two surveys in the food sector,[12] an in-depth study of the agro-food sector[13] and a further study on commercial distribution in Italy.[14]

[10] Law Decree no. 138 of 13 August 2011, converted into Law no. 148 of 14 September 2011.

[11] Law Decree no. 20 of 16 December 2011, converted with amendments by Law no. 214 of 22 December 2011.

[12] The first survey is the following: ICA "*Indagine sulla distribuzione agroalimentare*" (Survey on Agro-Food Distribution) – IC28 (order no. 14327 of 01/06/2005 – Beginning of survey/Order no. 16908 of 07/06/2007 – Ending of survey) (hereafter the "Survey on Agro-Food Distribution"); the second survey is the following: ICA, "Settore della Grande Distribuzione Organizzata" (Large scale retail sector) – IC43 (Order no. 21765 of 27/10/2010 – Beginning of survey/Order no. 24465 of 24/07/2013 – Ending of survey) (hereafter the "Survey on Large Scale Retail Sector").

[13] ICA, "*Meccanismi di trasmissione dei prezzi lungo la catena agro – alimentare: un esercizio di analisi sulla filiera della pasta alimentare secca*" (price transmission mechanisms along the agro-food chain: an analysis of dry pasta supply chain) – Studies and research no. 4 (August 2011) (hereafter the "Study of the Dry-Pasta Chain") in http://www.agcm.it/.

[14] ICA, "*Qualità della regolazione e performance economiche a livello regionale: il caso della distribuzione commerciale in Italia*" (Quality of the regulation and economic performance at

12.2.2.1 Market Studies of the Retail Grocery Sector

The Study of the Dry-Pasta Supply Chain was carried out in 2011 as part of a project by the ICA to monitor food product prices, with specific reference to the ways in which raw material fluctuations were transferred downstream by the operators at the various stages of the production and distribution chain.

Furthermore, the Study on the Commercial Distribution was carried out to examine the organisation and regulation of the commercial distribution sector. It describes how the Regions manage the powers given to them under national law.

In 2005, ICA conducted a Survey (IC28) on Agro-food Distribution on account of the increasing significance of the sector, in terms of volumes and costs, and the widespread perception that fruit and vegetable prices increased with the changeover from the Italian lira to euro on January 2002. Therefore, its aim was to check whether multiplying effects, if any, were somehow boosted by the change in currency and whether inefficient supply chain structures and/or related competition issues encouraged the adoption of speculative and/or anticompetitive practices by actors at the various stages of the supply chain.

In 2013, the ICA ended its Survey on Large Scale Retail Sector. This survey examined the following criticalities, often found in this sector: (1) on a horizontal basis, the competitive dynamics between large-scale retail operators when contractual restrictions require the pooling of one or more corporate functions (affiliation relationships, consortia, purchasing centres or super-centres, etc.) and, (2) on a vertical basis, the role of private labels in the establishment of contractual relations with suppliers and the nature and impact of increasing requests by large-scale retailers to suppliers for a contribution to the display, promotional and distribution activities that are separate from the purchase quantities and prices.

12.2.2.2 Conclusions and Recommendations

In the Study of the Dry-Pasta Chain,[15] the calculations made led to the following outcomes: (1) there was a surge in agricultural prices starting from the second half of 2007 causing—despite a slight delay—an increase in consumer prices that went well beyond the extent and period needed to permit the entire supply chain to recover the higher costs incurred; (2) the industrial transformation stage contributed most to that increase between prices of agricultural commodities and consumer prices, as it recorded a substantial average increase in its margins over the 3 years considered, compared to 2006 (period used as a benchmark); on the other hand, margins in the milling industry were generally stable, while the distribution area seems to have generally played a "virtuous" role in keeping prices down; (3) there was an especially noticeable increase in margins in the pasta sector in 2009, when

regional level: commercial distribution in Italy) – Studies and research No. 1 (March 2007) (hereafter the "Study on the Commercial Distribution") in http://www.agcm.it/.

[15] ICA, "*Meccanismi di trasmissione dei prezzi lungo la catena agro-alimentare: un esercizio di analisi sulla filiera della pasta alimentare secca*" (price transmission mechanisms along the agro-food chain: an analysis of dry pasta supply chain) – Studies and research no. 4 (August 2011).

both commodity and processing prices dropped, although the latter fell to a lesser extent.

Firstly, the Study on the Commercial Distribution[16] came to the following conclusions: (1) the regulatory environment related to the commercial sector is extremely diverse at regional level, and commercial federalism seems to have entered a stage of consolidation; (2) the greater freedom given to the Regions has not always resulted in greater deregulation; (3) the small-scale retail sector is competitive, with many entities and high turnover rates, and it is increasingly difficult—due to vertical integration dynamics—to distinguish retail distribution from wholesale distribution; (4) large-scale retailers are marked by an increasing concentration of groups, the creation of purchasing groups, the development of vertical integration structures between wholesale and retail sales, the appearance of distributor brands and the increasing internationalisation of groups and larger-sized chains.

Secondly, the Survey on Agro-Food Distribution[17] showed the following: (1) there are very different situations in the fruit and vegetable distribution supply chain due to the different types of products and also because of the number and characteristics of actors at the various stages, which often results in an excessively long distribution chain, making it easier to adopt speculative behaviour to increase profits; (2) large-scale retail outlets could have a decisive role to play in increasing the efficiency of the entire distribution chain, unlike neighbourhood outlets, which appear incapable of facing any type of innovation aimed at increasing the efficiency of the supply chain; local markets and street traders can continue to play a significant role in stimulating the reduction of distribution costs of fruit and vegetables; (3) large-scale retail outlets need to reorganise the upstream sectors of agricultural production and wholesale selling in accordance with the specific requirements of modern distribution and a correct competitive structure on a horizontal basis; (4) with reference to the agricultural supply, it is necessary to improve the level and quality of the commercial organisation, including by giving incentives to consortia and association type structures to amalgamate producers; (5) with reference to the wholesale distribution sector, a form of intermediation between production and distribution could be useful; (6) it would be advisable to concentrate this intermediation into one stage only, to shorten the distribution supply chain; an important role could be played by what were, until a few decades ago, wholesale markets, transformed into more modern and efficient agro-food centres; (7) finally, with reference to the terms that can guarantee proper horizontal competition between large-scale retail outlets, the need to remove certain problematic aspects in the regional implementation of commercial reform emerged, such as planning of commercial distribution on the basis of expected quantitative restrictions on

---

[16] Study entitled "*Qualità della regolazione e performance economiche a livello regionale: il caso della distribuzione commerciale in Italia*" (Quality of the regulation and economic performance at regional level: commercial distribution in Italy) in http://www.agcm.it/.

[17] Survey IC28 "*Indagine sulla distribuzione agroalimentare*" in http://www.agcm.it/.

entering the markets, unfair application of the rules aimed at blocking the entrance of new actors or the expansion of parties already on the market.

Finally, the Survey on Large Scale Retail Sector[18] showed the following results: (1) the degree of concentration in the large-scale distribution sector in Italy is not particularly high, especially if compared with that of the other major European countries; if the concentration is moderate at the national level (on January 2011, 90 % market share was held by about 18 operators, of which only 2 with a market share exceeding 10 % and only 6 with a share of more than 5 %), at the local level, however, there is a very high degree of concentration, which weighs on the power of the actors in the supply chain; (2) franchising weighs very significantly on the net sales area of many major distribution groups, representing also, for some of them, the prevailing way of management of its sales network[19]; (3) the number of the so-called *supercentrali di acquisto* (large group purchasing organisations) increased very significantly (there are 7 altogether, that aggregate 21 chains, with almost 80 % of the national retail sales); (4) there are conflicting relationships between producers and supermarket chains in relation to contributions paid by producers to obtain distribution and promotion services. Moreover, the ICA stated that besides the traditional instruments of antitrust intervention, it intends to make use of its powers in the field of abuse of economic dependence[20] and abuse of bargaining power.[21]

12.2.3 Regulations Applying to Retail Grocery Market Aside from Antitrust Italian Law

For the sake of completeness, it is necessary to highlight certain regulations applying to retail grocery market aside from Antitrust Italian Law in order to have a complete view of the main features of the said market.

[18] Survey IC43, "Settore della Grande Distribuzione Organizzata" in http://www.agcm.it/.

[19] It should be noted that in the Survey on Large Scale Retail Sector, it is stated that "the franchising or affiliation contracts used in the field of retail have a number of common features that substantially limit the scope for a full competition between the franchising stores of the same chain and the direct sales network of the same chain. All contracts, in fact, provide a set of very strict obligations on the part of the franchisee, especially regarding: methods of use of the sign and know-how the image, assortment, promotional and commercial policies, criteria on administrative and financial management, supply of accounting reports on sales and data for the economic management; in several cases, moreover, the requirements are also related to the methods for determining the selling prices and the granting of a right of pre-emption in the event of a sale of the assets and activities of the franchisee".

[20] Art. 9, Law no. 192, June 18, 1998.

[21] Art. 62, Law no. 27/24, March 2012.

12.2.3.1 Online Sales

E-commerce is subject to certain specific legal restrictions that must be scrupulously observed.

To start with, the "sale by correspondence, television or other forms of communication" covers all types of retail sales, including online.[22]

This rule provides certain restrictions on starting up commercial activities over the Internet (including the obligation to give prior notice to the Municipality where the operator resides if it is a physical person or where the registered office is if it is a legal person).

In addition, if the business is exercised in the food sector, the party that engages in that activity must hold one of the professional requirements specifically indicated by the aforesaid decree.

The modus operandi for online sales are also governed by a Legislative Decree,[23] issued on the basis of the authorisation provided in the EU law of 2001,[24] regarding certain legal aspects concerning information society services, and more especially e-commerce, in the internal market.

This decree establishes the principle whereby anyone who wishes to carry out e-commerce, or more generally intends to provide services within the information society, will have free access to that sector without having to get prior authorisation unless the sector is subject to specific rules (for example, postal services).

In addition, it imposes certain information and obligations to be complied with when entering into a contract and during the commercial relations, including an initial notice confirming the commercial nature of the communication, that it regards a promotional offer and the relative access conditions, with the name of the physical or legal person on whose behalf the commercial communication is sent.

Finally, e-commerce is subject to regulations aimed specifically at consumer protection, now contained in the Consumer Code,[25] and also to unfair practices with respect to consumers.

12.2.3.2 Prices Below Costs

A Presidential decree[26] prohibits selling below cost (*i.e.*, below the shopkeeper's purchase price).

More specifically, a business cannot sell below cost if, individually or together with others belonging to the same group, it holds more than 50 % of the overall sales area in the Province where the business has its registered office, with reference

[22] Art. 18, Legislative Decree no. 114 of March 1, 1998.

[23] Legislative Decree no. 70 of 9 April 2003.

[24] Directive 2000/31/CE of June 8, 2000.

[25] Legislative Decree no. 206, September 6, 2005: it governs the contracts entered into by computer and the right to withdraw without any penalties and without specifying the reason (Art. 64 of the Consumer Code).

[26] Presidential Decree no. 218, April 6, 2001.

to the commodity sector it forms part of. Below-cost sale regulations do not apply to certain businesses[27]: these are sales made through internal outlets; retail sales of products by automatic equipment, by correspondence or by television or by other means of communication, including e-commerce and to the homes of consumers. However, the aforesaid decree allows businesses to have three below-cost sales per year for periods that must not exceed 10 days for a maximum of 50 products.

Breaches of these provisions are punishable by fines of between € 516.46 and € 3,098.74. If the breach is particularly serious or is recurring, an additional sanction may be applied by closing the business for a period of no longer than 20 days.

In conclusion, the main purpose of the large-scale retail commerce regulation is to guarantee greater transparency and a more balanced relationship between the various operators of the agro-food supply chain, eliminating improper exploitation of positions of unfair bargaining power between the parties. Since the regulation was issued recently (2012), there are currently no judicial interpretations of the provisions of these laws.

12.2.3.3 Negotiating Practices of Large-Scale Retailers

The prohibited negotiating practices in themselves include management clauses of the product categories (known as category management), i.e., agreements between the supplier and the distributor whereby the supplier suggests how the distributor should organise/manage its shelves for a certain category of products, including both the suppliers' products and those of its competitors. These practices are more critical for the antitrust evaluation.[28] More specifically, the supplier indicates to the distributor which competitors' products must be on the shelves and which must be removed and also the single references by bar code; in the most invasive cases, they may even provide a profit table that the distributor must reach for that category. Another critical issue is represented by listing fees or slotting allowances, i.e., payments—often in advance—that the distributor requests from the supplier (especially small or medium-sized ones) in order to access the shelves. These payments are rarely requested or paid by the dominant supplier since it is also in the interest of the distributor to have the most known products on the shelves.

Then there is the hub-and-spoke situation consisting in orchestrated exchanges of sensitive information between suppliers through the distributors or exchanges of information between distributors through the suppliers. These practices are relatively rare in Italy to date. Even though single-branding cases are not common in the sector, the assortment obligation often imposed by the dominant supplier on the distributor to represent the entire range of products at the sale outlet—including those for which there is not much request, thereby taking space for other products

[27] Title VI of Legislative Decree 114, March 31, 1998.

[28] Order ICA n. 7804, *Pepsico Foods and beverages international– Ibg Sud Coca Cola Italia*; Order n. 9352, *Coop Italia – Conad/Italia Distribuzione*; Order n. 5276, *Procter & Gamble/ Tambrands*.

from the shelves, often at the expense of other smaller competing products—raises serious issues.

Finally, another practice that is forbidden is to impose long payment delays by the stronger contracting party.[29]

12.3 Competition Law Enforcement

12.3.1 Merger Control

There are no specific thresholds involving entities in the retail market sector. Indeed, the general thresholds[30] are applicable. They were revised in provision no. 24278 issued by the ICA on 20 March 2013 and are the following: (1) 482 million euro for turnover made on a nationwide basis from all the companies involved in the operation and (2) 48 million euro for companies to be acquired.[31]

The aforesaid increase is particularly important since it means that smaller concentration transactions fall outside the control of the Authority, such as those regarding smaller sized sales outlets that do not exceed the second threshold.

12.3.1.1 The Relevant Market

There are no specific regulations at national level that provide for a definition of relevant market: the ICA carries out its evaluations on the basis of the Commission's Communication on the definition of relevant market for the purposes of Community Competition law.[32]

Within the scope of "modern distribution", the ICA[33] distinguished the following sales outlet categories "for statistical purposes": (1) "superette" (including sales outlets with surface areas of between 200 and 400 m^2), (2) "supermarket" (including sales outlets with surface areas of between 4,000 and 10,000 m^2), (3) "hypermarket" (including sales outlets with surface areas of over 10,000 m^2), (4) "discount" (including sales outlets with surface areas of between 200 and 1,000 m^2).

According to the ICA, the differences in the quality and level of services offered by each type of sales outlet result in varying degrees of interchangeability between them so that interchangeability is limited to closer sales outlet categories only.

---

[29] Art. 62 of Law Decree no. 1. January 24, 2012.

[30] Art. 16, para. 1 of Law no. 287/1990.

[31] Pursuant to the amendment to Art. 16, para. 1 of Law no. 287/90 by Law Decree no. 1/2012, "taking effect from 1 January 2013", the aforesaid turnover thresholds became cumulative with the obligation to provide prior notification of the concentration if said thresholds were exceeded.

[32] OJ C 372 of December 9, 1997.

[33] Italian Competition Authority, Case C-3037, *Schemaventuno – Promodes/Gruppo GS*, Italian Competition Authority, Case A437 – *Esselunga/Coop Estense*.

The ICA established three relevant product markets according to the classification above: (1) the "hypermarket" market, comprising hypermarkets and supermarkets of over 1,500 m^2; (2) the "supermarket" market, comprising supermarkets, hypermarkets and superettes (therefore all large-scale retail sales outlets); (3) the "superette" market comprising superettes and small supermarkets, i.e., all sales outlets smaller than 400 square metres and small supermarkets smaller than 1,500 m^2.

In addition, on the basis of what the ICA found, even sales outlets managed in accordance with the discount formula can have interchangeability with other types of modern distribution sales outlets.[34]

As far as the geographical market is concerned, in the absence of specific criteria for identifying the relevant geographic market in the retail food sector, the criteria set out by the Commission in the Communication on the definition of relevant market are applicable.[35]

Apart from cases decided in less recent years in which the relevant market was identified on a common basis,[36] the ICA tends to identify the relevant market within the Province.[37]

12.3.1.2 Concentration of Grocery Retail Networks

The results of the recent Survey on Large Scale Retail Sector shows that in terms of the competitive dynamics, the companies belonging to the same chain appear to be characterised by an almost total lack of incentives to compete and by quite identical trade policies. In particular, all agreements of franchising actually used in the field of retail, although different between the chains, present elements that substantially reduce the degree of commercial autonomy of the franchisee so as to limit not only the competition between franchised outlets in the same chain but also the competition between the franchisee and the other sales point belonging to the chain.

In some cases, the high level of concentration in the retail food sector was given as the reason to justify concentration between food product suppliers. More specifically, the ICA authorised concentration between suppliers on account of the high purchasing power of the large-scale retailers. Indeed, the latter enjoy great bargaining power in negotiations and dealings with suppliers, thanks to their size, their commercial importance and their ability to access alternative supply sources if the supplier increases its prices. Because of their market power, large-scale retail operators were considered as price makers, as opposed to the selling parties forced to act as price takers.

In authorising these types of concentration, the ICA therefore considered the presence of numerous qualified competitors, unused production capacity and the lack of substantial barriers to access in addition to the significant ability of large-

[34] Italian Competition Authority, case I-397, *Discount development* and case C-10212, *Lidl Italia*.

[35] Official Journal C 372, 09/12/1997 P. 0005–0013.

[36] Italian Competition Authority, order no. 618/1992, case C526, *STANDA/ESSEBI*.

[37] Italian Competition Authority, case A437, *Esselunga/Coop Estense*.

scale retailers to take countermeasures owing to their role as main purchaser. All in all, such features were deemed to be "robust factors for countering the market power on the offer side, such as to allay any worries regarding the unilateral effect that could be caused by the merger in question".[38]

However, when facing a problematic concentration, the ICA defined specific remedies. In particular, the ICA authorised concentrations in the retail food sector in the last 5 years, subject to the following solutions: sale of a well-known brand name and relevant market presence,[39] structural changes such as divestiture of certain sales outlets,[40] reduction of the joint management period of the purchased company and introduction of a mixed price,[41] increased product presence in the retail channel,[42] purchase of certain sales outlets,[43] transfer of control over a specific branch.[44]

12.3.2 Recent Case Law

In order to better understand whether the ICA in Italy is efficiently meeting the challenges posed by the grocery retail market, it is necessary to analyse some relevant cases in the sector.

The most relevant case regarding the behaviour of food retailers in Italy in the last 5 years is the proceedings *Esselunga/Coop Estense*,[45] where ICA established that Coop Estense systematically interfered with the attempts of the competitor to start up new food sales outlets, in potentially suitable areas and shopping centres that were available to it, by making real interventions in the administrative procedures that had been initiated by Esselunga to obtain the necessary authorisations. The ICA stated that this strategy was carried out in a market environment that was already characterised by low availability of suitable areas and shopping centres and significant administrative barriers blocking entrance to the market. According to the ICA, this behaviour allowed Coop Estense to maintain—and actually strengthen—its dominant position in the markets in question, gaining increasing market share over time. In addition, by blocking an "efficient" competitor from accessing the market, Coop Estense damaged consumers in terms of higher prices and/or lower choice.

[38] Italian Competition Authority, case C8971, *Bolton Alimentari/Branch of Brands* and case C10109, *Bauli/Branch of Italian Nestle'*.

[39] Italian Competition Authority, Case n. 5408, *Cirio/Centrale del latte di Roma.*

[40] Italian Competition Authority, Case n. 6113, *Schemaventunopromodes/Gruppo GS.*

[41] Italian Competition Authority, Case n. 11040, *Società Esercizi Commerciali Iindustriali – s.e.c.i. – Co.pro.b. Finbieticola/Eridania.*

[42] Italian Competition Authority, Case n. 14390, *Koninklijke numico/Mellin.*

[43] Italian Competition Authority, Case n. 23542, *Conad del Tirreno/New branches of Billa.*

[44] Italian Competition Authority, Case n. 24102, *Bolton Alimentari/Simmenthal.*

[45] Italian Competition Authority, Order no. 23639, of 6 June 2012.

On 25 March 2014, the Supreme Administrative Court[46] confirmed the decision issued by the ICA on June 2012, imposing on Coop Estense a fine of 4.6 million euro and positive measures, i.e. the obligation to remove the obstacles it had set to Esselunga's entry to the relevant market, in order to open the market to an efficient competitor of Coop—Esselunga—for the consumers' benefit.

12.3.2.1 Horizontal Anticompetitive Practices at the Local Level

It is worth analysing whether horizontal anticompetitive practices at the local level (for example, a price-fixing agreement between the only two retail food stores in a small village) have been sanctioned by authorities and, if not, how such micro-violations could be sanctioned in Italy. To begin with, the ICA deals with all "the understandings between companies that intend to or result in consistently preventing, restricting or distorting competition within the domestic market or a significant part thereof".[47] The "significant part" of the domestic market referred to in Art. 2 of the law must be considered in relation to the significance of the local market for the consumer and the reasonable alternatives the consumer has[48]; therefore, if the conduct can distort competition in the market "at local level" each time to an appreciable degree, this will also fall within the range of the application of the antitrust laws. On the other hand, behaviour that has a negligible effect on the market will not be subject to the antitrust laws. For example, the ICA imposed sanctions on certain bread producers operating in the Province of Trento since they all increased the price of bread at the same time, applying equal end-sales prices.[49] This behaviour was considered to be a concerted action arranged among the companies by exchanging information and contacts and aimed at eliminating the competition in one of the most significant competitive variables, the sales price for the end consumer. Therefore, the Authority found that this behaviour had all the elements of an agreement to reduce competition pursuant to Art. 2 of Law no. 287/90. The bread consumption market was a local one, no bigger than the municipality, owing to the habits of consumers who tend to buy bread frequently, and therefore close to their homes. In this case, therefore, the unlawful concerted action was at local level, which, however, coincided with the market in question.

12.3.2.2 Horizontal Agreements Between Grocery Suppliers

It is important to mention, in particular, the case Consortium to Protect Grana Padano,[50] where the ICA decided that the decisions at association level is

[46] The so-called "Consiglio di Stato".

[47] Art. 2, para. 2 of Law 287/90.

[48] Regional Administrative Court of Lazio, Case n. 7444, 27 August 2002.

[49] Italian Competition Authority, case no. 7747 (I174B), *Bread prices in Trento*. November 24, 1999.

[50] Italian Competition Authority, case 1569, *Consorzio Grana Padano*, order no. 13300 of June 24, 2004.

equivalent in 2001 to an agreement to restrict competition within the production market[51]; more specifically, these decisions helped fix a quota for the supply of Grana Padano, significantly preventing a potential increase in the production of Grana Padano that year and helping to keep wholesale prices artificially high.

As regards the franchising relationships, the ICA considered, only in a few cases and following a specific assessment of the contents of the agreement, that these were suitable to constitute a *de facto* control of the franchisor on the franchisee, due to the substantial elimination of the commercial autonomy of the franchisee.

12.3.2.3 Recommended Resale Prices in the Retail Grocery Sector

There is no specific regulation regarding recommended sales prices in the food sector at national level. Therefore, reference is made to the Guidelines on Vertical Restraints[52], where the imposition of fixed or minimum sales prices ("resale price maintenance" or RPM) is prohibited in any form or manner under point 2.8 of the *Recommended prices and maximum resale prices*. The practice of recommending a resale price to a reseller or asking a reseller to abide by maximum resale prices may benefit from an exemption in accordance with the exemption rule by category when the market share of each of the parties to the agreement does not exceed a 30 % threshold on condition that this does not establish a minimum sales price or a price fixed in accordance with the pressure exercised or the incentives offered by any of the parties. The market position of the supplier is the most important factor in deciding whether there are any anticompetitive effects due to the maximum prices or recommended prices. The stronger the market position of the supplier is, the greater the risk that a maximum price or a recommended resale price will be applied as the resale price by most or all of the retailers.

Moreover, the ICA found that the Bakers' Association Union of Rome and the Province of Rome had established an agreement that restricted competition with respect to the preparation and disclosure of price suggestions for the different types of bread sold by the bread shops in the area, and the preparation and disclosure of cost analyses of the main types of bread, aimed at calculating the relative end prices.[53] The preliminary inquiry established that the Bakers' Association Union of Rome has held a number of meetings regarding bread prices since 2003, even preparing and publishing a list of "recommended prices" on September 2007. The price list gave indications regarding the sales prices (in a set range of prices) for the two main types of bread sold in the Province of Rome and "recommended" increases for all other types of bread. According to the ICA, by indicating minimum prices, the ICA encouraged alignment with higher price levels than those that would have been charged in an ordinary competition environment. In evaluating the

[51] Art. 2 of Law no. 287/90.

[52] Commission Communication of 13 October 2000: Guidelines on vertical restraints [COM(2000/C 291/01). OJ C 291 of 13.10.2000].

[53] Italian Competition Authority, case I695, *Bread price list*, concluded with Order no. 18443 of 4 June 2008 in http://www.agcm.it/.

seriousness of the agreement, the ICA considered the essential nature of the goods subject to the agreement and the fact that Bakers' Association Union of Rome was aware that it was not permitted to distribute price lists. The ICA imposed a fine on the Bakers' Association Union of Rome.

12.3.2.4 Reselling Below Cost, De-listing of Suppliers, Resale Price Maintenance and Abusive High Prices

Below-cost sales, even though not explicitly prohibited by competition law, could be subject to evaluation by the ICA if these practices have negative effects on consumers or change the rules of competition, for example by preventing the access of new operators to the market.

On the other hand, according to the competition rules, the imposition of improperly high prices is considered to be improper and therefore prohibited. This behaviour is considered by antitrust rules to be a typical exploitative abuse, through which a company, taking advantage of its dominant position and keeping its production levels the same, sets the price higher than that allowed in an open competition market, thereby maximising profit. A hypothetical "fair" price must be established in order to establish whether a price is excessive. Assessing whether a price is excessive further requires (1) the establishment of the company's costs and (2) the evaluation of the unfair character of the price with respect to the value of the economic performance.

12.4 Abuse of Economic Dependence

Regulations on the abuse of economic dependence are contained in the special law governing sub-contracting, Law no. 192 of 18 June 1998.[54]

More specifically, Art. 9 of the above-mentioned law contains two criteria to assess dependence: the excessive imbalance of rights and obligations and the real possibility for the abused party to find satisfactory alternatives on the market.

Even though this Article does not provide a precise definition of "abuse of economic dependence", it defines "economic dependence" as a "situation where a company can give rise to an excessive imbalance of rights and obligations in its commercial dealings with another company. Economic dependence is also evaluated by taking into account the real possibility that the party will not be able to find satisfactory alternatives on the market".

Dependence is not illegal itself but only when it involves restrictions to competition in the market in question. Specifically, Art. 9 prohibits companies from abusing a situation of economic dependence (exactly what happens in antitrust situations for the prohibition on the abuse of dominant position).

[54] "Law on sub-contracting in productive activities" (Law on Sub-contracting), which came into effect on 20 October 1998 and was subsequently amended by Law no. 57 of 5 March 2001, "Provisions on opening and governing markets".

Since the aforesaid Law on Sub-contracting does not define abuse of "purchasing power" or "dependence abuse" but defines only "economic dependence", this type of abuse has been defined by case law as the situation in which a company can establish an excessive imbalance in rights and obligations in commercial dealings with another company, noting that this status must be identified with regard also to the real possibility that the abused party will not be able to find satisfactory alternatives on the market.

The evidence used at the enforcement stage to define said abuse is therefore as follows: the existence of economic dependence due to the contractual or noncontractual behaviour (to be checked through market analyses or a survey aimed at showing the lack of satisfactory alternatives as a presumption of dependence) and the excessive imbalance between rights and obligations "considering the real possibility that the abused party will not be able to find satisfactory alternatives on the market".[55]

Art. 9 of the Law on Sub-contracting lists the behaviour that can be considered to be improper, and therefore unlawful, if found in a company in a situation of economic dependence. More specifically, it can be found in the following situations: (1) "refusal to sell or refusal to buy", (2) "imposition of unfairly oppressive or discriminatory contractual conditions" and (3) "arbitrary interruption of the trade dealings in place".

12.5 Conclusion and Perspective

There has been an increasingly meaningful development of consumer co-operatives and retail traders in Italy in recent years. Even though they have (formally) independent decision-making powers, with each co-operative being autonomous, they work through a complex coordination, control and monitoring system run by the consortium of co-operatives, a system that is based on targeted organisational decisions taken at a central level. The effect of this co-ordination is—for example—the territorial division of the markets created by the consortia, which means that they are not subject to competition from other consortia in their respective markets and that each of them is ensured of a position of potential leadership within their areas (this is what the ICA indirectly found happening at a factual level in Order A437 Esselunga/Coop Estense, in which it was shown how Coop Estense is the only co-operative of the Coop Italian system to operate in certain geographical areas). A further problematic issue from the standpoint of competition law, as much at national level as at local level, could be that these companies share aspects that are as delicate as they are strategic, such as advertising and prices, which are also shared at centralised levels.

[55] Landriscina, L'abuso di dipendenza economica tra violazione del canone di buona fede e abuso del diritto [The abuse of economic dependence between breach of the rules of good faith and abuse of law] note to order of the Court of Turin 11/03/2010, in *Giur. comm.* 2011, p. 1479.

Another distortion results from the tax advantages enjoyed by co-operatives operating as large-scale retailers. Almost all the consumer co-operatives define themselves as "cooperative a mutualità prevalente" (traditional co-operatives), i.e., mutual societies that carry out their activities mainly to benefit the consumer shareholders; since they are traditional co-operatives, they benefit from special laws and are certainly privileged compared to normal "società di capitali" (capital companies), their direct competitors in the large-scale retail sector. We would therefore hope that regulations on retail food distribution will be reviewed and will be applied by courts in a wider range of contexts for all actors in the sector to be granted equal market access and tax rights, as well as duties to be standardised.

Japan

13

Kenta Sugimoto, Noriko Itai, and Shigeshi Tanaka

13.1 Introduction

13.1.1 Economic Background

The national market structure at the main vertical levels in Japan is agricultural production, agricultural cooperative, wholesale dealer and grocery retail.

13.1.2 Legal Background

13.1.2.1 Competition Law

The competition law in Japan is the Antimonopoly Act (the "AMA"), which is an act on the prohibition of private monopolization and maintenance of fair trade.[1] It includes a ban on unfair competition, as well as the prohibition of anticompetitive practices. General rules are applied to the retail grocery market. There are some prohibitions as an example of the unfair trade practices.

The adopted provision mostly aimed at the retail market is the designation of specific unfair trade practices by large-scale retailers relating to trade with suppliers.[2] This is not law. This designates the examples of unfair trade practices by large-scale retailers to suppliers, unjust return of goods, unjust price reduction, unjust consignment sales contract, forcing of suppliers to lower prices for bargain

[1] Act No. 54 of 14 April 1947. Available at http://www.jftc.go.jp/en/legislation_gls/amended_ama09/index.html.

[2] Fair Trade Commission Notification No. 11 of 2005.

K. Sugimoto (✉) • N. Itai • S. Tanaka
Aoki, Sekine & Tanaka, Tokyo, Japan
e-mail: kenta.sugimoto@ast-law.gr.jp; n-itai@nifty.com; shigeshi.tanaka@nifty.com

P. Kobel et al. (eds.), *Antitrust in the Groceries Sector & Liability Issues in Relation to Corporate Social Responsibility*, LIDC Contributions on Antitrust Law, Intellectual Property and Unfair Competition, DOI 10.1007/978-3-662-45753-5_13

sales, refusal to receive specifically ordered goods, coercion to purchase, unjust assignment of work to employees of suppliers, unjust receipt of economic benefits, unfavorable treatment in response to refusal of requests and unfavorable treatment in response to notification to the Fair Trade Commission.

13.1.2.2 Other Laws and Regulations Applying to the Retail and Grocery Sector

One of the enacted specific laws (uniquely or primarily) aimed at controlling the structure of the grocery retail market or the behavior of large-scale grocery retailers outside of competition law is the Act on the measures by large-scale retail stores for preservation of living environment.[3] The material content is that a large-scale retail store should report to the prefectural government and keep the rules about traffic, noise and waste. This is not based on principles of fairness, correcting asymmetry in bargaining power, necessity to prevent inflationary pressure of grocery retail prices or other principles. But this law aims at controlling the living environment around the large-scale retail store.

Small and medium-sized retail business promotion act[4] also applies to the retail and grocery sector. The act requires franchise system business to explain to a person who is going to be a franchisee its membership fee or deposit in participation, sale conditions of goods to franchisees, matters regarding trademark or trade name to be used, matters regarding managerial instruction, term of franchise agreement or matters regarding renewal or termination of franchise agreement in order to improve properness of the management of franchise system and to modernize the management of small and medium-sized retail business.

The extent these acts limit the scope for competition in the retail grocery sector is rather small.

13.1.2.3 Exemptions from Competition Law Prohibitions

Some cooperative associations are partly exempted from competition law. The scope of these exemptions and their rationale are to protect small-scale entrepreneurs and promote fair and free competition.

For instance, agricultural cooperatives of small-scale farmers or cooperatives of retail suppliers of food product business that meet the requirements under the laws are exempted from AMA in collectively selling their products in order to counterbalance the buying power of large-scale distributors. However, this does not apply to cases where unfair trade practices are employed or where competition in any particular field of trade is substantially restrained, resulting in unjust increases of prices.

---

[3] Act No. 91 of 3 June 1998.

[4] Act No. 101 of 1973.

13.1.3 Market Studies

The competition authority in Japan, the Japan Fair Trade Commission (the "JFTC"), has done market studies of the retail grocery sector. The recent studies are as follows.

The Report on the Trade between Food Manufacturers and Wholesalers[5] was reported to understand the actual situation on the trades between wholesalers and manufacturers.

The survey results revealed the existence of some conducts in the past that might lead to the abuse of superior bargaining position between food manufacturers and wholesalers and some acts that wholesalers unreasonably requested the manufacturers due to the retailers' request to wholesalers, that is, the structure that the large retailers' conducts could be the source of the abuses in questions.

The JFTC will request related trade associations of wholesalers and larger retailers to make their umbrella organizations thoroughly understand the contents of Guidelines Concerning Abuses of Superior Bargaining Position under the Antimonopoly Act[6] and will take an active measure against the illegal abuses of superior bargaining position.

And the Fact Finding survey on the Trades between Large-Scale Retailers and Suppliers[7] was reported to understand the actual situation of unfair trade practices between large-scale retailers and suppliers that were designated by the Designation of Specific Unfair Trade Practices by Large-Scale Retailers Relating to Trade with Suppliers.

The JFTC examined how many suppliers had experienced requests or conducts by large-scale retailers that could lead to the abuse of superior bargaining position (8.4 % for payment of monetary contribution, 5.9 % for return of goods and 3 % for price reduction).

The percentage of the suppliers that bear all the cost due to the requests or conducts by the retailers is more than 70 %.

The JFTC will make every effort to promote fair trade between large-scale retailers and suppliers and to prevent the abuse of superior bargaining position. Furthermore, the JFTC requested the trade associations of large-scale retailers to take a voluntary action for the fair trade between large-scale retailers and suppliers.

---

[5] 19 October 2011. Available at http://www.jftc.go.jp/en/pressreleases/yearly-2011/oct/individual-000447.html.

[6] 30 November 2010. Available at http://www.jftc.go.jp/en/legislation_gls/imonopoly_guidelines.files/101130GL.pdf.

[7] 11 July 2012. Available at http://www.jftc.go.jp/en/pressreleases/yearly-2012/jul/individual-000491.html.

13.1.4 Pricing Regulations

Some grocery products are subject to price control in Japan. First, rice, barley and wheat are subject to price control under the Act for Stabilization of Supply, Demand and Prices of Staple Food,[8] which aims to help in the stabilization of supply and demand or prices of main food and thereby to contribute to the stabilization of the people's living or the national economy. Second, milk, butter and meat are subject to price control under the Act Concerning the Stabilization of Livestock Products,[9] which aims to ensure the stable supply of domestic sugar canes and starch from domestic potato and thereby to contribute to the stabilization of improvement of the people's eating habits. Third, sugar is subject to price control under the Sugar Price Adjustment Act,[10] which aims to help in the stabilization of supply and demand and prices of main food and thereby to contribute to the stabilization of the people's living.

13.2 Competition Law Enforcement

13.2.1 Case Law Related to the Conduct of Grocery Retailers

The following are the cases related to the conduct of grocery retailers in Japan in the last 6 years. All of them are cases on abuse of superior bargaining position described below.

(i) Cease and Desist Order against Marukyo Corporation

On 23 May 2008, the JFTC issued a cease and desist order against Marukyo Corporation ("Marukyo") operating grocery supermarkets (large-scale retailer), which conducted the following acts.

(a) Unjust return of goods

Marukyo set its own "sell-by" dates and returned goods whose "sell-by" date had passed to a supplier of the food products or general merchandise with whom Marukyo had an ongoing business relationship and over whom Marukyo enjoys a superior bargaining position on the ground that the "sell-by" life of the goods had expired, even though no conditions for return had been agreed in advance with the supplier.

(b) Unjust price reduction

Marukyo carried out discount sales on the ground that, variously, the goods concerned had a low turnover ratio; that a store was due to be closed; that the sales period for seasonal products had ended; or that

[8] Act No. 113 of 1994.

[9] Act No. 183 of 1961.

[10] Act No. 109 of 1965.

the goods were damaged as a result of, for example, falling from a shelf, and Marukyo returned goods to a supplier on the grounds that the goods had a low turnover ratio, etc., even though no conditions for return had been agreed to in advance with the supplier or coerced a supplier of goods subject to discount into accepting a reduction in the delivery price of those goods by the amount arrived at by multiplying 0.5 by the price before the discount.

(c) Unjust assignment of work to employees of suppliers

Marukyo coerced suppliers to dispatch their employees to Marukyo stores without having concluded prior agreements with such suppliers concerning the conditions for dispatching employees and without accepting liability for the costs normally incurred in dispatching employees.

(ii) Cease and Desist Order Against Eco's

The JFTC issued on 23 June 2008 a cease and desist order against Eco's Co., Ltd ("Eco's"), operating grocery supermarkets (large-scale retailer), which conducted the following acts.

(a) Unjust price reduction

Eco's coerced the suppliers to discount the supply prices of the goods decided to be discounted at the closing of the applicable stores or those first displayed at the opening of the applicable stores, although there was no reason attributable to the suppliers.

(b) Unjust assignment of work to employees of supplier

Eco's coerced the suppliers to dispatch their employees for display, restock and other work at the applicable stores that do not require the skill or ability of such employees although Eco's had not reached any agreement on dispatching conditions and did not bear the cost usually required to have temporary staff dispatched.

(c) Unjust receipt of economic benefits

Eco's had the suppliers supply specific goods delivered at the opening of the stores at prices lower than the usual supply prices without clearly explaining the calculated grounds and purposes in advance and thereby had the suppliers provide economic profit equivalent to the difference between such prices and usual supply prices.

(d) Unjust receipt of monetary contribution

At the opening of the stores of Eco's and its three subsidiaries, Eco's had the suppliers bear some money called "Cooperation money" without clearly explaining the calculated grounds and purposes in advance.

(iii) Cease and Desist Order against Seven-Eleven Japan

On 22 June 2009, the JFTC issued a cease and desist order against Seven-Eleven Japan Co., Ltd., ("Seven-Eleven Japan") managing franchising business for convenience stores (large-scale retailer). Seven-Eleven Japan deprived a franchise member of the opportunity to reduce its burden on its own management decision under the franchise system.

Seven-Eleven Japan is at a superior bargaining position over its franchise member (franchisees); its franchise system had a scheme where the amount equivalent to the costs of the disposed goods at the franchisee stores is entirely borne by the franchisees. Under this scheme, Seven-Eleven Japan forced some franchisees, which practice or intend to practice discount sales of daily goods among recommended goods, to stop such discount sales and thereby had them lose opportunities to reduce the loss of the amount equivalent to the cost of such disposed daily goods according to their own rational business judgment.

(iv) Cease and Desist Orders and Surcharge Payment Orders against K.K. Sanyo Marunaka

On 22 June 2011, the JFTC issued a cease and desist order and surcharge payment orders against K.K. Sanyo Marunaka ("Marunaka") operating grocery supermarkets (large-scale retailer), which conducted the acts of unjust return of goods, unjust price reduction, coercion to purchase, unjust assignment of work to employees of suppliers and unjust receipt of monetary contribution or economic benefits.

13.2.2 Competition Law Enforcement Against Anticompetitive Horizontal and Vertical Agreements

The JFTC deals with horizontal and vertical anticompetitive practices at the national level or at the local level.

Horizontal agreements between grocery suppliers to withdraw quantities in order to keep prices up have been sanctioned pursuant to Section 2(6) of AMA, although there do not seem to be such case in the last 5 years.

13.2.2.1 Internal Governance of Retail Networks

The internal governance of grocery retail networks (franchises, cooperatives, etc.) has been considered to be problematic from the point of view of competition in Japan. The law or guidelines that can be used to control this are as follows:

(i) AMA [particularly, abuse of superior bargaining power (Section 2 (9) (v), (vi))],
(ii) Guidelines concerning abuse of superior bargaining position under the antimonopoly Act,
(iii) Guidelines concerning the franchise system under the antimonopoly Act,[11]
(iv) Guidelines concerning the activities of agricultural cooperative under the antimonopoly Act, and

[11] 24 April 2002. Available at http://www.jftc.go.jp/en/legislation_gls/imonopoly_guidelines.files/franchise.pdf.

(v) Guidelines concerning the activities of trade associations under the antimonopoly Act.[12]

The JTFC has dealt with the internal rules of retail grocery networks such as franchises. For instance, as stated in Sect. 13.2.1 (iii) above, the JTFC ordered Seven-Eleven Japan to stop taking the action forcing some franchisees to stop discount sales and thereby had them lose opportunities to reduce the loss of the cost of such disposed goods.

13.2.3 Regulation of Large-Scale Food Retailing and Vertical Relationships Between Suppliers and Retailers

The contractual relationships between large-scale food retailers and small suppliers or small-scale retailers are regulated under the following:

(i) AMA [particularly, abuse of superior bargaining power (Section 2 (9) (v), (vi))],
(ii) designation of specific unfair trade practices by large-scale retailers relating to trade with suppliers,
(iii) Guidelines concerning designation of specific unfair trade practices by large-scale retailers relating to trade with suppliers,[13]
(iv) Guidelines concerning abuse of superior bargaining position under the antimonopoly Act,
(v) Guidelines concerning the franchise system under the antimonopoly act,[14] and
(vi) Guidelines concerning distribution systems and business practices.[15]

Further, in case the suppliers are subcontractors in contracts such as manufacturing contract, the act against delay in payment of subcontract proceeds to subcontractors[16] (the "Subcontract Act") may apply. The act regulates unfair acts of main subcontracting entrepreneurs against subcontractors, such as preventing a delay in payment of subcontract proceeds, to ensure that such transactions are fair and to protect the interests of the subcontractors.

The scope of such regulations is prohibition of unfair trade practices, including abuse of superior bargaining position by large-scale retailers in transactions with

[12] 30 October 1995. Available at http://www.jftc.go.jp/en/legislation_gls/imonopoly_guidelines.files/tradeassociation.pdf.

[13] 29 June 2005. Available at http://www.jftc.go.jp/en/legislation_gls/imonopoly_guidelines.files/guidelines_large_scale_retailers.pdf.

[14] 24 April 2002. Available at http://www.jftc.go.jp/en/legislation_gls/imonopoly_guidelines.files/franchise.pdf.

[15] 11 July 1991. Available at http://www.jftc.go.jp/en/legislation_gls/imonopoly_guidelines.files/distribution.pdf.

[16] Act No. 120 of 1956.

suppliers. The regulations that apply to large-scale retail food distributors refer explicitly or implicitly to the necessity to protect "fairness of transactions." There has not been any judicial interpretation of the content of the concept.

Some negotiating practices of large-scale retailers are prohibited per se. Designation of Specific Unfair Trade Practices by Large-Scale Retailers Relating to Trade with Suppliers specifies the ten categories of unfair trade practices by large-scale retailers: (i) unjust return of goods; (ii) unjust price reduction; (iii) unjust consignment sales contract; (iv) forcing suppliers to lower prices for bargain sales; (v) refusal to receive specifically ordered goods; (vi) coercion to purchase; (vii) unjust assignment of work to employees of suppliers, etc.; (viii) unjust receipt of economic benefits; (ix) unfavorable treatment in response to refusal of requests; and (x) unfavorable treatment in response to notification to the JTFC. The recent cease and desist order cases are mostly those of (vi) coercion to purchase, (vii) unjust assignment of work to employees of suppliers and (viii) unjust receipt of economic benefits.

The JFTC is in charge of implementing such regulations. In the enforcement of such regulations, the roles of the JFTC are (i) to investigate transactions suspected of violation of AMA or Subcontract Act conducting interrogatory, on-site inspection; inspection of books, documents and other materials; (ii) to remedy acts violating AMA by ordering cease and desist orders indicating measures necessary to eliminate the violation of AMA; and (iii) to remedy acts violating Subcontract Act by recommending the measures necessary to eliminate the violation of Subcontract Act. The JFTC also formulates various guidelines as preventive measures for violations of AMA or Subcontract Act in order to implement competition policies.

13.2.4 Resale Price Maintenance and Recommended Resale Prices

Resale price maintenance is prohibited under Section 2 (9) (iv) of AMA. Recommended resale prices in the retail grocery sector can be considered a violation of AMA on the ground that such recommended prices are bounding the retailers (for instance, if retailers do not resell the products at the recommended price, the retailers could be imposed undue disadvantage) may violate AMA.

The two recent important cases with regard to resale price maintenance are as follows.

One is a Cease and Desist Order Against Hamanaka Co., Ltd., issued on June 23, 2008. In the case, Hamanaka fixed the discount limit price for Hamanaka wool and requested that retailers sell the product at such discount limit price or higher and had the wholesalers request that retailers to which such wholesaler sold Hamanaka wool sell the product at the discount limit price or higher. In order to assure the actual effect of the request to the retailers, Hamanaka stopped shipment of Hamanaka wool to the retailer that did not satisfy such request or the wholesaler distributing the product to such retailer. JFTC ordered Hamanaka to stop the action and resolve with its board of directors that it would stop such action and would not take any similar action and so on.

The other is a Cease and Desist Order against Adidas Japan Kabushiki Kaisha of 2 March 2012, where Adidas Japan had caused retailers (i) to sell its shoes products EASYTONE at the discount limit price that Adidas Japan fixed or higher and (ii) to sell those at the suggested retail price that Adidas Japan fixed. The JFTC issued a cease and desist order against Adidas Japan.

13.2.5 Reselling Below Cost and Abusive High Prices

13.2.5.1 Reselling Below Cost

Reselling below cost may violate AMA. AMA prohibits supplying goods continuously for a consideration that is excessively below the cost without justifiable grounds, thereby tending to cause difficulties to the business activities of other entrepreneurs (Section 2 (9) (iii) of AMA).

The most relevant case with regard to reselling below cost in the last 5 years is Warning against Mitsubishi Shokuhin K.K. et al of 1 August 2012. In the case, three wholesalers of alcoholic liquors supplied a part of beer products, etc., to the retailers of alcoholic liquors continuously for a consideration that is excessively below the cost required for the supply and thereby were suspected of causing difficulties to the business activities of other retailers of alcoholic liquors around the stores managed by the said retailers of alcoholic liquors. The JFTC warned the wholesalers to stop and not to conduct such acts thereafter based on Section 2 (9) (iii) of AMA.

There do not seem to be any recent cases of small suppliers (for example, farmers) jointly retaliating against large grocery food retailers to punish the latter for selling low-priced imported agricultural products cheaply or collective boycotts by small food retail stores against suppliers selling to discounters. However, such practices may be punished under the competition law. If small suppliers refuse to supply to a large grocery store or restrict the quantity of goods to a certain grocery store concertedly with a competitor without justifiable grounds, such act may fall under Section 2 (9)(i) of AMA. If a small food retail store refuses to receive supplies of goods from a certain supplier concertedly with competitor without justifiable cause, such act may fall under Section 1 of Designation of Unfair Trade Practices.[17]

[17] Fair Trade Commission Public Notice No. 15 of June 18, 1982. Available at http://www.jftc.go.jp/en/legislation_gls/unfairtradepractices.html.

13.2.5.2 Abusively High Prices

Abusively high prices are punishable in case of abuse of superior bargaining position (Section 2 (9)(v)(vi) of AMA) or in case of discriminatory consideration (Section 2 (9)(ii) of AMA, Section 3 of Designation of Unfair Trade Practices).

13.2.6 Abuse of Buying Power

13.2.6.1 Legal Provisions Regarding Abuse of Buying Power

There is no statutory definition of what constitutes an abuse of "buying power" or abuse of dependency. However, AMA prohibits abuse of superior bargaining position that includes abuse of buying power or abuse of dependency. We answer to questions replacing abuse of buying power or abuse of dependency with abuse of superior bargaining position below.

13.2.6.2 Definition of Superior Bargaining Position

Superior bargaining position is defined as follows:

Party A has superior bargaining position over Party B if Party B is unable to avoid accepting Party A's request, etc., that is substantially disadvantageous for Party B on the grounds that Party B has difficulty in continuing the transaction with Party A and thereby its business management would be substantially impeded.

With regard to abuse of superior bargaining position, Guidelines Concerning Abuse of Superior Bargaining Position under the AMA of the JFTC provides as follows:

> When Party A has superior bargaining position over Party B, who is a transaction counterpart, it means such a case where if Party A makes a request, etc., that is substantially disadvantageous for Party B, Party B would be unable to avoid accepting such a request, etc., on the grounds that Party B has difficulty in continuing the transaction with Party A and thereby Party B's business management would be substantially impeded.
>
> In determining the presence or absence of superior bargaining position, the degree of dependence by Party B on the transactions with Party A, position of Party A in the market, the possibility of Party B changing its business counterpart, and other concrete facts indicating the need for Party B to carry out transactions with Party A are comprehensively considered.

13.2.6.3 Is Abuse of Superior Bargaining Position a *Per Se* Offense?

Abuses of superior bargaining position are prohibited only if they are likely to cause restriction on fair competition.

13.2.6.4 What Constitutes an Abuse of Superior Bargaining Position?

AMA enumerates acts that constitute abuse of superior bargaining position in items (v) and (vi) of Section 2(9).

Abuse of superior bargaining position requires that superior bargaining position was made use of "unjustly in light of normal business practices," which indicates that the presence or absence of abuse of superior bargaining position is determined case by case from the viewpoint of maintaining/promoting fair competition. In the Guidelines Concerning Abuse of Superior Bargaining Position under the AMA, JFTC provides which case should not be considered to meet "unjustly in light of normal business practices" by showing examples for each category of acts specified as abuse of superior bargaining position in the AMA.

13.2.6.5 Case Law on Abuse of Superior Bargaining Position

The following are typical practices that have been considered to be abuse of superior bargaining position in the case law. The recent cases are described in Sect. 13.2.1 above.

(i) Unjust receipt of monetary contribution, economic benefits

A distributor who is at a superior bargaining position over a supplier coerces the supplier to pay monetary contribution, etc., or to provide any economic benefits other than monetary contribution.

(ii) Unjust assignment of work to employees of suppliers

A distributor who is at a superior bargaining position over a supplier coerces the supplier to dispatch employees, etc., without paying the expenses for the dispatch.

(iii) Unjust return of goods

A distributor who is at a superior bargaining position over a supplier returns goods to the supplier even though no conditions for return had been agreed to in advance with the supplier.

(iv) Unjust price reduction

A distributor who is at a superior bargaining position over a supplier coerces a supplier into accepting a price reduction of the delivery price of goods purchased by the retailer, etc., after purchasing the goods from the supplier, except when the supplier accepts a reduction of the delivered price for any reason attributable to the supplier within a reasonable period from the date of receipt and to an extent deemed appropriate given the reason.

(v) Coercion to purchase

A distributor who is at a superior bargaining position over a supplier coerces a supplier into purchasing any goods or services.

13.3 Merger Control

There are not special thresholds for merger control in the retail (or the grocery retail) sector in Japan. The local office of the JFTC is in charge of controlling mergers at the local level.

13.3.1 Relevant Market

13.3.1.1 Product Market

Relevant product (or service) markets are defined by the perspective of product substitutability for users. Further, when necessary, substitutability for suppliers is also considered.

Different store formats are considered to belong to different markets.

In the case, Aeon Corporation acquired the share of Marunaka and Sanyo Marunaka in 2011; the JFTC concluded that the general supermarkets that sell not only groceries but commodity, clothing and so on and the grocery supermarkets that sell mainly groceries are both in the same relevant "supermarkets" market by the perspective of substitutability for consumers. The JFTC considered that consumers would select their store without distinction between general supermarkets and grocery supermarkets.

There are no statutory definitions of markets or what kind of test is applied by the court or enforcement agencies to delineate relevant markets. The Small but Significant and Non-transitory Increase in Price "SSNIP" test is applied.

13.3.1.2 Geographic Market

Relevant geographic markets are also determined from the perspective of substitutability for users between the products supplied in each area. There are no statutory definitions of what constitutes a relevant market. The SSNIP test is used by courts or enforcement agencies.

13.3.2 Concentration of Grocery Retail Sector

The growth or concentration of grocery retail networks (such as franchises or cooperatives) has been considered to be problematic in Japan. The legal instruments that can be used to control their growth or concentration is Article 17-2(1) of AMA.[18]

---

[18] Where there exists any act in violation of the provisions of paragraph (1) or (2) of Article 9, Article 13, Article 14 or the preceding article, the Fair Trade Commission may, pursuant to the procedures provided in Section 2 of Chapter VIII, order the person violating such provisions to dispose of all or some of his/her shares, resign from his/her position as an officer of the company or take any other measures necessary to eliminate such acts in violation of the said provisions.

The increasing level of concentration of the retail grocery sector has been offered as a reason for mergers among grocery suppliers. In the retail grocery sector, the concentration has been progressing and their competition gets keen. So the retail sector demands the wholesalers and their suppliers to discount and exercise competitive power.

There is no case that the JFTC imposed remedies for concentrations in the food retail sector in the past 5 years according to main case examples of concentrations officially published by the JFTC.

The Netherlands

14

Sarah Beeston, Jessey Liauw-A-Joe, and Suzan Lap

14.1 Introduction

The Dutch agricultural sector is becoming more concentrated. There are fewer farmers with larger businesses. Most farmers sell their produce via cooperatives to international traders. A large part of the production is then exported. National demand for agricultural products is largely supplied by supermarkets with strong buying power. The supermarkets are in fierce competition with each other with the result that there are 'price wars'. Consumers benefit from this competition and the lower retail prices. The strong buying powers of supermarkets lead, however, to a risk of exclusion of competitors and exploitation of suppliers. Market players have raised complaints about the behaviour of supermarkets. The Dutch government is therefore encouraging the industry to adopt a code of conduct. This code should ensure that the supermarkets do not abuse their strength and apply unfair conditions in their dealings with their trading partners. In the case of abuse or unfair trading, the general competition law and civil law rules apply.

14.2 Economic Background

The Dutch agricultural production sector comprises approximately 67,000 farmers. Since 2000, the number of farmers has decreased by 31 %. Over the same period, the reduction in the surface area used for agricultural purposes was only 7 %.

S. Beeston (✉) • J. Liauw-A-Joe
Van Doorne N.V., Amsterdam, The Netherlands
e-mail: beeston@vandoorne.com; LiauwAJoe@vandoorne.com

S. Lap
Sonos, Hilversum, The Netherlands
e-mail: Suzan.lap@sonos.com

P. Kobel et al. (eds.), *Antitrust in the Groceries Sector & Liability Issues in Relation to Corporate Social Responsibility*, LIDC Contributions on Antitrust Law, Intellectual Property and Unfair Competition, DOI 10.1007/978-3-662-45753-5_14

Farmers therefore run bigger businesses. The average turnover per producer has increased over this period by approximately 62 % to EUR 315,000. The increase in turnover differs per sector. The largest increase was in the livestock sector, followed by the horticultural business; it was relatively modest in arable farming (e.g., fruit, vegetables and potatoes). A significant part of agricultural production consists of dairy farms and livestock farms (25 %). Arable farming is the second-largest sub-sector (18 %).

Most producers are members of producers' associations or cooperatives, which sell the products on behalf of their members. Membership regulations generally require members to sell exclusively via the association or cooperative. Some producers' associations also act as traders at the secondary level. By way of example: there are 1,600 apple growers active in the Netherlands. Seventy-five percent of the apples produced by these growers are collected and distributed via either The Greenery or Fruitmasters, two producers' associations that also act as international traders.

Depending on the type of product, there may be one or more trading levels and/or processing activities involved. The level of market concentration at each trading levels varies per product and per activity. By way of example: after the sales at the initial wholesale level (including The Greenery and Fruitmasters), apples are delivered to the retail channel via a large number of service providers, the largest of which has a market share of 10–15 %. The secondary level has in international character. Seventy percent of the fruit and vegetables that have been produced in the Netherlands are exported, while 45 % of the fruit and vegetables consumed in the Netherlands have been imported.

The grocery retail level comprises approximately 13,000 retailers, operating from approximately 30,000 sales points. A total of 5,700 of these sales points are supermarkets, which distribute 75 % of grocery produce in the Netherlands. Although at the time of writing there are still very few hypermarkets, they are on the rise. The turnover of supermarkets in 2013 was approximately EUR 34.2 million. Of the money that consumers spend on groceries, over 50 % is spent in a supermarket.

Dutch supermarkets are in fierce competition. From 2003 until 2007, there was an outright 'price war'. This led to the demise of two supermarket chains and discussions on whether a prohibition of sales below cost would be desirable (see Sect. 14.5.3 below).

Currently, the top three retail purchasers represent approximately 85 % of the market: Albert Heijn (33.7 %), Jumbo (20–22 %) and purchasing cooperative Superunie (30 %). Discounters Aldi and Lidl are growing and currently have a market share of approximately 8 %.

14.3 Legal Background

14.3.1 Prohibition of Restrictive Agreements

The Dutch competition rules are set out in the Dutch Competition Act (the 'DCA'), which entered into force in 1998. The rules are modelled on and interpreted in accordance with the European competition rules. Article 6 DCA prohibits restrictive agreements. Article 24 DCA prohibits abuse of dominance. The DCA also contains a merger control regime. The Dutch competition authority, ACM, supervises compliance with competition law in all sectors.

The same restrictions that are considered hard-core restrictions under the EU rules will in general be considered hard-core restrictions under the Dutch competition rules. Having said this, during the consultation on the review of the Block Exemption Regulation on Vertical Restraints in 2009, the Dutch competition authority suggested that vertical price maintenance should be removed from the list of hard-core restrictions. This suggestion was not followed. Consequently and given that the EU block exemptions have direct effect under the Dutch competition rules, resale price maintenance remains listed as a hard-core restriction in the Netherlands. To date, however, the Dutch competition authority has not given any priority to enforcing resale price maintenance cases.

In addition, unlike the EU *de minimis* exemption from the prohibition on restrictive agreements, the Dutch statutory *de minimis* exemption also includes hard-core restrictions. Article 7 DCA exempts (1) all agreements, decisions and concerted practices that involve no more than eight undertakings whose combined turnover does not exceed EUR 5.5 million if they are involved in the sale of goods or EUR 1.1 million in all other cases and (2) all agreements, decisions and concerted practices between (potential) competitors provided that the combined market share of the parties involved does not exceed 10 % on any of the markets concerned. This second exemption was introduced in 2011. It aims to strengthen the position of small and medium-sized undertakings, including those dealing with large retailers.

Finally, there is a national block exemption that exempts certain price-fixing agreements (see Sect. 14.5.3 below). Like the EU competition rules, the DCA does not include provisions relating to unfair trading practices. Unfair practices by large retailers are a subject of debate in the Netherlands (see Sect. 14.3.4 below).

14.3.2 Merger Control

As mentioned above, the ACM is responsible for the supervision of mergers and other types of concentrations. Parties to a concentration are required to notify their transaction to the ACM if the following thresholds are met: (1) the combined worldwide turnover of the undertakings concerned exceeds EUR 150 million and (2) at least two of the undertakings concerned realised an individual turnover in the Netherlands of at least EUR 30 million. There are no specific thresholds for mergers in the grocery retail sector.

14.3.2.1 Relevant Market

The DCA does not contain a definition of the relevant (product and/or geographic) market, nor does it specify how to define markets. Markets are defined in accordance with the rules and principles set out in the EU competition rules.

In previous decisions, at grocery retail level, the ACM distinguishes separate product markets for

1. the sale of daily consumer goods via supermarkets (the 'supermarket market');
2. the procurement of daily consumer goods for sale via the retail market, in which account is taken of the differences between groups of products (however, to date the ACM has not defined separate markets for such product groups) (hereafter, the 'purchase market');
3. offering supermarket franchise services (hereafter, the 'franchise market').

The ACM takes into account the store size, calculating the market share of the merging parties on the basis of both turnover and 'sales surface'. Moreover, in some cases involving concentrations between large supermarkets, the ACM takes into account that small supermarkets (<less than 500 m^2) generally offer a limited product range and therefore do not constitute a full substitute for a large supermarket. Consequently, the ACM has excluded such small supermarkets from its assessment. The ACM considers that the supermarket market could potentially be split into a market for supermarkets, hypermarkets and discounters. It has however to date not adopted such narrow market definition.

The online activities of supermarkets have to date not been the specific subject of a competition law review.

The geographic scope of a market is established in accordance with the rules and principles set out in the EU competition rules.

In all cases to date, the most recent dating back to July 2012, the competition authority has refrained from drawing any definitive conclusions about the geographic scope of the supermarket market. ACM has held that the market has a local as well as a national dimension. As regards the local market(s), the ACM starts with the area within a 15-min drive of a supermarket. This area is subsequently limited to a village or city since consumers are generally not inclined to do their daily shopping outside their place of residence. Therefore, the local relevant market constitutes a 15-min radius within a *town*. An exception is made for situations where urban sprawl has wiped out town boundaries or for situations where the parties provide evidence that consumers are in fact inclined to visit a supermarket in another town. In those cases, the ACM assesses the 15-min radius area without taking account of town borders.

Besides, both the purchase market and the franchise market are considered national in scope.

14.3.2.2 Substantive Test

According to the DCA, the concentration control regime consists of one and possibly two phases. The relevant substantive test applied in the first phase is whether the concentration *could* significantly impede effective competition on the Dutch market, or a part of such market, particularly as a result of the creation of strengthening of a dominant position. If so, the ACM requires the parties to obtain a licence for the transaction. The ACM considers the parties' request for a licence in a so-called second-phase investigation.

In the second phase, the ACM assesses whether, as a result of the concentration, effective competition on the Dutch market or a part of it *would* be significantly impeded, specifically as a result of the creation or strengthening of a dominant position. If so, the ACM will refuse to grant a licence and the concentration will be forbidden.

The test is applied to mergers between competitors, parties on different levels on the supply chain and parties on unrelated markets.

14.3.3 Abuse of Dominant Position

The prohibition of abuse of a dominant position is set out in Article 24 DCA. The DCA does not give a definition of 'abuse'. The concept of abuse is interpreted in accordance with the EU rules.

Behaviour is considered abusive only if it has an exclusionary or exploitative effect. Therefore, there is no behaviour that is abusive *per se*. ACM does not have to show the actual effect of the behaviour. It is sufficient to make a reasonable case that the behaviour will or may have a restrictive effect on competition.

The test applied is rather vague. Acknowledging that there is no clear distinction between strong competition and the abuse of power, the ACM assesses whether the behaviour leads to the exclusion of market parties or whether the behaviour can be considered exploitative, for example because it is discriminatory or unjustified. Furthermore, the ACM assesses whether the behaviour causes harm to consumers. If there is sufficient competition on the downstream market, a buyer with market power is likely to pass on any advantages it has gained on the purchase market to its customers. In such case, it is unlikely that there will be abuse.

14.3.4 Retail and Grocery Specific Competition Law Rules and Exemptions

There are no specific competition rules for the grocery sector in the Netherlands. However, in addition to the EU block exemptions, two national exemption regulations apply. Both regulations are aimed at the retail sector. The government has considered but rejected a prohibition on sales below purchase price. It has encouraged the supermarket sector to adopt a code of conduct to avoid unfair trading.

The Decree on the Exemption of Cooperation Agreements in Retail exempts the following restrictions in 'franchise-like' networks: (1) maximum price agreements in relation to a temporary marketing action and, under certain conditions, (2) a purchasing obligation for a maximum period of 10 years. Given the broad scope of the exemption of the Block Exemption on Vertical Restraints, the decree is of little practical importance.

The Retail Exclusivity Agreements Decree exempts agreements in which the owner of a shopping centre grants a retailer of a particular type (for example, a shoe shop) exclusivity in the shopping centre for a period of 6 years. This exemption only applies to newly opened shopping centres. Consequently, like the Decree on the Exemption of Cooperation Agreements in Retail, its practical importance is limited.

In 2005, during the 'price war' between supermarkets, in response to parliamentary questions, the Ministry of Economic Affairs ordered two studies into the feasibility and desirability of introducing a statutory prohibition to sell products below purchase price. In addition, ACM submitted a letter to the Minister, stating that it saw no reason to start an investigation into whether the price war between the supermarkets constituted an abuse of dominance. ACM deemed the situation a sign of fierce competition between supermarkets, which led to a benefit to consumers in the form of lower prices. The Minister decided not to introduce a statutory prohibition to sell products below their purchase price.

Unfair business practices by retailers with buying power have been the subject of much public debate. Following complaints, particularly from suppliers in the agro-food sector, and subsequent questions in and motions from the parliament, the Ministry of Economic Affairs commissioned a number of studies investigating the extent to which suppliers in the Netherlands perceive buying power, the question whether the existing legal framework is sufficient to prevent and solve unfair practices by retailers with buying power and an exploration of the possibilities and feasibility of self-regulation in business-to-business relations. The reports conclude that there is, at least in the perception of suppliers, buying power and that the current legal framework—competition law and civil law—is insufficient to provide an effective solution. The Dutch government has chosen not to introduce legislation but wishes market parties to self-regulate via a code of conduct. The Minister of Economic Affairs has initiated two pilot projects for establishing a code of conduct, one involving the agro-food sector.

In the agro-food sector, alignment is sought with the European Supply Chain Initiative. Consequently, the Rules of Procedure for the Governance Group of the European Supply Chain Initiative apply to the Dutch pilot as do the European Framework, the Principles of Good Practice and the European dispute resolution system. A steering committee has been established in the Netherlands. Its members are the Dutch Federation for the Commodity Industry, an umbrella organisation for undertakings and trade associations in this industry; the Central Commodity Department, the professional representative for the supermarket branch and food service companies; and the arable farming and horticulture organisation, the undertakings' and employers' organisation for this sector. Their aim is to ensure that a future code of conduct could function effectively. The committee had all active supermarket organisations formally register with the European Supply Chain Initiative. Their business operations should be in line with the framework and principles of good practice within 6 months after registering. A number of commodity producers, such as Fruitmasters, have also now registered and become parties. There has been no actual dispute resolution through the specific procedure to date. The Minister concluded that the pilots are a growing success, but the familiarity with the principles and initiative should still increase.

The ultimate aim of the pilots is to come to a Dutch Code of Conduct that is part of self-regulation. It is likely that the code will be based on, or be similar to, the European Principles. In a market consultation, market parties have set out some criteria for drafting the code. According to these criteria, the provisions in the code should be concrete norms. Undertakings that have registered and are committed to the code should benefit from positive exposure. The possibility of anonymous complaints, when bundled, and sanctions when not applying with the code will lead to negative publicity.

By the end of 2014, a second review by the Minister will take place. He will then again report to the Senate. In the meantime, the Minister stays involved in the pilot, mainly as a facilitator.

14.4 Market Investigations and Advocacy

Like the Minister of Economic Affairs, the ACM regards the agro-food sector as one of its priorities, given the importance of this sector to consumers. ACM notes that the increasingly concentrated nature of the sector and the relatively homogenous nature of the products increase the risk of collusion. Furthermore, the ACM monitors the sector, taking account of complaints from producers, traders and trade associations alleging abuse by supermarkets of buying power.

In 2004, following a market consultation, the ACM published a paper setting out its vision on buying power. The ACM stated that buying power on the upstream market can be compensated by the position on the downstream market. In such cases, buying power can and will have a positive effect on the economy as a whole and for consumers. When assessing a concentration involving at least one party with buying power, the ACM takes account of the market position of the undertakings concerned, their position on their downstream market, the position of suppliers and the possibilities the concentration may create to exclude competitors or suppliers from the market. In the assessment of abuse of dominance by an undertaking with buying power, the ACM considers the alternative sales channels for suppliers, possible sales power and the position of the undertaking on the downstream market.

On December 2009, the ACM published a report on pricing in the agro-food sector. The assessment and conclusions in this report are based on interviews and research undertaken by the ACM and on the outcome of a large study by research institute, LEI. The report covered a selection of seven basic foodstuffs: eggs, apples, onions, cucumbers, bell peppers, bread and potatoes. It contained a description of the production and distribution chain per product, the development in prices, costs and margin per level in the chain over the period 2005–2008 and an (econometric) analysis of the price mechanism in the sector. On the basis of this analysis, a calculation could be made of the extent to which parties at a certain level of the chain are able on a long-term basis to improve their margins, and concentrations at the supermarket level will influence their purchase and sales prices.

The main conclusions of the study were that there are no indications that supermarkets are dominant in determining the price of foodstuffs. Prices at supermarket level are influenced by prices higher up in the chain, particularly by the prices at production level. Supermarkets cannot increase their margins on a lasting basis since such increase would be compensated by a price increase at wholesale level. The increased concentration at supermarket level only has a limited effect on supply and demand price. Asymmetrical price adjusting has a negligible effect on supermarket margins.

Finally, in 2011, the ACM commissioned a study of the fisheries sector. The report on this sector is descriptive and does not contain a competitive analysis. It only briefly refers to the retail sector.

14.5 Competition Law Enforcement

14.5.1 Restrictive Agreements

The ACM has sanctioned several cartels between suppliers at production level; three of these cartels included arrangements to limit production: the *shrimp* cartel and the two cartels involving *onions*. In 1999, the competition authority exempted a crisis cartel between *pig slaughterhouses*. In 2012, the ACM sanctioned associations of bell pepper producers for price agreements. These cases will be discussed below.

On January 2003, ACM imposed fines totalling EUR 13.8 million on Dutch, German and Danish producers' associations of shrimp fishers and shrimp wholesale traders (16 parties in total). The parties concerned had agreed on a weekly quota per boat and minimum price guarantees between traders and producers in the period between 1 January 1998 and 30 January 2000. Fishermen who deviated from the quota were sanctioned by the producers' associations. The highest appeal tribunal, the Administrative High Court for Trade and Industry, confirmed the infringement but reduced the fine, partly because of the lack of clarity about whether the actions concerned fell under a European exemption.

On May 2012, the Dutch competition authority fined five producers of silverskin onions (which represented 70 % of the EU production) for agreements concerning the maximum number of hectares (quota) that would be cultivated in the period from 1998 until 2010. From 1998 until 2003, the undertakings concerned had formed a cooperative that supervised the execution of the arrangements (the quota). After 2003, the arrangements continued without supervision by the cooperative. From 2006, the undertakings concerned also exchanged information on prices.

On February 2013, the Dutch competition authority fined seven producers of first-year onions (representing 80 % of the Dutch production) for agreements in 2009 and 2010 concerning a reduction of harvest in order to push up prices.

In 1999, the competition authority formally exempted an arrangement between pig slaughterhouses (representing 80 % of the market) to establish a fund that aimed to reduce overcapacity in the sector by buying and subsequently closing slaughterhouses. The authority assessed the arrangements under the rules for crisis cartels and granted an exemption for a period of 5 years. The authority did not approve of agreements reducing the production of the remaining capacity of the slaughterhouses.

Bell Peppers In 2012, the Dutch competition authority fined three cooperatives of pepper producers (representing a substantial part of Dutch production but a small percentage of EU demand) for agreements concerning prices. ACM imposed fines of EUR 14 million. On appeal, the court of first instance suggested that the ACM should reconsider its conclusions as to the undertakings concerned and reconsider the amount of the fine. The case is still pending.

The Dutch competition authority has not taken enforcement decisions involving grocery retailers over the last 5 years. Indeed, on several occasions, the authority has expressed the viewpoint that the fierce competition between the large grocery retailers in the Netherlands benefits consumers. In its opinion, if the pricing in the chain does not allow producers a viable income, there is overcapacity. Such overcapacity should not be solved by income protection or cartel agreements but by innovation, cost reduction and a shift in activities. To the extent that producers claim that the margins at the secondary level put (unacceptable) pressure on their income, the ACM points out that high margins should be a reason to enter a market. It refers to producers that have entered such market.

14.5.2 Merger Control

In the last 5 years, the competition authority has assessed eight concentrations in the retail grocery sector. In four of these cases, the authority raised concerns as regards the competition on a number of potential local supermarket markets. In these cases, the parties offered remedies in the first phase of the merger review procedure. On the basis of such remedies, the authority approved the transactions without requiring a second-phase investigation.

In all cases, remedies consisted of the divesture of (one or more) supermarkets (sales of owner-operated stores and transfer of franchise agreements). In three of the cases, the remedy included the appointment of a monitoring trustee. In two of these cases, in addition to the monitoring trustee, a sales trustee could be appointed if the parties were to fail to find a buyer themselves. In two cases, the remedies included a commitment from the acquirer to refrain, for a period of 10 years, from (re)gaining economic influence over the divested supermarkets.

14.5.3 Abuse of Dominance: Buying Power

There is no statutory definition of buying power in the Netherlands. In 2004, the Dutch competition authority published a vision paper on buying power. In this paper, the authority defines buying power as 'market power on the demand side of the market. This is the case if a party on the demand side can operate independently from the suppliers.'

To determine whether an undertaking has buying power, the competition authority determines (1) the relevant purchase market and (2) the position of the party on this market. It then (3) assesses the alternative sales channels for suppliers (i.e., other buyers) and (4) the existence of market power on the supply side of the market that would make it unlikely that the large purchaser can exercise buying power.

The paper on buying power suggests that exclusive supply agreements may constitute abuse of buying power. Other examples mentioned are the unilateral enforcement of certain exploitative conditions such as payment conditions, supply conditions and warranties. The paper notes that a refusal to negotiate the terms of a contract that has been submitted to a supplier does not necessarily constitute abuse.

There are no examples of buying power in case law concerning the grocery retail market. In fact, the Dutch competition authority has not taken any decisions concerning the abuse of buying power.

14.5.4 Pricing

Dutch competition law does not prohibit recommended resale prices, unless such recommended prices are combined with incentives not to deviate from such prices, as a result of which they have the effect of a fixed or minimum price. Reselling below cost and de-listing of suppliers are not prohibited as such under the DCA. Under circumstances, similar to those under the EU competition rules, it may qualify as an abuse of dominance. If so, they are incompatible with the DCA.

There is no strict standard determining which prices can be considered abusively high. An excessive margin, compared to the costs, may be an indication of excessive pricing. In addition, a comparison will be made with prices charged by suppliers. If no such suppliers are available in the Netherlands, an international tariff comparison may be made.

In line with the EU rules, resale price maintenance formally qualifies as a hard-core restriction of the competition rules. However, if the thresholds for this exemption are not exceeded, hard-core restrictions may benefit from the statutory de minimis exemption under the DCA. Moreover, as the ACM is of the opinion that resale price maintenance does not necessarily aim to restrict competition, it does not take proactive enforcement action in this respect. There is no case law of the Dutch competition authority on this subject.

One of the very few (published) civil court cases involving the grocery retail sector concerned a dispute in 2005 between Albert Heijn and a producer and supplier of gingerbread, Peijnenburg. The Peijnenburg gingerbread was used by the largest consumers' association in the Netherlands in its weekly price comparison between supermarkets. In light of this, Albert Heijn discounted this product well below the purchase price. Fearing that other supermarkets would follow Albert Heijn's lead, Peijnenburg ceased its supplies to Albert Heijn. Albert Heijn claimed that Peijnenburg could not terminate the relationship and that any attempt of Peijnenburg to have Albert Heijn increase its resale price would constitute prohibited resale price maintenance. The Court ruled that by the standards of fairness and reasonableness, Peijnenburg was entitled to terminate its relationship with Albert Heijn with immediate effect. As regards the competition law argument, the Court stated that this was for the competition authority to assess. The competition authority reacted to the ruling by issuing a press release stating that resale price maintenance is prohibited under national competition law. It did not, however, take any action.

14.6 Regulations

The main sector-specific regulations are mentioned here below. The Opening Hours Act regulates the opening hours of retail shops and until recently contained strict rules on opening on Sundays, including but not limited to a maximum of 12 Sundays a year and only in areas that should be designated as a 'tourist area'. These strict rules mainly aimed to protect smaller retailers. On February 2013, the Dutch government decided on a more flexible regime. It removed the conditions and delegated the authority for setting the rules on this subject to local authorities.

No specific permits or licences are required for grocery retail. Naturally, supermarkets are subject to food safety and hygiene regulations. These rules do not have a (significant) effect on competition. In addition, there are two collective labour agreements for the grocery sector: one applies to large grocery companies and one to franchise companies. The collective agreements apply automatically to all undertakings in the sector.

14.6.1 Civil Law

There are no specific rules regulating trading relations in the retail sector. Such relations are subject to the general rules of contract law, set out in the Dutch Civil Code (the '**DCC**').

These general rules embrace the principle of contractual freedom, particularly where it concerns B2B agreements. Parties are therefore free to determine the conditions of their cooperation. Given the dictum *pacta servanda sunt*, agreements cannot be unilaterally changed unless such right to unilateral amendment is provided for in the agreement. A defaulting party will have to reimburse another party to the contract for damage suffered as a result of the breach of contract.

Moreover, agreements are subject to the principles of fairness and reasonableness. Such principles can either impose additional rights and obligations or render unfair clauses unenforceable. More specifically, unreasonably burdensome conditions set out in general terms are voidable. Agreements that were concluded under the influence of threat, fraud or abuse of circumstance can be annulled. Unfair practices could also, under specific circumstances, constitute an unlawful act. As of March 2013, the DCC provides for maximum payment terms.

Finally, collective and therefore anonymous actions are possible under Dutch law.

Although Dutch civil law in theory provides for a fair level of protection for smaller suppliers, often such smaller suppliers do not make use of this protection. This is partly due to the fact that the above rules contain a lot of 'open norms', which will be assessed on a case-to-case basis. Suppliers do not start legal proceedings because they are costly and time consuming and, more importantly, may jeopardise the commercial relationship.

14.7 Conclusion

In the Netherlands, the grocery sector is subject to the general competition and civil law rules. The agricultural sector sells its produce through large cooperatives to international traders. Most of the produce is then sold abroad and to large supermarkets. Supermarkets acquire their supplies through large purchasing collectives, which account for approximately 85 % of demand on the Dutch market. This makes them powerful. Suppliers have raised complaints concerning the buying power of supermarkets. This has consequently become a subject of public debate. The Dutch competition authority has conducted several studies into pricing in the grocery sector and buying power in general. It concludes that the buying power of the supermarkets does not necessarily give rise to competition law concerns. Given that there is enough competition on the market on which the supermarkets are active, the buying power leads to lower prices for consumers. The buying power will only be cause for concern if it is exercised in a way to exclude competitors or exploit suppliers. The Minister of Economic Affairs also responded to the complaints from suppliers about the strength and behaviour of the supermarkets. It initiated a pilot in the agro-food sector in order to establish a code of conduct through self-regulation. The pilot is inspired by the European Supply Chain Initiative and their Principles of Good Practice. All supermarkets have registered with the Supply Chain Initiative. Their business operations will soon be in line with the Principles.

Romania

15

Anca Buta Muşat

15.1 The Evolution of the Grocery Market in the Market Economy Context

Prior to the political changes of 1989, agricultural production and sale of grocery products were the exclusive attribute of the State via its empowered agencies. With the agricultural reform of 1991,[1] individual property over agricultural lands was restored, but many individual owners sought different forms of joint ventures in order to make their ownership economically profitable. Thus, a large number of agricultural associations were established, mostly encouraged by the 1994 Law on the Lease of Agricultural Lands.[2] Following the 2005 Law on Land Reform[3] and the enabling of foreign citizens to acquire agricultural lands in Romania, more associations were established alongside large ownerships. Notwithstanding the above, the majority of large agricultural exploitations focus on grain cropping, due to the specific qualities of the soil in Romania; less interest is being manifested towards cropping of vegetables. This is also due to the fact that alongside the dissolution of the socialist agricultural property, in the very first years after 1990, the vast majority of facilities making up the national irrigation system—which is crucial to vegetable cropping—were rendered nonusable while the State (the owner thereof) did not perform any investments whatsoever in this particular respect.

[1] Performed via Land Law no. 18/1991, republished in Official Gazette no. 01/05 January 1998.

[2] Law no. 16/1994 on the lease of agricultural lands published in the Official Gazette no. 91/07 April 2005.

[3] Law no. 247/2005 on the reform in the fields of private ownership and justice and certain ancillary measures published in the Official Gazette no. 653/22 July 2005.

A.B. Muşat (✉)
Muşat & Asociaţii Attorneys-at-Law, Bucharest, Romania
e-mail: anca.buta@musat.ro

P. Kobel et al. (eds.), *Antitrust in the Groceries Sector & Liability Issues in Relation to Corporate Social Responsibility*, LIDC Contributions on Antitrust Law, Intellectual Property and Unfair Competition, DOI 10.1007/978-3-662-45753-5_15

On another hand, a considerable portion—if not the majority—of the Romanian agricultural land is still individually exploited for the purposes of satisfying individual consumption needs. However, the costs of individual exploitation of land for agricultural purposes usually exceed the economic power of its owners, and the Government consequently supports such exploitation via biannual subsidies aimed at partially (and, practically, insufficiently) financing the spring and autumn agricultural campaigns. As a result, much land is left unexploited, irrespective of legal provisions sanctioning the passivity of landowners.

As to the processing sector, the socialist units (such as farms, slaughterhouses and dairies) were privatized following the abandonment of the socialist economic model. Some of these units were privatized and converted into successful businesses, while others were simply closed down. A tendency that was noticeable at least in the last 15 years was the preference of private investors to invest in Greenfield processing sites. Nevertheless, not all socialist units were overlooked, but given their economically strategic locations and dimensions the acquisition, reconditioning and refurbishment thereof proved in many instances cheaper and more economically feasible than a Greenfield investment.

Lastly, the grocery retail sector has experienced in its own turn important changes as compared to the socialist period. While the 1990s was marked at first by the dissolution of state-held retail units and by the establishment of numerous privately held corner shops, the first decade of the twenty-first century was marked by the entry on the Romanian market of a series of large retailer chains at both cash & carry and retail (hypermarkets, supermarkets, discounters) levels. The late entry on the Romanian market of the modern forms of grocery retail has determined a strong competition at client level between the two. Pursuant to a 2009 Report of the Competition Council, in 2009, a majority of 60 % of Romanians preferred to acquire their grocery from a traditional trade unit (corner or neighborhood shop), while only 40 % preferred modern retail. However, the data and information comprised in said report might have changed with the expansion of different retail chains in Bucharest and the larger cities.

15.2 Impact of Competition Rules on the Grocery Sector

15.2.1 Romania's Competition Laws and Regulations

Competition is regulated in Romania via two major enactments.

The first and most important one is Competition Law no. 21/1996, as republished and further amended and supplemented (the "Competition Law").[4] The Competition Law captures under its ambit acts and facts perpetrated on the Romanian territory or possibly affecting the Romanian territory irrespective of the nationality of the natural or legal persons responsible thereof (pursuant to Article 2). The

[4] Republished in the Official Gazette no. 742/16 August 2005.

authority vested with enforcing the Competition Law is the Competition Council (the "RCC").

Article 5 paragraph (1) of the Competition Law contains a general prohibition of anticompetitive practices and does not distinguish between different industry sectors or fields of the economy. As such, the general prohibition of anticompetitive practices (be they horizontal or vertical) applies to all acts and facts that go against such prohibition (bid rigging, resale price maintenance, market sharing and limitation of output). Of the aforementioned, resale price maintenance deserves a special attention, as there is a fine distinction between recommended and imposed resale prices, an issue that is subject to scrutiny by both national and EU competition authorities.

Article 6 of the Competition Law sets forth a general prohibition of any abuse of dominance. Dominance is legally presumed to exist whenever an undertaking holds a market share of more than 40 %. Neither in respect of this particular prohibition does the Competition Law make any distinction as to specific conditions for its enforcement in respect of given sectors of the economy.

Similarly, the rules on merger control, laid down in Articles 10–15 of the Competition Law, are of general and mandatory application in all sectors of the economy, the RCC exposing a wide decision-making practice in mergers in the grocery retails sector.

The second major enactment is Law no. 11/1991 on the fight against unfair competition ("Law no. 11/1991").[5] It provides a general prohibition on unfair competition and exemplifies what acts or facts constitute unfair competition. However, given its broad and interpretable provisions, it was not practically enforced on a large scale. Currently, the RCC is vested with its enforcement (acting in such capacity as of 2010 when it took over from the Ministry of Finance) and has initiated a legislative process for the amendment thereof with a view to giving way to private enforcement of the law rather than a State-directed one.

15.2.2 Modernization of the Laws Governing the Sale of Perishable Goods in Romania

Although the Competition Law does not contain provisions particularly aimed at the retail market, the Competition Law was construed and developed by the RCC on the occasion of various decisions rendered in the field of retail. On a separate note, there are some enactments governing specific issues concerning competition in the retail market.

Government Ordinance no. 99/2000 on product commercialization and market services (the "GO no. 99/2000")[6] is one such example. It regulates both general aspects of conducting commercial businesses (functioning hours, public authority

[5] Published in the Official Gazette no. 24/30 January 1991.

[6] Republished in the Official Gazette no. 603/31 August 2007.

endorsements, the role of public authorities in the commercialization activity, etc.) as well as certain competition-related aspects such as the rules on different types of discounted sale. Specifically, Article 17 of GO no. 99/2000 prohibits predatory pricing practices. In the optic of the law, predatory pricing takes the form of sale of products at prices equal or inferior to the acquisition costs. Nevertheless, GO no. 99/2000 allows certain exceptions from such rules, one of them being in the case of perishable goods (food/grocery products).

In 2009, Parliament adopted Law no. 321/2009 on the commercialization of food products ("Law no. 321/2009")[7] in order to settle different dissonances between suppliers and the large retail chains. Essentially, it provides for specific rules on commercialization of groceries while also consecrating an entire chapter to prohibiting certain anticompetitive practices in the field such as (1) reciprocal obligations of sale and purchase of products to and from a specific third party, (2) charging and payment for services that are not directly related to the sale process, (3) charging and payment of fees aimed at supporting the expansion of the retailer's facilities, (4) the requirement by the retailer that the supplier not sell its products to other retailers at an equal or lower acquisition cost and (5) unlawful delisting of products by the retailer.

GO no. 99/2000 and Law no. 321/2009 are the only enactments governing the grocery retail sector. Nevertheless, there are sector-specific norms and regulations, all of which comply with the general rules laid down by the two aforementioned enactments.

As described above, the grocery retail sector is subject to the provisions of the Competition Law in the same manner as all other sectors and economy fields.

15.3 The Romanian Grocery Retail Market Under Scrutiny by the Competition Council

15.3.1 Background

Unsurprisingly, the RCC paid due attention to the grocery retail sector, given the tensions between modern and traditional forms of retail and between suppliers and retailers altogether, which existed in the sector after the year 2000 (landmark year for the consolidation of modern forms of retail in Romania). The RCC Chairman issued Oder no. 97/18.03.2008, whereby a sector inquiry was launched with a view to analyzing the food retail sector in Romania (the "Sector Inquiry"). The 200-page (annexes included) Sector Inquiry Report (the "RCC Report") was released to the public on September 2009 and proves to be a useful instrument for Competition Law enforcement in the grocery retail sector.

Before the RCC launching of the Sector Inquiry, there were certain points of contention between the retailers and the suppliers, which were brought to the

[7] Published in the Official Gazette no. 705/20 October 2009.

attention of the RCC. Moreover, the RCC was confronted with several merger control and individual exemptions (an institution now repealed under the current form of the Competition Law) that were taking place or were affecting the grocery retail sector. Officially, the RCC motivated its launching of the Sector Inquiry on the necessity for the authority to hold a clear image of the overall sector, and it covered the years 2005–2008.

15.3.2 Scope of the Sector Inquiry

Pursuant to the RCC Report, the Sector Inquiry covered six major aspects, as follows:

(i) the identification and assessment of the markets that make up the grocery retail sector;
(ii) the assessment of the application and practical functioning of the "most favored client" clause (the "MFN clause");
(iii) the analysis of slotting allowances as part of the contractual relationship between retailers and their suppliers;
(iv) the clarification and assessment of the concept of "category management";
(v) the identification of the manner in which costs are determined, prices are set and profits are achieved on the production–distribution–retail chain for certain important products;
(vi) the identification of potential competition law issues.

15.3.3 Conclusions and Recommendations Made by the Competition Council

As a preliminary remark, the period under assessment from the RCC was limited to 2008 (or, in some cases, 2007), and the conclusions thereof were made public on September 2009. Therefore, the below must be read while having in mind the aforementioned:

(i) The *scales of modern and traditional forms of trade* are clearly tipped in favor of the traditional ones (corner and neighborhood shops), which cover 60 % of consumer preferences as compared to 40 % covered by hypermarkets, supermarkets and discounters. Considering the period covered by the RCC Report, we deem that such results may have been altered due to different factors such as the proliferation of discounter chains on the Romanian market, price competition, variety of products, etc.
(ii) The *importance of sales via the cash & carry format has decreased* due to the significant number of entries by hypermarket/supermarket/discounter chains, consumers being more attracted by the easiness of access (cash &

carry stores require holding of a membership card as their target clients are resellers and not final consumers).

(iii) There is *no competition between the cash & carry format and small retailers*, given that (a) the latter generally procure their merchandise from the former (see (ii) above) and that (b) there are clear differences between the number and variety offered by the two formats to the final consumer.

(iv) *Modern forms of trade compete against traditional ones* based on the fact that the latter represent the initial form of trade present in the Romanian market. However, this conclusion is valid only until modern forms of trade will have a majority in the Romanian market, this particular point in time marking a shift in the behavior and preferences of the end consumer. After such moment will be reached, traditional forms of trade will no longer compete with the modern ones but will be perceived by the end consumer as complementary thereto.

(v) The *value of the Romanian trade of groceries* was estimated at the level of 2008 to be the following: (a) RON 83 billion (roughly EUR 21.2 billion) was the total value of current consumption goods, (b) RON 54.4 billion (roughly EUR 13.9 billion) was the total value of Romanian grocery trade, while (c) RON 22 billion (roughly EUR 5.6 billion) was the total value of Romanian modern grocery trade.

(vi) The assessment performed by the RCC's inspectors indicated that certain of the *slotting allowances* were not directly linked to the services provided by the retailers to their suppliers, while others presented such necessary connection. The RCC Report provides a nonexhaustive list of permitted and prohibited slotting allowances.

(vii) The analysis of the *MFN clause* led the RCC to recommend the elimination thereof from the retailer–supplier commercial relationships based on the existence of slotting allowances (permitted following the assessment in the RCC Report). For this specific reason, the RCC issued an endorsement concerning the 2009 amendment of the GO no. 99/2000, whereby it recommended the prohibition of the MFN clause in the grocery retail sector.

(viii) *Category management*—over the analyzed period, the increase in the sales of the competitors of category captains has exceeded the sales of the latter. Nevertheless, the RCC Report recommends that the responsibility for managing the shelf space be further assumed by the retailer and not by the category captain.

(ix) The *negotiation power* manifested by certain retailers in relation to their suppliers does not represent a point for consideration from the RCC as long as the retailer does not hold a dominant position on a given market. The RCC sees no point in a distinct and supplementary regulation of the abuse of superior negotiation power. The examples provided by the EU Member State show a scarce, if not totally absent, intervention by the State authority based on such provisions.

(x) At the moment when the RCC Report was issued, *private brands* held a mere 10 % share among the total number of brands commercialized by retailers, and as such they exercised no competitive pressure. This particular conclusion may have also been altered with the passage of time.

(xi) *Sales at loss and discounted sales* have also formed the object of the RCC's assessment. The RCC recommended that the Government repeal the prohibition on sales at loss (Article 17 of the GO no. 99/2000), but instead the Government opted to maintain unchanged said prohibition (with certain exceptions covering also the grocery retail activity).

(xii) The *increase of prices* charged by the retailers to the final consumers is consistent with the increases of the prices charged by the producers to suppliers in relation to the retail segment. The RCC points out that bread commercialization is a specific segment in which prices charged to end consumers rise more often than the prices charged in the upstream market. In fact, the RCC investigated two so-called bread cartels in the Maramures and Vrancea counties, following which significant fines for price fixing were imposed on bread producers, distributors and retailers.[8]

(xiii) Merger control is the best tool for prevention of potential competition distortion, given the entries of numerous retailers on the Romanian market.

(xiv) Following the finalization of the Sector Inquiry, the RCC launched four new investigations in the retail sector, cash & carry chains, retailers and suppliers being altogether subject to these proceedings. From the data and information available, the RCC is planning on finalizing the investigations in 2013.

15.4 Merger Control in the Grocery Sector

15.4.1 Turnover Thresholds that Trigger the Intervention of the Competition Council

The Competition Law provides for a double turnover threshold that needs to be met in case of an economic concentration operation in order for the latter to become subject to the RCC's clearance before implementation (subject to a standstill obligation). At present, these thresholds are as follows:

- the worldwide combined turnover of all the undertakings that are parties in the economic concentration operation exceeds the RON equivalent of EURO 10,000,000; and

[8] Decision no. 61 of 7.12.2009 concerning the infringement of Article 5 paragraph (1) of the Competition Law by 17 undertakings active on the bread market in the Maramures county; Decision no. 62 of 7 December 2009 concerning the infringement of Article 5 paragraph (1) of the Competition Law by 31 undertakings active on the bread market in the Vrancea county.

– at least two of the undertakings involved in the economic concentration operation individually achieve in Romania a turnover that exceeds the RON equivalent of EURO 4,000,000.

Such turnover values refer to the fiscal year prior to the one in which the merger takes place.

The RCC is the autonomous central administrative body in charge of the review and clearance of economic concentration operations that meet the above-mentioned thresholds. In such capacity, it issues a series of regulations and guidelines for the conducting of merger control notifications and the assessment thereof.

An innovation brought via an amendment to the Competition Law in 2011 refers to the power of the Country's Supreme Defense Council (the "CSDC") in merger control operations. When considerations of national safety so demand, it may request the Government to issue a decision prohibiting an economic concentration operation from taking place. This rule was detailed upon via CSDC Decision no. 73/2012 (the "CSDC Decision"), which provides that RCC is bound to inform the CSDC of all the merger notifications that it receives. Nevertheless, even if an economic concentration operation does not meet the above-mentioned thresholds, the CSDC still needs to be informed if the transaction takes place in one of the 13 sectors listed in the CSDC Decision. Although the grocery retail is not expressly listed therein, the protection of agriculture and environment is one of the mentioned sectors.

15.4.2 Defining the Relevant Market, a Cornerstone Task

The statutory definition and relevant steps for the assessment of the relevant product and geographic markets are laid down in the Guidelines on defining the relevant market enforced via Order no. 388/2010 of the RCC Chairman. Pursuant to this enactment, the relevant product market is to be defined as consisting of all products and/or services that the consumer deems interchangeable or substitutable due to their characteristics, prices and final use. The relevant geographic market consists of the area in which the concerned undertakings are involved in the request and demand of products and services, in which competition conditions are sufficiently homogenous and which can be delineated from neighboring areas due to the appreciable differences in terms of competition conditions.

The RCC's decision-making practice in merger control cases in the grocery retail sector deals with the taking over by well-established international retail chains of certain stores pertaining to their local competitors. Although quite extensive, this practice is marked by constancy, especially in what the definition of the relevant markets is concerned. As a rule, the RCC defined the relevant product market as being *the market for the retail of groceries via hyper/supermarkets, discounter stores and other similar shops (such as corner or neighborhood shops)*. As it results from this definition, the cash & carry stores are excluded from the definition of the relevant product market since—as the RCC puts it in both decisions and the above-cited Report—this trade format addresses other types of clients than end consumers. Moreover, in all the RCC decisions rendered in this particular field of the economy, the RCC opted to also define, in line with European Commission practice, a separate market for the *procurement of grocery for daily use*. The rationale behind this dual definition of the relevant product market consists in the different types of vertical relationships of the retailers (1) with their suppliers and (2) with their clients (end consumers).

The constancy indicated above in respect of defining the relevant product market was naturally maintained by the RCC when defining the dimension of the relevant geographic market in respect of such. Thus, the RCC considers, in line with the relevant European Commission decision-making practice, that the geographic dimension of the market for retail of grocery is usually local and is determined by the boundaries of a territory where the outlets can be reached easily by consumers (radius of approximately 10/20–30 min of driving time). As to the geographic dimension of the market for the procurement of grocery for daily use, the RCC adopted the European Commission position that it should be national in scope.

15.4.3 Market Evolution in Light of Recent Developments

The RCC Report indicates that at the level of 2008, there were 52 retailers engaged in activities of grocery retail at the level of Romania. This shows that—at least, at that time—no argument in favor of market concentration to the benefit of any of such retailers could have been made. Although some of the retailers have opted to expand their networks via different take-over of businesses (Profi, Mega Image) or via different cooperation agreements (Carrefour–Angst), the RCC has found that no such economic concentration operations posed any threats to the maintenance of a status quo normal competitive environment on the grocery retail market.

Nevertheless, should the RCC find—when analyzing a notified merger operation—that a dominant position on the grocery retail market is either created or consolidated thereby, it has the capacity to avoid such from occurring. Thus, the RCC may, under the terms of the Competition Law [Article 46 paragraph (4) letter c)], impose different remedies in respect of an economic concentration operation. The Guidelines on commitments in merger control operations, enforced via Order no. 688/2010 issued by the RCC Chairman, provide that the national competition authority may adopt either behavioral or structural remedies, i.e., it may either impose a given course of commercial conduct (setting up or terminating different supply relationships) or order the divesture of a given part of the business forming part of the economic concentration operation.

The Competition Law also provides that in case an economic concentration operation is implemented and that it is incompatible with a normal competitive environment or when it is implemented in disregard of a conditional clearance decision, the RCC has the power to order the parties to dissolve the economic concentration operation. As per the data and information that we hold, the RCC has not made use of such legal prerogative so far.

The RCC adopted one decision[9] specifically concerning the taking over by a large grocery supplier of the goodwill pertaining to smaller competitors thereof, but it does not insist on the grounds for merger. It nevertheless results that the rather insignificant impact of the operation on the relevant market was the main argument for the RCC's clearance, rather than the countervailing force of retailers. The other decisions passed by the RCC concerning mergers between grocery suppliers concern different change of control in the share capital of retailers active on the Romanian market.

As the Romanian retail market was marked by the late entry of the modern forms of grocery retail, the large retail chains opted for Greenfield investments and have only recently pursued the acquisition of preexisting brick-and-mortar shops. In the cases of Profi, Mega Image and Carrefour, all three retailers notified the RCC with respect to the acquisition of stores and goodwill that pertained to local competitors. On the other hand, in the case of Profi (having its national headquarters in Timisoara, a city in Western Romania), its acquisition of the "Albinuta" stores located in Bucharest represented the gateway into the largest urban retail market.

None of the RCC decisions rendered in the cases mentioned above has retained as grounds for clearance the need to counterbalance the increasing (negotiation) power of the grocery suppliers.

The RCC may either, on one hand, oppose and prohibit a merger or, on the other hand, clear it subject to behavioral or structural remedies. Although RCC has always benefitted from such power, in its entire 17-year history it opposed a single proposed economic concentration operation and imposed remedies on a limited number (under 10) of such operations. However, from the data and information that we hold, the RCC never imposed remedies in respect of economic concentration operation taking place in the grocery retail market.

Nevertheless, at the date hereof, the RCC assessed the proposed take-over by Auchan of all but four Real hypermarkets in Romania. The RCC held a public consultation on the matter and has rendered a much-debated conditional clearance in respect thereto.

From another perspective, the business of selling grocery via the Internet is rather novel to the Romanian market. There are several online platforms offering such services, but Romanian consumers usually prefer to purchase groceries from traditional brick-and-mortar stores. Moreover, at the moment of 2009, the RCC Report did not even take into consideration this particular form of modern trade when assessing the degree of competition between traditional and modern forms of retail or between different types of modern retail.

[9] Decision no. 247/22 December 2006 concerning the economic concentration operation achieved by the acquiring of joint control by S.C. Angst-Ro S.A. over S.C. Discovery Prodimpex S.R.L. and S.C. 2T Prod S.R.L.

Nevertheless, one has to consider the specific types of businesses conducted via Internet stores. If we are to refer to issues of fairness, there have been situations in which online stores were selling different branded products that were proven to be counterfeit or in respect of which IP rights protection was not exhausted. However, such incidents have been scarce and did not fall under the scope of the Competition Law so as to be reviewed by the RCC.

As mentioned above, the general legal framework applicable to the sale of grocery is consecrated in both GO no. 99/200 and Law no. 321/2009. Although they concern mainly the sale of grocery (and nonfood products) via the classic brick-and-mortar shops, their provisions must be applied *mutatis mutandis* to the activity of the Internet stores (e.g., sale at prices below costs or discounted sales).

15.5 Dominance and Abuse

15.5.1 Legal Framework

The Competition Law provides in Article 6 that the abuse of dominant position is prohibited. Paragraph (1) thereof exemplifies the forms that such an abuse may take, and among those forms is the "exploitation of a state of economic dependency of an undertaking that does not have an alternative solution under equivalent conditions." Although the RCC issued a series of guidelines and regulations for the application of the provisions of Article 5 (prohibiting anticompetitive practices) and merger control rules, a secondary legislation detailing the scope of Article 6, which prohibits abusive conducts, was enacted. Thus, there is no statutory definition of the buying power or of the exploitation of dependency. However, a number of the RCC's previous decisions follow the decision-making practice of the European Commission and the case law of the European Court of Justice.

For instance, in one of its landmark decisions on the abuse of dominance, concerning the National Post Company,[10] the RCC indicated (paragraph 193) that the prohibition of exploiting a state of dependency is incident inasmuch as alongside the general conditions that must be met for the identification of an abuse, certain cumulative conditions are also satisfied:

- the existence of a state of economic dependency of an undertaking towards another while the former does not have an alternative solution under equivalent solution, and
- the exploitation of such state of dependency.

Whether a state of dependency exists or not depends on the existence of an alternative solution under equivalent conditions for the company in question. The RCC further points out that the lack of an equivalent solution can be argued where

[10] Decision no. 52/16.10.2010.

the market does not provide for a supply source or where eventual substitutes compromise the competitiveness of the dependent undertaking. The RCC further points that the exploitation of the state of dependency is achieved via one of the conducts listed at letters a)–e) of Article 6, to which the termination of contractual relationships due to the undertaking's refusal to submit to unjustified commercial conditions is added. Consequently, the RCC indicates that the exploitation of dependency is absorbed in the content of the deeds listed under letters a)–e) of Article 6 and operates as a circumstance that qualifies the subject that performs the abuse. In other words, excessive pricing and discrimination absorb within their contents the exploitation of a state of economic dependency, fact that may be taken into account as an aggravating circumstance when sanctioning the abuse. As such, it could not be considered as a distinct misdemeanor.

The above-cited RCC decision is currently reviewed by the competent courts.

Article 6 paragraph (1) of the Competition Law is clear in providing that any abuse of dominance on the Romanian market or on a substantial part thereof is prohibited. Given such wording, there have not been any discussions on whether abuses of dominance are prohibited only in the cases in which they restrict competition on a given market. The general opinion of both RCC and courts is that abuses of dominance are per se prohibited under Article 6 of the Competition Law.

The only point of intense discussion is the recent enactment in the Competition Law [Article 6 paragraph (3)] of the rebuttable presumption that a market share of 40 % is a clear indication of dominance. Therefore, defining the relevant market and the allocation of the corresponding market share are points of debate in Article 6 cases.

There are no statutory definitions for the concepts listed above. Therefore, the RCC follows the decision-making practice of the European Commission and the case law of the ECJ.

15.5.2 Abuses of Buying Power or Dependency from the Perspective of the Competition Council

The following have been identified by the RCC as cases in which of economic dependency was exploited by a dominant company:

- the charging by the National Post Company to different publishing houses and other undertakings of unreasonably high prices for the services of delivering advertisements via post to end consumers,
- the increase by a producer of wooden products of increased prices to its clients on the Romanian market immediately after finalizing an economic concentration operation concerning to top Romanian producers of wooden products and the eventual acquisition of a dominant position of the market despite the conditional clearance of the merger operation by the RCC,

– the charging by an undertaking active on the market for natural-gas-related services of tariffs for issuing necessary endorsements for works undertaken by third parties that were ten times higher than the tariffs charged for similar work undertaken thereby.

15.5.3 Recommended Resale Prices & RPM

As a general rule, minimum and fixed resale prices are prohibited under Article 5 paragraph (1) of the Competition Law, in line with the rules laid down in the European Commission Guidelines on Vertical Restraints, which are of direct application by the RCC following the 2010 amendments to the Competition Law. Nevertheless, under the provisions of Article 5 paragraph (2) of the Competition Law (the national correspondent of Article 101(3) TFEU), price recommendations that are generally considered to be anticompetitive may theoretically be exempted when three cumulative conditions are met: (1) they contribute to the improvement of production while ensuring an advantage to the end consumer, (2) the restrictions imposed are indispensable for attaining such objective and (3) they do not give way to eliminating competition on the relevant market or on a part thereof. Although such a solution is not impossible, the RCC did not render any decisions in this respect.

Resale price maintenance (*RPM*) is a clear-cut prohibition under the Competition Law. Reselling below costs is a form of predatory pricing also prohibited under the Competition Law. Nevertheless, as previously mentioned, reselling below costs is also prohibited via GO no. 99/2000. It is also prohibited under Law no. 321/2009 via a text in the chapter on prevention of anticompetitive practices. Lastly, delisting of a supplier by a reseller is prohibited without just cause, such prohibition being laid down in the same chapter of Law no. 321/2009.

15.5.4 Treatment of Abusively High Prices Under Competition Law

Excessive pricing is regarded as a form of abuse of dominance under the provisions of Article 6 paragraph (1) letter e) of the Competition Law. It prohibits a company in a dominant position from charging excessive or predatory prices with a view to eliminating competition.

In determining whether prices charged by a dominant undertaking are excessive or not, the RCC follows in the footsteps of the European Commission as far as the applicable standards are concerned. For instance, in a 2004 decision,[11] the RCC found that an undertaking that has just achieved its dominant position on the Romanian market of wooden products (following a conditional clearance decision

[11] Decision no. 329/22 December 2004 concerning the infringement of Article 6 letter a) of the Competition Law by S.C. Kronospan Sepal S.A.

from the RCC itself) was charging excessive prices to its clients. In order to find that prices charged were excessive or not, the RCC proceeded to investigate whether the level of prices was supported by the level of production costs.

15.5.5 Confrontations Between Private Grocers and Large Retail Chains

Public records show no official complaints filed on such subject with the RCC. However, there have been different initiatives from associations (customarily referred to in Romania as "unions," although such is incorrect in terms of legal language) for the protection of Romanian producers against competition from lower priced imported grocery. From our information, such situations were to be found prior to 2009—the year when the Ministry of Agriculture launched the Code for Best Practices in the Trade of Grocery Products, an initiative later materialized in Law no. 321/2009.

Although the RCC has to our best knowledge no decision-making practice covering this particular aspect, applying *mutatis mutandis* other decisions, a few assertions can be made. An understanding aiming at limiting supply may be found to be restrictive of competition. It need not affect the entire Romanian market, the Competition Law being applicable even in the case where a substantial part of the national market is affected (the question of defining a substantial part of the market is to be determined on a case-by-case assessment). In such a case, the discussion from the perspective of competition law will most likely focus on whether it is a restriction of competition by object or by effect. Following the trend established by the European Commission and upheld by the ECJ, the effects of said practice should also be assessed in order to determine an infringement of competition rules.

15.6 Highlights of the Competition Council's Work

15.6.1 Grocery Sector

Apart from the two above-mentioned cases of "bread cartels," in the past 5 years the RCC has rendered a single decision relating to the behavior of grocery retailers.

Thus, in 2011, the RCC sanctioned[12] Profi (one of the main grocery retailers), Interfruct (a supplier of fresh fruit) and Albinuta Shops (a local retailer from Bucharest) for price fixing. Specifically, the RCC found that the fresh fruit supply agreements concluded by Interfruct with Profi and Albinuta Shops on March 2009 (for a duration of 8 months) contained a price-fixing clause whereby the shelf prices

[12] Decision no. 18/31 May 2011 concerning the infringement of the provisions of Article 5 paragraph (1) letter a) of the Competition Law by S.C. Interfruct S.R.L., S.C. Albinuţa Shops S.R.L. and S.C. Profi Rom Food S.R.L.

of the fruits supplied by Interfruct were to be determined by the latter. Following the expiry of said agreements and the launching of the investigation, the contracts were replaced and the price-fixing clause was eliminated. Nevertheless, the RCC sanctioned Interfruct and Profi (which in the mean time took over Albinuta Shops) with fines amounting to EUR 4 million.

The RCC launched four investigations in the grocery retail sector following the initiation of the Sector Inquiry. The outcome of these four proceedings, involving four of the major food retail chains in Romania (Metro, Selgros, Billa and Mega Image) and their suppliers investigated for alleged anticompetitive pricing practices, is expected in 2013.

Under the Competition Law, the RCC has the prerogatives of enforcing competition rules at any level and in any field of the economy. As such, it may deal with horizontal anticompetitive practices at local level.

Specifically, the RCC has undertaken two investigations on local markets for bread production and distribution in the Maramures and Vrancea counties of Romania, further to which sanctions have been imposed on a total number of 48 companies. The anticompetitive practices that were investigated concerned the price formation on the production–distribution–retail chain of bread products in the two counties.

As per the Competition Law, the RCC may act either *ex officio* or further to complaints being lodged therewith. In order to have a clear image of competition on the entire Romanian territory and for the purposes of prompt and coherent law enforcement, the RCC operates regional offices in all of Romania's 42 counties. Such offices may conduct investigation proceedings, may depose witnesses and may receive complaints.

15.6.2 Other Leading Cases Concerning Abuse of Dominance

In the past 5 years, the RCC rendered two decisions that are concerned with the issue of excessive pricing:

(i) *a decision of 2010, finding the National Post Company* (the "NPC") *guilty of abuse of dominance*[13]—the case was brought by seven undertakings alleging an abuse of dominance by the NPC on the market for internal delivery of advertisements via post—"Infadres," one of the charges brought against the NPC being that of excessive pricing for its dedicated services. The decision at hand contains an entire section dedicated to the issue of excessive prices and the RCC's standpoint in respect thereto. It is the RCC's view (based on the ECJ ruling in *United Brands Company and United Brands Continentaal BV v Commission of the European Communities*[14]) that "a price is excessive when

[13] Decision no. 52/2010.

[14] ECJ of 14 February 1978, case 27/76, *United Brands Company and United Brands Continentaal BV v Commission*, ECR 1978 207.

it is significantly higher than the level of effective competition or than the economic value of the product concerned." The RCC further cites the ECJ case law in *Case COMP/A.36.568/D3 – Scandlines Sverige AB v. Port of Helsinborg* and underlines that the method for determining the existence of an excessive price supposes two steps:

- the analysis of production cost-price, which ought to reflect the profitability of providing the service, and
- the assessment of the situation in which the price is either *per se* inequitable (either there is an unreasonable difference between the price charged and the economic value of the product/service concerned or such inequitable character derives via a comparison with the prices of other products).

In determining the economic value of the product, one has to consider both cost-related and non-cost-related elements deriving from the interaction between supply and demand in the context of existing market conditions. If there is a positive difference between the price and the production cost and such difference exceeds what can be considered a reasonable profit margin, that price is not excessive. This finding is conditional upon the existence of a reasonable relationship between said price and the economic value of the product/service.

Notwithstanding the above, it is the RCC's optic that it is not necessary to undertake the entire test should the completion of the first step indicate the existence of an excessive price.

(ii) *a decision of 2012 finding that a company active in several local markets for natural gas distribution, design of gas installations and execution of gas installations was abusing its dominant position via excessive prices charged for (i) the activity of endorsing projects for the execution of gas installations and (ii) for the activity of final reception of natural gas installations in three communes of the Prahova and Ilfov counties.*[15]

In this case, the RCC proceeded to the comparison of the tariffs charged by the investigated company for the endorsement of projects and the reception of works undertaken by its personnel with the same tariffs charged should the project and/or works had been performed by third parties. The RCC found that in the first case (endorsement) the tariffs were 3–18 times higher and in the second case—reception of works—they were 3–10 times higher if the services gas installation services were performed by third parties and not by the investigated company.

[15] Decision no. 50/05 September 2012 for the acceptance of commitments offered by S.C. PROGAZ P&D S.A. in the course of the investigation launched via Order no. 342/2010 of the Chairman of the Competition Council.

The case was settled via a commitment procedure without any fines being imposed.

15.7 The Intertwining Relationship Between Competition Laws and Regulations and the Enactments Governing the Sale of Groceries

15.7.1 Main Rules in the Grocery Retail Market Structures

The main general enactments governing the grocery retail sector are, as previously indicated, GO no. 99/2000 and Law no. 321/2009. On one hand, GO no. 99/2000 governs the general conduct of business on the retail market while containing certain competition law provisions necessary for the maintenance of a normal competitive environment, and, on the other hand, Law no. 321/2009 has a prominent competition law character, regulating certain specific behaviors from part of retailers in relation to their suppliers.

As detailed in the paragraphs above, the provisions of the Competition Law are of general application and, as such, manifest a public order character. Therefore, the legislator was always cautious so as not to derogate via sector enactments from the spirit of the regulations in the Competition Law. Therefore, the principles laid down in Articles 5 and 6 thereof were adapted so as to fit specific situations, as is the grocery retail.

GO no. 99/2000 provides for rules in the following fields of grocery retail: (1) criteria to be observed for the purposes of undertaking grocery trade; (2) hourly schedule for operation; (3) duties and obligations of public (regulating) bodies in respect of grocery retail; (4) commercial practices—covering the issue of discounted sales (such as timing, implementation or advertising); (5) rules on labeling, price indications, abusive clauses; and, lastly, (6) sanctions for the infringement of GO no. 99/2000. Of such principal lines of enactment, the following provisions are paramount:

- sales can be undertaken only by qualified personnel that has been duly authorized pursuant to the law;
- sales can be performed either from brick-and-mortar shops or from itinerant outlets;
- sale outlets may be open to the public on all weekdays;
- discounted sales can refer either to the retailer's entire merchandise or only to a part thereof (duly notified to the local authorities as such) and may take – *exempli gratia* – either one of the following forms: liquidation sales, seasonal discounted sales, sales via factory outlets, promotional sales. All such forms of sales abide by the prohibition of predatory price cutting (sale at loss), rule which admits several exemptions (liquidation sales, seasonal discounted sales, sales via factory outlets, sales of products subject to rapid deterioration etc.);

- all advertisements related to discounted sales must clearly indicate the period within which such are undertaken by the retailer;
- seasonal discounted sales may be undertaken only twice a year, each such period covering maximum 45 days and may only be undertaken by the retailer from the outlets it normally uses for the sale of its merchandise.
- certain commercial practices are prohibited: (i) pyramidal sales, (ii) snowball sales, (iii) any other type of sales that entail the offering of products/services by making the client believe that it will obtain them for free or at a price much lower than the real value thereof, while conditioning the sale by the placing of coupons (or other similar tickets) to third parties or by the collection of adhesions or subscriptions and (iv) the deed of proposing to a person to collect adhesions or to enlist by making such person hope for winnings pursuant to the growth of the number of recruited or enlisted persons.
- sales' networks are prohibited from requiring the adherent to pay a fee for the entry in the network.
- sale lotteries are admitted inasmuch as the participants are not required any expense supplementary to the price paid for acquiring the products/service.

The legal provisions detailed above, as well as the rules laid down in the Competition Law, are of general application, irrespective of the dimension and market power of the retailer.

Generally, Internet stores abide by the same rules as brick-and-mortar stores and itinerant outlets relating to the indication of prices and quantities, the restriction on sale lotteries, the prohibition of pyramidal sales and of the other unlawful commercial practices mentioned above, etc.

15.7.2 Sector-Specific Perspectives on Resale Below Cost, Delisting of Suppliers and RPM Practices

Reselling below costs is caught by all three major enactments that have been presented herein: the Competition Law, GO no. 99/2000 (which provides for the necessary exemptions from such prohibitions) and also Law no. 321/2009 (which refers to the provisions of GO no. 99/2000 and thus acknowledges the necessity—from the perspective of competition law—of the exemptions provided therein).

Delisting of suppliers is a practice caught as anticompetitive by the provisions of Article 7 of Law no. 321/2009. The practice was also indicated as such by the RCC Report, which indicated this practice as being abusive in the supplier–retailer relationship. Nevertheless, delisting of a supplier does not fall under a general prohibition, and it may be undertaken by the retailer for just cause. Delisting must be undertaken following a notification being served by the retailer to the supplier, with the exception of the case in which the supplier falls under contractual responsibility. Delisting must in any case be fair to the supplier, and thus the retailer is under the obligation of refunding the supplier with any moneys the latter has paid for the listing of its products as per the agreement concluded with the retailer.

In its turn, RPM is only caught by the provisions of the Competition Law.

15.7.3 Price Control

To our best knowledge, there are no regulations concerning price controls. The Government issued Decision no. 947/2000 concerning the manner of price indications on products offered for sale to consumers,[16] but this particular enactment contains provisions related only to the technical aspects of price display on food products.

As to the role of the RCC in such cases, under the procedure of adopting legislative texts, the point of view of the RCC—usually rendered by the latter in the form of an official consultative (and thus not binding) endorsement—must be sought on all economic regulations that are likely to impact the competitive environment in the Romanian marketplace.

15.8 Aspects Concerning Large-Scale Food Retailing and Vertical Relationships Between Suppliers and Retailers

15.8.1 No Statutory Limitation of Market Power in the Grocery Retail Sector

To our best knowledge, neither Parliament nor Government has issued regulations with regard to the contractual relationships between large-scale food retailers and small suppliers or small-scale retailers.

In the adoption of such rules, the role of the RCC would be that of rendering a nonbinding formal endorsement (which can be either in the positive or in the negative) with respect to the adoption of such enactments. In what the eventual enforcement of such legal provisions would be concerned, the RCC would not intervene should it not be empowered in that respect via such text of enactment.

Although rather specific to common law legal systems, the concept of "level-playing field" may be found in several texts of enactment of the Romanian legal system. Article 1 of Law no. 11/1991 provides that persons engaged in commercial activities (be they legal or natural persons) must undertake such activities in good faith, pursuant to honest commercial uses, also abiding by the interests of the consumers and the prerequisites of fair competition. Apart from being consecrated as a principle of commercial activities in the wake of the passage from socialist economy to market economy, "fairness of transactions" is also a guiding principle of Romanian Law, being a pillar for safeguarding the civil circuit of goods.

[16] Republished in the Official Gazette no. 643/09 September 2008.

The Competition Law makes no distinction whatsoever as to the addressees of its provisions. Nevertheless, in an economy such as the Romanian one, the need to foster individual private initiative and to stimulate individual production has determined the Government to render certain rules concerning the conducting of grocery retail inapplicable inasmuch as individual private producers are concerned.

Thus, Article 3 paragraph (3) of GO no. 99/2000 expressly provides that the provisions thereof are inapplicable inasmuch as the agricultural and food products sold by individual agricultural producers pursuant to a producer certificate are concerned. The producer certificate is an endorsement issued by the local public authority attesting to the fact that the individual retailer is a producer of the goods its sells.

From our perspective, such a provision enacted in the key legislative text for the retail sector ensures a public policy in favor of individual producers and retailers that are exempted from said rules.

15.8.2 Negotiating Practices and Unfair Trade Law

As previously mentioned, the Romanian enactment on unfair competition, Law no. 11/1991, was adopted by Parliament at the beginning of the transition of the Romanian economy to the level of market economy, and as such it misses out on certain relevant aspects of competition specific for the achievement of a normal competitive environment.

Article 5 of the Competition Law contains prohibitions on pricing practices that may prove anticompetitive (at either vertical or horizontal levels), as does Article 6 with respect to the conduct of dominant undertakings. Nevertheless, following the issuance of the RCC Report and the adoption by Parliament of Law no. 321/2009, a bit of light was shed upon the competition law regime of certain pricing practices.

Thus, Article 4 of Law no. 321/2009 provides that retailers are prohibited from requiring the suppliers to pay for services that are not directly linked to the sale operation. Moreover, the retailers are also precluded from requesting the payment of any fees or tariffs related to the expansion of the retailer's network, the development of its sale space or the operations and events for promoting the retailer's activity and (brand) image. Thus, from this perspective, slotting allowances that are not directly related to the services offered by the retailer are prohibited. The instrument that is to be used in determining the issue of permitted and prohibited slotting allowances is the RCC Report, which contains a comprehensive list thereof. Additionally, the RCC Report also recommended the elimination of the use of MFN clauses from the pricing practices of the retailers, given that certain slotting allowances are nevertheless permitted.

Article 8 of Law no. 321/2009 regulates the issue of payment terms in the supplier–retailer relationship. As a general rule, the payment term is subject to mutual agreement between the supplier and the retailer and consecrated via the supply agreement that the two parties conclude. The exception from such rule is represented by meat, milk, eggs, fruits, vegetables and fresh mushrooms in respect of which the payment term may not exceed, in any circumstance, 30 days. Delayed payment terms are subject to contractual liability.

15.9 Conclusion

Although it would be best to await the RCC's conclusions concerning the four investigations on the grocery retail and supply markets, there is at least one thing that needs more clarification in order to be consistently enforced.

Pricing practices at the supplier–retailer level are of paramount importance to the safeguarding of a normal competition environment in the relevant market. Therefore, we deem that it would be appropriate for the RCC to issue a set of guidelines on the matter of slotting allowances, MFN clauses and buying and negotiation power. Although the RCC argues in its Report that such should not acknowledge an overregulation, we deem that such guidelines—a tool of enforcement of the Competition Law nevertheless—would serve suppliers and retailers as well.

Sweden

16

Lars Henriksson

16.1 Economic Background

16.1.1 National Market Structure in Sweden

The retail grocery sector in Sweden can be categorised as an oligopoly comprising of four major retail chains. The four major players ICA, COOP, Axfood and Bergendahls dominate the market, and ICA is the strongest incumbent retailer and has increased its market share over the last 15 years. The three biggest retail chains have increased their joint market share from 60 to 80 % between 1997 and 2007. A recent study conducted in Sweden shows[1] that the margins or prices are no different at any level of the distribution chain in comparison to other countries in Europe on average.

There are significant economies of scale in the food processing industry, although there are about 3,000 companies in the food processing industry. Some 1,300 companies of those are self-employed sole proprietorships, and some 650 companies have less than ten employees. The Swedish food industry is therefore still quite concentrated as the bigger companies account for most of the sales in that level of the distribution chain. As a result, the suppliers are quite concentrated, as well as retailers. There appears to be a balance of selling and buying power in the middle of the distribution chain between suppliers and retailers. The introduction of private labels has increased retailer's bargaining power vis-à-vis the suppliers. Farmers are generally small companies however

[1] See the Swedish Competition Authority (Konkurrensverket, KKV), report *Mat och marknad – från bonde till bord*, Rapport 2011:3, April 2011.

L. Henriksson (✉)
Center for Business Law, Stockholm School of Economics, Stockholm, Sweden
e-mail: Lars.Henriksson@hhs.se

P. Kobel et al. (eds.), *Antitrust in the Groceries Sector & Liability Issues in Relation to Corporate Social Responsibility*, LIDC Contributions on Antitrust Law, Intellectual Property and Unfair Competition, DOI 10.1007/978-3-662-45753-5_16

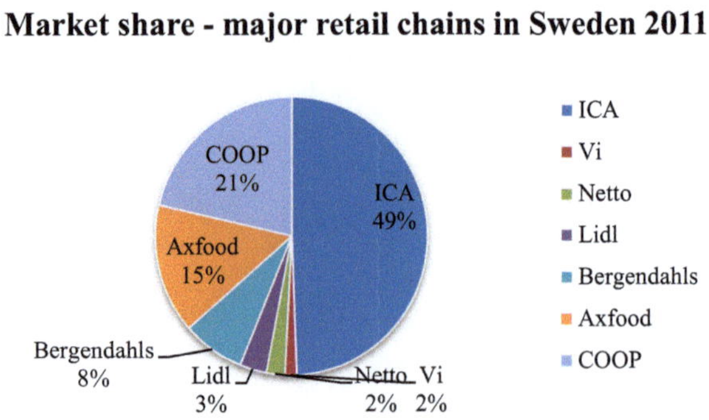

Fig. 16.1 Market shares of the retail grocery chains in Sweden 2011. *Source*: DI Dimension Nr 4, May 2013

organised in a primary agricultural associations in their roles as suppliers to the food industry.

Prices are most commonly negotiated by centralised negotiations between retail chains and suppliers, and the prices to end consumers appear generally to be determined by the state of competition between retailers.

Figure 16.1 shows the market shares of the retail grocery chains in Sweden in 2011.

16.2 Legal Background in Sweden

16.2.1 Scope of Competition Law with Respect to the Grocery Sector

There are currently no specific competition regulations in place in Sweden for the grocery retail sector. Generally, the industry is to date subject to the general competition rules enshrined in the Swedish 2008 Competition Act[2] and its EU counterparts. These national Swedish Rules on competition are essentially equivalent to the provisions of Articles 101 and 102 TFEU, save for the criterion of affecting trade between Member States. The Swedish Competition Authority, Konkurrensverket (the "KKV"), as well as private parties, is entrusted to apply Articles 101 and 102 TFEU when applicable in national litigation.

Unfair competition is, however, considered under Swedish law to be a broader concept, and a wider interpretation of the term would encompass several other legislative instruments directly or indirectly addressing the conditions of competition in different industries. Alongside the Competition Act, the Marketing Practices Act[3] deals with misleading, aggressive and unfair marketing practices, which arguably are important issues when taking a broader view on the market conditions and behaviour of undertakings. Rules on fair competition are essentially a long-

[2] SFS 2008:579.

[3] SFS 2008:486.

standing tradition in Sweden, and in this field there is currently a comprehensive bundle of rules aimed at unfair practices and consumer protection.[4]

16.2.2 Abolishment of the Specific Regulation for the Retail Market in Swedish Competition Law

There are currently no specific provisions applicable to the retail market regarding competition law. Previously, however, Sweden had a national block exemption for voluntary chains of retailers,[5] i.e. chain stores made up of independent retailers under common brand name, as opposed to corporate chains. Agreements or practices establishing the latter would normally escape the application of competition law, as such retailers normally are within the same economic unit, whereas Article 101 TFEU could be applicable to the former.

The old national block exemption was targeted at smaller chains holding up to 20 % market share, whereby joint purchasing and marketing, co-operation on the determination of prices in the common marketing, common accounting and calculation standards, exclusivity on purchased goods and co-operation regarding establishments, financial and administrative services for stores and staff development were exempted from the application of the Swedish 1993 Competition Act.[6] The ordinance also exempted horizontal co-operation on prices and accounting and calculation standards for chains holding 20–35 % market share. Odd as it may seem within the context of competition law today, special rules also applied for the calculation of market shares.

The ordinance had no counterpart in EU law and was not enacted on the basis of long-standing experience that lay behind the Commission's block exemption regulations. Instead, and in hindsight, it could be viewed as a practical way by the legislator to cope with the state of play in the Swedish retail sector, which indeed was made up of many of such voluntary chain stores at a time when a dramatic change in Swedish competition law occurred and entirely new principles were introduced. The ordinance was limited in time and was determined to expire on 1 July 2001. Another motivation behind the ordinance was the ongoing work in

---

[4] Amongst the most relevant legislative measure could be mentioned the Distance and Doorstep Sales Act (SFS 2005:59), The Consumer Contract Terms Act SFS (1994:1512), The E-sales Act (SFS 2002:562), the Consumers' Credit Act (SFS 2010:1846), The Consumers' Sales Act (SFS 1990:932), The Consumers' Services Act (SFS 1985:716), The Act on dangerous imitations of products that look like foodstuffs (SFS 1992:1328), The Price Indication Act (SFS 2004:347) and the Product Safety Act (SFS 2004:451).

[5] Government Ordinance (SFS 1993:80) on exemption according to Section 17 of the Competition Act (SFS 1993:20) for retail chains.

[6] The current 2008 Competition Act that replaced the 1993 Act significantly updated the procedural aspects and remedies available. However, the rules related to anti-competitive agreements and abuse of dominance have remained the same over the years.

the EU on group exemptions and that the Government, at that time, needed to clarify for undertakings the rules of the game in the marketplace.

The national block exemption regulation received negative critique on grounds that the market share calculation deviated from established practice within the EU competition law, that the exemption itself was an anomaly in relation to the then EU law and that the exemption could be questioned from a constitutional point of view.[7] The regulation was undoubtedly not built on a solid legal ground.

In a report from 2000, the KKV held that the national block exemption ordinance on horizontal co-operation in the retail sector might run afoul of EU rules, as it could entail a more favourable approach to individual exemptions than what followed from EU rules and case law. From a harmonisation point of view, this was consequently deemed potentially contrary to EU law. Equally important, the KKV held that the concentration level in the Swedish retail industry was quite high and the ordinance could prove counterproductive to enhance efficiency in the retail sector, strengthen even further the power of larger players and restrict competition. Therefore, the KKV advocated that the ordinance should not be extended and instead let it expire.

At the same time, the 2000 vertical agreement block exemption regulation entered into force,[8] and the block exemption regulations for certain horizontal agreements were under way.[9] Based upon the apparent overlapping regulation that this would result in, the Swedish Government found that the Ordinance should not be renewed, leaving the retail sector subject to general competition rules.

16.2.3 Laws Aimed at Controlling the Structure of the Grocery Retail Market or the Behaviour of Large-Scale Grocery Retailers Outside of Competition Law

Apart from the old national block exemption ordinance, which was applicable not only to the grocery retail sector, but also to voluntary chain stores in general, there has been no sector-specific legislation for the grocery retail sector. Food regulations

---

[7] See Wahl, N., *Rättsutlåtande rörande gruppundantagen för kedjor i detaljhandeln*, Konkurrensverkets rapportserie 1997:1, Wahl, N., *Application of Competition Rules in Sweden – The Swedish Competition Act and National Application of Community Competition Rules*, ERT 1999, p. 16. See also Wahl, N., *Gruppundantaget för kedjor i detaljhandeln* in Märkbara småföretag och konkurrens, 2000, p. 101 and Bernitz, U., *Konkurrensrätten på dagligvarumarknaden*, ERT 2004, p. 239.

[8] Regulation 2790/1999 of 22 December 1999 on the application of Article 81(3) of the Treaty to categories of vertical agreements and concerted practices, OJ 1999 L 336, p. 21.

[9] Regulation 1217/2010 of 14 December 2010 on the application of Article 101(3) of the Treaty on the Functioning of the European Union to certain categories of research and development agreements, OJ 2010 L 335, p. 36 and Commission Regulation 1218/2010 of 14 December 2010 on the application of Article 101(3) of the Treaty on the Functioning of the European Union to certain categories of specialisation agreements, OJ 2010 L 335, p. 43.

may potentially also have at least indirect effects on competition in the grocery sector, but such considerations are not the subject of this article.

Taking a more general view on grocery sector, there have been—and still are—legislative instruments that relate to the necessity to prevent inflationary pressure of grocery retail prices. In that regard, the Price Regulation Act[10] is still in force and applies to goods and services supplied in return for payment, as well as renting of residential apartments and commercial premises.

It was originally passed as part of legislative instruments to cope with macroeconomic challenges during and after World War II, whereby rationing and the interest to control escalation of prices as a result of shortages of supply were of prime interest. Following the oil crisis in the early 1970s and the high inflation in the 1980s, the act was used quite frequently, mirroring the macroeconomic policy of that time. Essentially, the act provided for the possibility of introducing maximum prices or to freeze or cap prices. Experience showed, however, that it was a blunt instrument that merely dealt with the symptoms of an underlying macroeconomic problem, and the price regulation activities decreased significantly at the end of the 1980s to come to a complete stop during the change in overall economic policies in the beginning of the 1990s. The introduction of the then EC-based 1993 Competition Act marked the definite ending of the general retail price regulation activities in Sweden.

A Commission of inquiry on rationing and price regulation, which was chaired by this rapporteur, proposed in 2009 that the price regulation act should be repealed altogether and that such actions should be reserved to a complement to rationing; however, no active steps have been taken in that direction yet.[11]

In summary, therefore, competition law is fully applicable to the retail grocery sector and subject to both national provisions on competition as well as the EU counterparts. The retail grocery sector does not receive neither beneficial nor unfavourable treatment by competition law.

16.3 Advocacy

16.3.1 Market Studies Commissioned by the Swedish Competition Authority of the Retail Grocery Sector

There have been several major studies over the years related to competition issues in the grocery retail sector. Following an assignment by the Swedish Government to assess the conditions of different levels of the distribution chain in the food sector,

[10] SFS 1989:978.

[11] Swedish Government Official Reports SOU 2009:3, Ransonering och prisreglering i krig och fred – delbetänkande av utredningen om översyn av ransoneringslagen och prisregleringslagen and SOU 2009:69, En ny ransonerings- och prisregleringslag – slutbetänkande av utredningen om översyn av ransoneringslagen och prisrelgeringslagen.

the KKV published in 2011 a comprehensive study of the grocery sector, concerning not only the retail level but also the whole distribution chain from farmers or growers to end consumers.[12]

Apart from this general assessment, the KKV has a permanent assignment to supervise and report twice a year to the Commission the retail monopoly for alcoholic beverages regarding its non-discriminatory function. This assignment stems from the accession treaty to the EU and the dispute between Sweden and the EU Commission on the legality of the Swedish retail monopoly. Such goods are not, at least from a Swedish viewpoint, treated as foodstuffs in general, and these reports are therefore forthwith treated as outside the scope of this article.[13]

In 2009, the KKV published a report on the state of competition in the grocery retail sector, which was authored by Copenhagen Economics. The assignment was to use qualitative and quantitative methods to describe the underlying factors that affect the price level of foodstuffs in Sweden in comparison to other countries in Europe.[14]

The competition authorities of the Nordic countries published jointly in 2005 the results and findings of a working group. The group was assigned with the task to identify, analyse and propose solutions to the competition problems in the Nordic food markets and provide recommendations on how to promote and ensure a competitive Nordic food market.[15]

---

[12] The main findings of the inquiry were published in the KKV report *Mat och marknad – från bonde till bord*, Rapport 2011:3. There were several underlying reports to the KKV findings; K. Olofdotter, J. Gullstrand, K. Karantininis, *Konkurrens och makt i den svenska livsmedelskedjan*, Agrifood Economics Centre, 2011; B. Berg-Andersson, O. Rantala, *Konkurrenstryckets och konkurrenskraftens inverkan på livsmedelskedjans prisbildning – Sverige i internationell jämförelse*, Näringslivets Forskningsinstitut Finland, 2011; J. Nilsson, *De lantbrukskooperativa företagens betydelse för konkurrensen inom livsmedelskedjan*, Agrifood Economics Centre, 2011; C. Jörgensen, *Lokalisering och konkurrens i dagligvaruhandeln*, Agrifood Economics Centre, 2011, Persson, M., *Pristransmission inom den svenska livsmedelskedjan*, Agrifood Economics Centre, 2011.

[13] See ECJ, case C-189/95, *Criminal proceedings against Harry Franzén*, ECR 1997, I-5909. The dispute arose out of criminal proceedings against a local grocery owner who attempted to sell wine in his shop. Although his action was illegal in Sweden, he invoked that the legislation was contrary to Articles 30 and 37 of the EC Treaty and that his actions therefore should not be deemed criminal. The preliminary ruling of the ECJ resulted in the discontinuing of Vin & Sprit's monopoly on imports of alcoholic beverages to Sweden; however, the monopoly for retailing of alcoholic beverages could be remain with the state-owned Systembolaget primarily on grounds of public health considerations.

[14] H. Ballebye Okholm, *Konkurrensen på dagligvarumarknaden*, Copenhagen Economics, Uppdragsforskning 2009:2, 2009.

[15] Fællessekretariet for Konkurrencenævnet & Grønlands Forbrugerråd, Konkurrencestyrelsen, Konkurrensverket, Konkurransetilsynet, Samkeppniseftirlitið, Kilpailuvirasto and Kappingarráðið, *Nordic Food Markets – a taste for competition*, Report for the Nordic competition authorities, No. 1/2005.

An overview of the Swedish grocery retail industry was published by the KKV in 2004. The report provided a contemporary description of the grocery sector and proposals for changes in the legislation.[16]

The Swedish Government assigned the KKV to conduct an in-depth investigation into the competition conditions in the retail grocery sector in 2002 and to analyse the price levels in comparison to other countries. The assignment resulted in two reports.[17]

Based upon statistics from Eurostat that Swedish food prices were in the region of 20–25 % higher than the EU average price level for groceries, the KKV published a study in 2001 that dealt with what could be done in order to bring prices down. Questions raised entailed what could increase competition result in that respect, what should be done and, lastly, who should act in order to reduce prices.[18]

The 2001 study had a forerunner in a major multi-industry survey covering several sectors in the economy. The Swedish Government had assigned the KKV to chart and analyse how competition conditions had developed on the Swedish market during the 1990s. One of the sectors that were given special attention was the grocery retail sector.[19]

16.3.2 Motivation of the Sector Inquiries or Market Studies Undertaken in Sweden

The common denominators of the studies undertaken is mostly related to concerns that food prices were higher in Sweden in comparison to the EU average and that it has constantly been a concern regarding the high concentration level in the grocery retail sector. However, the paradox appears to be that the output or quality of groceries has not been a major concern, and the establishment of discount retailers alongside incumbent super- and hypermarkets have so far implied both lower and higher prices spread on a wider range of products. The importance and impact of demand for locally organically produced food and groceries have not been the main concern in the market studies conducted despite the fact this appears to have attracted growing attention amongst consumers. Another important competition factor is the introduction and growth of private labels of the major retail chains. Further research on this topic appears to be needed.

---

[16] K. Lundvall, *Konsumenterna, matpriserna och konkurrensen*, Konkurrensverkets rapportserie 2004:2, June 2004.

[17] K. Lundvall, K. Viidas, *De svenska priserna kan pressas!*, Konkurrensverkets rapportserie 2002:5, December 2002 and J. Eliasson, C.-J. Hangström, *Dagligvaruhandeln – Struktur, ägarform och relation till leverantörer*, Konkurrensverkets rapportserie 2002:6, December 2006.

[18] K. Lundvall, R. Odlander, *Kan kommunerna pressa matpriserna?*, Konkurrensverkets rapportserie 2001:4, October 2001.

[19] Konkurrensverket, Konkurrensen i Sverige under 90-talet – problem och förslag.

16.3.3 Main Topics Covered by the Swedish Market Studies

The first study in 2000 was of general nature, whereby the task was to analyse the state of competition in general in eight important sectors of the economy in the light of the accession to the EU, internationalisation and consumption patterns. Furthermore, more than 30 different proposals were introduced in order to enhance competition and find more efficient instrument to combat restrictions of competition that ran contrary to the consumers' interest.

The 2001 study on the possibility for local communities to promote lowering of food prices covered mainly issues related to local rules on establishment and the application of the local planning/zoning procedures, i.e., general concerns related to the conditions for establishments.

In 2002, the KKV conducted a specific study of the grocery retail sector in Sweden in order to analyse the competition conditions in that sector. The Swedish Government assigned the KKV to present how the different players in the retail level of the distribution chain were organised in relation to ownership, way of organisation and existing co-operations. The ongoing centralisation of the industry should also be investigated in order to assess how that affected the business methods of the retail companies, especially regarding the product range, and what effects could be anticipated in the light of the changes in the industry. Another study in 2002 set out, firstly, to highlight the reasons to the high price levels in Sweden and, secondly, to generate proposals of measures to bring down price levels. Again, price levels appear to have been the prime concern.

The KKV presented a follow-up study in 2004, at which time it concluded that the competition had indeed intensified in the grocery retail sector, but there was still room for considerable improvements. Again, the KKV looked, *inter alia*, into the local planning rules and how new retail chains could be established.

The inter-Nordic study that presented jointly the Nordic competition authorities in 2005 examined the food markets in the Nordic region, again against the background that food prices tended to be higher in the Nordic countries than other countries in Europe. The more or less explicit apprehension was that grocery prices would be permanently higher than the EU average to the detriment of consumers.

Several years passed, and in 2009 the KKV decided to deepen the understanding of the driving forces of prices and factors underpinning the price mechanisms in Sweden in comparison to other countries in Europe. In doing so, the KKV therefore assigned Copenhagen Economics to undertake such a study based upon qualitative and quantitative methods. The study analysed the relationship between concentration and mark-ups and the relation between barriers and concentration and ended with a simulation of price impacts and connected all steps.

The most comprehensive study of the food sector in Sweden was undertaken in 2011 and encompassed the whole distribution chain from farmers/growers to end consumers. Like the older studies, the task assigned the KKV by the Swedish Government was to analyse competition conditions and other market factors in the food sector. However, this time the task was considerably broader compared to older studies as the whole distribution chain was covered. Apart from describing the food sector in terms of structure, market players, concentration levels, vertical integration, pricing in relation to other countries, the task was also to analyse entry barriers and the impact of locally and/or organically small-scale grown foodstuffs.

16.3.4 Main Conclusions and Recommendations of the Market Studies

The first major study dating back some 13 years did not result in any major recommendations in terms of competition policy. It did, however, contribute with a deepened understanding of the structure and market behaviour of the grocery retail sector and how this in general affected the state of competition in the sector. The study showed that there were three major chains dominating the market. In total, there were about 10,000 outlets of groceries in Sweden in 2000; however, only 6,500 outlets were actual grocery retail stores with a traditional range of products. The remainder consisted of specialised stores, food halls, tearooms, farmers' markets, service stations, etc. In 1998, the total private consumption of groceries amounted to about SEK 170 billion or about 18 % of total private consumption. The market shares were distributed as shown in Figs. 16.2 and 16.3.

An important conclusion of the study was that the higher prices in Sweden could at least be 50 % ascribed to macroeconomic factors: level of income, labour costs, taxes, density in population, consumption patterns and currency exchange rates. However, the remaining 50 % were ascribed to weak competition in many sectors of the economy. Enhancing competition would therefore be beneficial for consumers, the study concluded.

The 2001 study took the first steps in that direction, and some 16,000 local development plans/zonings for property development were analysed, thereby focusing on the conditions of new establishments. The study concluded that there was a clear relationship between higher prices and smaller retail space, i.e., the development of supermarkets and hypermarkets could bring price levels down considerably. However obvious this may seem from a mere economy of scale perspective, it also meant that the local municipalities had an important role to play in their capacity as city and local planners in granting building permits and to plan for such zones locally. Municipalities were urged to look favourably on such establishments, naturally in a transparent and non-discriminatory way. At the same time, however, its was acknowledged in the study that such major shifts in the planning procedure brought about trade-offs and difficult considerations in terms of impoverishment of the trade within the towns (especially old city centres), environmental aspects, road planning, etc., as new hypermarkets typically required new land to be utilised outside the old city centres. Therefore, the local municipalities were identified as a key player in bringing consumers' prices down.

The first 2002 study revealed that food prices were about 11 % higher in Sweden than the EU average in 2001, including VAT. Consumer prices in general were about 19 % higher than the EU average. The reasons for the generally higher prices

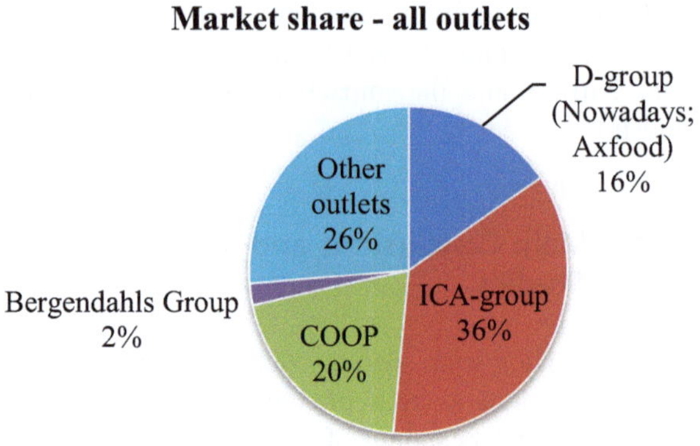

Fig. 16.2 Distribution of market shares by turnover in 1998. *Source*: KKV Study 2000

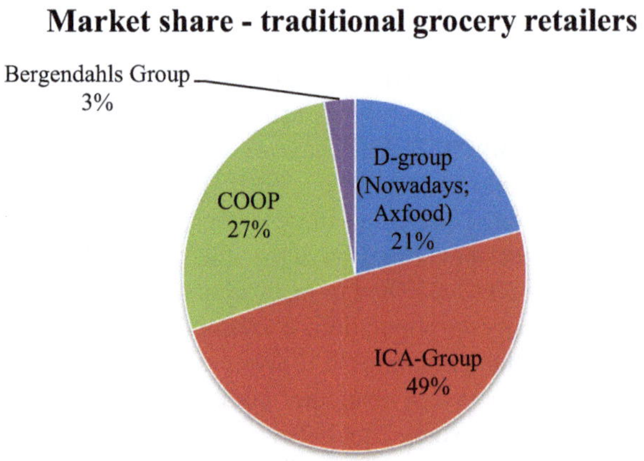

Fig. 16.3 Distribution of market shares by turnover 1998 for traditional grocery stores. *Source*: KKV Study 2000

in Sweden again highlighted weaker competition in Sweden in relation to other countries, and this could account for as much as 50 % of the price differences. Other factors were also considered, primarily the absence of significant grey import (parallel import), high transport costs, high gross national income (although that connection did not apply to Sweden), cost of labour and nominal currency exchange rates. Causes of actions suggested by the KKV were increased funding to the authority in order to combat cartels even more fiercely and to continue the re-regulation of several markets previously sheltered from competition: taxi, domestic air travel, post- and telecommunications, etc. Also, the remaining monopolies in the pharmacy industry should be discontinued, and the local competition plans should be drafted. A report from the Swedish Government[20] also suggested that entrepreneurship was lower in Sweden than in other comparable OECD countries, and the KKV held that entry barriers of different kinds should be minimised. On the macro-level, the KKV argued that remaining obstacle to intra-

[20] *Benchmarking av näringspolitiken 2002*, Näringsdepartementet, Ds 2002:20.

community trade must be enhanced in those sectors still not harmonised and that Sweden should introduce the euro as a currency in order to eliminate the exchange rate effect on prices. Moreover, the KKV held that consumers' surplus should be given special attention in the competition policy.

The parallel and more specific 2002 study into the grocery retail sector emphasised the increased concentration levels as a specific problem. The overall risks connected thereto that were considered were the difficulties of smaller manufacturers to access shelf space, local retailers having less room to adapt locally and product range not matching consumer demand. Presumably, this was an externality of the growing importance of private labels. The KKV therefore propagated the need for the introduction of new players on the market to remedy such concerns. Exactly how such actions would in fact have any adverse effects on private labels remains unclear. In order to achieve new establishments, the planning rules should be designed to look favourably on new establishments, and the competition interest should be "considered" in granting building permits and the overall planning work by municipalities and county councils. Again, it remains unclear exactly what should be changed either in the zoning regulations or in the practice of competent communal boards. It appears from the report as there is an underlying presumption that local communities had adopted a strict approach on permits to the detriment of newcomers and thereby indirectly counteracting the development of an increased competition. There are, however, no such supporting data to unequivocally draw such a conclusion. Instead, the fear of that this would be the case appears to motivate the measures proposed.

The 2004 study found that the introduction of international food chains had brought about enhanced competition, at least to some extent, whereby overall prices had been reduced. The gap to the EU average had dropped but was still considered too high. The growing importance of private labels was not seen as a problem but rather as a sign of increased competition. Again, the importance of local municipalities' planning activities was given special attention. It appears that inter-retailer competition (including that between private labels) were more important than the possibility of smaller producers to get access to shelf space in existing stores.

The inter-Nordic study in 2005 found that although food prices had decreased over the last 5–10 years, they were still between 12 and 24 % higher than the European average. However, increases in food prices were lower than elsewhere. Eliminating for VAT and the low promotional activities in the Nordic countries, the difference turned out to be lower, some 6–12 %, i.e., still significantly higher that the EU-15 average. Food supply was found to be narrower that in, e.g., France, although the general findings remain somewhat unclear.

Consumer demand was deemed notably heterogenic between the Nordic countries, despite the similar demographical characteristics. Consumers had displayed an increasing interest for "exotic" food but remained traditional in their demand as national dishes dominated the dinner tables in the Nordic countries. The nature of demand had also changed over the years as interest had been growing for quality, ethical considerations and sustainability in the food sector. Such products were growing in demand. The impact of these changes in demand in relation to competition has not been explored in further detail.

The study noted the growing importance for super- and hypermarkets as well as discount stores in the retail level of distribution. The overall concentration level had grown even further, which entailed a shift in the balance of market power to the benefit of large retailers. Concerns were raised that even though lower prices were envisaged, this might occur at the expense of product diversity in the store shelves. The increased concentration in the retail level was found to exhibit the hallmarks of stable tacit collusion, increasing the risk for reduced manufactures' prices not being passed on to consumers. Also, the cost structure was found to be less favourable in the retail sector as a result of wages in general being higher in the Nordic countries. The establishment of Lidl as a new player marked a change towards increased internationalisation of the trade, although the assortment and marketing remained national. Although only anecdotal evidence exists, milk products turned out to be especially difficult to sell in Sweden unless it had Swedish origin. Changes in zoning regulation and application of such rules allowing for the development of hypermarkets and other large self-service stores with a wide range of goods and a large car park, usually situated outside a town, had also contributed positively to the increased competition.

The study also showed that the increased downstream concentration had led to vertical integration upstream, whereby the role of previously independent wholesalers and other middlemen had been taken over by the retail grocery chains to a large extent. This could naturally result in increased bargaining power amongst the retailers and increase efficiency by reducing double marginalisation. The trend was generally considered to be beneficial to consumers, but on the other hand no guarantees were in place to ensure that the efficiency benefits would be passed on to consumers either in full or at least in part. Furthermore, the more powerful position of buyers would also affect the suppliers, as they would have to supply distribution centres rather than individual shops. It appears safe to say that the bargaining power of the retail grocery sector has increased over the last decade considerably, although distributed over a few major players. Such increased buying power is expected to have effects on the structure of the upstream suppliers.

The 2009 report from the KKV showed that the concentration level is an important determinant for the level of mark-ups and thereby general price levels. Across Europe mark-ups were in the region of 13 percentage points, whereas the sparsely populated Sweden with higher concentration levels in the retail sector amounted to up to 27 percentage points in mark-up. The size of the local market was found to be a very important factor for mark-ups. A larger market allows in general for more differentiated products, which could imply higher and lower prices, albeit the supply and range of products would be larger and wider, respectively. According to the study, emphasis should be on the local markets; establishments of newcomers would only have effects on prices if new shops were introduced locally. Also, in this report, the impact of the municipality planning regulations was underlined, and in general, it was demonstrated that strict regulation and discriminatory measures tend to increase concentration levels and thereby reduce competition and increase prices.

The most recent study from 2011 showed that the consumer prices had been brought down so much that Swedish consumers did not pay more than other consumers in comparable EU countries. Margins in the food supply chain were found to be no higher than in comparable EU countries. The KKV found, at the outset, that the competition in the food supply chain was essentially functioning efficiently and that any extensive regulatory reforms were not warranted. Still, however, the focus remained on the Planning and Building Act, and it was considered that there was yet work to be done in order to reform that regulation to allow for better planning standards allowing increased establishments and thereby competition.

Apart from reforming the EU agricultural policies to allow for increased import of food grown out with the EU, that Sweden as a member state cannot influence alone, focus was put on a proposed checklist for local municipalities. Consequently, it was suggested that the checklist cover

1. a pronounced objective to facilitate newcomers for daily consumer goods and being permissive in that role,
2. facilitation of establishment when food supply chains have reached the conclusion that establishments are commercially viable,
3. a procedure resembling that in public procurement in order to facilitate a fair process for awarding permits to stakeholders wishing to establish locally,
4. increased transparency in the application of planning rules, and
5. unification of the planning process and permit granting across communities in order to make application of rules more foreseeable.

To summarise, the studies conducted over the years have revealed an increased concentration and building up of buyer power in the retail grocery sector. At the same time, competition appears to be more efficient than before, offering consumers wider range of products and lower prices in general. This may seem paradoxical that increased concentration does not necessarily imply reduced effective competition. Also, this put existing co-operations in the retail grocery sector in another light. Co-operation that would normally be viewed as distrustful from a competition law point of view is not necessarily or inherently detrimental to consumers. This makes application of competition law in the retail grocery sector particularly difficult since enforcement against agreements that at face value are anti-competitive may have adverse effects on consumers and the efficiency of competition. This is, however, well in line with existing legislation as the conditions for exemption under Article 101(3) TFEU and its national counterpart may indeed be fulfilled. This could also explain the few cases so far related to abuse of dominance and anti-competitive behaviour, notwithstanding that the contrary could have been expected in the light of the serious concerns put forward in the different report over the last decade. There are, however, some unresolved issues related to the possibility of smaller and local producers' access to shelf space and whether the current state of the industry may mirror in supply the growing demand for locally produced and organic groceries and thereby satisfy a demand for true diversity.

16.4 Merger Control in the Grocery Retail Sector

16.4.1 Thresholds for Merger Control in the Retail (or the Grocery Retail) Sector

There are no special rules for concentrations in the retail sector in Sweden. Concentrations are instead subject to general rules enshrined in Section 4 on merger control of the Competition Act. There is a mandatory notification requirement according to Article 6 of the Competition Act for concentrations if the combined aggregate turnover in Sweden of all the undertakings concerned in the preceding financial year exceeds SEK 1 billion and at least two of the undertakings concerned had a turnover in Sweden the preceding financial year that exceeds SEK 200 million for each of the undertakings.

In case the second requirement is not fulfilled, the KKV may require a party to a concentration to notify the concentration, where particular grounds exist for so doing, or a party and other participants in a concentration may voluntarily notify a concentration. The competent authority to assess concentrations that do not have a community dimension is entrusted to the KKV alone.

16.4.2 The Legal Delineation of the Relevant Product (or Service) Markets in the Grocery Sector at the Retail Level

The relevant market is delineated according the exact same standards as those applied by the EU Commission. Therefore, the test relevant market comprising the relevant product market and relevant geographic market is based on the EU case law and the notice on the definition of the relevant market and applied in the very same as laid down by the EU Commission.[21] The definition of the relevant market will always take the prevailing market conditions into consideration, and there are therefore no presumptions regarding the store formats. Consumer demand will be the most important factor to consider, and as demand has shifted over the last decades it is not unlikely that this will have an impact on both product and geographic markets. There are no other statutory provisions in place in Sweden to define the market in any other way.

[21] Cf. Commission Notice on the definition of relevant market for the purposes of Community competition law, OJ 1997 C 372, p. 5. See also NJA 2008 p. 120, *Bornholmstrafikken* and MD 2013:5, *TeliaSonera*.

Some references have been made by the KKV to the Commission's decisional practice, and full range grocery retailers have been found to constitute an own product/service market where smaller shops (special shops, kiosks, petrol stations) are viewed as complements forming a distinct separate market from the full-range stores.[22]

Earlier case law has found the grocery retail market to be a distinct product market, at least in cases involving collusion on prices amongst retailers.[23]

16.4.3 Definition of the Geographic Markets for the Retail Grocery Sector?

Like the product market, there are no statutory provisions governing the definition of the relevant market, and the definition is done in accordance with the notice on the definition of the relevant market. There are very few cases on concentrations in the retail grocery sector. Some 40 cases have been notified in total; however, they cover the food industry as a whole, and only a few cases concern the retail level, and all have been cleared. No cases have been brought before the Swedish courts. The relevant market appears in general to be national at most and in same cases regional. However, the KKV decisional practice indicates even narrower geographical areas such as local municipalities or towns.[24]

Earlier case law has more in detail analysed the geographic market. In the *VIVO* case, the Swedish Market Court dealt with a calculation system that was shared amongst independent retailers. The court held that the starting point should be the area within which the retailers are conducting trade and where the co-operation has effect. The retailers were active in the greater Stockholm area, the island of Gotland and around the city of Södertälje (a major town some 35 km south of Stockholm). It was assumed that the retailers had their clientele and deposition within that area. At least it was not proven that any significant trade was done outside that area. Whether the market should be defined narrower, i.e. to the immediate nearby area of the individual shops, the Market Court held that the consumers' possibility to source groceries elsewhere, bearing in mind communication possibilities, did not

[22] KKV decision 747/2006, *ICA AB/Netto*. See also KKV Decision 744/2002, *Fri Mat ek. för. and Axfood AB (publ.)*. This was also in line with the Commission's decision in *Kesko/Tuko*, where the Commission held that "... the relevant market consists of the provision of a basket of fresh and dry food-stuffs, and non-food household consumables sold in a supermarket environment. The market does not include sales at specialised stores, kiosks and petrol stations. Instead these outlets provide a service that is complementary to those of supermarkets". See Commission decision of 20 November 1996, M.784, *Kesko/Tuko*, p. 20.

[23] MD 1997:11, *VIVO Stockholm ekonomisk förening and members of VIVO Stockholm ek. för. v Konkurrensverket*.

[24] KKV decision 747/2006, *ICA AB/Netto*.

imply that the market should be defined so narrowly. Instead, the market was defined as the greater region of Östergötland and the island of Gotland.[25]

16.4.4 The Swedish View on the Growth of Concentration of Grocery Retail Networks

The growing concentration has been viewed as problematic from a competition point of view. As indicated above in the reports commissioned by the KKV, about half of the price difference between Sweden and other comparable countries was ascribed to the weak competition, i.e., the oligopoly situation in Sweden. Lately, the concentration is even higher than before, but prices have decreased. Some new players are now active in the market, but despite the increased concentration the oligopoly has apparently been capable of yielding effective competition in the retail level of the distribution chain. Therefore, concentration levels as such do no longer appear to be a major concern. On the contrary, the KKV has concluded 2 years ago that the market is functioning efficiently.

16.4.5 Impact of Increasing Level of Concentration at the Retail Level in Relation to Mergers Amongst Grocery Suppliers

A few cases within the food industry have dealt with the concept of countervailing buyer power. In the *Arla/Milko* case,[26] the KKV considered the possible countervailing power of the retail chains vis-à-vis dairy companies. The KKV found that there was a mutual interdependence between the dairy companies and the retail grocery sector; however, most retailers, insofar as they had the possibility to source dairy products independently, did at most have two alternative suppliers of dairy products. Therefore, any countervailing bargaining power did not neutralise the restrictive effects of the concentration. A similar reasoning was applied in the *Carlsberg/Pripps Rignes* case.[27] Following the acquisition of biggest national brewery Pripps, the combined market shares of the parties in the concentration case would be more than 50 %. Such a strong position would, according to the KKV, enable Carlsberg to exert upward pricing pressure towards the retail sector, despite the existence of countervailing buyer power.

Stronger evidence for countervailing bargaining power has been found in other cases. In the *Cloetta/Leaf* case,[28] which concerned confectionary and chocolate

[25] MD 1997:11, *VIVO Stockholm ekonomisk förening and members of VIVO Stockholm ek. för. v Konkurrensverket*. Similar delineation of markets have been done in the KKV decision 570/95, *Kooperativa Detaljhandelsgruppen AB (KDAB)/Konsum Öst, ek.för.*

[26] KKV decision 445/2011, *Arla Foods amba/Milko ek. för.*

[27] KKV decision 615/2000, *Carlsberg A/S and Carlsberg Breweries A/Pripps Ringnes AB.*

[28] KKV decision 841/2011, *Cloetta AB publ/Leaf Holland B.V.*

products, the KKV held that retailers did have bargaining power, at least their position was described in a double negation in that the buyers did not possess insignificant buyer power. Also, in the concentration case *Fazer/Lantmännen Färskbröd*,[29] the KKV focused on the considerable buyer power possessed by the four major retail chains in Sweden, and it was held unlikely that the acquiring firm subsequent to the concentration would be in any position to exert selling power against the retailers. The KKV reached a similar conclusion in the *Swedish Meats/ SLP Pärsons* case,[30] which concerned a concentration for meat and meat products. Essentially, the same buyers were in focus, and the KKV held that alongside strong competition from imported meat and meat products, the countervailing buyer power from the retail chains would counteract the stronger upstream position that Swedish Meats would have after the concentration. The same findings have been put forward by the KKV for other suppliers to the retail grocery sector, the bread sector in the *Cerealia/Juvel* case,[31] as well as the milling industry for bakery flour.

Countervailing buyer power has proven to be a viable defence or at least an important factor to consider in concentration cases in Sweden. For most suppliers, the retail sector possesses significant bargaining power, as it has not been uncommon to observe that concentration's timely travel upwards in the distribution chain, i.e. the high concentration level in the retail level, is likely to trigger upstream mergers. Only when the upstream level is very concentrated, like the dairy industry, such countervailing bargaining power has been considered offset by the KKV.

16.4.6 Impact of Increasing Level of Concentration Amongst the Suppliers of Grocery Products in Relation to Mergers in the Grocery Retail Sector

In general, the countervailing buyer power argument has been raised as a "shield" against alleged problematic concentrations. However, there are no cases indicating the mirror image that the argument would be used as a "sword", i.e. an argument in support of creating buyer power. Concentration has generally not been driven by acquisition in Sweden, and growths of the chains are merely attributed to new establishments and closing down by competitors. Essentially, there are still the same three to four major players with increased joint market share, albeit market shares have changes amongst them.

[29] KKV decision 606/2008, *Fazer Bageri/Lantmännen Färskbröd AB*.

[30] KKV decision 123/2006, *Swedish Meats ek. för./SLP Pärsons AB*.

[31] KKV decision 694/2000, *Cerealia AB/Kvarn AB Juvel*.

16.4.7 Remedies Imposed in Case of Concentration in the Retail Grocery Sector

Concentration cases within the retail level of the distribution chain remain few in numbers. However, in the *ICA/Netto* case,[32] the KKV raised concerns about ICA's strong market position in the cities of Kumla, Uppsala, Enköping, Västerås and the municipality of Katrineholm. ICA voluntarily offered to divest 14 of the notified 21 stores in a non-discriminatory way. This undertaking was accepted by the KKV, and the acquisition was cleared. Similar remedies were considered in the upstream dairy sector in the *Arla/Milko* case. The acquiring dairy group Arla offered to divest several trademarks and to sell off one of the biggest dairy plants situated in mid-Sweden. The plant was subsequently acquired by the COOP. Thereby, the retail group reversed a long-standing strategy and integrated upstream further than the wholesale level to now encompass manufacturing as well.

16.4.8 Significance of Internet Stores in the Retail Grocery Sector

Groceries sold over the Internet are still not developed in Sweden. Although no official statistics has been found, it is estimated to be below one per cent of total sales.[33] The sector is, however, expected to grow rapidly, and there are several smaller players that have established business in home delivery systems for food. The major retailers such as ICA and COOP have launched such services recently.

In terms of regulation, the same rules apply for handling food sold over the Internet as for brick-and-mortar shops. The rules are mostly related to food safety, a harmonised area of law within the EU.[34]

---

[32] KKV decision 747/2006, *ICA AB/Netto*.

[33] Dagens Industri section 2, DI Dimension, Nr 4, May 16, 2013.

[34] See Regulation 178/2002 of the European Parliament and of the Council of 28 January 2002 laying down the general principles and requirements of food law, establishing the European Food Safety Authority and laying down procedures in matters of food safety, OJ 2002 L 31, p. 1. In addition, there are also a large number of detailed EU Regulations in several fields that have an impact on the Swedish food sector. The Swedish Food Act (Livsmedelslagen SFS 2006:804) complements the EU Regulations. It also contains rules on food control authorities and sanctions for violating the regulations. Furthermore, EU Directives are transposed into National Food Agency's (Livsmedelsverket) regulations and published in the NFA's own Code of Statutes, LIVSFS (previously SLVFS). The NFA has been authorised to issue legislation primarily as laid down in the Food Act and the Food Ordinance (livsmedelsförordningen, SFS 2006:813).

16.5 Abuse of Buying Power

16.5.1 Applicable Test Used by Enforcement Agencies or Courts

Abuse of market power, either in the form of monopoly or monopsony power, is regulated in the Competition Act, Section 2, Article 7, whereby any abuse by one or more undertakings of a dominant position on the market shall be prohibited. The prohibition is a national counterpart to Article 102 TFEU, and Sweden is applying the same rules on abuse of dominance as EU rules. Also, Articles 101 and 102 are directly applicable for national courts and the KKV. Therefore, the relevant EU case law, the concepts of dominance and abuse will be fully applicable in these cases.

The finding of a dominant position is in itself not a recrimination under Swedish law. Like in Article 102 TFEU, there are identical examples of abuses under Swedish law but no *per se* prohibitions on certain market conduct. Instead, one would have to rely upon any of the presumptions of abuse that has been laid down in EU case law. These do not, however, create a non-rebuttable *per se* finding of violation of competition law.

There are no cases on abuse of buyer power on file. However, dependency can be viewed in different ways. The mirror image of buyer power, i.e. selling power or the abuse of a position of a mandatory or essential trading party, has given rise to several cases, relating to several kinds of abuses like excessively high prices, discriminatory behaviour, etc.

16.6 Competition Law Enforcement in the Swedish Grocery Retail Sector

There are no cases related to the conduct of grocery retailers in the last 5 years from the Swedish courts or the KKV. The bulk of older cases relates to the application of individual exemptions or negative clearance for anti-competitive agreements. Subsequent to the abolishment of the notification of such agreements and making the national counterpart to Article 101(3) TFEU directly applicable for undertakings to rely upon, the strand of such cases came to a complete stop.

16.6.1 Application of Competition Law on Small Geographic Local Markets and Micro-Violations

In Sweden, as within the EU, there is a minimum threshold for the application of the competition rules. It is first and foremost a legal requirement that anti-competitive agreements or concerted practices must, to an appreciable extent, be capable of preventing, restricting or distorting competition. The Swedish *de minimis* rules state that companies with a turnover of less than SEK 30 million in the last fiscal year can jointly hold a market share of a maximum of 15 % without being subject to the application of the rules against anti-competitive agreements.[35] However, the existence of any blacklisted restrictions will set that exemption aside. Also, the definition of the relevant market will be very important. Micro-cartels typically imply a very narrow definition of the geographical market, on which smaller undertakings are active, or least involving a limited number of companies belonging to a larger chain. However, to date, very few examples of micro-cartels exist, although there are examples of smaller cartels being sanctioned.

A new instrument that is seemingly aimed especially at the smaller cartels is the fine order enshrined in Chapter 6, Article 16 of the Competition Act. Instead of instituting proceedings before the court of first instance regarding an administrative fine, the KKV may, in uncontested cases, order a company to pay such a fine. Several criteria must be met before such an order can be issued, and the violators must also concede to the order as the KKV otherwise would have to bring the case before the Court.[36]

16.6.2 Competition Concerns Related to the Internal Governance Structure of Grocery Retail Networks

In Sweden, there have been no cases involving an assessment of the internal governance of grocery retail networks insofar that would be problematic to a competition point of view. However, the largest retail player, ICA, is essentially made up of independent retailers in a complex structure of cross-ownership, vertical and horizontal restraints, which may or may not be subject to the competition rules. Paradoxically, such restraints have not generated any cases, seemingly because the internal structure of ICA has laid down a well-functioning incentive of local retailers and consistent market behaviour over a longer period that has been considered beneficial to consumers.

16.6.3 Recommended Resale Prices in the Retail Grocery Sector and Resale Price Maintenance in the Swedish Grocery Retail Sector

The Swedish rules on resale price maintenance (the "RPMs") in vertical agreements are in essence the same as the EU rules. It has been expected that the more lenient approach to RPM following the ruling in *Leegin Leather*[37] in the U.S. would bring

[35] Konkurrensverkets allmänna råd om avtal av mindre betydelse (bagatellavtal) som inte omfattas av förbudet i 2 kap. 1 § konkurrenslagen (2008:579), KKVFS 2009:1.

[36] See L. Henriksson, *Two Novelties in Swedish Competition Law: Fine Order and Trading Prohibition – A Critical Review*, in H.H. Lidgard, (ed.) National Developments In the Intersection of IPR and Competition Law, Swedish Studies in European Law, vol. 3, 2011, pp. 263–281.

[37] See U.S. Supreme Court ruling in *Leegin Creative Leather Products*, Inc. V. PKS, Inc., 551 U.S. 877.

about a change of the *per se* approach to other price maintenance measures than recommended prices and maximum prices. Therefore, the restriction of the buyer's ability to determine its resale price, without prejudice to the possibility of the supplier to impose a maximum sale price or recommend a sale price, provided that it does not amount to a fixed or minimum sale price as a result of pressure from, or incentives offered by, any of the parties, would be considered a hard-core restraint not possible to be exempted under Swedish law.[38] In general, obligations related to minimum or fixed prices are considered as hard-core restraints in vertical agreements.

The Swedish Market Court ruled in *Månpocket* that recommended prices pre-printed to the cover of books did not amount to actual recommended prices as it required from resellers to take active steps to remove the affixed retail price (if even possible) or to cover it with new labels. Most resellers did not do so, and the recommended price did in fact entail resale price maintenance in practice in violation of competition law.[39]

16.6.4 Reselling Below Cost, De-listing of Suppliers in Swedish Competition Law

The practice of selling low-priced products as such does not amount to a violation of competition law in Sweden, and there are no other available legal instruments to curb cheap import apart from macroeconomic measures. Selling at losses is not considered to be unlawful in Sweden, unless the pricing practice would meet the criteria for predatory pricing as laid down by the EU courts.[40]

De-listing of suppliers would in theory be the monopsonists' mirror image of refusal to supply. There have been no cases of de-listing of suppliers in the retail grocery sector. However, some 18 years ago, a dispute arose between ICA and one of its suppliers in the *Master Foods* case,[41] and the KKV assessed a de-listing practice of ICA, which was considered a collective boycott in violation of competition law. Uncertainty related to the application of the block exemption regulation

[38] Cf. Article 4.a of Commission Regulation 330/2010 of 20 April 2010 on the application of Article 101(3) of the Treaty on the Functioning of the European Union to categories of vertical agreements and concerted practices, OJ 2010 L 102, p. 1, in conjunction with Swedish Act (2008:581) concerning block exemption on vertical anti-competitive agreements. Generally about RPMs in Sweden, see further L. Henriksson, *Distributionsavtal – vertikala avtal och konkurrensrättsliga aspekter*, Norstedts Stockholm 2012, p. 126.

[39] MD 2002:5, *Svenska Bokhandlareföreningen v Månadens Bok, Bonnierförlagen AB/Norstedts Förlag AB/Bokförlaget Forum AB/Perigab AB HB*.

[40] Cf. ECJ, case C-62/86, *AKZO Chemie BV v Commission*, ECR 1991, p. I-3359; ECJ, case C-333/94 P, *Tetra Pak International SA v Commission*, ECR 1996, p. I-5951; ECJ, case C-202/07 P, *France Télécom SA v Commission of the European Communities*, ECR 2009, p. I-2369 and case CJEU, C-209/10, *Post Danmark A/S v Konkurrencerådet* (not yet published).

[41] KKV Decision 93/95, *ICA Handlarnas AB v Master Foods*.

led to the dismissal of the case, although the KKV envisaged its intention to sue for administrative fines if the practice would be repeated.

In general, refusal to purchase may amount, according to the KKV, to an abuse in some situations when the buyer enjoys a legal monopoly and without objective justification refuses to accept yet another supplier. The arguments are more or less the same as for essential facilities. Discontinuing an existing trading relationship with a supplier will be, nonetheless, treated differently, most likely as a discriminatory behaviour if undertaken by a dominant buyer.

16.6.5 Excessive Prices in Swedish Competition Law

Excessively high prices can at least in theory amount to an abuse of dominance. The legal standard for establishing this kind of exploitative abuse is in Sweden the same as established by the ECJ in the *United Brands* case,[42] i.e., charging a price, which is excessive because it has no reasonable relation to the economic value of the product supplied.

As lastly demonstrated in the *Helsingborgs Hamn* cases,[43] it is most difficult to practically draw the line between high—yet still legal prices—and illegally exorbitantly high prices. When considering cost measures, profitability and demand factors, this becomes even in theory a very difficult exercise indeed. In practice, excessive pricing has therefore mostly been related to cases where there also has been a restriction of intra-community trade.[44]

16.7 Few Regulations Aimed at the Retail Grocery Sector

There are no general sector-specific regulation to govern the structure of the retail grocery market structure in Sweden, apart from general competition law and the merger control regulation in the Competition Act. In addition to competition law, there is general legislation for marketing practices and unfair market practice. These regulations apply to all industries and do not directly affect the structure of the retail grocery sector. What does have a direct impact on retailers, on the other hand, would be the planning and zoning regulations, as mentioned above.

The way retailers are formally organised does not appear to affect constraints in general. However, the still ongoing vertical integration and development of

[42] ECJ, case 27/76, *United Brands Company and United Brands Continentaal BV v Commission of the European Communities*, ECR 1978, p. 207.

[43] Commission decisions of 23 July 2004, COMP/A.36.568/D3, *Scandlines Sverige AB v Port of Helsingborg*, and case COMP/A.36.570/D3, *Sundbusserne v Port of Helsingborg*.

[44] See, e.g., N. Wahl, *Exploitative high prices and Europan competition law – a personal reflection*. In: The Pros and Cons of High Prices, KKV 2007, pp. 47–64; L. Henriksson, *Konkurrensrättsöverträdelser – Ekonomisk analys i den juridiska processen*, Norstedts, 2013, p. 213.

distribution centres at strategic geographical locations have become an important competitive factor for the retail chains. To withstand the increased competition and be able to offer even more favourable prices, the logistic function has become strategically important.

16.7.1 Consumer Protection Rules Applying to Internet Retail Stores in Relation to Brick-and-Mortar Stores

Internet grocery stores are subject to complementary legislation in order to deal with the challenges that stem from the fact that purchasing is not done at the seller's premises. When Contracting between sellers (undertakings) and consumers over the Internet Distance and Door-to-Door sales Act will apply, which, *inter alia*, entails a right for consumers to cancel the contract within a fortnight period. However, foodstuffs are not covered by that legislation for obvious reasons, as many of the products are perishable. Other than that, the same rules apply for Internet retail stores.

As mentioned above, increasing prices has traditionally been a major concern of the legislator. Already mentioned above, the general Price Control Act[45] is still in force, although the act was originally intended to be used during wartime or at risk of war to complement the rules on rationing. In the 1970s and the 1980s, it was also used as a macroeconomic tool to curb inflation, including prices for grocery retail goods. A fundamental change in the overall macroeconomic policy at the end of the 1980s marked the end of the application of that law, although it is still in force. There is currently no price control on any grocery products in Sweden, and it appears highly unlikely that price control would be used in the grocery retail sector unless exceptional circumstances will arise.

16.7.2 Regulation of Large-Scale Food Retailing and Vertical Relationships Between Suppliers and Retailers

There is no specific Swedish market regulation in force to actively achieve a level-playing field or to ensure fairness in general, apart from the competition law. In contract law, on the other hand, there are two acts that govern unfair contract terms in B2C and B2B settings, respectively.[46] The two laws complement Article 36 of the Contracts Act, according to which unfair contracts or contract terms may be adjusted or nullified. Again, these provisions are generally applicable and not aimed at any particular industry.

[45] SFS 1989:978.

[46] Lag (1994:1512) om avtalsvillkor i konsumentförhållanden and lag (1984:292) om avtalsvillkor mellan näringsidkare.

Special rules do, however, apply to farmers if they are members of what is called a "primary agricultural association". Such organisations are under Section 1, Article 7 of the Competition Act defined as an economic association, whose members are individual farmers or other undertakings engaged in agriculture, horticulture or forestry. If associations of such undertakings are members of an association, the latter is, however, only regarded as a primary agricultural association providing that such associations only contain local associations of undertakings operating activities of the kind specified. The Act[47] on the meaning of the terms agricultural, horticultural and forestry produce, as used in the Competition Act, contains special provisions on what is meant by such produce.

According to Section 2, Article 4 of the Competition Act, the prohibition against anti-competitive agreement does not apply to those agreements within a primary agricultural association, or its subsidiaries, that concern co-operation between the members of the association on

1) the production, collection, processing, sale or related activities such as the use of jointly owned facilities, storing, preparation, distribution or marketing of agricultural, horticultural or forestry produce, or
2) the purchase of goods or services for such activity as is referred to in 1).

The first paragraph does not, however, apply to agreements that have as their object or effect the prevention or impairment of free mobility of a member on the market with respect to choosing a buyer or a supplier, to the possibility of leaving the association, in other respects of equivalent importance or where selling prices are directly or indirectly fixed for goods when the sale takes place directly between the member and a third party.

Other than these sector-specific rules for upstream producers, the grocery sector is subject to the full application of the general competition rules.

16.8 Looking Ahead: Recommended Improvements to the Competitive Landscape in the Grocery Retail Sector

Currently, there appears to be very little room for new sector-specific regulation in the grocery retail sector in Sweden. Over the years, very little has been voiced about the need for special regulation, and focus has been on facilitating entry to the market—especially on local markets. Market concentration has been viewed both as a threat to consumers; however, large players have also meant fierce competition between the oligopolists, and the trade has evolved considerably over the last years as the product range has widened and prices have been lowered in general. The introduction of large international discount retailers has put pressure on the incumbent retail chains.

[47] SFS 2000:1025.

Although vertical integration and large-scale purchasing are very important factors for the retailers, competition is still manifested locally and the role of local municipalities is crucial in the development of competition. It is not possible in Sweden for incumbents to enter into exclusivity agreements with local communities on grounds of non-discrimination obligations on local government. Incumbent firms do own considerable amount of real estate and buildings, however mostly for internal needs. Renting to third parties is very limited in scope, although, e.g., ICA Fastigheter (part of the ICA group) has become a major player as a landlord for commercial premises—especially around the new developed hypermarkets sites.

In 2011, changes were introduced in the Building and Planning Act,[48] and it is now mandatory for local authorities to pay special attention to economic growth and the development of competition in the planning or zoning procedures. How exactly this should be done in individual matters remains unclear. At the very least, however, the authorities cannot ignore these factors in their decisional practice.

There are still challenges to be dealt with, like abuse of appeal of planning decision in order to delay or oust competitors to the incumbents, long handling procedures and non-consistent procedures between communities. All in all, there appears currently not to be any pressing needs for major legislative reform to boost competition in the retail grocery sector. Fine-tuning of the existing administrative rules appears to be more in focus. There is still, however, room for improvement and better efficiency and consistency in the application of the rules that directly and indirectly affect the competitive situation.

[48] SFS 2010:900.

Switzerland 17

Bernhard C. Lauterburg

17.1 Introduction

This report addresses the characteristics of competition on the food retail market in Switzerland and the legal framework competition is subject to. As will be outlined below, the Swiss food retail market is largely dominated by two large retailers that are organized as cooperatives. Despite the high degree of concentration, acquisitions by the two large retailers have occurred in the past and were not considered to harm efficient competition. Furthermore, market entries of foreign retailers, namely the German Lidl and Aldi retailers, could be observed in the past.

While there are no provisions generally taking precedence over the Swiss Law on Cartels (the "LCart")[1] in the food retail sector, hence limiting competition, the food retail sector is affected by a multitude of norms limiting its *competitiveness*, such as high degree of protection in the agricultural sector (e.g., import quotas, regulations and agreements with respect to the price of milk on the manufacturer and supplier level), technical barriers to trade (e.g., labeling regulations) or higher labor costs.

17.2 The Food Retail Market in Switzerland

The food retail market is largely dominated by the two large retailers Migros and Coop with a combined market share of roughly 80 % on the retail market. Private labels account for a large share of the product range of both Migros and Coop. Other

[1] Federal Law of 6 October 1995 on Cartels and other Restraints on Competition (Law on Cartels, LCart; SR 251).

B.C. Lauterburg (✉)
Prager Dreifuss Ltd., Berne, Switzerland
e-mail: bernhard.lauterburg@prager-dreifuss.com

P. Kobel et al. (eds.), *Antitrust in the Groceries Sector & Liability Issues in Relation to Corporate Social Responsibility*, LIDC Contributions on Antitrust Law, Intellectual Property and Unfair Competition, DOI 10.1007/978-3-662-45753-5_17

retailers include Aldi, Lidl, Denner (recently acquired and now owned by Migros), Spar, Primo/Vis-à-Vis, Volg and others. Switzerland historically has a high degree of concentration in the grocery retail sector. The two largest retailers are organized as cooperatives with a history dating back to the end of the nineteenth century (Coop, 1890) and early twentieth century (Migros, 1925).

In 2007, Accenture undertook a study of the Swiss retail market, which was referred to by the competition authorities in the case Coop/Carrefour in 2008. According to the study, a large majority purchase goods for daily use at either Migros or Coop and participate in their loyalty program. Swiss consumers attach great importance to accessibility and a choice of fresh products and regional products and such from ecological and sustainable production.[2] While Aldi and Lidl pursued an aggressive market entry strategy, recent research by Credit Suisse reveals a slowdown of their expansion within Switzerland but notes in the context of shopping tourism their strong position at the German–Swiss border.[3] The combined market share of Aldi and Lidl, however, remains low, at 5 %.[4]

17.3 Legal Framework

17.3.1 The Law on Cartels

The LCart sets out the fundamental provisions on behavioral and structural control in order to prevent the harmful economic or social effects of cartels and other restraints of competition and for this purpose aims at promoting competition in the interests of a liberal market economy.[5] The retail grocery sector is subject to the behavioral[6] and structural provisions set forth in the LCart to the extent that there are no other statutory provisions, such as provisions that establish an official market or price system, taking precedence over the LCart. We are not aware of such provisions taking precedence over the LCart.[7]

To date, there are no per se prohibitions in a strict sense under the LCart, neither in relation to behavioral nor merger control. Hence, in each single case, the competition authority must establish the subjective and objective elements of the concerned provision and determine whether the conduct in question can be justified. The proposed amendment to the LCart, which is currently discussed in Parliament,

[2] Coop/Carrefour, RPW/DPC 2008/4, pp. 593 *et seq*., paras. 146 *et seq*.

[3] Credit Suisse, Retail Outlook 2013, pp. 19–20.

[4] Credit Suisse, Retail Outlook 2013, p. 20.

[5] See Article 1 LCart.

[6] The LCart does not include provisions on unfair competition. The LCart governs horizontal and vertical agreements, abuse of dominance and merger control. Unfair competition is dealt with in the Federal Law of 19 December 1986 on Unfair Competition (Law on Unfair Competition, LUC; SR 241).

[7] *Cf*., CoopForte, RPW/DPC 2005/1, pp. 146 et seq., paras. 20 and 34.

provides for a directly effective prohibition of certain horizontal and vertical agreements (price fixing, agreement on quantities or territorial allocation) and a shift in the burden of proof from the competition authorities to the undertakings.

Pursuant to Article 45(1) LCart, the competition authority shall constantly monitor the status of competition. In this context, the competition authority may conduct informal market observations that may or may not result in a preliminary investigation (Article 26 LCart) or a formal investigation (Article 27 LCart). In a preliminary investigation, the competition authority may propose measures to eliminate or prevent restraints of competition (Article 26(2) LCart). While the details of market observations are normally not revealed, the competition authority releases information on the number of market observations and the products covered, such as in 2011 gluten-free products[8] and whether it found any indications of potentially anticompetitive conduct. The outcome of preliminary investigations as well as formal investigations is published in a report or, respectively, a decision.

17.3.2 The Competition Authority's Eyes on the Retail Grocery Sector

In the past, the competition authorities repeatedly examined the retail grocery sector on the occasion of concentrations involving the two large retailers Migros and Coop.[9] In *CoopForte*,[10] the competition authorities examined the structures on the supply market in the context of an alleged abuse of buying power by Coop.

With the high euro/CHF exchange rate, the passing on of currency exchange benefits to consumers has been placed on the agenda of competition enforcement agencies and consumer advocacy organizations. The Competition Commission even established a subsection on this issue on its website,[11] and the Price Supervision Authority noted in a report that retailers—with some delays—largely pass on currency exchange benefits to consumers but that Switzerland for structural reasons will remain a nation with a high price level.[12] Credit Suisse noted in their market research that the price level for grocery products decreased by 6 % in the last 3 years.[13]

[8] *See* Annual Report of the Competition Commission, RPW/DPC 2012/1, p. 4.

[9] Given the high degree of concentration in the retail grocery sector involving the two large retailers Migros and Coop, virtually all relevant case law involves these entities. In 2003, Coop acquired Waro, which at that time was owned by the parent company of Denner. In 2008, Migros acquired Denner, the then largest discounter in Switzerland, however subject to significant remedies, and Coop acquired sole control over the operating company of the Swiss Carrefour stores with Carrefour withdrawing from the Swiss market.

[10] CoopForte, RPW/DPC 2005/1, pp. 146 et seq.

[11] http://www.weko.admin.ch/aktuell/01054/index.html?lang=de.

[12] Report of the Price Supervision Authority of 20 September 2012.

[13] Credit Suisse, Retail Outlook 2013, p. 10.

17.4 Merger Control

17.4.1 Thresholds

The retail grocery sector is subject to the same threshold levels as all other industries. Accordingly, transactions are subject to notification if the undertakings concerned together reported a turnover of at least 2 billion Swiss francs, or a turnover in Switzerland of at least 500 million Swiss francs, and at least two of the undertakings concerned each reported a turnover in Switzerland of at least 100 million Swiss francs (Article 9(1) LCart). In addition to these numerical criteria, notification shall exceptionally be mandatory if one of the undertakings concerned has been held to be dominant in a market in Switzerland in proceedings under this Act in a final and nonappealable decision and if the concentration concerns either that market or an adjacent market or a market upstream or downstream thereof (Article 9(4) LCart). Currently, Migros is subject to this exception.[14]

17.4.2 Product Market

The product market comprises all those goods or services that are regarded as interchangeable by consumers on the one hand and by suppliers on the other hand with regard to their characteristics and intended use (Article 11(3)(a) MCO).[15] Hence, authorities distinguish between a market for sales (downstream) and a market for supply (upstream).

On the downstream market, the authorities base their assessment on a range of products that typically include fast-moving consumer goods. According to the decision in *Migros/Denner*, the range of products would typically include food, near-food and nonfood products for daily use, with an emphasis the basis of a one-stop shopping approach.[16] Excluded from the relevant product market were specialty and convenience stores,[17] although it was not excluded that such store formats may have a certain disciplinary effect on traditional retailers.[18] Also excluded from the relevant product market was "shopping tourism."[19]

In *Migros/Denner*, the competition authorities noted that the retail grocery sector cannot generally be considered the only distribution channel for manufacturers of

[14] *See* Migros/Denner, RPW/DPC 2008/1, pp. 129 et seq., para. 4 of the operative part of the decision.

[15] Ordinance of the Swiss Federal Council of 17 June 1996 on the Control of Concentrations of Undertakings (Merger Control Ordinance, MCO; SR 251.4).

[16] *See* Migros/Denner, RPW/DPC 2008/1, pp. 129 et seq., para. 164.

[17] *See* Migros/Denner, RPW/DPC 2008/1, pp. 129 et seq., para. 166 et seq.

[18] *See* Migros/Denner, RPW/DPC 2008/1, pp. 129 et seq., para. 185.

[19] *See* Migros/Denner, RPW/DPC 2008/1, pp. 129 et seq., para. 197 et seq. The authorities, however, did not exclude that "shopping tourism" may have a disciplinary effect on the retail sector.

retail business goods; however, the competition authorities hitherto left open whether gastronomy, hospitals, specialty stores, convenience shops and exportation should be considered a part of the relevant product market.[20]

In *Coop/Waro*,[21] *Migros/Denner*[22] and *Coop/Carrefour*,[23] the following food product markets were defined on the upstream market:

- dairy products, eggs;
- bread and pastry products;
- meat;
- frozen food products;
- traiteur/convenience (fresh and chilled);
- vegetables/salads;
- fruits;
- canned food/sauces;
- soups/cooking ingredients;
- basic foodstuffs/baking ingredients;
- hot beverages/cereals;
- confectionery/biscuits;
- snacks/apéro;
- pet food/pet supplies;
- alcoholic beverages;
- soft drinks.

In *Migros/Denner*, the competition authorities further had to determine whether the Migros-owned manufacturing businesses should be considered a part of the supply market.[24] The competition authorities determined that retailers consider products from integrated and independent manufacturers as substitutes (although the Migros-owned industries are normally favored over independent manufacturers), for which reason the Migros-owned industries belong the to relevant supply market.[25]

[20] *See* Migros/Denner, RPW/DPC 2008/1, pp. 129 et seq., para. 211.

[21] Coop/Waro, RPW/DPC 2003/3, pp. 559 et seq., para. 43.

[22] Migros/Denner, RPW/DPC 2008/1, pp. 129 et seq., para. 208.

[23] Coop/Carrefour, RPW/DPC 2008/4, pp. 593 et seq., para. 82.

[24] Note that Migros owns and operates various manufacturing businesses such as Jowa (bakery products), Bischofszell (convenience food), Midor (biscuits), Chocolat Frey (chocolate bars, confectionary), Aproz (mineral water), Delica (the largest coffee roaster in Switzerland), Mibelle (cosmetics). A full list is available at http://www.migros.ch/de/migros-gruppe.html.

[25] Migros/Denner, RPW/DPC 2008/1, pp. 129 et seq., paras. 224 et seq.

17.4.3 Geographic Market

The geographic market comprises the area in which, on the one hand, consumers purchase and, on the other hand, suppliers sell the goods or services that constitute the product market (Article 11(3)(b) MCO).

Referring to EU practice,[26] the competition authorities in *Migros/Denner* and *Coop/Carrefour*, as well as earlier in *Coop/EPA*, distinguished between a local market and a national market on the downstream market. The market radius of small retail stores was estimated at ca. 10 min, for medium retail stores at 15 min and for large-scale hypermarkets at 20 min.[27] Although the competition authorities considered that the relevant geographic market is local from a consumer perspective, pricing and sales policy of the large retail chains are coordinated on national level; hence, competition for consumers occurs on a national level.

As regards the upstream market, the competition authorities considered that it is at least national with a possibility that for nonperishable goods not subject to local consumer habits the relevant geographic market could be international.

17.4.4 Competition Analysis

17.4.4.1 Clearance Despite High Degree of Concentration

Concentrations that are subject to notification may be prohibited or authorized subject to conditions and obligations if the investigation indicates that the concentration creates or strengthens a dominant position liable to eliminate effective competition and does not improve the conditions of competition in another market such that the harmful effects of the dominant position can be outweighed.[28]

In both *Migros/Denner* and *Coop/Carrefour*, the authorities noted that the conditions for collective market power by Migros and Coop were satisfied and that disciplinary effects from the German discounters Aldi and Lidl on the *Migros/Coop* duopoly should not be overestimated.[29] The competition authorities determined that high market entry barriers existed in Switzerland. In *Migros/Denner*, the competition authorities distinguished among three types of market entry barriers: (1) structural entry barriers, (2) administrative entry barriers and (3) strategic entry

[26] Migros/Denner, RPW/DPC 2008/1, pp. 129 et seq., para. 236; Coop/Carrefour, RPW/DPC 2008/4, pp. 593 et seq., para. 103. Reference was made by the Swiss competition authorities to Rewe/Meinl (Commission Decision of 3 February 1999, M.1221), Rewe/Billa (Commission Decision of 27 August 1996, M.803), Ahold/Superdiplo (Commission Decision of 23 October 2000, M.2161) and Carrefour/Promodes (Commission Decision of 25 Janvier 2000, M.1684).

[27] Migros/Denner, RPW/DPC 2008/1, pp. 129 et seq., paras. 237 et seq.; Coop/Carrefour, RPW/DPC 2008/4, pp. 593 et seq., paras. 104 et seq.

[28] Article 10(2) LCart.

[29] Migros/Denner, RPW/DPC 2008/1, pp. 129 et seq., paras. 419 et seq.

barriers.[30] As regards structural barriers, the competition authorities noted that establishing a new retail network would require considerable investments due to the already high density of retail stores in Switzerland and the multilingualism prevalent in Switzerland. As regards administrative barriers, the competition authorities particularly referred to strict zoning and planning laws, nontariff barriers (Swiss-specific standards and prescriptions on product declaration), the high degree of protection in the agricultural sector (import restrictions). As regards strategic barriers, the competition authorities particularly noted the limited availability of prime retail locations as well as possible imbalances on the supply market.

Despite high market entry barriers, low existing and potential competition, the competition authorities cleared the transactions involving Migros and Denner on the one hand and Coop and Carrefour on the other hand, however, subject to certain remedies:

- In *Migros/Denner*,[31] where Migros acquired the discount chain Denner, substantial behavioral remedies were imposed on Migros. E.g., Migros was enjoined from integrating Denner, hence was obliged to operate Denner legally and organizationally independent entity with its own policy regarding pricing, product range and sales, loyalty programs of both Migros and Denner could not be integrated and/or merged, both Migros and Denner were enjoined from jointly procuring goods intended for resale and Migros was enjoined from acquiring any other retailers in Switzerland. In addition, Migros was ordered to waive exclusivity in relation to any product suppliers. With respect to the notification requirement, Migros was put under an obligation to notify any concentration on the grocery retail market independent of the threshold amounts (Article 9 (4) LCart).
- In *Coop/Carrefour*,[32] Coop was enjoined from acquiring any other retailers in Switzerland for a duration of 6 years, divest some of its retail space in certain areas. Same as in *Migros/Denner*, Coop was ordered to waive exclusivity in relation to any product suppliers.

In both cases, Migros and Coop could apply to waive or amend the remedies starting 1 January 2010[33] provided that the conditions on the retail market substantially changed (i.e., new market participants Lidl and Aldi operate a combined number of 250 retail stores in Switzerland). To our knowledge, Migros recently

[30] Migros/Denner, RPW/DPC 2008/1, pp. 129 et seq., paras. 383 et seq.; *see also* Coop/Carrefour, RPW/DPC 2008/4, pp. 593 et seq., paras. 313 et seq.

[31] Migros/Denner, RPW/DPC 2008/1, pp. 129 et seq.

[32] Coop/Carrefour, RPW/DPC 2008/4, pp. 593 et seq.

[33] Migros/Denner, RPW/DPC 2008/1, pp. 129 et seq., para. 1.12 of the operative part of the decision; Coop/Carrefour, RPW/DPC 2008/4, pp. 593 et seq., para. 1.6 of the operative part of the decision.

filed an application in this regard, and Credit Suisse states that by the end of 2012, Aldi and Lidl combined operate 250 stores.[34]

17.4.4.2 "Countervailing Force" of Retailers as an Argument to Put into Perspective the Emergence of Market Power

In various merger decisions concerning producers of retail products, the competition authorities touched on the issue of buying power by the large retailers. In this context, the competition authorities used the "countervailing force" of retailers as an argument to put into perspective the emergence of market power on certain producer markets as a result of such mergers amongst producers.[35]

17.4.4.3 Competitive Pressure by Internet Stores?

Although both large retailers operate Internet stores (Migros: LeShop; Coop: Coop@Home), Internet commerce to date only plays an insignificant role in the retail grocery sector. Both Internet stores achieved a combined turnover of approximately CHF 250 million, which represents only a small fraction of the overall retail turnover in the grocery sector (e.g., in 2012, Coop achieved an overall turnover in the food sector of more than CHF 12 billion). Internet and brick-and-mortar retail stores are subject to the same laws and regulations concerning grocery retail.

---

[34] Credit Suisse, Retail Outlook 2013, p. 20.

[35] *Cf.*, *e.g.*, Bell AG/SEG-Poulets AG (RPW/DPC 1998/3, pp. 392 et seq); Toni AG/Tochtergesellschaften der Säntis Holding AG (RPW/DPC 1999/1, pp 93 et seq); Unilever/Bestfoods (RPW/DPC 2001/4, pp. 701 et seq); Gemeinschaftsunternehmen The Coca-Cola Company/Nestlé (RPW/DPC 2001/4, pp. 746 et seq).

In "Bell AG/SEG-Poulets AG", the competition authorities noted the extraordinary vertical integration of Coop and Migros with respect to the slaughtering and distribution of poultry and the market power that came along with it. In other decisions, such as "Toni AG/Tochtergesellschaften der Säntis Holding AG" (concerning milk processing and the sale of milk products with combined market shares up to 75%) and "Gemeinschaftsunternehmen The Coca-Cola Company/Nestlé" (concerning soft drinks with combined market shares up to 55%), the competition authorities also noted and used as an argument the vertical integration of retailers to put into perspective the increase of market shares resulting from the concentrations. Furthermore, the market power of the retailers was explicitly used to answer in the negative the potential emergence or increase of a dominant position resulting from the concentration. In "Toni AG/Tochtergesellschaften der Säntis Holding AG", the competition authorities held that the concentration with market shares up to 75% would create a countervailing power to the high degree of concentration on the retail market. In "Unilever/Bestfoods" the competition authorities equally noted that the market shares of up to 60% resulting from the concentration on certain food-markets would not lead to a dominant position as the principal competitors Nestlé, Migros and Coop would account for sufficient competition. Moreover, Coop (being active on both the supply and the retail market) noted that its own position would be strong enough so as to permit the substitution of Unilever/Bestfoods products with other products.

17.5 Anticompetitive Practices

17.5.1 Abuse of Buying Power, Abuse of Dependency

17.5.1.1 Definition of Buying Power

Buying power is relevant under competition legislation if it involves a dominant position of the buyer. Pursuant to Article 4(2) LCart, dominant undertakings are one or more undertakings in a specific market that are able, as suppliers or consumers, to behave to an appreciable extent independently of the other participants (competitors, suppliers or consumers) in the market.

Referring to an opinion of the French *Conseil de la Concurrence*,[36] the competition authorities for the first time applied the principle of buying power in *CoopForte*. Accordingly, a supplier is deemed dependent if two criteria are satisfied: (1) there are no comparable customers on the market for the concerned goods, and additional demand by other customers would not suffice to cover the suppliers fixed costs, and (2) production-specific assets may not be used or adjusted to be used with reasonable efforts to manufacture other goods.[37] Later, in *Denner/PickPay*[38] and, in particular, in *Migros/Denner*,[39] the competition authorities held that the two criteria need not be satisfied cumulatively but alternatively. Furthermore, in *Migros/Denner*, the competition authorities distinguished between suppliers of branded products and suppliers of store brands. The criteria for both groups of suppliers are the following:

a) Suppliers of branded products:

- The supplier achieves more than 30 % of its turnover on the retail market with Migros and Denner; and
- The bargaining power of the supplier is not sufficient so as to avoid that Migros and Denner can unilaterally impose their terms and conditions on the supplier, which in particular the case when the supplier is not an important participant on the market, the supplier is unable to export its products and the supplier does not offer "leader brands" or offers products which can be easily replaced; and
- There are no alternate supply channels within and beyond the retail sector but Migros and Denner, i.e. the supplier's existence would be in jeopardy the supply channel through Migros and Denner would be lost within a year.

[36] Avis n° 97-A-04 of 21 January 1997 regarding various questions concerning a concentration in the distribution in the retail sector ("Avis du 21 janvier 1997 relatif à diverses questions portant sur la concentration de la distribution).

[37] CoopForte, RPW/DPC 2005/1, para. 98.

[38] Denner/Pick Pay, RPW/DPC 2006/1, p. 138, para. 57.

[39] Migros/Denner, RPW/DPC 2008/1, pp. 129 et seq., para. 607. The same criteria were later confirmed and applied in Coop/Carrefour, RPW/DPC 2008/4, pp. 593 et seq., para. 479.

b) Suppliers of store brands:

- The supplier made specific investments in order to supply Migros and/or Denner; and
- The supplier did not enter into long-term or exclusive agreements with Migros and/or Denner which would allow the amortization of its investments; and
- The amount of switching costs necessary to adjust production to alternate markets would jeopardize the supplier's existence.

Accordingly, in order to be dependent, a supplier must cumulatively satisfy the conditions under either (a) or (b) and dependency must not result from a strategic decision of the supplier that later proves unfortunate, i.e., dependency must result without fault on account of the supplier from the market conditions.

To the extent that buying power is not captured by competition law, remedies may exist under contract law (e.g., Article 21 CO, unfair advantage).

17.5.1.2 Is Abuse of Buying Power a Per Se Violation of Competition Law?

In this context, it may be useful, by way of introduction, to set out the pertinent substantive provision of Article 7 LCart. Both in relation to terminology and taxonomy, Article 7 LCart is based on Article 102 TFEU. The provision consists of a blanket clause (para. 1) and a nonexhaustive catalogue of examples that may be deemed to constitute abusive practices provided that the conditions of the blanket clause are satisfied.[40] The practices listed in para. 2 of Article 7 LCart do not constitute *per se* abusive practices; rather, they are subject to a case-by-case analysis.[41]

Pursuant to Article 7(1) LCart, dominant undertakings behave unlawfully *if by abusing* their position in the market they hinder other undertakings from starting or continuing to compete or disadvantage trading partners, such as by imposing of disproportionate prices or other disproportionate conditions of trade (Article 7(2) (c) LCart). Hence, in order for Article 7 LCart to apply, a causal link between dominance (Article 4(2) LCart) and abusive conduct is necessary.[42] Furthermore, competitors or upstream or downstream market participants must not have means to oppose to or avoid a dominant undertaking's conduct.[43]

The conduct of a dominant undertaking amounts to an abuse only and is subject to the legal consequences set forth in Article 49a LCart (prohibition order and sanctions)[44] if it has anticompetitive effects in that other undertakings are hindered

---

[40] Jürg Borer, Wettbewerbsrecht I, Kommentar, N 4 on Article 7 KG, with further references.

[41] *Cf., e.g.,* Roland von Büren, Eugen Marbach, Patrik Ducrey, Immaterialgüter- und Wettbewerbsrecht, 3rd. ed. (2008), para. 1520.

[42] *Cf.*, Supreme Court of 11 April 2011, case 2C.343/2010, pt 4.3.4.

[43] *Ibid.*

[44] Pursuant to Article 49a(1) LCart, any undertaking that behaves unlawfully pursuant to Article 7 shall be charged up to 10 per cent of the turnover that it achieved in Switzerland in the preceding

from starting or continuing to compete or trading partners are suffering disadvantages and if it cannot be justified by legitimate business reasons. Accordingly, it cannot be said that abuses of buying power or dependency are prohibited *per se*.

17.5.1.3 Case Law

In *CoopForte*, the competition authorities held that conditions of trade are disproportionate if there is a disparity to the economic value of the benefits offered by the dominant undertaking[45]; however, it ultimately remained open whether Coop's practices amounted to an abuse of buying power as Coop made concessions that eventually resulted in the case being discontinued. The concerned practice that led to the investigation was the following: Coop considered that a realignment of its business would provide certain benefits to its suppliers, for which Coop deducted an amount of 0.5 % from all supplier invoices.

End of 2008, Lidl filed a complaint with the competition authorities alleging that Coop would exercise pressure on certain Swiss manufacturers of branded products to decline supplying Lidl. No formal proceedings were initiated; however, the competition authorities discovered that Coop had threatened some of the concerned manufacturers with retaliatory measures in case they would supply Lidl. Although the competition authorities did not find a causal link between Coop's conduct and the nonsupply of Lidl by the concerned manufacturers, the competition authorities admonished Coop.[46]

17.5.2 Resale Price Maintenance and Price Recommendations

Resale price maintenance is considered unlawful. According to Article 5(4) LCart, the elimination of effective competition is presumed in the case of agreements between undertakings at different levels of the production and distribution chain regarding fixed or minimum prices. The presumption in Article 5(4) LCart may be rebutted by the undertakings concerned.

Recommended resale prices are not generally unlawful in Swiss competition law. Pursuant to sec. 15 of the Notice on the Treatment of Vertical Agreements under Competition Law (the "Notice"),[47] price recommendations are considered relevant (qualitative relevance) if as a result of coercion or measures reducing the resellers' and retailers' incentive to lower the resale price they have as their effect

---

three financial years. The amount is dependent on the duration and severity of the unlawful behavior. Due account shall be taken of the likely profit that resulted from the unlawful behavior.

[45] CoopForte, RPW/DPC 2005/1, para. 147.

[46] Annual Report 2009 of the Competition Commission to the Federal Council, p. 17.

[47] Pursuant to Article 6 LCart, the Competition Commission may publish general notices on Categories of agreements affecting competition that are deemed justified. These notices are not considered legislative acts such as Regulation 330/2010; rather, such notices are similar to the guidelines published by the EU Commission.

that of a fixed or minimum price. Whether this applies to a particular price recommendation must be examined on a case-by-case basis. Similar as the EU Commission's Guidelines on Vertical Restraints, the Notice provides that such price recommendations may give rise to competition concerns (threshold criteria), in particular, when price recommendations are not disclosed to the public but are restricted to resellers and retailers, or are not designated as such, or when the price level of the products affected is significantly higher than for comparing products in neighboring countries or if price recommendations are adhered to by a significant part of resellers and retailers.

17.5.3 Reselling Below Cost

Reselling below cost is not per se prohibited by competition law; it may be an issue under the Law on Unfair Competition. However, the undercutting of prices by a dominant undertaking is considered unlawful under Article 7 LCart if the dominant undertaking, by abusing its position in the market, hinders other undertakings from starting or continuing to compete or disadvantages trading partners.[48]

17.5.4 Delisting of Suppliers

Delisting of suppliers may be an unlawful practice under Article 7 LCart, if used, for instance, as a threat by dominant retailers to obtain lower prices. Discussions with respect to the delisting of suppliers came up when retailers delisted certain products from international brand manufacturers (such as Ferrero, Kinder Schokolade) in order to obtain lower prices. Although the Swiss Brand Manufacturer Association called on the competition authorities to investigate the matter, no formal investigation is known to date; however, on October 2012, the competition authorities sent a questionnaire to Migros and Coop concerning their pricing policy in relation to branded products and potential withholding of foreign currency exchange gains.[49] Whether delisting may be unlawful must be determined in a two-tier analysis: firstly, the dominant undertaking must exclude the suppler from a given market or hinder the supplier in pursuing its business; secondly, the retailer's conduct must be weighed against reasons that may justify the conduct in question.[50]

[48] Jürg Borer, supra n 33, N 24 on Article 7 LCart.

[49] *Cf.*, Handelszeitung of 18 November 2012.

[50] *Cf.*, Jürg Borer, supra n 33, N 12 on Article 7 LCart.

17.5.5 Pricing of Products and Abusively High Prices

Apart from Article 7 LCart,[51] the following provisions should be observed:

- The Ordinance on Price Disclosure requires retailers to advertise with and indicate only actual prices the consumer will have to pay (i.e., including all taxes) so as to allow for direct price comparison. Misleading price information is prohibited.
- The Law on Price Supervision (the "LPS") provides that participants of competition agreements and dominant undertakings may voluntarily submit an envisaged price increase to the Price Supervision Authority for preemptive price control.

Prices may be subject to investigations by the Price Supervisory Authority (in particular, in the utility sector, public transportation, radio and television and state-administered prices). Only to the extent that inappropriate prices are the result of a dominant market position, they are captured by the LCart.

Article 13 of the LPS lists certain criteria in order to assess whether prices are inappropriate. These criteria are often referred to by analogy also in competition law[52]:

- the development of prices on comparable markets (as-if concept[53]);
- the necessity to achieve reasonable profits;
- the development of costs;
- particular entrepreneurial achievements, such as innovations and risk taking;
- particular circumstances on the concerned market.

17.5.6 Collusion at Local Level?

Only agreements that significantly restrict competition or eliminate effective competition will be considered by the competition authorities. Given the high density of retail stores, the high degree of mobility and other factors, such agreements would likely not be deemed to significantly restrict competition in the Swiss "Mittelland" (which comprises the large agglomerations). However, the situation could be different in remote alpine valleys where the density of retail stores might be lower and the distances between possible alternative retail stores are bigger.

---

[51] E.g., para. (2)(c), any imposition of unfair prices or other unfair conditions of trade.

[52] Marc Amstutz, Blaise Carron, N 301 on Article 7 LCart, in: Amstutz, Reinert, eds., Basler Kommentar zum Kartellgesetz.

[53] Adrian Künzler, Roger Zäch, N 3 on Article 13 LPS, in: Oesch, Weber, Zäch (eds.), Wettbewerbsrecht II; Marc Amstutz, Blaise Carron, N 302 on Article 7 LCart, in: Amstutz, Reinert (eds.), Basler Kommentar zum Kartellgesetz, with further references.

Note, however, that the purpose of the LCart is to "prevent the harmful economic or social effects of cartels and other restraints of competition and, by doing so, to promote competition in the interests of a liberal market economy" (Article 1 LCart). In this regard, it may be questionable whether the competition authorities would indeed examine and potentially sanction "micro-violations" as described above; rather, the competition authorities may refer the claimant to the civil courts.

17.5.7 Synthesis

To the extent that competition matters are concerned, large-scale retailers are subject to competition legislation irrespective of their legal or organizational form.[54] Whether certain conduct is captured by and relevant under the LCart depends on the effects on the competitive environment (such as effects on the upstream or downstream market) and is the result of a case-by-case analysis. Hence, there are no per se prohibitions.

The LCart as well as related statutes, namely the LUC and the LPS, apply independently of the store format. The same applies to statutes concerning the admission of a product to the market (e.g., labeling) and food safety.

While the LCart only governs behavioral and structural aspects of competition from a view of safeguarding the institute of competition, contractual relationships are generally governed by the Code of Obligations (the "CO") to the extent that the parties did not agree otherwise and the CO permits the parties to do so. Contractual provisions that contravene the provisions set forth in the LCart are deemed invalid.

17.6 Conclusions and Prospective

Although the grocery retail sector is historically characterized by a high degree of concentration, legislative changes aimed at reversing or dismantling the structures currently existing in Switzerland are not warranted. While in their decisions concerning Migros/Denner and Coop/Carrefour the competition authorities cautioned not to overestimate the market entries of Aldi and Lidl and imposed remedies on both Migros and Coop, recent developments indicate that the Migros/Coop duopoly is exposed to fierce competition from Aldi and Lidl with notably Aldi creating an image of retailer selling local products and thus directly "attacking" Coop and Migros with their slogans "from the region for the region" (Migros) and seeking for downtown shop units. Only recently, at least Migros sought to withdraw certain of these remedies as a result of a changing landscape in the retail grocery sector.

[54] Pursuant to Article 2(1bis) LCart, undertakings are all consumers or suppliers of goods or services active in commerce regardless of their legal or organizational form.

Currently, the Swiss legislator discusses far-reaching—ill-founded—amendments to the LCart. Within the scope of this questionnaire are, namely, the proposed amendments providing for a directly effective prohibition of certain types of agreements (thus departing from the internationally recognized effects-based approach) and—in order to address the high level of prices in Switzerland—a supply obligation of foreign suppliers to supply Swiss retailers at the same conditions as foreign retailers. The *Council of States* approved the proposed amendments, while the *National Council* rejected to consider the matter and sent it back to the Council of States for reconsideration.

The Swiss competition authorities will have taken note of the EU Commission's "Green Paper on Unfair Trading Practices in the Business-to-Business Food and Non Food Supply Chain in Europe." To the extent that possible changes in the Commission's enforcement practice or amendments to the Commission's guidelines emerge, the Swiss authorities will likely assess the matter and—if necessary—follow the Commission with some delay.

Ukraine

18

Timur Bondaryev and Lana Sinichkina

18.1 Introduction

As food prices are both highly volatile and highly visible, the grocery retail market is the object of intense scrutiny by governments and competition authorities, particularly in periods of price instability of agricultural products. Competition authorities, either spontaneously or at the urging of government, have in many countries engaged in market studies or sector inquiries of the food and/or the grocery sector to better understand the pricing of foodstuff. The pricing of milk, bread, oil, flour, sugar, shrimps, mussels, meat, fruits, bananas, vegetables, beer and wine has been analyzed in a variety of countries.

The structure of the retail grocery sector is, in most countries, evolving structurally. Small traditional stores increasingly have to coexist with retail chains, commercial groupings and large-scale stores, and market concentration in the distribution of grocery products is often on the rise both locally and nationally. Also, "non-structural aggregations" of firms, such as retailers' cooperatives, retailers' voluntary associations, franchising contracts and alliances by companies to undertake joint purchasing and logistics functions, have considerably expanded in the last 20 years. Furthermore, recently we have witnessed the emergence of Internet food retail distributors competing with brick-and-mortar distributors.

At the vertical level, there have been, first, concerns that the most powerful retail chains are able to enter into agreements with the largest suppliers, which may increase barriers to entry and restrict both interbrand and intrabrand competition, for example, through category management agreements that reserve access to sensitive market information to a few partners or make access to shelf space more difficult for the competitors of the category captains. Second, in a number

T. Bondaryev (✉) • L. Sinichkina
Arzinger Law Office, Kiev, Ukraine
e-mail: Timur.Bondaryev@arzinger.ua; Lana.Sinichkina@arzinger.ua

P. Kobel et al. (eds.), *Antitrust in the Groceries Sector & Liability Issues in Relation to Corporate Social Responsibility*, LIDC Contributions on Antitrust Law, Intellectual Property and Unfair Competition, DOI 10.1007/978-3-662-45753-5_18

of countries, there has been a more general concern that large distributors may abuse their buying power vis-a-vis small suppliers and impose unfair terms and conditions on them, such as abusively low buying prices or abusively long payment delays or the imposition of upfront access payments, "pay to stay" fees, listing fees, slotting allowances or other unilaterally set contractual conditions. Third, the functioning of purchasing alliances and the multilayered negotiations between suppliers and various levels of intermediaries has also attracted scrutiny. Fourth, the conditions of cooperation between suppliers and large retailers in the launching of private labels and the competitive impact of such labels have also been investigated.

At the horizontal level, there are concerns about increasing concentration in the retail grocery sector because of the sustained merger and acquisition movement that has made the collective exercise of market power on the selling side by the most powerful grocery retail chains easier by, inter alia, facilitating the coordination of their policies, as well as the coordination of their marketing promotions policy and the exchange of sensitive commercial information among them. But beyond this, there has also been a concern in some countries that commercial estate management and affiliation contracts between independent retailers and retail chains, franchises and cooperative, which include "golden shares" aimed at blocking chain switching, exit fees for distributors wanting to leave a chain, long postagreement nonreaffiliation and noncompete clauses of long duration, as well as overlapping opaque contractual obligations of excessive duration, entry fees and the like, constitute barriers to changing chains and therefore restrict competition.

Even though competition authorities have tended to aggressively use their traditional enforcement instruments—such as merger control to fight excessive concentration of retail, control of abuse of dominance by retailers or sanctioning price fixing by grocery retailers and/or grocery product manufacturers or exchange of information among them—their enforcement actions have occasionally been considered ineffectual to redress some of the most obvious perceived competition problems in the retail grocery sector, such as the rapidly rising price of food products at certain periods, the disappearance of traditional small-scale grocers and the increase in concentration at the local level or the concentration of supply of grocery products in reaction to the increased concentration at the retail level.

As a result, in many countries, the retail grocery sector is subject not only to traditional competition law but also to regulations that tend to create barriers to entry for large-scale retailers. For example, planning laws may regulate the size and location of shops. In addition, specific sectoral laws restrict various aspects of the strategic freedoms of large-scale retailers with respect to their suppliers or competitors, through bans on resale below cost or the imposition of minimum resale prices for foodstuff. It is argued that such laws constitute better means of preventing monopoly pressure on suppliers and guarantee fair competition. The question of whether the standardization of contracts between food growers and retailers could alleviate both the instability of prices and the risk of unfair treatment of small farmers has also been debated in the number of countries.

Competition authorities have in general used their competition advocacy tools to try to discourage governments from adopting laws or provisions deemed to be potentially anticompetitive and/or to fight the proposals to exempt the food sector from competition law—thus allowing, for example, small farmers or fishermen to collectively negotiate with the powerful retailers—but more often than not such advocacy has fallen on deaf ears.

When such provisions are part of the competition law, competition authorities may have difficulties enforcing them because they tend to be loosely worded and seem to be based on concepts of "fairness" or "level-playing fields," which have, in some cases at least, the potential of being at odds with the logic of efficiency that underlies traditional competition law. There is an abundant jurisprudence when the sectoral laws related to the retail grocery sector are enforced by courts or by bodies other than competition authorities, but the risk of contradiction between this body of jurisprudence and the approaches followed by competition authorities is more pronounced.

Overall, the important and controversial questions are whether competition law can in itself be a powerful enough instrument to achieve efficiency in the retail grocery sector, whether competition failures not easy to handle through competition law require that regulation specific to the retail sector or to the grocery sector exist to complement competition law, whether other socioeconomic goals than the pursuit of economic efficiency justify regulatory intervention in the retail grocery sector and, if there are competing goals, whether there are mechanisms to ensure that inconsistencies between competition law and sector-specific regulations are kept at a minimum.

18.2 Economic and Legal Background

18.2.1 Economic Background

According to the information of the Antimonopoly Committee of Ukraine (the "AMCU") for 2008, in 2005–2007 the number of companies has decreased in several sectors of the national economy, in particular agriculture, together with hunting and forestry—by 5.6 %; production of foodstuff, beverages and tobacco products—by 8.9 %; retail—by 5.7 %.[1]

In accordance with the report of the AMCU for 2009, reduction of competition was reported by executives of retailers interviewed. In particular, in the first quarter of 2009, only 40 % of companies felt strong competition compared with 65 % in early 2005 and 53 % in early 2008.[2] At the same time, only 2 % of retailer executives interviewed in 2009 considered that there are no competitors on the

[1] Annual report of the Antimonopoly Committee of Ukraine for 2008, section 1.

[2] Annual report of the Antimonopoly Committee of Ukraine for 2009, section 1.

market at all.[3] In the agricultural sector, the competition decreased in the first and second quarters of 2009 compared to previous periods—by 3 %. In this sector, unlike all other, external competition was the same, or even higher, than internal competition.

Pursuant to the AMCU's report for 2010, there was strong reduction of production volumes in a number of industries with competitive market structure, in particular in retail, in Ukraine this year. The interviews with executives about how the competition influences their market behavior show that the diminution in demand due to the financial and economic crisis did not increase much the manufacturers' competition for their consumers on internal markets. Instead, the majority of retailers noted that competition decreased in 2010 compared to 2009.[4] Only the agricultural sector showed some strengthening of the competition.

Besides, in 2010, the situation on the internal market began to stabilize. Specifically, preliminary assessment of the State Statistics Committee showed that the GDP in Ukraine grew by 4.5 % compared to 2009, volume of industrial production by 11 %, including processing industry—by 13.5 % and retail—by 7.6 %.[5]

In early 2011 compared to 2010, the most competitive markets were retail and intermediary services, with 82 % of the gross sales volume, and the agroindustry, with 68.1 % of the gross sales volume in the sector.[6] That year, attention of the AMCU in the agroindustry was focused on the price abuse of the monopoly (dominant) position on the grocery market, principally bread and flour, eggs, milk and butter. During the year, over 50 of such infringements were detected and ceased in Volyn, Zaporizhzhia, Ivano-Frankivs'k, Kiev, Kirovograd, Poltava, Sumy, Kharkiv, Khmelnyts'k, Cherkassy, Chernigiv regions, the AR Crimea and Kiev.[7]

In 2012, some positive trends of monopolization decrease were seen on the markets of grocery, textile and wood, rubber and plastic industries, metallurgy, manufacture of machines and equipment, coke, construction, vehicle sales and repair, etc. The best structural conditions for competition remain in retail—75.4 % of goods are sold on markets with competitive structure. Positive structural preconditions for competition remain in the agriculture industry, where 59.1 % of goods, works or services are sold on markets with competitive structure.[8]

It should be mentioned that circulation and sale of foodstuff in Ukraine has three main phases: *production*, *processing*, *retail/wholesale*.

---

[3] Ibid, section 1.

[4] Annual report of the Antimonopoly Committee of Ukraine for 2010, section 2.

[5] Available at http://www.ukrstat.gov.ua/.

[6] Annual report of the Antimonopoly Committee of Ukraine for 2011, section 2, available at http://www.amc.gov.ua/control/main/uk/publish/article/89514.

[7] Ibid, section 3.3.

[8] Annual report of the Antimonopoly Committee of Ukraine for 2012, section 2, available at http://www.amc.gov.ua/amku/doccatalog/document?id=95114&.

18.2.1.1 Production

The production phase is currently in transition. During Soviet times, there was only one state procurer that united the production in the whole USSR and sold all the products to consumer unions that ensured equal distribution of the products.

According to information as of 2011, after liquidation of the previous system, the production volume has fallen temporarily by 17 % compared to the production level at the moment of the USSR's collapse,[9] still at the moment the competition is developing and new market participants are emerging.

In general, the following entities produce groceries: business companies, private enterprises, agricultural production cooperatives, state agricultural enterprises, farms, husbandries.

At this, husbandries take 49 % of the market and all companies share 51 % of the market, which means that there are many small husbandries and few industrial enterprises.[10]

18.2.1.2 Processing

According to information for 2011, the value of the foodstuff processing market is USD 19,500,000.[11]

According to information for 2011, export of processed foodstuff amounts to 25 % of Ukraine's general export volume, which is more than the same in EU countries. At the same time, the imported goods make up 10 %, which corresponds to the common European index. Direct foreign investments into the foodstuff processing industry amount to USD 2,070,000,000.[12]

It should be mentioned that at the time of the USSR's collapse, foodstuff producers sold 96 % of their goods to processing enterprises. According to the information for 2011, this index amounts to 16 % only. The majority of goods go to the secondary market.[13]

Production of meat products almost completely satisfies the needs of the internal market in the country. The total production volume of meat products in in-kind equivalent amounted to 6 % of the gross foodstuff production in 2010. Export of

---

[9] Kyryliuk, Ievheii and Proschalykina, Alina. 2013. Transformation of the structure of the economic relations on the agrimarket of Ukraine. Available at http://www.economy.nayka.com.ua/?operation=1&iid=1323. Accessed 30 May 2014.

[10] Deryvedmid, Sergiy. 2011. Analysis of the retail Market of Ukraine. Available at http://web.znu.edu.ua/herald/issues/2011/eco_2011_1/2011_1/108-115.pdf.

[11] Yevtushenko, Sergiy and Vacht, Vladimir. 2013. Food processing industry in Ukraine. Available at http://investukraine.com/wp-content/uploads/2012/11/Food-processing-in-Ukraine_WWW.pdf. Accessed 30 May 2014.

[12] Ibid, section 1.1.

[13] Kyryliuk, Ievheii and Proschalykina, Alina. 2013. Transformation of the structure of the economic relations on the agrimarket of Ukraine. Available at http://www.economy.nayka.com.ua/?operation=1&iid=1323. Accessed 30 May 2014.

meat and edible by-products amounts to less than a quarter of import for the same period. The most exported goods are cattle meat, poultry meat and edible by-products. The most imported goods based on import volume in money equivalent are pork meat and poultry.

Production of dairy products is clearly seasonal. The maximum volumes are produced in the second and third quarters of a year. Production of liquid milk and cream is dominant based on production volumes in in-kind equivalent. Export of dairy products in 2010 exceeded the import by four times. The main part of the imported goods makes cheese of any kind—45 % of the industry's import in monetary equivalent. Twenty-nine percent of import covers butter and milk fat. Condensed milk, condensed cream and sour milk drinks, such as buttermilk, yoghurt or kefir, make 10 % of the import each. The remaining milk products make 6 % of the import in monetary equivalent.

Production of alcoholic beverages makes up 16 % of the general volume of the produced goods in 2010. Eighty-four percent of the gross volume of alcoholic beverages makes malt beer. The second largest group of alcoholic beverages is vodka—74 % of all alcoholic beverages, except beer. Liquors, ratafia, infusions make 20 %, brandy—6 %.[14]

18.2.1.3 Wholesale and Retail

The modern commercial formats did not arise in Ukraine at once. Already in USSR there was a centralized network that united over 800,000 grocery stores, supermarkets, pavilions in the whole Soviet Union, and 116,000 of them were located in Ukraine.

After USSR's collapse, this system was basically ruined. Alternative forms of retail market began to emerge: kiosks, where everything was sold—from chocolate to haberdashery; grocery markets; combined grocery and nongrocery goods markets. Then kiosks started to specialize, and in 2000 first supermarkets for mass consumers began to open. It was between 2000 and 2008 that the volume growth in retail circulation started to enhance by 8–29.5 % compared to previous years.

Retail evolution stages in Ukraine: legacy of the centralized store chains of the USSR; emergence of small business elements, such as kiosks and markets; emergence of first "elite" supermarkets; emergence of modern retailers for mass consumers, development of Internet stores; etc.

According to the State Statistics Committee, the total volume of the commodity circulation in Ukraine in January–October 2012 grew by 15 % and amounted to UAH 650,380,000,000 (approximately USD 79,850,000,000 or EUR 61,110,000,000). The circulation of commodities in enterprises grew by 13.9 %

[14] Yevtushenko, Sergiy and Vacht, Vladimir. 2013. Food processing industry in Ukraine. section 3.1. Available at http://investukraine.com/wp-content/uploads/2012/11/Food-processing-in-Ukraine_WWW.pdf. Accessed 30 May 2014.

and amounted to UAH 329,000,000,000 (approximately USD 40,390,000,000 or EUR 32,920,000,000) in the same period, which makes about 51 % of the total commodity circulation.[15] In 2011, foodstuff made 39 % of the commodity circulation.

Taking into account the retail market structure in Ukraine, it shall be noted that according to research conducted by analytical organizations, such as Roland Berger Strategy Consultants, the market is dominated by big organized marketing companies (70 %), but retail chains come short in this volume with 44 % of the organized marketing market.[16]

Based on the form of activity, there are the following groups of chain retailers: supermarkets, 37 %; Cash & Carry, 16 %; hypermarkets, 15 %; discounters, 14 %; grocery (convenience) stores, 13 %; others, 5 %.[17]

As for 2009, the retail market in Ukraine is dominated by national operators: international operators, 14 % of the market; national operators, 51 %; regional operators, 17 %; local operators, 18 %. Therefore, local and national grocery retailers are the main driving force in the development of the retail market in Ukraine. In late 2009, 50 biggest retail chains in Ukraine were named, among which discounters, convenience stores, supermarkets and Cash & Carry.[18]

In conclusion, it must be said that the share of retail chains in the organized marketing amounts to 45 %. The most popular format for retail shops at the moment is supermarket, but it is expected that in the next future more discounters will appear. National operators whose share amounts to 51 % of the Ukrainian market remain the main driving force for the development of the retail market.[19]

18.2.2 Legal Background

18.2.2.1 General Review

The competition law in Ukraine, in particular the Law of Ukraine "On Protection of the Economic Competition"[20] and the Law of Ukraine "On Protection against Unfair Competition,"[21] is applied to the grocery sector to the fullest. It includes a ban on unfair competition, as well as the prohibition of anticompetitive practices.

---

[15] Available at http://www.ukrstat.gov.ua/.

[16] New opportunities of investment to Europe's fastest growing retail market of Ukraine. 2009. section A. Available at http://www.rolandberger.ua/media/pdf/Roland_Berger_Retail_Investment_opportunities_Eng_20090221.pdf.

[17] Ibid.

[18] Retail market of Ukraine is growing. 2009. Available at http://www.retail.ru/articles/top_ukraine_retailers/.

[19] Deryvedmid, Sergiy. 2011. Analysis of the retail Market of Ukraine. Available at http://web.znu.edu.ua/herald/issues/2011/eco_2011_1/2011_1/108-115.pdf.

[20] Available at http://zakon2.rada.gov.ua/laws/show/2210-14.

[21] Available at http://zakon4.rada.gov.ua/laws/show/236/96-%D0%B2%D1%80.

The Law of Ukraine "On Protection against Unfair Competition" prohibits unfair competition, in particular:

i) illegal use of company's business reputation, such as illegal use of denotations, illegal use of goods produced by other manufacturer, copying the trade dress and comparative advertising;
ii) creation of obstacles for other business entities in competition and obtaining illegal competitive advantages, such as defamation, coercion to boycott, coercion to discrimination of a buyer (client), bribing supplier's employees or officers, bribing buyer's (client's) employees or officers, obtaining illegal competitive advantages or dissemination of misleading information;
iii) illegal gathering, disclosure or use of commercial secrets, such as illegal gathering of commercial secrets, disclosure of commercial secrets, coercion to disclosure of commercial secrets or illegal use of commercial secrets.

The Law of Ukraine "On Protection of Economic Competition" prohibits both anticompetitive concerted actions and abuse of the monopoly (dominant) position on the market.

Pursuant to Article 6 of this Law, anticompetitive concerted actions but not limited to, the following but not limited to, the following:

i) maintaining prices or other terms for purchase or sale of goods;
ii) restricting manufacture, commodity markets, technical and technological development, investments or control of the same;
iii) allocation markets or supply sources according to territory, assortment of goods, sales or purchase volumes, circle of sellers, buyers or consumers or according to other characteristics;
iv) bid rigging during auctions and tenders;
v) removing from or limiting access to the market or withdrawal from the market of other business entities, buyers, sellers;
vi) applying different terms to equivalent agreements with other business entities creating competitive disadvantages for them;
vii) entering into agreements provided other business entities undertake additional obligations which according to their substance or fair business and trade practices are not related to the subject of such agreements;
viii) limiting considerably competitiveness of other business entities on the market without objectively justified reasons.[22]

Pursuant to Article 13 of the Law of Ukraine "On Protection of the Economic Competition," abuse of the monopoly (dominant) position includes

[22] Ibid.

i) establishing such prices or other terms for purchase or sale of goods which would be impossible provided considerable competition on the market;
ii) applying different prices or terms to equivalent agreements with other business entities, sellers or buyers without objectively justified reasons therefor;
iii) entering into agreements provided other business entities undertake additional obligations which according to their substance or fair business and trade practices are not related to the subject of such agreements;
iv) limiting production, markets or technological development which incurred or may incur damages by another business entities, buyers, sellers;
v) partial or complete refusal to purchase or sell commodities if there are no alternative sources of sale or purchase;
vi) limiting considerably competitiveness of other business entities on the market without objectively justified reasons;
vii) creating obstacles for the market access or market withdrawal for or removing from the market other business entities.

The list of practices prohibited as anticompetitive concerted actions of business entities or as abuse of the monopoly (dominant) position on the market is not exhaustive.

Pursuant to Article 6 of this Law, anticompetitive concerted actions in form of "establishment of prices or other terms for purchase or sale of goods" are prohibited, in particular, for the retail grocery market. The term "establishment of prices" is widely interpreted in the legal practice and refers to any concerted horizontal or vertical practices of business entities that directly or indirectly influence the pricing. Therefore, it is prohibited to establish prices for purchase or sale of goods or to maintain any components of the pricing, including discounts.

There is an exception for the resale price maintenance as provided in Article 8 of the Law of Ukraine "On Protection of the Economic Competition." In particular, vertical price maintenance, namely concerted actions in relation to supply when one participant of concerted actions sets limitations for another participant of concerted actions as to the price and/or other terms of a contract on supply of the delivered goods to other business entities or consumers, is prohibited only if such concerted actions

i) result in the substantial restriction of competition on the whole market or in its significant part, including the monopolization of the relevant markets;
ii) limit the entry of other economic entities into the market;
iii) result in the economically unjustified raise in prices or the growth in product deficit.

18.2.2.2 Specific Regulations Aimed at the Retail Market

It should be noted that Ukraine has not yet adopted any provisions specifically aimed at the retail market in the Ukrainian competition law. Moreover, at the moment, Ukraine has no specific laws aimed at controlling the structure of the grocery retail market or the behavior of large-scale grocery retailers.

Still, some specific provisions of the current laws partially regulate these issues. In particular, provisions of Article 3 of the Law of Ukraine "On State Support of the Agriculture in Ukraine" set forth the state price regulation for the following types of agricultural products: hard wheat, soft wheat, corn, barley, winter rye, spring rye, pea, buckwheat, panic grass, oat, soya, sunflower seeds, rapeseeds, flax seeds, hope cone, granulated sugar (beet), wheat flour, rye flour, meat and poultry, including by-products, milk powder, butter, sunflower oil.[23]

The Law of Ukraine "On State Support of the Agriculture in Ukraine" sets forth the following specific provisions for the products subject to the state price regulation above[24]:

i) For products subject to the state price regulation there is a maximum 20 % mark-up (surcharge) of the manufacturer's wholesale price (customs value) for the final consumer.
ii) Manufacturers (suppliers) of the products subject to the state price regulation, wholesale and retail enterprises and their affiliated persons are prohibited to enter into agreements which set forth any other financial obligations except for sale and purchase relations in respect to agricultural products.
iii) Wholesale and retail enterprises are obliged to pay suppliers of products subject to the state price regulation not later than within 7 banking days upon receipt of proceeds from sale of such goods.

The Law of Ukraine "On state regulation of manufacture and circulation of ethyl, cognac and fruit alcohol, alcoholic beverages and tobacco products" authorizes the Cabinet of Ministers of Ukraine to set minimum wholesale and retail prices for alcoholic beverages.[25] In particular, the Resolution of the Cabinet Ministers of Ukraine "On setting forth minimum wholesale and retail prices for certain types of alcoholic beverages" is currently in force.[26]

The Law mentioned above specifically provides that the manufacturer or the importer sets the maximum retail price for tobacco products.[27]

Furthermore, legislators have already many times elaborated special bills aimed at controlling the structure of the grocery retail market or the behavior of large-scale grocery retailers.

On 22 January 2013, the Parliament of Ukraine registered bill No. 2067 "On Incitements for the Development of the Internal Market of the Domestic

---

[23] Available at http://zakon2.rada.gov.ua/laws/show/1877-15.

[24] Ibid, para. 3.3.4.

[25] Available at http://zakon4.rada.gov.ua/laws/show/481/95-%D0%B2%D1%80.

[26] Available at http://zakon4.rada.gov.ua/laws/show/957-2008-%D0%BF.

[27] The maximum retail price for tobacco products set by the manufacturer or the importer shall be printed on the package, box or gift box for tobacco products, along with the manufacture date.

Foodstuff," elaborated by a Ukrainian people's deputy.[28] The explanatory note to the bill says that passing of this bill is required due to the necessity to take urgent measures for the development of the national grocery market, measures against monopolization of the grocery market by single chains and measures for the increase of the domestic foodstuff production. Moreover, it was stated that the lack of actual governmental support for small and middle-sized businesses in the foodstuff sector and concentration of the internal market under the control of big retail chains allows big retailers to dump prices, squeezing out private entrepreneurs and small enterprises from the grocery market.

In conclusion, it should be underlined that the retail grocery sector is not exempted from competition law either in full or in part. Thus, the competition law of Ukraine is applied to all economic activities exercised in Ukraine.

18.2.2.3 Abuse of Buying Power, Abuse of Dependency and Concentrated Actions

There is no specific statutory definition of buying power or dependency in the competition legislation of Ukraine.

Given that, abuses of buying power and dependency are prohibited only in case they restrict competition, limit market access by other business entities or cause an economically unjustified price increase or a deficit in a commodity.

Nevertheless, a kind of prototype of the term "abuse of dependency" is provided by Article 19 of the Law of Ukraine "On Protection of Economic Competition."[29] Specifically, the seller of certain commodities is deemed to depend on the buyer if such a buyer receives from such a seller a special remuneration, apart from traditional discounts or other bonuses, which other similar buyers do not receive. In practice, such privileges may be quantitative, for example considerable discounts or very low prices, or qualitative, such as additional services or special privileges. Moreover, to be deemed dependent on the buyer, the seller shall (1) be a small or a medium enterprise, taking into account relations of control, i.e., to have the annual turnover of EUR 500,000 and (2) have no alternative sources of supply.

It is prohibited for buyers under the above circumstances to establish restrictions for economic activity of business entities (suppliers) that, as a rule, do not apply to other business entities (suppliers) or to apply without objective reasons different approaches to different business entities (suppliers).

Within the period of last 5 years, Ukrainian competition authority paid its attention mostly to the conduct of retail chains, namely to

i) increase of prices for chicken eggs;
ii) application by the retail chains of similar mechanisms that might have led to an economically unjustified increase of grocery prices and 15–60 % increase of

[28] Available at http://w1.c1.rada.gov.ua/pls/zweb2/webproc4_1?pf3511=45523.

[29] Available at http://zakon2.rada.gov.ua/laws/show/2210-14.

prices for milk products; noodles, sunflower oil, cereals, meat and fish were increased by 15–60 % in 2011 and early 2012;

iii) sugar price increase by 17.1 % in the period from September to December 2010;

iv) increase of prices for milk products, such as milk, sour cream, butter and hard cheese and poultry meat;

v) increase of wholesale prices for lemon, garlic and onion. Specifically, in some retail chains, the retail prices for lemons grew 1.6–2.3 times; at this, retail mark-ups in some companies increased 2–2.7 times and amounted to 260–300 %; in some cases, prices for garlic grew between 1.6 and 2 times.

There are also some restrictions regarding the recommended resale prices in the retail grocery sector. Pursuant to Article 8 of the Law of Ukraine "On Protection of the Economic Competition," concerted actions mean that one participant of concerted actions sets restrictions for another participant of concerted actions regarding the establishment of prices or other terms of a contract on sale of the goods delivered to other business entities or consumers.

Anticompetitive concerted actions include such concerted actions that sufficiently restrict the competition on the whole market or its major part, including result in monopolization of the respective markets; limit market access for other business entities; lead to economically unfeasible price increases or commodity deficiency.

Pursuant to Article 10 of the Law of Ukraine "On Protection of Economic Competition," concerted actions may be allowed by respective bodies of the Antimonopoly Committee of Ukraine if their participants can prove that such actions facilitate improvement of production; purchase or sale of goods; technical and technological, economic development; development of small or medium entrepreneurs; export or import optimization; elaboration and application of unified technical specifications or standards for goods; rationalization of production.

Concerted actions cannot be allowed by the bodies of the Antimonopoly Committee of Ukraine if they sufficiently restrict the competition on the whole market or its major part.

The Cabinet of Ministers of Ukraine may allow concerted actions that have not been approved by the Antimonopoly Committee of Ukraine pursuant to part two of this article if participants of the concerted actions prove that the positive effect for the public interests outweighs negative consequences of the competition restriction.

Approval of the Cabinet of Ministers cannot be provided if participants of concerted actions apply restrictions that are not necessary for the concerted actions, restriction of competition threatens the system of the market economy.

Anticompetitive concerted actions are prohibited until obtaining the approval of the bodies of the Antimonopoly Committee of Ukraine or the Cabinet of Ministers of Ukraine.

Besides, pursuant to Article 11 of the Law of Ukraine "On Protection of the Economic Competition," coercion of a supplier to discriminate a purchaser (client), as an act of unfair competition, shall be the incitement of the supplier by a competitor of the purchaser (client), directly or through third persons, to apply disadvantageous terms for such purchaser (client) compared to other competitors of the purchaser (client).

Besides, laws of Ukraine do not prohibit reselling below cost.

Import of goods is subject to the Law of Ukraine "On protection of the domestic manufacturer from damping import."[30] Pursuant to this Law, damping is import of goods to the customs territory of Ukraine at prices that are lower than the reference prices for the similar goods in the country of export that damages the domestic manufacturer of similar goods.

As to the delisting of suppliers, it may be an infringement of the competition law in cases regarding clients that have monopoly (dominant) position on certain markets. Thus, pursuant to Paragraph 5 Part 2 Article 13 of the Law of Ukraine "On Protection of Economic Competition," partial or complete refusal to purchase or to sell goods if there are no alternative sources of sale or purchase is deemed to be abuse of dominance on the market. In the meantime, there is no direct legislative prohibition of delisting of suppliers in other cases.

18.2.2.4 Regulation of the Pricing and Pricing Policy, Price Controls

Under Ukrainian law, it is prohibited to establish such prices as would be impossible provided considerable competition on the market exists. The liability constitutes a fine in an amount of up to 10 % of the business entity's income (revenues) from sale of the goods, works and services in the last reporting year preceding the year of the fine imposition.

Moreover, Part 2 Article 6 of the Law of Ukraine "On Protection of Economic Competition" prohibits anticompetitive concerted actions regarding establishment of prices or other conditions for sale or purchase of goods. As the practice shows, coordination shall not refer to the price per se. Anticompetitive concerted actions often concern only component of the pricing, e.g., discounts. But this restriction is applied to all business entities without limitation to big retailers only.

It is important to mention that some groceries in Ukraine are subject to price regulation. The reasons are explained in Article 12 of the Law of Ukraine "On Prices and Pricing."[31] Specifically, it states that state price regulation is applied to commodities that have decisive influence on the general price level and dynamics and are socially important and to commodities produced by entities with monopoly (dominant) position on the market.[32] The state price regulation may also be introduced for commodities of business entities that violate requirements of the law on economic competition protection. Article 12 of this Law establishes that prices regulated by the state are changed according to the procedure and terms determined by authorities responsible for the state price regulation according to this

[30] Available at http://zakon2.rada.gov.ua/laws/show/330-14.

[31] Available at http://zakon4.rada.gov.ua/laws/show/5007-17.

[32] See Sect. 18.2.2.2 above.

law. The prices regulated by the state may be changed due to change of production or sale conditions that do not depend on the economic activity of the business entity.

Subject to the approval of the AMCU are decisions on the procedure for establishment of prices and tariffs, maximum profitability indexes for products subject to the antitrust regulation, which is stated in the provision for obtaining approvals from the Antimonopoly Committee of Ukraine for decisions of government authorities, bodies of administrative and economic management and control, self-government authorities as to demonopolization of the economy, competition development and antitrust regulation as approved by Order of the AMCU as of 01 April 1994 No. 4.[33] At this, term "decision" means "drafts of orders, decrees, instructions, provisions, rules, methodical instructions or other acts passed by government authorities, bodies of administrative and economic management and control, self-government authorities; drafts of regulatory decisions made by regional, district, city, city district or village Councils."

18.2.2.5 Regulation of Large-Scale Food Retailing and Vertical Relationships Between Suppliers and Retailers

In general, contractual relationships between large-scale food retailers and small suppliers or small-scale retailers are not regulated in Ukraine.

Still, single special provisions of current legislative acts govern these issues partially. In particular, paragraph 3.3.1 Article 3 of the Law of Ukraine "On State Support of the Agriculture in Ukraine" defines the following agricultural products (goods) as subject to the state price regulation: hard wheat, soft wheat, meslin, corn, barley, winter rye, spring rye, pea, buckwheat, panic grass, oat, soya, sunflower seeds, rapeseeds, flax seeds, hope cone, granulated sugar, wheat flour, rye flour, meat and poultry, including by-products, milk powder, butter, sunflower oil.[34]

The same article of the respective Law stipulates the following special provisions concerning the products above subject to the state price regulation:

i) Manufacturers (suppliers) of the products subject to the state price regulation, wholesale and retail enterprises and their affiliated persons are prohibited to enter into agreements which set forth any other financial obligations except for sale and purchase relations in respect to agricultural products.
ii) Wholesale and retail enterprises are obliged to pay suppliers of products subject to the state price regulation not later than seven days after receipt of proceeds from sale of such goods.

The above concerns, though, not only big retailers.

As to the exemption of the small-scale farmers and suppliers of food products, the competition law of Ukraine does not contain any exemptions on collective sale

[33] Available at http://zakon4.rada.gov.ua/laws/show/z0078-94.

[34] Available at http://zakon2.rada.gov.ua/laws/show/1877-15.

of products by small-scale or medium entities. The only provision giving some privileges for small-scale and medium entities is set forth in Article 7 of the Law of Ukraine “On Protection of Economic Competition” and exempts any voluntary concerted actions of small-scale and medium entities as to collective purchase of goods from the general prohibition set forth by Article 6 of the Law.[35] At this, such exemption is explained by the fact that such actions do not result in considerable restriction of competition and increase the competitiveness of small-scale and medium entities.

Moreover, Article 1 of the Law defines a small-scale or a medium entity as a business entity with income (revenues) from sale of goods, works or services in the last financial year or the value of assets not exceeding in equivalent EUR 500,000 based on the exchange rate of the National bank of Ukraine on the last day of the fiscal year provided there are competitors with much bigger market shares on the markets of such business entity’s operation.

18.2.2.6 Market Research of the Retail Grocery Sector and Recommendations of the Competition Authority

The sector inquiries and market research were not once undertaken by the Antimonopoly Committee of Ukraine Ukrainian competition authority. The necessity in their conduct is caused by the price movements and possible competition failures, price differentials in retail chains and specialized shops. The retail market is often investigated as a part of the supply chain from the manufacturer to the final consumer in order to determine actual reasons for overpricing. The AMCU pays special attention to prices for the so-called socially important groceries, i.e., the most necessary items in the market basket.

On January 2014, the press service of the AMCU notified of the new investigation of the activities of Ukrainian retail chains (19 brands) regarding parallel conduct in dealing with national and foreign suppliers. The investigation also involved vast market analysis.

For example, on September 2012, the press service of the AMCU informed that the AMCU investigated the retail market. The AMCU began to analyze the activity of retail chains in Kiev (under 15 brands) as to compliance with legislative requirements. The reason for this was application by these retail chains of similar mechanisms that may have led to economically unjustified increase of grocery prices. In particular, prices for milk products, noodles, sunflower oil, cereals, meat and fish were increased by 15–60 % in 2011 and early 2012. At the same time, the consumer price index in Kiev grew by 13.5 %. In AMCU’s opinion, such actions of retail chains may have signs of anticompetitive concerted actions.[36]

---

[35] Available at http://zakon2.rada.gov.ua/laws/show/2210-14.

[36] AMCU Press release, 10 September 2012, available at http://www.amc.gov.ua/amku/control/main/uk/publish/article/88930;jsessionid=ADA7C31FD6DFD132C8DB8054432AAAA7.

In autumn 2009, the AMCU investigated the price increase for lemon, onion and garlic. During that time, the flu epidemics triggered high demand for these products as they are traditionally used for flu prevention. Due to this, the prices for these products grew considerably, which would have been impossible provided essential competition on the market exists. Thus, though prices for lemon import to Ukraine on October to early November 2009 remained unchanged, single wholesale suppliers increased wholesale prices 1.5–2.3 times, and in some retail chains the lemon retail prices grew 1.6–2.3 times; at this, retail mark-ups in some companies were increased 2–2.7 times and amounted to 260–300 %. Garlic prices grew 1.6–2 times in some cases.

In spring 2009, upon results of the above investigation, the AMCU delivered decisions in nine cases on infringement of the competition law on these markets, namely, in the city of Kiev, Dnipropetrovs'k, Donetsk, Lviv and Lugans'k regions. The infringers were fined with UAH 170,400 (approximately USD 20,920 or EUR 16,010 at the time) in total. Moreover, business entities received 110 recommendations regarding prevention of dominance abuse and anticompetitive concerted actions; 90 of them were provided to retailers and 20 to wholesalers and related to increasing prices for lemon, garlic and onion to an economically feasible level. In fulfillment of these requirements, lemon prices were lowered in Vinnitsa, Dnipropetrovs'k, Donets'k, Ivano-Frankivs'k, Cherkassy and other regions and in the city of Kiev. In cases of nonfulfillment of recommendations or if illegal practices had caused considerable damages, the AMCU initiated proceedings on violation of the competition law.

On October 2012, Donetsk regional territorial department of the AMCU, taking into account the trends for increase of chicken eggs' prices, recommended the regional poultry farms and owners of retail chains working in the region to refrain from establishing economically unfeasible wholesale prices for this product. As a result, the prices for chicken eggs in retail chains were reduced. This price reduction was achieved due to reduction of wholesale prices for chicken eggs by manufacturers and nonincrease of the retail mark-ups. Thus, as of November 2012, the price for chicken eggs was step by step reduced in the retail chain Brusnytsia (up to UAH 1.20 for 10 eggs—approximately USD 0.15 or EUR 0.11) and in the retail chain Obzhora (up to UAH 1.30 for 10 eggs—approximately USD 0.16 or EUR 0.12).[37]

On February 2011, the AMCU concluded that the analysis of the economic situation on the market shows no objective reasons for considerable increase of sugar prices. Thus, from September to December 2010, the sugar price grew by 17.1 %. According to the analysis of the demand and supply balance forecast for the new marketing year, it was established that the volume of internal sugar consumption did not grow and remained on the level of 2009/2010 marketing year (1,840,000 tons). Moreover, the period from September to December, inclusive,

[37] AMCU Press release, 10 November 2012, available at http://www.amc.gov.ua/amku/control/don/uk/publish/article/80281.

is not the period of seasonal sugar price increase. At the same time, according to the Ministry of Agricultural Policy of Ukraine, there was big enough stock of sugar owned by plants without taking into account sugar stored.

The AMCU obliged sugar market players to bring wholesale and retail prices to an economically feasible level. This requirement concerned 8 groups of sugar plants, 11 sugar manufacturers not part of any group, 9 big sugar wholesale suppliers and 8 biggest retail chains: Foodmarket Ltd, ECO Ltd, Metro Cash & Carry Ukraine, Furshet CJSC, Ashan Ukraine Ltd, Fozzy Group trade and industrial corporation, PAKKO-Holding Ltd and Adventis Ltd. The AMCU obliged eight biggest retail chains (1) to bring sugar retail prices to an economically feasible level, (2) to facilitate conclusion of direct sugar sale contracts between retail chains and manufacturers, (3) to refrain from economically unjustified increase of sugar price, (4) to refrain from increasing retail mark-ups, (5) to refrain from creating the deficiency of sugar sold by weight through complete transition to selling the packed sugar only.[38]

18.3 Merger Control

Foremost, it should be noted that the competition law of Ukraine does not contain any specific provisions regulating the issuance of merger clearances or concerted actions clearances in the retail sector or in the grocery retail sector by public authorities.

The legal act that stipulates legal grounds for support and protection of economic competition and restriction of monopolism in Ukraine is the Law of Ukraine "On Protection of Economic Competition."[39] This law sets forth general thresholds meeting, which obliges market players to apply for merger clearance to the specially authorized pubic agency—the Antimonopoly Committee of Ukraine—should they make the respective decision.

In particular, pursuant to Part 1 Article 24 of the Law of Ukraine "On Protection of Economic Competition," concentration is prohibited until obtaining a respective merger clearance from the Antimonopoly Committee of Ukraine upon simultaneous fulfillment of the following conditions:

– the aggregate asset value or the aggregate turnover of merger participants, taking into account control relations, has exceeded in equivalent EUR 12,000,000 in the last fiscal year, including abroad, and
– the aggregate asset value or the aggregate turnover, including abroad, of each of at least two merger participants, taking into account control relations, exceeds in equivalent EUR 1,000,000, and

[38] AMCU Press release, 02 February 2011.

[39] Available at http://zakon2.rada.gov.ua/laws/show/2210-14.

– the aggregate asset value or the aggregate turnover in Ukraine of at least one merger participant, taking into account control relations, exceeds in equivalent EUR 1,000,000.

Moreover, irrespective of meeting financial thresholds by the business entities as stated above, a merger clearance of the Antimonopoly Committee of Ukraine is required if the market share of any of the merger participants or the aggregate market share of the merger participants, taking into account control relations, exceeds 35 % and the merger takes place on the respective or the close-related market.

The only state agency authorized to consider applications for merger clearance of business entities and to make respective decisions is the Antimonopoly Committee of Ukraine, the status and powers of which are set forth in the Law of Ukraine "On the Antimonopoly Committee of Ukraine." The applications for approval of concerted actions may be considered by the territorial departments of the Antimonopoly Committee of Ukraine. As a rule, the competence is divided based on the size of the territory where a participant of concerted actions is active or on the market conditions under which such concerted actions take place—dominance of a business entity on the market, national security assurance or defense issues.

Pursuant to Part 2 Article 31 of the Law of Ukraine, approval of the bodies of the Antimonopoly Committee of Ukraine for concerted actions or merger may depend on whether participants of the merger or concerted actions fulfill certain requirements or obligations that eliminate or mitigate the negative influence of such concerted actions or the merger on the competition. Such terms or obligations may, in particular, concern property management or disposal restrictions or obligation of a business entity to alienate the property. Still, the list above is not exhaustive, and bodies of the Antimonopoly Committee of Ukraine are entitled to establish respective terms at their own discretion.

Besides that, there are no specific laws or bylaws in Ukraine regulating the issuance of merger clearances; depending on whether business entities fulfill certain obligations in the grocery retail sector, general approaches as stated above are applied.

18.3.1 Definition of the Market in the Grocery Sector

The markets are defined based on the Methodology for determination of a monopoly (dominant) position of business entities on the market, as approved by order of the Antimonopoly Committee of Ukraine, registered with the Ministry of Justice of Ukraine on 1 April 2002 under No. 317/6605 (hereinafter—the Methodology).[40] The Methodology was elaborated based on the Laws of Ukraine "On Protection of Economic Competition" and "On the Antimonopoly Committee of Ukraine."

[40] Available at http://zakon4.rada.gov.ua/laws/show/z0317-02.

The definition of markets may include actions such as determining the object of analysis, in particular a business entity, a specific commodity (product, work or service) manufactured, supplied, sold, purchased, consumed or used by such business entity; making a list of goods or services having features of one commodity or a commodity group; making a list of main sellers (suppliers, manufacturers), purchasers or consumers of the commodity or the commodity group; defining commodity borders of a market; defining territorial borders of a market; defining time borders of a market; defining volumes of a commodity circulating on the market; calculating market shares of business entities; making a list of sellers (suppliers, manufacturers), purchasers (consumers) of a commodity (commodity group)—potential competitors, purchasers who may sell (supply, manufacture), purchase (consume, use) the same and/or a similar commodity (commodity group) on the market; defining market entry barriers for business entities that sell (supply, manufacture), purchase (consume, use) or can sell (supply, manufacture), purchase (consume, use) the same and/or a similar commodity (commodity group) on the market.

Geographic borders of a market for a certain commodity (commodity group) are defined by determining the minimum territory beyond which, from the consumer's point of view, purchase of a commodity (commodity group) belonging to a group of interchangeable commodity (commodity group) is impossible or inexpedient. Upon the final definition of territorial (geographic) borders of a market, the lesser ability of displacement of either demand or supply shall be decisive.

18.3.2 Internet Grocery Retail Stores

About 44 % of the Ukrainian population is Internet users; 10 % of them shop online, according to the information for January–September 2012. According to the forecast from GfK Ukraine till 2015, the share of Internet stores will grow up to 20–25 % in the general trade volume.[41] Still, according to the Ukrbusiness research, the grocery retail sector on the Internet amounts only to 5 % of the general number of Internet users.

This sector is very promising, as there is still little competition on the Internet grocery market, and the number of customers in Internet stores grows constantly.

Nonetheless, at the moment, there are no specific regulations applying to Internet retail stores. Moreover, currently the laws of Ukraine have no definition for "an internet store." The Law of Ukraine "On Protection of Consumer Rights" envisages a possibility to conclude an agreement remotely.[42] A remotely concluded agreement is an agreement concluded between the seller and the consumer by means of long-distance communication, including Internet. Pursuant to this Law, decree of

[41] GfK Ukraine Press Release, available at http://joom.org.ua/post/gfk-yak-rozvyvaetsya-ukrayynskyy-rynok-internet-torgivli.

[42] Available at http://zakon4.rada.gov.ua/laws/show/1023-12.

the Ministry of Economy No. 103 approves Rules for the sale of goods on order and outside of sales or office premises (hereinafter—the Rules).[43] According to the Rules sale of commodities on order is a type of trade when the consumer concludes a sale and purchase agreement with the seller by means of long-distance communication or preorders them directly by the seller. Therefore, Internet stores have to follow the requirements of these Rules.

These Rules determine relations between the consumer and the business entity-seller that sells commodities based on an order and outside of sales or office premises based on a sale and purchase agreement concluded remotely or outside of sales or office premises and regulate requirements as to proper quality, safety and service provision.[44]

With regard to attention of supervisory authorities to the Internet grocery retail sector, the Antimonopoly Committee of Ukraine has not yet conducted any investigations of this market sector yet. Thus, no infringements on this market have been revealed now.

18.4 Prospective and Recommendations

The Ukrainian grocery market faces imbalances in bargaining power of retailers and suppliers, as well as anticompetitive practices in the food chain. The aforesaid imbalances cause the following issues:

i) additional financial "contributions"/payments that are imposed by retailers on suppliers; to those, specifically, belong upfront access payments, "pay to stay" fees, listing fees, promotion and transport fees, fees for placing products/services linked to the use of shelf space, as well as other unilaterally set contractual conditions;
ii) retroactive contract changes, for example, envisaging deductions from the invoiced amount to cover promotion fees, unilateral discounts, which have not been previously agreed upon in a due course;
iii) long payment delays;
iv) unfair transfer of commercial risk to the other party, for example, transfer of the retailer's responsibility for stolen or spoilt goods to the supplier, demanding investment in new outlets or obligations to compensate for losses incurred by a retailer;
v) ambiguous contract terms.

[43] Available at http://zakon4.rada.gov.ua/laws/show/z1181-07.

[44] Para. 1.2. of these Rules state: "Remote trade is a form of sale of commodities outside of sales or office premises at which selection and order of goods do not coincide in time with the actual transfer of the selected commodity to the consumer."

We recommend that the Antimonopoly Committee of Ukraine should take an active part in promoting the following tools aimed at solving the aforesaid issues:

i. to establish a dialogue with the main stakeholders of the grocery market of Ukraine, namely, retailers, suppliers and producers;
ii. to facilitate mechanisms of self-regulation, including but not limited to elaboration of code of conduct for retailers and suppliers.

In order to solve the most essential problems related to forcing up the suppliers to enter into the supply agreements with retailers on unfavorable terms, for example, payments for shelves, pay-to-stay fees, it is recommended to elaborate such self-regulation mechanism as a code of conduct for retailers and suppliers directly prohibiting such discriminatory actions.

Besides, from a procedural point of view, in order to improve the competitive landscape in Ukraine and enhance effectiveness of antitrust enforcement, we would recommend the following amendments:

- firstly, to envisage a possibility for conclusion of an amicable agreement between an offender and the AMCU;
- secondly, to separate powers between units of the AMCU so that investigations are conducted by one working group and the imposition of fines is made by another working group;
- thirdly, to envisage a fine determination mechanism providing for the base amount of fine that can be corrected based on different criteria in each particular case;
- fourthly, to prohibit further investigation by the AMCU as regards a matter reviewed by a court where there was a decision to close a case for failing to prove the violation;
- lastly, to limit the term for conducting investigations by the AMCU to 6 months.

United Kingdom

19

Daniel Piccinin

19.1 Introduction

A draft version of this report was circulated to members of the Competition Law Association (the "CLA") on April 2013. This report reflects the views expressed by CLA members at a meeting held on 9 May 2013 to discuss the draft.

In summary, the view of the CLA members in attendance was that the United Kingdom's competition law regime has, in recent years, handled the food distribution sector well and that further legislation is not needed. As explained below, the sector has come in for detailed scrutiny, in particular in the form of a market investigation that produced a number of significant remedies. We note, however, that in the absence of such a regime, other jurisdictions may well find that specific legislation is needed to deal with the sector effectively.

19.1.1 Economic Background

The structure of the grocery production, processing and retailing markets in the United Kingdom is similar to that of many other developed countries, in that primary agricultural production markets are generally characterised by very low levels of concentration, whereas grocery retailing is characterised by relatively high levels of concentration, at both the national and local levels. Intermediate steps in

In addition to receiving helpful comments from the wider Competition Law Association, the Reporter is especially grateful for comments from last year's National Reporter, David Bailey, on an early draft. All errors and omissions remain those of this year's Reporter, however.

D. Piccinin (✉)
Brick Court Chambers, London, UK
e-mail: daniel.piccinin@brickcourt.co.uk

P. Kobel et al. (eds.), *Antitrust in the Groceries Sector & Liability Issues in Relation to Corporate Social Responsibility*, LIDC Contributions on Antitrust Law, Intellectual Property and Unfair Competition, DOI 10.1007/978-3-662-45753-5_19

the supply chain (including processors and wholesalers) feature varying levels of concentration from product to product.

By way of (very crude) illustration, the United Kingdom's Department for the Environment, Food and Rural Affairs (the "Defra") publishes annual statistics on various aspects of the food chain, including the total number of undertakings involved at each level. Needless to say, these data do not accurately reflect economic concentration levels because (1) they say nothing about the distribution of market shares between those undertakings, (2) they are not broken down by product market and (3) they do not reflect the fact that primary producers can in some cases group together to market their products collectively (as noted below). However, they provide a broad overview of the UK food sector. Defra's latest figures, from 2011, are as follows:

1. farmers and primary producers: 222,668 enterprises;
2. food and drink manufacturing: 7,356 enterprises;
3. food and drink retailers: 52,124 enterprises.[1]

Some more detailed data are also available for particular segments of the food sector. In particular, the Competition Commission analysed the food supply chains for four types of food in the course of its investigation into "The supply of groceries in the UK" (the "2008 Groceries Investigation Report"), discussed in detail below: (1) red meat, (2) pig meat, (3) milk and (4) fruit. Its findings, based on data from 2005, are summarised in Table 19.1.

As for the retail level, although there were 93,000 grocery stores in the United Kingdom in 2009, 85 % of grocery sales are accounted for by the eight large grocery retailers, and two-thirds of sales are accounted for by the four largest grocery retailers (Asda, Morrisons, Sainsbury's and Tesco).[2]

Finally, it should be noted that the levels of concentration described above do not necessarily provide a completely accurate reflection of the bargaining power and economic strength of the various levels of the supply chain. Although the primary production markets generally feature very low levels of concentration, it is common for producers to market their produce jointly through large cooperatives. In particular, the EU's common agricultural policy provides for "producer organisations" for certain types of produce (including fruit and vegetables, as well as milk and milk products) whose objectives are to plan production, increase the concentration of supple, optimise production costs and stabilise producer prices.[3] Furthermore,

[1] Defra, *Agriculture in the United Kingdom 2011*, Chart 7.2, p. 61, available at http://www.defra.gov.uk/statistics/files/defra-stats-foodfarm-crosscutting-auk-auk2011-120709.pdf.

[2] Department for Business, Innovation and Skills, *Groceries Code Adjudicator: Impact Assessment*, May 2011, pp. 8–9.

[3] See Council Regulation 1234/2007 of 22 October 2007 establishing a common organisation of agricultural markets and on specific provisions for certain agricultural products (as amended), Article 122. See also Case C-500/11 *Fruition* (opinion of 23 April 2013, not published) pts 23–32, for an account of their role in the common agricultural policy over time.

Table 19.1 Food supply chains

Food type	Primary production	Processors
Red meat	80,000 cattle holdings 87,000 sheep holdings[a]	300 abattoir companies Largest 22 accounting for 59 % of cattle slaughtering Largest 19 accounting for 45 % of sheep slaughtering[b]
Pig meat	10,000 holdings[c]	Six integrated pig processors[d]
Milk	20,000 holdings[e]	Over 200 processors Largest three accounting for more than 90 % of milk sold to grocery retailers[f]
Fruit	500 holdings[g]	Four marketing agents accounting for 80 % of UK-produced fruit sold to large grocery retailers[h]

[a]2008 Groceries Investigation Report Annex 9.4, §4
[b]Ibid, §22
[c]2008 Groceries Investigation Report Annex 9.5, §6
[d]Ibid, §11
[e]2008 Groceries Investigation Report Annex 9.3, §3
[f]Ibid, §11
[g]2008 Groceries Investigation Report Annex 9.6, §13
[h]Ibid, §19

farmers have proven able to exert industrial and political pressure on processors and retailers through other forms of collective action. By way of example, as discussed below, the Office of Fair Trading found that in 2002, pressure from dairy farmers for an increase in the "farm gate" price of milk was so intense (including blockades of depots)[4] that grocery retailers and dairy processors implemented an across-the-board retail and processor price increases for the purpose of passing back an increase in the farm gate price of milk.[5] Far from being an isolated incident, similar incidents have occurred regularly, and again as recently as this year.[6] Finally, it is fair to say that at least some consumers in the United Kingdom have a preference for purchasing food that supports farmers, and this in turn is reflected in grocery retailers' efforts to demonstrate that they are farmer friendly in their practices.

19.1.2 Legal Background

19.1.2.1 Overview of UK Competition Law

There are four principal elements of competition law in the United Kingdom, all of which apply to grocery retailing:

[4] See OFT Decision of 26 July 2011, *Dairy retail price initiatives*, §§ 5.29–5.36.

[5] Ibid, §5.27, although the OFT noted that it could not establish whether the various dairy pricing initiatives had any lasting, appreciable impact on farm gate prices.

[6] Financial Times, *Morrisons Depots Blocked by Farmers*, 23 April 2013, p. 20.

1. the market investigation regime (discussed in Sect. 19.2 below),
2. competition law enforcement (discussed in Sect. 19.3 below),
3. merger control (discussed in Sect. 19.4 below).

Each of those elements is discussed in turn below. It should be noted, however, that the United Kingdom's competition law regime is in the process of undergoing substantial institutional reform. Whereas there were until recently two general competition law authorities - the Office of Fair Trading (the "OFT") and the Competition Commission - these two institutions merged into a single Competition and Markets Authority, which commenced work on 1 April 2014.[7] Various changes will be made to competition law procedures, and some changes to aspects of the substantive regimes, but little that is material to the issues discussed in this report will change.[8] In what follows, this report therefore discusses the current regime and the ways that it has been applied to this sector in recent years.

The first of those elements, the market investigation regime, is, to the reporter's knowledge, unique in global competition law. It combines the wide-ranging powers of investigation and reporting that are common in market study/sector inquiry regimes in other jurisdictions with the extensive remedial powers that more commonly arise in the context of merger control or antitrust enforcement. The regime operates as follows:

1. The OFT[9] has the power to refer a market to the Competition Commission for investigation where it has "reasonable grounds for suspecting that any feature, or combination of features, prevents, restricts or distorts competition in connection with the supply or acquisition of any goods or services in the United Kingdom or a part of the United Kingdom".[10] The term "feature" is defined very widely to include market structure or the conduct of suppliers or customers.[11]
2. Where such a reference has been made, the Competition Commission must decide whether any feature of the relevant markets prevents, restricts or distorts competition.[12] It is allowed 2 years to investigate and publish its final report.[13]
3. Where the Competition Commission identifies features of the market that restrict competition, it must also consider what measures it should take, or what

[7] Enterprise and Regulatory Reform Act 2013, Part 3.

[8] Enterprise and Regulatory Reform Act 2013, Part 4.

[9] The various sectoral regulators (e.g., for energy or telecommunications) can also make references in respect of markets in their sectors. However, grocery markets do not fall within the jurisdiction of any sectoral regulators, so those regulators are not considered further in this report.

[10] Section 131(1) EA. The relevant government minister can also refer a market for investigation, but to date that power has not been used.

[11] Section 131(2) EA.

[12] Section 134(1) EA.

[13] Section 137(1) EA.

measures it should recommend that others take, to remedy those features and any detrimental effect on consumers resulting from them.[14]
4. The Competition Commission has extremely wide-ranging remedial powers, including the power to prohibit agreements, mandate various forms of conduct, order divestitures or prohibit acquisitions.[15]
5. It should also be noted that Competition Commission market investigation references are very resource intensive, not just for the Competition Commission but also for the private parties involved. Given the expense involved and the risk of adverse outcomes (from the parties' perspective), the mere threat of a reference can have an impact on parties' behaviour and market outcomes.

The market investigation regime applies to grocery retailing markets in the same way as it does to other markets. Indeed, as discussed in Sect. 19.2 below, the Competition Commission published a market investigation decision on the grocery sector in 2008, which followed an earlier investigation under the predecessor regime in 2000.

The second element, merger control, is also somewhat distinctive. The Enterprise Act provides for "relevant merger situations" (broadly, acquisition of control or "material influence" over another undertaking) that satisfy either a turnover test (GBP 70 m for the target) or a market share test (25 % combined share of supply) to be reviewed by the OFT and Competition Commission. Because the market share test can be applied in relation to local, regional or national markets, even very small mergers (such as the acquisition of a single grocery retailer store) can be reviewed.[16]

Unlike many other jurisdictions, the United Kingdom's merger control regime features voluntary notification, combined with a 4-month deadline (measured from when the fact that the merger has completed has been "made public") for the OFT to decide whether to refer the merger for in-depth investigation by the Competition Commission. As a result, it is possible for some small or inconspicuous acquisitions to escape scrutiny altogether if they do not come to the OFT's attention.[17]

The substantive test for review is whether the merger gives rise to a "substantial lessening of competition". In addition, the relevant minister can intervene in a case and take the final decision on wider public interest grounds if the merger engages

[14] Section 134(4) EA.

[15] Sections 138, 161 and Schedule 8 EA.

[16] See, for example, Competition Commission decision of 28 November 2007 *Tesco/Co-op Store in Slough*.

[17] See, for example, OFT decision of 2 February 2004 *Tesco/Co-op Store in Slough* under the heading "*jurisdiction*", in which the OFT recorded that Tesco had recently acquired three Co-op grocery retailing stores, only one of which fell within the four-month deadline and therefore could be investigated.

one of the defined public interests set out in the legislation. Although there are not currently any public interests specified in relation to the grocery sector, in principle the government of the day could change that position in the course of a merger investigation if it saw it fit to do so.[18]

The remaining two elements of competition law in the United Kingdom follow broadly the same pattern as other EU jurisdictions: a prohibition on anticompetitive agreements (the Ch I Prohibition/Article 101 Treaty on the Functioning of the European Union) and a prohibition on abuses of a dominant position (the Ch II Prohibition/Article 102 Treaty on the Functioning of the European Union). Both are enforced by the OFT, in conjunction with the national courts. Breaches of either provision can result in substantial financial penalties.

In principle, both prohibitions can be applied in the grocery sector, although to date only the Ch I prohibition has been (as will be discussed below). Both prohibitions require proof of an effect on trade within the United Kingdom (Ch I and II Prohibitions) or between Member States of the EU (Articles 101 and 102 TFEU).

19.1.2.2 Retail and Grocery-Specific Competition Law Rules and Exemptions

The United Kingdom's competition law regime described above is (for the most part) generally applicable across all sectors. There are no sector-specific exemptions or special provisions in respect of their application to grocery retailing.

However, one of the remedies imposed by the Competition Commission in the 2008 Groceries Investigation Report was the establishment of the Groceries Supply Code of Practice (the "GSCOP"), which regulates the relationship between large grocery retailers and their suppliers. In particular, it imposes a general obligation of fair dealing, in addition to a number of specific requirements in relation to various aspects of the supplier–retailer relationship. At the time of the 2008 Groceries Investigation Report, the Competition Commission required the retailers to seek to agree to the appointment of an Ombudsman to enforce the GSCOP. However, they failed to reach an agreement, and so Parliament decided to legislate for a new role of Groceries Code Adjudicator to act as an enforcer for GSCOP.[19] Because it resulted from a market investigation rather than as a sui generis piece of competition legislation, the GSCOP is discussed in more detail in Sect. 19.2 below.

---

[18] Section 42 EA. For example, during the *Lloyds/HBOS* banking merger, the Government designated a new public interest of "the stability of the UK financial system" during the course of the OFT's review, with the result that the minister could intervene and approve the merger without the need for an in-depth review by the Competition Commission. See, to that effect, Lord Mandelson's decision of 31 October 2008 *Lloyds/HBOS*.

[19] The Groceries Code Adjudicator Act received Royal Assent on 25 April 2013.

19.2 Market Investigations and Advocacy

19.2.1 Overview

As discussed in Sect. 19.1.2.1 above, one of the unique features of the competition law regime in the United Kingdom is its market investigation regime, which empowers the Competition Commission to impose wide-ranging remedies to address any features of markets that it considers to be undesirable from a competition perspective. One such recent investigation concerned the grocery sector, which is discussed in Sects. 19.2.2–19.2.4 below.

19.2.2 Background to the 2008 Groceries Investigation

As explained in Sect. 19.1.2.1 above, the Competition Commission can only conduct a market investigation where the OFT (or other relevant body) refers a market to it for investigation. The reference that gave rise to the 2008 Groceries Investigation was made by the OFT in 2007 but was the product of many years of competition concerns in relation to the sector.

In 1999–2000, the predecessor to the Competition Commission, known as the Monopolies and Mergers Commission (the "MMC"), had conducted an inquiry into the grocery sector under the competition legislation that was in force at that time (the Fair Trading Act 1973) (the "MMC Investigation"). That legislation provided for a market investigation regime that is similar to that which is found in many other jurisdictions, in that the MMC had powers of investigation but could only make recommendations as to what the Government or others should do to remedy any concerns that it identified.

The MMC Investigation arose out of concerns in the 1990s about high prices and profits in the grocery sector in the United Kingdom. Those concerns reflected a broader concern that consumer prices were higher in the United Kingdom than in continental Europe and the US, which the popular press dubbed "Rip off Britain".[20] The MMC Final Report identified a number of competition concerns, falling into two broad categories: (1) concerns about grocery retailers' pricing strategies (in particular, below-cost pricing and "price flexing", whereby higher prices were charged in some stores than others)[21] and (2) concerns about grocery retailers' conduct towards their suppliers.[22] It decided not to recommend any action in relation to the pricing concerns, however, because it considered that the potential remedies (such as a prohibition on below-cost selling or on price variations across stores) would either have too many unintended consequences (such as prohibiting desirable price cutting or differential pricing that reflects regional cost differences)

[20] MMC Investigation §2.5. See http://en.wikipedia.org/wiki/Rip_Off_Britain for an account of the wider "Rip off Britain" phenomenon.

[21] MMC Investigation §§2.435–2.436.

[22] Ibid, §§2.548–2.550.

or be too difficult to implement.[23] In relation to the concerns about supplier practices, the MMC recommended the adoption of a Supermarkets Code of Practice for all grocery retailers with a national market share in excess of 8 %. Such a code (the "SCOP") was drawn up and adopted by the four largest grocery retailers at the time.

In the years that followed, complaints continued to be made to the OFT about grocery retailers' treatment of suppliers, in particular, and also about competition in the sector, more broadly. The OFT conducted a general review of SCOP in 2004 and commissioned and published a detailed audit of compliance with SCOP in 2005. At the same time, the OFT sought submissions on the effectiveness of competition in the grocery retail markets but concluded on August 2005 that a further reference to the Competition Commission for a market investigation was not warranted because the SCOP and competition generally were both working well.[24] On October 2005, however, that decision was challenged by the Association of Convenience Stores (the "ACS"), which considered that competition was not working well at all. The OFT conceded that its decision had not been properly reasoned, consented to the quashing of that decision by the Competition Appeal Tribunal and undertook to investigate and consider the issues again.[25] On 9 May 2006, the OFT referred the market to the Competition Commission for investigation, citing concerns about (1) the operation of the planning system, (2) barriers to entry raised by large grocery retailers' landholdings, (3) grocery retailers' imposition of restrictive covenants when selling land and (4) the same retail pricing and supplier relationship practices that the MMC had found problematic in the earlier MMC Inquiry.[26]

19.2.3 The 2008 Groceries Investigation Report

The 2008 Groceries Investigation ran for nearly 2 years (9 May 2006–30 April 2008) and covered a comprehensive range of competition issues:

1. competition between large grocery retailers and smaller convenience and specialist stores,
2. concentration in local markets for grocery retailing,
3. barriers to entry or expansion,
4. possible collusion or coordination between grocery retailers, and
5. competition issues in the grocery supply chain.

Its findings in relation to each topic are summarised below.

[23] Ibid, §§2.558–2.577.

[24] OFT decision of 3 August 2005, *Supermarkets: The Code of Practice and other Competition Issues*, OFT807.

[25] *ACS v OFT* [2005] CAT 36.

[26] OFT decision of 9 May 2006, *The Grocery Market: The OFT's reasons for making a reference to the Competition Commission*, OFT845.

19.2.3.1 Competition Between Large Grocery Retailers and Smaller Convenience and Specialist Stores

As explained above, the 2008 Groceries Investigation only came about because of pressure from the convenience store sector based on their concerns that large grocery retailers were squeezing them out of the market. But for their intervention, the 2008 Groceries Investigation would not have happened. The ACS actively participated in the Investigation as well, submitting 16 documents over the course of the Investigation. As explained below, however, although the Competition Commission investigated a number of the concerns raised by the ACS, in each case the Competition Commission concluded that there was no restriction of competition.

First, the Competition Commission investigated the so-called waterbed effect, whereby large grocery retailers exercise their buyer power to obtain low-cost prices for themselves, with the result that suppliers need to charge higher cost prices to smaller grocery retailers in order to recover their costs. As a consequence, large grocery retailers are able to offer more competitive retail prices, which in turn allows them to increase their market shares at the expense of smaller retailers and thereby reinforces their buyer power. Ultimately (according to the theory), consumers are harmed by the reduction in competitive constraint posed by small retailers.

Although the Competition Commission's investigation confirmed the accuracy of ACS' complaint that large grocery retailers pay less for their supplies than their smaller competitors, and although the Competition Commission accepted that the "waterbed effect" theory was logically coherent, the Competition Commission found that there was no such effect in the United Kingdom grocery markets. In that regard, the Competition Commission placed weight on (amongst other factors) (1) evidence suggesting that there is a limit to the extent to which growth in the size of a retailer translates into lower supply prices[27] and (2) the fact that because competition between large grocery retailers is intense, any reductions in supply prices that they achieve are likely to be passed on to consumers.[28]

Second, the Competition Commission considered the argument that the closure of some convenience stores was leading to a "tipping point" in the viability of the wholesalers that supply them as those wholesalers become unable to recover their fixed costs from a more limited customer base. The Competition Commission rejected that argument, however, on the basis that both the convenience store sector and the wholesaler sector were growing rather than declining, and in any event any decline in customer base would be more likely to lead to consolidation amongst wholesalers rather than resulting in a "tipping point" for the viability of the whole sector.[29]

[27] 2008 Groceries Investigation Report §5.31.

[28] Ibid, §5.29.

[29] Ibid, §5.51.

Third, the Competition Commission investigated whether below-cost pricing by large grocery retailers might foreclose competition from specialist and convenience grocery stores. Although the Competition Commission found that large grocery retailers *do* sell products below cost, unlike the MMC in the MMC Investigation, the Competition Commission did not consider this to be problematic from a competition perspective. In particular, the Competition Commission rejected the suggestion that the below-cost pricing might be an attempt to "predate" smaller stores, not least because the Competition Commission found that such smaller stores do not in general place a competitive constraint on larger stores.[30] Similarly, the Competition Commission rejected the suggestion that the foreclosure of convenience and specialist stores might be an "unintended consequence" of below-cost selling because the evidence showed that the local entry of a large grocery retailer (which tends to engage in below-cost pricing) had no impact on the rate of entry or exit of convenience stores or off-licence alcohol retailers.[31] Finally, the Competition Commission also rejected the argument that below-cost selling by large retailers might "mislead" consumers into believing that such retailers were better value than small retailers across the board. The Competition Commission considered that the evidence showed that consumers take into account a broad range of factors, rather than just the price of a select few items, in determining where to shop.[32]

Fourth, the Competition Commission considered the argument that local discount voucher campaigns by large grocery retailers (and in particular Tesco) might be part of a predatory strategy to exclude smaller retailers from the market. The Competition Commission rejected that argument on the basis that the evidence did not show any impact of those strategies on the entry or exit of convenience stores and because local voucher campaigns were not used extensively in any event.[33]

Finally, the Competition Commission considered the entry by Tesco and Sainsbury's (two of the largest grocery retailers) into the convenience store sector. However, the Competition Commission concluded that their efforts to compete in this sector were pro-competitive and did not provide any evidence of predation.[34] It should be noted, however, that the Competition Commission's findings that there had not been predation and that competition from large grocery retailers was pro-competitive do not provide a complete answer to concerns that the expansion of large grocery retailers might be socially undesirable for other reasons (i.e., reasons that do not relate to competition). For example, the Competition Commission could not consider in its investigation the question of whether diversity in high

[30] Ibid, §5.58.

[31] Ibid, §§5.65–5.66. The Competition Commission pointed out that, because alcohol was one of the items that was regularly sold below cost by large grocery retailers, it might be expected that any impact that such below-cost selling would have would be felt by alcohol specialist retailers.

[32] Ibid, §5.67.

[33] Ibid, §§5.81 and 5.86.

[34] Ibid, §§5.88–5.98.

streets across the country is desirable in its own right irrespective of the impact on competition. As the Competition Commission explained, that and a wide range of other public policy issues were outside of its remit under the United Kingdom's market investigation regime.[35]

19.2.3.2 Concentration in Local Markets for Grocery Retailing

The Competition Commission conducted an in-depth investigation of the extent to which competition between grocery retailers in highly concentrated local markets might be restricted. In contrast to the situation at the time of the MMC Investigation, by 2006–2008, most large grocery retailers had stopped engaging in "price-flexing" and had rather adopted uniform national pricing policies pursuant to which prices only varied between stores according to their overall size.[36] Moreover, most large grocery retailers took a similar approach to other aspects of their retail offering, including product range and the use of promotional discounts.[37]

Nevertheless, the Competition Commission was concerned that a lack of competition at the local level could manifest itself in one or both of two ways: (1) a deterioration in the quality of those parts of the retail offering that were determined at a local, store level (i.e., opening hours, stock levels, cleanliness, quality of service) and (2) influencing the overall pricing and quality decisions applied by the retailers across the board. As explained below, the Competition Commission found evidence of both forms of anticompetitive harm.

First, the Competition Commission analysed the extent to which retailers might soften their competitive efforts in local markets in which they faced reduced competition. Although the Competition Commission conceded that it could not measure this directly, it could analyse store level profit margins, and the evidence showed that profit margins were higher in highly concentrated local markets. The Competition Commission concluded that those higher profit margins reflected the deterioration of the retailer's local competitive efforts.[38]

Second, the Competition Commission concluded that, when setting national price levels, retailers would take into account the extent to which they faced competition in the various local markets in which they compete. Because the Competition Commission found that a significant proportion of grocery stores were located in highly concentrated local markets (11–27 % for large stores and 10–22 % for mid-large stores), it stood to reason that retailers would take that into account and set higher national prices than they would have if more of their stores were located in highly competitive local markets.[39]

[35] Ibid, §§2.11–2.18.

[36] Ibid, §6.31.

[37] Ibid, §6.32.

[38] Ibid, §§6.60–6.63.

[39] Ibid, §6.73.

19.2.3.3 Barriers to Entry or Expansion

The Competition Commission investigated a number of potential barriers to entry or expansion in grocery retailing, both in general and in local markets that are currently highly concentrated. In particular, the Competition Commission considered three potential barriers: (1) cost advantages held by large grocery retailers, and Tesco in particular; (2) the planning system; and (3) large grocery retailers' land banks.

In relation to cost advantages, the Competition Commission found that large retailers (and in particular Tesco) had such advantages but that they did not give rise to material barriers to entry. The evidence showed that other retailers successfully acquired and developed new sites notwithstanding their cost disadvantages.[40]

In relation to the planning system, the Competition Commission noted that it necessarily has the effect of restricting entry and expansion, both because it constrains retailers' freedom to choose where to build new stores or enlarge existing ones and because the planning approval process itself is costly and time consuming.[41] Further, the Competition Commission noted that the system favours incumbents, both because it is easier to obtain approval for expansions of existing stores than for building new stores and because the existing large grocery retailers have more expertise and resources for dealing with the process than new entrants would have.[42] However, the Competition Commission considered that the planning system only gave rise to a material barrier to entry in respect of large stores because medium and smaller stores could more easily be established in areas that are not subject to planning restrictions.[43]

The Competition Commission also identified material barriers to entry arising from large grocery retailers' holdings of land and the restrictive covenants and exclusivity arrangements that attach to those holdings. Although the Competition Commission accepted that none of the retailers pursued a strategy of using those holdings to exclude competition, it found that the presence of such holdings in highly concentrated local markets had the effect of restricting competition in those local markets.[44]

19.2.3.4 Coordination Between Grocery Retailers

The Competition Commission also investigated the possibility that large grocery retailers might collude or coordinate with each other. It noted that the OFT was in the process of conducting a number of cartel investigations involving the sector, which are discussed in Sect. 19.3 below. It also noted that the conditions that make collusion or tacit coordination possible were evident in the sector, although it found no evidence of such behaviour taking place.[45]

---

[40] Ibid, §§7.115–7.117.

[41] Ibid, §7.118.

[42] Ibid, §§7.118–7.119.

[43] Ibid, §7.120.

[44] Ibid, §7.121.

[45] Ibid, §8.40.

19.2.3.5 Supply Chain Issues

Finally, the Competition Commission considered whether large grocery retailers have significant buyer power and whether they use that power in a way that distorts competition.

The Competition Commission concluded that large grocery retailers do have buyer power[46] but that this is not in itself problematic from a competition perspective because the lower supply prices that their buyer power makes possible are passed on to consumers.[47] In particular, the Competition Commission rejected the suggestion that retailers exercised their buyer power by withholding demand, which (if it had been established) would have had adverse effects on consumers.[48] However, the Competition Commission drew a distinction between the normal exercise of buyer power to obtain better trading terms and the use of buyer power to "transfer excessive risks or unexpected costs to their suppliers through practices involving retrospective adjustments to supply agreements or giving rise to moral hazard on the part of the grocery retailer".[49] According to the Competition Commission, such conduct "is likely to lessen suppliers' incentives to invest in new capacity, products and production processes ... [and] will be detrimental to the interests of consumers".[50] Particular examples of retrospective conduct that the Competition Commission identified included imposing price changes on suppliers after goods had been ordered or delivered or requiring them to contribute to the costs of promotions that had not been agreed upon in advance.[51] Examples of excessive risk transfer giving rise to moral hazard included the practice of making suppliers liable for losses arising from goods being lost or stolen in store.[52]

In addition to its investigation of buyer power and supply chain practices, the Competition Commission also investigated whether the sale by retailers of "own label" products alongside branded products gave rise to distortions of competition by reason of the retailers acting as both customers and competitors of suppliers of branded products. The Competition Commission rejected the suggestion that their privileged position gave retailers a substantial competitive advantage, however, because the evidence did not show that own-label products had been consistently growing at the expense of branded products.[53]

19.2.3.6 Remedies

As explained above, the Competition Commission identified four features of the relevant markets that distort competition: (1) high levels of concentration in some

[46] Ibid, §9.21.

[47] Ibid, §9.41.

[48] Ibid, §§9.68–9.69.

[49] Ibid, §9.41.

[50] Ibid.

[51] Ibid, §9.45.

[52] Ibid, §9.48.

[53] Ibid, §§9.74–9.75.

local markets, (2) the planning system, (3) retailers' landholdings and (4) supply chain practices. In each case, the Competition Commission found that the features gave rise to detrimental effects on consumers, and accordingly the Competition Commission had a statutory duty to impose remedies.[54]

The Competition Commission decided to impose a package of remedies to address those concerns, including

(i) a recommendation that a new "competition test" be incorporated in the planning regime, which would block the development of new large grocery stores or the extension of existing ones where the operator of the new store would have a local market share in excess of 60 %[55];
(ii) measures in relation to restrictive covenants and exclusivity arrangements
    (1) requiring the release of restrictive covenants in highly concentrated local markets;
    (2) imposing a prohibition on new restrictive covenants that restrict grocery retailing;
    (3) prohibiting the enforcement of exclusivity arrangements in highly concentrated local markets beyond a period of 5 years;
    (4) recommending that the then existing exemption from competition law for Land Agreements should be amended to exclude exclusivity arrangements that restrict grocery retailing[56];
(iii) the establishment of a Groceries Supply Code of Practice ("**GSCOP**"), based on the existing SCOP, but amended to include a general requirement of fair dealing and specific prohibitions of the retrospective and excessive risk transferring forms of conduct considered above, together with a requirement that retailers should enter into binding arbitration to resolve any disputes arising under the GSCOP[57]; and
(iv) a recommendation that unless the retailers themselves established a GSCOP Ombudsman to monitor and enforce compliance with the GSCOP, that the Government should establish such an ombudsman.[58]

19.2.4 Implementation of the 2008 Groceries Investigation Report

Although the findings and remedies made, recommended and imposed by the Competition Commission were quite clear and detailed, the implementation of those remedies has been far from smooth.

[54] Ibid, §§10.13–10.17.

[55] Ibid, §§11.437–11.441.

[56] Ibid, §§11.442–11.444.

[57] Ibid, §11.445.

[58] Ibid, §§11.446–11.448.

First, Tesco challenged the Competition Commission's decision to recommend the introduction of a "competition test" in the planning regime. The Competition Appeal Tribunal upheld that challenge on the basis that (1) the Competition Commission had failed to investigate to what extent it would be effective at reducing concentration in highly concentrated local markets[59] and (2) the Competition Commission had failed to take into account the extent to which the remedy itself would harm consumers by preventing the expansion of incumbents in highly concentrated local markets.[60] Both points were based on the proposition that the direct effect of the competition test could only be to *prevent* the building of new capacity, which would (in the absence of prompt entry or expansion by a competitor) harm consumers. So the desirability of the competition test depended critically on the extent to which the expansion that was blocked by the competition test would be offset by new entry or expansion by smaller competitors in the highly concentrated local markets. Although this was crucial to the analysis, the Competition Appeal Tribunal found that the Competition Commission had not investigated it sufficiently and so quashed and remitted the decision to the Competition Commission for reconsideration.

The Competition Commission then reconsidered the desirability of the competition test remedy, focussing on the question of how long it would take for competitors to replace any expansion by incumbents that was blocked by the test. The Competition Commission concluded that the benefits substantially outweighed the costs and therefore reinstated its recommendation that it should be implemented, subject to only to the introduction of a *de minimis* exception whereby small extensions could be made by incumbents without needing to pass the competition test.

By the time the new recommendation had been made (October 2009), however, the then Labour Government's term in office was coming to an end. The Government did not have time to decide whether or not to accept the Competition Commission's recommendation before the election on May 2010 that led to a change in Government. The new Conservative/Liberal Democrat coalition has not implemented the competition test, and at the time of writing there do not appear to be any proposals to do so.[61]

The other remedies have fared better but have also been affected by delays:

1. The GSCOP came into force on 4 February 2010 (i.e., nearly 2 years after the Competition Commission decided it should be implemented),[62] and legislation providing for an enforcement mechanism was enacted on 25 April 2013.[63]

[59] *Tesco v Competition Commission* [2009] CAT 6 §§111–128.

[60] Ibid, §§144–165.

[61] House of Commons Library, *Supermarkets: competition inquiries into the groceries market*, 2 August 2012, p. 34.

[62] See s 1(2) of the Groceries (Supply Chain Practices) Market Investigation Order 2009.

[63] In the intervening period, the OFT has played a limited monitoring role as set out in its guidance document, *Monitoring and Enforcement by the Office of Fair Trading of the Groceries (Supply Chain Practices) Market Investigation Order 2009*, first published in August 2009 and then updated through to August 2012.

2. The remedies in relation to restrictive covenants and exclusivity arrangements were implemented in the Groceries Market Investigation (Controlled Land) Order 2010, which was issued on 10 August 2010 (i.e., more than 2 years after the Competition Commission decided that the remedies should be implemented).
3. The recommendation that exclusivity arrangements restricting grocery retailing should be removed from the exemption from competition law that land agreements enjoyed at the time was effectively implemented by the revocation of that exemption in its entirety as of 6 April 2011.[64]

19.3 Competition Law Enforcement

19.3.1 Enforcement Against Anticompetitive Agreements

There has been a significant degree of antitrust enforcement activity in the food (and other grocery) distribution sector in recent years, although it is fair to say that (1) it mostly concerned conduct that took place much longer ago (reflecting the lengthy nature of antitrust investigations in the United Kingdom) and (2) very few of the allegations that have been made by the OFT have resulted in findings of infringement that have withstood the scrutiny of the Competition Appeal Tribunal.

In particular, there have been three separate investigations involving large grocery retailers and a fourth involving allegations of collusion between upstream producers:

1. The *Tobacco* case: this is a case in which the OFT found that two major tobacco manufacturers (Imperial and Gallaher) had entered into bilateral agreements with several grocery retailers beginning in the mid-1990s and running up to the OFT's investigation in 2003 that effectively linked the retail prices of each manufacturer's product at a particular retailer to the retail price of the other manufacturer's product at the same store.[65] The OFT considered that those agreements had the object of restricting competition between the manufacturers (i.e., inter-brand competition).[66] The OFT imposed fines of GBP 225 m in total on the manufacturers and retailers. A number of parties (including Imperial and several retailers) appealed to the Competition Appeal Tribunal. During the course of the appeal, the OFT's case collapsed (i.e., it considered that it could no longer support the findings of infringement it had made in light of the evidence), with the result that the decision was quashed as against the appealing parties.[67] Gallaher and some other retailers have since applied for permission to appeal out of time, and their appeals remain outstanding at this stage.[68]

[64] Competition Act 1998 (Land Agreements Exclusion Revocation) Order 2010/1709.

[65] OFT Decision of 15 April 2010 in *Tobacco*.

[66] Ibid, §1.13.

[67] *Imperial Tobacco and Ors v OFT* [2011] CAT 41.

[68] *Gallaher v OFT* [2013] CAT 5.

2. The *Dairy* case: in this case, the OFT found that in 2002/2003 a number of milk processors and dairy product manufacturers orchestrated an increase in the retail price of dairy products so as to fund an increase in the cost price (i.e., the price paid by grocery retailers to processors/manufacturers).[69] The background to that case was that the price paid to dairy farmers for milk was extremely low and farmers were protesting and blockading processor and retailer depots to put pressure on them to increase prices. In response to that pressure, the processors/manufacturers acted as conduits for the exchange of future pricing intentions among the retailers to increase their confidence in their ability to increase retail prices (and therefore be in a position to pay increased cost prices) without being undercut by rivals and therefore losing market share. This is referred to as a "hub and spoke" infringement. Initially, the OFT alleged that this occurred in five separate initiatives (1) fresh liquid milk in 2002, (2) cheese in 2002; (3) fresh liquid milk in 2003, (4) cheese in 2003 and (5) butter in 2003. Indeed, all of the alleged participants in those alleged infringements admitted that they occurred as alleged, with the exception of Tesco (the largest grocery retailer) and Morrisons[70] (another large grocery retailer). Notwithstanding those admissions, however, the OFT ultimately accepted the position put forward by Morrisons and Tesco in relation to the alleged fresh liquid milk collusion in 2002 (point (1) above)[71] and the position put forward by Tesco in relation to the alleged fresh liquid milk and butter collusion in 2003 (points (3) and (5) above). Indeed, in relation to fresh liquid milk in 2002 and butter in 2003, the OFT felt unable to conclude that even the parties that had admitted being involved in collusion had actually done anything wrong. The OFT did ultimately find infringements had taken place in relation to cheese in 2002 and 2003 (involving Tesco, amongst others) and in relation to fresh liquid milk in 2003 (not involving Tesco) and imposed fines totalling GBP 50 m. Tesco appealed, however, and the Competition Appeal Tribunal quashed the entirety of the cheese 2003 infringement finding and most of the OFT's findings in relation to 2002.[72] What was left was a finding that Tesco's cheese buyer had exchanged future pricing intentions in relation to cheese with Tesco's competitors (via its suppliers) on three occasions in 2002 but that, contrary to the OFT's case, there was no overall plan to coordinate retail prices.[73] As an aside, it is also noteworthy that the *Dairy* case gave rise to the *Safeway v Twigger* litigation, in which one of the Dairy infringers (Safeway) sued its former employees and directors for damages (including the penalties imposed by the OFT). That claim failed, however, on

[69] OFT Decision of 10 August 2011 in *Dairy*.

[70] Morrisons was only accused of being involved in the fresh liquid milk collusion in 2002.

[71] As a result, the OFT accepted that Morrisons had not been involved in any dairy product collusion in that period.

[72] *Tesco v OFT* [2012] CAT 31.

[73] Ibid, §202.

the basis of the English law principle (which is also common to many other jurisdictions) of *ex turpi causa*.[74]

3. The *Scottish Milk* case: between 2001 and 2008 the OFT investigated allegations of price fixing between Scottish milk processors. It ultimately concluded, however, that the evidence did not support a finding of infringement and that further investigation was not an administrative priority.[75]
4. The *Other Groceries* case: between 2008 and 2010, the OFT also investigated allegations that suppliers of a wide range of grocery products had been acting as conduits for the exchange of future retail pricing intentions between retailers in the years 2005–2008 (i.e., a hub-and-spoke infringement). Several parties admitted having acted unlawfully, but the OFT ultimately decided on administrative priority grounds not to pursue the investigation to a conclusion one way or the other.[76]

Several interesting features emerge from that selection of cases. First, none of them involve anything that could be described as classic cartel conduct between grocery retailers. Nor is that merely a matter of form rather than substance. The *Tobacco* case was really about a restriction of competition between different brands of tobacco products (i.e., inter-brand competition) rather than a restriction of competition between retailers of the same product (i.e., intra-brand competition). Similarly, although the *Dairy* case involved indirect sharing of future retail price intentions between retailers, that was a means of facilitating the satisfaction of farmers' demands for an increase in the upstream price of milk. There was no evidence that the retail price increases that retailers were coordinating were higher than would normally be expected as a market response to the cost price increases that were being imposed by their suppliers: on the contrary, the evidence was that retailers were being encouraged to *restrain* the extent of their retail price increases.[77]

Second, as noted above, the *Dairy* case in particular provides an example of a highly fragmented upstream market (dairy farmers) bringing enormous and ultimately irresistible pressure to bear on the more highly concentrated dairy processing and grocery retailing markets. While traditional economic models may predict that more highly concentrated levels of the market are likely to have greater market (or negotiating) power, the logistical consequences of their concentration (for example, large and strategically important depots) leave them exposed to

[74] *Safeway v Twigger* [2010] EWCA Civ 1472.

[75] OFT case closure summary of October 2008 in *Scottish Milk*.

[76] OFT case closure summary of November 2010 in *Other Groceries*.

[77] *Tesco v OFT* [2012] CAT 31 §202, in which it was noted that Dairy Crest, a cheese supplier, had proposed "that there be a GBP 200 per tonne cost price increase for cheese and a *concomitant* retail price increase, which should, in Dairy Crest's view, *be limited to cash margin maintenance*".

industrial action from the politically powerful and highly motivated farmer lobbies. As noted above, the behaviour of the dairy farmers in 2002 has been repeated at regular intervals since then as well. Although competition law does in principle apply to farmers as well,[78] there is a wide exemption for farmers set out in paragraph 9 of Schedule 3 to the Competition Act, which protects, *inter alia*, agreements between farmers within the United Kingdom concerning the production or sale of agricultural products, so long as there is no obligation on farmers to charge identical prices. Although it is not clear whether that would cover agreements to engage in what amounts to industrial action, and although the OFT retains a power to disapply the exemption, no enforcement action has ever been taken by the OFT against farmers. Nor have intermediate processors or retailers yet found any other way to protect themselves from such action.

Third, both the *Tobacco* and *Dairy* cases illustrated the tendency of suppliers to want to influence retail prices. Resale price maintenance is generally treated as a "hardcore" restriction "by object", meaning that competition authorities do not need to prove that it has anticompetitive effects in order to establish an infringement and that a sceptical approach is taken to attempts by suppliers or retailers to justify their use of it.[79] Thus, while it is perfectly lawful for suppliers and retailers to discuss (on a purely bilateral basis) the current or future retail prices for the suppliers' products, or for a supplier to seek to persuade a retailer to adopt a particular retail price, the retailer must always retain an unfettered discretion as to its own retail prices. What those cases also show, however, is that the grey area in which suppliers seek to influence retail prices while leaving retailers ultimate discretion is a very dangerous place indeed. It is natural that suppliers will seek to give retailers comfort that they can accept a cost price increase by commenting on how other retailers would be likely to respond. But, as in the *Dairy* case, that can easily slip into anticompetitive territory if it results in future retail pricing intentions effectively being communicated from one retailer to another. It is also unsurprising that suppliers should be concerned about the relationship between retail prices for their own products and those of their competitors, as in *Tobacco*. More generally, they are likely to be concerned by the overall positioning (including physical positioning on shelves) of their products relative to their competitors. But the extent to which suppliers can actually set targets for retailers to achieve for their products by reference to competitors remains unclear. All of this gives rise to material challenges both for suppliers and for retailers in finding ways to carry out their day-to-day business while ensuring that all of their staff complies with this complex aspect of competition law.

[78] See the OFT's guidance paper, *How competition law applies to co-operation between farming businesses: Frequently asked questions*, November 2011.

[79] EU Commission Guidelines on Vertical Restraints, OJ 2010, C 130, p. 1, para. 223.

19.3.2 Enforcement Against Abuse of Dominance

As noted above, competition law in the United Kingdom treats abuses of buyer power or dependency as part of the wider category of abuses of dominant positions, which is one of the two antitrust prohibitions. However, the prohibition of abuses of dominant positions is of little or no application to the food distribution sector because the threshold for dominance is so high. In practice, it is difficult to establish dominance with market shares (in this case, purchasing market shares) below 40 %. None of the large grocery retailers in the United Kingdom have market shares close to that level. Although there may be pockets of very high concentration further up the chain (i.e., for manufacturers of specific products), only one of those has ever featured in an abuse of dominance investigations in the United Kingdom, and that did not concern buyer power.[80]

19.4 Merger Control

As noted above, the food distribution sector (including grocery retailing) is subject to exactly the same merger control regime as every other sector of the economy. The jurisdictional thresholds are twofold: (1) that the target's turnover in the United Kingdom exceeds GBP 70 m[81] *or* (2) that the parties' combined share of supply (or purchase) for any goods or services in respect of which they overlap exceeds 25 % in the United Kingdom or a substantial part thereof.[82] It should be noted that the "share of supply" test is *not* a market share test, in that the competition authorities have the flexibility to define product and geographic combinations that would not amount to relevant markets for antitrust purposes. There is no fixed definition of a "substantial part" of the United Kingdom either, although in practice it has been given a wide interpretation. By way of example, in the *Slough* case referred to above, the Competition Commission said that the Borough of Slough (population c. 140 k) was a substantial part of the United Kingdom.[83] As a result, even very small acquisitions can qualify.

The position is even more extreme in respect of Tesco's largest grocery retailer, Tesco. Because the OFT considers that Tesco accounts for more than 25 % of supply across the United Kingdom, even the acquisition of a single store by Tesco anywhere in the United Kingdom (i.e., even in a local market in which Tesco's market share would be less than 25 %) satisfies the share of supply test.[84]

The substantive approach that the United Kingdom authorities take to investigating grocery retail mergers is relatively flexible. As with the jurisdictional

[80] See *Claymore Dairies v OFT* [2005] CAT 30.

[81] Section 23(1)(b) Enterprise Act.

[82] Section 23(2)(b) Enterprise Act.

[83] Competition Commission decision of 28 November 2007 *Tesco/Co-op Store in Slough* §4.6.

[84] See, for example, OFT decision of 14 July 2009 in *Tesco/SPAR*.

thresholds, there are no special statutory rules applicable to market definition or measuring competition in the grocery sector. That said, the authorities have developed a relatively detailed methodology through their decisional practice while retaining the flexibility to adjust it to the particular features of the case at hand. Their methodology is broadly reflected in the guidance that they have published in relation to the appraisal of mergers in the retail sector.[85]

Although the authorities do take a standard market definition-based approach to evaluating mergers, they do not apply the resulting market definition strictly, but rather they take account of competition both within and outside of the defined markets. The main function of the initial market definition is to act as a filter (by reference to a fascia count and simple "indicative price rise" calculations based on diversion ratios and profit margins) to identify the local markets that require more detailed investigation.

In terms of product market definition, broadly speaking, the OFT and the Competition Commission distinguish between the following three types of grocery retailers:

1. **One-stop stores**: those with a net sales area of 1,400 m^2 or above. These stores form their own product market and are not materially constrained by any other stores.
2. **Mid-size stores**: those with a net sales area between 280 and 1,400 m^2. These stores are also constrained by one-stop stores and so should be assessed by reference to a combined one-stop/mid-size market.
3. **Convenience stores**: those with a net sales area of less than 280 m^2. These stores are constrained by all grocery stores and so should be assessed as part of a wider market, including one-stop stores and mid-size stores as well.[86]

In addition to defining the market by store size, the authorities also distinguish between stores according to the range of groceries that they sell. In particular, when assessing competition from the perspective of the large grocery retailers, the market excludes frozen food retailers, specialist retailers (such as butchers, bakers, etc.) and limited assortment discounters (which tend to sell fewer than 1,000 products, compared with the 5,000–10,000 sold by larger grocery retailers in stores of a similar size).[87] The authorities' approach is flexible enough to recognise, however, that when a large grocery retailer acquires (for example) a limited assortment discounter, there may be an asymmetric loss of competitive constraint from the large grocery retailer to the discounter.[88]

[85] OFT and Competition Commission, *Commentary on retail mergers*, March 2011.

[86] See OFT decision of 15 January 2009 in *CGL/Somerfield*, §10.

[87] Ibid, §§13–15.

[88] See OFT decision of 9 March 2011 in *Asda/Netto*.

In terms of geographic market definition, the starting point is usually as follows:

1. **one-stop stores**: 10-min drive time in urban areas and 15-min drive time in rural areas;
2. **mid-size stores**: 5-min drive time in urban areas and 10-min drive time in rural areas, but these stores are also constrained by one-stop stores within a 10-min drive time in urban areas or 15 min in rural areas; and
3. **convenience stores**: 5-min drive time in all areas (and 1 mile as a sensitivity), but these stores are constrained by one-stop stores within a 10-min drive time in urban areas (or 15 min in rural areas) and by mid-size stores within a 5-min drive time in urban areas (or a 10-min drive time in rural areas).

The most significant grocery retailer merger investigation of the past 5 years was the 2008/2009 investigation of the Cooperative Group's acquisition of Somerfield (the "*CGL/Somerfield*").[89]

The *CGL/Somerfield* case saw the merger of two large national grocery retailers. CGL had 2,228 stores at the time, of which 59 were "one-stop", 452 were "mid-size" and 1,717 were "convenience stores". Somerfield had 877 stores, of which 40 were "one-stop", 616 were "mid size" and 221 were "convenience stores". Notwithstanding that they were both large retailers, however, their combined share of total grocery sales in the United Kingdom was less than 8 %, so the merger was not thought likely to have a significant negative effect on competition at the national level. On the contrary, the OFT said that "it is reasonable to consider that CGL will in effect become a stronger fifth rival to the UK's four largest supermarket operators".[90] The investigation therefore focussed on the local markets in which the two retailers overlapped. There were 295 Somerfield stores that overlapped with CGL stores, although only 139 called for any real investigation because the others were in geographic markets in which at least three other competitors already operated.[91] There were 153 CGL stores that overlapped with Somerfield stores, but only eight of those were in areas that required investigation in addition to the areas in which the 139 Somerfield overlap stores were located.[92]

The OFT then reduced the list of markets to investigate further by applying a simply economic test for "illustrative price rises" based on diversion ratios and profit margins.[93] That reduced the number of markets to investigate to 98.[94] Further qualitative investigation reduced the number to 94.

[89] OFT decision of 15 January 2009, *CGL/Somerfield*.

[90] See OFT decision of 15 January 2009 in *CGL/Somerfield*, §27.

[91] Ibid, §51.

[92] Ibid, §53.

[93] See OFT and Competition Commission, *Commentary on retail mergers*, March 2011, section 4, for an explanation of those simple economic tests.

[94] Ibid, §56.

In addition, the OFT identified a further 32 areas in which competition concerns arise because of overlaps between Somerfield and other cooperatives that are closely affiliated with CGL.[95] CGL was therefore required to divest a total of 126 stores to obtain clearance for its acquisition of Somerfield.[96] Subsequently, that figure was increased by seven to account for various calculation errors that the OFT had made,[97] by a further four to account for an additional acquisition that CGL made before it had implemented the divestments required by the *CGL/Somerfield* case[98] and then reduced by five to reflect material changes in circumstances (entry of new competitors or exit of either CGL or Somerfield) in some of the areas in the course of the period in which CGL was to divest stores.[99]

There have been a significant number of other grocery retailer merger investigations over the past 5 years as well, many of which concerned the divestments that CGL was required to make as a result of the *CGL/Somerfield* case. That is one of the features of merger control in the United Kingdom's grocery retail markets: because local markets are so highly concentrated, even divestments made to satisfy the conditions of a merger control clearance frequently raise their own merger control issues because the acquirers also have stores that overlap with the divestment stores. It is fair to say, however, that the scale of the divestments required in the *CGL/Somerfield* case was exceptional: the Chief Executive of the OFT at the time said that it was "the largest divestiture package [ever] accepted in UK merger control".[100]

Most grocery merger cases following *CGL/Somerfield* have concerned very small acquisitions of no particular significance. One exception, however, was the recent *Asda/Netto* case, in which the OFT approved the acquisition by Asda (one of the big four) of Netto, one of the largest limited assortment discounters with 194 stores across the United Kingdom, subject to an obligation to divest 47 stores.[101]

There have also been a number of merger investigations further up the food distribution chain.[102] Given the diversity of upstream markets, however, the issues raised vary greatly between cases. One common theme, however, is the extent to which the countervailing bargaining power that the large grocery retailers enjoy downstream negates the possibility of an upstream merger giving rise to

[95] Ibid, §§121–122.

[96] Ibid, §178.

[97] Ibid, endnotes.

[98] OFT decision of 13 May 2009 in *CGL/LBA*.

[99] OFT decision of 21 December 2009 in *CGL/Somerfield*.

[100] OFT press release of 20 October 2008, OFT considers grocery store divestments in Co-op/Somerfield merger.

[101] OFT decision of 9 March 2011 in *Asda/Netto*.

[102] For example, the Competition Commission's decision on 19 April 2013 to approve the merger between two "cash and carry" wholesalers, Booker and Makro, and its decision on 8 October 2008 to approve the merger of two Stilton suppliers, Long Clawson Dairy and The Millway.

anticompetitive effects. One case in which a merger was cleared in part because of retailers' buyer power was *Cott/Macaw*, in which two suppliers of own-label plastic-bottled carbonated soft drinks merged. Although their combined market share of 65 % (with a 25 % increment)[103] might otherwise have been thought to be quite substantial, the Competition Commission cleared the merger, citing the importance of retailer bargaining power that would be likely to continue post-merger.[104] More recently, the Competition Commission approved the *Kerry Foods/Headlands Foods* frozen ready meals merger on the basis that evidence of customers actually finding new suppliers in response to the merger proved that the merger did not limit competition.[105] It is fair to say, however, that retailer bargaining power is far from a "silver bullet" for upstream merging parties. The egg merger case of *Clifford Kent/Deans Food* provides an example of the Competition Commission rejecting that argument.[106]

19.5 Regulation

As noted above, the most prominent forms of regulation for the grocery sector that are relevant from a competition perspective are those that have been put in place as a result of the 2008 Groceries Investigation, and in particular the GSCOP. In addition, that investigation also considered the competitive effects of other important forms of regulation, most notably the planning system, which is also discussed above. The two main forms of regulation that were not discussed in those sections relate to (1) consumer protection, where there has been important enforcement activity by the OFT in relation to misleading promotions, and (2) public health, where there has been actual (in Scotland) and proposed (in England and Wales) legislation for minimum prices or prohibitions on below-cost selling in relation to alcohol. These are discussed in turn below.

The legislative framework for the OFT's relevant consumer protection powers are principally set out in the Consumer Protection from Unfair Trading Regulations 2008 (the "CPUTR"). Regulation 3 CPUTR sets out a broad prohibition on unfair commercial practices, which includes both misleading actions and misleading omissions.

On January 2012, the OFT had been concerned that grocery retailers were taking a variety of different approaches to presenting their promotions that might give rise to confusion amongst consumers. Although it did not reach any conclusions as to whether any unlawful conduct had occurred, the OFT did set out some principles for retailers to follow in respect of "internal reference pricing" (e.g., "Was GBP

[103] Competition Commission Decision of 28 April 2006 in *Cott/Macaw* Table 4 on p. 35.

[104] Ibid, §§7.5–7.7.

[105] Competition Commission Decision of 2 December 2011 in *Kerry Foods/Headlands Foods* §§ 7.49–7.50.

[106] Competition Commission Decision of 20 April 2007 in *Clifford Kent/Deans Food* §6.73.

3, Now GBP 2" labels) and "pre-printed value claims on packs" (for example, "Bigger Pack, Better Value"). Those principles were as follows:

1. Prices should never be artificially manipulated so that future planned discounts are made more attractive.
2. Where a price has been marketed as a discount price for longer than the period of time for which the higher selling price was initially charged, retailers should generally consider that the value of the product is now established at the lower price and that it is no longer appropriate to describe this as a discount.
3. References to previous selling prices should only be used where they give a relevant and meaningful basis for comparison.
4. Where packaging carries best/better value claims, they should be objectively accurate. In particular, there should exist no cheaper way of buying the same volume of the identical good in the same store.[107]

In relation to alcohol prices, there have for many years now been concerns about the impact of low alcohol prices on public health, in particular, through binge drinking and the effects of alcoholism, in general. In Scotland, those concerns resulted in the Scottish legislature passing the Alcohol (Minimum Pricing) (Scotland) Act 2012, which will set a minimum retail price of 50 p per unit of alcohol.[108] That minimum price has not yet come into force, however, and the Government has said it will not bring it into force until the result of certain legal challenges (brought by, amongst others, the Scottish Whisky Association) is known. Those legal challenges recently failed at the first instance but could be subject to appeal.[109]

Similar measures have been considered by the Westminster Parliament as well, but so far legislation has not been forthcoming. The Coalition Agreement between the Conservatives and the Liberal Democrats on May 2010 said, "We will ban the selling of alcohol below cost". On July 2010, the Home Office consulted on amending the Licensing Act 2003 to introduce such a prohibition. No such amendment was forthcoming, however. Instead, on March 2012, the Government published a new strategy that proposed the establishment of a minimum alcohol price, similar to (but lower than) the Scottish approach. On November 2012, the Government consulted on plans to establish a minimum alcohol price of 45 p per unit.[110] The Home Office (which is the responsible government department) is now considering the responses, but it appears that certain members of the Cabinet

[107] OFT, *Principles on food pricing display and promotional practices* 30 November 2012.

[108] Note that in the United Kingdom, an alcoholic unit is defined as 10 ml by volume or 8 g by weight of pure ethanol. A single 25 ml shot of spirits (with a strength of 40 %) therefore amounts to a single unit.

[109] [2013] CSOH 70.

[110] Home Office, *A Consultation on delivering the Government's policies to cut alcohol fuelled crime and anti-social behaviour* November 2012.

(including the Home Secretary) have scuppered that policy, notwithstanding strong support from the Prime Minister.[111]

As explained above, one of the competition concerns that had been raised in the 2008 Groceries Investigation was that supermarkets were selling alcohol below cost, with the result that specialist alcohol retailers and convenience stores were struggling to compete. Although the Competition Commission agreed that supermarkets did engage in below-cost selling, it said that the evidence did not establish that below-cost selling foreclosed those smaller competitors. Even so, if minimum alcohol pricing or a prohibition of below-cost selling were to be introduced for public health reasons, it stands to reason that those smaller retailers (not to mention pubs) would benefit.

Finally, it should also be noted that the pressure that farming lobbies exert through industrial action (as discussed above) also sometimes finds expression in legislative proposals to increase the regulation of supermarkets' relationships with farmers. On one such occasion, the Conservative MP for Shrewsbury and Atcham (a largely rural constituency) proposed a specific piece of legislation to give the OFT specific powers to investigate what supermarkets pay for their milk.[112] Although that legislation never came to pass, it illustrates the ongoing political sensitivity of the topic of supermarket–supply chain relations in the United Kingdom.[113]

19.6 Conclusion

The view of the CLA members that assembled to discuss this report is that the United Kingdom's competition law regime is working well in relation to the food distribution sector and that there is no need for the introduction of further specific rules to deal with the sector. There is a general sense that competition in the sector is improving, perhaps in part due to the various competition investigations in recent years that are discussed in this report.

---

[111] See, for example, "Plans for minimum alcohol pricing reportedly dropped after cabinet revolt", The Guardian, 13 March 2013, available at http://www.guardian.co.uk/society/2013/mar/12/alcohol-health.

[112] Hansard, *Commons* Debates, 25 July 2007: Columns 884–886.

[113] It also illustrates the colourful means by which farmers often bring their political pressure to bear. In the MP's words: "The greatest publicity came not just from us politicians, but from a single individual [Women's Institute] member from Gloucestershire who came on a very cold January morning wearing nothing but a bikini. People were pouring bottles of milk all over her as she sat in a bath just outside the House of Commons. That went down very well, I have to say, and got us a great deal of publicity. I applaud her for doing that on such a cold day and for being prepared to be photographed in a bikini with all that milk being poured all over her".

The CLA members note, however, that part of the reason why we do not consider that further legislation is needed in this area is that the Competition Commission's market investigation report in 2008 (combined with support from Parliament to implement some of its remedies) has already investigated the need for special rules in respect of grocery retailing and has implemented some such rules. Of particular note in that regard is the GSCOP. It may be that in other jurisdictions that do not have a comparable market investigation regime, specific competition rules for the sector may add value.

United States of America 20

Katherine Mereand-Sinha, Howard Bergman, and Donald I. Baker

20.1 Introduction

The US food distribution market, and particularly the grocery retail sector, is dynamically competitive and innovative today. As a result, apart from hyperlocalized issues, food distribution and marketing do not seem likely to be a priority area for public antitrust enforcement or even private antitrust litigation in the next decade or so.

This situation represents a marked difference from many markets in Europe, where quite a few national competition authorities (the "NCAs") are devoting considerable attention and resources to the grocery sector. Ideologically, the difference seems to be that today the US tends to be less concerned about the outcome of "fair" competition, even if it means the elimination of competitors; Europeans tend to be more concerned about "fairness" of the outcome among businesses, even if it means restricting competition. The US has traveled some of the roads that Europe is traveling and faced many of the same questions in an earlier area.

This difference of enforcement emphasis in the US appears to be due to divergent regulatory approaches and market fundamentals. Less overall sector regulation, a more liberal business climate, more technological and supply chain R&D and innovation, effective cartel enforcement, relatively light restrictions on vertical arrangements, limited intervention in mergers, and a few other factors

K. Mereand-Sinha (✉)
District of Columbia Department of Consumer and Regulatory Affairs, Washington, DC, USA
e-mail: katherine@mereand-sinha.com

H. Bergman
Qian & Nemecek, Alexandria, VA, USA
e-mail: hjbergman@yahoo.com

D.I. Baker
Baker and Miller LLC, Washington, DC, USA
e-mail: DBaker@bakerandmiller.com

P. Kobel et al. (eds.), *Antitrust in the Groceries Sector & Liability Issues in Relation to Corporate Social Responsibility*, LIDC Contributions on Antitrust Law, Intellectual Property and Unfair Competition, DOI 10.1007/978-3-662-45753-5_20

combine to make grocery retail, and retail overall, a vibrant and competitive segment of the American economy that offers a rich variety of products with a diverse range of quality and prices.

Nonetheless, the US antitrust agencies (the Department of Justice Antitrust Division, the "US DOJ," and the Federal Trade Commission, the "FTC") continue to monitor sections of the industry to put industry players on notice and ensure that unexpected problems do not crop up. We detail these factors below.

20.1.1 Modern American Regulatory Environment

Less regulation is obviously a relative measurement. The US has both less competition-specific regulation and less overall regulation when compared with many of our European counterparts. While the less regulation exhortation may sound like a broken American record, things like the myriad Sunday shopping laws, or blue laws,[1] and town center zoning regulations that occur in many other countries can depress overall prices and sales and create barriers to entry for large and small market players.

These examples are underscored by the long-term work of the OECD in assessing indicators of product market regulation. The most recent indicators from 2008 reflect how the common law countries in general, and the US in specific, have a significantly more liberal approach to both labor (employment protection laws) and product market regulation. The net effect is that even after extensive liberalization in Europe, primarily between 1998 and 2003, the US still has far more incentive-based regulation than prohibitions and has lower barriers to entrepreneurship.[2]

To some extent, the US approach is due to an established pillar of our national, constitutional law, a doctrine known as the Dormant (or negative) Commerce Clause that with a few exceptions prevents states and municipalities from responding to local merchants' political pressure to erect discriminatory and protectionist regulatory barriers against interstate (or foreign) enterprises. In most industries, only Congress may create regulations that restrict trade and investment, and we can see the impact of the doctrine because traditionally liquor is exempt

[1] While Sunday shopping laws that have a secular purpose are constitutional in the US, *McGowan v. Maryland* 366 US 420 (1961), between 1966 and today many states and municipalities have repealed those laws or had them overturned for a variety of issues related to the Establishment Clause, jobs creation, consumer preference, retail sales lobbying, etc. *See* Section 2 of *Does Church Attendance Cause People to Vote? Using Blue Laws' Repeal to Estimate the Effect of Religiosity on Voter Turnout*, by Alan Gerber, Jonathan Gruber, and Daniel M. Hungerman, Working Paper 14303, http://www.nber.org/papers/w14303.

Further, collective agreements among retailers to shut down on Sundays or other days have been struck down on antitrust and other grounds. *FTC v. Detroit Auto Dealers*, see summary at http://www.ftc.gov/opa/1997/03/dada-97.shtm.

[2] *Ten Years of Product Market Report in OECD Countries, Insights from a Revised PMR Indicator*, by Anita Wölfl, Isabelle Wanner, Tomasz Kozluk and Giuseppe Nicoletti OECD Economics Department Working Papers No. 695, at 12, available at http://www.oecd.org/eco/42779045.pdf.

from the doctrine under the 21st Amendment of the Constitution of the United States repealing Prohibition.

Alcohol sales are the exception that may prove the rule. For many years, shipping wine or other alcohol between States without the State boards' involvement and control was prohibited by local laws that only permitted producers to sell their products to wholesalers (the three-tiered distribution system). Only recently is that regime starting to liberalize due to efforts like a 2005 Supreme Court decision that permitted direct-to-consumer sales.[3] While some would hold that the protection created a cushion for local alcohol industries, it appears that the recent flourishing of craft beer, non-California wineries, and even craft distilleries—throughout the country—owes its genesis to a loosening of protectionist regulation in many states that was led by the demand of Internet retailers to ship wine and beer directly to consumers.

20.1.2 Prior Examinations of the US Grocery Sector

The US Federal Trade Commission has conducted studies of the retail grocery sector at different times. Sometimes a study is through a staff or agency-sponsored report, but more recently in 2007 the FTC held a conference in which it invited scholars to discuss their individual research and findings.[4] The papers included the following:

- *Neighbourhood Effects and Trial on the Internet: Evidence from Online Grocery Retailing*, by David R. Bell and Sangyoung Song[5];
- *The Dynamics of Retail Oligopoly*, by Arie Beresteanu and Paul B. Ellickson[6];
- *The Diffusion of Wal-Mart and Economies of Density*, Thomas J. Holmes.[7]

Earlier efforts included 2003 and 2001 staff reports on slotting fees, also known as "pay-to-stay" fees paid by manufacturers,[8] and a 1990 literature review.[9]

[3] *Granholm v. Heald*, 544 U.S. 460 (2005) (a Dormant Commerce Clause decision allowing small wineries to ship directly to consumers).

[4] Conference agenda, transcript, presentations, and presented papers are accessible at http://www.ftc.gov/be/grocery/.

[5] Published at Quantitative Marketing and Economics, 2007, vol. 5, issue 4, pages 361–400.

[6] *See* http://www.ftc.gov/be/grocery/docs/copeland.pdf/.

[7] *See* http://www.ftc.gov/be/grocery/docs/holmespapaer.pdf.

[8] *The Use of Slotting Allowances in the Retail Grocery Industry. A Report from the Staff of the Federal Trade Commission* (November 2003) http://www.ftc.gov/os/2003/11/slottingallowancerpt031114.pdf. See also http://www.ftc.gov/os/2001/02/slottingallowancesreportfinal.pdf and http://www.aae.wisc.edu/fsrg/publications/wp2004-2.pdf.

[9] For earlier studies, *see A Review of Structure-Performance Studies in Grocery Retailing*, Keith B. Anderson, June 1990: this is a review of the literature on the effects of grocery retailing concentration on market performance. The review generally concludes that the existing structure-performance studies of this industry contain methodological and econometric weaknesses. Response History: http://www.fmpc.uconn.edu/publications/rr/rr13.pdf.

The reports on slotting fees resulted in theories for how such arrangements, where manufacturers pay retailers for premium shelf space, would be anticompetitive. However, the 2003 report was not able to find data and economic models that conclusively determined antitrust harm or injury that resulted from slotting fees.

20.1.3 Recent Cases of Competition Enforcement Against the US Grocery Sector

Grocery retailer conduct cases have been sparse in the US in the last 5 years. However, a recent set of consolidated grocery wholesaler cases did wend through the US Courts.

In *In re Wholesale Grocery Products Antitrust Litigation*,[10] two of the largest wholesale grocers allegedly agreed to not compete in the other's primary region. The five direct purchaser plaintiffs claim that this agreement artificially raised prices. The wholesalers attempted and failed to escape the litigation through arbitration agreements, but more recently several claims were dismissed on a finding that the retailers could not prove antitrust injury under a Rule of Reason analysis.

The US DOJ and FTC rarely are involved in hyperlocal antitrust enforcement outside of market remedies for larger mergers that affect small markets. Policing anticompetitive practices can happen through the State Attorneys General, through state or applied Federal law, or through private cases, though those are rare. Enforcement by the State Attorneys General varies greatly across the states.

Revenue Sharing One of the more recent cases of local anticompetitive practices was a 2004 revenue-sharing agreement by three grocery stores in California that were together facing labor renegotiations. The California Attorney General led this case with assistance from the US DOJ. Through appeals and litigation, the court case regarding this dispute is ongoing.[11]

Monopolization Similarly, the California Attorney General also brought a case, with assistance from the US DOJ, in the same year requiring divestiture of a supermarket store where 6 years earlier Vons purchased both supermarkets in a small island community.[12] In this case, California was able to demonstrate a direct rise in local grocery prices.

Abusively high consumer prices by a single firm are generally clear evidence of monopoly power and thus can support a charge of monopolization of a market

[10] A Multi-District combination of: *King Cole Foods, Inc., et al. v. SuperValu, Inc., et al.* (11-3768), *Blue Goose Super Market, Inc., et al. v. SuperValu, Inc., et al.* (11-3773) and *DG, Inc. v. SuperValu, Inc., et al.* (13-1297). For details, see the MDL Court's description: http://www.mnd.uscourts.gov/MDL-Wholesale/introduction.shtml.

[11] *See*, e.g., *California ex rel. Harris v. Safeway, Inc.*, 651 F. 3d 1118 (9th Circuit 2011).

[12] *California ex. rel. Lockyer v. The Vons Companies, Inc.* (C.D. Cal CV 05-8972 DSF January 03, 2006).

under US antitrust law if coupled with other exclusionary conduct by a defendant. Similarly, abusively high prices by several competitors could be important evidence supporting a finding that a price-fixing conspiracy among competitors has occurred. Such conspiratorial price fixing, however, is generally illegal *per se*, regardless of whether the prices were reasonable or abusive.

Research did not reveal any major cases beyond *California ex. rel. Lockyer v. The Vons Companies, Inc.*,[13] which involved retail grocery monopolization of a small California town. The plaintiff state, California, was able to demonstrate across-the-board price increases following monopoly control.

20.1.3.1 Resale Price Maintenance

Slightly further back one finds the leading case on resale price maintenance (the "RPM") in the US, the 2007 Supreme Court decision in *Leegin*,[14] which overturned the *per se* presumption leaving RPM under the Rule of Reason. The result has been a flowering of contradictory RPM decisions in the lower courts.[15]

Reselling below cost, delisting suppliers, or RPM are not *per se* violations of American antitrust law. Research did not reveal major US antitrust cases on these topics.

20.2 Economic Landscape of the US Grocery Sector

20.2.1 National Market Structure of the Vertical Levels of Grocery Competition

There are four main levels of the US food/grocery market: (1) agricultural production, (2) secondary production (processing), (3) wholesaling, and (4) grocery retail.

20.2.1.1 Agricultural Producers

Agricultural production in the United States is vast and varied, but it remains strongly marked by the cooperative structure.[16] Farming cooperatives have limited immunity from antitrust scrutiny by the 1922 Caper–Volstead Act.[17] Note,

[13] *California ex. rel. Lockyer v. The Vons Companies, Inc.* (C.D. Cal CV 05-8972 DSF January 03, 2006).

[14] *Leegin Creative Leather Products v. PSKS, Inc.*, 127 S. Ct. 2705 (2007).

[15] See, generally, Surinder Tikoo and Bruce Mather, *The changed legality of resale price maintenance and pricing implications, Resale Price Maintenance (RPM): The U.S. and E.U. perspectives Journal of Retailing and Consumer Services* 19 (5), pp. 537–544, http://dx.doi.org/10.1016/j.bushor.2010.12.001.

[16] The National Council of Farm Cooperatives indicates that American farming employs over 21 million employees, making it the number one employer in the nation. More than 2 million US farmers belong to one or more of the 2,500 farm marketing and/or supply cooperatives.

[17] The United States Department of Agriculture Rural Business Cooperative Service developed a comprehensive report about the Capper Volstead Act (http://www.rurdev.usda.gov/rbs/pub/cir59.pdf).

however, that the antitrust immunity has not necessarily resulted in economic stability or prosperity for many small farmers. Median farm income in 2012 was in the red.[18]

It is debatable today whether Capper–Volstead antitrust immunity ultimately benefits most farmers or simply benefits the corporate heads of large cooperatives, though the issue largely has been dropped.[19] Several recent consolidated antitrust cases discussed herein have challenged what downstream purchasers believed were cooperatives restricting supply to maintain higher prices for producers.[20]

At the production level, the price and quantity of corn, which are heavily impacted by the price of oil,[21] in turn impact the price of animal products such as beef, poultry, and dairy. There is a phenomenon by which small family farms, while banded together through coops, nonetheless are unable to exercise sufficient pricing control for inputs or outputs; thus, many small producers operate at a loss and rely on outside income, tax benefits, and government support.[22] Thus, despite 2012 being the highest income year for American farmers on record, the benefit of higher prices did not uniformly support producers.[23]

20.2.1.2 Food Processing

The processing industry is not covered by Capper–Volstead and historically was frequently regional due to the perishability of products and high cost of overland

[18] "Despite high prices for many crops, 2012 was no exception, with median farm income projected to be −USD 2,799. Most farm households earn all of their income from off-farm sources—median off-farm income is projected to increase by 3.4 percent in 2012, to USD 55,229 and by 3.9 percent in 2013, to USD 57,378." *See* http://www.ers.usda.gov/topics/farm-economy/farm-household-well-being/farm-household-income.aspx#.UcsuJfk3tJ4.

[19] *See* http://www.themilkweed.com/Pete's_speech.htm, http://www.atg.state.vt.us/assets/files/2010-1-6%20Act%2048%20Report.pdf, http://www.watertowndailytimes.com/article/20100509/NEWS02/305099964.

[20] *See, generally, In re: Processed Egg Products Antitrust Litigation*, MDL No. 2002 08-md-02002 (E.D. Pa) (http://www.eggproductssettlement.com/); *In re Southeastern Milk Antitrust Litigation*, 2:08-MD-1000 (E.D. Tenn.) (http://www.southeastdairyclass.com/); *In re: Fresh and Processed Potatoes Antitrust Litigation*, 4:10-MD-2186-BLW (D. Idaho); and *In re: Mushroom Direct Purchaser Antitrust Litigation*, case number 06-0620 (E.D. Penn.).

[21] Oil prices affect corn prices in several ways: fertilizer prices, direct energy use for farm equipment, and the impact of ethanol as a replacement for gas all closely tie corn to oil prices.

[22] The USDA Economic Research Service tracks median family farms and commercial farms separately. The 2012 family farm household median income from farming was −USD 2,799 compared to a commercial farm median household income from farming of USD 84,649. *See* http://www.ers.usda.gov/topics/farm-economy/farm-household-well-being/farm-household-income.aspx#.UZFH4rU3unw.

[23] "Despite high prices for many crops, 2012 was no exception, with median farm income projected to be −USD 2,799. Most farm households earn all of their income from off-farm sources—median off-farm income is projected to increase by 3.4 percent in 2012, to USD 55,229 and by 3.9 percent in 2013, to USD 57,378." *See* http://www.ers.usda.gov/topics/farm-economy/farm-household-well-being/farm-household-income.aspx#.UcsuJfk3tJ4.

shipping. Concentration has been increasing for decades, however, as processers focus on new technology, economies of scale, and low energy costs as key drivers of economic viability.[24] The United States Department of Justice and the Department of Agriculture have been investigating processing industries for signs of monopsony in recent years through public workshops because concentration levels in the major segments are high.[25,26] Many larger processors have successfully insulated themselves from the recent global pricing shocks through commodity hedging.[27]

The 2007 Economic Census found almost 30,000 food and beverage processing plants in the US owned by about 24,500 companies in 2007. However, 77 % of all processed foods were made by the largest 12 % of processors.[28]

20.2.1.3 Food Wholesaling

Food wholesaling in the United States is in decline. The US Census identifies three main types of wholesalers: (1) merchant or third-party wholesalers, which accounted for 57 % of grocery wholesaling in 2007; (2) manufacturers' sales branches and offices (the "MSBOs") that help manufacturers market their own products accounted for 23 % of wholesaling; and (3) brokers and agents who do not handle products accounted for the final 20 %.[29] Both manufacturers and supermarkets are looking to cut wholesalers out of the supply chain. The market contraction for failed wholesalers is driving concentration,[30] and recent litigation marks retailers' concern about wholesaler monopsony pricing.[31] There has also been vertical integration of the wholesaling function into retailing and manufacturers and wholesalers moving to direct-to-consumer marketing.[32]

---

[24] Structural Change in the Meat, Poultry, Dairy, and Grain Processing Industries, available at http://www.ers.usda.gov/media/850597/err3.pdf.

[25] Competition and Agriculture: Voices from the Workshops on Agriculture and Antitrust Enforcement in our 21st Century Economy and Thoughts on the Way Forward, The 2012 report following a series of joint USDA/DOJ producer workshops held in 2010, available at http://www.justice.gov/atr/public/reports/283291.pdf. Recent criticism suggests that little of the relief farmers sought through the workshops was gained.

[26] CR_4 levels for processing industries are frequently between 50 and 80 %. See http://www.foodcircles.missouri.edu/07contable.pdf.

[27] "Hedging helps foodmakers through uncertainty," Financial Times 2010: http://www.ft.com/intl/cms/s/0/88d1f506-a63b-11df-8767-00144feabdc0.html#axzz2TCf8RvWL.

[28] *Id.*

[29] USDA Economic Research Service data on Retailing & Wholesaling, from the 2007 Economic Census, available at http://www.ers.usda.gov/topics/food-markets-prices/retailing-wholesaling/wholesaling.aspx#.Ucs26vk3tJ4.

[30] "IBIS World estimates the Grocery Wholesaling industry was the second most active-industry in the United States for merger and acquisition activity between 2004 and 2008." Kelly, Doug, IBIS World Industry Report 42441 Grocery Wholesaling in the US (December 2012) at 8.

[31] *In re Wholesale Grocery Products Antitrust Litigation*, No. 11-3768, 8th Cir (2012), available at http://media.ca8.uscourts.gov/opndir/13/02/113768P.pdf.

[32] IBIS World Industry Report 42441 Grocery Wholesaling in the US (December 2012).

20.2.1.4 Food Retailing

Food retailers exist in a changing and nationally competitive market that may nonetheless be subject to regional or submarket dominance and control. In particular, lower income communities throughout rural and urban areas and those found increasingly in suburban locations frequently lack the level of competition and variety available to middle and higher income communities in the United States.[33] Antitrust authorities, however, rarely consider market segmentation based upon income levels of the consumers, and therefore little has been written about this lack of competition in antitrust literature.

In 2011, the US had 212,000 traditional food stores, which sold USD 571 billion of retail food and nonfood products.[34] Grocery stores, including supermarkets, accounted for 91 % of food store sales.[35] USDA Economic Research Service data show that the top 4 retailers account for 37.3 % of the retail market, the top 8 retailers account for 50.5 %, and the top 20 account for 63.7 %.[36]

As the latest ERS data show, "The longer term trend shows an increasing concentration of sales among the Nation's largest grocery retailers."[37] "One contributing factor to such increases over the past decade has been the rapid growth of Wal-Mart Supercenters. Their food and non-food grocery sales amounted to an estimated $109.4 billion in 2011, making it the largest U.S. retailer of grocery products. In comparison, second-place Kroger, the largest traditional grocery retailer, had sales of USD 71.1 billion in 2011."[38]

20.2.2 Geographic and Consumer-Led Markets

The grocery market in the US, as in Europe, is complicated because many of the consumer markets are geographically small with sales competition occurring at a local level. Nationally, concentration in the US grocery market seems low, with the top 20 retailers accounting for 63.7 % of the market. However, many of the retail chains are regional or local and do not participate in all geographical markets. As a result, concentration in specific markets may be higher.[39]

---

[33] FOOD DESERTS, USDA, available at http://apps.ams.usda.gov/fooddeserts/foodDeserts.aspx. *See Appendix A, American Food Deserts.*

[34] USDA Economic Research Service data on Retailing & Wholesaling, from the 2007 Economic Census, available at http://www.ers.usda.gov/topics/food-markets-prices/retailing-wholesaling/wholesaling.aspx#.Ucs26vk3tJ4.

[35] *Id.*

[36] *Id.*

[37] *Id.*

[38] *Id.*

[39] For example, in the geographical market area of Southeast Georgia and Northeast Florida, including the Jacksonville, Daytona Beach and Tallahassee, Albany and Brunswick, the three largest chains hold 77.9 percent of the market: Wal-Mart (30.1 %), Publix (29.7 %), and Winn-Dixie (18.1 %).

Nonetheless, in the main, the shape of the US grocery consumer markets allow for an easy mix of national and regional chains that benefit from considerable foreign direct investment and ownership. Consolidation in US grocery chains is rising as it does in most mature industries, but it remains low with the top four retailers holding 37 % of the market.[40] The market has been shaped by consumer demand (for store hours, location, product variety, prices, quality, etc.) and will likely become ever more segmented based upon the type of consumer (i.e., deep discount, convenience, specialty, high end).

Even as the market continues to mature, barrier entry into the market at various levels remains relaxed. For small and medium enterprises, nonrestrictive local zoning and relatively little land use restrictions have allowed niche providers like green grocers, gourmet food stores, and organic markets to enter urban and high-income areas in proliferation. At the same time, Wal-Mart has grown quickly in rural areas to openly compete with local and regional chains that previously faced little competition.

While the growth of Wal-Mart and other hypermarkets and warehouse stores has led to various other public policy concerns (mainly labor issues), regarding competition among retail grocery providers, anticipated changes to the market may displace most concerns about Wal-Mart gaining regional monopoly or national and international monopsony powers in grocery retail or retail overall.

For antitrust purposes, retail grocery markets have been defined in terms of the local geographic areas where a consumer could reasonably turn for alternatives. But this may be changing. The FTC in the 2007 Whole Foods case, a specialty grocery store merger, argued that "organic" markets were a distinct product market from main retail grocery stores, displaying a more nuanced view of shoppers' behavior.[41]

Beyond redefinition by the agencies, the retail market in the US is undergoing organic, innovative change. Leading online retailer Amazon is poised to enter the grocery market with refrigerated delivery, and much like Wal-Mart, Carrefour, or other "grocery" retailers will offer a product mix that covers much of the basic retail landscape. With an already formidable brand, logistical operation, and customer base, Amazon's entry into grocery retail is another example of how competition can keep the market moving quickly. Other major grocery chains are expected to follow suit in providing delivery options creating a new dynamic in terms of customer engagement and allowing for new players to vie for customer attention and loyalty.

[40] USDA Economic Research Service data on Retailing Wholesaling available at http://www.ers.usda.gov/topics/food-markets-prices/retailing-wholesaling/wholesaling.aspx#.Ucs26vk3tJ4.

[41] *FTC v. Whole Foods Market, Inc.* 548 F. 3d 1028 (D.C. Cir. 2008) (also notable for a prolonged appeals process resulting in divestment after the merger took place).

20.2.3 Technology and Innovation

Some aspects of grocery retailing in the US are similar to many other countries, given that it is a low margin business. The low margins coupled with low regulatory barriers incent retailers towards ever more efficiency and innovation to shave costs.

Innovation takes many forms, but many of the more recent innovations have been in business process and inventory control that reduce unnecessary overhead and speed up decision making. Through this grocery retailing again is morphing from being about the product (groceries) to being more about the distribution systems and customer engagement (and simply merging with broader retail). Importantly, however, much of the technological innovation appears to rely on sufficient scale to invest in technology like RFID inventory control, better computer modeling and consumer studies, etc. Interestingly, US-based companies spending on R&D in this sector outstrips EU spending by a third or more.[42]

While there is recognition that Internet grocery retail presents an interesting area of growth, market entry, and specialization, there are no substantially different competition laws applied to online grocery retailers. In many cases in the US, online retailers are subsidiaries of well-established brick-and-mortar stores.

Online grocery retail occurs mostly for dry groceries and nongrocery (home and beauty) items.[43] As of 2012, 46 % of shoppers said that they never or rarely shop for grocery items online.

In most cases, however, online sales are small enough, with the slow adoption of the service by consumers, that these institutions have not drawn the attention of the agencies. In particular, in the dry groceries and nongrocery space, Amazon, Inc. continues to be a major market player, but currently little public attention has been paid to Amazon's potential impact in the grocery sector.

20.3 Impact of Legal Factors on the US Grocery

20.3.1 Effective Antitrust Cartel Enforcement

One reason that US-facing firms may spend more on innovation is the need to gain a competitive edge in a tough market, a consideration that is less critical to companies engaging in traditional cartels. The American approach to anticartel enforcement (with its heavy emphasis on directly punishing individuals with incarceration and fines) appears to have done a reasonable job of deterring domestic cartels. As result, we haven't seen recent investigations or cases, public or private, in the grocery retail or larger good sector based on cartel theories.

[42] *Data Trends of the European Food and Drink Industry* (2012), FoodDrink Europe, at 9, available at http://www.fooddrinkeurope.eu/uploads/publications_documents/Data__Trends_%28interactive%29.pdf.

[43] *See* http://www.icn-net.com/docs/12086_FMIN_Trends2012_v5.pdf.

In contrast, the 2012 European Competition Network ECN Food Sector Report lists that half of all European NCA antitrust inquiries in the food sector between 2004 and 2007 concerned cartel activities.[44] There are no specific negotiating practices that are banned by unfair trade or competition laws. US antitrust law has swung away from *per se* presumptions. Negotiating practices in vertical relationships would not violate any *per se* rules.[45]

The US has had cartel and other competitive concerns in the food sector in the past, and these have been dealt with through strong enforcement in an earlier era. For example, under the 1922 Capper Volstead Act, farming cooperatives were granted limited antitrust exemptions to allow small farmers to band together to purchase supplies and sell their products. However, an agricultural cooperative loses its exemption if it includes nonfarmers in horizontal agreements concerning prices or output.[46] Historically, there was a considerable amount of US DOJ criminal antitrust enforcement against milk producers and cooperatives for engaging in nonexempt activity.[47]

However, for at least 30 years, cartel enforcement in the domestic food sector has no longer been necessary. There do not seem to have been any prosecutions against groceries for cartel activity, since 1972, when the US DOJ prosecuted a group of small, independent grocers that organized to compete against larger chains. However, the Justice Department has brought cases against food processors for price fixing. In one recent case, the president of a large food company was sentenced to 6 years in prison for bribing customers to purchase tomatoes at an inflated price. More recently, concerns of producer collusion and price fixing have been addressed through private cases like chocolate and potato growers.

20.3.2 Abuse of Monopsony Status

Technically, abuse of buying power is prohibited in the US under the major antitrust laws, although very few cases alleging monopsony are seen in the US Courts.[48]

---

[44] *ECN Activities in the Food Sector: Report on competition law enforcement and market monitoring activities by European competition authorities in the food sector*, at 6 (May 2012) available at http://ec.europa.eu/competition/ecn/food_report_en.pdf (detailing competition inquiries across the food sector and finding cartel behavior for some retailers and many upstream suppliers).

[45] As Commissioner Joshua Wright of the FTC wrote in 2007, "Perhaps the Chicago School's most important and visible victory has been the continual narrowing of the *per se* rule, which, after *Leegin* lifted the prohibition on minimum resale price maintenance, exists only in naked price-fixing cases and, in a weakened form, in tying cases." *The Roberts Court and the Chicago School of Antitrust: The 2006 Term and Beyond*. Competition Policy International, Vol. 3, No. 2, pp. 24–57, 30, Autumn 2007; George Mason Law Economics Research Paper No. 07-41. Available at SSRN: http://ssrn.com/abstract=1028028.

[46] *National Broiler Marketing Assn. v. U.S.*, 436 U.S. 816 (1978).

[47] *US v. Borden*, 370 U.S. 460 (1962).

[48] Peter C. Carstensen, *Buyer Power, Competition Policy, and Antitrust: The Competitive Effects of Discrimination among Suppliers*, 53 Antitrust Bull. 271, 272 (2008) (finding that "the merger

The leading case law on monopsony or oligopsony power is the 2007 Supreme Court case *Weyerhaeuser Co. v. Ross-Simmons Hardwood Lumber Co., Inc.*, 549 U.S. 312 (2007).

In *Weyerhaeuser*, the Court used a Rule of Reason analysis to place the burden on plaintiffs to prove that potential monopsonists not only have market power but also have "a dangerous probability of recouping the losses incurred [. . .] through the exercise of monopsony power." This heightened burden goes beyond the monopolist's predatory pricing Rule of Reason analysis in US case law to further suggest that buyer power, to the extent that it benefits consumers with lower prices, may not pose an antitrust harm under the US law.[49]

Any case list where a court found a buyer to be exercising undue buyer power in the US will be short, although a recent case exists in the food sector: *United States v. George's Foods, LLC*.[50] In this rather unusual case for the DOJ, the US challenged the acquisition of a chicken processing plant on the ground that the capacity of the merged plants would be less than the preexisting independent plants. Reduced production capacity was expected to adversely affect chicken farmers who had developed their business practices to meet a specific demand. The resolution, also unusual for US DOJ, was a behavior remedy to make improvement to the plant to increase capacity.

Case law and theory regarding the operation and harms of monopsony power, which scholars are beginning to believe is not a complete inverse of monopoly power, are noted to be underdeveloped in US antitrust law.[51]

Conduct antitrust enforcement in the retail grocery store sector has been limited. A few state-led actions and a few private class actions exist, but enforcement in this area does not fit well into an American antitrust context. The various types of competition concerns listed in the questions below can be used to demonstrate antitrust injury under a rule of reason analysis, but success is rare. This is due both to the shape of the US antitrust law as well as the politics of the food and agricultural markets in the US.

20.3.3 Permissive Approach to Vertical Restrictions

A more fundamental antitrust difference is that the United States has been more permissive on vertical restraints than most other countries. In 1977, the Supreme Court overruled an 11-year precedent holding that vertical territorial restrictions in

enforcement decisions by the courts and agencies have failed to appreciate the buyer power issues presented in some merger cases").

[49] *Weyerhauser*, 529 U.S. at 324.

[50] *United States v. George's Foods, LLC*, Civ. Act. No. 5:11-cv-00043-GEC, complaint available at http://www.justice.gov/atr/cases/f270900/270983.pdf.

[51] Maurice E. Stucke, *Looking at the Monopsony in the Mirror* (2013) at 4. Law Publications and Other Works: http://trace.tennessee.edu/utk_lawpubl/59.

distribution agreement were *per se* illegal,[52] and since then there have been virtually no challenges to such restraints under the so-called Rule of Reason requiring a court to consider all relevant factors. By contrast, the European Commission has seen vertical territorial restraint as a significant impediment to market integration and always attached significance to enforcement against them.

In 2005, the US Supreme Court moved still further when it repealed the 94-year-old *per se* prohibition on vertical pricing agreements.[53] By comparison, the 2012 ECN Food Sector Report lists that nearly 20 % of antitrust inquiries [by European NCAs] in the food sector between 2004 and 2007 were vertical resale price maintenance (RPM) questions.

The impact of the American view is twofold. First, by allowing no pricing refuge, it keeps the competitive ratchet at the large end of the spectrum moving, incenting the big players to continue to innovate to hold onto market share. Second, it leaves our antitrust regulators with more time to concentrate on other forms of market distortions (like anti-price-fixing enforcement). It may be that the US lucked out because resale price maintenance was never an important factor in food distribution (unlike distribution of pharmaceutical products) and the de facto absence of an RPM prohibition does not seem to be a significant barrier to consumers getting competitive prices in the retail grocery field.

Part of the US legacy may be that for many years the US enforced RPM to protect smaller service-oriented retailers and image-creating manufacturers against free riding by big price cutters that did not provide much in the way of point-of-sale (the "POS") services. Since RPM was never particularly important in grocery retailing, it is not clear whether removing effective RPM prohibitions has been procompetitive or commercially irrelevant in this sector. Either way, there is little evidence that it has been anticompetitive in the main.

20.3.4 Limited Merger Intervention

The basic enforcement system in the U.S. makes it substantially less likely that the FTC (or the Justice Department) would seek to shape or prohibit a grocery merger that seems to be true under the administrative enforcement systems that prevail in Europe. The numbers bear this out. Between 2004 and 2011, the NCAs conducted over 400 grocery retail merger inquiries, and 25 or so were required commitments from the parties.[54] In that same period, the US FTC

---

[52] *Continental T.V. v GTE Sylvania, Inc.*, 433 U.S. 36 (1977) (overruling *United States v. Arnold, Schwinn Co.*, 388 U.S. 365 (1967)).

[53] *Leegin Creative Leather Products, Inc. v. PSKS, Inc.*, 551 U.S. 877 (2007) (overruling *Leegin Creative Leather Products, Inc. v. PSKS, Inc.*, 551 U.S. 877 (2007)).

[54] *ECN Activities in the Food Sector: Report on competition law enforcement and market monitoring activities by European competition authorities in the food sector*, at 45 (May 2012) available at http://ec.europa.eu/competition/ecn/food_report_en.pdf.

required divestment in only four mergers, one of which was the novel Whole Foods case discussed herein.[55]

In order to block a merger before consummation, the FTC (which does most of the antitrust reviews of grocery mergers) must bring a case before a Federal Judge (most frequently in the District of Columbia) and, in an expedited proceeding, persuade the Judge both (1) that the government would be likely to prevail after a full trial on the merits and (2) that the harm to the public interest outweighs the likely loss to the companies and their shareholders of having their transaction held up for an extended period of time. Given this reality, the government agencies tend to end up with a half-a-loaf merger settlement—especially in a close case—rather than try to block the whole transaction, even where the parties are leading competitors with fairly high market shares. In the grocery retail business, a typical settlement involves requiring the parties to spin off some stores overlapping areas to new or smaller competitors approved by the government.

Where there is no settlement and the FTC or US DOJ has to obtain a preliminary injunction, the District Court's decision on the injunction is often the end of the case. If the government wins, the parties tend to abandon the merger. If the defendant wins and consummation occurs, the government will more often than not abandon its effort.

The preliminary injunction process is generally hazardous and uncertain for both government enforcers and merging parties. This is well illustrated by what happened to the FTC's last effort to prohibit a grocery merger. In 2007, in *FTC v. Whole Foods*, the FTC was attempting to block a merger between two grocery retail chains that catered to higher end shoppers with gourmet and organic products at a premium price. However, the District Judge refused to accept the FTC's novel "premium national and organic supermarkets" market definition and thus ruled in favor of the defendants. After the merger had been consummated, the FTC appealed to the Court of Appeals, which reversed the decision of the District Judge. However, by then the eggs were thoroughly scrambled and the FTC had to settle for what seemed to be some relatively inconsequential divestitures of 32 of the acquired stores.

US antitrust laws do not provide for remedies for problematic concentration outside of merger divestitures. Since 2007, the FTC has required divestiture in four retail supermarket mergers: (1) Whole Foods/Wild Oats in 2007 (discussed above), (2) Great Atlantic Pacific Tea Company/Pathmark stores in 2007, (3) Tops/Penn Traffic in 2010, and (4) Giant Food/Genuardi's in 2012. Remedies included divestiture of 1–32 stores.

20.3.5 Geographic Market Evaluations

The 2010 Horizontal Merger Guidelines counsel the antitrust agencies, and reviewing courts should they choose to follow the guidelines, to assess relevant

[55] *Enforcement Actions in Industry/Sector: Retail – Grocery/Supermarkets (FY1996-FY2013)*, available at http://www.ftc.gov/bc/caselist/industry/cases/retail/RetailGrocery.pdf.

product and geographic market structures and dynamics in a fact-intensive way on a case-by-case basis. Recent FTC actions in the grocery/supermarket sector suggest, however, the following market definitions:

Product Market "Supermarkets provide a distinct set of products and services and offer consumers convenient one-stop shopping for food and grocery products. Supermarkets typically carry more than 10,000 different items, typically referred to as stock-keeping units (the "SKUs"), as well as a deep inventory of those items. In order to accommodate the large number of food and non-food products necessary for one-stop shopping, supermarkets are large stores that typically have at least 10,000 square feet of selling space."[56]

Geographic Market "Customers shopping at supermarkets are motivated by convenience and, as a result, competition for supermarkets is local in nature." "Customers shopping at supermarkets are motivated by convenience and, as a result, competition for supermarkets is local in nature."[57]

While these definitions appear to be consistent over the last three supermarket mergers for which the agencies brought complaints, the market definition in a critical 2007 case, *FTC v. Whole Foods*, was a major turning point in complicated agency litigation. From the FTC's original complaint, merging parties Whole Foods and Wild Oats were considered to be "premium natural and organic supermarkets."
As the FTC indicated:

Product Market The operation of premium and natural organic supermarkets is a distinct "line of commerce" within the meaning of Section 7 of the Clayton Act, 15 U.S.C. § 18.

Geographic Market "Unlike conventional supermarkets, which tend to draw their customers from within a radius of three or four miles, premium natural and organic supermarkets tend to draw their customers from within a radius of five or six miles. As a result, areas as small as approximately five or six miles in radius from premium and natural organic supermarkets or as large as a metropolitan area are distinct "sections of the country" within the meaning of Section 7 of the Clayton Act, 15 U.S.C. § 18."

The *Whole Foods* litigation and market definition was contentious in the US Courts with disagreement about whether premium, organic groceries constituted a separate product market. While ultimately the FTC's theory that the market was distinct prevailed, the US has not yet seen an attempt to use the inverse market

[56] COMPLAINT. *In the Matter of Koninklijke Ahold N.V./Safeway Inc.*, File No. 121-0055 (http://ftc.gov/os/caselist/1210055/120817konkinlijkecmpt.pdf).

[57] Koninklijke Ahold, supra.

definition of discount groceries used in an antitrust enforcement setting. That may be due to the fact that the concentration of discount retail groceries has occurred mostly through natural Wal-Mart Supercenter growth that edges smaller, more regional providers out of local markets instead of through mergers. Growth, as opposed to mergers and acquisitions, does not receive antitrust agency enforcement scrutiny.

20.4 American Culture and Politics of Food

While regulation and antitrust law greatly affect competitiveness of markets, other factors also impact the overall shape of a market in ways that can be difficult to measure.

20.4.1 Culture and Labeling

Though harder to evaluate or describe, the US has what may be a unique history in the development of the culture of food that no doubt impacts consumer demand, and, in a consumer-led market, such impacts can matter. One major difference in the US has been the approach to both organic and genetically modified foods. There has been no real central government regulation of what constitutes "organic" or "low" calorie food. Organics and lower calorie are reflected in brands not a classification, allowing for more privately generated options and consumer-led decisions regarding product mix. This branding is contributing to the consumer segmented market definition referred to above as organic becomes a premium brand that has also contributed to a renewed flourishing of small businesses such as farmers' markets, community-supported agriculture shares, and green groceries in denser population centers.

20.4.2 Politics of Farming

Similarly hard to fully measure is the politics of food product. The agriculture lobby is powerful in the U.S., but apparently less so than in Europe. Here many agricultural products are outside the reach of political protection. Perhaps most importantly, while the government continues to support farmers in many ways, the US has largely moved away from price controls and other efforts to ensure farm gate prices.

These alternative solutions may have other downsides but have helped create a competitive market for food. Producer subsidies, which undeniably have their international impacts, have not had a negative effect on domestic prices because they are encouraging more production, as well as more export sales. While environmental resource questions are starting to be a concern, continued availability of low-cost water on a priority basis for farmers in Western United States is a classic example of supporting farmers, as are federally subsidized crop and flood insurance.

The US has developed less anticompetitive means of supporting a critical sector of the economy than involving itself in the question of pricing or relative bargaining power throughout the supply chain, though notably exceptions do exist. Domestic producers of some agricultural products (such as sugar) have been able to politically obtain price controls or other barriers to lower cost production from abroad.

20.5 Some Competitive Issues and Sectoral Concerns on the Horizon

Some possible competitive concerns and major changes for the US grocery-retailing sector do exist, and the antitrust agencies are monitoring these.

20.5.1 Processor Consolidation and Wholesaler Death

While grocery consolidation is rising, it is still low at the national level and is not likely to be an antitrust concern at the national level in the near future. Local or regional grocery retailing markets may sometimes be of greater antitrust concern, but where this occurs in a merger context, the parties may settle such investigations by agreeing to spin off a few stores to a new entrant or smaller competitor.

Greater antitrust concerns may well be generated by rising concentration at the food processor and manufacturing level in some markets. Due to rapid technological growth in the 1970s, the processors consolidated heavily to now have a top four concentration measure of 50–80 % in most of the processing markets.

To monitor this concern, the US DOJ and the United States Department of Agriculture held a series of workshops in 2010. While their monopsony enforcement has been low, they continue to monitor producer/processor markets and have been involved in a few cases in poultry to begin to set the stage for such enforcement actions in the future. At the same time, the antitrust agencies have been cautious about being protectionist in supply chain issues, allowing for the creative destruction of wholesalers that are holding on but have begun to outlive their productive value.

20.5.2 Sector Convergence and Customer Segmentation

More certain than any of the other factors likely to affect this sector in the short term is an industry transformation—fed by technological growth and permitted by light regulations—that could have painful short-term effects but dynamic long-term outcomes.

Many commentators have been concerned about the growth of Wal-Mart Supercenters.[58] A 2006 study found that the entry of a Wal-Mart into a local market leads to a significantly increased grocery retail concentration[59]; state and local studies generally lead to similar conclusions.[60] It is noted that the impact of Wal-Mart Supercenters on concentration tends to be in more rural, lower income communities.[61] In counterpoint, however, Wal-Mart frequently offers lower cost groceries than competitors and forces many competitors to lower prices in response.[62]

In addition, some researchers have found flaws in the data used to assess Wal-Mart's size and impact on the grocery retail market.[63] Estimates of market share vary between 10 and 23 %.

By offering lower prices, Wal-Mart generally escapes US antitrust notice under the prevailing US theory of consumer welfare. Nonetheless, the long tail of discount retail concentration through Wal-Mart's growth is as of yet unknown.

Wal-Mart's natural growth has been fast, and it may come to dominate food and nonperishable channels in some local or regional markets. Many onlookers are concerned that Wal-Mart will or already has gained effective monopolies in poor rural communities and has exhibited monopsony power in many products. We believe that such control will be offset in the long term through the entrance of major players like Amazon that do not conform to traditional geographic markets and can and do provide a platform for small batch and niche products. Nonetheless, the speed of such change in the communities most dominated by Wal-Mart today may be slow, as infrastructure like high-speed wireless and home amenities like computers lags. Additionally, as firms like Wal-Mart and Amazon create infrastructure that the retail market begins to rely on, possible duopoly, duopsony, and essential facility concerns have the potential to develop. It remains too early to predict, however, how the layers of infrastructure will develop.

The entrance of Amazon into grocery retailing will complete the already underway international transformation of grocery retailing to general retailing. Unnecessary middlemen like wholesalers, and possibly shipping companies, may exit entirely. The end result may be that the major market segmentation for retail will shift dramatically from the way that antitrust agencies in the US typically see them (as product and geographic markets) to being primarily customer segmented

---

[58] Watch Wal-Mart grow: http://money.cnn.com/magazines/fortune/storysupplement/walmart_spread/index.html.

[59] Martens, Bobby J.; Dooley, Frank J.; Kim, Sounghun, The Effect of Entry by Wal-Mart Supercenters on Retail Grocery Concentration, available at http://ageconsearch.umn.edu/bitstream/21101/1/sp06ma03.pdf [hereinafter Wal-Mart Entry].

[60] Volpe, Richard J., Lavoie, Nathalie, The Effect of Wal-Mart Supercenters on Grocery Prices in New England, Review of Agricultural Economics, 2008, vol. 30, issue 1, pages 4–26.

[61] Wal-Mart Entry, supra.

[62] *See* http://aepp.oxfordjournals.org/content/30/1/4.short and http://onlinelibrary.wiley.com/doi/10.1111/j.1530-9134.2009.00235.x/full.

[63] *See* Ellickson at 15, available here: http://www.econ.psu.edu/~plg15/SuperEmpDist.pdf.

markets. While not having a completely settled doctrine for how to approach such dramatically new and shifting market definitions, US antitrust regulators have presaged this change with the 2007 Whole Foods merger case, in which the agency vigorously defended a market definition that was limited to a small, high-end customer profile.

20.5.3 Cascading Concentration Incentives

To a limited extent, concentration is a defense of supplier mergers, as is "wholesaler bypass" whereby wholesalers are being cut out of the market by direct agreements or integration between retailers and manufacturers.[64] While wholesaling and supplier mergers have not faced significant enforcement actions from the antitrust agencies, it is estimated that the 83 grocery wholesaler mergers occurred between 2003 and 2008.[65] What's more, grocery wholesaling is estimated to have been the second most active US industry for MA activity in the US between 2004 and 2008.[66]

Contraction of the wholesale industry happened in part due to a need to deal with consolidated retailers. However, this is also potentially the long-term effect of major, structural processor consolidation and contraction that has occurred in the processing sector starting in the early 1970s.[67] It is predicted that the wholesaling industry has come to the end of its life cycle and will continue to decline. Processing and manufacturing concentration, which is already high, is expected to continue.

20.5.4 Unlikely Legislative Remedies

The retail grocery sector does not exist in isolation, but it also does not suffer from significantly different competitive concerns from most major US sectors. Narrow legislative changes aimed directly at grocery retailers do not make sense without major consideration of upstream suppliers, low-income consumers, and the whole structure of US agricultural policy.

Before legislative changes applied narrowly or broadly can be explored realistically, US antitrust needs to determine whether to value harm to upstream suppliers and downstream purchasers, whether access to product variety and quality across income segmentation of the market matter, and whether concentration and monopoly through natural growth can ever be a concern.

---

[64] IBIS World Reports US Grocery Retailing December 2012.

[65] *Id.*

[66] *Id.*

[67] USDA Economic Research Service data available at http://www.ers.usda.gov/media/850597/err3.pdf.

The harms in US food production, namely market abuse of producers and a lack of quality and variety available to low-income communities, are not universally seen as antitrust harms in the US.

However, given the current structure and focus of US antitrust law, which denies seeing such harms, the limited antitrust protections guaranteed to farmers under Capper–Volstead may be creating market distortions that harm those that the act seeks to protect. Such protections for small entities should be either extended up through the vertical layers of food production or removed entirely to create more balance in the competitive landscape from farm to table.

20.6 Abandonment of a Protectionist and Populist Antitrust Legacy

The US has had a rather rich history of antitrust activity in the grocery sector during the 1930s–1970s, but the famous antitrust decisions of that that era have come to be regarded as populist relics of limited (or no) relevance in a subsequent era where antitrust decisions by courts and enforcement agencies have come to be driven by moderate-to-conservative economic thinking.

The Federal Robinson–Patman Act, dealing with price discrimination, was enacted in 1936 at the behest of the independent grocery wholesalers that were being bypassed by the newly emerging supermarkets (principally AP, the first of the supermarkets). This protectionist law made it more difficult for larger retailers to solicit or receive price concessions and was intended to make it harder for them to offer consumers lower prices. It was vigorously enforced by the Federal Trade Commission until the 1960s and then was increasingly criticized by the DOJ, economists, and others in the 1970s. Since the 1980s, the Robinson–Patman Act, while still on the books, has ceased to be enforced and therefore ceases to be a significant restraint on efficient markets in grocery products. This reality is underscored by the fact that the Robinson–Patman Act generated numerous Supreme Court decisions prior to 1980 (and none since then). The Act simply became regarded as a populist barrier to vigorous price competition and has ceased to generate cases or investigations, even though it has never been repealed.

During the so-called Warren Court period on the US Supreme Court (in the 1950s and 1960s especially), the Court generated several grocery industry decisions that are no longer treated as relevant. The high water mark of populist antimerger enforcement was a 1966 decision in U.S. v. Von's Grocery, striking down a merger involving two supermarket chains with less than 10 % of a still unconcentrated grocery market in Los Angles.

In 1964, the Supreme Court sustained against an antitrust claim a collective bargaining agreement that prevented a supermarket chain from selling meat on Sundays. Such clauses no longer exist in grocery market where unionized stores face vigorous competition from nonunionized ones.

In 1972, the Supreme Court struck down as per se illegal under Section 1 of the Sherman Act a territorial restriction in a joint venture agreement among small-to-medium size supermarkets. These stores had created a national private label brand called "Topco" for use on standard grocery products, and each joint venture member was given an exclusive license to sell Topco-branded products in a defined service territory.[68]

In their day, these were important rules and decisions that occupied a significant amount of time and attention among grocery and other retailers and their counsel, as well as enforcement agencies. Today they no longer matter in practical terms (which illustrates how US antitrust law can evolve without old statutes being repealed or old court decisions being explicitly overruled by courts or Congress.)

20.7 Conclusion

Many of the changes that we see underway in the US find parallels in Europe because technology and consumers are leading both markets in that direction, and businesses operating internationally naturally converge on certain practices. However, the transition in the US may be smoother because our system is set up to incentivize the transformation that is underway.

At the moment, we do not anticipate market, enforced,or legislative changes that are likely to generate substantial amounts of new antitrust enforcement in the grocery sector in the US.

[68] *United States v. Topco Assocs., Inc.* – 405 U.S. 596 (1972).

Part II

Liability Issues in Relation to Corporate Social Responsibility

International Report

21

Guy Tritton

21.1 Introduction

In economically advanced countries with sophisticated and well-educated consumers, where effective competition has meant that many products are similarly priced and of similar quality, undertakings often seek to differentiate themselves from their competitors in other ways, apart from price and quality. Increasingly, it is recognised that the "reputation" of an undertaking affects the purchasing decisions of consumers. One important facet of the reputation of an undertaking is whether it has a corporate social responsibility ("CSR") policy and, if so, its nature. Good evidence of the importance of CSR policies in such decisions is that despite the price of Fair Trade coffee being materially higher than non-Fair Trade coffee, consumers will buy Fair Trade coffee even though the same coffee is sold unbranded for a lower price. Furthermore, CSR policies do not just affect consumer decisions. Surveys have shown that employees increasingly wish to work for companies with CSR policies. Thus, in one survey, 35 % of interviewees said that they would take a 15 % pay cut to work for a company committed to CSR.[1]

Good evidence of the importance of CSR policies is that Starbucks has adopted an elaborate and detailed set of standards (appropriately named C.A.F.E![2]) that it complies with when sourcing coffee beans. This standard requires its coffee growers to comply with certain minimum social and environmental standards. Starbucks endorses this policy in its promotional material.

[1] See http://netimpact.org.

[2] Coffee and Farmer Equity practices.

G. Tritton (✉)
Hogarth Chambers, London, UK
e-mail: gtritton@hogarthchambers.com

P. Kobel et al. (eds.), *Antitrust in the Groceries Sector & Liability Issues in Relation to Corporate Social Responsibility*, LIDC Contributions on Antitrust Law, Intellectual Property and Unfair Competition, DOI 10.1007/978-3-662-45753-5_21

This international report examines the increasingly important issue of CSR. In particular, it considers how the laws of those countries that have provided national reports (hereafter "the Reporting Countries") control and regulate the use by undertakings of CSR as an adjunct to the marketing and promotion of the goods or services of those undertakings.

21.2 CSR Policies and Legal Overview

The national reports show that there are no *sui generis* laws that are aimed specifically at the legal control of CSR policies adopted by undertakings. The nearest to a *sui generis* law is, in the European Union, the enactment of the Unfair Commercial Practices Directive ("UCPD").[3] This is discussed below.

Invariably, the laws of the Reporting Countries do not seek to regulate or provide legal remedies if an undertaking does not comply *per se* with a voluntarily adopted CSR policy. However, where the undertaking fails to comply with such a policy *and* advertises and promotes that policy, then the law may intervene. In general, the relevant laws are the following:

- unfair competition (encompassing consumer protection laws), and
- competition law.

However, CSR policies are also encouraged via a number of alternative legal mechanisms. Thus, public procurement laws in Europe permit objectives of sustainable development to be taken into account when awarding public contracts.[4]

Moreover, self-regulation is encouraged, and the legal framework for this is a multipartite contractual mechanism. Organisations that promote particular CSR policies to businesses will often require contractual adherence to a code of conduct before businesses can promote their policies. These codes of conduct have contractual force and usually provide for dispute resolution mechanisms to deal with non-compliance. This has a self-disciplining effect.

[3] Directive 2005/29/EC of the European Parliament and the Council of 11 May 2005 concerning unfair business-to-consumer practices in the internal market OJ 2005, L149, p. 22.

[4] Directive 2004/18 of the European Parliament and the Council of 31 March 2004 on the coordination of procedures for the award of public works contracts, public supply contracts and public service contracts, OJ 30.4.2004, L134, p. 114 and EC Directive 2004/17 of the European Parliament and the Council of 31 March 2004 coordinating the procurement procedures of entities operating in the water, energy, transport and postal services sectors, OJ 30.4.2004, L134, p. 1.

21.3 Analysis of Reporting Countries' Laws Regarding CSR

21.3.1 Unfair Competition

The law most relevant to the wrongful advertisement or promotion of CSR is the law of unfair competition. Thus, all the laws of Reporting Countries prohibit commercial practices that involve unfair competition in the context of business to consumer communications (B2C).

21.3.1.1 European Union: UCPD

The UCPD is a directive that seeks to harmonise the laws of the European Union on unfair commercial practices harming consumers' economic interests.[5] The notion of "unfairness" is clearly very dependent on a wide range of factors, including cultural, social and ethical norms, which themselves vary throughout the European Union (although Recital 7 of UCPD makes it clear that it is not intended to deal with matters of taste and decency). In particular, some Member States have a rich tradition of unfair competition, whereas countries like the United Kingdom have not historically favoured such laws, save in very limited circumstances. Thus, very recently, the Court of Appeal of England and Wales has held that in general, there is no justification for implying a "good faith" term into a contract.[6]

However, even in the United Kingdom, it is recognised that the law of contract is ill-fitted to controlling B2C relationships and contracts whereby the consumer has little or no power to influence the contractual terms and many transactions are done over the Web.[7]

The UCPD thus seeks to redress the balance of power towards the consumer by ensuring that unfair commercial practices are outlawed. The structure of the UCPD is as follows:

- It applies only to B2C unfair commercial practices. However, competitors are able to complain about unfair B2C practices of undertakings.[8] Furthermore, in the case of CSR codes, such are aimed at the consumer.

[5] Art. 1, UCPD.

[6] *Compass Group UK and Ireland Ltd (t/a Medirest) v Mid Essex Hospital Services NHS Trust* [2013] EWCA Civ 200.

[7] Indeed, this problem is very real in relation to online contracts. In one well-known example, Gamestation, a UK company, inserted a term that the purchaser's soul would belong to the company for eternity and never received any comment from any purchaser (see http://scrambledeggsblog.blogspot.co.uk/2010/04/7500-customers-sell-their-soul-to.html).

[8] Art. 11, UCPD ("such means shall include legal provisions under which persons or organisations regarded under national law as having a legitimate interest in combating unfair commercial practices, including competitors, may (a) take legal action against such unfair commercial practices…").

- A commercial practice is unfair if (a) it is contrary to the requirements of professional diligence and (b) it materially distorts or is likely to materially distort the economic behaviour of consumers.[9] "Professional diligence" is defined as the "standard of special skill and care which a trader may reasonably be expected to exercise towards consumers, commensurate with honest market practice and/or the general principle of good faith in the trader's field of activity".[10]
- Without prejudice to the generality of the above, the UCPD states that commercial practices that are misleading (as set out in Arts. 6 and 7) and aggressive (as set out in Arts. 8 and 9) are to be considered unfair.
- Finally, Annex 1 of the UCPD deems certain commercial practices to be unfair.

Of particular relevance is the notion of a misleading commercial practice. A threshold requirement is that the practice must be misleading in some way *and* cause or be likely to cause the average consumer to "take a transactional decision that he would not have taken otherwise". A narrow interpretation of this provision would be that *but for the misleading statement*, the average consumer would have taken a different decision regarding the purchase of products or services, i.e., he would not have bought the product if the misleading statement had not been made but would have bought it when accompanied by the misleading statement. However, this interpretation would be difficult to prove and ignores the fact that it is rare that there is any *one* factor that causes a consumer to buy a product. Rather, the decision to buy a product arises from a combination of factors. It is sufficient if the commercial practice is "likely to cause the average consumer", which suggests that it need only be an influential factor if not a decisive factor. Moreover, many of the deemed misleading practices in Annex 1 are unlikely to be decisive to a purchaser as whether to buy or not, but all may be considered influential. This is important because it may be difficult to show that a CSR policy is critical to a purchaser's decision to buy products from an undertaking.

Another issue is the definition of "commercial practice". This is defined as "any act, omission, course of conduct or representation, commercial communication including advertising and marketing, by a trader, *directly connected* with the promotion, sale or supply of a product to consumers".[11] As commented on in the Austrian report, it is unclear how close the nexus between the breach of the relevant CSR code and the undertaking's indication to be bound by the code must be for it to fall within these provisions. Thus, the Austrian report asks whether it is necessary that the code and the breach appear in the same advertisement. The definition of "commercial practice" underlines the fact that the UCPD does not prohibit breaches of CSR codes *per se*. Rather, it must be shown that the CSR policy is used as a "sales tool" for selling goods or services. Whilst the CJEU has emphasised that

[9] Art. 5, UCPD.

[10] Art. 2(h), UCPD.

[11] Art. 2(d), UCPD.

"commercial practices" in the UCPD should be given a "particularly wide definition",[12] not *every* aspect of a CSR policy is directly connected with the sales or promotion of goods. Thus, it may be difficult to show that an undertaking of a general obligation to give away 1 % of a company's income to a charity is directly connected with the promotion, sale or supply of a product. If such a fact is used in advertising or promotional material for such products, it would be difficult for the company to deny that it is using such a fact to promote its goods. However, where such a fact is merely recorded on a company's website under the headline "charitable activities", it may be difficult to show the necessary "direct connection" to trigger the application of the UCPD.

The UCPD deals specifically with unfair commercial practices relating to "codes of conduct" that clearly are relevant to CSR policies. Thus, non-compliance by a trader with "commitments contained in codes of conduct by which the trader has undertaken to be bound where (i) the commitment is not aspirational but is firm and capable of being verified and (ii) the trader indicates in a commercial practice that he is bound by the code" is prohibited, provided such causes or is likely to cause the average consumer to take a transactional decision that he would not have taken otherwise.[13] In the context of these provisions, the Belgian report says that the intention of the legislator is to sanction only breaches of a code of conduct that have an actual impact on the consumer. This may be another way of analysing whether a commitment is aspirational or firm. In general, consumers pay little attention to aspirational commitments (e.g., "eco-friendly") but do to firm commitments (e.g. "wood sourced only from forests certified as sustainable by the Teak Sustainable Forestry Organisation"). The latter has an actual impact on the consumer's purchasing decisions, but the former does not.

Annex 1 of the UCPD sets out that the following practices are deemed to be unfair. Of particular relevance are practices whereby an undertaking:

- claims to be a signatory to a code of conduct when the trader is not;
- displays a trust mark, quality mark or equivalent without having obtained the necessary authorisation;
- claims that a code of conduct has an endorsement from a public or other body that it does not have; and
- claims that a trader (including his commercial practices) or a product has been approved, endorsed or authorised by a public or private body when he/it has not or is making such a claim without complying with the terms of the approval, endorsement or authorisation.[14]

[12] CJEU Case C-304/08 *Zentrale zur Bekämpfung unlauteren Wettbewerbs eV v Plus Warenhandelsgesellschaft mbH* ECR 2010 I-217, ¶36.

[13] Art. 6(2)(b), UCPD.

[14] Annex 1, Clauses 1 to 4, UCPD.

"Code of conduct" is defined as "an agreement or set of rules not imposed by law, regulation or administrative provision of a Member State which defines the behaviour of traders who undertake to be bound by the code in relation to one or more particular commercial practices or business sectors".[15] In Germany, this has generated some academic debate as to whether this requires more than one party to the code of conduct with the report suggesting that provided other businesses have the possibility to sign up to the code, it is sufficient if only one undertaking has undertaken to be bound by the code.[16] However, if the promotion of a CSR policy involves misleading information, then such debate is academic because the UCPD prohibits such promotions regardless of whether such relates to a code of conduct as defined.

The UCPD also prohibits misleading *omissions*.[17] Thus, where a commercial practice omits *material* information that the average consumer needs to take an informed transactional decision and thereby causes or is likely to cause the average consumer to take a transactional decision that he would not have taken otherwise, then such is an unfair commercial practice. In the case of an invitation to purchase a product, the "main characteristics to an extent appropriate to the medium and the product" are deemed material by the UCPD and thus must be included.[18] The German national report takes the view that the UCPD does not force undertakings to inform the consumer about their CSR policies, although some authors in Germany take the view that it does.[19] However, it should be remembered that the "main characteristics" provision is simply a deeming provision. Its absence is not fatal to a finding of misleading omission. In considering the issue of whether it is or is not misleading to omit to refer to a CSR policy, a possible approach is to consider the converse position—whether it would be misleading to promote the policy if the undertaking did *not* comply with the policy. If such is found to be the case, then, as a matter of logic, it must follow that the CSR policy has caused the consumer to make a transactional decision that he would not have taken otherwise and thus it would be a material omission *not to inform* the consumer about the CSR policy. For instance, if an undertaking has a CSR policy of sourcing its foodstuffs from sustainable farming and breaches such a policy, such is very likely to be held to be an unfair commercial practice. It thus follows that a CSR policy of sourcing from sustainable farming is a practice that is likely to cause a consumer to make a transactional decision he or she would not otherwise make and not informing the consumer of such is a misleading omission within the meaning of UCPD. However, the *failure* to inform a consumer of a CSR policy can hardly be considered to be *unfair* as such can only work to the disadvantage of the undertaking with the CSR policy rather than the consumer. In other words, taking the above example, a failure

[15] Art. 2(f), UCPD.

[16] Para. 2(b) (p. 6 and p. 7), German Report.

[17] Art. 7, UCPD.

[18] Art. 7(4)(a), UCPD.

[19] Para. 2(e) and footnote 35, German Report.

to inform consumers that foodstuffs bought by consumers from an undertaking have been grown using sustainable farming can hardly be a matter of complaint by consumers, save the most diehard curmudgeon.[20]

However, what if a company is one of the few or the only undertaking *not to have* a CSR policy? For instance, if a clothing manufacturer is one of the very few (or possibly the only one) that sources its clothing from a third-world manufacturer that uses child labour where the children are paid very little? Is the *failure* to draw the consumer's attention to such a misleading omission? Many consumers may say that they would not wish to buy clothing that has been made using child labour, and therefore such is highly material to their purchasing decisions. Whilst such may not be a *main characteristic*, such a practice is likely to be considered material information that the *average consumer* needs to take an informed transactional decision.[21] If such is the case, the fact that the CSR policy does not relate to the main characteristics of the product is not fatal to the application of the UCPD.[22]

The UCPD does not seek to prohibit self-regulation by organisations responsible for compliance with codes provided such is in addition to the ability to seek redress before the courts or in administrative proceedings.[23] Normally, self-regulation is via the enforcement of multipartite contracts or undertakings agree voluntarily to abide by the decisions of organisations that administer self-regulatory code and the sanctions or remedies that such codes permit.

Up and until 12 June 2013, Member States of the European Union were able to continue to apply national provisions within the field approximated by the UCPD that were more restrictive or prescriptive. However, as such a date has now expired, the substantive law of Member States in this area should now be harmonised.[24]

Outside the European Union, there also exist unfair competition laws that are relevant to the promotion of CSR policies. Thus:

- Brazil has a Consumer Code of Protection that prohibits the provision of false information where either such refers to a characteristic of the product or such information could be interpreted as a factor that attracts the consumer to the product or service. This is likely to include promotion of CSR policies.
- Ukraine has a law on protection against unfair competition and a law on protection of consumer rights that prohibits unfair business practices that mislead the consumer and the presentation of information that is untrue and/or

[20] A lovely English word that describes a person who is ill-tempered and full of resentment and stubborn notions—particularly towards modern fashions and ways of thinking—and is very "contrary" in his or her thinking. Such a person may despise the whole notion of CSR in the same instinctive sense that he or she despises any form of human rights or anti-discrimination laws!!

[21] Art. 7(1), UCPD.

[22] Art. 7(4), UCPD—this is a deeming provision. It does not set the test.

[23] Art. 10, UCPD.

[24] Art. 3(5), UCPD. This does not apply to unfair competition practices relating to financial services.

incomplete so as to prevent them from making a conscious, competent and free choice as to the selection of products or services.

21.3.2 Laws Other than Unfair Competition

Reporting Countries also have laws that are not strictly unfair competition laws but that are relevant to CSR policies. Thus:

- Germany has laws relating to the advertisement of food where such is promoted as being organic or sustainably harvested.[25]
- In France, under the French Commercial Code, directors may incur civil liability where ethical standards are infringed, as mismanagement is defined with regard to social interests.
- In the Italian Civil Code, the use directly or indirectly of any means that is "not compliant to professional fairness principles and suitable to cause damage to another business" is considered unfair competition.[26]
- In the United Kingdom, the law of passing off is relevant. This permits "class" actions whereby undertakings that collectively own goodwill in a particular symbol or logo (i.e., Fair Trade farmers) could bring an action against an undertaking that uses such a symbol or logo but in a manner that is inconsistent with the public's understanding of what the symbol denotes. Whilst it might be thought that such adds nothing to the UCPD, in the United Kingdom, the domestic legislation that implements the UCPD does not permit competitors or consumers to enforce it.[27] Proceedings can only be brought by regulatory authorities.

The adoption of CSR policies are often heavily encouraged by governments. This is often done by incorporating them in "standards" that can be voluntarily adopted by undertakings with the latter advertising that they are standard compliant. Thus, in Austria, the Austrian Standard Institute has published certain standards (ONORMEN) that can be considered as economic ethical policies. Austrian law on

[25] S. 11 German Law on Food and Food Safety (*Lebensmittel- und Futtermittelgesetzbuch*). It should, however, be emphasised that Germany does have a general B2C law of unfair competition.

[26] Art. 2598(3), Italian Civil Code.

[27] The Consumer Protection from Unfair Trading Regulations 2008 (SI 2008/1277). It is of note that on November 2008, the Law Commission of the United Kingdom considered whether there should be a private right of redress for unfair commercial practices. Whilst it held that such had its attractions, it was clear that there were concerns that such would radically change United Kingdom law, make a dramatic difference between consumer contracts and commercial contracts and create a large number of small claims that would have a negative effect on businesses (see http://lawcommission.justice.gov.uk/docs/rights_of_redress_advice1(2).pdf).

standards prohibits the usage of ONORMEN or confusingly similar signs by undertakings who do not comply with ONORMEN standards.[28] However, this can be seen as a type of unfair competition law as its essence is that undertakings must not mislead the consumer.

Often, the consumer may have a contractual remedy. Thus, in France, the principle of estoppel imposes a responsibility on a party not to occasion detriment to another party by acting inconsistently with an understanding concerning their contractual relationship, which it has caused that other party to have and upon which that other party has reasonably acted in reliance. This could include the promotion of a CSR policy. Under UK law, such could amount to a pre-contractual misrepresentation, which entitles the purchaser to avoid the policy. In France, there is a similar doctrine based on the "defects of consent" principle. Whilst consumers will be unlikely to bring such actions, a trade purchaser that has purchased produce following a misrepresentation about its ethical characteristics, i.e. the produce had been grown in an environmentally sustainable way, may be more inclined to bring an action (particularly if downstream purchasers or consumers discover such facts and boycott the produce).

Ultimately, all of the above laws are concerned with the prohibition of misleading or unfair communications directed at consumers. It does not matter whether the CSR policy is an external policy (i.e., Fair Trade) or a unilateral policy adopted by the undertaking.

However, in certain cases, the adoption of a CSR policy may give rise to a liability even if not used in connection with advertisement or promotion to consumers. Thus, in France, under natural law,[29] a policy voluntarily adopted by a business can acquire a binding force. Thus, as held by the Cour de Cassation, a unilateral commitment to execute a natural obligation, when taken in full knowledge, is transformed into a legal duty. Also, as said by the French national report, CSR policies voluntarily adopted by directors on behalf of their company create a legal duty on the company. It is unclear whether this duty exists regardless of whether the company advertises or promotes such a policy.

In summary, the importance of CSR policies in the twenty-first century means that an undertaking that adopts a CSR policy and promotes or advertises such a policy cannot, with impunity, breach the policy. Such will, in all the Reporting Countries, normally amount to an unfair commercial practice or unfair competition.

However, it is important to emphasise that the *remedy* is not that the undertaking must comply with the CSR policy (a point made clearly by the Ukrainian report) but that the undertaking must not promote goods or services by reference to the CSR policy where it does not comply with such a policy. Thus, the laws are intended to prevent consumers from being deceived or confused by advertising or promotional campaigns rather than requiring the undertaking to comply with the CSR policy.

---

[28] S. 8 Law on Standards 1971 (*Normengesetz 1971*). However, this can only be enforced by Austrian administrative authorities.

[29] *Théorie des obligations naturelles.*

21.4 The Undertakings that Can Enforce Unfair Competition Law

Reporting Countries were asked to consider whether the above unfair competition laws could be enforced by regulatory authorities, consumers, competitors and suppliers and purchasers of the goods or services (e.g. the supplier of Fair Trade coffee).

In this respect, the answers from the Reporting Countries vary, and it is useful to put the information in a tabular format (see Table 21.1). In some reports, the issue is whether a class action can be brought by a group of consumers, and thus this is also dealt with where mentioned.

It can be seen from the above that there is considerable variety as to who can enforce unfair competition laws. In some countries (e.g., Ukraine and Hungary), the only requirement for *locus standi* is that the suing party is aggrieved, i.e., affected adversely by the practice complained of. In contrast, the United Kingdom does not permit the enforcement of unfair competition laws other than by regulatory or statutory authorities.[30] This UK provision has had some strange consequences. For instance, in the context of comparative advertisements (potentially a form of unfair competition), aggrieved competitors have brought actions for trademark infringement where their registered mark is used, and in such circumstances, the CJEU has held that European unfair competition laws concerning comparative advertising are a complete defence if the conduct falls within such laws.[31] This depends arbitrarily on whether the defendant has used a registered trademark in the advertisement. In contrast, in Germany, there is no regulatory authority to enforce the German unfair competition law, but instead its enforcement is left to powerful consumer associations or other associations such as the Wettbewerbszentrale (which is an independent institution of German industry whose aim is to ensure that companies compete fairly in the marketplace).

Many countries report that it would be unusual for consumers to bring an action even though they have *locus standi* because of the cost and uncertainty of such actions. However, as a counterbalance, consumer associations play an important role in protecting the consumer against unfair competition. However, because consumer associations are not themselves injured by the actions, certain countries, e.g. Hungary, do not permit them to bring actions to enforce unfair competition laws. In such circumstances, the non-CSR-compliant undertaking does not have to fear the award of damages against it.

[30] Unfair Trading Regulations 2008.

[31] E.g., see CJEU C-533/06 *O2 Holdings v 3G UK Ltd* ECR 2008 I-4231.

Table 21.1 Who can enforce unfair competition laws in Reporting Countries

	Regulatory authority	Competitor	Class action	Consumer/ Consumer associations	Supplier	Purchaser
Austria	Yes[a]	Yes[b]	Debated[c]	Yes	Yes[d]	Yes[f]
Belgium	Yes[e]	Yes (provided it has an interest)	No[f]	Yes (provided he has a direct and personal interest)	Yes	Yes
Brazil	Yes[g]	Yes	NK	Yes/ Consumer associations can enforce	Yes	Yes
France	Yes[h]	Yes	NK	No[i]/ Consumer associations can enforce	Yes	Yes
Germany	No[j]	Yes	No	No[k]/ Consumer associations can enforce[l]	No	No
Hungary[m]	Yes[n]	Yes	Yes[o]	Yes/No[p]	Yes	Yes
Italy	Yes[q]	Debated[r]	Yes	Yes/ Consumer associations can enforce	Yes[s]	Yes[t]
Ukraine	Yes[u]	Yes	NK	Yes	Yes	Yes
United Kingdom[v]	Yes[w]	No	No	No	No	No

[a]The Austrian Unfair Competition Act is enforceable by the Federal Competition Authority but only where such is likely to distort competition significantly to the detriment of enterprises. It is not clear that there is a specific regulatory authority that is there to protect consumers (as opposed to enterprises); [b]Provided the competitor is "directly affected"; [c]See ¶2.2.2.2, Austrian National Report; [d]Provided the supplier or purchaser is directly affected; [e]Minister of Economic Affairs and the Director General of the Federal Public Service of Economic Affairs; [f]Intended to be brought in and being discussed in Parliament; [g]Public prosecutor; [h]The main authority is L'Autorité de Régulation Professionelle de la Publicité ("AARP"); [i]Where the legal cause of action is unfair competition claims; [j]The UWG (*Gesetz gegen den unlauteren Wettbewerb*) permits business associations, chambers of commerce and industry or craft chambers to bring an action, but there is no actual regulatory authority tasked with enforcement of the UWG. However, the *Wettbewerbs-zentrale*, although not a state body, is a highly influential independent association whose main role is to enforce the law against unfair competition; [k]There is some debate on this issue, but the prevailing view is that the UWG is not a *Schutzgesetz* (protective law)—see p. 16, German Report; [l]E.g., the German federal consumer organisation (*Verbraucherzentrale Bundesverband*) or consumer centres in the German Länder; [m]In general, any legal entity that can show it has suffered may enforce the unfair competition laws; [n]The UCP Act (which implements the UCPD) is primarily enforced by the National Consumer Protection Authority ("NCPA"), but the Hungarian Competition Authority has the right to enforce the law on misleading and comparative advertising. The HCA may issue a "class action" on behalf of a class of consumers in the courts provided it has

(continued)

Table 21.1 (continued)

commenced its own competition supervision proceedings; [o]Provided that the claimants' interests are sufficiently aligned to each other. See also previous table footnote; [p]A consumer association does not have *locus standi* as it is not itself an injured party; [q]Autorita Garante della Concorrenza a del Mercato ("AGCM"); [r]This is the subject of academic debate, but as pointed out by the Italian National Rapporteur, Art. 27, Consumer Code indicates that "any subject or organisation having interest" can seek enforcement against a misleading practice; [s]If they have a "relevant interest"; [t]Although there is some debate whether an association of suppliers can bring an action; [u]Antimonopoly Committee of Ukraine ("AMC"); [v]In implementing the UCPD, the United Kingdom has not conferred a private cause of action for breach of the directive. As the United Kingdom does not have any other laws of unfair competition, a competitor or consumer would have to rely upon other laws, e.g., passing off, malicious falsehood, trademark infringement or contract law, which are much more limited in scope; [w]This will be enforced by either the Office of Fair Trading or local authority trading standards officers

Art. 11 UCPD requires Member States to ensure that persons or organisations regarded *under national law* as having a *legitimate interest* in combating unfair commercial practices, including *competitors*, may take legal action against such unfair commercial practices and/or bring proceedings before an administrative authority competent to decide on complaints or to initiate legal proceedings.[32] There is an interesting issue whether such gives Member States complete discretion as to which persons or organisations have *locus standi* to enforce domestic legislation implementing the UCPD in a private action. The German reporter considers that such gives significant discretion to Member States with regard to who can bring enforcement proceedings. This may indeed be a correct analysis. On the other hand, the wording of Art. 11 UCPD suggests that if under national laws on unfair competition laws that existed *prior* to the implementation of the UCPD permitted, an undertaking was entitled to bring an action against an other undertaking for unfair commercial practices, then Member States must ensure that the same undertaking also has an equivalent right of action under the UCPD. Apart from the United Kingdom, where no private action can be brought at all for breach of domestic legislation implementing the UCPD, in the other Reporting Countries, private actions can be brought, and in general, such includes both competitors and consumers where such have a legitimate interest. In the case of the United Kingdom, neither competitors nor consumers have *locus standi*. Either may inform administrative authorities and encourage them to initiate appropriate legal proceedings, but neither can compel them to bring such actions (and indeed such authorities will prioritise according to their limited resources). It is highly arguable that the United Kingdom's enforcement of the UCPD in this regard is deficient. However, there is considerable discretion given to Member States under the UCPD as to how to implement the directive.

[32] Art. 11, UCPD.

21.5 The Courts and Tribunals that Can Enforce Unfair Competition Laws and the Available Remedies

In general, unfair competition laws concerning CSR policies can be enforced in the courts of Member States. However, in certain countries, unfair competition laws can be enforced in administrative proceedings before an administrative tribunal, which may itself also have the ability to enforce unfair competition laws in civil courts. In this sense, such organisations are similar, in the field of competition law, to the European Commission, which acts as both enforcer and a first instance administration tribunal.

It is useful to set out the differences in the Reporting Countries regarding the existence of administrative tribunals for enforcing unfair competition laws and the remedies available to them (the position regarding *competition* laws, i.e., abuse of dominant position/anti-competitive conduct is not considered; see Table 21.2).

Table 21.2 Enforcement by regulatory authorities in Reporting Countries

Austria	Public administrative authorities such as BWB and those responsible for enforcement of standards may issue cease and desist orders, but their jurisdiction is limited.[a]
Belgium	The Minister of Economic Affairs may conduct an investigation and issue a warning requiring that the undertaking cease practice. However, it has no right to levy fines (although non-compliance with an injunctive order is punishable by fines). If the warning is not complied with, the matter may be referred to the Public Prosecutor. If pursued through the criminal courts, then available fines range from €250 to €10,000.
Brazil	Enforcement only through courts.
France	The AARP can bring proceedings before the Jury de Déontologique Publicitaire (JDP): such cannot order fines or imprisonment but may request the withdrawal of the disputed advertisements.[b]
Germany	No regulatory or administrative tribunal for enforcement of unfair competition laws. Enforcement is through the courts.
Hungary	The National Consumer Protection Authority ("NCPA") and Hungarian Competition Authority ("HCA") may injunct the offending practices and/or issue fines (between €50 and €6.5 million or 10 % of the net turnover of the undertaking in the previous business year).
Italy	The AGCM can enforce unfair competition and issue prohibitory orders and issue fines (€5,000 to €500,000). The AGCM can act *ex officio* or at requests of any subject or organisation having an interest (e.g., competitors, consumers).
Ukraine	The AMC may issue cease and desist orders and fines (up to 5 % of annual turnover of undertaking in the previous financial year). The consumer protection authority may also impose fines (up to 30 % of the relevant sales revenue).
United Kingdom	There is no administrative authority that can issue cease and desist orders or fines for breach of unfair competition. Enforcement by regulatory authorities is through the courts.

[a]Thus, it does not extend to all unfair commercial practices—see ¶2.3.1.1, Austrian Report
[b]It is not clear whether the JDP has any legal powers to prohibit advertisements or promotions or is, instead, a self-regulatory organisation that relies upon organisations complying with its rulings. It would appear the latter is the case

21.6 Enforcement Through Courts

As discussed above, there is considerable variety as to whether private undertakings (e.g., competitors) can bring civil proceedings under the laws of the Reporting Countries for breaches of CSR policies. The UCPD specifically envisages that competitors be able to bring proceedings.

However, as with any civil proceedings where the proceedings are brought not by a body tasked with enforcement of particular legislation but rather by a private individual, a claimant will usually need to show that it has sufficient interest in the subject matter of the proceedings and that it has suffered damages.

In general, where there is a breach of a CSR policy, it will not be difficult for a consumer who has purchased products where there has been an overt breach of the policy to show that he was misled and that he is entitled to compensation. However, aside from "class" actions by consumers, such proceedings are rare. In general, the interests of the consumers are protected by consumer associations or regulatory organisations.

In the case of competitors, an undertaking that breaches its well-publicised CSR policy may indeed be harmful to a competitor. For instance, an undertaking that misleads the public by saying that teak (tropical wood) furniture has been sourced from forests where sustainable forestry is practised when in fact such is not the case will have a competitive advantage over those undertakings that do source from sustainable forestry as wood sourced from the latter will invariably be more expensive.

In the case of CSR policies, Reporting Countries were asked to consider three different scenarios in the context of a competitor being able to obtain relief against an undertaking that has not complied with its CSR policy:

- coffee marketed with a Fair Trade label that was not sourced from Fair Trade coffee farmers (**Scenario 1**);
- coffee marketed by a business that has imported coffee using ships that emit excessive carbon dioxide that do not comply with a business's "green" CSR policy (**Scenario 2**); and
- coffee marketed by a business that advertises its CSR policy of providing 2 % of all sales revenue to educating children in the third world but, upon audit, is found not to have complied with that policy (**Scenario 3**).

Whilst it might be thought that, within the European Union, the ability to recover is harmonised, such is not the case. The UCPD does not harmonise the procedural aspects of enforcing the UCPD other than to require that Member States "shall ensure that adequate and effective means exist to combat unfair commercial practices". The modality of enforcement is very much left to the Member States.

These three scenarios were chosen because they differ widely in the degree of *nexus* between the products being bought (coffee) and the offending practice. Plainly, the first scenario has the closest nexus, although it should be emphasised that a failure to comply with the first scenario does not mean *necessarily* that the

Table 21.3 Remedies in civil courts in Reporting Countries

	Scenario 1	Scenario 2	Scenario 3
Austria	Injunction and damages if capable of being proven.		
Belgium	Injunctive relief and damages.	Probably too vague for any relief.[a]	Injunctive relief but difficult to prove damage.
Brazil	Injunction and damages if capable of being proven.		
France	Remedies can include injunction or award of damages depending on the circumstances of case. A competitor would be unlikely to be able to prevent Scenario 3.		
Germany	Injunction in all three cases. Damages are also available if competitor can prove that damage was caused by violation of the UWG (unfair competition law) and the acts were done intentionally or negligently. In practice, it is easier to prove such in Scenarios 1 and 3 as opposed to 2. Under German law, no business can request disgorgement of profit.		
Hungary	Injunction/damages—dependent on competitor proving damage.		
Italy	Injunction/damages.	Depending on proof of harm to competitor, injunction and damages.	Dependent on proof of harm to competitor, injunction and damages.
Ukraine	The nexus between the CSR statement and the products/services of the CSR offender is "of paramount importance" for a competitor to obtain both injunctive and financial relief.		
United Kingdom	Injunctive relief and damages (action in passing off or trademark infringement).	Nexus is too weak—no relief.	Nexus is too weak—no relief.

[a]See judgment of Commercial Court, 19 December 1996 (*Gand* DCCR 1997/52), where "bio" was considered very general and thus not an unfair practice (see para. 2.4.2.2, Belgium Report)

coffee's *physical characteristics* are any different. This is because Fair Trade conditions relate to social as well as environmental conditions.

In Table 21.3, the responses of the Reporting Countries are set out in tabular form as to whether a competitor could obtain injunctive or financial relief where another undertaking breaches its CSR policy.

It can be seen from the above that, in large part, Reporting Countries do permit undertakings to sue their competitors for breach of CSR policies. Their right to do so is largely dependent on their ability to show that the breach of the CSR policy has caused them damage. In other words, *locus standi* is determined by whether the undertaking concerned has suffered loss or damage from the breach of the CSR policy. Clearly, such is much easier in the case of Scenario 1 than Scenarios 2 and 3. Moreover, it would presumably be easier to demonstrate *locus standi* if the complainant undertaking itself has a CSR policy the same as or similar to the one that it alleges has not been complied with by a competitor. Thus, suppliers and distributors of Fair Trade coffee will be in a better position to complain about another competitor that falsely claims that it is distributing Fair Trade coffee than an undertaking that does not distribute Fair Trade coffee. However, there is no reason in principle why the latter could not complain if it can be shown that it has lost market share to the defendant by reason of the latter's false claim.

Scenarios 2 and 3 are clearly much more difficult for a complainant undertaking to demonstrate loss. It is less clear from the national reports whether the need to show that the undertaking has suffered damage is a prerequisite to *injunctive* relief or merely damages. In other words, if an undertaking cannot show that he has suffered damage but can show that it has "sufficient interest", it is not clear whether such an undertaking would be entitled to injunctive relief.

21.7 Ability to Obtain Information

In many cases, it will be difficult to show that an undertaking has or has not complied with its advertised CSR policy. By its very nature, a breach of a CSR policy is not obvious to the purchasing consumer. He is highly unlikely to know whether the coffee has indeed been purchased from Fair Trade coffee growers or whether the undertaking does contribute a percentage of its sales revenue to educating children in the third world.

The recent European scandal on the inclusion of horsemeat in pork and beef by suppliers demonstrates the need for full investigatory powers and the ability to obtain information. In general, investigation into these will not be the province of consumers but that of regulatory organisations and consumer associations. However, undertakings may also wish to obtain information from competitors that they suspect of misleading the public with regard to their CSR policies and/or their compliance.

Art. 12 of the UCPD requires Member States to confer upon courts or administrative authorities the power to require traders to furnish evidence as to the accuracy of factual claims in relation to a commercial practice if such appears appropriate on the basis of the circumstances of a particular case. Thus, as the Belgian report shows, this can be implemented by shifting the burden of proof onto the defendant to show compliance with its CSR policy. As Art. 12(b) of the UCPD says, if the evidence provided is not furnished or is deemed insufficient, then the court or administrative authority may consider that the factual claim is inaccurate.

Again, differences emerge from the Reporting Countries, which is best shown in tabular form (see Table 21.4).

The above demonstrates that it may be very difficult for private concerns to demonstrate breach of CSR policies in civil proceedings unless there is some evidence giving rise to a *prima facie* case of breach of the CSR policy. Within the European Union, this suggests that Art. 12 has not been implemented in a proper manner. In countries where disclosure of documentation is not ordered and the burden of proof remains with the complainant, proof of non-compliance with a CSR policy may be difficult. As said by the German national report, "violations of CSR policies are difficult to detect".

Conversely, however, regulatory authorities appear to have wide-range investigative powers to discover unfair competition practices.

Table 21.4 Obtaining information in Reporting Countries

Austria	No ability for private or public concerns to obtain information. However, in civil proceedings, the CSR business may have the burden to prove the correctness of an allegation of fact, as opposed to the complainant needing to prove that such is false.
Belgium	The Minister of Economic Affairs can conduct investigations to detect infringements. Consumers and competitors have little means to obtain information, although under Belgian law the judge can shift the burden of proof onto the defendant to show no breach of CSR policy.
Brazil	Public bodies tasked with enforcement have wide-ranging investigative powers. In the case of civil proceedings, there is a limited ability to obtain information prior to the issue of proceedings.
France	Not answered.
Germany	Limited (particularly where such information is required to show a violation of German unfair competition laws).
Hungary	No ability for private or public concerns to obtain information directly from businesses, but they can submit complaints to the HCA, which can investigate and order the provision of information (if in competition supervision proceedings).
Italy	The AGCM can request information (or upon request to the AGCM by competitors, consumer associations, etc.) about the compliance of a business with its CSR policy.
Ukraine	Limited for private concerns. The AMC (regulatory authority) has powers where there is "reasonable suspicion" that a possible non-compliance with a CSR policy may amount to an offence actionable by such authority or the court.
United Kingdom	Public bodies tasked with enforcement have wide-ranging investigative powers. In the case of civil proceedings, there is limited ability to obtain information prior to the issue of proceedings.

21.8 Are Laws of Reporting Countries Fit for Purpose?

In general, the Reporting Countries reported that they considered that their laws were satisfactory and able to deal with breaches of CSR policies by undertakings. There is a need to distinguish here between (a) whether the existing law is fit for purpose to deal with breaches of CSR policies and (b) whether, in practice, the law is being properly enforced.

In relation to the first part, despite the lack of existence of *sui generis* laws, the Reporting Countries demonstrate that breaches of CSR policies are capable of being dealt with adequately within the framework of existing laws—particularly, unfair competition laws. Thus, there is no request for *sui generis* laws to deal with breach of CSR policies. However, as noted by the Austrian report, ultimately for a breach of a CSR code to fall within the UCPD as an unfair commercial practice, it must be shown that the practice is directly connected with the promotion, sale or supply of a product to consumers. Thus, it may be difficult to show that general obligations stated by companies to support charities that are breached fall foul of the UCPD.

Many countries reported the need to strengthen the ability to obtain information and also the right to introduce "class actions". In relation to the latter point, the European Commission is alive to this. Thus, on June 2013, it issued a non-binding recommendation that Member States introduce "collective redress mechanisms" to improve access to justice.[33]

In particular, many of the national reports said that there is no ability to audit compliance with the CSR policies. Thus, the Belgian national report complained of the lack of transparency with regard to implementing CSR policies. It suggested that such could be detected in a number of ways, e.g., encouraging the adoption of standards (e.g., ISO 26000[34]) and thus leaving the issue of compliance to the authorities administering the standard, use of "labels" that can only be used where the undertaking complies with the conditions of such labels, social rating agencies, and annual reports.[35] The idea here is that regulatory organisations that administer the use of such standards, labels, etc., can limit the use of such indicia to those undertakings they have investigated. However, as recognised by the Belgian report, such depends on active involvement by these organisations.

The need for transparency of large companies and groups with regard to their CSR policies has been recognised by the European Commission in its communication "A renewed strategy 2011–2014 for Corporate Social Responsibility".[36] In this, it recommended that Directives 78/660/EEC and 83/349/EEC[37] as regards disclosure of non-financial and diversity information of large companies and groups be amended to include a non-financial statement containing information relating to at least environmental, social and employee matters; respect for human rights; anti-corruption and bribery matters, including the following:

1. a description of the policy pursued by the company in relation to these matters,
2. the results of these policies, and
3. the risks related to these matters and how the company manages those risks.[38]

[33] Communication from the Commission to the European Parliament, the Council, the European Economic and Social Committee and the Committee of the Regions "Towards a European Horizontal Framework for Collective Redress" COM (2013) 401/2 (http://ec.europa.eu/justice/civil/files/com_2013_401_en.pdf).

[34] Guidance on how business and organisations can operate in a socially responsible way.

[35] Since 1995, Belgian companies must file a "bilan social", which is a social report that includes information on environmental and social issues.

[36] COM (2011) 681 final of 25th October 2011.

[37] Fourth Council Directive 78/660 on 25th July 1978 based on Art. 54(3)(g) of the Treaty on the annual accounts of certain types of companies OJ 14.8.1978, L222, p. 11; Seventh Council Directive 83/349 of 13 June 1983 based on Article 54(3)(g) of the Treaty on consolidated accounts OJ, 18.7.1983, L193, p. 1.

[38] The proposal is that Art. 46 Directive 78/660/EC and Art. 36 Directive 83/49/EEC are amended (see Art. 1 of the draft amending directive).

Indeed, the proposal requires large companies[39] that do *not* pursue such policies to provide an explanation of why they do not. Thus, a large company may not choose the path of silence! Of significance is that the annual report must, where appropriate, include both financial and non-financial key performance indicators "to the extent necessary for an understanding of such development, performance or position".[40]

The ability to enforce compliance with unfair competition laws will often rest on administrative organisations that have to prioritise. Thus, as noted by the Italian report, enforcement before the AGCM is not that effective due to the workload of the authority.

When considering the need for sanctions for breaches of voluntary CSR policies, it is important not to deter their adoption in the first place. There is a balance to be struck between deterring companies from breaching such policies and encouraging them to adopt them in the first place. The world is a better place if companies do adopt CSR policies but intermittently breach them than if companies are discouraged by "heavy handed" enforcement from adopting them in the first place. It should be remembered that in many cases, the power of investigative journalism and the ability to "name and shame" are a more powerful deterrent than recourse to legal proceedings. After all, companies adopt CSR policies because they know that their reputation is important and that consumers are sensitive to environmental-social concerns. They will not lightly risk losing that reputation. So, in the same sense that a company has a self-interest in ensuring that its trademark is not used for poor quality products but there is no law to prevent them from doing so, it might be said that a company with a CSR policy will not lightly risk its reputation being destroyed by breaching its own CSR policy. However, that consideration is lessened if it is difficult to prove a breach.

In this sense, one may consider that unfair competition laws where the promotion of CSR policies must be connected with the promotion, sale or supply of products strike the right balance. A company that deliberately uses its CSR policy as a "sales promotional tool" should not expect many favours from the law if it breaches such a policy. On the other hand, if a company adopts a CSR policy to donate a proportion of its general revenue (as opposed to revenue from sales of a particular product) to a charity but, upon investigation, is found to have failed to do so, and there is no evidence that it has sought to rely upon such a fact in promoting its products, it may legitimately say that no one has suffered as a result.

[39] Defined as a company whose average number of employees exceed 500 and whose balance sheet exceeds €20 million or a net turnover of €40 million.

[40] Ibid. Although not wholly clear, it seems that such should relate to the CSR policies.

21.9 Competition Issues

Reporting Countries were asked whether CSR policies raised any competition issues (as opposed to unfair competition issues). A particular concern arises where a number of competing undertakings agree to commit to a CSR policy. In such cases, there will often be a trademark or a symbol that can only be used by such undertakings to demonstrate their adherence to such a CSR policy. A good example is the "dolphin-friendly tuna" symbol below which is a registered trademark[41]:

Because of consumer pressure, a number of undertakings that are competitors may be parties to a common CSR code. Such a code will be contractual in nature and will set out rules and conditions that must be complied with regarding, say, the catching of tuna that minimises the risk of dolphins being accidentally killed. Such will have the effect of co-ordinating behaviour at a horizontal level.

The European Commission has analysed standardisation agreements and issued Guidelines concerning Horizontal Cooperation Agreements.[42] In general, provided any undertaking is free to accede to such standards or code, it is difficult to see how any issues of competition law arise. Para 280 says:

> Where participation in standard-setting is unrestricted and the procedure for adopting the standard in question is transparent, standardisation agreements which contain no obligation to comply with the standard and provide access to the standard on fair, reasonable and non-discriminatory terms will normally not restrict competition within the meaning of Article 101(1).

In general, NGOs and private organisations that encourage the adoption of a particular environmental standard operate in a manner that is consistent with the above approach. Such organisations have little interest in preventing undertakings from having access to such standards, and indeed the nature of such organisations

[41] In fact, in the United States, the Dolphin Protection Consumer Information Act describes the conditions in which a tuna product may be labelled dolphin safe.

[42] Guidelines on the applicability of Article 101 of the TFEU to horizontal cooperation agreements, OJ 14.11.2011, C 11, p. 1.

(which tend to be not for profit) is that they would wish to encourage as many undertakings as possible to adopt such codes.

It is rare that a CSR policy can ever be considered a true barrier to entry such that competition is not feasible by companies that operate outside the CSR policy. As said by the German national report, it is likely that there are a lot of consumers who are not willing or able to buy expensive tuna. Invariably, the adoption of a CSR policy means higher prices, and those consumers who are more concerned about price than social or environmental factors will not buy such tuna.

Concerns may arise where the CSR policy has become a *de facto* standard in a market sector. This will be the case where it is shown that, in large part, there is effective consumer resistance to buying goods that do not adhere to a particular CSR code. In such cases, the CSR policy may be considered akin to an "essential facility" and to which access is necessary in order for an undertaking to compete in a particular market. However, as pointed out in the French report, the Commission Guidelines on the application of Art. 101(3) of the TFEU do not prohibit *de facto* standards as within the standard, suppliers may compete on price, quality and product. This is undoubtedly the case with CSR policies where such does not seek to control such primary characteristics of products but much more indirect characteristics, e.g., the nature of production of those products. Indeed, a review of supermarket shelves demonstrates that of dolphin-friendly tuna, there is considerable variety in price.

However, it is notable that Art. 101(3) does *not* mention that factors to be considered are environmental or social benefits arising from an agreement that falls within Art. 101. It is notable that in certain domestic competition laws, equivalent provisions do mention environmental protection. Thus, Art. 17 of the Hungarian Competition Act, which in large part replicates Art. 101(3), includes within the first condition not only technical or economic development but also "environmental protection". Given the importance of the environment, it is considered that the Hungarian approach is preferable to the purely economic approach of Art. 101(3).

Outside the European Union, the Brazilian and Ukrainian national reports did not identify any particular issues with competition law and CSR policies. Whilst they did not rule out that the application of standard competition laws could give rise to issues, no specific ones were identified. However, in the case of horizontal agreements that do lead to establishment of standards protected by IPRs that are adhered to by undertakings with a collective substantial market share, the Brazilian report states that there may be a need for fair, reasonable and non-discriminatory ("FRAND") licensing.

As said by the Italian report, particular competition concerns may arise where the CSR policy is a *de facto* standard and is associated with a collective mark in the control of a single organisation. That said, it is rare that a mark *per se* can be an effective barrier to entry to a market. Organisations are free to use other marks that signify dolphin-friendly tuna if the conditions imposed by the single organisation are too onerous. This distinguishes itself from technical standards that are protected by patents where an organisation may have no alternative but to use the protected technology. Furthermore, as already said, organisations that own collective or certification marks that can only be used by undertakings that agree to abide by the codes governing methods of production will generally not wish to restrict access to the use of those marks provided that the undertaking agrees to comply with the associated code of conduct.

In summary, the national reports do not identify any specific issues relating to the adoption of CSR policies by a number of competitors. Furthermore, there is no suggestion that competition laws should be adapted to deal with issues raised by the adoption of CSR policies.

21.10 Conclusions and Proposals

The adoption of CSR policies by businesses is obviously to be encouraged. A heavy-handed approach by the law that deters the adoption of CSR policies is to be discouraged. There was no suggestion from the Reporting Countries that non-compliance with CSR policies was a substantial problem or that their existing laws, although not *sui generis* laws enacted specifically to deal with non-compliance with CSR policies or CSR abuses, were not suitable or fit for purpose. Thus, any proposal or recommendation should proceed with care for fear of causing more problems than it solves. Thus, this paper proposes some "fine tuning" of the laws of Reporting Countries as follows.

Firstly, an analysis of the laws of the European Union and the Reporting Countries demonstrates that breaches of CSR policies will generally only give rise to a right of legal action where such are used in close connection with the promotion or advertisement of goods or services, In the case of the UCPD, there is the threshold requirement that such use must be "directly related" to the promotion of goods. It is considered that the concept of "directly related" sets the threshold too high. CSR policies will often influence consumers to buy goods even if such CSR policies are not directly related to their promotion. A company that has a robust and strong CSR policy will often generate a "feel good" feeling about that company, which subtly and indirectly influences a consumer to buy its goods. In some respect, this can be considered similar to the way that a brand image subtly influences a consumer to buy goods bearing that brand. Such brand image may bear little relationship to the characteristics of the product itself (a good example is the positive "feel good" brand image of the Virgin brand) but still materially affects the consumer decision to purchase the goods or services of a company.

However, the *mere* fact that a company has breached a publicised CSR policy should not give rise to a cause of action. Such could positively discourage companies from adopting CSR policies. Thus, a balance needs to be struck. The focus should be on whether the breach of the CSR policy is material in some way to a consumer's decision to purchase goods of the company.

It is necessary thus to put forward a "nexus" test for determining whether a breach of CSR policy should be actionable. It is proposed that the test should be that the breach of the CSR policy would "materially influence" the reasonable consumer's decision to purchase goods or services of the undertaking promoting the said CSR policy. The above test avoids arguments as to whether *but for* the CSR policy in issue, the consumer would have bought the goods—a test that would be very difficult to satisfy and that sets the threshold too high. Furthermore, the resort to the legal fiction of the "reasonable consumer" ensures that the courts are not bound by evidence from consumers who said that they were materially influenced when such evidence appears to be an unreasonable conclusion.

Secondly, there is considerable diversity amongst the Reporting Countries as to who can enforce unfair competition laws. This is unsatisfactory. Regulatory authorities will often not have the resources to deal with breaches of CSR codes. Consumers will rarely bring direct action (as opposed to complaining to the relevant organisation). Interestingly, it would appear that the most effective enforcers are consumer associations and competitors, e.g., in Germany, the Wettbewerbszentrale.

A distinction needs to be drawn between the right to sue (*locus standi*) and the cause of action. In relation to the latter, CSR policies are aimed and focussed at consumers and not at suppliers or competitors. Thus, the cause of action should always be related to the effect of the CSR policy (and thus its breach) on consumers. This has already been discussed. In relation to the right to sue, the question is whether a wider class of persons other than consumers should be able to bring a private action.

It is clear that the businesses of suppliers, purchasers and competitors can be materially affected by breaches of CSR policies where consumers are likely to make purchasing decisions based on those CSR policies. Thus, a coffee distributor that supplies Fair Trade coffee is likely to be adversely affected by a competing coffee supplier that promotes its adherence to a Fair Trade coffee code of conduct but does not comply with it. Equally, Fair Trade coffee producers in developing countries will suffer as well (by reason of a reduction in coffee being bought from them) as a result of the offending undertaking.

In such circumstances there is no rational basis for restricting the right to sue to just consumers or indeed leaving enforcement to regulatory organisations. Indeed, such is recognised in Art. 11 of the UCPD. It is tempting to say that those who have suffered damage should have the right to sue. In other words, *locus standi* should be based on the ability to prove that the undertaking has suffered damage as a result of the offending undertaking's conduct in breaching its CSR policy. However, such would mean that the issue of *locus standi* could not be determined until conclusion of proceedings, which is unsatisfactory. Furthermore, in certain cases, it may be difficult for a competitor, supplier or producer to prove that it has suffered damage. A good example of this would be where a Fair Trade coffee producer or supplier is one of many qualifying Fair Trade coffee producers or suppliers and a retail coffee chain is failing to comply with its publicised policy of buying Fair Trade coffee. The coffee producer or supplier may find it very difficult to establish that it has suffered any loss of sales (e.g., because the retail coffee chain did not historically buy from the suing coffee producer or supplier when the retail coffee chain did comply with its CSR policy). However, that Fair Trade coffee producer or supplier may be the only producer or supplier with sufficient financial resources to bring a claim against the retail coffee chain.

In such circumstances, it is proposed that any undertaking (including any natural person) that can satisfy the court that he, she or it has "sufficient interest" should be applied. Such a test has considerable flexibility, is a concept familiar in law and permits a court or tribunal to take account of a wide range of factors and not just whether the suing undertaking has suffered damage. In particular, it is proposed that such a test should be satisfied where an undertaking that is a member of a group can establish that the group, *considered as a whole*, has been materially affected by the offending undertaking's breach of its CSR policy.

Thirdly, as discussed above, there is variety in the laws of the Reporting Countries as to the ability to bring consumer class actions against undertakings that have breached CSR policies. The European Commission has recommended their introduction but subject to restraints to prevent their abuse. In this respect, as commented in the European Commission recommendation, the Commission has proposed that contingency fees and punitive damages should be prohibited as these are seen as creating an industry for abusive class actions.[43]

The need for class actions is mitigated where there are active associations that will protect consumers' interests (such as the Wettbewerbszentrale in Germany) or effective enforcement authorities. However, these organisations invariably have limited resources and must prioritise those resources. Class actions (or, to use the more European terminology, "collective redress" actions) have a disciplining effect on undertakings that fail to comply with their publicised CSR policies but which have little to fear from individual actions.

The issue of whether to permit class actions is, of course, not unique to CSR and raises a host of issues as to how they should be regulated—for instance, one particular issue is whether there should be an "opt-in" or "opt-out" approach to persons who fall within the class.

It is not considered prudent to make detailed recommendations as to how class actions in breach-of-CSR policy actions should be controlled and conducted—particularly to prevent abusive litigation. Such issues are not specific to such actions and should be considered at a wider level. However, it is recommended that in principle, class actions should be permitted where an undertaking has breached a publicised CSR policy.

Fourthly, in civil proceedings, as identified in this report, it is often difficult to prove that an undertaking has breached a CSR policy. Such facts and information as necessary to prove such will normally only be in the possession of the undertaking. The UCPD seeks to address this by requiring companies to provide information and/or reversing the burden of proof where they do not. On the other hand, it would be disproportionate and potentially damaging to undertakings if speculative claims could be brought against them that require them to divert resources to prove that

[43] Communication from the Commission to the European Parliament, the Council, the European Economic and Social Committee and the Committee of the Regions "Towards a European Horizontal Framework for Collective Redress" Para. 30, COM (2013) 401/2 (http://ec.europa.eu/justice/civil/files/com_2013_401_en.pdf).

they comply with their CSR policies. Thus, it is considered that the appropriate balance to be struck is that a complainant should be required to establish a *prima facie* case that the defendant undertaking has breached its CSR policy. If such is established, then the defendant undertaking should be required to adduce information that it has not.

Fifthly, as discussed above, there appear to be few (if any) concerns about CSR policies giving rise to anti-competitive concerns. However, it is unsatisfactory that when considering competition concerns raised by CSR policies, a narrow economic approach should be taken to determining whether such comply with competition law. For example, when considering a CSR code promoted by an independent not-for-profit organisation, to which undertakings representing more than 50 % of the relevant market have adhered to, it would be wrong in principle if analysis of any anti-competitive effects caused by horizontal cooperation was not entitled to take into account the beneficial effects to the environment and social working conditions that adherence to such a code may have. At the heart of competition law is whether conduct by one or more undertakings is such as to have a detrimental effect on consumers' interests. When considering whether such is the case, the twenty-first century consumer's interests extend beyond mere price and quality. Thus, it is considered that the Hungarian approach that allows consideration of such factors when deciding whether to exempt *prima facie* anti-competitive agreements should be adopted. Accordingly, it is proposed that when considering the application of competition laws to CSR policies, the beneficial effect on the environment and social working conditions should be taken into account.

21.11 Recommendations

The final recommendations adopted in Kiev were as follows:

21.11.1 Nexus

Where an undertaking commits a breach of a CSR provision that is promoted or advertised directly or indirectly in connection with the sale of its goods or services, such shall be actionable as an unfair commercial practice if the CSR provision would materially or is likely to materially influence the average consumer's decision to buy those goods or services of the undertaking.

21.11.2 Locus Standi

In principle, any person who is materially and adversely affected by a breach of a CSR provision, without exclusion to other persons, including trade or consumer associations, shall be entitled to bring an action for unfair competition.

21.11.3 Disclosure of Information

Where an arguable case is made out that an undertaking has breached a publicised CSR policy, a court shall have the power to order that the undertaking provide information that is relevant to the allegation that is in its possession and that be located by the undertaking conducting a reasonable search.

21.11.4 Competition Law

In considering the application of competition laws to CSR policies, the beneficial effect on the environment and social working conditions shall be taken into account.

Austria

22

Max W. Mosing

22.1 Introduction

The (non-legal) discussion of sustainable development and its economic impact started in Austria in the late 1980s and has therefore a longer tradition than the discussion around corporate social responsibility (CSR); as many other Austrian approaches, the Austrian CSR activities build upon the long-lasting Austrian tradition of broad stakeholder involvement within the so-called "social-partnership," which is the common dialogue platform between the main social partners[1]: in the 1990s, Austrian companies learned to deal with environmental and social friendliness and, last but not least, with the term "sustainability."

Nowadays, 95 % of the Austrian companies declare to have been involved by one or more measures for society; for eight out of ten Austrian companies, social commitment is part of their entrepreneurial self-understanding, meaning that they are providing money, labour, and material resources for measures in the context of social responsibility.[2]

However, there are "practical differences" between declaring to do good and actually really doing good—which leads to consider what should be the legal consequences in Austria if such differences appear in the context of commercial practices.

The final version of this report incorporates the views expressed by the Austrian LIDC members at a meeting held on May 2012 ("Austrian Group").

[1] Strigl, Corporate Social Responsibility in Austria, http://oin.at/_publikationen/PublikationenALT/Fachartikel/Strigl%202004%20csr%20in%20austria.pdf.

[2] See, on this, http://juliusraabstiftung.at/resources/files/2014/6/6/974/jrs-studienergebnisse-unternehmerische-verantwortung-2014-medieninfo-final.pdf.

M.W. Mosing (✉)
GEISTWERT Rechtsanwälte Lawyers Avvocati, Vienna, Austria
e-mail: max.mosing@geistwert.at

P. Kobel et al. (eds.), *Antitrust in the Groceries Sector & Liability Issues in Relation to Corporate Social Responsibility*, LIDC Contributions on Antitrust Law, Intellectual Property and Unfair Competition, DOI 10.1007/978-3-662-45753-5_22

22.2 The Different Types of CSR Policies and the Law

Basically, there is no clear definition of CSR policies in Austria, and therefore it cannot be distinguished between different types of CSR policies—definitely not in terms of the Austrian laws. However, CSR policies can—depending on the actual circumstances—be subsumed under the below-listed legal terms:

(I) CSR policies could fall under "codes of conducts" ("*Verhaltenskodex/ Verhaltenskodizes*") mentioned by the Austrian laws in two forms, namely that such code of conduct (a) must be issued and adopted,[3] especially in the context of specific rules governing regulated professions[4] (*e.g.*, Austrian medical doctors,[5] Austrian attorneys at law,[6] Austrian Pharmacies,[7] etc.) or that it (b) can voluntarily be issued and adopted. As case (a) is out of the scope of this contribution, only case (b) will be covered in this paper.

The Austrian Act against Unfair Competition ("*UWG*")[8] defines—in the context of commercial practices—the term "code of conduct" as "an agreement or set of rules not imposed by law, regulation or administrative provision of a Member State of the European Union and which defines the behaviour of enterprises who undertake to be bound by the code in relation to one or more particular commercial practices or business sectors."[9]

Because of this broad definition corporate social responsibility ("CSR") policies—at least those used in connection with consumers—can be easily subsumed under "code of conduct" in terms of the UWG. However, the term is much broader.

In the context of "codes of conducts," the Codex Alimentarius Austriacus ("*Österreichisches Lebensmittelbuch – ÖLMB*")[10] has to be mentioned, firstly, because of its practical impact and, secondly, because of its "special legal status": although it is published by the Austrian Federal Ministry for Health, it is not as such legally binding. The ÖLMB is "only" a "qualified experts' opinion" on certain aspects in the food industry, especially the labelling with certain signs. Although it is not legally binding, not "complying" with the ÖLMB could be a breach of the UWG, as consumers might be misled: where the consumer does not know the specifics of a product, *e.g.* what it contains, how it is produced, where it comes from, etc., it is possible that such consumer relies purely on what (ingredients, way of production, origin, etc.) experts in the field of such product demand as necessary

[3] *E.g.*, Sec 7 of the Lobbying Transparency Act ("*Lobbying- und Interessenvertretungs-Transparenz-Gesetz*"); Sec 4 para 8 Austrian Broadcasting Act ("*ORF-Gesetz*").

[4] Compare Art 3 para 8 Unfair Commercial Practices Directive.

[5] "*Richtlinie 'Arzt und Öffentlichkeit'*" by the Austrian Chamber for Medical Doctors.

[6] "*Richtlinie für die Berufsausübung*" by the Austrian Chamber for Attorneys At Law.

[7] "*Berufungsordnung*" by the Austrian Chamber of Pharmacies.

[8] Bundesgesetz gegen den unlauteren Wettbewerb – UWG.

[9] Sec 1 para 4 no 4 UWG.

[10] See http://www.lebensmittelbuch.at/.

("referring consumer perception"/"*verweisende Verbrauchervorstellung*").[11] Therefore, not complying with the ÖLMB could be a "misleading commercial practice" in terms of Sec 2 UWG.[12] This case law developed in the context of the ÖLMB could be also of relevance regarding CSRs—see also (III)(b) below regarding "Private Seals of Quality" ("*Gütesiegel bzw Gütezeichen*").

(II) As the case might be, CSR policies could fall under "Austrian standards" ("ÖNORMEN") that are issued by the Austrian Standards Institute.[13] ÖNORMEN are regulated by special Austrian laws[14] and again can be[15] (a) legally obligatorily issued and adopted[16] or (b) voluntarily issued and adopted.

Among the literally hundreds of ÖNORMEN, which generally refer to nearly every area of (business) life, some could be considered as "economic ethical policies," respectively CSR policies, *e.g.*, "Guidance on social responsibility" (ISO 26000:2010)[17] and "Risk Management for Organizations and Systems—Part 1: Guidelines for embedding the risk management in the management system" (Implementation of ISO 31000).[18] These ÖNORMEN are not obligatory CSR policies but can be voluntarily adopted by businesses.

(III)(a) In the context of CSR policies, the Austrian laws providing for a "Seal of Quality" ("*Gütesiegel*")[19] and an "Official Test or Guarantee Sign" ("*Prüf- und Gewährzeichen*")[20] have to be mentioned. However, these legally issued seals and signs are—as indicated above—not subject to this paper.

(b) On the other hand, "Private Seals of Quality" ("*Gütesiegel bzw Gütezeichen*") can, being qualified as "codes of conducts,"[21] be of relevance in the context of CSR policies. "Private Seals of Quality" can have an "economic ethical" respectively "CSR background." The "seals" as such can also be protected as trademarks.[22]

According to Austrian Consumers' Association ("*Verein für Konsumenteninformation – VKI*"), more than 90 "Seals of Quality" exist only in the sector of the

[11] Austrian Supreme Court 12.08.1996, 4 Ob 2131/96b.

[12] See below, Sect. 22.3.

[13] See http://www.as-institute.at.

[14] Based on Law on Standards 1971 ("*Normengesetz 1971*").

[15] Sec 5 Normengesetz 1971.

[16] *E.g.*, ÖNORMEN for electronic technology ("*ElektrotechnikV*") or for packaging ("*VerpackungsV*").

[17] Preview: https://www.astandis.at/shopV5/Preview.action?preview=&dokkey=379631&selectedLocale=de.

[18] Preview: https://www.astandis.at/shopV5/Preview.action?preview=&dokkey=347215&selectedLocale=de.

[19] Regulation on Seal of Quality for Accredited Companies ("*Meisterbetrieb GütesiegelV*").

[20] Several Regulation on Test or Guarantee Signs (also from foreign countries). See also Sec. 4, 6 Trademark Act ("*MarkenschutzG*").

[21] See item (I) above.

[22] Compare Wiltschek, Smaragd®, Federspiel® und Steinfeder®. Qualitätsmarken als Herkunftskennzeichen, ÖBl 2011, 292.

food industry.[23] A study by the Austrian Chamber for Labour ("*Arbeiterkammer*") considered that "only" one out of 27 tested "Seals of Quality" in the food industry was misleading.[24]

However, in several cases pertaining to "Private Seals of Ecological Quality," the Austrian Supreme Court has stated that "statements about the natural or environmental impact of a product are highly suited to influence the buying decision of the consumer. As desirable as such information may be if it is true, it may be dangerous if it is linked to the emotional sphere of the consumer and thereby is likely to mislead the consumer."[25] "The question of whether advertising regarding environmental protection is suitable to mislead has to be assessed in a similar strict manner as those regarding health promotions."[26]

22.3 Prevention and Sanctioning in Case of Breach of a Voluntarily Adopted CSR Policy

The Austrian Unfair Competition Act ("*UWG*") provides special provisions for the prevention and sanctioning in the context of misuse of, respectively breach of, a "code of conduct" ("*Verhaltenskodex*")[27] voluntarily adopted by a business. CSR can, as the case may be - as shown under Sect. 22.2 - , be subsumed under the legal term of "code of conduct" ("*Verhaltenskodex*"):

(I) Sec 2 para 3 UWG reads as follows: "A commercial practice shall also be regarded as misleading if it is able to cause a market participant to take a transactional decision that he would not have taken otherwise, and which involves the following: [. . .] non-compliance with commitments, which the entrepreneur has in the framework of a code of conduct undertaken to be bound, insofar as: a) the commitment is not aspirational but is firm and is capable of being verified, and b) the entrepreneur indicates in a commercial practice that he is bound by the code."

There is no case law on this provision. Consequently, it remains unclear how close the *nexus* between (a) the verified breach of the code of conduct and (b) the entrepreneur's indication to be bound by the code has to be for Sec 2 para 3 UWG to be infringed: does the entrepreneur have to refer to the code and to breach it in the course of the same commercial practice, *e.g.*, in the same advertisement? Is the reference to be bound by the code on the business' website sufficient that every breach of the code in (another) commercial practice falls under Sec 2 para 3 UWG?

---

[23] See http://www.konsument.at/cs/Satellite?pagename=Konsument/MagazinArtikel/Detail&cid=318882281653&pn=1.

[24] http://www.arbeiterkammer.com/bilder/d136/B_2011_LebensmittelGuetezeichen.pdf.

[25] Austrian Supreme Court 09.10.1990, 4 Ob 132/90 and 18.05.1993, 4 Ob 38/93 and 28.11.2012, 4 Ob 202/12b.

[26] Austrian Supreme Court 28.11.2012. 4 Ob 202/12b.

[27] See above the broad legal definition of this term.

Furthermore, it is worth mentioning that "commercial practice" is defined in the UWG as "any act, omission, course of conduct or representation, commercial communication including advertising and marketing of an enterprise, directly connected with the promotion, sale or supply of a product." It could therefore be argued that a breach of a "code of conduct" that is not directly connected with the promotion, sale or supply of a product would not fall under Sec 2 para 3 UWG.

(II) Another special provision is Annex 1 lit. 1 UWG, which lists "[t]he false declaration of an entrepreneur claiming to be a signatory to a code of conduct" as a "misleading commercial practice." Reference is made to the above-cited definition of a "commercial practice" and the argument that a "code of conduct" that is not directly connected with the promotion, sale or supply of a product would not fall under the provision.

(III) But the Austrian UWG provides even more provisions in the context of codes of conducts in the broadest sense: (a) Annex 1 lit 2 UWG qualifies "displaying a trust mark, quality mark or equivalent without having obtained the necessary authorisation" as a "misleading commercial practice." (b) Pursuant to Annex 1 lit 3 UWG, "the false claim that a code of conduct has an endorsement from a public or other body" is a "misleading commercial practice."

Ad (I) and (II): In the context of the application of Sec 2 para 3 UWG (non-compliance with the code of conduct) and Annex 1 lit 1 UWG (false declaration to be a signatory to a code of conduct), Sec 1 UWG has to be taken into account:

> (1) Anyone who in the course of business 1. resorts to an unfair commercial practice or another unfair practise which is likely to distort not only insignificantly the competition to the detriment of enterprises or 2. uses an unfair commercial practise contrary to the requirements of professional diligence and [which] is with regard to the respective product suitable to materially distort the economic behaviour of the average consumer whom it reaches or to whom it is addressed, may be sued for a cease-and-desist order and in case of fault for payment of damages.
>
> [...]
>
> (3) Unfair commercial practices shall be in particular those, which are 1. aggressive in the sense of Section 1.a. or 2. misleading in the sense of Section 2.

Ad (III): In connection with the above-cited Annex 1 lit 1 to 3 UWG, Sec 2 para 2 UWG reads as follows:

> In any case the commercial practices mentioned in the annex under lit 1 to 23 are deemed to be misleading.

(IV) The Austrian Unfair Competition Act ("*UWG*") provides also general provisions for the prevention and sanctioning in the context of a breach of statements or commitments voluntarily issued or adopted by a business:

Sec 2 UWG reads as follows and could be applied on the breach of a CSR policy being a code of conduct:

(1) A commercial practice shall be regarded as misleading if it contains false information (Section 39)[28] or otherwise is able to deceive a market participant in relation to the product on one or more of the following elements in such a way that he will be caused to take a transactional decision that he would not have taken otherwise:

[. . .]

2. the main characteristics of the product or the material features of tests or checks carried out on the product;
3. the extent of the commitments of the enterprise, the motives for the commercial practice, [. . .] any statements or symbols in relation to direct or indirect sponsorship or approval of the enterprise or the product;

[. . .]

6. the person, the attributes or rights of the enterprise or his agent, such as his identity and assets, his qualifications, status, approval, memberships or relations as well as ownership of industrial, commercial or intellectual property rights or his awards and distinctions;
7. the rights of the consumer from warranty and guarantee or the risks he may face.

Again, reference is made to the above-cited definition of a "commercial practice" and the argument that a "code of conduct"/CSR policy that is not directly connected with the promotion, sale or supply of a product would not fall under the provision. However, this argument could in the context of the general provisions against "misleading practices" be overcome by the possible "referring consumer perception" ("*verweisende Verbrauchervorstellung*") based on codes, policies, etc., as explained above in Sect. 22.2.

(V) Pursuant to Sec 8 of the Law on Standards 1971, the usage of the sign ÖNORM (or confusingly similar signs) without fulfilling the regarding requirements for using the sign ÖNORM is punishable with an administrative fine of up to EUR 2,180.

22.4 Enforceability

22.4.1 By Public or Regulatory Authorities

Fines under the Law on Standards 1971 can only be imposed and enforced by the Austrian administrative punitive authority. However, a breach of the Law on Standards 1971 can also be seen as a breach of the Austrian Unfair Competition Act in terms of unfair competitive advantage due to a breach of law.

Public respectively Regulatory Authorities have certain rights to file actions under the Austrian UWG: pursuant to Sec 14 UWG in the case of a "misleading (commercial) practice" or "breach of law, which is likely to significantly distort the

[28] "(1) Allegations and representations within the meaning of this Act shall also include illustrations and other activities which are designed and suitable to substitute verbal representations. (2) Any addition, omission, restriction, change or other activity of such kind or form as to escape observation or notice if no special attention is observed shall not preclude application of this Act in the event of any action prohibited under this Act."

competition to the detriment of enterprises"—like a breach of Law on Standards 1971—a petition for, *inter alia*, a cease-and-desist order may, *inter alia*, be filed with the Austrian courts by the Federal Competition Authority ("*BWB*") as a public authority and the following "regulatory authorities": the Federal Chamber of Labour, the Federal Economic Chamber, the Presidential Conference of the Austrian Chambers of Agriculture and the Austrian Trade Union Federation.

22.4.2 By Consumers

In the case of a "misleading commercial practice" contrary to the Sec 2 UWG petition for, *inter alia*, a cease-and-desist order[29] may be filed by any consumer directly affected when the undertaking is at fault for the damages sustained by the consumer.[30]

In the absence of case law on this issue, the main commentators disagree as to whether or not directly affected consumers should also be entitled to file for a "popular action" pursuant to Sec. 14 UWG, which could be raised irrespective of any fault of the undertaking.[31] Pursuant to Sec 14 UWG in the case of a "misleading commercial practice," actions for, *inter alia* (for details, see Sect. 22.5), a cease-and-desist order may also be filed with the courts by (*inter alia*) the Austrian Consumers' Association ("*Verein für Konsumenteninformation – VKI*"). Furthermore, any of the bodies and organisations of another European Union Member State in terms of Art 4 (3) of Directive 98/27/EC on injunctions for the protection of consumers' interests can file such claims with the Austrian courts.

22.4.3 By Competitive Businesses

In the cases of a "misleading (commercial) practice" and "breach of laws leading to an unfair advantage"—like a breach of Law on Standards 1971—which are likely to significantly distort competition to the detriment of enterprises, petition for, *inter alia*, a cease-and-desist order and in case of fault for damages—including loss of profit[32]—may be filed by every directly affected person, including competitors.[33]

Pursuant to Sec 14 UWG (also) in those cases, a suit for, *inter alia* (for details, see Sect. 22.5), a cease-and-desist order may be filed by (a) any entrepreneur who manufactures or markets goods or services of the same or a similar kind (competitor) or (b) associations to promote the economic interests of entrepreneurs, provided that such associations represent interests that are affected by the offence (so-called *Schutzverbände*).

[29] For details, see below, Sect. 22.5.

[30] Kodek/Leupold in Wiebe/Kodek UWG^2 § 14/69, and references.

[31] Kodek/Leupold in Wiebe/Kodek UWG^2 § 14/101 et seq.

[32] Sec 16 UWG.

[33] Kodek/Leupold in Wiebe/Kodek UWG^2 § 14/69 and references.

Competitors and *Schutzverbände* are also entitled to start penal proceedings if in the course of business for competitive purposes knowingly (!) misleading business practices are applied in a public announcement or in a media; the offender shall be sentenced by the penal court to a fine of up to 180 *per diem* rates ("*Tagessätze*"), calculated on the actual economic situation of the convicted.[34]

22.4.4 By Vertically Connected Businesses, e.g. Suppliers to and Purchasers/Dealers of the Goods or Services of the Business (e.g., the Farmers of Fair Trade Coffee to a Dealer/Coffee Shop that Fails, Contrary to Its Well-Publicised CSR Policy, to Buy and Sell Fair Trade Coffee)

While competitors are explicitly mentioned by the Austrian UWG and thus by law are entitled to raise claims (see Sect. 22.4.3), enterprises on a different (distribution) level, therefore not being competitors, are not explicitly mentioned. However, as mentioned above, pursuant to case law, every directly affected person may file with the courts actions for, *inter alia*, a cease-and-desist order and in case of fault also for payment of damages based on the UWG. This includes suppliers and purchasers, which are directly affected by a breach of a CSR policy when there is a "link" between the supplier, respectively purchaser, and the business being in breach of the policy.

Regarding the example in the heading, not every farmer of Fair Trade coffee is directly affected if a dealer/coffee shop fails, contrary to its CSR policy, to buy and sell Fair Trade coffee because complying with the CSR policy does not automatically mean that the dealer/coffee shop would buy the coffee from the regarding farmer. Therefore, it seems difficult to show that such farmer is directly affected. However, e.g., if a coffee shop advertising its fair trade policy has several supplying farmers and one or more of the farmers are not supplying Fair Trade coffee, the other farmers meeting the policy might be directly affected.

22.5 Causes of Action and Range of Remedies Available to Regulatory Authorities

22.5.1 Injunctive Relief Against Businesses that Market Goods or Services in Breach of Their CSR Policy

The public authority ("BWB") and the quasi-regulatory authorities mentioned in Sect. 22.4.1 are in the case of a "misleading commercial practice" or "breach of law, which is likely to significantly distort the competition to the detriment of enterprises"—like a breach of Law on Standards 1971—pursuant to the UWG

[34] Sec 4 UWG.

entitled to raise claims with Austrian courts for (1) cease and desist, (2) information,[35] (3) elimination of a condition that is contrary to the law[36] and (4) publication of the decision.[37] The mentioned claim for a cease and desist may be secured with preliminary injunctions[38] issued by Austrian courts following applications by persons/institutions named in Sect. 22.4 above.

---

[35] Sec 14a UWG: "(1) Entrepreneurs, who offer postal or telecommunication services and who process for their commercial service activities names and addresses received by their users, are – upon written request (para 2) of one of the bodies capable to file suits according to Section 14 para 1 second and third sentence or the Schutzverband gegen unlauteren Wettbewerb, in case of a reasonable suspicion of an unfair practice of that user according to Sections 1, 1a or 2 – obliged to render this data in writing in an appropriate period of time. These [entrepreneurs] are only obliged to render information insofar as such data is without further inquiries available and is connected with a domestic mailbox or a domestic telephone number not registered in a listing of participants which is commonly accessible. (2) The party requiring information has – by otherwise loss of his right to receive information – to state in his request the reasons for his suspicion and has to lay down that he needs the data mentioned in para 1 for the prosecution of his rights against unfair commercial practices according to Sections 1, 1a or 2, that he [will] use such only in this respect and cannot receive such through commonly accessible means of information. (3) The party requiring information with the exception of the Federal Competition Authority has to reimburse appropriate costs for the rendering of information to the provider of services. He has also to hold him harmless for all possible claims of users that may arise from the rendering of information. He has to store a copy of the written request for the period of three years."

[36] Sec 15 UWG: "The claim for a cease-and-desist order shall also include the right to demand from the liable [party] the elimination of a condition which is contrary to the law, to the extent that the liable [party] has the disposition thereof."

[37] Sec 25 UWG: "(1) In the cases of Sections 4 and 10, publication of the sentence may be ordered at the expense of the sentenced party. (2) In the cases of Sections 4 and 10, the court may, upon application by the acquitted party, authorise such party to have the acquittal published at the expense of the plaintiff in the private prosecution within a specified period of time. (3) Where, except in the cases of Sections 11 and 12, a suit for a cease-and-desist order is undertaken, the court shall, upon application, authorise the prevailing party, if such [party] has a legitimate interest in it, to have the sentence published at the opposing party's expense within a specified time limit. (4) The publication shall comprise the wording of the sentence. The manner of publication shall be defined in the sentence. (5) In civil proceeding[s], the court may, upon application by the prevailing party, define a text of the publication which varies from or supplements the scope or wording of the sentence. Such application shall be filed not later than four weeks after the sentence has become final. If such application is only filed after the end of the [first instance] hearing, it shall be decided by the court of first instance by an order after the sentence has become final. (6) Upon application of the prevailing party, the court of first instance shall specify the costs of publication and shall order the opposing party with the reimbursement. Upon application of the prevailing party, [the court] can order the loosing party to a prepayment of the presumable costs for publication in a period of four weeks. From an order of prepayment of [publication] costs has to be refrained if the loosing party certifies that the circumstances of its income and property do not suffice such a payment for the time being. The course of the time period for the publication of the sentence shall be stayed by the application for the deposit of the presumable costs of publication until the day of the arrival of the prepayment or the dismissal of this application. After publication was effected the prevailing party has under notification of the actual accrued costs to refund to the loosing party an exceeding amount including interest. (7) Publication based on a final sentence or another enforceable writ of execution shall be made by the media entrepreneur without any unnecessary delay."

[38] Sec 24 UWG.

22.5.2 The Right of Regulatory Authorities to Impose Fines

A breach of the CSR policy may fulfil the conditions for the criminal offense of fraud.[39]

Furthermore, the breach of the requirements regarding an ÖNORMEN can lead to fines by administrative penal authorities.

The criteria for the fine are, *inter alia*, previous convictions, the size of infringement and the quality of fault.

Codes of conduct, etc., might also include and impose their own "private regulatory authority" that is entitled to impose "fines" on businesses that breach the "code." These "fines" are based on the contractual obligation between the involved parties. Of course, imprisonment, etc., cannot be imposed by such "private regulatory authority." Please note in this context that (*inter alia*) the Code of Conduct[40] of the Association of the Austrian Pharmaceutical Industry—PHARMIG[41]—and its legal impact (outside the self-imposed "regulatory authority") were the subject matter of several Supreme Court decisions. However, the Supreme Court always avoided to decide on the questions (1) if such code of conduct, whereas nearly all Austrian pharmaceutical companies are members of the PHARMIG and therefore bound by the code, has legal impact *erga omnes* (also on pharmaceutical companies that are not members of the PHARMIG) and (2) if a breach of the Code of Conduct automatically leads to a breach of the UWG.[42]

22.6 The Causes of Action and Available Remedies to Private Entities (e.g., Competing Businesses)

Pursuant to the UWG and in the case of a "misleading commercial practice" or "breach of law which is likely to significantly distort the competition to the detriment of enterprises"—like a breach of Law on Standards 1971—competitors and directly affected persons are entitled to raise claims for (1) cease and desist, (2) information,[43] (3) elimination of a condition that is contrary to the law[44] and (4) publication of the decision,[45] and in case of fault of the business for (5) damages, including loss of profits.

The claim for cease and desist may be secured with preliminary injunctions.[46]

[39] Sec 146 et seq Austrian Penal Act.

[40] In English: http://www.pharmig.at/uploads/19VHC2009_Englisch_10_5694_DE.pdf.

[41] http://www.pharmig.at.

[42] Austrian Supreme Court 22.5.2007, 4 Ob 58/07v; 13.11.2007, 4 Ob 174/07b, wbl 2008,148/68 = EvBl 2008, 281 = ÖBl-LS 2008/41, 42, 46, etc.

[43] Sec 14a UWG – see above.

[44] Sec 15 UWG – see above.

[45] Sec 25 UWG – see above.

[46] Sec 24 UWG.

For example, where a business can prove that it has lost substantial business to an entrepreneur promoting chocolate sourced from Fair Trade farmers, it may recover compensation/lost profit if it is proven that, in fact, the entrepreneur was not selling chocolate so sourced. If Fair Trade cocoa farmers have *locus standi* depends on the circumstances, i.e., whether they are directly affected. Consequently, if—but only if—they are directly affected, they can bring such claims.

22.6.1 The Proximity (Nexus) Required Between a Commercial Practice Which Breaches a CSR Policy and the Goods Produced or Services Supplied by the Business with the CSR Policy for the Private Business to Be Able to Obtain Relief

Assuming that all above-mentioned measures are (a) likely to significantly distort the competition to the detriment of enterprises and/or (b) with regard to the respective product suitable to materially distort the economic behaviour of the average consumer whom it reaches or to whom it is addressed,[47] they have to be considered as "unfair commercial practice," and thus the above remedies are applicable under the Austrian UWG. When the undertaking is at fault and the damages caused by the measures, including loss of profits, can be proven, the faulty undertaking has to indemnify the injured party, irrespective of how close the *nexus* between the commercial practice and the goods produced or services supplied are.

22.7 The Powers of Private or Public Concerns to Obtain Information from Businesses with CSR Policies

There is no general power by private or public concerns to obtain such information in Austria.

However, if a claim for a cease-and-desist order or for damages is raised, pursuant to Sec 1 para 5 UWG, the defending undertaking might bear the burden of proof if—due to the circumstances of the single case—such shift of the burden of proof is appropriate. Such shift seems generally to be appropriate whenever questions regarding compliance with CSR policies arise.

In this context, it is worth mentioning that the Austrian Supreme Court has stated for claims regarding the environmental impact of the product that such claims may only be used if they are clearly proven and such claims are absolutely unlikely to mislead the consumer. If unspecific terms are used, the advertiser is obliged to clarify those terms.[48]

[47] Compare Sec 1 UWG – see above.

[48] Austrian Supreme Court 28.11.2012, 4 Ob 202/12b.

22.8 De Lege Ferenda Questions

The Austrian Group considers the laws in Austria to be sufficient to deal with commercial practices where a business commits a breach of its own CSR policy.

Nevertheless—at least at the moment—it remains unclear whether Sec 2 para 3 UWG covers all relevant breaches of such policies because it remains unclear what *nexus* is needed between the breach of the policy and the indication by the business to be bound by the code. In our opinion, as nobody is "forced" to voluntarily adopt a code of conduct, etc., it should be sufficient that the business refers (wherever) to the fact that it is bound by the code/policy, for each such breach of the code/policy to be considered to be a breach of Sec 2 para 3 UWG.

Furthermore, it could be argued by undertakings being in breach of their CSR policy that their CSR policies and their breach do not fall under "commercial practices" if the CSR policy is not directly connected with the promotion, sale or supply of a product, e.g., the CSR policy is "only" mentioned on the website but not in the actual promotion of the undertaking. The Austrian Group is of the opinion that the UWG must not be interpreted in such a "formal manner," namely that the CSR policy and its breach have to be directly connected with the promotion, sale or supply. This is especially because the Austrian Group is of the opinion that one promotion might affect the consumers' perception of another promotion of the same undertaking.

As shown on the example of the food sector, there are dozens of voluntarily adopted seals, policies, codes of conduct, etc., and only a few of them seem to be misleading respectively to be breached. Nevertheless, there seems to be a hype in nearly every area of business to adopt seals, policies, codes of conduct, etc. The Austrian case law has already addressed this issue (at least regarding environmental claims and health claims) and has a very strict approach regarding all those claims.

Although we are of the opinion that there should be sufficient enforcement regarding the non-compliance with policies etc., it has to be also stressed that policies etc. could lead to a technocratic system of (*de facto* obligatory) rules lacking legitimate democratic background; furthermore, (CSR) policies will not and cannot substitute the need of laws in the regarding areas.[49] Therefore, we are of the opinion that not every breach of every (CSR) policy should lead to legal consequences—there has to be an evaluation in every specific case. Therefore, we are of the opinion that the UWG and, especially, the "competitor as a regulator" are a good tool to deal with breaches of (CSR) policies. In this context, the Austrian Group suggests "Transparency Rules for CSR Policies" to provide the consumers with the necessary information to enable the enforcement of breaches—for details, see Sect. 22.10.

On the other hand, in our opinion, it has to be stressed that (CSR) policies can present advantage for consumers: "Good" (CSR) policies lead to "good" products

[49] Compare Lachmayer, Technokratische Rechtssetzung Privater, juridikum 2013, 109.

and services that can be bought by the consumer "with clear and social conscience." Therefore, there could be—not only from a cartel law perspective—"objective justification/reasons" for strict (CSR) policies, and in those cases there has to be an effective (legal) way to enforce them—again a reason for a suggestion by the Austrian Group that "Transparency Rules for CSR Policies" should be implemented.

22.9 Consumers' and Businesses' Concerns About Non-compliance with CSRs

The concerns of consumers about non-compliance with any kind of policy seem to differ depending on the sector of business or the affected values: ecology, health, fairness, politics. While consumers seem to be very sensitive regarding policies in the food sector, it seems that in other business sectors consumers are not paying so much attention to policies, e.g., in the sector of e-commerce. Nevertheless, we have the feeling that in Austria consumers generally demand that businesses comply with their policies, etc. Our feeling is that Austrian consumers demand a legal sanction for businesses not complying with their policies, especially if there is organisational fault. In this context, it is again worth mentioning that all claims—but the claim for compensation—based on the UWG are not subject to any fault. This could be considered as very tough.

However, it seems that the number of available seals, (CSR) policies and codes of conduct and their exact contents, respectively implication, overburden most of the consumers. Generally—also in Austria—it is as a matter of fact difficult and sometimes even impossible for the individual consumer to check if the businesses are in compliance with their policies. However, the Austrian Consumers' Association ("*Verein für Konsumenteninformation—VKI*") and the Austrian Chamber for Labour ("*Arbeiterkammer*"), for example, reviewed seals based on codes of conducts or policies in the food sector. This proves our general feeling that consumers (and "their" organisations) want to make sure that policies are not misleading and that businesses are in compliance with them: the "demand" of consumers in terms of compliance seems to be higher if businesses refer or even stress these policies in their advertisements. Nevertheless, the VKI does not only focus on advertised CSR, but it also has indeed conducted more than 100 "business ethic test" in nearly all areas of business, irrespective if a CSR policy is in force or advertised.[50]

[50] http://www.konsument.at/cs/Satellite?pagename=Konsument%2FPage%2FSuchergebnis&cid=1188229659865&_charset_=utf-8&q_queryterm=ethik-test.

22.10 The Extent to Which Austrian Laws Fail to Meet These Private and Public Concerns

Although the Austrian Group is of the opinion that the Austrian laws generally meet the concerns regarding (CSR) policies, etc., it seems that the amount of policies, etc., overburdens most of the consumers.

Therefore, there seems to be a demand for more transparency in relation to (CSR) policies, and the Austrian Group suggests to impose an obligation that (a) the (CSR) policies (at least those used in advertising and/or on products) have to meet certain minimum requirements regarding transparency and "prima facie evidence" that they are met, (b) the (CSR) policies are named and filed with a trustworthy authority (e.g., a ministry) and (c) the filed (CSR) policies are published by the authority on the Internet (maybe also further information, even decisions, on a breach of the policies, etc.).

In the Austrian Groups' opinion, the law cannot compensate the fact that it is difficult and sometimes even impossible for individual consumers to check if businesses are in compliance with their policies. Nevertheless, the Austrian consumer protection organisations, especially the VKI, are very active regarding "ethic-tests," and it seems that they obtain sufficient information to accomplish such tests.

Nevertheless, to the Austrian Group it does not seem balanced that businesses are more or less free to issue and adopt "quality seals," including CSR policies, and are not—at least not in the first place—obliged to provide sufficient information showing that they are indeed in compliance with "their" policy. Only if someone raises an action will the businesses have to prove compliance. The Austrian Group suggested that "transparency measures" could be a step towards balancing the interests.

22.11 Competition Law Issues in Relation to CSR Becoming Recognised Standards

As long as no undertaking is excluded as a result of (also *de facto*) discriminatory conditions from the CSR policy, there seem to be no issues under Austrian competition law even if a (substantive) number of undertakings in a horizontal relationship agree to voluntarily commit to a CSR policy imposed, e.g., by a NGO. However, a voluntary commitment to the CSR policy must not be combined with further—not "objectively justified/unreasonable"—anticompetitive practices, e.g., agreements on exclusivity, prices, limitation or control of production, sources of supply, etc. Therefore, e.g., also statutes of collective marks must not contradict the (general) Austrian cartel law and the Austrian Federal Law on the Improvement of Local Supply and Competition.[51]

[51] Bundesgesetz vom 29. Juni 1977 zur Verbesserung der Nahversorgung und der Wettbewerbsbedingungen – NahversorgungsG.

If involved undertakings have a substantial market share or are in a collectively dominant position, the above only changes insofar as the cartel law rules on the abuse of market dominance (additionally) apply. Irrespective of a substantial market share or (sole/joint) dominance, pursuant to the Austrian Federal Law on the Improvement of Local Supply and Competition, behaviour of entrepreneurs in business are prohibited if they are likely to jeopardise the performance-based competition ("*Leistungswettbewerb*"). The Law states that such behaviour is, e.g., fulfilled if different conditions are offered to customers and those different conditions are not objectively justified. Anybody granting in identical circumstances discriminatory conditions may be sued for cease and desist (generally in front of the Cartel Court). It can be argued that this applies also to, e.g., NGOs "offering" the granting of "Seals," etc., based on (CSR) policies.

22.12 IPR Law Issues in Relation to CSR Policies Which Have Become *De Facto* or *De Jure* Standards (Private or Government Encouraged) for Trade in Goods or Services

CSR policies might be connected with signs, logos, etc. ("CSR logo"), protected by IPR, especially by trademark and/or copyright laws. To be able to use the IPR-protected CSR logo could be of vital interest to undertakings if the CSR logo and its underlying CSR policy, respectively, have become a *de facto* or *de jure* standard and consumers are only purchasing goods labelled with the CSR logo. This leads to the issue of granting the (IP) right to label the CSR logo on goods:

As shown above, it could be argued in Austria that, e.g., NGOs issuing/offering CSR policies are obliged to do so under non-discriminate conditions and by not including any anticompetitive clauses. It can also be argued that this applies to IPRs protecting, e.g., a logo referring to the CSR policy. In other words, IPR licences have to be granted under non-discriminate conditions and without anticompetitive clauses.

Additionally, the Austrian cartel law, generally determined in the Austrian Cartel Act,[52] applies the "essential facility doctrine," and it could be argued that—in specific case—this doctrine also applies to CSR policies and CSR logos being *de facto* or *de jure* standards and when there is no reasonable alternative to the regarding CSR policy. Furthermore, as outlined above, CSR policies can be also challenged if the CSR (with/without IPR) is offered on discriminating terms. Under these (strict) conditions, compulsory licences regarding the CSR logos/CSR policies could be enforced via Austrian (Cartel) courts (based on the Austrian Cartel Act).

[52] Bundesgesetz gegen Kartelle und andere Wettbewerbsbeschränkungen (Kartellgesetz 2005 – KartG 2005).

Belgium

23

Laurie Caucheteux and Michaëla Roegiers

23.1 Introduction

In Belgium, CSR policies concern different areas of business. Firstly, we will analyse the different laws concerning CSR policies. Then we will examine if Belgian law prevents or sanctions a business that carries out commercial practices that breach a CSR policy voluntarily adopted. Secondly, we will consider whether Belgian laws adequately address commercial practices when a business is breaching its own CSR policy. Finally, we will point out competition aspects of CSR standards and if issues are raised by Belgian competition law when undertakings in a horizontal relationship agree voluntarily to commit to a CSR policy.

23.2 Definition and Context of CSR in Belgium

In Belgium, CSR policies concern different areas of business. At federal level, the Commission of the interdepartmental of sustainable development (hereinafter: CIDD) has adopted an action plan on 21 December 2006[1] (hereafter "the Action

The authors want to thank Alex Tallon for his comments on an earlier draft of this paper. The content of this report remains the authors' sole responsibility.

[1] CIDD, "Plan d'action fédéral. La responsabilité sociétale des entreprises en Belgique," 25/10/2006.

L. Caucheteux (✉) • M. Roegiers
Praetica, Brussels, Belgium
e-mail: lc@praetica.com; mr@praetica.com

P. Kobel et al. (eds.), *Antitrust in the Groceries Sector & Liability Issues in Relation to Corporate Social Responsibility*, LIDC Contributions on Antitrust Law, Intellectual Property and Unfair Competition, DOI 10.1007/978-3-662-45753-5_23

Plan"), which aims at promoting CSR policies and at stimulating companies to integrate those policies in their management.[2] This Action Plan is not binding.

This Action Plan defines a CSR as "a continuous improvement process where the undertakings include in a voluntarily way social, environmental and economic considerations in their management."

Furthermore, we have different laws directly related to CSR policies:

- The law of 28 April 2003 regarding the additional/complementary pension and its tax system and some advantages in the sector of social security schemes that compel pension funds to take into account social, environmental and ethical considerations in their investment strategy;[3]
- The law of 13 January 2006 modifying art. 96, 1° of the Companies Code imposing to include in the management report not only financial devices of performance but also non-financial indices such as environmental and social information;[4]
- The law of 27 February 2002, which promotes socially responsible production by creating a social label.[5]

In addition, some business sectors have created their own code of conduct,[6] including CSR policies, thereby auto-regulating themselves. For instance, the association of pharmaceutical companies follows its own code of conduct regarding drug advertising.[7] The jury of ethical advertisement, which is the self-regulatory body of Belgian advertising industry, examines the conformity of an advertising message in the media in relation to a code of conduct.[8] The industrial food sector[9] and the association of cosmetic producers[10] have also their own code of conduct.

[2] At the regional level, in Brussels, there is an "*Ordonnance*" of 04/09/2008 promoting CSR in Belgian businesses and, in particular, the granting of the "Bruxelles label" delivered by the Government of *Bruxelles-Capitale* to the business socially responsible. There are also similar initiatives in the other Belgian regions.

[3] Loi du 28 avril 2003 relative aux pensions complémentaires et au régime fiscal de celles-ci et de certains avantages complémentaire en matière de sécurité sociale, *M.B.*, 15/05/2003, available at http://www.ejustice.just.fgov.be/loi/loi.htm.

[4] Loi du 13 janvier 2006 modifiant le Code des sociétés, *M.B.*, 20/01/2006, 03118.

[5] Loi du 27 février 2002 visant à promouvoir la production socialement responsable, *M.B.*, 26/02/2002.

[6] The code of conduct is defined as "an agreement or set of rules not imposed by law, regulation or administrative provision of a Member State which defines the behaviour of traders who undertake to be bound by the code in relation to one or more particular commercial practices or business sectors" (art. 2, 31° LPMC; art. 2, f Directive 2005/29/EC).

[7] See http://pharma.be/.

[8] See http://www.jep.be/fr/, the consumer has to make his claim to the jury of Ethical advertisement.

[9] See http://www.fevia.be.

[10] See http://www.detic.be/pages/FR/detic.asp.

Some codes of conduct have been negotiated between consumers and professional organisations within the council of consumption.[11] These so-called *co-regulation* codes include the code on ecological advertisement, the charter for the customer, the code of conduct on the advertisement and marketing toward young people for bank services and products.

However, these codes are currently not binding, as they have to be enacted in a royal decree to enter into force.[12] For that to happen, the council of consumption would have to unanimously approve the binding force of such a code. Experience showed that it will be difficult to build such a majority inside the council of consumption.

23.3 Relevant Legislation Sanctioning a Business Which Carries Out Commercial Practices in Violation of Its Own CSR

We have to distinguish between the financial compensation remedy provided by Article 1382 of the Civil Code and the law of the 6 April 2010 on market practices and consumer protection, which provides injunctive relief (hereinafter: "LPMC").

23.3.1 Injunctive Relief

The LPMC draws a difference between the business-to-consumer practices (Arts. 83–94) (transposing the EU unfair commercial practices Directive[13]) and the unfair practices taking place between undertakings (Arts. 95–99).

23.3.1.1 Consumers' Protection

The Law

In order to guarantee consumers' protection, the Directive established a list of commercial practices that are deemed unfair (Annex I of the Directive 2005/29/EC).

This "black list" has been implemented into Belgian law by Article 91 LPMC, which provides that some commercial practices towards the consumer are, under any circumstances, considered as being unfair. These include the following:

---

[11] This Council has been created by the Royal Decree of 20 February 1964; its mission is to give recommendations to the Minister of Economic Affairs and the government in relation to consumers' protection. See http://economie.fgov.be/fr/spf/structure/Commissions_Conseils/Conseil_Consommation/#.UYPzWaKmGSo.

[12] Art. 105 LPMC.

[13] Directive 2005/29/EC of the European Parliament and of the Council of 11 May 2005 concerning unfair business-to-consumer commercial practices in the internal market, OJ L 149, 11.6.2005, p. 11 (hereafter "the Directive").

(i) claiming to be a signatory to a code of conduct when the trader is not;
(ii) displaying a trust mark, quality mark or equivalent without having obtained the necessary authorisation;
(iii) claiming that a code of conduct has an endorsement from a public or other body which it does not have;
(iv) claiming that a trader (including his commercial practices) or a product has been approved, endorsed or authorised by a public or private body when he/it has not or making such a claim without complying with the terms of the approval, endorsement or authorisation.[14]

Article 91 does not apply to the non-compliance by an undertaking of its own CSR policies.[15]

However, the violation of CSR policies by an undertaking could be sanctioned by Article 89, 2° LPMC, which provides that "A commercial practice shall also be regarded as misleading if, in its factual context, taking account of all its features and circumstances, it causes or is likely to cause the average consumer to take a transactional decision that he would not have taken otherwise, and it involves non-compliance by the trader with commitments contained in codes of conduct by which the trader has undertaken to be bound, where:

(i) the commitment is not aspirational but is firm and is capable of being verified and;
(ii) the trader indicates in a commercial practice that he is bound by the code."[16]

The Applicants

The Minister of Economic Affairs (hereafter "the Minister") and the General Director of the Federal Public Service of Economic Affairs can obtain an injunctive relief against an undertaking that breaches the provisions of the LPMC pertaining to the protection of consumers, except in cases involving Article 95 LPMC et seq. concerning unfair practices between undertakings (Art. 113, al. 1, 2°, LPMC).[17] The Minister does not have to prove any interest in order to obtain an injunctive relief before the Court.

In case of unfair practices in a business-to-consumer relationship, the consumer may apply for injunctive relief against an undertaking (Art. 113, al. 1, 1° LPMC). The consumer must be affected by the unfair practice and must have a direct and

[14] See above FN 13.

[15] H. Jacquemin "Les pratiques déloyales à l'égard des consommateurs ou des entreprises," in Les pratiques du marché : une loi pour le consommateur, le concurrent et le juge, dir. Laurent De Brouwer, Bruxelles, Larcier, 2011, 83.

[16] Which corresponds to Art. 6 Directive 2005/29/EC.

[17] A. Tallon, "La procédure : nouveautés et sanctions," H. Jacquemin "Les pratiques déloyales à l'égard des consommateurs ou des entreprises," in Les pratiques du marché : une loi pour le consommateur, le concurrent et le juge, dir. Laurent De Brouwer, Bruxelles, Larcier, 2011, 138.

personal interest (Arts. 17 and 18 of the Judicial Code). However, it can also be a preventive action.[18]

A consumers' association may also apply for injunctive relief against an undertaking (Art. 113, al. 1, 4°, LPMC; Art. 2 RPLPMC[19]). The consumers' association needs to have a legal personality and has to be represented in the council of consumption or has to be approved by the Minister for Economic Affairs. The association's purpose, as reflected in the articles of association, must be devoted to the protection of the interests of consumers. The association would have to prove a collective advantage but not a direct interest such as the one that is provided for the consumer (Art. 113, al. 2 LPMC) (see above). The consumers' association may not introduce a proceeding in case of an unfair practice between undertakings[20] (Art. 113, al. 1, 4° LPMC).

23.3.1.2 Prohibition of Unfair Competition Between Undertakings

The Law

In order to prohibit unfair practices between undertakings, Article 95 LPMC provides: "Is prohibited all act contrary to the unfair competition by which an undertaking shall affect the interest of one or more undertakings."

The concept of unfair competition practice is not defined by the law. This notion implies a behaviour that breaches a law or that must be considered as being unfair according to the minimum standard of loyalty between undertakings.

In the latter case, a violation by an undertaking could be considered as an unfair practice between undertakings if two conditions are fulfilled:

1. the behaviour of the undertaking must be unfair taking into account the business sector, the circumstances of the case;
2. the commercial practices must be considered as being unfair regarding the minimum standard of loyalty between undertakings and the due professional care.[21] In this context, the judge may find in the CSR policies the definition of this standard of the prudent and careful professional care.[22]

---

[18] J. Ligot, et alii, Les pratiques loyales, dir. A. Tallon, 2ème éd., Bruxelles, Larcier, 2012, 299.

[19] Regulation regarding the proceeding concerning the law on market practices (hereinafter "RPLMPC").

[20] Liège, 26/01/2007, *D.C.C.R.*, 2008, p. 73. By its decision dated 26 January 2007, the Court of Appeal of Liège has admitted that the association of consumers Test Achat is competent to introduce a case because it has a collective interest. However, the Court said that the practice has not to concern all the consumers.

[21] H. Jacquemin "Les pratiques déloyales à l'égard des consommateurs ou des entreprises," in Les pratiques du marché : une loi pour le consommateur, le concurrent et le juge, dir. Laurent De Brouwer, Bruxelles, Larcier, 2011, 102.

[22] J. Ligot, et alii, Les pratiques loyales, dir. A. Tallon, 2ème éd., Bruxelles, Larcier, 2012, 299.

In addition, the non-compliance by an undertaking to the business-to-consumer practices under the LPMC may also be in violation of Article 95 LPMC if:

(i) the commercial practice affects not only consumers protection but also one or more undertakings;
(ii) the commercial practices is unlawful under the provisions of the LPMC concerning consumer protection (Article 83 et seq.).

In view of the above, the non-compliance by an undertaking with its own code of conduct within the meaning of Article 89, 2° LPMC could be considered as being an unfair practice between undertakings within the meaning of Article 95 LPMC.

Furthermore, non-compliance by an undertaking of a code of conduct endorsed by the council of consumption may be sanctioned under Articles 93 and 94 LPMC.

The Applicants

A competing company may bring a legal action against unfair competition on the basis of Article 95 (Art. 113, al 1, 1° LPMC). The undertaking, just as the consumer, would have to prove an interest according to Articles 17 and 18 of the Judicial Code. A potential breach of Article 95 LPMC might still happen.[23] However, an undertaking cannot bring an action *ad futurum*.[24]

When a business faces an unfair practice carried out by another undertaking, a professional group may have an interest to introduce a case of injunctive relief (Article 113, al. 1, 3°, LPMC). This professional group, just like a consumer association, has to prove a collective interest but not a direct interest unlike individual consumers or undertakings (see above). This collective interest has to be integrated in the articles of association.

The suppliers and the purchasers of the goods or services of a business may bring an action against unfair practices on the basis of Article 95 LPMC if they are considered as an undertaking in the sense of Article 2, 1° LPMC, *i.e.*, "a physical person or a legal entity with an economic goal." As mentioned above, a risk of a violation of Art. 95 LPMC might be sufficient to bring a legal action. The supplier or purchaser may be Belgian or not.[25]

The Minister can bring a legal action following a complaint from a consumer or at the request of the Public Prosecutor regarding an infringement of the LPMC (Arts 123 et seq. and 133 et seq., LPMC). The Minister has the power to conduct an investigation in order to detect an infringement to the LPMC (Art. 133 LPMC). The Minister may issue a warning so that the undertaking ceases its practices (Art.

---

[23] Article 2, al. 2, RPLMPC.

[24] Comm., Bruxelles, prés. 18/02/1994, Prat. Comm., 1994, 437.

[25] A. Tallon, "La procédure : nouveautés et sanctions," H. Jacquemin "Les pratiques déloyales à l'égard des consommateurs ou des entreprises," in Les pratiques du marché : une loi pour le consommateur, le concurrent et le juge, dir. Laurent De Brouwer, Bruxelles, Larcier, 2011, 67.

123 LPMC). If the undertaking does not comply with the warning, the Minister may transfer the case to the Public Prosecutor.

Usually, the Minister will offer a settlement. If the undertaking accepts this settlement, no action will be introduced by the regulatory authority.

All unfair practices carried out against the consumer are likely to trigger a criminal fine from EUR 250 to EUR 10,000 (Art. 124, 13° LPMC). If an undertaking acts in bad faith, it could be sanctioned by a criminal fine from EUR 500 to EUR 20,000. The concept of bad faith is discussed by the doctrine. According to the jurisprudence, bad faith is proven if the undertaking that has been subject to an injunctive relief order commits an unfair practice in another business sector.[26]

In addition, non-compliance with an injunctive judgment may be sanctioned by a criminal fine of EUR 1,000 up to EUR 20,000 (Art. 126, 1°, LPMC).

23.3.2 Financial Compensation

23.3.2.1 The Law

The violation of CSR policies by a company could also be sanctioned under civil law by using the standard of the prudent and careful trader in the same circumstances of the case (Art. 1382 Civil Code). An undertaking or a consumer may bring an action for damages when an undertaking breaches its own CSR policies if they can prove the existence of damage and a causal link between the fault and the damage. The judge could find in the CSR policies the definition of the standard of the prudent and careful trader.[27] The objective of Art. 1382 is to grant compensation for damages; on the contrary, the main purpose of the LPMC is to put an end to an unfair practice.[28]

23.3.2.2 The Applicants

In Belgium, public authorities do not have *locus standi* to claim damages on the basis of Article 1382 Civil Code.[29]

A consumer may also bring a legal claim based on Article 1382 Civ. Code. He must prove a fault (violation of the LPMC), a damage, and a causal link. If there is a

[26] Mons, 6/03/1985, J.T., 1985, 717.

[27] E. de Cannart d'Hamale, La responsabilité sociale des entreprises, soft law ou hard law ? J.T., 2007, liv. 6267, 420.

[28] H. Jacquemin "Les pratiques déloyales à l'égard des consommateurs ou des entreprises," in Les pratiques du marché : une loi pour le consommateur, le concurrent et le juge, dir. Laurent De Brouwer, Bruxelles, Larcier, 2011, 105.

[29] A. Tallon, "La procédure : nouveautés et sanctions," H. Jacquemin "Les pratiques déloyales à l'égard des consommateurs ou des entreprises," in Les pratiques du marché : une loi pour le consommateur, le concurrent et le juge, dir. Laurent De Brouwer, Bruxelles, Larcier, 2011, 168.

judgement of injunctive relief on the basis of the law of LPMC, the fault is proved by this judgement.

Few consumers will file suit because of the costs of such a proceeding.

In Belgium, the class action does not yet exist.[30] However, the Government has the intention to introduce this type of legal action in our legal system. This type of action could be brought by non-profit organisation and professional associations. There have been several proposals from the Parliament on this subject.[31]

An undertaking may claim damages on the basis of Article 1382 Civ. Code. It has to prove a fault (violation of the LPMC), a damage and a causal link. If there is a judgement of "stop order" on the basis of the LPMC, the fault is proved by this judgement.

The judge has to evaluate the loss of profits of the undertaking harmed and linked to this fault.[32] The good faith of the undertaking is not a criterion to assess the damage. It is often difficult for the undertaking to prove its disgorgement of profits.[33]

If the judge cannot accurately assess the damage, he will set the compensatory damages ex *aequo et bono.*

In Belgium, class action does not exist yet.[34] But there have been several proposals from the Parliament on this subject (see above). A professional association has, just like a consumers' association, to prove its own damages and interests. This will rarely be the case (see above).

However, if the association is a professional union in the sense of the provisions of the law of 31 March 1898, it could file suit on behalf of several members harmed by the unfair practice in order to recover the damages.[35]

Under Article 1382 Civ. Code, the suppliers and purchasers of the company have to prove a fault, a causal link, and a damage. The proof of a damage caused by an undertaking that breaches its own CSR policy is more complicated. In conclusion, the suppliers and purchasers have more chances to bring an action for injunctive relief than to obtain some financial compensation.

[30] Cass., 9/12/1957/, *R.C.J.B.*, 1958, 247.

[31] Wetsvoorstel van M. Gerkens, R. Landuyt, S. Van Hecke, wetsvoorstel tot tot wijziging van het Gerechtelijk Wetboek teneinde verenigingen een vorderingsrecht toe te kennen ter verdediging van collectieve belangen, 22/02/2008, doc 52/0872/001; wetsvoorstel, M. Stefaan Van Hecke, Ronny Balcaen, wetsvoorstel tot wijziging van het Gerechtelijk Wetboek wat het instellen van een collectieve rechtszaak betref, doc 532035001, 6/02/2012, www.chambre.be; see also, P. Hifströssler, "Waarom een "class action" in België? Krijtlijnen van het voorstel van de orde van Vlaamse Balie," De orde van de dag, Kluwer, 2011, nr 54, 95.

[32] Bruxelles, 30/04/1953, Ing. Cons., 1953, 138.

[33] A. Tallon, "La procédure : nouveautés et sanctions," H. Jacquemin "Les pratiques déloyales à l'égard des consommateurs ou des entreprises," in Les pratiques du marché : une loi pour le consommateur, le concurrent et le juge, dir. Laurent De Brouwer, Bruxelles, Larcier, 2011, 172.

[34] Cass., 9/12/1957/, R.C.J.B., 1958, 247.

[35] Cass., 28/06/1968, *JT*, 1968, 579.

23.3.3 Case Law

We will analyse in our case law the power of interpretation of the judge when a business breaches its CSR policy in order to determine how close the connection is between the commercial practice that breaches the CSR policy and goods produced or services supplied by the business.

According to the national case law, in a judgement dated 4 June 2010, the President of the commercial court of Turnhout decided that the placing on the market of a product with a quality mention while the product does not come from that producer is considered as an unfair practice between undertakings. The undertaking had no power to control the product that is sold with a quality label.[36] The undertaking claimed to have the quality label but without having obtained a quality label. In that case, the judge had no power of interpretation.

In a judgement dated 19 December 1996, the President of the commercial court decided that in absence of any legal directive, the term "bio" is very general. The use of the term "bio" on a product by an undertaking cannot be considered as constituting unfair practices.[37] The judge has first to analyse if a CSR exists and what is the content of it. When there is a general term that has no specific content, it will be difficult for the judge to appreciate if this practice is considered as unfair.

In a judgement dated 16 September 2011, the President of the commercial court of Gent decided that the advertisement made by a professional association of tiled floor and its members who were selling tiled floor under a label of quality (quality on the tiled floor, quality on the client service) is not considered as an unfair practice. Indeed, the fact that there is no inspection agency does not prove that the use of a quality label misleads the consumer.[38] The commitments of an undertaking regarding a label or a code of conduct need to have a content in order to be considered as an unfair practice.

23.4 Efficiency of the Belgian Laws, a Question of Transparency of CSR Policies

Having examined in detail the relevant legislation applicable in Belgium, its effectiveness remains to be examined.

In other words, we will consider whether Belgian laws adequately address commercial practices where a business commits a breach of its own CSR policy.

The answer to that question depends on the context in which CSR policies are developed and their transparency on the market.

[36] Voorz. Kh. Turnhout, 4 juni 2010, Jaar. Markt., 2010, 524.

[37] Gand, 19 décembre 1996, DCCR, 1997, 52.

[38] Voorz. Kh. Gent, 16 september 2011, Jaar. Hand., 2011, 217.

23.4.1 Transparency of CSR Policies

As explained above, a CSR policy essentially remains a voluntary process that is largely promoted in Belgium. This voluntarism implies that it is not necessarily communicated to other involved parties, except in the obvious situation where a company uses it to promote its corporate image.

There is currently no legal audit available to check businesses' compliance with CSR policies, or in other words their sincerity, regularity, conformity and suitability to reflect a loyal corporate image.

In this way, transparency does not prevail at the time of CSR policy implementation.

This being said, the increased promotion in Belgium of CSR policies and the constant reminder of its voluntary character unfortunately have also as a consequence that they become, with time, a catch-all notion without a real evaluation tool—except evaluation systems that companies are forced to draw up and develop themselves.

These evaluation systems are, in general, internal ones.[39] For instance, in the pharmaceutical sector, pharma.be has created a deontological code of conduct that provides with an examination in case of violation of the code and sanctions[40] (cessation of activity, reprimand, corrective measure, etc.).[41]

Nevertheless, we would like to draw the attention on the fact that, in our opinion, breaches by companies of their CSR policy can be detected and certain measures can be taken against these companies on the basis of the following tools:

ISO 26000: "provides guidance on how businesses and organizations can operate in a socially responsible way. This means acting in an ethical and transparent way that contributes to the health and welfare society."[42] ISO 26000 cannot be certified, unlike some other well-known ISO standards, to the extent that it is a process voluntarily introduced by companies. However, this ISO standard suggests guidelines to implement in order to improve CSR. So it is a comprehensive and qualitative tool. Moreover, this tool can be subject to a certification in order to obtain a label (see below).[43]

Labels: they are made of words and symbols applied on products and they are designed to inform consumers about their characteristics. Thanks to these labels, companies try to influence consumers' shopping habits. However, because of proliferation of heterogeneous labels and the absence of external control,

[39] Advice of 18/05/2006 of council of consumption on the reference framework about CSR in Belgium, 7.

[40] There are three types of examinations: the proceeding of control ex post of the written communication, the proceeding of ex ante visa and the proceeding of complaint (in this last proceeding, everybody may introduce a complaint, including the consumer).

[41] This code is available on www.pharma.be/assets/files/1162/1162_129785162531886268.pdf.

[42] http://www.iso.org/iso/home/standards/iso26000.htm?=.

[43] Interview of Oriane de Vroey, CSR partner, Business & Society Belgium.

consumers may lose confidence in labels.[44] A Belgian society "netwerk bewust verbruiken" has realised an inventory of labels in order to stimulate dialogue and encourage awareness and formation of labels. Every label is catalogued and evaluated. The objective of this evaluation is to facilitate consumers' choice between the different labels on sustainability. This is made possible by comparing the inspection and transparency of all the labels and by evaluating social and environmental criteria.[45] Such a system and the corporate image that certain labels acquires among the public induce a certain transparency and guarantee the respect of criteria bound to certain fields of CSR. Particularly in Belgium, the "label social belge" (Belgian social label) aims at promoting a socially responsible production, and the kinds of labels such as "fair trade" and "ecocert" are credible labels of quality because they are subject to an external inspection.

Social rating agencies: these agencies determine the level of companies' responsibility, including social responsibility, with regard to sustainable development. Their objective is to help investors pick out more responsible companies in relation to environmental and social aspects. There are two such agencies: Deminor Ratings and Forum Ethibel.[46] Their intervention is however (1) costly and (2) conditioned by the advertisement of CSR policy because it is based on public documents, questionnaires and results of interviews with heads of companies.

Annual reports: since 1995, Belgian companies have been required to include in their annual report a "bilan social" (social report) that consists of data on the nature and the evolution of employment in their companies (i.e., workforce, fluctuations, training). Under the recent law of 13 January 2006, companies have to add in their annual report an analysis of their business evolution, of financial provisioning decisions and on indicators of their financial performance relating to their specific activities, notably information about environmental and social questions.[47]

Investigation powers: the Minister has the power to conduct investigations in order to detect infringements of the LPMC by an undertaking (Art. 123 LPMC). This leads to a letter of notice addressed to an undertaking that does not respect its own code of conduct. If the undertaking does not comply with the order given by the regulatory authority, the latter will introduce an injunctive relief action. Consumers may introduce a complaint before the Minister (see above). The Minister decides autonomously to investigate the violation by a undertakings of its own CSR policies. Furthermore, according to Article 103 LPMC, the judge dealing with the injunctive relief application may shift the burden of proof. In order words, the undertaking that breaches the LPMC has to produce the proof that there is no unfair practices. Apart from this complaint, consumers or competing undertakings have few tools to obtain information from the companies that breach their own CSR

---

[44] Reference framework "La responsabilité sociétale des entreprises en Belgique," 29/03/2006, available on rse.wallonie.be/apps/spip/IMG/pdf/CadreRefRSE2006-3.pdf.

[45] See www.infolabel.be.

[46] See www.financite.be.

[47] Article 5, Loi du 13 janvier 2006 modifiant le Code des Sociétés.

policies if the latter do not publicly communicate the result of the implementation of these CSR policies.

In our opinion, those different kinds of tools generate a certain transparency and may detect breaches of CSR policies of an undertaking.

But these tools are based on a law or are initiated by a third party; in order words, no real assessment tool currently exists.

Action n° 8 of the above-mentioned Action Plan foresees a dialogue with stakeholders on CSR policies in order to exchange points of view and reach a consensus. So this dialogue may create a certain degree of transparency.

But this action does not seem to have any impact, as some consumers anticipated it.[48]

However, although a violation of its CSR policy by an undertaking is not actually yet deemed to constitute a breach of the law in Belgium, the voluntary nature of CSRs and the promotion made about them led to demands by consumers for more transparency.

Indeed, because—as explained above—some undertakings use what they have at their disposal, one faces situations where companies use a CSR policy as a complementary mean for advertising in order to communicate with consumers and improve their corporate image. On the other hand, consumers fear that their fundamental right to access to information will be violated: an undertaking could display an image of being a socially responsible undertaking only on the basis of a skilfully elaborated marketing plan. Therefore, consumers consider that inspections have to be conducted by an independent inspection body related to producers/distributors and that is entrusted for this type of inspection with public powers in order to objectively exert a control over information, avoid that the CSR concept is tarnished by these kinds of bad practices and ensure a real transparency.

Moreover, consumers would prefer that this type of inspection assesses the situation and establishes a report that is based not only on the statements of undertakings but also on a set of pre-established criteria.

Nevertheless, representatives of manufacturers, distributors and middle classes are opposed to establishing a unique inspection tool. They reminded that CSR initiatives are a dynamic process, that requests for inspection will lead to hindering the voluntary nature of the CSR concept.[49]

But since these issues have been communicated in an advice issued by the council of consumption in 2006, neither an inspection tool nor a possible sanction—except on basis of laws studied above—is currently discussed.

[48] CIDD, "Plan d'action fédéral. La responsabilité sociétale des entreprises en Belgique," 25/10/2006, 30; advice of 05/02/2007 of Council of consumption on the draft of action plan on CSR in Belgium, 4.

[49] Advice of 18/05/2006 of council of consumption on the reference framework about CSR in Belgium, 3–8.

23.4.2 Conclusion and Proposals

First of all, a distinction should be drawn where the undertakings make their CSR policies available to the public or not. In other words, the question arises as to whether there is a sufficient level of transparency or not.

In case the undertakings make their CSR policies *public*, they have to comply with Article 89, 2° LPMC, which provides that "the non-compliance by a trader with commitments contained in codes of conduct shall be a misleading commercial practice if:

(i) the commitment is not aspirational but is firm and is capable of being verified and;
(ii) the trader indicates in a commercial practice that he is bound by the code."[50]

On the basis of this provision, consumers may bring a legal action for injunctive relief against the undertaking that does not comply with its own CSR policies or lodge a complaint before the council of consumption. However, as it is mentioned above, few consumers will bring an action to recover financial loss against an undertaking that breaches its own CSR policies because they won't have any *locus standi*.

Our legislation gives the possibility to the undertakings to bring a legal action on the basis of the LPMC. Nevertheless, they are not going to use it, but they will rather wait for sanctions coming from the market (adverse comments through the press . . .).

Regarding the public concerns, as mentioned above, the Minister of Economic Affairs has a power of investigation. It can also obtain an injunctive relief, but it cannot obtain any financial compensation because there is not yet a collective action in Belgium.

If there is no sufficient transparency, there is no issue, no tool to know whether the undertakings are complying with their own CSR policies, and the law cannot meet those private and public concerns.

The lack of transparency is precisely at the heart of the criticism faced by CSR policies and constitutes the problem of effectiveness of Belgian law.

So, in our opinion, if CSR policies are considered as only being an internal regulation tool, there is no (private or public) interest to make it available to the public.

However, if undertakings are using these CSR policies as corporate image and without any transparency about the content of their CSR policies, the consumers and regulatory authorities should have access to information on these policies.

In this context, we suggest that the law should require undertakings to disclose their CSR policies and their precise content.

[50] Article 89, 2°, LPMC.

Moreover, an external inspection should be set up in order to assess if undertakings are complying with their own CSR policies.

Under this approach, the Belgian law would be entirely satisfactory.

23.5 Competition Aspects of CSR Standards

This topic aims to know if issues are raised by Belgian competition law when a number of undertakings in a horizontal relationship agree voluntarily to commit to a CSR policy.

The Belgian competition law is essentially composed of Articles 2, 3 and 6 to 10 of the law of 10 June 2006 on the protection of economic competition (hereinafter "LPCE").[51]

Under Belgian competition law, anticompetitive horizontal "relationships" are prohibited on the basis of Articles 3 and 4 of the LPCE.[52]

It should be noted that Belgian competition law extensively reproduces the principles stated in Articles 101 and 102 of Treaty on the Functioning of the

[51] Law of 10/06/2006 on the protection of economic competition, *M.B.*, 29/06/2006, 32755; see also Law of 15/09/2006 on the protection of economic competition, *M.B.*, 29/06/2006, 50613.

[52] Those Articles stipulate:

- Article 3: "§ 1er. Sont interdits, sans qu'une décision préalable soit nécessaire à cet effet, tous accords entre entreprises, toutes décisions d'associations d'entreprises et toutes pratiques concertées qui ont pour objet ou pour effet d'empêcher, de restreindre ou de fausser de manière sensible la concurrence sur le marché belge concerné ou dans une partie substantielle de celui-ci et notamment ceux qui consistent à:

1° fixer de façon directe ou indirecte les prix d'achat ou de vente ou d'autres conditions de transaction;

2° limiter ou contrôler la production, les débouchés, le développement technique ou les investissements;

3° répartir les marchés ou les sources d'approvisionnement;

4° appliquer, à l'égard de partenaires commerciaux, des conditions inégales à des prestations équivalentes en leur infligeant de ce fait un désavantage dans la concurrence;

5° subordonner la conclusion de contrats à l'acceptation, par les partenaires, de prestations supplémentaires qui, par leur nature ou selon les usages commerciaux, n'ont pas de lien avec l'objet de ces contrats.

§ 2. Les accords ou décisions interdits en vertu du présent Article sont nuls de plein droit. (...)".

- Article 4: "Est interdit, sans qu'une décision préalable soit nécessaire à cet effet, le fait pour une ou plusieurs entreprises d'exploiter de façon abusive une position dominante sur le marché belge concerné ou dans une partie substantielle de celui-ci.

Ces pratiques abusives peuvent notamment consister à:

1° imposer de façon directe ou indirecte des prix d'achat ou de vente ou d'autres conditions de transaction non équitables;

2° limiter la production, les débouchés ou le développement technique au préjudice des consommateurs;

3° appliquer à l'égard de partenaires commerciaux des conditions inégales à des prestations équivalentes, en leur infligeant de ce fait un désavantage dans la concurrence;

European Union (hereinafter "TFEU"). The Belgian legislator made indeed an excellent implementation of the principles of European competition law into the Belgian legal order.

Moreover, since Belgian competition law does not provide Guidelines or Communications, most of the time Belgian courts refer to principles contained in Articles 101 and 102 of the TFEU rather than to Articles of the LPCE in order to rule on disputes involving the application of competition law.[53] In a similar way, when national courts apply provisions of Belgian competition law, they underline that, as far as their construction of the law is concerned, they refer to the implementation and corresponding construction of Articles 101 and 102 as it is resulting from the case law of the CJUE.

This being said, in order to know whether the type of agreement encompassed by the present subject matter has as its object the prevention, restriction or distortion of competition, it is necessary to take into account the following factors to evaluate an eventual restriction in accordance with the case law of the European courts: the terms of agreement, the objectives that this agreement is seeking to achieve, the context in which this agreement was concluded, the effective behaviour of parties and the proof of the subjective intention of the parties to restrain competition.

On the other hand, concerning the restrictive effects of an agreement on competition, the Belgian competition council (hereinafter "the council") evaluates these effects on the basis of the Commission guidelines concerning the application of Article 81, § 3 of the TFEU,[54] which states:

> For an agreement to be restrictive by effect it must affect actual or potential competition to such an extent that on the relevant market negative effects on prices, output, innovation or the variety or quality of goods and services can be expected with a reasonable degree of probability.

Therefore, we have to consider an agreement in its context, which involves determining the relevant product market in order to assess whether the parties to the agreement are in (actual or potential) competition with each other and the appreciable effect on the market.[55]

4° subordonner la conclusion de contrats à l'acceptation, par les partenaires, de prestations supplémentaires, qui, par leur nature ou selon les usages commerciaux, n'ont pas de lien avec l'objet de ces contrats."

[53] D. Grisay, Introduction au droit belge de la concurrence, Bruxelles, Larcier, 2009, 112–113; Court of Appel of Brussel, 03/11/1998, Ann. prat. comm. & conc., 1998, 747; Court of Appeal of Brussels, 24/05/1996, *D.C.C.R.*, 1996, 262.

[54] Communication from the Commission – Guidelines on the application of Article 81(3) of the Treaty, OJ, C 101, 27.04.2004, p. 97.

[55] It is necessary to refer to the definition given by European case law and to the Commission notice on the definition of relevant market for the purposes of Community competition law, OJ, C 372, 09.12.1997, p. 5.

The geographical market is by essence limited to the Belgian territory or at least to a substantial part of it.

According to European case law, different factors have to be taken into account to verify if a horizontal agreement is likely to restrict competition by object or by effect or if, on basis of Article 2, § 3, it can benefit from an exemption.[56]

This exemption allows to escape the prohibition contained in Article 2, § 1 of the LPCE if the conditions contained in the Article are met. To apply this exemption, there should be a reference to European case law.

It is considered that agreements of horizontal co-operation organised between companies create a distortion of competition when they notably generate negative effects on factors such as prices, production, innovation or diversity and quality of products offered to users and final consumers.

However, they may also induce positive effects, notably in matters of environmental protection, normalisation, access to quality labels ... which is especially targeted by certain CSR policies.

By doing so, the Belgian doctrine considers that, in general, horizontal agreements targeted by this paper (agreements in virtue of which companies voluntarily adopt a CSR policy) are less likely to contain restrictions about price or production.

Indeed, potential negative effects that this kind of agreements may generate rather touch upon innovation or product diversity, and they may also raise issues of market foreclosure.[57]

---

[56] This Article provides:

> § 3. Toutefois, les dispositions du § 1er ne s'appliquent pas:
> 1° à tout accord ou catégorie d'accords entre entreprises,
> 2° à toute décision ou catégorie de décisions d'associations d'entreprises, et
> 3° à toute pratique concertée ou catégorie de pratiques concertées qui contribuent à améliorer la production ou la distribution ou à promouvoir le progrès technique ou économique ou qui permettent aux petites et moyennes entreprises d'affermir leur position concurrentielle sur le marché concerné ou sur le marché international, tout en réservant aux utilisateurs une partie équitable du profit qui en résulte et sans toutefois :
> a) imposer aux entreprises intéressées des restrictions qui ne sont pas indispensables pour atteindre ces objectifs;
> b) donner à ces entreprises la possibilité, pour une partie substantielle des produits en cause, d'éliminer la concurrence.

[57] See footnote, 136.

23.5.1 Substantial Market Share or Collectively Dominant Position

As mentioned above, in order to be forbidden, an agreement must generate a restriction of competition of a certain magnitude; the effects must be appreciable on the Belgian market.

Examination of the "appreciability" is based on Commission Notice of 2001, which establishes a "de minimis" rule,[58] and the criterion used is the market share threshold of companies.

The cumulated market share allows to compute the position of the parties on the market; if this position is weak, it is less likely that their co-operation produces restrictive effects.

When an agreement affects the market in a negligible way, in consideration of the weak position that operators hold on the relevant product market, this agreement cannot be prohibited.

Nevertheless, if parties hold a strong position on the market, their agreement is likely to maintain, acquire or reinforce a market power, thanks to the co-operation they establish, that is to say, that they are able to produce negative effects on the market concerning prices, production, innovation or variety or quality of proposed goods and services.

However, and as it is already explained *supra*, the fact that parties active on the market concerned by the CSR standard hold very important market shares, does not necessarily lead to the conclusion that their agreement has such an appreciable effect in order to produce restrictive effects on competition. Indeed, these agreements produce also positive effects that are more effective proportionally by the application of a CSR policy.

If parties hold collectively a dominant position, their agreement is more likely to appreciably restrict competition, but it is only the case if the abuse that is committed by these companies is forbidden, in accordance with Article 3 of the LPCE (stated *supra*).

23.5.2 Case of *De Facto* or *De Jure* Standard

As it is described above, Belgian competition law reproduces principles developed under European competition law, which provides that in such case, only market share are of interest to analyse whether an agreement between companies eradicates competition.[59]

[58] Commission Notice on agreements of minor importance which do not appreciably restrict competition under Article 81(1) of the Treaty establishing the European Community (de minimis), OJ, C 368, 22.12.2001, p. 13–15.s.

[59] Guidelines on the applicability of Article 101 of the Treaty on the Functioning of the European Union to horizontal co-operation agreements, OJ, C 11, 14.01.2011, n. 324.

From a geographical point of view of the market definition, this computation operation will be conducted regarding Belgian territory.

When the CSR standard is protected by intellectual property law, there is obviously a conflict between owner's rights and usage by others.

No decision currently exists under Belgian competition law, and neither are there some about FRAND engagement.

However, it is according to European case law that these kinds of—potentially restrictive—practices will be examined, and this will always be so on the basis of the Articles mentioned above.

23.6 Conclusion

In Belgium, we have a legislation that can be applicable to the commercial practices when undertakings breach their CSR policies.

In this sense, the violation of CSR policies by a company could be sanctioned by injunctive relief or financial compensation.

The judge has a large power of appreciation to consider if a commercial practice is unfair, regarding the following elements: the company uses its CSR policies as a marketing tool, it makes it public by an advertisement and there is a control on its CSR policies.

But the lack of transparency is precisely at the heart of the criticism faced by CSR policies and constitutes the problem of effectiveness of Belgian law.

If undertakings are using these CSR policies as corporate image and without any transparency about the content of their CSR policies, the consumers and regulatory authorities should have access to information on these policies.

In this context, we suggest that the law should require undertakings to disclose their CSR policies and their precise content.

Moreover, an external inspection should be set up in order to assess if undertakings are complying with their own CSR policies.

Under these conditions, the Belgian law would be entirely satisfactory.

Regarding competition law, issues, already developed at European level, are raised by Belgian law in case of horizontal relationship. This kind of agreement may have negative effects on the Belgian market (innovation, product's diversity and problems of market foreclosure) and also positive effects (in matters of environmental protection, normalisation, access to quality labels . . .).

Brazil

24

Paulo Parente Marques Mendes

24.1 Introduction

The issue of the legal liability of businesspeople who advertise that they voluntarily adopt socially responsible practices but do not actually implement them is extremely new and, to our knowledge, has never been discussed in Brazil.

This issue has neither reached public discussion forums in Brazil, nor is there any news of a pending law that might deal specifically with such liability.

However, exactly as it should be, our legislation does not let businesspeople who claim to have a social conscience in an attempt to fool the general public, especially consumers, go unpunished.

24.2 The Different Types of CSR Policies Existing in Brazil

In the wake of global trends, Brazilian legislation, trade practices, as well as the influence of NGOs and government policies, have been introducing objective social responsibility duties into the field of relevant market values, to be fulfilled by businesspeople on account of their carrying out such an activity.

In our country, the principle of the social function of private and company property is covered by the Constitution. Our economic order is governed by the following principles (Article 170 of the Constitution):

- national sovereignty;
- private property;
- social function of property;

P.P. Marques Mendes (✉)
Di Blasi, Parente & Associados, Rio de Janeiro, Brasil
e-mail: paulo.parente@diblasi.com.br

P. Kobel et al. (eds.), *Antitrust in the Groceries Sector & Liability Issues in Relation to Corporate Social Responsibility*, LIDC Contributions on Antitrust Law, Intellectual Property and Unfair Competition, DOI 10.1007/978-3-662-45753-5_24

- free competition;
- consumer protection;
- environmental protection, also through differentiated treatment according to the environmental impact of products and services and their preparation and provision processes;
- reduction of regional and social inequalities;
- pursuit of full employment; and
- preferential treatment for small businesses incorporated under Brazilian law and that have their headquarters and management in the country.

Within this framework, there are several laws that provide obligations or give incentives to businesspeople so that they might adopt socially responsible positions. The most common projects and measures voluntarily adopted in our country are as follows:

- environmentally sustainable measures that go beyond the basic requirements of environmental law;
- granting of benefits and assistance to workers and their families who live in impoverished areas (in the case of industries that exploit the agricultural region, for example);
- use of technology and "green" products;
- use of organic raw materials;
- selection of suppliers in accordance with socioenvironmental criteria;
- adoption of recycling measures that go beyond that required by law;
- reduction in the use of water;
- reduction in the use of energy per manufactured product;
- donations and support for social and charitable acts;
- support for cultural events in situations where the sponsored element is weak or inexistent (events that are not seen by the target public of the products or services);
- support for sport, especially the training of children in poorer regions, without being characterized as sponsorship (incentivized sponsorship); and
- a final product with less environmental impact.

24.3 Brazilian Laws Permitting the Prevention or Sanctioning of a Business that Carries Out Commercial Practices that Breach a CSR Policy Voluntarily Adopted by the Business

Brazil does not have a law that deals specifically with the violation of social responsibility commitments voluntarily assumed by a businessperson. Nor are our regulatory bodies concerned about this: they only monitor and restrain conduct that directly violates a legal obligation or one created by a specialized provision.

Nevertheless, there is a set of laws that is applicable in the repression of this type of behavior.

There is first the Consumer Protection Code,[1] which prohibits, *inter alia*, false advertising. Under Article 37 of the Code, the provision of any false information by a supplier of products and services is considered a violation of consumer rights, especially when this information

- refers to a characteristic of the product or service, or
- can be interpreted as a factor that attracts the consumer to the product or service.

If the false information is about a characteristic of the product (the use of organic materials, biodegradable packaging, etc.), the supplier may face criminal prosecution (Article 66 of the Consumer Code of Protection) without prejudice to appropriate remedial measures, even if no actual injury has been caused.

Even if the information does not pertain to a characteristic of the product or service, the supplier can be punished criminally if such information is used in advertising (thereby constituting false advertising).

Further, deceitful information surrounding social responsibility of a company can be the subject of civil proceedings.

In this case, and based on Consumer Law, the following people have standing to file a lawsuit:

- private consumers,
- consumers' associations (of a private nature),
- the Public Prosecutor (public body).

According to some Brazilian scholars, competitors themselves could, based on the Consumer Code of Protection, file a lawsuit against businesspeople who do not in practice follow the socially responsible conduct that they have adopted voluntarily. However, this group is in a minority in our country.

Competitors could in any case take legal measures based on the Industrial Property Law[2] (IPL), which is also the basis for the repression of acts of unfair competition (passing off, misrepresentation).

Inasmuch as the adoption of a set of socially responsible measures affords a company a competitive advantage, noncompliance can constitute "diversion of clientele by fraud," an act punishable as a crime (Article 195, III of the IPL).

Also, the law punishes the attribution to himself, for advertising purposes, of awards that have not been obtained. Prizes, medals, honours, etc., that reflect a social concern fit into this definition of "award" (Article 195, VII of the IPL).

Please note that the violation of a social responsibility program taken on voluntarily, in reflecting an undue advantage from a competitive point of view, can be punished as a civil offense without the need for it to be characterized as a crime.

[1] Law 8.078/1990 of September 11, 1990.

[2] Law No. 9.279/1996, of May 14, 1996 as amended by Law 10.196/2001 of February 14, 2001.

The IP Law affords the victim injunctive relief, provided that there is a strong likelihood that the claim is genuine and there is a risk of injury that is irreparable or difficult to repair.

The injunction would primarily consist of an order to compel the defendant to make the correct information known on their page or to cease from passing false information or to be subject to a fine. Our understanding is that it is very difficult or unlikely for a judge to oblige a defendant to comply with its social responsibility policy if its items do not reflect legal obligations.

The difficulty in obtaining injunctions in such cases is to convince the judge that the plaintiff, as a competitor, is being so heavily injured that, if no measure is quickly implemented, it could suffer irreparable damage or damage that is difficult to repair.

Although, depending on the market, the information that a certain competitor adopts socially responsible policies can undoubtedly represent a considerable advantage, only in specific cases could this cause serious injury to the other competitors.

Another possible interested party is the holder of a certification mark duly registered at the National Institute of Industrial Property (INPI), a type of mark that exists in Brazil, which, meeting certain parameters, can be used by businesspeople. If an undertaking uses a certification mark to obtain an advantage without having first proved that it meets the requirements, or if, failing to meet the requirements, it continues to use the certification mark, it may answer for the crime of trademark infringement without prejudice to any civil reparations.

Other economic agents (lenders, suppliers, sponsors, etc.) may have standing to bring proceedings against the undertaking only if they prove that they entered into a contractual relationship with the undertaking *because of* its social responsibility policy or that this was at least an essential element in their decision. However, the penalty in a similar case would be limited to the cancelation of the contract or the correction of the irregularity thereof and, possibly, reparation for losses and damages.

As previously stated, this issue is new in Brazil, and, until now, there has been no court decision involving such specific situation, to our knowledge.

24.4 Brazilian Law and Its Relationship to Commercial Practices

As has already been mentioned, the issue is new and has not been debated in Brazil. Therefore, there is not a set of opinions or sufficient concrete cases so that we can indicate a trend.

It seems, in a merely hypothetical context, that legislation that protects consumers combined with the Industrial Property Law is enough to prevent and repress the abuses of businesspeople who advertise that they voluntarily adopt socially responsible practices.

In our opinion, a specific law on the theme could be of general benefit, provided that freedom of initiative is safeguarded and it does not imply an exaggerated intervention by the state in the economy.

We would question the constitutionality of a law that might, for example, provide a court measure that forces a company to comply with its own social responsibility policy, when this policy is freely adopted (that is, it does not reflect compliance with legal obligations). After all, a social responsibility policy is not a signed contract with society and consumers. At best, this company should be obliged to remove the information (or the policy) from media and print a retraction.

Finally, in our view, if the violation of the social responsibility policy itself reflects a crime against consumers, the means of investigation provided by criminal law are broad and, in general, sufficient. However, if it only results in a civil offense, this investigation is much more limited.

24.5 Issues Raised by Brazilian Competition Law Where Undertakings in a Horizontal Relationship Agree Voluntarily to Commit to a CSR Policy

Brazil's Council for Economic Defense (*Conselho Administrativo de Defesa Econômica*, hereinafter, CADE)—The Brazilian Antitrust Authority—has not yet analyzed any kind of relationship of horizontally related companies part of a CSR policy or an NGO organization.

In this context, a differentiation should be made between *i*) NGOs and CSR Codes developed by independent entities with no relation to the players and (*ii*) NGOs and CSR Codes developed and managed by the players in the market.

In the first case, the imposition by the organizations of conducts may be considered a barrier to entry in the market, though we do not understand that it could be considered an unlawful conduct, once the initiative for the restrains created by the organizations should have no relation to the players' interests. Ultimately, CADE could use its advocacy function to recommend the organizations to review their standards.

In the second case, if the market players are part of the organizations, an analogy can be made with trade associations. Depending on the object of the organization restraints, CADE may identify an anticompetitive conduct by the organizations and the players. In relation to what may be considered unlawful conducts in trade associations, CADE identified, *e.g.*, price lists, code of ethics, standardization and certification, accession criteria, and nonmembers' treatment as relevant issues. In those cases, when the practice leads to the exclusion of players or price and sales conditions, the authority may identify them as unlawful conducts.[3]

[3] In this regard, please see the brochure "Combate a Cartéis em Sindicatos e Associações (2009)" created by the Brazilian Antitrust Authority, available (in Portuguese) at http://portal.mj.gov.br/services/DocumentManagement/FileDownload.EZTSvc.asp?DocumentID={2FBB0E91-BAA6-4173-A5F6-A8B97A3A0A74}&ServiceInstUID={2E2554E0-F695-4B62-A40E-4B56390F180A}. Last access: 07/14/2014.

24.5.1 Role of Market Share in Finding Infringement

The case where the organizations are developed and managed by the market players (case *ii* above) may raise a competitive concern with CADE. At this point, the market share of the parties involved in the organization could be considered a key factor for the analysis.

When nevertheless there is an intention to harm, the authority may disregard the players' market share. This happened in some CADE's recent decisions about gas station trade associations in Brazil.[4] In those cases, the intention of the parties was identified, and CADE determined that those illegal conducts should be analyzed by their object (to collude), independently of the effects (and dominant position of the parties). In the mentioned decisions, CADE made clear that the market share of the parties held liable for an anticompetitive conduct or part of an anticompetitive scheme, and the sum of their shares, does not affect the result of the decision.

24.5.2 Compulsory IPR License

According to Article 36, XIV of the Brazilian Competition Law,[5] the misuse of IPRs may be considered an unlawful conduct and, thus, subject to the intervention of CADE. Accordingly, the recommendation for compulsory license of IPRs is provided as a possible penalty applied by CADE, according to Article 38, IV, a) of the Brazilian Competition Law. Note, however, that CADE has powers only to recommend the compulsory license, not to impose it.

The National Institute of Industrial Property (henceforth "INPI") has powers to impose the compulsory license according to Article 68 of the IPL.[6]

In case the denial for use of the CSR Code and IPRs is conduced as a market exclusion tool by the organizations developed and managed by market players, CADE may intervene in order to cease the conduct. However, in cases of independent (case *i* above) or governmental organizations, we understand that CADE could, in the limit, recommend a policy change as an advocacy measure, but it has no powers to impose any modification.

[4] *E.g.*, Administrative Procedure no. 08012.010215/2007-96, 08700.000547/2008-95, 08012.001003/2000-41.

[5] Law No. 12.529/2011 of November 30, 2011.

[6] Law No. 9.279/1996, of May 14, 1996 as amended by Law 10.196/2001 of February 14, 2001.

France

25

Véronique Sélinsky and Linda Arcelin Lécuyer

25.1 CSR French Policies

Since 2001 and the enactment of the NRE Statute (Loi NRE[1]), research on CSR policies has been conducted about governance issues in the social and environmental fields. It led to the introduction in the French Statute of these two new concerns, first in the field of public procurements and then, more broadly, with the enactment of the Grenelle I[2] and Grenelle II[3] laws.

25.1.1 In the Field of Public Procurement

In 2006, Council Directive (EC) 2004/18/EC on the coordination of procedures for the award of public works contracts, public supply contracts and public service contracts[4] and Council Directive (EC) 2004/17/EC coordinating the procurement procedures of entities operating in the water, energy, transport and postal services

[1] Loi n° 2001-420 du 15 mai 2001 relative aux nouvelles régulations économiques.

[2] Loi n° 2009-967 du 3 août 2009 de programmation relative à la mise en œuvre du Grenelle de l'environnement (loi Grenelle 1).

[3] Loi n° 2010-788 du 12 juillet 2010 portant engagement national pour l'environnement (loi Grenelle 2).

[4] Directive 2004/18/EC of the European Parliament and of the Council of 31 March 2004 (O.J. L134/114).

V. Sélinsky
Independent Practitioner, Paris, France
e-mail: selinsky@wanadoo.fr

L.A. Lécuyer (✉)
Université de la Rochelle, la Rochelle, France
e-mail: linda.arcelin@wanadoo.fr

P. Kobel et al. (eds.), *Antitrust in the Groceries Sector & Liability Issues in Relation to Corporate Social Responsibility*, LIDC Contributions on Antitrust Law, Intellectual Property and Unfair Competition, DOI 10.1007/978-3-662-45753-5_25

sectors[5] were implemented, leading to a remake of the French Public Procurement Code (all state agencies and regional/local authorities can now include CSR clauses in a public call for tender and enforce the dispositions of the *Charte de l'environnement* Legislation of 2005).

Article 5 of the French Public Procurement Code (*Code des marchés publics*) provides:

> The nature and extent of the needs to be met shall be precisely ascertained before launching any competitive public tender or negotiation not preceded by a competitive public tender. Objectives of sustainable development must be taken into consideration. The only purpose of Public Procurement(s) or framework agreement(s) concluded by the contracting authority is to meet these needs.[6]

Article 14 of the French Public Procurement Code provides:

> Public Procurement(s) or framework agreements performance clauses can contain elements of social or environmental nature which take into consideration the objectives of sustainable development by balancing business with environmental protection and promotion, and social progress.[7]

Article 53 of the French Public Procurement Code provides:

> A Public Procurement shall be awarded to the applicant who proposes the most advantageous economically offer. The contracting authority shall base its decision on the items listed hereinafter:
> 1. Either in respect of a plurality of non-discriminatory criteria related to the subject matter of the Public Procurement, including the quality, the price, the technical merit, the aesthetic and functional characters, the performance in the fields of environment protection and employability, the life-cycle costs, the profitability, the innovative character, the after-sales service and technical assistance and the delivery date and time. Other criteria can be taken into consideration if they are justified by the subject matter of the Public Procurement;
> 2. Or, given the subject matter of the Public Procurement, on the sole criterion of price.

In 2007, the French Government adopted a national plan for sustainable Public Procurement.[8]

On 9 April 2008, the French Government decided that the use of social clauses should be equal to 10 % of the State's markets. Social clauses are seen as a tool to fight against exclusion and unemployment. They integrate with the social aspects of sustainable development and are leverage for the promotion of employment.

On 3 December 2008, a ministerial circular clarified the concept of *exemplarité de l'Etat* (exemplarity of the State), which is based on a concrete application of the principles of environmental and social responsibility.

---

[5] Directive 2004/17/EC of the European Parliament and of the Council of 31 March 2004 (O.J. L134/1).

[6] The emphasis is ours.

[7] The emphasis is ours.

[8] Achats publics durables – PNAAPD.

Between 2009 and 2011, the integration of social clauses in public call for tender has increased by more than 200 %, from less than 2,000 to more than 4,000.

Since 2009, reduction of energy consumption must be taken into consideration in Public Procurement. Article 5 of Law no 2009-967 of 3 August 2009 provides:

> In order to take into account the reduction of energy consumption, when it offers to enter into a public procurement, the contracting authority shall resort to an energy performance contract, in the form of a global market bringing together the design, operation or maintenance and provided that the improvements of energy efficiency are contractually guaranteed.

On 11 March 2010, a Circular of the Prime Minister on the incentive financial facilities reaffirmed the priority of the exemplary administrations plans supplemented in 2012.[9]

25.1.2 In the NER Field

Since 2001, the French companies listed on a regulated market (NYSE Euronext) shall publish their data management annual report in order to evaluate "how they take into consideration the social and environmental impacts of business." The New Economic Regulations Statute of 15 May 2001[10] defines the requirement to be met for the publication of social and environmental data in annual management reports.

Then the Decree of 20 February 2002 set a list of information to be provided: the internal social data collection (workforce, schedule, vocational training, hygiene, security, parity, disability, *etc.*), the territorial impact (subsidiaries, subcontractors, territory link) and the environmental effects of the business activity (emissions into the air, the water and the ground, *etc.*).

The Decree of 30 April 2002 defined the information on serious polluting discharges (emission of greenhouse, emission into the air, the water or the ground of certain substances. . .).

The implementation of paragraph b of section 1–14 of the Council Directive (EC) 2003/51/EC,[11] on the annual and consolidated accounts of certain types of companies, banks and other financial institutions and insurance undertakings, by Order No. 2004-1382 of 22 December 2004, supplemented the existing scheme.

Henceforth, to the extent necessary for the understanding of the business evolution, the financial performance or the overall condition of the company (or the companies included in the consolidation), the analysis of the annual report includes (. . .), if any, a key indicator of non-financial nature performance relating to the "specific activity of the company (or the companies included in the consolidation), including information relating to environmental and staffing matters."[12]

---

[9] Administrations exemplaires.

[10] Loi NER.

[11] Directive 2003/51/EC of the European Parliament and of the Council of 18 June 2003 (O.J. L178/16).

[12] Art. L225-100 Code de commerce.

25.1.3 In the Grenelle I and II Fields

An action plan on governance issues was established by the "Grenelle I" Act in order to

- enhance social and environmental information provided by companies to their stakeholders (shareholders, salaries, NGOs, residents, *etc.*);
- involve employee representative bodies in business and sustainable development issues;
- develop sectorial development benchmarks;
- support the development of "labels," in order to give recognition to companies with good social and environmental practices;
- promote socially responsible investments;
- support the creation of Community social and environmental standards.

The "Grenelle II" Act introduced in the French legislation both Article 224 on socially responsible investment and Article 225 on corporate social responsibility.

These two articles have respectively been supplemented first by the Decree of 30 January 2012 relating to the information provided by Asset Management Companies in connection with social, environmental and governance quality criteria taken into account in their investment policy[13] and then the Decree of 24 April 2012 relating to the obligations of transparency of companies in terms of social and environmental issues.[14]

Corporate social responsibility is also present in the national strategy for sustainable development[15] adopted on 27 July 2010 by the Interministerial Committee for Sustainable Development for 2010–2013.[16] To ensure effective social responsibility, the tools and levers are the following:

- the companies' promotion of their environmental and social achievements (socially responsible investment, accession to the European Eco-Management and Audit Scheme (EMAS), nonfinancial reporting based on environmental societal and governance criteria, *etc.*);
- the companies' involvement of representative bodies in the elaboration of the sustainable development strategies and the environmental and social Reports;
- the involvement of services providers (accountants, auditors, accounts, social auditing firm, *etc.*);

[13] Décret n° 2012-132 du 30 janvier 2012 relatif à l'information par les sociétés de gestion de portefeuille des critères sociaux, environnementaux et de qualité de gouvernance pris en compte dans leur politique d'investissement (JORF n°0026 of 31 January 2012 p. 1776).

[14] Décret n° 2012-557 du 24 avril 2012 relatif aux obligations de transparence des entreprises en matière sociale et environnementale (JORF n°0099 of 26 April 2012 p. 7439).

[15] Stratégie nationale de développement durable - SNDD.

[16] http://www.developpement-durable.gouv.fr/IMG/pdf/SNDD-3.pdf.

- the adaptation of sustainable development tools to SMEs (development of standards/simple labels adapted to eco-responsible SMEs);
- the development of ecolabels (NF Environment and European ecolabel).

The Government's Ecological Transition Roadmap of September 2012 made a number of significant announcements regarding corporate social responsibility and socially responsible investment, including the creation of a platform for CSR policies or of a socially responsible investment label.

With the Preparatory Document at the french national level for the development of the corporate social responsibility (CSR) of January 2013,[17] the French Government answered to the Communication from the EU Commission of 25 October 2011 on a renewed EU strategy 2011–2014 for Corporate Social Responsibility. This white paper presents a current state of government commitments and actors of the French nation as they could be identified in late 2012. They are divided into the following chapters:

- A consistent and pro-active CSR Policy in respect of International and European Agreements;
- Creation, for big business, of mandatory reportings based on social, environmental and economic criteria, in order to harmonize the European standards;
- Promotion of standardization and voluntary libeling programs;
- Concertation, social dialogue, vocational training and research promotion;
- The State, the central responsible economic player for CSR Policy;
- French promotion and support of socio-economic development at the European and international levels.

25.2 General and Specific Laws Dealing with Violation of Voluntary Commitments

25.2.1 Absence of Specific Penalties

Article L. 225-102 para. 7 of the French Commercial Code provides that "social and environmental information included or to be included with regards to legal and regulatory duties are investigated by an independent body. This verification leads to a notice forwarded to the shareholders or associates' meeting at the same time as the Board of Directors or the Management's report." But companies' liability is, in fact, very limited.

Foremost, the Act provides no specific penalty for violation of commitments. Under these circumstances, only the shareholders to whom the audit report is transmitted can take a decision. In this case, they can probably sue the offending

[17] Document préparatoire au plan national francais de développement de la responsabilité sociétale des entreprises (RSE).

officer. Indeed, Articles L. 223-22 and L. 225-251 of the French Commercial Code penalize mismanagement. However, as it is underlined by the doctrine, "infringements of ethical standards are likely to incur directors' civil liability since mismanagement is defined with regards to social interest and, under the influence of the so-called 'corporate governance', voluntary codes of conduct must be respected."

Besides, it appears that internal controls are, in fact, nonexistent and shareholders or the directors cannot effectively play their oversight role.

25.2.2 Enforcement of General Rules

According to principles of natural law,[18] a policy voluntarily adopted by a business can acquire binding force. On the face of it, a natural obligation is only a moral duty, not legally binding, and its breach cannot therefore be repaired through damages or specific performance. However, it can turn into a legal duty when one unilaterally commits to perform. Thus, for the French "Cour de cassation," "a unilateral commitment to execute a natural obligation, when taken in full knowledge, is transformed into a legal duty." Under such conditions, "CSR policies voluntarily adopted by Directors on behalf of their company, create a legal duty supported by the company."

Moreover, CSR policies voluntarily adopted could be qualified as unilateral commitments, even if French law barely resorts to this notion.

Finally, the "defects of consent" theory can be applied when a party enters into a contract on account of ethical commitments. Nullity of a contract for deception can be obtained if the disputed agreement, which was taken in consideration of environmental CSR commitments, actually remained unfulfilled. According to Article 1116 of the French Civil Code, such decisive considerations are not presumed and must be proven.

Outside contractual relationships, principles of tort law can apply (Articles 1382 and 1383 of the French Civil Code). Thus, an operator who falsely claims to meet, in an advertisement, a voluntarily adopted CSR policy, could be sued for unfair competition. But the French "Cour de cassation" held that infringements to a code of conduct (which is not legally binding) do not automatically equal a civil wrong. The same position should be adopted for CSR policies' infringements.

25.2.3 Enforcement of Consumer Legislation

Article 6(2)b) of Council Directive (EC) 2005/29/EC on unfair business-to-consumer commercial practices in the internal market[19] provides:

[18] Théorie des obligations naturelles.

[19] OJEU n° L 149, 6/11/2005, p. 22.

> A commercial practice shall also be considered as misleading if, in its factual context, with all its features and circumstances, it causes or is likely to cause the average consumer to take a transactional decision that he would not have taken otherwise, and it involves (b) non-compliance by the trader with commitments contained in Codes of Conduct by which the trader has undertaken to be bound, where (i) the commitment is not aspirational but is firm and is capable of being verified, and (ii) the trader indicates in a commercial practice that he is bound by the code.

Voluntary commitments deriving from codes of conduct are relevant for the implementation of CSR policies. European law does not seem to distinguish between companies' internal codes of conduct and collective codes of conduct, derived from companies' self-regulation.

However, the French implementation legislation[20] does not exactly reflect the wording of the Directive. Article L. 121-1-1° of the French Consumer Code only provides:

> Shall be deemed misleading, within the meaning of Article L. 121-1, business practices designed to:
>
> 1. for a trader, falsely claim to be a signatory to a Code of conduct;
> 2. falsely display of a label, a quality certification or equivalent;
> 3. make a consumer or a user, believe that a product or a service has been certified when it is not;
> 4. falsely present any product or service which has been certified as being guaranteed by the government or by a public body.

Thus, in French law, only voluntary commitments arising from a collective code of conduct are taken into consideration.

However, a commercial practice that infringes CSR policies could be prohibited under Articles L. 121-1 and L. 120-1 of the French Consumer Code. There is indeed a hierarchy between the above-mentioned provisions. According to the "Cour d'appel de Reims":

> The legal framework on business practices is defined in Chapter 1 of Title II, Book 1 of the legislative section of the French Consumer Code;
>
> A preliminary chapter, entitled "unfair commercial practices", precedes this first chapter. It encompasses Article L. 120-1 par. 1 which prohibits any business practice that, in breach of professional diligence, causes detrimental effects on an average consumer's decision-making power.
>
> While the conditions for unfair commercial practices are laid down in Article L. 120-1 of the French Consumer Code, Article L. 121-1-1 sets a list of practices deemed to be unfair according to Article L. 121-1.
>
> Thus, when he/she assesses the validity of a commercial operation, the Judge shall first answer to the question whether the litigated practice equals to one of the 22 practices deemed to be unfair, set out in Article L. 121-1-1.
>
> If not, the Judge shall determine whether the practice is misleading in accordance with the criteria set out in Article L. 121-1. If not, he/she shall complete his/her analysis and

[20] Lois Châtel du 3 janvier 2008 et Loi de Modernisation de l'économie – LME- du 4 aout 2008.

> assess the case as a general unfair practice (Article L. 120-1 of the French Consumer Code).[21]

Therefore, the assessment of a commercial operation involves a two-step approach: whether the commercial practice meets the standards set out in Article L. 121-1-1 and, if not, whether the conditions listed in Article L. 121-1 are fulfilled.

Article L. 121-1 of the French Consumer Code provides:

> 1.- Any commercial practice shall be considered as unfair when:
> 1. It causes confusion between one's mark, product or service, brand, business name, or any other distinctive marks and those of a competitor;
> 2. It is based on information or presentations, in any form whatsoever, which are false or likely to mislead, where the latter cover one or more of the items listed hereinafter:
>   a) either in respect of the existence, availability or nature of goods or services;
>   b) or on the composition, the substantial qualities, the accessories, the origin, the quantity, the mode and date of manufacture, the properties, the conditions for their use, the results which may be expected from their use, the sale or service provision procedures;
>   c) or on the price, the manner in which the price is calculated, the element of promotional nature of the price and sales, the arrangements for payment, the delivery conditions of goods or services;
>   d) or on the after-sale services, the need of a service, the spare parts, the replacement and repair conditions;
>   e) or on the scope of the obligations undertaken, the nature and the reason for the sale or service;
>   f) or on the identity, the qualities and professional rights of the competitor;
>   g) or on the claim handling and the consumer rights;
> 3. It is impossible to identify the service or product provider.

If the practice is not deemed to be unfair according to the above-mentioned criteria, the Judge will rely on the two general criteria set forth in Article L. 120-1 of the French Consumer Code.

Article L. 120-1 provides:

> Unfair commercial practices shall be prohibited. A commercial practice shall be unfair when it is contrary to the requirements of professional diligence, and materially distorts or is likely to materially distort the economic behavior with regard to the product or service of the average consumer whom it reaches or to whom it is addressed, or of the average member of the group when a commercial practice is directed to a particular group of consumers.

Thus, an infringement shall be contrary to both the requirements of professional diligence and the interests of the consumer whose economic behavior could be materially distorted. Nevertheless, it is likely that all infringements of a CSR policy will not fulfill these two criteria: if the first criterion can be demonstrated, the second criterion implies that the consumer is aware of the CSR policy, which is, in fact, impossible as we will see.

---

[21] CA Reims, 13 nov. 2012, *SA Atol c/SAS Hans Anders France*.

Article L. 213-1 of the French Consumer Code provides:

> Anyone, whether or not they are party to the contract, who may have deceived or attempted to deceive the contractor, by any procedural means whatsoever, even if this is through the intermediary of a third party, shall be punished by two years imprisonment and a € 37,500 fine:
>
> 1. either in respect of the nature, species, origin, material qualities, composition or content in terms of useful principles of any merchandise;
> 2. or on the quantity of items delivered or on their identity by delivery of merchandise other than the determined item to which the contract relates;
> 3. or on the fitness for use, the risks inherent in use of the product, the checks carried out, the operating procedures or precautions to be taken.

The infringement must be contrary to the requirements of professional diligence and must substantially alter the economic behavior of consumers.

25.2.4 Is It Possible to Be Creative and to Innovate to Ensure CSR Effectivity?

A new solution based on the estoppel principle may be considered.

The principle of estoppel imposes a responsibility on a party not to occasion detriment to another party by acting inconsistently with an understanding concerning their contractual relationship, which it has caused that other party to have and upon which that other party has reasonably acted in reliance (a CSR policy for instance). It is a general application of the principle of good faith and fair dealing.

Derived from international law (Art. 18 of the Unidroit Principles of International Commercial Contracts of 2010), the estoppel principle has been incorporated in French law by the French "Cour de cassation" in its decision of 20 September 2011.[22]

25.3 Implementation of the Rules

25.3.1 Implementation by Public and Private Regulatory Authorities

A majority of the previously mentioned articles come under the remit of the general law for their enforcement and are subjected to Administrative Courts for Public Procurements and Civil Courts.

Regulatory authorities encompass both independent public authorities (such as the French Competition Authority[23] and the French Financial Markets Authority[24]) and associations with regulatory or oversight legal powers (such as the ARPP).

[22] Cass.com. n° 852, 20 Sept. 2011 (10-22.888).

[23] Autorité de la concurrence (competition authority).

[24] Autorité des marchés financiers (financial markets authority).

25.3.1.1 Advertising Self-Regulation Authority[25](ARPP)

The ARPP can bring proceedings for breach of a recommendation before the "Jury of advertising ethics"[26] ("JDP"). The European Commission, in its Communication on a renewed EU strategy 2011–2014 for Corporate Social Responsibility of 25 October 2011, encourages the improvement of self- and coregulation processes as a mean to create and enhance responsible business behaviors. The ARPP's Recommendations "développement durable" of June 2009 and "commerce équitable" of December 2011 have set a framework for advertisers.

25.3.1.2 The Competition Authority

The contentious jurisdiction of the French Competition Authority ADLC is limited to anticompetitive practices (cartels, abuse of a dominant market position) and mergers. The ADLC cannot rule on unfair competition claims.

In this case, the ADLC will likely be seized for its consultative prerogatives when CSR policies imply competition issues.

25.3.1.3 Financial Markets Authority (AMF)

The AMF cannot order any penalties or sanctions. However, it can make recommendations or reporting on business reporting obligations.

25.3.2 Implementation by Consumers

Any consumer can seize a Court on the basis of all the above-mentioned provisions, except for issues concerning corporate law and unfair competition claims, which can only be brought by consumer associations. Besides, only an association can bring an action in front of the ADLC.

25.3.3 Implementation by Competing Businesses

Competitors can either bring an action in front of Courts for unfair competition (Articles 182 and 1383 of the Civil Code) or on the basis of Article L. 121-1-1 of the Consumer Code or seize the ADLC.

25.3.4 Implementation by Suppliers and Purchasers

Suppliers and/or purchasers can bring an action on the basis of the provisions of the French Consumer Code. Besides, they can alert public authorities and seize the ADLC.

---

[25] Autorité de régulation professionnelle de la publicité (ARPP).

[26] Jury de déontologie publicitaire.

25.4 Causes of Action and Range of Remedies Available to Regulatory Authorities

25.4.1 Injunctions

If the "Jury de déontologie publicitaire" ("JDP") may request the withdrawal of the dispute advertisement, it cannot order it. However, the collective discipline effect can, in fact, insert such authority to the JDP's requests.

When it intervenes as part of its contentious prerogatives, the ADLC can order injunctions. But being also an advisory body, it can propose recommendations for businesses or public authorities.

25.4.2 Fines and Imprisonment

The JOP cannot order fines or imprisonment when operators infringe voluntary CSR policies.

The "ADLC" can only impose fines for anticompetitive practices.

However, only a Judge can order imprisonment, and only he/she is faced with a specific criminal offense.

25.5 Causes of Action and Remedies Available to Private Entities

25.5.1 The Role of Unfair Competition and the Repair of the Harm

When the offender wrongly asserts that a product or service gets certified according to national or international standards, the victims are both competitors and producers:

- competitors can rely on parasitism theory (commercial free-riding/leeching), defined as "the fact for a third party to place itself in the wake of another and take advantage of the efforts he/she made, his/her reputation, name or products";
- producers can bring an action for unfair competition, which does not require the demonstration of a competitive link between the parties (Cass. Com., 30 mai 2000 no 98-15549).

In all cases, the victim has to provide proof of a fault, a damage and a causal connection.

The harm can, for instance, arise from consumer poaching or an unnecessary investment (such as advertising campaign).

The plaintiff shall, in any case, demonstrate his prejudice and the causal connection between the injury suffered and the defendant act. But, in fact, this will be difficult.

The cocoa producer falsely appending a label causes a prejudice to the certifying authority by reducing consumers' confidence and lowering the label's reputation.

25.5.2 Relationship Between Infringement and Goods Procured or Services Provided

25.5.2.1 Deception by Means of a False Fair Trade Label

In Case of Label Noncompliance

Firstly, the authority awarding a label and/or a logo can withdraw them if the product or service does not actually comply with the specifications. Such withdrawal can have a significant impact on the corporate image and can therefore be a useful deterrent sanction.

Secondly, competitors can bring an action for unfair competition if the offender makes believe that a product or a service has been labelized when it is not.

In Case of Internal CSR Policy Noncompliance

Brought to the notice of the consumer, CSR policies confer a competitive advantage. In case of fictional commitment to a CSR policy, offenders do not bear any additional cost and their products/services are more attractive.

Competitors shall define the loss they suffered. One again, such loss will be difficult to prove, essentially because customer turnover can be explained by many factors.

25.5.2.2 Deception by Means of a Not Applied CSR Green Policy

The preliminary issue is to assess whether or not it can be detected by stakeholders.

If so, previous findings may apply. If not, the unfair behavior is not subject to direct sanction.

25.5.2.3 Deception by Means of a False CSR

It represents the amount of the sum kept by the infringing competitor, while scrupulous ones, who respect the CSR policy, actually do pay 2 % of all their sales revenue to education.

There is no direct penalty. Only information campaigns could try to hinder such practices.

Remedies can either be the award of damages or an order for specific performance, depending on the circumstances of the case.

25.6 Assessment of French Legislation

When businesses voluntary infringe CSR policies, they are not directly liable. According to the French legislation, it is up to the market ("the consumers – the intermediaries – the suppliers") to sanction these infringements.

French consumers being not able to arbitrate, public authorities should take over and impose appropriate sanctions.

French legislation should, first, strengthen control procedures (self-monitoring or control by independent bodies) and, second, improve consumers' information and introduce class actions.

On March 2014, a new law has been passed in order to set up a "class action" relating to consumer collective claims: this new provision will allow to repair economic damages, including those deriving from competition law infringement.[27]

However, French legislation is still not efficient enough. Greater transparency of CSR policies and their fulfillment toward consumers, and not only towards companies' internal organs, is needed. For instance, an annual report for consumers, or for consumers and environmental associations, could be published on companies' websites.

If the information is not voluntarily provided and a doubt arises as to the company's CSR commitments, victims may seek the data presentation.

Indeed, an inquiry can be ordered by the Judge to assess whether a company complies with its CSR commitments. Thus, an "expertise in futurum" (preparatory inquiry) may be ordered to obtain the relevant documents in order to establish the misconduct of the undertaking before any trial.

Thus, Article 145 of the French Civil Procedure Code provides:

> If there is a legitimate reason to preserve or to establish, before any legal process, the evidence of the facts upon which the resolution of the dispute depends, legally permissible preparatory inquiries may be ordered at the request of any interested party, by way of a petition or by way of a summary procedure.

The applicant may request the delivery of documents held by third parties (Article 138) or by other parties at the trial (Article 142). Article 146 also provides that "a preparatory inquiry on a fact may be ordered only if the party who pleads it does not have sufficient material to prove it." However, the applicant must convince the Judge of the usefulness of the inquiry by providing some elements/material because no preparatory inquiry may be ordered "for the sake of making up a party's deficiency to produce evidence" (Article 146 para 2).

The Judge can also commission a technician (Article 232) or an expert (Article 263).

These measures may facilitate the proof of the failure. However, they do not make up for the difficulties due to the absence of specific sanctions for infringements of CSR policies.

[27] LOI n° 2014-344 du 17 mars 2014 relative à la consommation.

25.7 The Special Case of CSRs Becoming Standards

In some cases, a particular CSR policy (e.g., dolphin-friendly tuna) becomes so important to consumers that a company that does not accede to such a policy risks losing substantial business. In short, a business that does not comply with the corresponding CSR policy is unable to compete effectively in the market (e.g., for tuna) because the policy has become a standard. In most cases, there can be no concerns about market foreclosure because any fishing business can adopt dolphin-friendly fishing techniques and any supplier of tuna can choose only to buy from such businesses. However, when these CSR "standards" are protected by IPRs, e.g. certification marks that are in the control of NGOs, without the ability to display the corresponding certification marks, a business may not be able to stay in the market despite otherwise complying with the CSR standard. Equally, in some cases, a CSR "standard" may be strongly supported by governmental legislation (which may give preferential treatment, e.g., tax breaks to adopters of the CSR standard) that although a business may choose not to adopt it, such a business will suffer as a result.

25.8 Enforcement of Competition Law in Relation to CSRs that Became Standards

In relation to the issue of enforcement of competition law, it may be useful to consider the following example:

Fifty percent of suppliers of fresh fish into your national market are persuaded by an NGO to agree to only buy fish from fishing fleets that abide by a CSR Code promoted by an NGO. The code is intended to ensure that those fleets only use environmentally friendly sustainable fishing practices, including, e.g., not fishing for certain endangered species, not using banned equipment (e.g., nets with very small mesh or boats that are painted with certain chemicals), etc. In general, the perceived wisdom is that this CSR Code is good for the marine environment and should be encouraged. However, there are certain concerns that the CSR Code is "over the top" and that some requirements are too onerous with little benefit to the environment (e.g., some of the so-called endangered species are considered by many fishing experts to be actually plentiful). The CSR Code has a logo that is protected as a collective registered mark 13. Only those who agree to abide by the *whole of the* CSR Code are licensed by the NGO to display the logo. Market research surveys show that intense marketing campaigns by the NGO have resulted in consumers showing a marked preference for fish that displays the logo despite the extra cost and that suppliers of fish that are not licensed to use the logo are experiencing very considerable reduction in business. Indeed, there has developed a "shame culture" among the buying public about those who buy fish that do not display the logo.

The French competition authority in Opinion 06-A-07 dated 22 March 2006 relating to the examination, in terms of competition law, of the operating conditions of the fair trade sector in France questioned the efficiency of the prohibition on cartels with regard to standard requirements and economic regulations.[28]

A cartel on standards agreements does not automatically infringe the law. Thus, "a technical standard aimed at ensuring the interoperability of certain products or establishing technical or qualitative classification is less likely to have an anticompetitive object or effect than other standards, even technical or quality, or by any other objectives, which leads to a limitation of the production (for instance, by a quotas system) or a price harmonization" (pt. 65).

Then the mandatory or voluntary nature of a commitment to a standard shall be taken into consideration. In principle, unlike mandatory commitments, voluntary commitments should not have any anticompetitive effect on the market. However, the French competition authority notices that "even optional standards can derive from anti-competitive agreements, regardless of their actual effects, that is to say regardless of whether standards are more or less followed by traders if their object is to promote traders' parallel or aligned anticompetitive behavior on the market" (pt. 68).

Incentive may be even stronger if the Government legitimizes and recognizes the certifying power of the authorities involved. "Public recognition of some fair trade traders, on the basis of their compliance with rules unable to guarantee the reality of fair trade initiatives would give these traders a substantial competitive advantage to the ones who, while relying on other rules, guarantee the same quality" (pt. 84). "Restriction of competition can occur, in particular, if this recognition leads to the creation of a central authority (pt. 85). Such restriction can reduce or suppress competition between certifying bodies, or between distributors by reducing their opportunities to market products originated from fair trade concepts or rules but different from the criteria used for certification" (pt. 75).

For instance, Max Havelaar is the main actor of labelization on the fair trade market. The logo "Max Havelaar" is granted to brands that comply with the label's criteria and pay a license fee. Such license fee, even if it does materially distort the competition, can be exempted according to Article 101 para. 3 of the Treaty on the Functioning of the European Union (TFEU). The Guidelines on the application of Article 81(3) of the Treaty of 27 April 2009 provide:

> The fact that the agreement substantially reduces one dimension of competition does not necessarily mean that competition is eliminated within the meaning of Article 81(3). A technology pool, for instance, can result in an industry standard, leading to a situation in which there is little competition in terms of the technological format. Once the main players in the market adopt a certain format, network effects may make it very difficult for alternative formats to survive. This does not imply, however, that the creation of a de facto industry standard always eliminates competition within the meaning of the last condition of Article 81(3). Within the standard, suppliers may compete on price, quality and product features. However, in order for the agreement to comply with Article 81(3), it

[28] Avis n° 06-A-07 du 22 mars 2006 relatif à l'examen, au regard des règles de concurrence, desmodalités de fonctionnement de la filière du commerce équitable en France.

must be ensured that the agreement does not unduly restrict competition and does not unduly restrict future innovation (pt. 152).[29]

On March 2014, the European Commission has adopted new rules for the assessment of technology transfer agreements under EU antitrust rules. The purpose of such agreements is to enable companies to license the use of patents, know-how or software held by another company for the production of goods and services. The revised rules facilitate such sharing of intellectual property, including through patent pools, and provide clearer guidance on licensing agreements that stimulate competition. At the same time, they aim to strengthen incentives for research and innovation.

[29] OJEU n° C 101, 4/27/2004.

German Report

26

Susanne Augenhofer

26.1 CSR Policies in Germany and Legal Concerns

In Germany, there are various kinds of CSR policies. As the introduction to this book already suggests, CSR policies may be adopted by or together with NGOs, business associations or consumer organisations, and they may address questions of external (e.g., eco/social sponsoring, eco/social-friendly branding) or internal policy (e.g., treatment of employees).

With regard to legal consequences, the main distinction depends on whether or not a CSR policy falls within the definition of a code of conduct (*Verhaltenskodex*) according to Section 2 subsection 1 No. 5 of the Act Against Unfair Competition (*Gesetz gegen den unlauteren Wettbewerb*,[1] UWG). This provision states that codes of conduct "shall mean an agreement or set of rules which defines the conduct of entrepreneurs who have undertaken to be bound by the code in relation to business sectors or individual commercial practices, without such obligations having been imposed by statutory or administrative provisions".[2] By contrast, the definition of CSR is broader, encompassing any social or environmental issue a business

The author would like to thank Carmen Appenzeller for help with editing this report. The report was written in May 2013 and has only been slightly updated for publication. References are kept to a minimum.

[1] Any German legislation cited in this report is available at http://www.gesetze-im-internet.de/.

[2] In this country report, the English translation of the UWG provided by the German government is used. It is available at http://www.gesetze-im-internet.de/.

S. Augenhofer (✉)
Professor for Civil Law, European Private Law, Comparative Law and Market Regulation through Consumer Law and Competition Law, Humboldt-University, Berlin, Germany
e-mail: susanne.augenhofer@rewi.hu-berlin.de

P. Kobel et al. (eds.), *Antitrust in the Groceries Sector & Liability Issues in Relation to Corporate Social Responsibility*, LIDC Contributions on Antitrust Law, Intellectual Property and Unfair Competition, DOI 10.1007/978-3-662-45753-5_26

addresses without being legally obliged to do so.[3] Consequently, while all codes of conduct can be CSR policies, not all CSR policies are codes of conduct according to the definition of the UWG. For example, the statement by an enterprise that a certain percentage of its profit is donated to charity can be qualified as a CSR policy but not as a code of conduct (cf. the definition of codes of conduct supra).

Within these two main categories, CSR policies can be found in practice with different variations, such as codes of conduct adopted with or without the involvement of public authorities or organisations. As an example of the former may serve the code for quality and safety regarding the online sale of cars and motorbikes (*Kodex für Qualität und Sicherheit beim Fahrzeughandel im Internet*).[4] This code was developed jointly by the Centre for Protection Against Unfair Competition (*Zentrale zur Bekämpfung unlauteren Wettbewerbs e.V.*, abbrev. *Wettbewerbszentrale*), the German motor industry, the German automobile club and two online selling platforms. Other examples of CSR in the form of codes of conduct are the advertising regulations published by the German advertising self-regulation body (Advertising Standards Council, *Werberat*).[5] Generally speaking, one can note that the reference to CSR policies in commercial practices has increased over the last years. CSR policies are used more often, especially with regard to organic food and environmental issues.[6] Most supermarket chains in Germany refer on their homepage to the social and ecological factors under which their products are manufactured. But one can also find CSR policies involving donations to charities or other external activities, e.g., a supermarket claiming that it will plant a tree for every 10 EUR spent by a customer.

In addition, CSR policies are more frequently the subject of public statements in the aftermath of crises. As an example, one can refer to the collapse of factory buildings in Bangladesh in May 2013. Soon after, clothing companies—including

---

[3] See the definition of CSR in the Communication of 22 March 2006 from the Commission to the European Parliament, the Council and the European Economic and Social Committee "Implementing the Partnership for Growth and Jobs: Making Europe a Pole of Excellence on Corporate Social Responsibility" (COM (2006) 136 final) p. 2: corporate social responsibility (CSR) is "a concept whereby companies integrate social and environmental concerns in their business operations and in their interaction with their stakeholders on a voluntary basis. It is about enterprises deciding to go beyond minimum legal requirements and obligations stemming from collective agreements in order to address societal needs. Through CSR, enterprises of all sizes, in cooperation with their stakeholders, can help to reconcile economic, social and environmental ambitions." Cf. also the new, broader definition used in Communication of 25 October 2011 from the Commission to the European Parliament, the Council, the European Economic and Social Committee and the Committee of the Regions "A renewed EU strategy 2011–14 for Corporate Social Responsibility" (COM (2011) 681 final), p. 6: "responsibility of enterprises for their impacts on society"; cf. also the recent Directive 2014/95/EU of the European Parliament and of the Council of 22 October 2014 amending Directive 2013/34/EU as regards disclosure of non-financial and diversity information by certain large undertakings and groups, OJ L 330 of 15.11.2014, p. 1, recital 3; cf. Schrader, *Nachhaltigkeit in Unternehmen*, ZUR 2013, pp. 454 et seq.; Lanfermann, *EU-Richtlinienvorschlag zur Offenlegung von nicht-finanziellen Informationen: Ist eine Pflicht notwendig?*, BB 2013, pp. 1323–1325.

[4] The German version is available at https://www.wettbewerbszentrale.de/de/branchen/ecommerce/pressemitteilungen/_pressemitteilung/?id=237.

[5] The German version is available at http://www.werberat.de/verhaltensregeln.

[6] Cf., for the relevance of CSR policies in environmental protection, www.bmub.bund.de/P407/.

German enterprises—published statements and/or codes of conduct aiming to ensure that their clothes are produced respecting the fundamental rights of their workers, particularly regarding adequate safety and working hours. Once again, we can observe the above-mentioned distinction between CSR in the (narrow) form of codes of conduct and CSR policies more broadly: some businesses have signed a code of conduct, the Bangladesh Safety Accord,[7] which was developed, i.a., by IndustrieALL and UNI Global Union,[8] while others have developed their own CSR policies with regard to worker safety. As will be analysed in the following paragraphs, the UWG is capturing all CSR policies—or rather their violation—regardless of their specific form as long as they can be qualified as "commercial practices" (cf. Section 2 subsection No. 1 UWG). However, different sections of the UWG—with different preconditions—will apply.

26.2 Prevention of and Sanctions for Breaches of CSR Policies Under German Law

26.2.1 Relevant Legislation

26.2.1.1 The UWG: General Remarks

The law applicable to breaches of CSR policies in Germany—as long as they can be qualified as commercial practices (Section 2 subsection 1 No. 1 UWG)[9]—is the above-mentioned UWG. As a result of this broad definition, it is hard to imagine CSR policies that do not fall within this definition as all CSR policies aim at the creation of a positive impression of a business and thereby the enhancement of sale.[10]

As the first act against unfair competition was already enacted in 1896,[11] it is fair to say that the law against unfair competition/commercial practices has a long tradition in Germany. The current UWG was adopted in 2004[12] but was amended in

[7] Accord on Fire and Building Safety in Bangladesh of May 13, 2012, available at http://www.laborrights.org/creating-a-sweatfree-world/resources/bangladesh-fire-and-building-safety-agreement.

[8] Cf. for a list of participating companies, mostly from Europe, http://www.industriall-union.org/bangladesh-accord-on-fire-and-building-safety-released.

[9] "'Commercial practice' shall mean any conduct by a person for the benefit of that persons or a third party's business before, during, or after, the conclusion of a business transaction, which conduct is objectively connected with promoting the sale or the procurement of goods or services, or with the conclusion or the performance of a contract concerning goods or services; 'goods' shall be deemed to include immovable property as well, and 'services' also rights and obligations".

[10] For a different view, pointing out that CSR policies are made on a voluntary basis and therefore should not entail any legal consequences; cf. the references in Balitzki, *Werbung mit ökologischen Selbstverpflichtungen*, GRUR 2013, p. 671 at n. 16. It has to be noted that voluntariness is no longer part of the new definition put forward by the Commission in COM (2011) 681 final, p. 6. Cf. also Directive 2014/95/EU (n. 3) which imposes a duty to provide a non-financial report on companies meeting a certain threshold. Member States have to implement the Directive until December 2016.

[11] Of 27.05.1896, RGBl. p. 145.

[12] Of 03.07.2004, BGBl. I, p. 1414.

2008,[13] when Germany had to implement the Unfair Commercial Practices Directive (UCPD).[14] The UWG generally applies to B2C and to B2B commercial practices as it aims at the protection of competitors, consumers and other market participants, as well as at the protection of the public's interest in undistorted competition (cf. Section 1 UWG). However, as a result of the implementation of the UCPD—which applies to B2C commercial practices only—there are slightly different rules applicable to B2C relations. For example, Annex I of the UCPD was implemented only with regard to B2C relations (cf. Section 3 subsection 3 UWG).

It is important to note already at this point that a violation of CSR policies—regardless of whether it can be qualified as a code of conduct or not—is not *per se* unfair.[15]

While today references to CSR policies are allowed in commercial practices unless they are misleading, aggressive or unfair under the general clause of Section 3 subsection 2 UWG (for details, cf. the following paragraphs), such statements were considered unfair—and consequently prohibited—under the German law of unfair competition for a long time. Courts held that statements referring to facts that were not directly connected to the characteristics of the advertised product or service would influence consumers in an inappropriate way by putting them under pressure, thus deterring competition on the merits.[16] An advertisement by McDonald's, stating that a certain percentage of profits from all Big Macs sold on a specific date would be donated to a German charity organisation, was held unfair under this former approach.[17]

26.2.1.2 CSR in the Form of Codes of Conduct

As stated above, the main distinction—regarding the legal consequences of a business's breach of its CSR policy—has to be drawn between codes of conduct and CSR policies that do not fit into the definition of codes of conduct provided for

---

[13] Of 22.12.2008, BGBl. I, p. 2949. Cf., e.g., Köhler, *Die Umsetzung der Richtlinie über unlautere Geschäftspraktiken in Deutschland*, in Augenhofer (ed), *Die Europäisierung des Kartell- und Lauterkeitsrechts*, 2009, pp. 101–116. The UWG has been amended several times since then. Currently there is a proposal for another amendment as it has been noted that the implementation of the UCPD (n. 14) did not take into account all requirements set out in the Directive, cf. WRP 2014, 1373. The proposal is not dealt with in this paper.

[14] Directive 2005/29/EC of the European Parliament and of the Council of 11 May 2005 concerning unfair business-to-consumer commercial practices in the internal market and amending Council Directive 84/450/EEC, Directives 97/7/EC, 98/27/EC and 2002/65/EC of the European Parliament and of the Council and Regulation (EC) No 2006/2004 of the European Parliament and of the Council ('Unfair Commercial Practices Directive'), OJ L 149 of 11.6.2005, p. 22. Note that the definition of commercial practice given in Art. 2 lit. d UCPD varies from the one in Section 2 subsection 1 No. 1 UWG in that it requires a direct connection between the commercial practice and the promotion, sale or supply of a product to a consumer.

[15] Cf. BGH GRUR 2011, p. 432 – *FSA-Kodex*.

[16] Cf., e.g., BGH GRUR 1991, p. 545 – *Tageseinnahmen Mitarbeiter*; BGH GRUR 1995, p. 595 – *Kinderarbeit*; BGH GRUR 1995, p. 742 – *Arbeitsplätze bei uns*.

[17] BGH GRUR 1987, p. 534 – *McHappy-Tag*.

in Section 2 subsection 1 No. 5 UWG.[18] This definition was adopted from Article 2 lit. f UCPD when the directive was implemented into German law. As a result, Section 2 subsection 1 No. 5 UWG has to be interpreted in light of the UCPD. To be qualified as a code of conduct, a CSR policy consequently must meet the following criteria: agreement or set of rules, in relation to commercial practices, and voluntariness.

Agreement or Set of Rules

Codes of conduct under Section 2 subsection 1 No. 5 UWG require an agreement or a set of rules. From the term "agreement", it is concluded that there must be more than one party to a code of conduct.[19] However, it is sufficient that one party has already undertaken to be bound by the code as long as other businesses have the possibility to sign the code as well.[20] It has rightly been pointed out that for the qualification as codes of conduct, it is of no importance what kind of legal nature an agreement or set of rules has and how it is labelled.[21] In addition, the qualification as a code of conduct has to be made regardless of the process by which the agreement was developed.[22]

It has been discussed whether the definition in Section 2 subsection 1 No. 5 UWG requires the code of conduct to have external effects. This discussion seems to be rather hypothetical as codes of conduct used as CSR policy will always have external effects in the sense that it will be made available to the public. Consequently, when a business refers to its having adopted, e.g. the German Corporate Governance Code,[23] it has to be regarded as code of conduct in the sense of Section 2 subsection 1 No. 5 UWG as well.[24]

[18] Cf. on codes of conducts under the UWG Kopp/Klostermann, *Vorsicht Falle: Verhaltenskodizes im reformierten Lauterkeitsrecht des UWG*, CCZ 2009, pp. 155–159.

[19] Cf., e.g., Birk, *Corporate Responsibility, unternehmerische Selbstverpflichtungen und unlauterer Wettbewerb*, GRUR 2011, p. 199.

[20] Cf., e.g., Alexander, *Verhaltenskodizes im europäischen und deutschen Lauterkeitsrecht*, GRUR-Int. 2012b, p. 967.

[21] Cf., e.g., Alexander, *Verhaltenskodizes im europäischen und deutschen Lauterkeitsrecht*, GRUR-Int. 2012b, p. 967.

[22] Cf. Keller, in Harte-Bavendamm/Henning-Bodewig (eds) *Gesetz gegen den unlauteren Wettbewerb*, 2013, § 2 para 165. The term "code owner" (Article 2 lit. f UCPD) was not implemented into German law but still has to be considered. According to Article 2 lit. f UCPD, authorities or organisations, e.g. consumer organisations, can also be code owners. However, as pointed out earlier, it is not required that such organisations are involved in the adoption of a code.

[23] With German Corporate Governance Code, we refer to the Corporate Governance Code, which was adopted by the Governance Commission and introduced by the German Ministry of Justice; cf. http://www.dcgk.de/de/.

[24] For a different opinion, cf. Alexander, *Verhaltenskodizes im europäischen und deutschen Lauterkeitsrecht*, GRUR-Int. 2012b, p. 968; Bornkamm, in Köhler/Bornkamm (eds) *Gesetz gegen den unlauteren Wettbewerb*, 2015, § 5 para 5.163. In the view of the latter author, the corporate governance code is not a code of conduct as it is not the result of an agreement between businesses. However, according the definition used in the UCPD, as well as in the UWG, a set of rules developed by a code owner – which can be any entity – can be a code of conduct as well.

In Relation to Commercial Practices

The code of conduct must regulate the behaviour of businesses with regard to commercial practices. The term commercial practices is defined in Section 2 subsection 1 No. 1 UWG and has been introduced into the UWG when implementing the UCPD. It follows from this definition, as well as from the jurisprudence of the Court of Justice of the European Union (CJEU), that the term "commercial practices" has to be understood in a broad sense.[25] Consequently, the scope of application of codes of conduct is rather wide, basically comprising all activities before, during or after the conclusion of a business transaction, connected with the promotion, the sale or the procurement of goods or services.

Regarding the subject of codes of conduct, they can have rather different contents. As it has to go beyond the already legally binding standard,[26] a code of conduct may deal with subjects outside the scope of application of the UCPD. Therefore, codes of conduct may regulate commercial practices in B2B relations[27] or questions of taste or decency,[28] which are not addressed by the UCPD. It has been discussed whether codes of conduct must not contain commercial practices violating the law.[29] Especially, their relationship with the Act Against Restraints of Competition (*Gesetz gegen Wettbewerbsbeschränkungen*, GWB) was disputed. One must know that Section 24 GWB allows for the establishment of competition rules. Codes of conduct may be qualified as such competition rules under Section 24 GWB, but the concept of competition rules is narrower compared to the definition of codes of conduct, as the former can be published only by trade and industry associations as well as by professional organisations. Competition rules are furthermore restricted in their scope of regulation, as they have to promote fair and effective competition (cf. Section 24 subsection 2 GWB).

Voluntariness

It follows from the very nature of a code of conduct that it is not sufficient to merely reproduce the state of the law but that it must go beyond that. The definition also seems to require that a business has undertaken to be bound by the code of conduct. However, this requirement is not fundamental for the qualification as a code of conduct but rather for the legal consequences applicable.

---

[25] CJEU, joined cases C-261/07, *VTB-VAB*, and C-299/07, *Galatea BVBA*, ECR 2009 I-02949; CJEU, case C-304/08, *Plus Warenhandelsgesellschaft*, ECR 2010 I-00217 ; CJEU, case C-540/08, Mediaprint, ECR 2010 I-10909.

[26] Keller, in Harte-Bavendamm/Henning-Bodewig, *UWG*, 2013, § 2 para 159.

[27] Cf. Article 2 UCPD.

[28] Cf. Recital 7 UCPD.

[29] Cf., e.g., Hoeren, *Das neue UWG und dessen Auswirkungen auf den B2B-Bereich*, WRP 2009, p. 793; for a different view cf. Alexander, *Verhaltenskodizes im europäischen und deutschen Lauterkeitsrecht*, GRUR-Int. 2012b, p. 970.

26.2.1.3 Codes of Conduct Under Annex I UWG

No. 1 and No. 3 of Annex I of the UWG especially address codes of conduct. Annex I of the UWG lists the 31 commercial practices of Annex I of the UCPD, which are to be regarded as unfair under any circumstances.[30] Under No. 1 of Annex I of the UWG, the false statement by an entrepreneur that she is a signatory to a code of conduct is prohibited. It is argued that the business must actually make such statement and that it is not enough that such impression is created by the business as No. 1 of Annex I of the UCPD uses the term "claiming", whereas, e.g., No. 7 explicitly encompasses "creating the impression".[31] However, the false creation of such impression will be covered by Section 5 UWG in any case.

In addition, according to No. 3 of Annex I of the UWG, it is also prohibited to make "the false statement that a code of conduct has an endorsement from a public or other body". An example of such an unfair commercial practice would be a business falsely claiming that the signed code was endorsed by the German Federal Consumer Organization (*Verbraucherzentrale Bundesverband e.V.*) or the Centre for Protection against Unfair Competition.[32]

Besides these two provisions which directly refer to codes of conduct, No. 2 of Annex I of the UWG might also be of relevance for CSR policies, including those that cannot be qualified as codes of conduct. No. 2 of Annex I of the UWG refers to commercial practices related to quality signs and trademarks and prohibits the display of "a trust mark, quality mark or the equivalent without having obtained the necessary authorization". This provision may capture situations in which a business falsely refers to a quality sign that promotes, e.g., sustainability or the eco-friendliness of a product. One might also think of applying No. 2 of Annex I of the UWG to the misleading use of test results, especially of *Stiftung Warentest* and *Öko-Test*, two German foundations carrying out tests that shall provide consumers with objective information on product quality and safety. However, it is said in German literature that No. 2 of Annex I of the UWG does not refer to test results[33] but only to trust marks and quality marks conferred by organisations. Misleading advertising with such test results is prohibited by Section 5 subsection 1 UWG. Indeed, Section 5 UWG, which generally prohibits misleading commercial practices, is of great importance for the regulation of CSR.

[30] However, it has included No. 26 of Annex I of the UCPD into Section 7 subsection 2 UWG; thus, the Annex of the UWG only contains 30 practices.

[31] Bornkamm, in Köhler/Bornkamm (eds) *Gesetz gegen den unlauteren Wettbewerb*, 2015, Anhang zu § 3 Abs 3 Nr. 1 para 1.4.

[32] It has to be noted that none of the organisations referred to actually endorses codes of conduct.

[33] Cf., e.g., Dreyer/Weidert, in Harte-Bavendamm/Henning-Bodewig (eds) *Gesetz gegen den unlauteren Wettbewerb*, 2013, Anh. § 3 Abs. 3 No. 2 para 3.

26.2.1.4 CSR Policies Under Sections 3, 5 UWG[34]

According to Section 5 subsection 1 sentence 2 UWG, any commercial practice containing information that is untruthful or otherwise suited to deceive regarding the circumstances enumerated in No. 1-7 *leg. cit.* shall be deemed misleading. Consequently, all CSR policies containing untruthful statements are prohibited under Section 5 UWG, regardless of whether they were made in connection with a code of conduct or not. A CSR statement prohibited under this provision would be a declaration that 10 % of the daily profits are donated to charity when the actual donation is only 5 %.

The second alternative of Section 5 subsection 1 sentence 2 UWG especially addresses codes of conducts as No. 6 refers to deceptive information regarding "compliance with a code of conduct by which the entrepreneur has undertaken to be bound when he makes reference to such commitment". As Section 5 subsection 1 sentence 2 No. 6 UWG—as well as especially Article 6 subsection 2 UCPD—requires that the business declared to be bound by a code of conduct, it is assumed that such declaration is not part of the definition of a code of conduct in Section 2 subsection 5 UWG but only a requirement for Article 6 subsection 2 UCPD/Section 5 subsection 1 sentence 2 No. 6 UWG.[35]

It has been questioned if this provision is in line with the UCPD as Article 6 subsection 2 UCPD in contrast to Section 5 subsection 1 sentence 2 No. 6 UWG only requires that the non-compliance with a code of conduct causes the consumer to take a transactional decision that he would not have taken otherwise, but not that the commercial practice be deceptive.[36]

Aside from No. 6 *leg. cit.*, Section 5 subsection 1 sentence 2 variation 2 UWG also addresses CSR policies that cannot be qualified as codes of conduct. Of special importance in this regard will be No. 1 *leg. cit.*, which refers to the essential characteristics of the goods or services, including, *inter alia*, test results. The same is true for No. 4 *leg. cit.*, which refers to "any statement or symbol in relation to direct or indirect sponsorship or approval of the entrepreneur or of the goods or services".

[34] It has to be noted that where commercial practices towards consumers are concerned, Section 5 UWG has to be applied in conjunction with Section 3 subsection 2 UWG (instead of in conjunction with Section 3 subsection 1 UWG). Sentence 1 of Section 3 subsection 2 UWG reads as follows: "Commercial practices towards consumers shall be illegal in any case where they do not conform to the professional diligence required of the entrepreneur concerned and are suited to tangible impairment of the consumer's ability to make an information-based decision, thus inducing him to make a transactional decision which he would not otherwise have made." To ensure that the UWG is in line with the UCPD, the first requirement of Section 3 subsection 2 UWG (breach of professional diligence) may not be applied to Section 5 UWG; cf. for a different view (Section 3 subsection 1 UWG) Köhler, in Köhler/Bornkamm (eds) *Gesetz gegen den unlauteren Wettbewerb*, 2015, § 3 para 8, 8f.

[35] Cf. Birk, *Corporate Responsibility, unternehmerische Selbstverpflichtungen und unlauterer Wettbewerb*, GRUR 2011, p. 198.

[36] Köhler, *Richtlinienumsetzung im UWG – eine unvollendete Aufgabe*, WRP 2013, p. 407.

26.2.1.5 CSR Policies Under Sections 3, 5a UWG

In addition to the provisions already cited, the prohibition of misleading omissions in Section 5a UWG may be relevant for CSR policies. While Section 5a subsection 1 UWG applies to B2C as well as B2B relations, Section 5a subsections 2–4 UWG implement Article 8 UCPD and are restricted to B2C relations. Prior to the implementation of the UCPD, it had been ruled by the German Supreme Court (*Bundesgerichtshof*, BGH) that a business' promise to support a charity in exchange for the purchase of its goods or services does not oblige the business to inform customers about the donation in detail unless the advertisement causes a misconception.[37] While it seems to be the prevailing opinion that there is still no general and absolute duty to inform unless a—legal or contractual—duty of disclosure exists,[38] it has been disputed whether businesses have to inform consumers about their CSR policies under Section 5a subsections 2–3 UWG. Such a duty may especially be discussed under Section 5a subsection 3 UWG. This provision specifies which information has to be regarded as material for commercial practices qualifying as an invitation to purchase. *Inter alia*, a business has to inform about "all main characteristics of the goods or services to an extent appropriate thereto and to the communication medium used" (Section 5a subsection 3 No. 1 UWG). In the view of some authors, CSR policies fall under "main characteristics", and they will also influence a consumer's ability to take a decision, making Section 5a subsection 2 UWG applicable.[39] In our view the wording of Section 5a UWG and Article 7 UCPD does not force businesses to inform about their CSR policies unless they want to do so. However, the UCPD only states—even with regard to commercial practices that establish an invitation to purchase—that information about the main characteristics of the good or service has to be given "to an extent appropriate to the medium and the product". This means that there is no general duty to inform about every aspect of the advertised product or, e.g., its environmental impact unless there do exist legal obligations to provide such information.[40] Therefore, neither the wording of Section 5a UWG nor Article 7 UCPD requires businesses to provide information about their CSR policies unless they choose to do so.

As soon as a business refers to its CSR policies, it has to ensure that consumers are given all the information necessary to take an informed decision. This might seem harsh as it requires businesses actively referring to their CSR policies to provide more information than businesses that remain silent in the first place. However, those businesses referring to CSR also enjoy the advantage of attracting

---

[37] BGH GRUR 2007, p. 247 – *Regenwaldprojekt I.*

[38] Birk, *Corporate Responsibility, unternehmerische Selbstverpflichtungen und unlauterer Wettbewerb*, GRUR 2011, p. 203; Bornkamm, in Köhler/Bornkamm (eds) Gesetz gegen den unlauteren Wettbewerb, 2015, § 5 para 4.176.

[39] Wiebe, in Fezer (ed), *Lauterkeitsrecht – Kommentar zum Gesetz gegen den unlauteren Wettbewerb*, Vol. 1, 2010, § 4-S2 para 38.

[40] For a different view, cf. Fezer, *Das Informationsgebot der Lauterkeitsrichtlinie als subjektives Verbraucherrecht*, WRP 2007, p. 1029; Wiebe, in Fezer (ed), *Lauterkeitsrecht – Kommentar zum Gesetz gegen den unlauteren Wettbewerb*, Vol. 1, 2010, § 4-S2, para 94.

customers with their CSR policies. Eventually, the full potential of Section 5a UWG—or rather the underlying Article 7 UCPD—will only be discovered over time, when it is interpreted by the CJEU.[41]

26.2.1.6 Other Relevant Provisions of the UWG

Other relevant provisions of the UWG with regard to CSR policies are Section 4 No. 1 and No. 2 UWG in conjunction with Section 3 UWG, as well as the general clause of Section 3 subsection 1 UWG. Section 4 No. 1 UWG states that "commercial practices that are suited to impairing the freedom of decision of consumers or other market participants through applying pressure, through conduct showing contempt for humanity, or through other inappropriate, non-objective influence" shall be regarded as unfair. According to Section 4 No. 2 UWG, "commercial practices that are suited to exploitation of a consumer's mental or physical infirmity, age, commercial inexperience, credulity or fear, or the position of constraint to which the consumer is subject" are prohibited as well. Section 4 No. 1 UWG was the main provision applied to CSR policies before the implementation of the UCPD. As stated earlier, German jurisprudence used to regard commercial practices referring to CSR policies without direct link to the characteristics of the advertised product as unfair, as it was argued that such commercial practices unduly influenced the ability of a consumer to make a rational choice.[42] As noted above, the BGH has abandoned this jurisprudence in 2007, holding that such commercial practices were not *per se* establishing a violation of Section 4 No. 1 UWG.[43] Within the scope of application of the UCPD, any other view would contradict the model of the rational average consumer as defined in the jurisprudence of the CJEU—since a reasonably circumspect consumer should be able to recognise CSR policies as commercial practices. Furthermore, the UCPD aims at full harmonisation (Article 3 subsection 5 UCPD). Accordingly, only the commercial practices listed in Annex I of the UCPD can be regarded as unfair without considering any further circumstances.[44] Consequently,

---

[41] So far, there is only one decision by the CJEU regarding the interpretation of Article 7 UCPD; cf. CJEU, case C-122/10, *Ving Sverige*, ECR 2011 I-03903. There is one preliminary ruling pending regarding the definition of "invitation to purchase", cf. case C-476/14, submitted by the BGH in October 2014.

[42] Cf. on the legal situation before e.g., Kort, *Zur wettbewerbsrechtlichen Beurteilung gefühlsbetonter Werbung*, WRP 1997, pp. 526–531; cf. on the use of CSR policies relating to pharmaceutical products Heil/Klümper, *Die Werbung mit der sozialen Verantwortung – "Social Sponsoring" im Bereich der Arzneimittelwerbung*, PharmR 2008, p. 226.

[43] BGH GRUR 2007, p. 247 – *Regenwaldprojekt I*; Seichter, *Das Regenwaldprojekt – Zum Abschied von der Fallgruppe der gefühlsbetonten Werbung*, WRP 2007, pp. 230–237; cf. also BGH GRUR 2006, p. 75 – *Artenschutz*, where the BGH held that "environmental sponsoring" was permitted under unfair competition law; cf. Hartwig, *Der BGH und das Ende des Verbots "gefühlsbetonter Werbung"*, NJW 2006, p. 1326; cf. on the permissibility of "shocking advertisement" BVerfG GRUR 2001, p. 170; Hartwig, *Image Advertising Under Unfair Competition Law and the Benetton Campaign*, IIC 2001, pp. 777–794; Wassermeyer, *Schockierende Werbung*, GRUR 2002, pp. 126–134.

[44] CJEU, case C-304/08, *Plus Warenhandelsgesellschaft*, ECR 2010 I-00217; CJEU, case C-540/08, *Mediaprint*, ECR 2010 I-10909.

Section 4 No. 1 UWG cannot render all CSR policies unfair but is applicable only to situations in which pressure was put on the consumer in a way that can be qualified as aggressive under Articles 8, 9 UCPD.[45]

In addition, CSR policies might also fall under the general clause of Section 3 subsection 1 UWG or—with regard to B2C relations—Section 3 subsection 2 UWG, which prohibits any commercial practice that is contrary to the requirements of professional diligence and is "suited to tangible impairment of the consumers' ability to make an information-based decision, thus inducing him to make a transactional decision which he would not otherwise have made". Even though this general clause has the function of a safety net, it does not seem likely in practice that many CSR policies fall under Section 3 subsection 2 UWG seeing that Nos. 1–3 of Annex I of the UWG, as well as Section 5 and Section 5a UWG, are the more specific—and therefore prevailing—provisions. As pointed out earlier, the violation of a CSR policy as such is not per se unfair, but only if it is misleading, aggressive or can be deemed unfair under the general clause.[46] On the other hand, codes of conduct do not provide for a safe harbour because they can be prohibited under specific provisions. CSR policies in the form of codes of conduct, however, can help to interpret the general clause when applied to other CSR policies.[47]

26.2.1.7 Other Legislation

Provisions Within the Framework of Unfair Competition Law

There are laws outside the UWG that also establish bans on misleading practices. For instance, rules regarding food can be relevant within the context of CSR when food is promoted as organic or sustainably harvested. Those laws, like Section 11 of the German Law on Food and Feed Safety (*Lebensmittel- und Futtermittelgesetzbuch*, LFGB) or Article 16 of the General Food Safety Regulation,[48] are applicable beside Sections 5, 5a UWG.

---

[45] Cf., generally, on the implementation of Art. 8, 9 UCPD in Section 4 No. 1 UWG e.g. Köhler, in Köhler/Bornkamm (eds) *Gesetz gegen den unlauteren Wettbewerb*, 2015, § 4 para 1.7.

[46] A violation of a code of conduct does not lead to a violation of Section 4 No. 11 UWG either; cf. below Sect. 26.2.2.1.

[47] First Report on the application of Directive 2005/29/EC of the European Parliament and of the Council of 11 May 2005 concerning unfair business-to-consumer commercial practices in the internal market and amending Council Directive 84/450/EEC, Directives 97/7/EC, 98/27/EC and 2002/65/EC of the European Parliament and of the Council and Regulation (EC) No 2006/2004 of the European Parliament and of the Council ('Unfair Commercial Practices Directive'), COM (2013) 139 final, p. 23; it is disputed in Germany whether the violation of a code of conduct can have indicative effects or not; cf. Köhler, in Köhler/Bornkamm (eds), *Gesetz gegen den unlauteren Wettbewerb*, 2015, § 2 para 115.

[48] Regulation (EC) No 178/2002 of the European Parliament and of the Council of 28 January 2002 laying down the general principles and requirements of food law, establishing the European Food Safety Authority and laying down procedures in matters of food safety, OJ L 31 of 01.02.2002, p. 1 as last amended by Regulation (EU) No 652/2014 of the European Parliament and of the Council of 15 May 2014 laying down provisions for the management of expenditure

General Civil Law

CSR policies that influence the decision of the buyer (not necessarily a consumer) to purchase a certain product or service that then does not live up to the statements made can constitute a defect according to Section 434 subsection 1 sentence 3 German Civil Code (*Bürgerliches Gesetzbuch*, BGB).[49] Misleading CSR policies may also create a mistake or violate the pre-contractual obligation not to infringe upon the other party's interests. However, the law on the sale of goods in general precedes the law of mistake (at least with regard to Section 119 subsection 2 BGB) and pre-contractual duties.[50] But within the framework of CSR policies, this hierarchy must be the subject of further examination. Finally, Section 826 BGB can be taken into account, which states that a "person who, in a manner contrary to public policy, intentionally inflicts damage on another person is liable to the other person to make compensation for the damage". However, due to the exigent requirement to prove the intentional infliction of harm, Section 826 BGB will not be of great importance in practice with regard to CSR policies.

26.2.2 Enforcement of the Relevant Laws

26.2.2.1 Public Authorities and Private Organisations

Foremost, it has to be noted that in Germany, there is no public authority in charge of the enforcement of the UWG (in contrast to the law against restraints of competition, where such a public authority—the Federal Cartel Office (*Bundeskartellamt*)—does exist). Rather, enforcement lies in the hands of competitors and those private organisations that were granted standing in Section 8 UWG. According to Section 8 subsection 3 No. 1 UWG, competitors, business associations meeting the criteria set out in Section 8 subsection 3 No. 2 UWG,[51] entities meeting the criteria set out in the Injunctions Directive,[52] as well

relating to the food chain, animal health and animal welfare, and relating to plant health and plant reproductive material, amending Council Directives 98/56/EC, 2000/29/EC and 2008/90/EC, Regulations (EC) No 178/2002, (EC) No 882/2004 and (EC) No 396/2005 of the European Parliament and of the Council, Directive 2009/128/EC of the European Parliament and of the Council and Regulation (EC) No 1107/2009 of the European Parliament and of the Council and repealing Council Decisions 66/399/EEC, 76/894/EEC and 2009/470/EC, OJ L 189 of 27.06.2014, p. 1.

[49] Cf., e.g., Schrader, *Nachhaltigkeit in Unternehmen*, ZUR 2013, p. 452.

[50] Cf., e.g., Armbrüster, in *Münchener Kommentar zum BGB*, Vol. 1, 2012, § 119 para 29.

[51] "Associations with legal personality which exist for the promotion of commercial or of independent professional interests, so far as a considerable number of entrepreneurs belong thereto, and which distribute goods or services of the same or similar type on the same market, provided such associations are actually in a position, particularly in terms of their personnel, material and financial resources, to pursue the tasks, under their memoranda of association, of promoting commercial or independent professional interests, and so far as the contravention affects the interests of their members."

[52] Directive 2009/22/EC of the European Parliament and of the Council of 23 April 2009 on injunctions for the protection of consumers' interests, OJ L 110 of 01.05.2009, p. 30.

as the chambers of commerce and industry or craft chambers, may bring a claim for elimination[53] and for an injunction.

It has to be noted that Section 8 UWG requires that Section 3 UWG or Section 7 UWG has been violated. Consequently, Section 8 UWG is applicable to all the above-stated provisions of the UWG, which can be of importance for CSR provisions.

Before bringing an action before the court, plaintiffs will try to get an undertaking (*Unterlassungserklärung*), including a penalty clause, signed by the business to amend or cease the unfair commercial practice. The organisations that in practice are most likely to bring a claim under Section 8 UWG are the Centre for Protection against Unfair Competition[54] and the Federation of German Consumer Organisations (*Verbraucherzentrale Bundesverband*) or one of the 16 consumer centres in the German federal states (*Verbraucherzentralen*).

In contrast, those organisations will not have standing to bring a claim under civil law if Section 434 BGB is violated as they are not a party to a contract. However, under Section 4 No. 11 UWG, commercial practices infringing "a statutory provision that is also intended to regulate market behaviour in the interest of market participants" are unfair and consequently prohibited. It has been discussed whether remedies for defective goods according to civil law are statutory provisions in the sense of Section 4 No. 11 UWG.[55] The German Supreme Court ruled that the laws of warranty may be qualified as such statutory provisions.[56] However, it is questionable whether Section 4 No. 11 UWG is in line with the UCPD as it basically introduces additional *per se* prohibitions.[57] As long as Section 4 No. 11 UWG is upheld in German law, the organisations named in Section 8 UWG, as well as competitors, will have the possibility to sue for an elimination and injunction when warranty claims are violated. In addition, those organisations—but not competitors—may sue for an injunction under Sections 2, 3 of the German Injunctions Act (*Unterlassungsklagengesetz*, UKlaG).

26.2.2.2 Consumers

The German UWG does not explicitly grant consumers standing. In 2004, when a new German act against unfair competition law was adopted, there was a discussion on whether a right to redress for the individual consumer should be introduced.[58]

[53] Elimination means a claim to stop an unfair commercial practice (*Beseitigungsanspruch*).

[54] Cf., for the procedure followed by the Centre for Protection against Unfair Competition, http://www.wettbewerbszentrale.de/media/getlivedoc.aspx?id=32204 at p. 3.

[55] Lorenz, in Säcker/Rixecker (eds), *Münchener Kommentar zum BGB*, Vol. 3, 2012, § 477 para 15; cf. Ohly, in Piper/Ohly/Sosnitza, *Gesetz gegen den unlauteren Wettbewerb*, 2014, § 4 para 11/7b.

[56] BGH GRUR 2011, p. 638 – *Werbung mit Garantie*.

[57] Köhler, in Köhler/Bornkamm (eds), *Gesetz gegen den unlauteren Wettbewerb*, 2015, § 3 para 8e; cf. Köhler, *Richtlinienkonforme Gesetzgebung statt richtlinienkonforme Auslegung: Plädoyer für eine weitere UWG-Novelle*, WRP 2012, p. 257.

[58] Cf., e.g., Fezer, *Das wettbewerbsrechtliche Vertragsauflösungsrecht in der UWG-Reform*, WRP 2003, pp. 127–147.

It has been disputed whether the UWG can be qualified as protective law (*Schutzgesetz*), which would give consumers at least the right to sue for damages under Section 823 subsection 2 BGB in conjunction with the UWG. However, the prevailing opinion does not qualify the UWG as such a protective law,[59] despite the fact that Section 1 UWG states that it aims at the protection of consumers as well.

Consumers, however, have remedies under civil law when a good or service is defective as defined in Section 434 BGB. They have the right to have the defective good repaired or exchanged, or—as repair or exchange will most likely not be possible when a CSR policy is misleading—to reduce the price or to rescind the contract if the defect is not only minor (Section 437 BGB[60]).

It should be noted that consumers have the possibility to turn to the regional consumer centres for advice and may also cede any claims resulting from a violation of CSR policies to allow for enforcement by the consumer centre.[61]

26.2.2.3 Competitors

As stated above, competitors[62] can sue for elimination and bring a claim for an injunction under Section 8 UWG as long as they are direct competitors of the business infringing the UWG. In addition, competitors may sue for damages under Section 9 UWG if the business violating the UWG acted with intent or negligence. Competitors may also sue for injunctions or damages when a business violates other statutes than the UWG and those statutes fall under Section 4 No. 11 UWG (cf. above 26.2.2.1.).

26.2.2.4 Suppliers and Purchasers

As suppliers and purchasers are not competitors, they do not have standing under the UWG. A purchaser—regardless of whether it is a consumer or another business—will have contractual rights when a misleading CSR leads to a defect (Section 434 BGB) of the product or service.[63]

Suppliers may have specific distribution agreements in their contracts, stating that purchasers are only allowed to buy fair trade coffee if they are serving it in an eco-friendly environment. Without such specific agreement, suppliers may be

[59] Köhler, in Köhler/Bornkamm (eds), *Gesetz gegen den unlauteren Wettbewerb*, 2015, Einleitung para 7.5, but exempting criminal provisions from this limitation; Ahrens, in Harte-Bavendamm/Henning-Bodewig (eds.) *Gesetz gegen den unlauteren Wettbewerb*, 2013, Einleitung G para 135.

[60] Westermann, in Säcker/Rixecker (eds), *Münchener Kommentar zum BGB*, 2012b, § 437 para 1; Westermann, in Säcker/Rixecker (eds), *Münchener Kommentar zum BGB*, 2012a, § 434 para 19. If the seller acted with fault, the buyer can also claim damages.

[61] Cf., generally, on the cessation of claims to consumer centres Piekenbrock, in Vorwerk/Wolf (eds.), *BeckOK ZPO*, 2014, § 79 paras 13 et seq.

[62] According to Section 2 No. 2 UWG, "'Competitor' shall mean any person who has a concrete competitive relationship with one or more entrepreneurs supplying or demanding goods or services".

[63] Cf. Söbbing, *Außerordentliche Kündigung wegen Verletzung eines Code of Conduct?*, GWR 2014, pp. 78–82.

eligible to sue under Section 826 BGB. However, it will be difficult to prove causation, intent and also the amount of damage suffered.

If CSR policies are part of a code of conduct, suppliers, purchasers, competitors and also consumers may be able to report the breach of a CSR policy to the self-regulation body established in the framework of the code of conduct. For example, a breach of the advertising rules published by the German advertising self-regulation body (*Werberat*) can be reported to the *Werberat* itself, which then will start a "naming and shaming" procedure. However, it has to be noted that self-regulatory enforcement cannot substitute the enforcement of the UCPD by Member States (Article 10 UCPD). It is also important to point out that codes of conduct are not qualified as statutory provisions in the sense of Section 4 No. 11 UWG[64] and that not all codes of conduct set out a self-regulatory body in charge of its enforcement.

26.2.3 The Role of Regulatory Authorities

As noted above (cf. 26.2.2.1.), the UWG is not enforced by a regulatory authority. Criminal law does not play a major role in unfair competition law either. From the few provisions of the UWG dealing with criminal law, only Section 16 subsection 1 UWG may be of importance with regard to CSR policies. Section 16 subsection 1 UWG provides for imprisonment of up to 2 years or a fine. While there are some overlaps with Section 5 UWG as both provisions address misleading commercial practices, Section 16 subsection 1 UWG is the narrower provision capturing only commercial practices directed towards a wider audience, which contain false information, thereby creating the impression of a favourable offer, and in addition requires intent.[65] In practice, Section 16 UWG is not applied very often. Unlike the rest of the UWG, Section 16 subsection 1 UWG is regarded as a protective law, enabling parties suffering a loss to sue for damages under Section 16 subsection 1 UWG in conjunction with Section 823 subsection 2 BGB.[66]

In this context, Section 263 Penal Code (*Straftgesetzbuch*, StGB), fraud, is also applicable as long as all its prerequisites are met. In addition, Section 59 LFGB also establishes a criminal sanction for the violation of Section 11 LFGB.

Finally, while consumer organisations and business associations (Section 8 subsection 3 No. 2–4 UWG) may not impose fines, they may bring a claim for disgorgement of profits under Section 10 UWG. In practice, however, Section 10 UWG is not of great importance, *inter alia*, because the infringing business must

---

[64] Köhler, in Köhler/Bornkamm (eds), *Gesetz gegen den unlauteren Wettbewerb*, 2015, § 4 para 11.30; BGH GRUR 2006, p. 773 – *Probeabonnement*; BGH GRUR 2011, p. 431 – *FSA-Kodex*.

[65] Cf., e.g., Bornkamm, in Köhler/Bornkamm (eds), *Gesetz gegen den unlauteren Wettbewerb*, 2015, § 16 para 7.

[66] Bornkamm, in Köhler/Bornkamm (eds), *Gesetz gegen den unlauteren Wettbewerb*, 2015, Einleitung para 7.5.

have acted with intent, which may be difficult to prove. Furthermore, the suing organisation bears the full risk of losing in court but will not profit if it wins because the ill-gotten gains have to be surrendered directly to the Federal budget.[67]

26.2.4 Causes of Action and Remedies Available for Private Undertakings

As pointed out above, competitors may sue for damages under Section 9 UWG. This provision requires that the business violating Section 3 or Section 7 UWG acted with intent or negligently, and the competitor has to prove that the damage suffered was caused by the violation of the UWG. The amount of damages is established in accordance with Sections 249–252 BGB and includes lost profits (Section 252 BGB). In practice, competitors sue for damages less often than for injunctive relief, as the suing competitor bears the burden of proof, and despite Section 287 Code of Civil Procedure (*Zivilprozessordnung*, ZPO)—which allows for the judge to estimate the damage—this requirement is often difficult to meet.

Under German law, businesses cannot ask for a disgorgement of profits (for Section 10 UWG, cf. above).

26.2.5 Access to Information

The UWG explicitly addresses information issues only in Section 8 subsection 5 UWG, referring to Section 13 UKlaG. According to Section 13 UKlaG, the organisations and associations allowed to bring a claim under Section 8 subsection 3 UWG (but not the competitor) have a right to obtain information from telecommunication services. However, this right encompasses only the name and address of a business and exists only if the information cannot be obtained through other means.[68]

In addition, jurisprudence grants a right to obtain information based on Section 242 BGB.[69] However, this right depends on the main claim for injunction or damages and consequently exists only once the suing party has been able to show that the sued business violated the UWG.[70]

[67] For a detailed analysis of Section 10 UWG, cf., e.g., Alexander, *Nutzen und Zukunft der Gewinnabschöpfung in der Diskussion*, WRP 2012a, pp. 1190–1197; Goldmann, in Harte-Bavendamm/Henning-Bodewig (eds), *Gesetz gegen den unlauteren Wettbewerb*, 2013, § 10 para 5.

[68] Köhler, in Köhler/Bornkamm (eds), *Gesetz gegen den unlauteren Wettbewerb*, 2015, UKlaG § 13 para 4.

[69] For details cf. Bergmann/Goldmann, in Harte-Bavendamm/Henning-Bodewig (eds), *Gesetz gegen den unlauteren Wettbewerb*, 2013, Vorbemerkungen zu §§ 8 ff. para 13.

[70] For details, cf. Bergmann/Goldmann, in Harte-Bavendamm/Henning-Bodewig (eds), *Gesetz gegen den unlauteren Wettbewerb*, 2013, Vorbemerkungen zu §§ 8 ff. para 13.

26.3 Evaluation of the Legal Situation in Germany

26.3.1 Compliance of Businesses with Their CSR Policies

According to the Centre for Protection against Unfair Competition, hardly any violations of CSR policies are reported. In the view of the Federation of German Consumer Organisations, on the contrary, violations of CSR policies do play some role in practice. However, making a precise statement seems tricky as violations of CSR policies are difficult to detect. In our view it is safe to state that CSR policies are becoming increasingly important as consumers are paying more and more attention to them. As evidence for this assumption, one can refer to the protests against clothing companies not willing to sign the Bangladesh Safety Accord mentioned above.[71] While it has to be emphasised again that it is difficult to determine to what extent businesses are violating their CSR policies, we are under the impression that there are no significant policy issues arising from businesses not complying with their own CSR policies.

26.3.2 Compliance from the Perspective of Consumers and Competitors

Generally speaking, consumers and businesses, as well as consumer organisations and trade associations, will be concerned about violations of CSR policies. But as we already noted, it is often difficult to monitor whether businesses are obeying their CSR policies or not. Consumer awareness—and the call for imposing stricter sanctions—tends to be higher in the aftermath of an event that makes the need for efficient CSR visible. This may be either a (well-publicised) discovery of a violation of a CSR or even a disaster such as what happened in the Bangladeshi garment industry. The publication of judgements can be part of the legal sanctioning process in Germany (cf. Section 12 subsection 3 UWG), so we would assume that consumers prefer to have a combination of legal sanctions and commercial sanctions. It also has to be noted that consumers these days are expressing their view on the behaviour of businesses via modern media, e.g., Facebook and companies like "rank a brand"[72] are trying to give consumers information about CSR policies of businesses.

[71] Cf., e.g., http://www.cbc.ca/news/canada/toronto/story/2013/06/29/toronto-bangladesh-protest.html.

[72] http://rankabrand.org/.

26.3.3 Recommendations for Improving the Legal Situation in Germany

We do not think that German substantive law is failing to meet private and public concerns with regard to CSR policies.[73] One might consider the fact that No. 1 of Annex I of the UWG applies only to situations in which an explicit reference to a code of conduct was made as unsatisfying. The same is true for the fact that No. 2 of Annex I of the UWG is not applied to the misleading use of test results. However, these situations are easily captured by Sections 3, 5, 5a UWG. If there are any shortcomings, they concern remedies and enforcement.[74] In the view of the reporter, it is unsatisfactory that consumers do not have standing under the German UWG. In addition, as already pointed out, it is difficult to discover violations of CSR policies because extensive monitoring—which is costly and difficult[75]—would be necessary. The injunction system of the German UWG is regarded as highly effective. However, with regard to damages, competitors have standing, while consumer organisations and trade associations can only apply Section 10 UWG. As we already noted, Section 10 UWG, unfortunately, is not effective in practice. Consequently, as suggested elsewhere,[76] other forms of collective redress should be considered.[77]

26.3.4 Difficulty to Access Information and Burden of Proof

Neither consumers nor consumer organisations, trade associations or competitors have a general power to investigate or ask for the disclosure of documents and/or internal information. Aside from a general duty to inform based upon Section 242 BGB (cf. 26.2.5.), which complements Section 8 and Section 9 UWG and Section 8 subsection 5 UWG, which refers to Section 13 UKlaG, there are no specific discovery provisions. However, under the general rules of civil procedure, the

[73] But cf. critically, e.g., Kocher/Wenckebach, *Recht und Markt*, KJ 2013, p. 24, in the context of working conditions.

[74] Cf., for a recent discussion of the legal situation and enforcement mechanisms, Henning-Bodewig/Liebenau, *Corporate Social responsibility (CSR) – verbindliche Standards des Wettbewerbsrechts?*, GRUR Int 2013,756.

[75] Even Ökotest points out that it is not able to take CSR policies fully into account as it is not able to monitor compliance; cf. http://www.oekotest.de/cgi/index.cgi?artnr=10591&gartnr=91&bernr=04.

[76] Cf., e.g., Augenhofer, *Some questions on enforcement and individual redress – the example of Regulation (EC) No 261/2004*, in Geimer/Schütze/Garber (eds.), *Europäische und internationale Dimension des Rechts*, Festschrift für Daphne-Ariane Simotta, LexisNexis, 2012, pp. 39–56, with further references.

[77] Cf., in this regard, the Communication from the Commission to the European Parliament, the Council, the European Economic and Social Committee and the Committee of the Regions "Towards a European Horizontal Framework for Collective Redress", COM(2013) 401/2 of 11.06.2013.

court may ask the parties to provide the court with certain documents (cf. Section 142 ZPO). As this possibility only exists after legal proceedings have been initiated, it does not help at the pre-trial stage.

26.4 CSR Policies and German Competition Laws

26.4.1 Importance of Market Share and a Collectively Dominant Position Resulting from Horizontal CSR Agreements

As mentioned before, competition law is regulated in Germany in the GWB, the Act against Restraints of Competition. The GWB, however, is based on European competition law and resembles to a large extent Article 101, Article 102 Treaty on the Functioning of the European Union (TFEU).[78]

The European Commission has analysed standardisation agreements in its guidelines on the applicability of Article 101 of the Treaty on the Functioning of the European Union to horizontal co-operation agreements.[79] These guidelines also help to interpret the relevant provisions of the GWB.[80] According to paragraph 280 of the guidelines, "where participation in standard-setting is unrestricted (1) and the procedure for adopting the standard in question is transparent (2), standardisation agreements which contain no obligation to comply (3) with the standard and provide access to the standard on fair, reasonable and non-discriminatory terms will normally not restrict competition within the meaning of Article 101 subsection 1 TFEU".[81] According to the Commission, the third requirement is not met "if the standard-setting agreement binds the members to only produce products in compliance with the standard, the risk of a likely negative effect on competition is significantly increased and could in certain circumstances give rise to a restriction of competition by object".[82] This means that CSR policies may result in a restriction of competition, leading to market foreclosure, as it will be rather difficult for some, especially small and medium-sized businesses to meet the standards set by an NGO. High standards set in the CSR policy are also likely to lead to a price increase for consumers. For instance in the case of tuna fishing

[78] Cf., e.g., Zimmer, in Immenga/Mestmäcker, *Wettbewerbsrecht: GWB*, 2007, § 1, para 2; for the relationship between antitrust law and CSR cf. Lübbig, *Nachhaltigkeit als Kartellthematik*, WuW 2012, pp. 1142–1155.

[79] Guidelines on the applicability of Article 101 of the Treaty on the Functioning of the European Union to horizontal co-operation agreements, OJ C 11 of 14.01.2011, p. 1, hereafter "Guidelines".

[80] Bechtold, *Leitlinien der Kommission und Rechtssicherheit – am Beispiel der neuen Horizontal-Leitlinien*, GRUR 2012, p. 108. It also has to be taken into account that according to para 310 of the Guidelines (n. 79), "[a]greements for testing and certification go beyond the primary objective of defining the standard and would normally constitute a distinct agreement and market".

[81] For a critical assessment of the non-application of Article 101 TFEU, cf. Schweitzer, *Standardisierung als Mittel zur Förderung und Beschränkung des Handels und des Wettbewerbs*, Anm. zu EuGH 12.07.2012, C-171/11, EuZW 2012, p. 770.

[82] Guidelines (n. 79) para 293.

(cf. the example given in the introduction to this book), other means of fishing will have to be applied that are more costly compared to the forbidden ones. These negative results of such behaviour are more likely to occur when the companies involved have a substantial or even a dominant market share.[83] On the other hand, the CSR policy regards only one feature of the product, which means that competition in regard to other features—e.g., packaging of the tuna, taste of the tuna, price—will remain possible. In addition, while we agree that CSR policies are influencing the decisions of consumers, there are most likely a lot of consumers who are not willing or able to buy more expensive tuna.

Furthermore, a standardised agreement that violates Section 2 GWB or Article 101 subsection 1 TFEU might be justified under Article 101 subsection 3 TFEU (Section 2 GWB), provided that it "contributes to improving the production or distribution of goods or to promoting technical or economic progress, while allowing consumers a fair share of the resulting benefit", and the counter-exceptions of Article 101 subsection 3 lits. a and b TFEU do not apply. The CSR policy may lead to the development of new fishing means, thereby facilitating innovation within the fishing industry, which in the long run could lead to more competition and cheaper prices. While in the meantime prices for consumers probably will increase (at least for tuna sold by undertakings that have adopted the CSR policy), eventually consumers may be provided with more choice because of the CSR policy.[84]

It has been discussed whether reasons outside competition itself—e.g., the protection of the environment—can be taken into account under Article 101 subsection 3 TFEU or Section 2 GWB.[85] While the Commission in an earlier decision has weighted the protection of the environment as an important factor,[86] the guidelines seem to have abandoned that opinion.[87] Also, the German *Bundeskartellamt* seems to refrain from such a broader approach to Section 2 GWB.[88]

[83] Cf. also Guidelines (n. 79) para 296.

[84] On the other hand, CSR policies may also lead to less choice due to the fact that those companies not complying with the CSR could be forced out of the market as the majority of the consumers won't buy their products anymore given this non-compliance with environmental standards set in the CSR.

[85] Cf., e.g., Ellger, in Immenga/Mestmäcker, *EU Wettbewerbsrecht*, 2012, Artikel 101 Abs. 3 AEUV, paras 513 et seq.; Nordemann, in Loewenheim/Meessen/Riesenkampff (eds), *Kartellrecht*, 2009, § 2 GWB, paras 138 et seq.

[86] Commission Decision of 24.01.1999, 2000/475/EC – *CECED*, OJ L 187 of 26.07.2000, p. 47, paras 52 et seq.

[87] Cf. Guidelines (n. 79) para 18 at n. 14. These guidelines do not contain a separate chapter on "environmental agreements", as had been the case in the previous guidelines. Standard setting in the environment sector, which was the main focus of the former chapter on environmental agreements, is more appropriately dealt with in the standardisation chapter of these guidelines. In general, depending on the competition issues, "environmental agreements" are to be assessed under the relevant chapter of these guidelines, be it the chapter on R&D, production, commercialisation or standardisation agreements. Also making this point, cf. Lübbig, *Nachhaltigkeit als Kartellthematik – Ein Beitrag über die zunehmende Verrechtlichung eines diffusen, aber bedeutsamen Begriffs*, WuW 2012, p. 1153.

[88] Cf., e.g., Bundeskartellamt, WuW/E DE-V pp. 1392, 1402 – *Altglas*.

To sum up, whether CSR policies will lead to a violation of Article 101 subsection 1 or not and whether such agreements are still justified under Article 101 subsection 3 have to be decided on a case-to-case basis.

Besides Sections 2 and 3 GWB, which as noted resemble Article 101 TFEU, Section 20 subsection 6 GWB especially refers to, *inter alia*, quality mark associations and states that such associations "shall not refuse to admit an undertaking if such refusal constitutes an objectively unjustified unequal treatment and would place the undertaking at an unfair competitive disadvantage". Consequently, Section 20 subsection 6 GWB only establishes a duty to not discriminate, which can be already deduced from Article 101, Article 102 TFEU.

26.4.2 CSR Policies as *De Facto* or *De Jure* Standards

In our view the example stated in the FRAND jurisprudence—while generally accepted in Germany[89]—does not apply where a logo indicating compliance with the CSR Standard is a registered trade mark or collective mark. Such a fact pattern is different from the one that can be found in FRAND cases: in the given example, businesses are—unlike in FRAND cases—still free to either create their own standard or to accept the CSR standard provided by the NGO and to join it. Consequently, businesses already have access to the CSR policy at fair, reasonable and non-discriminatory conditions, while in FRAND cases or in cases dealt with under the essential facilities[90] doctrine, the question is whether the patent owner or the owner of the essential facility has to grant a licence or access in the first place.[91]

References

Ahrens H-J (2013) Einleitung G. Stellung des Wettbewerbsrechts im Gesamtsystem. In: Harte-Bavendamm H, Henning-Bodewig F (eds), *Gesetz gegen den unlauteren Wettbewerb*, 3rd edn. C.H. Beck, München

Alexander C (2012a) *Nutzen und Zukunft der Gewinnabschöpfung in der Diskussion*. WRP 10: 1190–1197

Alexander C (2012b) *Verhaltenskodizes im europäischen und deutschen Lauterkeitsrecht*. GRUR-Int. 11: 965–973

[89] Cf., e.g., Nägele/Jacobs, Zwangslizenzen im Patentrecht, WRP 2009, pp. 1062–1074; cf. also OLG Karlsruhe MMR 2011, p. 469 – *UMTS Standard*.

[90] For the application of the essential facilities doctrine by the CJEU, cf., e.g., CJEU, case C-241/91, *Magill*, ECR 1995 I-00743; CJEU, case C-418/01, *IMS Health*, ECR 2004 I-05039; for the application by the BGH, cf., e.g., BGH NJW 2013, p. 1095 – *Fährhafen Puttgarden II*.

[91] One might also have to distinguish the facts in the decision CJEU, case C-385/07, *Der Grüne Punkt*, ECR 2009 I-06155, from those in the example given in 26. 4.2. since in the case before the CJEU, the undertaking was charging a service fee that was disproportionate with regard to the economic value of the service provided.

Armbrüster C (2012) § 119. In: Säcker F-J, Rixecker R (eds), *Münchener Kommentar zum BGB* Vol. 1, 6th edn. C.H. Beck, München

Augenhofer S (2012) *Some questions on enforcement and individual redress – the example of Regulation (EC) No 261/2004*. In: Geimer R, Schütze R, Garber T (eds), *Europäische und internationale Dimension des Rechts*, Festschrift für Daphne-Ariane Simotta, LexisNexis, Vienna, pp 39–56

Balitzki A (2013) *Werbung mit ökologischen Selbstverpflichtungen*. GRUR 7: 670–675

Bechtold R (2012) *Leitlinien der Kommission und Rechtssicherheit – am Beispiel der neuen Horizontal-Leitlinien*. GRUR 2: 107–112

Bergmann A, Goldmann M (2013) Vorbemerkungen zu §§ 8 ff. In: Harte-Bavendamm H, Henning-Bodewig F (eds), *Gesetz gegen den unlauteren Wettbewerb*, 3rd edn. C.H. Beck, München

Birk A (2011) *Corporate Responsibility, unternehmerische Selbstverpflichtungen und unlauterer Wettbewerb*. GRUR 3: 196–203

Bornkamm J (2015) § 5, Anhang zu § 3. In: Köhler H, Bornkamm J (eds), *Gesetz gegen den unlauteren Wettbewerb*, 33rd edn. C.H. Beck, München

Dreyer G, Weidert S (2013) Anh. § 3 Abs. 3 No. 2. In: Harte-Bavendamm H, Henning-Bodewig F (eds), *Gesetz gegen den unlauteren Wettbewerb*, 3rd edn. C.H. Beck, München

Ellger R (2012) Artikel 101 Abs. 3 AEUV. In: Immenga U, Mestmäcker E-J (eds), *Wettbewerbsrecht Volume 1: EU/part 1*, 5th edn. C.H. Beck, München

Fezer K-H (2007) *Das Informationsgebot der Lauterkeitsrichtlinie als subjektives Verbraucherrecht*. WRP 9: 1021–1030

Fezer K-H (2003) *Das wettbewerbsrechtliche Vertragsauflösungsrecht in der UWG-Reform*. WRP 2: 127–143

Goldmann M (2013) § 10. In: Harte-Bavendamm H, Henning-Bodewig F (eds), *Gesetz gegen den unlauteren Wettbewerb*, 3rd edn. C.H. Beck, München

Hartwig H (2006) *Der BGH und das Ende des Verbots "gefühlsbetonter Werbung"*. NJW 19: 1326–1329

Hartwig H (2001) *Image Advertising Under Unfair Competition Law and the Benetton Campaign*. IIC 7: 777–794

Heil M, Klümper M (2008) *Die Werbung mit der sozialen Verantwortung – "Social Sponsoring" im Bereich der Arzneimittelwerbung*. PharmR 5: 226–236

Henning-Bodewig F, Liebenau D (2013) *Corporate Social responsibility (CSR) – verbindliche Standards des Wettbewerbsrechts?*. GRUR Int 8–9: 753–757

Hoeren T (2009) *Das neue UWG und dessen Auswirkungen auf den B2B-Bereich*. WRP 7: 789–794

Keller E (2013) § 2. In: Harte-Bavendamm H, Henning-Bodewig F (eds), *Gesetz gegen den unlauteren Wettbewerb*, 3rd edn. C.H. Beck, München

Kocher E, Wenckebach J (2013) *Recht und Markt. Ein Plädoyer für gesetzliche Pflichten von Unternehmen zur Offenlegung ihrer Arbeits- und Beschäftigungsbedingungen*. KJ (Kritische Justiz) 1: 18–29

Kopp R, Klostermann E A (2009) *Vorsicht Falle: Verhaltenskodizes im reformierten Lauterkeitsrecht des UWG*. CCZ 4: 155–159

Kort M (1997) *Zur wettbewerbsrechtlichen Beurteilung gefühlsbetonter Werbung*. WRP 6: 526–531

Köhler H (2015) Einleitung, §§ 2, 3, 4 and UKlaG. In: Köhler H, Bornkamm J (eds), *Gesetz gegen den unlauteren Wettbewerb*, 33rd edn. C.H. Beck, München

Köhler H (2013) *Richtlinienumsetzung im UWG – eine unvollendete Aufgabe*. WRP 4: 403–416

Köhler H (2012) *Richtlinienkonforme Gesetzgebung statt richtlinienkonforme Auslegung: Plädoyer für eine weitere UWG-Novelle*. WRP 3: 251–260

Köhler H (2009) *Die Umsetzung der Richtlinie über unlautere Geschäftspraktiken in Deutschland*. In: Augenhofer (ed), *Die Europäisierung des Kartell- und Lauterkeitsrechts*, Mohr Siebeck, Tübingen, pp 101–116

Lanfermann G (2013) *EU-Richtlinienvorschlag zur Offenlegung von nicht-finanziellen Informationen: Ist eine Pflicht notwendig?*. BB 22: 1323–1325

Lorenz St (2012) § 477. In: Säcker FJ, Rixecker R (eds), *Münchener Kommentar zum BGB Volume 3*, 6th edn. C.H. Beck, München

Lübbig T (2012) *Nachhaltigkeit als Kartellthematik – Ein Beitrag über die zunehmende Verrechtlichung eines diffusen, aber bedeutsamen Begriffs*. WuW 12: 1142–1155

Nägele T, Jacobs S (2009) *Zwangslizenzen im Patentrecht – unter besonderer Berücksichtigung des kartellrechtlichen Zwangslizenzeinwands im Patentverletzungsprozess*. WRP 9: 1062–1075

Nordemann J (2009) § 2 GWB. In: Loewenheim U, Meessen K, Riesenkampff A (eds), *Kartellrecht*, 2nd edn. C.H. Beck, München

Ohly A (2014) § 4. In: Piper H, Ohly A, Sosnitza O (eds), *Gesetz gegen den unlauteren Wettbewerb: UWG*, 6th edn. C.H. Beck, München

Piekenbrock A (2014) § 79. In: Vorwerk V, Wolf C (eds), *Beck'scher Online-Kommentar ZPO*, 15th edn. C.H. Beck, München

Scherer I (2013) *Massiver Irrtum bei Nr. 17 der "Schwarzen Liste" des UWG-Anhangs?*. WRP 2: 143–146

Schrader C (2013) *Nachhaltigkeit in Unternehmen – Verrechtlichung von Corporate Social Responsibility (CSR)*. ZUR 9: 451–458

Schweitzer H (2012) *Standardisierung als Mittel zur Förderung und Beschränkung des Handels und des Wettbewerbs*. EuZW 23: 765–770

Seichter D (2007) *Das Regenwaldprojekt – Zum Abschied von der Fallgruppe der gefühlsbetonten Werbung*. WRP 3: 230–237

Söbbing T (2014) *Außerordentliche Kündigung wegen Verletzung eines Code of Conduct?*. GWR 4: 78–82

Wassermeyer A (2002) *Schockierende Werbung*. GRUR 2: 126–134

Westermann H (2012a) § 434. In: Säcker F J, Rixecker R (eds), *Münchener Kommentar zum BGB Volume 3*, 6th edn. C.H. Beck, München

Westermann H (2012b) § 437. In: Säcker F J, Rixecker R (eds), *Münchener Kommentar zum BGB Volume 3*, 6th edn. C.H. Beck, München

Wiebe A (2010) § 4. In: Fezer K-H (ed), *Lauterkeitsrecht: UWG Volume 1*, 2nd edn. C.H. Beck, München

Zimmer D (2014) § 1. In: Immenga U, Mestmäcker E-J (eds), *Wettbewerbsrecht Volume 2: GWB*, 5th edn. C,H. Beck, München

Hungary

27

Ádám Liber, Gusztáv Bacher, Lilla Cs. Tóth, Orsolya Hambalkó, Anikó Keller, Ágnes Komári, Tamás Kostyánszki, and Katalin Szamosi

27.1 Corporate Social Responsibility in Hungary

"CSR" refers to an undertakings' commitment to conduct business in a way that has a positive impact on the environment, consumers, employees, communities, stakeholders and all other members of the public sphere[1]; however, its notion has no clear and accepted definition.[2]

Members of the Working Committee: Gusztáv Bacher; Lilla Cs. Tóth; Orsolya Hambalkó; Anikó Keller; Ágnes Komári; Tamás Kostyánszki; Katalin Szamosi.

[1] See http://en.wikipedia.org/wiki/Corporate_social_responsibility, last visited on 15 May 2013.

[2] Antony Page/Robert A. Katz – Is Social Enterprise the New Corporate Social, Responsibility? – Seattle University Law Review 2011, Vol. 34:1351, p. 1351.

Á. Liber (✉)
Bogsch & Partners, Budapest, Hungary
e-mail: adam.liber@bogsch.hu

G. Bacher • A. Keller
Partner at Szecskay Attorneys at Law, Budapest, Hungary

L.Cs. Tóth
Managing Partner of Cs. Tóth Law Firm, Budapest, Hungary

O. Hambalkó
Case Handler at the Hungarian Competition Office, Budapest, Hungary

Á. Komári
PhD candidate at ELTE Law Faculty, Budapest, Hungary

T. Kostyánszki
Senior Compliance Associate at UniCredit Bank Austria AG, Vienna, Austria

K. Szamosi
Managing Partner of SBGK Law Office, Budapest, Hungary

P. Kobel et al. (eds.), *Antitrust in the Groceries Sector & Liability Issues in Relation to Corporate Social Responsibility*, LIDC Contributions on Antitrust Law, Intellectual Property and Unfair Competition, DOI 10.1007/978-3-662-45753-5_27

Based on local surveys,[3] it can be generally stated that CSR has been present in the activities of Hungarian top-tier and multinational companies only in the past 10 years. In Hungary, CSR is treated as a communication tool and considered as part of the image communication; therefore, CSR programs are supervised by the PR/marketing departments. Surveys reflect that CSR is already an integral part of the strategy planning of leading firms; however, CSR activities are only rarely represented at the top management level of local companies.[4] In contrast to multinationals that conduct CSR activities—that is more or less influenced by group level CSR commitments—small and mid-size undertakings in Hungary do very rarely conduct CSR activities.

Remarkably, only a very little (but growing) proportion of local consumers find the seller's CSR activities as an important/a determining factor of their purchase decision,[5] as it is the purchase price that is of utmost importance for the Hungarian average consumer.[6]

The types of local CSR programs range between voluntary work (Provident), employment of persons with disabilities (Telenor), child support (Raiffeisen Bank), equal opportunities (Magyar Telekom), selective waste collection (Electrolux), donation/sponsorship (Audi Hungaria), education programs (Kürt), shelter programs (McDonald's), etc. CSR commitments may be reflected in drawing up codes of conduct, in developing policies and initiatives, as well is in implementing mechanisms for the supervision of such commitments.

The Hungarian Group believes that only those CSR policies that refer to a specific commitment of its publisher (advertiser) might give rise to legal concerns. For instance, if a CSR policy refers to the fact that its signatory does not use any child labor in connection with the production of goods it sells but, in fact, the producer of the goods does employ children, this may be qualified as a misleading unfair commercial practice for which the signatory would be liable. In contrast, general declarations and mission statements in CSR policies such as "we are committed to environmental sustainability" does not reflect any specific commitment; therefore, such statements are unlikely to trigger the trader's liability.

[3] See http://csr.braunpartners.hu/files/sharedUploads/B_P%20Research%20Notes/2011/20110809_BP_Research%20Notes.pdf. The Research of B&P Braun & Partners was based on a survey conducted with 53 companies; see the CSR research of Donor's Forum at http://www.donorsforum.hu/hu/component/content/article/142-archivum/492-maf-top200-kutatas-eseti-tamogatasok-a-hazai-nagyvallalatok-tamogatasi-gyakorlataban; visited on 15 May 2013.

[4] See Katalin, Szilágyi – Jó ügyek mellé állnak a vállalatok – CSR-körkép itthon – HR Poral – http://www.hrportal.hu/hr/jo-ugyek-melle-allnak-a-vallalatok-csr-korkep-itthon-20121001.html, visited on 15 May 2013.

[5] See http://www.hrportal.hu/c/csr-pr-fogas-vagy-felelos-mukodes-20090910.html, last visited on 15 May 2013.

[6] The Hungarian average consumer is particularly price sensitive, which is also acknowledged in the practice of the Hungarian Competition Authority; see the Lidl Magyarország case, decision Vj/012-017/2011, section 18.

We note in advance that there is no relevant practice available in the Hungarian jurisdiction regarding the prosecution/breach of CSR commitments; thus, in practice, CSR policies did not give rise to any specific legal concerns in Hungary, yet.

Legal concerns might arise in the context of *sponsorship* of certain undertakings and relating to certain products: the Hungarian Act on Business Advertising[7] specifically prohibits[8] sponsorship activities relating to tobacco products if it concerns events or activities involving or taking place in several Member States of the European Economic Area or otherwise having cross-border effects, events in connection with sporting and cultural events or events or activities relating to health care. Further, tobacco companies are also required to publish the amount of their spending on sponsorship during the current year on their website and in at least two national daily newspapers. Regarding the prosecution of the tobacco sponsorship ban, BAT Hungary has been fined with HUF 10 million (approximately EUR 30,000) by the National Consumer Protection Authority (NCPA) in 2009 for awarding the "BAT Publicum's Prize" at the National Theatre of Pécs.[9]

In the context of *media services*, the Act CIV of 2010 on the freedom of the press and the fundamental rules on media content generally prohibits[10] surreptitious advertising in the media content. This prohibition refers to any commercial communications the publication of which deceives the audience about the true nature of the communication. In relation to CSR programs, Act CLXXXV of 2010 on Media Services and Mass Media (Act on Media Services) provides[11] that in media services, information concerning the corporate social responsibility of an undertaking shall not qualify as a surreptitious commercial communication, but such reports may only contain the name, logo and trademark of the undertaking and its product or service, if it is closely connected to its social responsibility. The slogan of the undertaking or any parts of its commercial communication may not appear in the report, and the information may not expressly encourage the purchase of the product or the use of the service offered by the undertaking.

27.2 Prevention and Sanctioning of Commercial Practices Breaching a CSR Policy

27.2.1 Relevant Legislation

In Hungary, there are no special *sui generis* laws in force that address specifically the breach of CSR policies. However, there are legislative acts that are more general in nature but applicable if an undertaking breaches its own self-imposed CSR

[7] Act XLVIII of 2008 on the Basic Requirements and Certain Restrictions applying to Commercial Advertising Activities.

[8] Under Article 20 (1).

[9] See the Press Release of the Anti-Smoking NGO Füstírtók, available at http://www.google.com/hostednews/epa/article/ALeqM5iuNAjCnLBocIOL1EmjFPxpvlPXTQ, visited on 15 May 2013.

[10] Under Article 20 (3).

[11] Under Article 32 (9).

policy, which may constitute a violation of the provisions of the Competition Act,[12] the UCP Act[13] (implementing the EU Unfair Commercial Practices Directive) or the Act on Business Advertising.

If the undertaking breaches its own self-imposed CSR policy, the provisions of the UCP Act[14] would be applicable to such conduct, provided such breach could be considered as a commercial practice potentially affecting the transactional decision of any consumer in the territory of Hungary. Under the UCP Act, consumers are exclusively natural persons.

According to Article 5 of the UCP Act, codes of conduct shall not encourage unfair commercial practices.

Moreover, the Annex of the UCP Act (the so-called blacklist) also lists those conducts that are specifically *ex lege* unfair. According to the first and the second paragraphs of the blacklist, claiming to be a signatory to a code of conduct when the undertaking is in fact not as well as claiming that a code of conduct has an endorsement from a public administrative authority or other body vested with public administrative authority, which it does not have, are specifically unfair and therefore prohibited.

The Act on Business Advertising applies to any business advertising performed by persons in their capacities as advertisers, advertising service providers or publishers of advertisements, to sponsorship as well as to codes of conduct relating to them. The CSR breach would be considered as a misleading advertising—subject to the provisions of the Act on Business Advertising—if its addressees were exclusively undertakings (nonnatural persons) acting for purposes that do not relate to their respective independent professions and economic activities.[15] Thus, the pertaining provisions of the Act on Business Advertising apply only to B2B relations.

Article 2 of the Competition Act lays down a general clause that prohibits unfair economic activities, which infringe or jeopardize the legitimate interests of competitors, trading parties or consumers or is contrary to the requirements of business fairness. Further, Article 8 of the Competition Act might be also applicable in relation to the breach of CSR commitments. This provision generally prohibits deceiving trading parties (business partners) in economic competition. Paragraph 2 sets out some particular cases of deception of trading parties, which are prohibited according to that Article.

Summarizing the above:

- If a CSR breach is considered as a commercial practice (such as advertising) affecting any consumer (including any kind of business-to-consumer communications), the UCP Act would be applicable.

[12] Act LVII of 1996 on the Prohibition of Unfair and Restrictive Market Practices.

[13] Act XLVII of 2008 on the Prohibition of Unfair Commercial Practices against Consumers.

[14] Article 2 a) of the UCP Act.

[15] Article 2 of the Act on Business Advertising.

- If the CSR breach is committed by advertising (e.g., misleading advertising), which does not concern any consumer (but trading parties/business partners), the provisions of the Act on Business Advertising would apply to such conduct.
- In contrast, if the CSR breach could not be qualified as "advertising" but similarly deceives/unfairly influences trading parties (business partners), this conduct would be subject to the provisions of the Competition Act.

27.2.2 Enforceability of the Relevant Laws

27.2.2.1 By Public or Regulatory Authorities

The UCP Act is enforced by three public authorities in Hungary.

The *National Consumer Protection Authority* (NCPA) and its local inspectorates have general competence to proceed against unfair commercial practices. However, if the commercial practice concerned relates to an activity of the undertaking that is supervised by the *Hungarian Financial Supervisory Authority* (HFSA), such as banks, insurance companies, and financial service providers, the HFSA shall also prosecute unfair commercial practices by such entities. If the commercial practice is capable of materially affecting competition, the *Hungarian Competition Authority* (HCA) has the power to proceed.[16] The provisions on misleading and comparative advertising *vis-a-vis* business partners, as well as the provisions of the Competition Act, are also enforced by the HCA.

27.2.2.2 By Consumers, Competitive Businesses or Suppliers to and Purchasers of the Goods or Services of the Business

Any person (including suppliers, consumers and competitors) may submit a (formal) complaint or an informal complaint to the HCA if she observes a conduct that infringes the Competition Act or the Act on Business Advertising (misleading of business partners, unfair manipulation of consumer choice, misleading advertising falling within the competence of the HCA). This may result, subject to the decision of the HCA, in the introduction of a competition supervision proceeding. The lodging of both formal complaints and informal complaints is free of charge. Upon request of the complainant or of the person making an informal complaint, the HCA does not disclose the identity to the undertaking concerned. A formal complaint shall be made by the use of the form published by the HCA, whereas informal complaint may be submitted without any formal requirements. Hence, even handwritten notes or letters or e-mails can be used for making informal complaints.

Consumer protection proceedings of the HFSA and NCPA can also be launched on the basis of a consumer complaint, but these authorities are also entitled to launch proceedings on their own initiative. Consumer complaints to the HFSA and NCPA are reviewed within the framework of administrative proceedings.

Article 15 (1) of the UCP Act provides that proceedings conducted under the Act shall not prevent injured parties from enforcing civil law claims, which are based on

[16] Article 10 of the UCP Act.

the unfairness of a commercial practice, directly before a Court. Accordingly, local consumers and businesses may file a court action for compensation of damages they have sustained. The burden of proof of the accuracy of factual claims in relation to the commercial practice shall rest with the undertaking. Further, both consumers and business partners may file court action based on the infringement of Article 2 of the Competition Act (the general clause) and claim damages as well as restitution for such infringement.[17]

27.2.3 Causes of Action and Range of Remedies Available to Regulatory Authorities

27.2.3.1 Injunctive Reliefs

According to the Competition Act, the Competition Council may, by an interim measure, prohibit by its order to continue the engagement in an illegal conduct or order the elimination of the unlawful situation if prompt action is required to protect the legal or economic interests of the interested persons or if the formation, development or continuation of economic competition is threatened.

Article 27 of the Act on Business Advertising also used to empower authorities and courts in the past to prohibit the disclosure of an advertisement that has not been published before if publication had breached the provisions of Act on Business Advertising. The Hungarian Constitutional Court established that the respective provision of the Act disproportionately restricted the freedom of the press and free speech, so it has been nullified as being unconstitutional in 2010.[18]

27.2.3.2 Causes of Action

The causes of action and the competence for the prosecution of infringement by Hungarian public authorities have been described in detail under Sects. 27.2.1 and 27.2.2.1, respectively, above.

27.2.3.3 Range of Remedies

The Competition Council of the HCA may in its decision

- establish that the conduct is unlawful;
- order a situation violating competition laws to be eliminated;
- prohibit the continuation of the conduct that violates the provisions of any of the Acts mentioned in item Sect. 27.2.1;
- where it finds that there is an infringement of the law, impose obligations;
- order a corrective statement to be published with respect to untruth information.

[17] See Sect. 27.2.4 below.

[18] Decision of the Constitutional Court Nr. 23/2010 (III.4) AB.

The NCPA is entitled to

- order the termination of the unlawful situation;
- impose a ban of the unlawful conduct;
- order the business entity to terminate the deficiencies and disparities exposed within the deadline;
- ban, restrict or impose conditions regarding the supply of the goods until the infringement is eliminated;
- order the temporary closure of the commercial establishment affected until the infringement is eliminated, where deemed necessary for the protection of human lives, health, physical integrity or for the prevention of dangers posing significant threats to a broad range of consumers; or
- impose a consumer protection fine.

The HFSA may in administrative proceeding

- issue a notice to terminate the deficiencies and comply with the law;
- order the termination of the unlawful situation;
- impose a ban of the unlawful conduct;
- order to terminate the deficiencies and disparities exposed within the deadline, as well as to subsequently notify the Authority on the introduced measures;
- ban, restrict or impose conditions on the activity until the infringement is eliminated; or
- impose a consumer protection fine.

According to Article 92 of the Competition Act, the HCA may file an action to enforce civil law claims of consumers where the infringing activities concern a large group of consumers that can be defined based on the circumstances of the infringement. The HCA is empowered to file the action only where it has commenced competition supervision proceedings with respect to the infringement in question. No action may be filed after the end of 3 years following the date when the infringement was committed—regarding the time limit, the duration of the competition supervision proceedings shall not be taken into account. If the legal basis and content of the claim, as well as the amount of damages, can be clearly determined without considering the individual situation of the adversely affected consumers, the HCA may request the court to award such claims and order the business entity in question to satisfy these claims, or failing this, the HCA may request the court to establish by declaratory judgement that infringement occurred concerning all consumers indicated in the claim. If according to the court's decision the violation was established to affect all consumers indicated in the claim, the consumers may file charges against the business entity and are required to verify only the amount of damages and the fact that the damage is the direct result of such infringement. The court's decision shall specify the consumers who are affected by the violation, and therefore are entitled to demand compensation of damages based on the judgment, and shall determine the data required for their identification. In its ruling, the court may authorize the HCA to publish the court's decision in a national daily newspaper (at the expense of the infringer) or to make it available to the general public (by means consistent with the nature of the violation). If the court's decision, apart from having established the violation, also orders the business entity to provide satisfaction for a specific claim, the infringer shall be required to satisfy the claim of the consumer on whose behalf the judgment was awarded. If the consumer's claim is not satisfied voluntarily, the consumer may request judicial enforcement. The court shall probe the consumer's entitlement in its proceedings for the issue of an enforcement order.

Similar to the HCA, the NCPA[19] and the HFSA[20] are also entitled to file court actions for the enforcement of consumers' civil law claims where the infringing activities concerns a large group of consumers not individually identified, provided that the infringement of consumer protection laws have been established by the authority proceeding in the case. The enforcement of the claims of the HCA, NCPA and HFSA does not prejudice the right of consumers to take individual action by themselves against the infringers under the general provisions of civil law.

27.2.3.4 Setting of Monetary Fines

As it is the competence of Hungarian criminal courts to impose punishment for criminal acts, consequently, public authorities cannot impose imprisonment for the criminal breach of the above-identified legal provisions.

Nonetheless, if breaching the CSR policy leads to the infringement of the above-mentioned provisions,[21] local regulatory authorities may impose monetary fines.

NCPA: in the event of a violation of consumer protection regulations, the NCPA may impose a fine by resolution that may range between HUF 15,000 (EUR 50) and 5 % of the net sales revenue of the undertaking in the preceding business year. The fine may not exceed HUF 2 billion (EUR 6.5 million) for the most serious violations of the law (or if the infringement concerns the lives, health or physical integrity of a broad range of consumers or results in substantial financial injury to a broad range of consumers). In connection with setting the fine, the NCPA shall consider the circumstances of the case, with particular emphasis on the sphere and gravity of damages caused to consumers, the duration of the violation and repeated offense and the advantage gained by such violation. In case of mid-size and small undertakings, no fine can be imposed in case of first-time violation of consumer protection provisions,[22] unless the breach concerns a broad range of consumers.

HFSA: in the event of a violation of consumer protection laws by financial organizations, the HFSA may impose a fine between HUF 100,000 (EUR 300) and HUF 2 billion (EUR 6.5 million).[23] When determining the amount of the fine, the HFSA shall consider (1) the gravity of the infringement; (2) the effect of the

[19] See Article 38 of the Act CLV of 1997 on Consumer Protection.

[20] See Article 116 of the Act CLVII of 2010 on the HFSA.

[21] See Sect. 27.2.1.

[22] Article 12/A of the Act XXIV of 2004 on SME's.

[23] Article 62 (1) of the Act on the HFSA.

unlawful conduct on the market or safety of operation; (3) the effect on other market operators and clients; (4) the effects on other participants of the financial sector; (5) the risk perpetrated by the conduct, the amount of damages caused and voluntary restitution of the damages; (6) the cooperation of responsible persons of the infringer with the HFSA; (7) the good faith or bad faith of the person subject to the authority's measure and the material advantage obtained by them in connection with the conduct; (8) the concealment of information or the attempt thereof; and (9) repeated infringement.

HCA: according to Article 78 of the Competition Act, the proceeding Competition Council of the HCA may impose a fine on persons violating the provisions of the Act. The maximum fine shall not exceed ten percent of the net turnover, achieved in the business year preceding that in which the decision establishing the violation is reached; of the undertaking; or, where the undertaking is member of a group of undertakings that is identified in the decision, of that group of undertakings. The maximum fine imposed on social organizations of undertakings, public corporations, associations or other similar organizations shall not exceed ten percent of the total of the net turnover in the preceding business year of the member undertakings. The Competition Act also lays down the criteria to be taken into account by the proceeding competition council to determine the amount of the fine. It shall be established with respect to all circumstances of the case taken into account, in particular the gravity of the violation, the duration of the unlawful situation, the benefit gained by the infringement, the market positions of the parties violating the law, the imputability of the conduct, the effective cooperation by the undertaking during the preceding and the repeated display of unlawful conduct. The gravity of the violation shall be established, in particular, on the basis of the threat to economic competition and the range and the extent of harm to the interests of consumers and trading parties.

The HCA has published Notice No. 1/2007 on the method of setting fines in cases of unfair influence on consumer decisions.[24] The notice describes the basic principles of the practice of the HCA, summarizes past experience and outlines the practice to be followed in the future. In general, as a starting point, the HCA first refers to the advertising expenses of the undertaking and presumes that the company intended to realize a profit that exceeds its expenses. Second, the HCA examines the aggravating factors (effect on the market; the nature of the product (health care products); the intensity of the communication, including the scope of the consumers at which the advertising was directed, and the application of the complex communication campaign; the duration of the illegal conduct; the advantage gained by the illegal conduct; etc.) and the extenuating circumstances of the case (first proceedings launched; although the violation of competition law rules shall be established on the basis of objective criteria, professional diligence may decrease the degree of responsibility; cooperation with the HCA in the course of the investigation, provided that the scope of such cooperation exceeds the legal duty of

[24] The Notice is available at http://gvh.hu//data/cms1022256/jogihatter_magyarpiac_kozlemenyek_2007_1_fogybirsag_m.pdf, last visited on 15 June 2014.

the undertaking to provide information to the HCA). It shall be emphasized that the weight given to each of the above-mentioned factors is at the discretion of the HCA. Furthermore, the HCA also evaluates whether the amount of the fine shall have an appropriate deterrent effect, both for the undertaking under investigation and other market participants.

27.2.4 Causes of Action and Remedies Available to Private Entities

Although there is no relevant practice available in Hungary regarding the breach of CSR commitments, in theory, breaching CSR policies may be considered as violating the prohibition on unfair competition as set forth in the general clause of Article 2 of the Competition Act, which provides that "it is prohibited to conduct economic activities in an unfair manner and, in particular, in a manner which violates or jeopardizes the lawful interests of competitors, business partners and consumers, or in a way which is in conflict with the requirements of business integrity."

This general clause establishing the general prohibition on unfair competition in Section 2 is a so-called subsidiary provision. If the market practice subject to the litigation does not fall under any specific provisions (denigration and discrediting of competitors, passing off, acts infringing trade secret, prohibitions of calls to boycott and unfair influencing of a bidding process), it shall be evaluated under this subsidiary provision and Section 2 can be used as an independent legal ground.

The Competition Act does not define unfairness. Therefore, in the lack of a normative definition, it is the task of the judge to define the concept of "fairness" in light of the specific behaviors subject to the legal dispute. Fairness is interpreted as the prevalence of "good morals" among competitors. In the course of adjudicating whether a practice is fair, in particular social expectations, usages and standards will be decisive factors. However, the alleged unfairness must have an impact on competitors that is equal to the expressly named incidences. Causing confusion, discrediting a competitor and making false allegations about a product are pretty harmful practices, and in order for any commercial conduct to be prohibited directly under the general clause, it has to be equally serious and harmful to competitors.[25]

According to the court practice, if, for example, the competitor uses a product name that does not comply with the legal requirements for using such a name, this constitutes unfair market practice. The basis of the unfairness is that the infringing party gains a competitive advantage over his competitors who comply with legal rules, and he saves on the investment costs necessary for the production of goods complying with the legal requirements.[26]

---

[25] Gusztáv Bacher, Unfair Competition – Country report on Hungary, in: Henning-Bodewig (ed): International Handbook on Unfair Competition VERLAG C.H.BECK, 2013 (copublished by Hart Publishing and Nomos), 2013.

[26] BDT 2005.1087.

On the basis of the breach of the prohibition of unfair competition (Section 2 of the Competition Act), the injured party may demand:

(i) declaratory relief (the violation of the law to be established);
(ii) the cessation of the violation of the law and to enjoin the infringing party from any further violation of the law;
(iii) that the infringing party gives satisfaction (makes an apology) by making a statement or by another appropriate manner, and, if necessary, that sufficient publicity be given to the satisfaction (apology) on the part or at the expense of the party violating the law;
(iv) to terminate the infringement, the *restitution in integrum*, and to deprive the goods – manufactured or placed on the market through the violation of the law – of their offending character, or, if this is not possible, the destruction thereof, and the destruction of any special devices and facilities used for the manufacture thereof;
(v) compensation for damages in accordance with the rules of tort law, and
(vi) that the defendant disclose information about the parties participating in the manufacturing and marketing of the products involved in the case as well as information about the business relations it has established to distribute such products.

The court has also the competence to impose a fine.

As a general rule, pursuant to Section 156(1) of the Hungarian Civil Procedure Code,[27] a court may issue a preliminary injunction in order to (1) prevent imminent damage, (2) maintain the status quo during a legal dispute or (3) protect the claimant's rights requiring special protection. This stands as long as the burdens imposed by such a measure do not exceed the benefits that may be gained by it. The facts relating to the reasoning of the request for a preliminary injunction must be of a probable nature.

The civil law remedies that are not irreversible can be requested by way of interim relief.

Damages may be claimed if it can be proven that the aggrieved party suffered loss of business due to the action or omission of the other party, in other words there is a causal relationship between the damages and the infringing conduct (e.g., the claim that chocolate is sourced from Fair Trade farmers). This causal connection can arise out of an active conduct or passive omission and can be either direct or indirect.

The party causing the damages may be exempted from liability if it proves that the causing of damages was not illegal or that it acted in a way that can generally be expected under the given circumstances.

Under Hungarian law, it is the injured party only who is entitled to enforce its claim. The right to initiate an action cannot be assigned. Thus, any association of traders cannot start action on behalf of its members. It has *locus standi* only if the association is the injured party itself.

[27] Act No III of 1952 of the Civil Procedure Code.

Two or more claimants can initiate a joint action if any of the following applies:

- The subject matter of the claim is a joint right or obligation that can only be judged uniformly, or the judgment will affect the claimants jointly irrespective of one of the claimants' absence from the procedure.
- The claimants' claims are based on the same legal relationship.
- The claimants' claims have similar legal and factual bases, and the same court has jurisdiction for all defendants.

27.2.5 Right of Information

Private and public actors do not have power to obtain information directly from the businesses failing to meet CSR commitments. However, private and public concerns may submit a complaint or an informal complaint to the HCA or file an action before the court; moreover, consumer representative associations may initiate administrative procedure before NCPA or before HFSA, in which procedures the breach of CSR may be proved as follows.

HCA: the procedure before the HCA comprises two phases: (1) investigatory procedure, (2) competition supervision proceedings. Upon the complaint or the informal complaint, the investigator of the HCA shall have authority to obtain the data necessary for examination of the notification, to conduct a hearing of the parties concerned. If the party affected refuses to cooperate in this investigatory phase, no administrative penalty may be imposed, nor may any means of coercion be used. The documents of the case may not be inspected by the complainant. Upon the complaint or the informal complaint, the HCA may initiate a competition supervision proceeding *ex officio*; therefore, the complainant and the person making an informal complaint do not become parties, not even when the HCA initiates its proceeding based on the document that they submitted. During the competition supervision proceeding, the HCA has the possibility to use the investigative measures as follows: request for information, hearing of witnesses, access to documents, onsite inspection, seizure, sealing or the making of forensic images about the computer database. In this second phase, administrative penalty may be imposed if the affected business entity refuses to cooperate.

When no administrative proceeding is initiated by the HCA on the basis of the complaint, the complainant may turn to the Municipal Court of Budapest for legal remedy. In the course of court proceedings, the provisions of the Hungarian Civil Procedure Code[28] on administrative actions shall be applied. In the course of the lawsuit, the burden of proof shall lie upon the party claiming the infringement.[29] Means of proof shall, in particular, include testimonies, opinions of experts, inspections, documents and other physical evidence. The court may order to launch

[28] Chapter XX of the Civil Procedure Code.

[29] Article 88/B Section 7 of the Competition Act.

the inquiry within 30 days. Contrary to a case of formal complaint, if the HCA does not initiate any competition supervision proceeding, the person making the informal complaint may not turn to the court for legal remedy.

In case of misleading advertising, the procedure differs as follows: upon the complaint or informal complaint, the HCA may request the advertiser to furnish evidence as to the accuracy of factual claims in advertising. In the absence of compliance by the advertiser, factual claims shall be deemed not to be accurate.[30] The investigator does not have any choice; he shall issue an order opening an investigation in case the infringement is likely rendered.[31]

In cases involving unfair manipulation of consumer choice falling within the competence of the HCA, the procedure differs as follows: upon the complaint or informal complaint, the HCA may request the undertaking to produce evidence as to the accuracy of factual claims in relation to the commercial practice. In the absence of compliance by the undertaking, factual claims shall be considered to be inaccurate.[32] The investigator does not have any choice; he shall issue an order opening an investigation.[33]

NCPA: in cases involving unfair manipulation of consumer choices falling within the competence of the NCPA, under the Act on Consumer Protection,[34] consumer representative associations are entitled to initiate as well as to participate in the administrative proceedings as clients of the procedure, which position permits applications for evidence taking in the matter. The complaint of the consumer representative association shall be inquired in 30 days by NCPA. The following evidentiary measures may be used in NCPA's procedure: request for information, hearing of witnesses, access to documents and other physical evidences, seizure, inspection, and opinions of experts.

Court: consumer representative associations are entitled to file an action against the manipulative undertaking if several consumers are concerned.[35] In such court procedures, the general rules of the Act on the Code of Civil Procedure shall be applied. The burden of proof shall lie upon the party required to produce evidence, so mainly on the applicant. Means of proof shall, in particular, include testimonies, opinions of experts, inspections, documents and other physical evidence.

Regarding private actors, it is the injured party of the misleading advertising or the person adversely affected by the unfair manipulation of consumer choices who may file an action in court. In court proceedings, the burden of proving the accuracy of factual claims in advertising shall rest on the advertiser/undertaking.[36]

---

[30] Article 29 of the Act on Business Advertising.

[31] Article 30 Subsection 1 of the Act on Business Advertising.

[32] Article 14 of the UCP Act.

[33] Article 26 Subsection 1 of the UCP Act.

[34] Article 46 Subsection 2 a) of the Act on Consumer Protection.

[35] Article 39 of the Act on Consumer Protection.

[36] Article 15 Subsection 1–2 of the UCP Act and Article 24 Subsection 5 and Article 29 Subsection 2 of the Act on Business Advertising.

27.3 Local Practice and Consumer Expectations Relating to the Breach of CSR Commitments

There is no relevant practice available regarding the breach of CSR policies in Hungary. To the best knowledge of the Hungarian Group, no breach of CSR policies has been established, yet.

According to local surveys, Hungarian consumers show very little interest/concerns in consumer protection matters.[37] No relevant survey is available on consumer expectations relating to the breach of CSR commitments. The Hungarian Group believes that there is *no gap* in the relevant laws of Hungary.

27.4 Competition Restriction and CSR

27.4.1 Horizontal Cooperation Issues

One of the typical manifestations of CSR policies can be realized when (potential) competitors, operating on the same market level, act similarly or in the same way. It is generally stated that the relationship between actual or potential competitors may be commonplace and economically beneficial, and even necessary too. However, problems may arise in connection with the implementation of CSR measures if this potentially involves a cooperation between competitor undertakings that have as their object or potential or actual effect the prevention, restriction or distortion of competition, such as

- the direct or indirect fixing of prices or business terms and conditions;
- the limitation or control of production, distribution, technical development or investment;
- the allocation of sources of supply or the restriction of their choice, as well as the exclusion of a specified group of consumers from purchasing certain goods;
- the allocation of markets, exclusion from sales or restriction of the choice of marketing possibilities;
- the hindering of market entry;
- discriminatory practices; or
- making the conclusion of contracts subject to the acceptance of obligations, which, by their nature or according to commercial usage, do not belong to the subject of such contracts.

Cooperation between market participants might have significant achievements, including innovation, cost savings, risk sharing, improved product quality and

[37] Tudatos Vásárlók Egyesülete – Survey on Consumer Protection – May 2010 – http://tudatosvasarlo.hu/sites/tudatosvasarlo.hu/files/tve_fogyasztovedelmi_kutatas_2010.pdf, Survey on consumer protection problems in convergence regions (November 2009); see http://www.akontroll.hu/userfiles/file/dok/t-unio09_091209.pdf, last visited on 19 April 2013.

selection. There is a need that certain cooperation forms are excluded from the scope of the general prohibition of competition restriction, such as agreements that support the reasonable and harmonic economic development. Accordingly, the Competition Act provides under Article 17 that prohibition on agreements restricting or distorting the competition shall not apply to an agreement if it complies with all of the following requirements:

- it contains facilities to improve the efficiency of production or distribution, or to promote technical or economic development, or the improvement of means of environmental protection or competitiveness;
- a fair part of the benefits arising from the agreement is conveyed to the consumer or the business partner;
- the concomitant restriction or exclusion of economic competition does not exceed the extent required for attaining the economically justified common goals;
- it does not contain facilities for the exclusion of competition in connection with a considerable part of the goods concerned.[38]

The above general test is also applicable with regard to the adoption of CSR policies or CSR standards by competitors or associations/organizations of undertakings that operate with the participation of competitor undertakings. In its practice, the HCA, which is responsible for the enforcement of the prohibition of competition restrictive agreements, also considers the Communication of the European Commission on horizontal cooperation agreements,[39] which lists the main aspects of beneficial horizontal cooperations. The Hungarian group believes that CSR having a significant positive impact on the environment, consumers, employees or communities could potentially benefit from the exemption under Article 17 of the Competition Act if restrictions of competition are outweighed by such beneficial effects. The Hungarian Group notes that there is no relevant practice available on horizontal cooperation competition issues of CSR in Hungary.

27.4.2 Abuse of a Dominant Position

CSR policies might under certain circumstances also trigger liability under the general prohibition of abuse of a dominant position, which is prohibited by Section 21 of the Competition Act.

CSR undertakings might be linked to the use of a certification mark by undertakings. If the holder of such mark refuses to grant a license, this conduct might be considered as an abuse of a dominant (economic) position. The

[38] Article 17 of the Competition Act.

[39] COMMUNICATION FROM THE COMMISSION Guidelines on the applicability of Article 101 of the Treaty on the Functioning of the European Union to horizontal cooperation agreements (Text with EEA relevance) (2011/C 11/01).

Competition Act prohibits the abuse of a dominant position, which covers, in particular, the following conducts:

- refusing to establish or maintain business relations adequate for the nature of the transaction without any justification,
- hindering competitors from entering the market in any other unjust manner, or
- creating a market environment that is unreasonably disadvantageous for the competitors or influencing their business decisions for the purpose of gaining unjustified benefits.

However, the refusal to grant a license and limitations on the scope of license granted cannot be considered as in and of themselves *per se* infringements of competition law.[40] If we apply the doctrine of abuse of dominant position to intellectual property rights, we are in effect placing an external competition law limitation on the given rights.

There is no relevant practice available on abusive practices specifically relating to the CSR of undertakings having a dominant position of the relevant market.

27.4.3 CSR Standards Protected with IPRs

In practice, the companies adopting the CSR use a specific logo that indicates to the consumers compliance with the CSR Standard. This logo can be a registered trademark or, in particular, certification mark.

The Hungarian Trademark Act[41] provides that certification marks are trademarks that distinguish goods or services of specified quality or of other characteristics from other goods or services by attesting to such quality or characteristic (Article 101(1)). The holder himself may not use the certification mark for the purpose of certification; however, he shall authorize its use for such purpose with respect to the goods or services complying with the prescribed quality requirements or with other characteristics.

It shall be noted that Article 21 of the TRIPS Agreement sets forth that compulsory licenses may not be granted for trademarks. In respect of trademarks, we refer to the fact that there are numerous limitations on the trademark right holder's exclusive right of use, based on competition policy:

- use of indications of the characteristics of the goods or service;
- indicators for the proper use of the goods or service, particularly in the case of accessories or spare parts;
- use of the trademark in comparative advertising.

[40] Cf. CJEC, judgment of 5 October 1988, in case C-238/87, *AB Volvo v. Erik Veng* (E.C.R. 6211).

[41] Act XI of 1997 on the Protection of Trademarks and Geographical Indications.

We refer to the fact that LIDC has analyzed in detail the issue of compulsory access to IP and network facilities. Competition law limitations on intellectual property rights, under the heading of abuse of a dominant position, can only be allowed upon the existence of special circumstances in the cases of functional, industrial creations (software, nonunique original databases). Even in these cases, they can only be allowed if it can be proven that the subject of protection is an indispensable (essential) facility. The use of a logo cannot be considered as an essential facility.

27.5 Summary

In Hungary, CSR activities are generally conducted by top-tier and multinational companies, and it includes various range of programs and initiatives of undertakings mainly focusing on values outside business. CSR is part of the image communication of companies; therefore, such programs are eligible to influence the purchase decision of consumers. However, as a general rule, only those CSR might give rise to problems, which formulate specific commitments instead of more general mission statements of companies.

The Hungarian legal framework already addresses the issue of voluntary commitments by undertakings, as well as noncompliance with such commitments. Prosecution of breach of such commitments—depending on the material effect on competition or scope of activity of the undertaking—is delegated to three public authorities, including the Hungarian Competition Authority, the National Consumer Protection Authority, as well as the Hungarian Financial Supervisory Authority. Competitors could enforce the general clause on the prohibition of unfair competition before Hungarian courts, which may order injunction, award damages or, in principle, impose a fine if the unlawful conduct can been established. The burden of proof always lies on the publisher that its statement/commitment is true.

The Hungarian Group established that there is no legal gap regarding the relevant laws on CSR in Hungary since Hungarian law provides several causes of action/remedies in case of breach of CSR commitments, including damage claims. There is no relevant practice available in the Hungarian jurisdiction regarding the prosecution and breach of CSR commitments, as CSR policies did not give rise to any specific legal concerns in Hungary, yet.

Due to the growing importance of CSR in the context of commercial communications, the Hungarian Group recommends that CSR be treated as a commercial practice if it reflects specific commitments of undertakings. However, the Hungarian Group believes that there is no need to address the issues raised by CSR with *sui generis* legal regulations.

Italy

28

Linda Brugioni

28.1 CSR Policies Adopted by Italian Undertakings

The corporate social responsibility ("CSR") policies adopted by most Italian undertakings can be divided into two types.[1]

The first group deals with the internal dimension of CSR (focusing on benefits for employees and/or shareholders), which includes benefits and allowances for the human resources (such as facilities for employees, fiscal benefits/loans for employees, flexible working hours), projects for a higher standard of health and safety in the workplace compared to the compulsory legal requirements, and adoption of codes of conduct in order to increase transparency regarding activities of social interest performed by the undertaking dedicated to employees or shareholders.

The second group deals with the external dimension of CSR (focusing on benefits for suppliers and customers), which includes environmental protection, ethical control of the supply chain, and funding of nonprofit organizations.

Within this last group, a widely used code of conduct aimed at setting criteria for ensuring fair and nonmisleading advertising is the Commercial Communication Self-Disciplinary Code ("CAP").[2]

[1] UNIONCAMERE, Camere di Commercio di Italia, La responsabilità sociale delle imprese e gli orientamenti dei consumatori, 2006, p. 64, available at www.unioncamere.it.

[2] *Codice di Autodisciplina della Comunicazione Commerciale* ("CAP"). In particular, the first release of CAP dates back to 12 May 1966 and the last release, the 56th, was published on 31 December 2012. CAP is available at http://www.iap.it/it/codice.htm.

L. Brugioni (✉)
Bird & Bird, Milan, Italy
e-mail: linda.brugioni@twobirds.com; lindabrugioni@gmail.com

P. Kobel et al. (eds.), *Antitrust in the Groceries Sector & Liability Issues in Relation to Corporate Social Responsibility*, LIDC Contributions on Antitrust Law, Intellectual Property and Unfair Competition, DOI 10.1007/978-3-662-45753-5_28

The CSR policies involving the most delicate topics are sometimes distinguished by certification marks and/or included in schemes such as technical standards.[3]

28.2 Sanctions for Breaches of Voluntary Codes of Conduct Under Italian Law

28.2.1 The Implementation of Directive 2005/29/EC on Unfair Commercial Practices

Codes of conduct or CSR policies may be breached by the businesses adopting them as a result of several commercial practices (such as marketing, supply, and advertising).

Generally speaking, advertising can be considered as the practice most likely to give rise to litigation.

Italian undertakings mainly adopt codes of conduct as an additional commercial promotion method. In other words, the principal aim of a company adopting a code of conduct is to increase its appeal to the public since by means of codes of conduct, the company demonstrates its compliance with higher standards (in terms of product quality/ethical awareness) than the mandatory legal ones.[4]

Therefore, the communication of codes has been crucial for companies.

It is quite significant that the need to regulate advertising also led to one of the first voluntary codes of conduct and self-regulation successfully applied in Italy, the CAP, which provides a system of nonstatutory rules aimed at preventing and sanctioning misleading advertising.[5]

In addition to this "private" self-regulatory system, several pieces of legislation have been passed over the years to punish unlawful conduct performed by businesses through advertising.

However, no specific regulation has been drafted with the aim of punishing advertising in breach of a voluntary code of conduct.

---

[3] The best known are the Social Accountability 8000 standard (known also as SA 8000), which strikes a balance between employment law and human rights; ISO 14001 on environmental protection, issued by the International Organization of Standardization; and the GRI (Global Reporting Initiative) Guidelines on economic matters. On this point, see L. Bussoli, Responsabilità sociale, codici di condotta e pratiche commerciali sleali, in La responsabilità sociale dell'impresa: idee e prassi, a cura di Perulli A., 2013.

[4] P. Fabbio, I codici di condotta nella disciplina delle pratiche commerciali sleali, in Giurisprudenza Commerciale, Rivista trimestrale di diritto e procedura civile, July–August 2008, p. 726.

[5] Despite the voluntary nature of CAP, which is only binding on those entities that have accepted it, Italian case law states that its rules should be considered as parameters for evaluating the commercial fairness of practices performed by Italian undertakings. See Corte di Cassazione (Supreme Court), 15 February 1999, in Annali Italiani del Diritto d'Autore [AIDA], 1999, p. 407.

Nor has any specific legislation been drafted that sanctions other commercial practices, such as marketing, distribution, production, breaching codes of conduct.[6]

A specific mention of breaches of codes of conduct is made in Directive 2005/29/EC concerning business-to-consumer commercial practices in the internal market[7] (the "Directive").

The Directive concerns both unfair commercial practices and misleading advertising. The Directive was implemented in Italy by two legislative decrees.[8]

In particular, one of said decrees,[9] implementing the provision of the Directive on unfair practices, has been transposed within the Italian Consumer Code, specifically Articles 18–27-*quarter*. This latter rules deal with breaches of a code of conduct in more detail. Specific reference is made to Articles 21.2.b) and 23 of the Consumer Code.

Before examining possible violations and enforcement, the Consumer Code, in Article 18,[10] provides a definition of "code of conduct".

That definition states that a code of conduct can be either *i)* an agreement between undertakings, which could be adopted by other companies later, or *ii)* a set of rules unilaterally issued by an association of businesses or by a single business. In both situations, the code of conduct is adopted on a voluntary basis.[11]

With reference to the breach by a company of its own voluntarily adopted code of conduct (or CSR policy), Article 21.2.b) states the conditions upon which said breach could constitute a misleading practice: "Misleading practices are defined as practices which, having taken into account all the characteristics and factual circumstances, lead or are liable to lead the average consumer to take a commercial

[6] Other regulations mention codes of conduct, but they only highlight the importance of the role of voluntary codes of conduct in reducing the workload of the courts or helping businesses to demonstrate their compliance with legal standards. See, for instance, Directive 2000/31/EC on electronic commerce, implemented in Italy by the Legislative Decree of 9 April 2003, no. 70. However, no regulations that punish breaches of voluntary codes of conduct have been passed.

[7] Directive 2005/29/EC of the European Parliament and of the Council of 11 May 2005 concerning unfair business-to-consumer commercial practices in the internal market and amending Council Directive 84/450/EEC, Directives 97/7/EC, 98/27/EC and 2002/65/EC of the European Parliament and of the Council and Regulation (EC) No 2006/2004 of the European Parliament and of the Council ("Unfair Commercial Practices Directive"), OJ L 149, 11.6.2005, pp. 22–39.

[8] The first is the Legislative Decree of 2 August 2007, no. 145 on misleading and comparative advertising; the second Legislative Decree of 2 August 2007, no. 146 on unfair commercial practices, the latter transposed to the Italian Consumer Code, Articles 18–27-*quater* (Legislative Decree no. 206/2005, the "Consumer Code"). For a recent overview of this topic, see L. C. Ubertazzi, Le PCS ed il futuro dell'autodisciplina in Il Diritto Industriale [Dir. Ind.] 4/2010, p. 374.

[9] The Legislative Decree of 2 August 2007, no. 146 on unfair commercial practices.

[10] According to Article 18, paragraph 1.f) of the Consumer Code, a code of conduct is "an agreement or a set of rules which is not imposed by the law, regulations or administrative provisions of a Member State and which defines the conduct of the business that undertakes to comply with such code in relation to one or more commercial practices or one or more business sectors." Article 18 of the Consumer Code corresponds to Article 2.f) of Directive 2005/29/CE.

[11] G. de Cristofaro, A. Zaccaria, Commentario Breve al Diritto dei Consumatori, 2010, p. 125.

decision that he or she would have not taken otherwise and involve: . . . b) disregard by the business owner of a commitment included in a code of conduct which he or she has undertaken to comply with, if he or she did so in a firm and verifiable manner and if he or she indicated in a commercial practice that he or she is bound by it."

In other words, a breach of a code of conduct is considered to be an unfair practice (specifically, a misleading practice) only if the following conditions are fulfilled: *a)* the breach of the code of conduct is liable to lead the average consumer to take a commercial decision that s/he would not have taken otherwise, *b)* the commitment of the business to the code is "firm and verifiable," and *c)* the commitment was clearly indicated by the business in a commercial practice.

Therefore, the intention of the legislator is to sanction only breaches of a code of conduct that have an actual impact on consumers.[12]

In addition to the general provision contained in Article 21.2 of the Consumer Code, other misleading practices listed under Article 23.1 may be relevant. Although not specifically referring to breach of a code of conduct, they include the situation where a business claims the application of and commitment to a code of conduct in a misleading manner.

Reference is specifically made to the false statement by a business owner about the adoption of a code of conduct (para. a), the production of a quality or certification mark without the necessary authorization (para. b), and the false statement that a code of conduct has obtained the approval of a public body or other authority (para. c).

Legislative Decree no. 145/2007 on misleading advertising applies when advertising cannot be considered as a commercial practice aimed at promotion, sale, or supply to consumers (i.e., commercial practices included in the scope of the provisions of the Consumer Code relating to unfair commercial practices) but only relates to other competitors.[13]

No express reference to codes of conduct is made in this case.

[12] P. Fabbio, I codici di condotta nella disciplina delle pratiche commerciali sleali, in Giurisprudenza Commerciale, Rivista trimestrale di diritto e procedura civile, July–August 2008, p. 707. The legislator's decision to punish only conduct having the characteristics mentioned is designed to avoid discouraging business operators from adopting codes of conduct.

[13] Should the advertising also entail an unfair commercial practice under Article 21.2.b) of the Consumer Code (i.e., "lead[s] or is liable to lead the average consumer to take a commercial decision that he or she would have not taken otherwise"), the advertising could be sanctioned both by the terms of the Consumer Code governing unfair commercial practices and by Legislative Decree no. 145/2007 on misleading advertising. G. de Cristofaro, La disciplina 'generale' della pubblicità contenuta nel d. lgs. 2 agosto 2007, n. 145, in G. de Cristofaro, Pratiche commerciali scorrette e Codice del Consumo, 2008, p. 491.

28.2.2 Statutory Provisions Governing Unfair Competition

Finally, another set of rules, though not specifically focusing on breaches of codes of conduct, may apply, due to their broad general scope: the unfair competition rules contained in Article 2598 onwards of the Italian Civil Code.[14]

In particular, reference is made to Article 2598.3, which states that "without prejudice to the application of the rules for the protection of distinctive signs and patent rights, whoever ... 3) directly or indirectly uses any other means not compliant with the principles of professional fairness and liable to cause damage to another business performs acts of unfair competition."[15]

28.2.3 Parties Entitled to Take Proceedings for Breach of Codes of Conduct

The provisions sanctioning breach of a code of conduct are enforced differently, depending on whether the complainant relies on the rules governing unfair commercial practices included in the Consumer Code, the rules on misleading advertising (Legislative Decree no. 145/2007), or the unfair competition legislation.

Therefore, when examining which parties are entitled to take proceedings against a breach of codes of conduct, where appropriate, it will be stated which legislative provisions allow proceedings to be taken by respectively regulatory authorities, consumers, competitors, or suppliers of the business breaching its own code of conduct.

28.2.3.1 Proceedings Initiated by the Regulatory Authority, AGCM

The Italian Competition and Market Authority ("AGCM")[16] is the regulatory authority with power to rule, from a regulatory point of view, on claims relating to unfair commercial practices governed by the Consumer Code and claims relating to misleading advertising governed by Legislative Decree no. 145/2007.

AGCM holds broad powers, including the power to file *ex officio* proceedings against businesses performing unfair commercial practices and businesses performing misleading advertising.[17]

[14] L. Bussoli, Responsabilità sociale, codici di condotta e pratiche commerciali sleali, in La responsabilità sociale dell'impresa: idee e prassi, a cura di Perulli A., 2013, p. 172.

[15] G. de Cristofaro, La disciplina 'generale' della pubblicità contenuta nel d. lgs. 2 agosto 2007, n. 145, in G. de Cristofaro, Pratiche commerciali scorrette e Codice del Consumo, 2008, p. 172.

[16] *Autorità Garante della Concorrenza e del Mercato.*

[17] See Article 27 of the Consumer Code and Article 8 of Legislative Decree 145/2007.

28.2.3.2 Proceedings Initiated by Consumers

Unfair Commercial Practices Governed by the Consumer Code

With reference to breaches of a code of conduct entailing an unfair commercial practice under the Consumer Code, consumers may file proceedings before the administrative regulatory authority, i.e. the AGCM, or before the civil courts.

With reference to proceedings before the AGCM, Article 27 of the Consumer Code states that "any party or organization having an interest" can file a claim before the AGCM.

This implies that consumer associations[18] are among the parties entitled to start such proceedings.

Moreover, according to Article 27-*ter* of the Consumer Code, consumers have the option of starting proceedings before the AGCM or under the self-regulatory system of enforcement provided by the code of conduct, if any. In the system illustrated by the Directive,[19] enforcement under the self-regulatory system is suggested as preliminary to starting proceedings before the AGCM, in order to reinforce the role of codes of conduct and reduce the workload of the administrative authority. However, this suggestion has not been fully implemented in the Italian legislation since preliminary proceedings before the self-regulatory body are subject to the agreement of the parties (i.e., the consumer and the business involved), which is usually unlikely to be obtained.

In addition to proceedings before the AGCM, consumers can file proceedings in the civil courts.

In particular, consumer associations may seek relief entailing discontinuance of the unfair practice and an injunction to prevent the continuation of said practice and may also claim damages (in a class action pursuant to Article 140-*bis* of the Consumer Code).

It is debatable whether an individual consumer would actually be successful in filing an action before the civil courts (by filing an action in tort pursuant to Article 2043 of the Italian Civil Code), as it would be quite difficult to prove that the consumer has a concrete legal interest in obtaining an injunction and to prove the actual loss suffered.[20]

Breaches of Unfair Competition Rules

Article 27.15 of the Consumer Code expressly provides for proceedings to be filed in the "ordinary courts pursuant to Article 2598 of the Italian Civil Code..." in addition to proceedings based on the provisions of the Consumer Code.

[18] According to Article 27, paragraph 2, of the Consumer Code, "The Authority, ex officio or upon the request of any party or organization having an interest, may issue an injunction prohibiting the continuation of the unfair practice...."

[19] See Article 11, Directive 2005/29/EC. See also G. Floridia, Il coordinamento fra controllo autodisciplinare e controllo amministrativo delle pratiche sleali, in Dir. Ind. 2/2009, p. 175.

[20] A. Ciatti, "Gli strumenti di tutela individuale e collettiva," in G. de Cristofaro, Pratiche commerciali scorrette e Codice del Consumo, 2008, p. 422.

As mentioned, those rules sanction conduct that constitutes unfair competition.

Although, in principle, the application of the unfair competition rules is subject to the condition that a competition relationship must exist between the parties to the proceedings (and no such relationship obviously exists between the consumer and the business performing the unfair competition), some Authors[21] consider that consumers' associations can also file proceedings under Article 2598 of the Italian Civil Code.

Breaches Entailing Misleading Advertising

The terms of Legislative Decree no. 145/2007 relating to misleading advertising are specifically intended to protect competitors, not consumers, from misleading advertising.

Therefore, in principle, consumers are excluded from the application of these provisions.[22]

However, misleading advertising of a code of conduct that has the characteristics of an unfair commercial practice is punishable under the relevant provisions of the Consumer Code, as mentioned in the first paragraph of this section.[23]

28.2.3.3 Proceedings Initiated by Competitors

Unfair Commercial Practices Governed by the Consumer Code

With reference to competitors, some Authors state that competitors are not entitled to invoke the provisions of the Consumer Code concerning breach of codes of conduct (i.e., Articles 21 onwards) because those provisions are only intended to protect consumers.[24]

According to Article 21, breach of a code of conduct only constitutes a misleading practice if "it is liable to induce the average consumer to take a commercial decision s/he would not have taken if the breach had not occurred."

---

[21] P. Auteri, La disciplina della pubblicità, in Diritto Industriale, Proprietà Intellettuale e concorrenza, 2012, p. 404.

[22] G. de Cristofaro, La disciplina 'generale' della pubblicità contenuta nel d. lgs. 2 agosto 2007, n. 145, in G. de Cristofaro, Pratiche commerciali scorrette e Codice del Consumo, 2008, p. 516.

[23] See Sect. 28.2.3.2. Enforcement by consumers – Unfair Commercial Practices governed by the Consumer Code.

[24] L. Bussoli, Responsabilità sociale, codici di condotta e pratiche commerciali sleali, in La responsabilità sociale dell'impresa: idee e prassi, a cura di Perulli A., 2013, p. 175. According to this perspective, competitors are not entitled to enforce a breach of a code of conduct since the Directive provides two parallel systems, one intended to protect consumers and the other intended to protect competitors. Accordingly, the two systems are governed in Italy by two different Decrees and a parallel system, one for protecting consumers (i.e., the provisions relating to misleading practices contained in Legislative Decree no. 146/2007, included in the Consumer Code) and one for protecting competition and competitors on the market (i.e., the provisions on misleading advertising contained in Legislative Decree no. 145/2007). Thus, according to this interpretation, competitors are only entitled to protection according to the misleading advertising legislation and cannot file claims under the unfair practices legislation.

The focus on "consumers" would exclude competitors from taking proceedings under these provisions.

However, another interpretation[25] gives the provisions a broader scope and also allows competitors to take proceedings against breach of a code of conduct.

Article 27 states that "any party or organization having an interest" can seek enforcement against a misleading practice; there is no doubt that the breach of a code of conduct liable to divert the commercial decisions of consumers has an adverse impact on competition and on business competitors, thus entitling them to start proceedings before the AGCM.

Breaches of Unfair Competition Rules

With reference to enforcement according to the unfair competition rules, especially those relating to acts of unfair competition (Article 2598 no. 3 of the Italian Civil Code), competitors can file proceedings in the civil courts if the necessary conditions are fulfilled (such as the existence of a competition relationship between the parties, the existence of an act of unfair competition, and the ability of such act to harm the competitor's business).

Breaches Entailing Misleading Advertising

Should the breach of the code of conduct be performed through advertising, competitors can either start proceedings before the AGCM or file a claim in the civil courts.

28.2.3.4 Proceedings Initiated by Suppliers

Unfair Commercial Practices Governed by the Consumer Code

Suppliers, purchasers, or other businesses not directly competing with the business performing the unlawful activity may start proceedings before the AGCM under the terms of the Consumer Code governing misleading practices, claiming breach of Article 21 and 23. As already stated in the case of competitors, "any party or organization having an interest therein" may start proceedings before the AGCM.

Breaches of Unfair Competition Rules

With specific reference to the unfair competition rules, the condition that a competition relationship must exist between the parties also applies where the businesses do not operate at the same level, e.g., supplier versus producer. A competition relationship would exist anyway since "the end result of the activities of both undertakings will concern the same group of consumers, thus the actions performed by one would poach customers attracted to the products of the other business."[26]

---

[25] P. Auteri, La disciplina della pubblicità, in Diritto Industriale, Proprietà Intellettuale e concorrenza, 2012, p. 384 onwards, in particular p. 403.

[26] A. Vanzetti, Manuale di Diritto Industriale, 2009, p. 16.

Therefore, suppliers are also entitled to start proceedings against the undertaking breaching its own code of conduct pursuant to Article 2598 of the Italian Civil Code.

Breaches Entailing Misleading Advertising
Suppliers may also start proceedings according to the rules on misleading advertising, both before the AGCM and before the civil courts. As this system is designed to protect the interests of businesses (not consumers), it can be assumed that other entities in the supply chain of the breaching business in question are also included in the said definition.

28.2.4 Causes of Action and Remedies Available to the AGCM

As stated, according to Article 27 of the Consumer Code, the AGCM can start *ex officio* proceedings against a business performing a misleading practice, such as breach by said business of a voluntarily adopted code of conduct, according to Articles 21.2.b) and 23 of the Consumer Code.

The causes of action on which the AGCM can rely are that the practice violating the code is liable to lead the consumer to make a decision that he or she would not have taken if the misleading practice had not occurred, the business has made a firm and verifiable commitment on the adoption of the code, and, finally, the business has indicated in a commercial practice that it is bound by the code.

Other causes of action are those set out in Article 23.1.a), b), c) of the Consumer Code, included in the "blacklist" of misleading practices (see Sect. 28.2.1. above).

The remedies that can be granted by the AGCM are an injunction and an order reestablishing the situation prior to the misleading practice (Article 27.2), which can be preceded by suspension of the misleading practice in urgent cases.

Moreover, AGCM can order the publication of the decision in the press or a declaration aimed at preventing the further spread of the effects of the misleading practice (Article 27.8).

If the unfair commercial practice is not considered very serious, AGCM can request a formal undertaking from the business to stop the misleading practice or to remedy the effects of the misleading practice (Article 27.7).

Finally, together with the inhibitory order, AGCM can impose fines ranging from EUR 5,000 to EUR 500,000.00. The applicable fine, in principle, depends on the seriousness and duration of the breach.[27]

The same remedies and range of fines are available to the AGCM in relation to misleading advertising according to Legislative Decree no. 145/2007.[28]

[27] For the criteria applying to the fines imposed by the AGCM, see AGCM decision of 21 August 2009, no. 18782, in Dir. Ind. 2009, p. 378.

[28] Article 8, Legislative Decree 145/2007.

28.2.5 Causes of Action and Remedies Available to Private Undertakings

As mentioned above, private undertakings, such as competitors, are also entitled to take proceedings against misleading practices performed by another business in breach of its code of conduct.

In proceedings before the AGCM,[29] competitors can rely on the same causes of action and request the same remedies as granted *ex officio* by AGCM.[30]

Therefore, the competitor is entitled to obtain an injunction prohibiting the misleading practice and publication of the order and to request the regulatory authority to impose a fine.

Private undertakings are also entitled to claim the remedies provided for by Article 2598 of the Italian Civil Code on unfair competition if they can prove a competition relationship with the business to which the proceedings relate and that the breach entails a violation of the principles of fair competition according to Article 2598.3 of the Italian Civil Code.

The remedies available under the Italian Civil Code are the injunction referred to in Article 2599 of the Italian Civil Code,[31] damages, and publication of the decision pursuant to Article 2600 of the Italian Civil Code.[32]

28.2.5.1 Damages and Criteria for Their Calculation

With specific reference to damages, the requirements for obtaining monetary compensation are (1) subjective, i.e. intentional or negligent harm to one business by another (although in the case of negligence, an assumption operates: a ruling of unfair conduct implies negligence, and the victim is not bound by the very difficult burden of proof), and (2) objective, i.e. the existence of actual unlawful harmful conduct (and not just the likelihood of prejudice[33]) and its causal link to the loss suffered by the complainant.

Calculation of the compensation is not straightforward, due to the difficulty of effectively establishing the extent to which the effects of the unfair competition have spread.

---

[29] As mentioned, said procedure applies both to breach of Articles 21 onwards concerning unfair practices and to misleading advertising according to Legislative Decree 145/2007. The proceedings before the AGCM and the corresponding remedies are described in Article 27 of the Consumer Code on unfair commercial practices and Article 8 of the Legislative Decree 145/2007 on misleading advertising.

[30] See Sect. 28.2.4.

[31] Article 2599 states that "the decision ascertaining the acts of unfair competition will include an injunction preventing their continuation and additional measures designed to eliminate their effects."

[32] Article 2600 states that "if the acts of unfair competition are performed wilfully or negligently, the party who committed them is liable for damages. In such case, the court may order publication of the decision. Having ascertained the acts of unfair competition, negligence is assumed."

[33] A. Vanzetti, Manuale di Diritto Industriale, 2009, p. 129.

In principle, damages include both actual loss and potential loss suffered by the complainant.

Actual loss is easier to calculate; it usually includes the cost of the advertising required to counteract the effects of the unfair competition.

Potential loss, which is more difficult to calculate, generally corresponds to the net profits lost by the complainant, which can be causally linked to the conduct in dispute. In practice, it is often calculated as the profit earned by the defendant, which is usually easier to establish on the basis of its profit and loss account from its books of account.[34]

The difficulty of proving the exact amount of the loss could be overcome by asking the court to calculate an equitable sum as damages on the basis of the evidence produced and the legal arguments, which can be inferred from the pleadings submitted to the court.

28.2.5.2 The *Locus Standi* of Collective Organizations of Suppliers

Collective organizations of suppliers enacting a CSR policy may also file proceedings against a business breaching the CSR policy it has voluntarily adopted.

Foremost, they can start proceedings before the AGCM according to Article 27 of the Consumer Code since, as already stated, anyone having an "interest" is entitled to start proceedings.

As indicated, if such kind of action is filed, injunction can be obtained but not damages.[35]

With reference to the unfair competition regulation, there has been a great deal of discussion as to whether organizations of suppliers (or business associations in general) are entitled to take proceedings against a producer performing acts of unfair competition (constituted, in the present case, by the breach of the CSR policy by said businesses).

The legal framework is based on Article 2601 of the Italian Civil Code, which states that "when unfair competition prejudices the interests of a category of businesses, unfair competition proceedings can be taken by associations of businesses and by the bodies representing them."

Although the majority of the legal literature[36] recognizes the *locus standi* of organizations of businesses to claim unfair competition pursuant to Article 2601 of the Italian Civil Code, courts in a number of decisions have been quite reluctant to recognize the *locus standi* of said collective organizations.

---

[34] A. Vanzetti, Manuale di Diritto Industriale, 2009, p. 130.

[35] Article 27 of the Consumer Code protects the public interest by defending consumers against misleading practices and upholding fair competition on the market. The remedy of damages is linked to the regulation of unfair competition aimed at protecting private interests. G. de Cristofaro, Commentario Breve al Diritto dei Consumatori, 2010, comment on Article 27, p. 220.

[36] See, for example, A. Vanzetti, Manuale di Diritto Industriale, 2009, pp. 20–22, G. Ghidini, Della concorrenza sleale, in Il Codice Civile – Commentario diretto da Piero Schlesinger, p. 453, L.C. Ubertazzi, Commentario breve alle leggi su proprietà intellettuale e concorrenza, 2012, p. 1234.

In particular, the *locus standi* of organizations of businesses to take proceedings for unfair competition has been denied on the ground that the organization lacks a commercial purpose.[37] This, in particular, was claimed against the body regulating the use of a collective trademark used by a number of businesses.[38]

In another fairly old decision, the Supreme Court denied the *locus standi* of an association of retailers because, instead of claiming breach of a specific collective interest protected by the association, it claimed breach of the general principles of commercial fairness. Breach of commercial fairness can certainly be claimed in a business-to-business claim, but an association of businesses should, instead, claim the protection of the specific collective interest it is intended to represent.[39]

On the other hand, several decisions have clearly affirmed the *locus standi* of associations of businesses to claim unfair competition. In some of them, *locus standi* is taken for granted,[40] whereas in some others, it was expressly confirmed,[41] even in connection with foreign associations of businesses.[42]

28.2.5.3 The Connection Between the Unfair Commercial Practice and the Product Supplied: Actions and Remedies in Context

As we shall discuss in the next section, within the Italian system, the enforcement of CSR policies or voluntary codes of conduct is not considered to be of great importance by either private undertakings or consumers. The legislative system, though suggesting the importance of codes of conduct, neither effectively

---

[37] The doubt, also discussed by A. Vanzetti, Manuale di Diritto Industriale, 2009, p. 21, is whether Article 2601 of the Italian Civil Code entails a different type of unfair competition from those concerning conflicts between single undertakings referred to in Article 2598. One interpretation states that Article 2601 of the Civil Code merely allows an organization to bring a single action to protect an interest shared by many producers, instead of having to file many single actions relating to the same violation. Therefore, the organization would act as a sort of representative of the producers. Another interpretation considers the organization as having its own interest, corresponding to the collective interest of the members. According to this second interpretation, the organization is entitled to claim damages only for the violation of its own interest.

[38] Corte di Cassazione (Supreme Court), 29 August 1995, no. 9073 in Giurisprudenza Annotata di Diritto Industriale [GADI] 1995, p. 202. Similarly, Court of Appeal of Milan, 8 May 1992, in GADI 1992, p. 617.

[39] Corte di Cassazione (Supreme Court), 20 December 1996, no. 11404 in GADI 1996, p. 19.

[40] Court of Appeal of Bologna, 26 May 1994, in GADI 1994, p. 752, where the *locus standi* of the Prosciutto di Parma Consortium, which does not produce the product but performs supervisory activities relating (*inter alia*) to the correct use of the geographical indication and the collective trademarks managed by it, was taken for granted both by the counterparty and by the Court.

[41] Court of Milan, 5 May 2005 in GADI 2005, p. 895; Court of Appeal of Milan, 30 June 1999, in Dir. Ind. 2000, 2, p. 141.

[42] The *locus standi* of foreign associations is specifically contemplated by Article 10-*ter*/2 of the Paris Convention. Principle confirmed by the case law: Corte di Cassazione (Supreme Court), 15 November 1984, n. 5772, in GADI 1984, p. 80. See also L.C. Ubertazzi, Commentario breve alle leggi su proprietà intellettuale e concorrenza, 2012, p. 2135, A. Vanzetti, Manuale di Diritto Industriale, 2009, p. 22.

emphasizes their role nor provides for a system of transparency regarding breaches of codes of conduct by businesses that have adopted such codes.[43]

As a consequence, specific case law on the topic is not available in the Italian system, and thus it is not easy to determine how close the connection between the unfair practice breaching the CSR policy and the relevant product or service produced or rendered by the breaching business should be, for another business to be entitled to file suit.

In order to provide some elements for evaluation, the following three scenarios will be considered:

(i) *Action taken by a coffee producer against a competing coffee producer marketing its coffee under a Fair Trade logo or label, although the coffee is not sourced from Fair Trade coffee makers*

In this scenario, the competing business could claim misuse of the Fair Trade logo as a misleading practice[44] according to the Consumer Code (if the conditions laid down by Article 21 and/or Article 23.a) or b) are fulfilled) and would thus be entitled to file a claim before the AGCM. However, as already discussed, in proceedings before the AGCM, the complainant is not entitled to claim damages and s/he is entitled only to obtain an injunction.

Further remedies, such as damages, would be available according to the unfair competition legislation for breach of the principles of commercial fairness under Article 2598.3 of the Italian Civil Code. In particular, the competing business would need to prove that the misuse of the Fair Trade logo constitutes a breach of the principles of commercial fairness.

It may be claimed that since trademarks, and especially collective marks and certification marks (which usually function as a badge of origin from a specific geographical area or a product quality indicator[45]), such as a Fair

---

[43] P. Morara, F. Vella, I codici etici: dalla teoria all'esperienza concreta, in Fondazione Unipolis (a cura di), Governance e responsabilità sociale. Analisi sull'applicazione dei codici etici in Italia, in "I quaderni di Unipolis," 1, 2009, p. 51.

[44] See, for instance, the terms of Article 21.1.c) of the Consumer Code, which defines as misleading practice "a practice containing information which is false or otherwise liable to induce the consumer to a take a commercial decision that he or she would not have taken otherwise, on the basis of: . . . c) the extent of the business's commitment, the reasons for the commercial practice and the nature of the sale process, any declaration or sign relating to the promotion or direct or indirect approval of the business or product." In particular, AGCM has already considered as misleading communication the misuse of expressions such as "environment-friendly" or "100% disposable" and the related marks on the packaging of products (AGCM decision, 11/01/2006, no. 15104, in Giustizia Civile, 2006, 6, p. 1371).

[45] Article 11 of the Italian Intellectual Property Code (Legislative Decree of 10 February 2005, no. 30) contains an express exemption to the prohibition on registering a trademark consisting of an indication of the "quality" or "geographical origin" of the product it distinguishes. This kind of trademark, more than noncollective trademarks, has the function of communicating a message to the public (e.g., the quality/geographical origin of the product concerned). G. Sena, Il Diritto dei Marchi, 2007, p. 47.

Trade logo, convey a message to the public,[46] the misuse of a mark could be equivalent to misleading and false advertising, considered as a breach of the principles of commercial fairness punished by Article 2598.3 of the Italian Civil Code.[47]

However, in order to claim successfully that misuse of the Fair Trade logo actually constitutes a breach of the principles of commercial fairness and unfair competition, the competing business would need to prove that the misuse of the Fair Trade logo would lead to specific prejudice to its commercial activity. In other words, the competing business would not be entitled to take unfair competition proceedings if the misuse of the Fair Trade logo, though contrary to the general principle of commercial fairness, does not affect its own activity in any manner.[48]

The case law has already established that the competitor may be successful if it also uses the Fair Trade logo and complies with the relevant CSR policy. In such a scenario, the competing business would be successful in claiming under Article 2598.3 for breach of the principles of commercial fairness and Article 2598.2[49] for passing off, as the specific prejudice to its business is straightforward.

As regards remedies, those mentioned in Sect. 28.2.5 apply to proceedings taken by private entities.

(ii) *Action taken by a coffee producer against a competing coffee producer advertising that 2% of its sales and revenues are donated to charity, although an audit demonstrates noncompliance with the said policy*

The arguments and remedies (in particular, damages) indicated in the previous scenario may also apply to this scenario since the unlawful practice would entail misleading advertising. As a consequence, the competitor that can prove it was affected by the misleading advertising could seek said remedies, including damages pursuant to Article 2600 of the Italian Civil Code.

(iii) *Action taken by a coffee producer against a competing coffee producer importing coffee using ships emitting carbon dioxide in excess of the amount allowed by its CSR policy*

The likelihood that a competing business will obtain relief in this scenario would depend on whether the coffee maker made its CSR policy available to the public and the market (i.e., "advertised" it). Should this be the case, the

[46] G. Sena, Il Diritto dei Marchi, 2007, p. 51.

[47] Court of Modena, 11 March 2010 in GADI 2010, p. 481, which states that marketing of products bearing a mark indicated in an ISO technical standard but not compliant with said standard constitutes unfair competition, as well as misleading advertising. For a similar ruling, see Court of Brescia, 2 December 2008, in GADI 2010, p. 88.

[48] G. Ghidini, Della concorrenza sleale, in Il Codice Civile – Commentario diretto da Piero Schlesinger, p. 294.

[49] Article 2598, no. 2 of the Civil Code states that "any party that . . . passes off its own products and business activity as those of a competitor" commits unfair competition.

above reasoning would also apply in this case if the competing business successfully proves that the breach of the CSR policy would constitute an act of unfair competition liable to harm its business.

28.2.6 Powers of Private or Public Entities Relating to Information Disclosure

AGCM, when starting proceedings *ex officio*, or other private entities (e.g., competitors, consumers' associations, or associations of other businesses or suppliers), upon request to AGCM, can ask for information about the compliance of a business with its own code of conduct (or CSR policy) in order to establish whether a breach thereof has occurred. Such a request can be addressed to undertakings, bodies, or parties holding said information.[50] Such a request can also be addressed to the business involved in the proceedings, which is required to provide evidence about the correctness of the factual circumstances relating to the unfair practice.

28.3 Breaches of Codes of Conduct: The Approach of the Italian Legislator and the Perception of Italian Businesses and Consumers

28.3.1 An Assessment of the Activity of the Italian Legislator Relating to Punishment of Breaches of Codes of Conduct

As already stated, the legislative framework most specifically relating to breaches of codes of conduct by the business that voluntarily adopted them is mainly based on the implementation of the Directive within the Italian system, as well as the general legislation governing unfair competition.

Article 11 of the Directive sets out general principles and guidelines on combating unfair practices (including breach of voluntary codes of conduct). In particular, it requires that *a)* it is possible to take legal action against those practices, *b)* actions can be brought before an administrative authority provided with the powers of deciding complaints and taking action, *c)* the authority can require the discontinuance of the disputed practice or the prohibition of imminent practices, *d)* the authority may order publication of the decision and/or a corrective statement issued by the breaching entity.

By comparing the text of the Directive and the relevant Article of the Consumer Code (Article 27), it appears reasonable to state that the scope of the Directive has been implemented.

[50] According to Article 27.3 of the Consumer Code and Article 8.2 of Legislative Decree 145/2007 on misleading advertising.

Within said framework, it is indeed possible for the regulatory authority and/or other entities having an interest therein to stop the breach/prohibit imminent breaches and to require publication of the decision, thus making breach of a code of conduct highly inadvisable for the business that adopted it.

Moreover, enforcement is accompanied by a set of quite heavy fines that would oblige the business to "think twice" before breaching its own voluntary code of conduct.

However, in practice, the enforcement of codes of conduct is quite problematic.

A first concern relates to the fact that enforcement by the AGCM may not be very effective due to the workload of the Authority.[51]

A second issue concerns the fact that the Italian legislation does not provide for effective coordination between the activity of the AGCM (or the civil courts) and the self-regulatory enforcement system provided by codes of conduct.

In fact, the Italian legislation does not fully implement the suggestion included in the Directive that preliminary proceedings under the self-regulatory enforcement system should be compulsory before the AGCM is called in. This has tended to undermine confidence in codes of conduct and their implementation by the businesses adopting them.

This circumstance has been criticized by some Authors,[52] with specific reference to the CAP. As already stated, this code of conduct has been established within the Italian system for years and has been recognized by businesses and institutions alike as an authoritative self-regulatory system. Therefore, the suggestion contained in the Directive that prior proceedings before the self-regulatory body should be mandatory was seen as a good opportunity to enhance the role of codes of conduct (especially CAP) and reduce the workload of the regulatory authority. However, this expectation was frustrated: the Italian legislator only allows prior proceedings under the self-regulatory system if the parties agree and only allows the suspension of the corresponding proceedings already started before the AGCM if the regulatory authority, "having evaluated all the circumstances," deems it opportune to do so.

This has tended to undermine confidence in codes of conduct (especially those that do not have such a long-standing reputation as CAP) and their implementation by the businesses adopting them.

The decision not to give codes of conduct, and their internal enforcement system, the importance and relevance set out in the Directive (as indicated in Article 10) is probably due to the fact that self-regulatory enforcement systems

---

[51] According to G. de Cristofaro, L'attuazione della direttiva 2005/29/CE nell'ordinamento italiano: profili generali, in G. de Cristofaro, Pratiche commerciali scorrette e Codice del Consumo, 2008, p. 86, the legislative decision to indicate the AGCM as the sole regulatory authority to impose fines for unfair commercial practices could indeed paralyze the activity of the AGCM if it receives a huge number of requests for intervention against unfair commercial practices.

[52] G. Floridia, Il coordinamento fra controllo autodisciplinare e controllo amministrativo delle pratiche sleali, in Dir. Ind. 2/2009, p. 175.

(apart from CAP) are still not efficiently organized in Italy and are not sufficiently trustworthy in terms of implementation of sanctions.[53]

Finally, from a different point of view, it should be noted that Italian businesses have recently been compelled to adopt codes of conduct following the entry into force of Legislative Decree no. 231/2001 concerning the administrative liability of enterprises. The provisions of said Decree state that in the event of compliance with codes of conduct (which Article 6 of the Decree defines as "modelli organizzativi"—organization models) by the business adopting them, it will be presumed that the business (and its executives) is not liable for the criminal and administrative offenses to which the Decree relates.

However, the aim of said codes of conduct (the nature of which is basically mandatory) seems to imply that, for the time being, only mandatory codes of conduct deserve proper enforcement in the event of breaches, whereas breaches of voluntary codes of conduct, which in theory convey the philosophy and ethical principles of a business, are not deemed particularly important, either by consumers or the legislator.[54]

28.3.2 The Attitude of Consumers and the Business Environment to Noncompliance with Codes of Conduct

The Italian business community represented by the Association of Chambers of Commerce recently conducted research into the perceptions of CSR policies among the public and businesses.

The outcome of the research is that CSR policies are reasonably well known to Italian consumers and businesses.[55]

However, awareness relating to breaches of a code of conduct and CSR policy is still not very high, with the exception of a few isolated activities.[56]

---

[53] L. Bussoli, Responsabilità sociale, codici di condotta e pratiche commerciali sleali, in La responsabilità sociale dell'impresa: idee e prassi, a cura di Perulli A., 2013, p. 163. Similarly, P. Morara, F. Vella, I codici etici: dalla teoria all'esperienza concreta, in Fondazione Unipolis (a cura di), Governance e responsabilità sociale. Analisi sull'applicazione dei codici etici in Italia, in "I quaderni di Unipolis," 1, 2009, p. 53.

[54] P. Morara, F. Vella, I codici etici: dalla teoria all'esperienza concreta, in Fondazione Unipolis (a cura di), Governance e responsabilità sociale. Analisi sull'applicazione dei codici etici in Italia, in "I quaderni di Unipolis," 1, 2009, p. 51.

[55] UNIONCAMERE, Camere di Commercio di Italia, La responsabilità sociale delle imprese e gli orientamenti dei consumatori, 2006, p. 179 onward, available on www.unioncamere.it, where it is stated that consumers are well aware of policies such as social accountability and environmental accountability. Awareness is higher when the policy is accompanied by certification, such as SA 8000.

[56] Such as the "Clean Clothes Campaign" ("*Campagna Abiti Puliti*") and the "Businesses on Trial" ("*Imprese alla Sbarra*") project. Source: http://www.unimondo.org/Guide/Politica/Codici-di-condotta/(desc)/show.

In particular, it is believed that breach of a code of conduct still does not influence the commercial decisions of consumers.[57] This is probably due to the fact that consumers are still quite sceptical about CSR policies; in other words, they believe that an undertaking only uses a code of conduct as an advertising tool, and the statements it contains are therefore not to be taken very seriously.

This perception is probably strengthened by the fact that little information is published by the press or institutions about breaches of codes of conduct.

For instance, the Ministry of Economic Development, after an initial rush of enthusiasm for codes of conduct, resulting in a dedicated page on its website with the aim of publishing information about the codes of conduct adopted by undertakings and breaches thereof, eventually did not include such information.[58]

28.3.3 Difficulty of the Italian Legislation in Enhancing the Role of Codes of Conduct and Ensuring Their Enforcement

Consumers still do not trust the correct implementation of codes of conduct by businesses, and the Italian legislator appears to share their mistrust.

According to some opinions,[59] the Italian legislator prefers to impose heavy fines for breach of codes of conduct (such as those imposed by Article 27 of the Consumer Code and Article 8 of Legislative Decree no. 145/2007), instead of leaving more room for the creation of a self-enforcement system that could gain more trust from businesses and consumers and could effectively reduce the workload of the administrative and civil authorities.

Another failure of the Italian legislation is the lack of coordination of enforcement of codes of conduct between the AGCM and the civil courts. Proceedings before the AGCM are certainly an important tool, but, for instance, they cannot grant damages.

In order to obtain damages, it is necessary to start an action before the civil courts, which apply the general principles of civil law. Such general principles, in situations like breaches of codes of conduct, place a heavy burden of proof on consumers or competitors in order to obtain damages (such as proving that the defendant willfully/negligently prejudiced the consumer/competitor and that there

---

[57] L. Bussoli, Responsabilità sociale, codici di condotta e pratiche commerciali sleali, in La responsabilità sociale dell'impresa: idee e prassi, a cura di Perulli A., 2013, p. 163. P. Fabbio, I codici di condotta nella disciplina delle pratiche commerciali sleali, in Giurisprudenza Commerciale, Rivista trimestrale di diritto e procedura civile, July–August 2008, p. 730.

[58] L. Bussoli, Responsabilità sociale, codici di condotta e pratiche commerciali sleali, in La responsabilità sociale dell'impresa: idee e prassi, a cura di Perulli A., 2013, pp. 175–176. See also F. Ghezzi, Codici di condotta, autodisciplina, pratiche commerciali scorrette. Un rapporto difficile, in Rivista delle Società, 2010, n. 4, p. 680.

[59] G. Floridia, Il coordinamento fra controllo autodisciplinare e controllo amministrativo delle pratiche sleali, in Dir. Ind. 2/2009, p. 175.

was a causal connection between the breach and the prejudice to the consumer/competitor).[60]

28.3.4 Possible Amendments to the Legislation

In the light of the above factors, possible changes in the legislation could be, according to substantive law, the start of an action under the private enforcement system prior to the action filed before the AGCM and/or the civil courts.

Some Authors[61] criticized the strong powers given to AGCM to punish unfair practices, which deprives the self-enforcement system under codes of conduct of any independence and of a "proper" role. In other words, breaches of voluntarily adopted policies would be better dealt with on a private basis, under the rules laid down in the codes of conduct.

With specific reference to remedies, amendments could be made in order to make it easier for consumers (both individually and jointly as consumer associations) to obtain damages for breach of codes of conduct by businesses. Amendments should also include methods of terminating agreements that consumers entered into because they were misled by the "false promises" of businesses declaring (but not complying with) their CSR commitments.[62]

28.3.5 Monitoring by Consumers and the AGCM of Compliance by Businesses with Their Own CSR Policies. The Broad Powers of the AGCM

In proceedings before the AGCM (which can be started either *ex officio* or on request by consumers or other entities), the authority has wide powers of investigation.

As mentioned, under Article 27 of the Consumer Code, AGCM can request information from third parties that may be aware of the existence and extent of a breach.

The AGCM can access the premises of the business investigated and call on the assistance of the Finance Police (*Guardia di Finanza*).[63]

---

[60] See the comment on this point by G. de Cristofaro, L'attuazione della direttiva 2005/29/CE nell'ordinamento italiano: profili generali, in G. de Cristofaro, Pratiche commerciali scorrette e Codice del Consumo, 2008, p. 92.

[61] G. Floridia, Il coordinamento fra controllo autodisciplinare e controllo amministrativo delle pratiche sleali, in Dir. Ind. 2/2009, p. 175. L.C. Ubertazzi, Le PCS ed il futuro dell'autodisciplina, in Dir. Ind. 4/2010, p. 374.

[62] G. de Cristofaro, L'attuazione della direttiva 2005/29/CE nell'ordinamento italiano: profili generali, in G. de Cristofaro, Pratiche commerciali scorrette e Codice del Consumo, 2008, p. 91.

[63] Article 27.2 of the Consumer Code.

In the civil courts, the powers of consumers to obtain information about the existence and extent of the breach would be limited, and would depend on an assessment on a case-by-case basis, mainly aimed at verifying the actual, specific legal interest of the consumer in obtaining such information.[64]

28.4 Conflict Between Codes of Conduct and Competition Law

Codes of conduct adopted by several undertakings inevitably coordinate the conduct of said undertakings on the market and lead to a modification in competition.

Therefore, in principle, codes of conduct may be considered as an agreement between undertakings relevant to competition law.[65]

In these respects, the Italian legal literature has considered the possible conflicts between the competition law and the CAP code of conduct.

Several Authors agree that CAP constitutes an agreement liable to affect competition.[66]

However, they consider CAP to be one of the agreements or agreed practices that would not raise concerns under competition law since it "allows consumers a fair share of the resulting benefit,"[67] in other words, since it pursues an interest that the system considers worth protecting.

The above statement is confirmed by the fact that the case law[68] considers CAP as a tool for providing guidance on the interpretation of the fairness principle under the unfair competition legislation, which is useful to establish whether a breach of the principles of commercial fairness has occurred. This further function indicated by the case law can be considered as a sort of statutory approval of the interest

---

[64] For instance, it may be evaluated on a case-by-case basis whether an application for the preliminary investigations laid down by Article 696 and 696-*bis* of the Italian Civil Procedural Code could be made. If intellectual property rights (such as a trademark) are involved in the breach (for instance, where the breach of the code of conduct includes infringement of the collective trademark associated with said code), it could be evaluated whether an application for a *descrizione giudiziale* (judicial inspection) aimed at collecting evidence of the infringement and unlawful conduct may be requested on a case-by-case basis.

[65] The definition of "agreement" under competition law is set out in Article 2.2. of Statute no. 287/1990, substantially corresponding to the definition provided in Article 101 of the Treaty on the Functioning of the European Union (TFEU).

[66] G. Floridia, Autodisciplina e funzione arbitrale, in Rivista del Diritto Industriale [Riv. Dir. Ind.] 1991, I, p. 5; A. Pedriali, Profili soggettivi dell'autodisciplina pubblicitaria, in Riv. Dir. Ind. 1992, I, p. 136; M.S. Spolidoro, Le sanzioni del codice di autodisciplina pubblicitaria, in Riv. Dir. Ind. 1989, I, p. 58, G. Manfredi, Giurì di autodisciplina, autorità indipendenti e autorità giudiziaria, in Dir. Ind. 1/2011, p. 61. As regards case law, Court of Milan of 22 January 1976, in Riv. Dir. Ind. 1977, II, p. 91, sets out the principles shared by the literature on this topic.

[67] Article 4 of Statute 287/1990 and Article 101.3 of the TFEU.

[68] Supreme Court (Corte di Cassazione), 15 February 1999, no. 1259, in AIDA 1999, p. 407.

protected by CAP, thus excluding it from the definition of an agreement in restraint of trade.

It could be claimed that the above argument also applies where the undertakings that agree to comply with CAP hold a substantial market share.

The above reasoning could therefore concern all codes of conduct that pursue an interest that the State considers worth protecting, and "which allows consumers a fair share of the resulting benefit,"[69] as CAP does.

28.4.1 Possible Abuse of Dominant Position

If the undertakings agreeing to a CSR policy are in a collectively dominant position, legal issue under competition law would not necessarily arise.

When determining whether an abuse of said dominant position has taken place, the general principles of competition law would apply (i.e., if undertakings impose prices, set predatory prices, or perform excluding, discriminatory, and tying practices).

The situation would differ if an intellectual property ("IP") right (e.g., a collective trademark) is associated with compliance with a code of conduct and that IP right is owned by one or more companies in a dominant position. As we shall see in the next section, the exclusion of other undertakings from the use of said IP right could be considered as an abuse of dominant position, specifically entailing an excluding practice as defined in Article 102 TFEU and Article 3 of Statute no. 287/1990.[70]

28.4.2 Conflict Between Competition Law and Collective Trademarks: Licensing Issues

It is not unusual for CSR policies or codes of conduct to be associated with a registered collective trademark.

The use of collective trademarks by third parties is subject to compliance with the use regulations submitted with the application for the collective trademark (Article 11 of the Italian IP Code).

However, the law does not oblige the owner of the collective trademark to grant a license to use said trademark to any party that meets the requirements laid down by the collective trademark regulation.

Some Authors[71] have investigated the consequences of denial of access to the use of collective trademarks from a competition law standpoint. This is because

[69] G. Ghidini, Profili evolutivi del diritto industriale, 2008, p. 182.

[70] Statute of 10 October 1990, no. 287, on rules of the protection of the competition and the market.

[71] M. Ricolfi, Marchi di servizio, non registrati e collettivi, in Diritto Industriale Proprietà Intellettuale e Concorrenza, 2012, pp. 167–168.

collective trademarks, like other IP rights, are liable to create a dominant position or monopoly for the owner of said rights.

In particular, a distinction has been made between the situation where an association or consortium owns the collective trademark and the situation where the owner of the collective trademark is a single business.

Only in the first situation would denial of access to the use of the collective trademark be legitimate, if the use regulations require the potential licensee to be a member of the association/consortium and the requesting business is not.

In the second situation, refusal by the collective trademark owner would be unlawful because it would be in restraint of trade.

Moreover, should the CSR policy or code of conduct distinguished by said collective trademark becomes popular with the public and businesses (or a *de facto* standard), the risk of competition law litigation would be even greater.

Although Italian law does not include any specific provisions on this topic, it may be argued that in a similar situation, the principles of the "essential facilities doctrine"[72] could be applicable.

According to that doctrine, refusal by the owner of the collective trademark to grant a license, or refusal to grant it under fair, nondiscriminatory conditions, would be unlawful if the facility (or in our case, the policy distinguished by the trademark) is difficult to replicate and refusal impedes the development of new products/new services and forecloses competition at the bottom level.

The condition relating to the difficulty of replicating the policy should be evaluated partly in terms of the economic burden that the business wishing to use the collective trademark in question would incur in order to implement a similar policy.

Therefore, the difficulty of replicating the policy may be understood as the obstacle in terms of the economic burden involved in obtaining the same commercial appeal and reputation among consumers as gained by the collective trademark associated with a specific CSR policy.[73]

Should such conditions be fulfilled, the business owning said collective trademark would be in a dominant position and, in order not to abuse said dominant position, would be obliged to grant licenses under fair, nondiscriminatory conditions to other businesses wishing to enter the market in question and thus wishing to use the collective trademark in dispute.

[72] G. Olivieri, L'abuso di posizione dominante, in Diritto Industriale Proprietà Intellettuale e Concorrenza, 2012, pp. 481–482.

[73] G. Ghidini, Profili evolutivi del diritto industriale, 2008, p. 210.

Poland

29

Agnieszka Wiercińska-Krużewska and Aleksandra Wędrychowska-Karpińska

29.1 Introduction

In recent years, the adoption of CSR policies has gained popularity in Poland amongst NGOs and businesses, mainly as a part of their marketing strategies. Nonetheless, it may happen that the businesses do not follow voluntarily issued or adopted CSR policies. This contribution aims to answer the question if there are appropriate legal grounds and remedies in Poland to challenge what can be considered as unfair practices. The concept of CSR is relatively new in Poland, although it is attracting more and more attention of businesses[1] and also of nongovernmental organizations ("NGOs") and the government.

[1] There are many Polish businesses adopting their own CSR policies, not only in terms of relations with their employees or the society at large but also in terms of environmental protection or promotion of fair market practices. For example, a medium-sized construction company provides financial support to its workers and their families for the purposes of their cultural, educational and sporting activities. Community CSR can be seen, for example, in the case of a small Polish PR firm that acts *pro bono* for a nongovernmental organization promoting Polish-Jewish dialogue. The firm provides assistance in media relations, press conference organization and website design. In terms of environmental protection, a medium-sized Polish motor company maintains environmentally friendly waste policies in that both their manufacturing wastes and the waste products they collect from their customers are recycled and used for the manufacture of new products. What is more, the company ensures that its production processes are free from materials containing asbestos or heavy metals. When it comes to market-oriented CSR, there is a business engaged in the wholesale of bathroom and kitchen accessories that has offered an extended 7-year warranty and allows its customers to use charge-free technical support.

A. Wiercińska-Krużewska (✉)
Wierciński Kwieciński Baehr, Warsaw, Poland
e-mail: agnieszka.wiercinska@wkb.com.pl

A. Wędrychowska-Karpińska
Wierciński Kwieciński Baehr, Poznan, Poland
e-mail: aleksandra.wedrychowska@wkb.com.pl

P. Kobel et al. (eds.), *Antitrust in the Groceries Sector & Liability Issues in Relation to Corporate Social Responsibility*, LIDC Contributions on Antitrust Law, Intellectual Property and Unfair Competition, DOI 10.1007/978-3-662-45753-5_29

In order to promote the idea of CSR, the Polish government created, in 2009, a CSR consultative working group,[2] chaired by a representative of the Minister of Economy, consisting of representatives of several other ministries and agencies, as well as social partners and civil society representatives (entrepreneurs, NGOs, etc.). The task of the CSR working group is to prepare recommendations for the government in respect of CSR promotion and, in particular, to suggest suitable means of coordinating CSR actions of different public administration bodies, gather CSR information on good practices and enhance the dialogue among social partners.[3]

In order to promote the adoption of ethical or professional standards among businesses, NGOs are developing codes of conduct intended to be implemented by their members. For example, the "Credible Company" (*Wiarygodna Firma sp. z o. o.)* grants certificates to the companies that comply with its code of conduct[4]; the Advertising Council[5] (*Rada Reklamy*), an association bringing together organizations representing entities operating in the advertising market, grants a license to use its trademark "I advertise ethically" to companies that comply with its code of conduct; the Conference of Financial Companies in Poland (*Konferencja Przedsiębiorstw Finansowych w Polsce*) grants membership to businesses that undertake to be bound by its code of conduct[6]; and the Polish Bank Association (*Związek Banków Polskich*)[7] has enacted "the Rules of Good Banking Practice" (*Zasady Dobrej Praktyki Bankowej*), setting forth policies on such matters as contacts with clients and relations with local communities. The Polish Chamber

[2] See www.csr.gov.pl. The website promotes the idea of CSR and the CSR working group's activities.

[3] As an example, the Ministry of Economy has published a CSR guidebook, addressed to SMEs and describing CSR tools and practices.

[4] The "Credible Company" is a program to promote business ethics and companies that are committed to complying with the code of conduct, which calls for compliance with labor and consumer laws, with duties towards public authorities and other businesses and for the protection of the national environment.

[5] Advertising Council has as its task to promote and protect rules of conduct for businesses and others engaged in advertising activities in Poland and to protect advertising audiences and beneficiaries. The Advertising Code of Conduct focuses on ensuring that advertising is not misleading and provides protection against unethical and unfair advertising messages. Violations of the Code may be complained against by consumers and businesses to Advertising Board's Ethics Committee.

[6] The Conference of Financial Companies in Poland currently associates 39 key institutions active on the Polish Consumer Finance market (banks, financial advisors and intermediaries, money lending companies, economic information bureaus, debt management companies and insurers). It joined the European Federation of Finance House Associations—EUROFINAS—which is the main voice of the specialized consumer credit industry at European level.

[7] The Polish Bank Association is a self-government organization of banks, which membership is voluntary and open for all banks created under the Polish law, as well as for foreign credit institutions branches operating in Poland. The statutory tasks of the Association include, i.a., representing and protecting common interests of member banks, also with respect to legal regulations related to banking; participating in legislative work of legislatory commissions of the Parliament; supporting the standardization of banking products and services; conducting conciliatory proceedings and amicable judicature for banks.

of Commerce (*Krajowa Izba Gospodarcza*) has also enacted a code of ethics for entrepreneurs.[8]

Regarding banking services, the Financial Supervision Authority (*Komisja Nadzoru Finansowego*) may issue recommendations about the good practices of cautious and sustainable bank management. According to Recommendation H (covering, in particular, internal supervision/audit), a bank's board of directors, management and supervisory board are responsible for promoting high ethical standards.

For media services, the National Radio and Television Broadcasting Council (*Krajowa Rada Radiofonii i Telewizji*) is competent to initiate and support self-regulation and coregulation of media services.[9]

In addition, there are the so-called codes of deontology adopted by certain professions, such as lawyers, notaries, bailiffs, patent attorneys, doctors, etc.

29.2 Relevant Polish Laws in Regard to CSR Policies

In Poland, there are no laws specifically addressing CSR policies. Neither the notion of CSR nor the breach of CSR policies has been defined in Polish law. Therefore, the laws that are more general in nature are applicable to such practices.

The breach of a CSR policy may be treated in most situations as an unfair competition act or an unfair commercial practice. Hence, the prevention and sanctioning of a business that engages in commercial practices that breach a CSR policy voluntarily adopted by the business are addressed in Poland by the laws that combat unfair practices in B2B relations (the Act of 16 April 1993 on Combating Unfair Competition—*Ustawa o zwalczaniu nieuczciwej konkurencji*—hereinafter "CUCA") and B2C relations (the Act of 23 August 2007 on Combating Unfair Commercial Practices—*Ustawa o przeciwdziałaniu nieuczciwym praktykom rynkowym*,[10] hereinafter "CUCPA").

[8] Polish Chamber of Commerce founded in 1990 is the largest economic self-government institution in Poland, which groups above 150 business organizations. PCC promotes social responsibility of business by organizing trainings and conferences. PCC cares about entrepreneurs in the international arena. PCC is also a member of EUROCHAMBRES, the Association of the European Chambers of Industry and Commerce, which groups the European chambers of commerce and the International Chamber of Commerce (ICC) in Paris.

[9] The National Broadcasting Council is a state authority for supervision of radio and television broadcasting. It controls broadcasters' activities and sets subscription fees and license charges. The Council has the authority to grant radio and television broadcasting licenses, as well as the right to appoint members of supervisory boards and program councils in public radio and television stations.

[10] The CUCPA transposes into Polish law the Directive 2005/29/EC of the European Parliament and of the Council of 11 May 2005 concerning unfair business-to-consumer commercial practices in the internal market and amending Council Directive 84/450/EEC, Directives 97/7/EC, 98/27/EC and 2002/65/EC of the European Parliament and of the Council and Regulation (EC) No 2006/2004 of the European Parliament and of the Council ("Unfair Commercial Practices Directive") (O.J. L 149/22).

An unfair commercial practice may negatively affect the interests of competing businesses as well as consumers. Said unfair practice may thus be prohibited by both above-mentioned laws (CUCA and CUCPA). Accordingly, commercial practices that breach CSR policies will usually be prohibited by both CUCA and CUCPA. Both acts prohibit actual and threatened unfair practices.

The CUCPA specifically addresses the consequences of the breach of a code of conduct (which may include a CSR policy), which is regarded as an unfair commercial practice. Pursuant to Article 2.5 of CUCPA, a "code of conduct"[11] is defined as a set of rules, such as ethical or professional standards, in respect of the behavior of entrepreneurs who have undertaken to be bound by them in relation to one or more specific commercial practices. A code of conduct is construed as an instrument of self-regulation. Therefore, in order for a particular set of rules to be called a code of conduct within the meaning given to that term in the CUCPA, it may not be imposed by law or regulation or any other administrative provision.

The CUCPA specifically prohibits the following practices:

- creating an unlawful code of conduct (Article 11.2 of CUCPA),
- using an unlawful code of conduct (Article 4.2, 11.1 of CUCPA),
- misrepresenting as to compliance with a code of conduct by a business (Article 5.2.4 of CUCPA),
- misrepresenting as to acting as a signatory to (or otherwise being bound by) a code of conduct (Article 7.1 of CUCPA),
- falsely claiming that a code of conduct has been approved by a public authority or another entity (Article 7.3 of CUCPA).

Even if the targeted CSR policy is not a code of conduct, the above rules may be applicable *per analogiam*.

The CUCA may also be applicable to the above-mentioned misconducts insofar as they meet the general definition of an unfair competition act, *i.e.*, infringe the interests of other businesses.

Furthermore, the CUCA may be applicable to the breach of a CSR policy amounting to one of the following practices:

- misleading designation (labeling) of products (Articles 5 and 10.1 of CUCA),
- misleading advertising (Article 16 of CUCA).

[11] This is the term used in the Directive. However, the literal translation of the term used in CUCPA is "code of good practices" (*kodeks dobrych praktyk*).

29.3 Enforcement of Applicable Laws

29.3.1 Enforcement by Public and Regulatory Authorities

In case of an unfair commercial practice prohibited by the CUCPA or an act of unfair competition prohibited by the CUCA that negatively impacts the collective interests of consumers, the President of the Office of Competition and Consumer Protection (hereinafter referred to as the President of the OCCP) may commence administrative proceedings against the infringing undertaking.

The relevant laws may also be enforced by the Chief Pharmaceutical Inspector,[12] the Financial Supervision Authority[13] and the Commercial Inspection Authority.[14]

29.3.1.1 Range of Remedies Available to Public and Regulatory Authorities

The President of the OCCP may order an unfair commercial practice or an act of unfair competition to be discontinued and prescribe additional measures, *e.g.*, enjoin the infringing undertaking to publish, once or several times, a declaration that content and form would be set out in the decision. Usually, the decision orders that such declaration informs about the infringement and that the business was committed to stop it.

In some cases, sector-specific laws give industry regulators (authorities) oversight competences to ensure compliance of businesses with the law (*e.g.*, CUCPA and/or CUCA).

The Chief Pharmaceutical Inspector (*Główny Inspektor Farmaceutyczny*) or, in the case of veterinary drugs, the Chief Veterinary Officer may order an advertisement not to be displayed or conducted if it is not compliant with the applicable law. These authorities may also order publication of their decision in places where such advertisement has been displayed and the issuance of a *corrigendum.*[15]

If a bank is engaged in an unlawful conduct, the Polish Financial Supervision Authority (*Komisja Nadzoru Finansowego*) may, following a written admonition:

[12] The Chief Pharmaceutical Inspector is the central institution of government administration executing tasks of the Pharmaceutical Inspection and holds supervision over manufacturing and import conditions of medicinal products for human and veterinary use. It supervises compliance with the regulations of Pharmaceutical Law Act in the scope of advertisement.

[13] The Financial Supervision Authority supervises the financial services industry in Poland. This includes credit institutions, insurance firms, investment companies, exchanges, pension scheme, as well as payment institutions and credit unions. The aim of financial market supervision is to ensure regular operation of this market, its stability, security and transparency, confidence in the financial market, as well as to ensure that the interests of market actors are protected.

[14] The Commercial Inspection Authority is a supervisory body that aims to ensure protection of the consumers' interests and rights, as well as the state's commercial interests.

[15] Article 62.2. of the Pharmaceutical Law Act.

- request the appropriate body of the bank to dismiss the president, vice president or other management board member directly responsible for the noncompliance;
- suspend the responsible board member until dismissal;
- limit the scope of operations of the bank or of any of its internal units;
- impose on the bank a financial penalty of up to 10 % of its revenues as per the most recent audited financial statements but in any case no more than PLN 10,000,000 (about EUR 2,300,000);
- withdraw the bank's license authorization.

The Commercial Inspection Authority (*Inspekcja Handlowa*) has also the powers to investigate the way traders conduct their business, including misleading labeling.[16]

29.3.1.2 Fines or Imprisonment for Breaching Voluntary CSR Policies

In case of breach of voluntary CSR policies that affects consumers' interests, the main authority to take action and impose a fine is the President of the OCCP. Sector-specific regulators are also potentially empowered to impose financial penalties in case of false advertisement or misleading practices by the entities acting under their supervision, however it is uncertain if in practice they would be ready to undertake any action in cases involving CSRs.

Where a business breaches a voluntary CSR policy, thereby infringing CUCPA and/or CUCA with an impact on the collective interests of consumers, it may be subject to a penalty of up to 10 % of the revenue of the previous year. However, the fine does not usually exceed 1 % of the revenue. What is more, the President of the OCCP may impose a fine of an equivalent of up to EUR 10,000 for each day of delay in the execution of the authority's decision.

In case a participant of the financial market breaches either the CUCPA or the CUCA, the Polish Financial Supervision Authority may impose a fine at a maximum of 10 % of the participant's year revenue but in any case no more than PLN 10,000,000 (about EUR 2,300,000).

29.3.2 Enforcement by Consumers

Under the CUCPA, consumers are entitled to bring actions to courts against businesses that engage in unfair commercial practices.

Pursuant to Article 12.1 of the CUCPA, the consumer whose interest has been jeopardized or violated may request that

- such a practice be discontinued;
- the effects of such a practice be removed;

[16] Article 3 of the Commercial Inspection Authority Act.

- a single or multiple statement of appropriate content and appropriate form be made;
- the damage as per general terms and conditions be redressed and, in particular, to request that the contract be cancelled and the benefits mutually returned and the costs associated with the purchase of the product be reimbursed by the trader;
- an adequate amount of money be adjudicated for a specific social cause related to supporting the Polish culture, national heritage or consumer protection.

The consumer shall only make plausible, and not necessarily prove, that the targeted commercial practice constitutes an unfair market practice.

Such court action may also be brought by the Commissioner for Civil Rights Protection, a national or regional organization whose statutory objective is to protect consumer interests or a district (municipal) consumer ombudsman.

Consumers may also notify the President of OCCP that a business is in breach of a CSR policy. In the case where such breach constitutes an unfair commercial practice that infringes collective consumer interests, the President may (but does not have to) proceed against the business in accordance with the procedure described above (Sect. 29.3.1).

29.3.3 Enforcement by Competitive Businesses

If the breach of a CSR policy results in an unfair competition conduct, a competitor (whose interests have been infringed or threatened) may bring an action to common court against the (potential) infringer on the basis of CUCA.

Pursuant to Article 18.1 of CUCA, the remedies available to the competitor include

- cessation of the prohibited practices;
- removal of the effects of the prohibited practices;
- the making of one or repeated statements of appropriate content and form;
- reparation of the damage pursuant to general rules laid down in the Polish Civil Code;
- disgorgement of unjustified benefits pursuant to general rules laid down in the Polish Civil Code (*i.e.* the rules referring to unjust enrichment); and/or
- the payment of an appropriate sum of money in support of a social cause relating to support for the Polish culture or protection of national heritage.

A competitive business may also notify the President of OCCP that a business is in breach of CSR commitments and such breach is at the same time an unfair commercial practice that infringes collective consumer interests. In such a case, the President of OCCP may commence administrative proceedings against such offending business. However, in our experience, it appears that the President of OCCP is not inclined to act on notifications from competing businesses and tends to advise such complainants about the opportunity to file a lawsuit under unfair competition law.

29.3.4 Enforcement by Suppliers to and Purchasers of the Goods or Services of the Business

If a CSR policy adopted by a supplier relates to the origin or other specific features of the products, the supplier's noncompliance with the CSR policy may in some cases lead to the supplier's breach of contract. In such case, the purchaser may be entitled to reject the products, to withdraw from the contract, and/or to claim damages for breach of contract. The particular claims available may depend on the facts related to the conclusion of the contract and both parties' intent or contract wording, in particular if specific features of the product as described in the CSR policy were offered by the supplier.

If it is the buyer that is in breach of a CSR policy, *e.g.* in the example above, the supplier may be entitled to claims for breach of contract if the buyer contractually agreed to abide by the policy.

In addition to claims in contract, both the buyer and the supplier might be entitled to unfair competition claims, in particular under CUCA provisions prohibiting false or misleading information about products and/or activities.

29.3.5 The Possibility for Undertakings to Obtain Financial Compensation Against Competing Businesses that Breach Their CSR Policies

It appears that all of the above-mentioned remedies (see Sect. 29.3.3) may not be successfully pursued in case of breach of CSR policy.

In particular, it may be impossible for undertakings to claim damages. In an action for damages under CUCA, the aggrieved business needs to prove (1) that the act of unfair competition has been committed by another business, (2) that it has incurred an actual loss and (3) that there is a causal relationship between the act and its own loss. The act causing the loss must have been done "with fault." Further, the aggrieved business must prove the precise amount of the loss it incurred due to CSR breach.

In most cases, a breach of CSR representations will not cause a loss that remains in an adequate causal relationship with the breach.

For instance, a CSR breach that involves misrepresentation of the product's origin (*e.g.*, a business promoting chocolate sourced from Fair Trade farmers when, in fact, the business is not selling chocolate so sourced) falls under Articles 10.1 and 16 of CUCA as an act of unfair competition consisting in misleading information in relation to, among other things, the origin, quality and manufacturing process of the goods or services. Therefore, any other business whose interests have been jeopardized or infringed by such market practice may bring an action on the basis of CUCA against the infringing undertaking. However, showing proof of an actual loss would be quite difficult.

In the "Fair Trade" example, the business that promotes and sells chocolate sourced from "Fair Trade" farmers may gain a competitive advantage, insofar as the "Fair Trade" label may attract more customers and direct their choice towards "Fair Trade" products instead of other competing chocolates. Since there are many producers and distributors of chocolate on the market, "Fair Trade" label promotion may negatively impact chocolate sales of many different businesses. If the "Fair Trade" label appears to be falsely applied, competitors may, whether acting jointly or individually, be able to secure injunction(s). But the loss suffered by each individual competitor in such case is hard to quantify. The aggrieved businesses would rather not be able to prove by what exact amount their sales decreased as a direct consequence of the CSR breach and no other cause. Chocolate sales depend on various other circumstances, and there may be no direct connection between the sales of "Fair Trade" chocolates and the competing chocolates.

The situation is even more complex where "Fair Trade" products are promoted without being sold. In such case, it may happen that such promotion affects the goodwill of the competing businesses, in particular if the customers have come to believe that the competing businesses did not meet "Fair Trade" standards. The loss of each competing entity is also hard to quantify.

29.3.6 The Connection (Nexus) Between the Commercial Practice that Breaches the CSR Policy and the Goods Produced or Services Supplied by the Business with the CSR Policy

To be able to obtain injunctive relief, the connection (nexus) between the commercial practice breaching a CSR policy and the goods produced or services supplied by the business with the CSR policy seems irrelevant. In most cases, the unfair commercial practice remains illegal, irrespective of whether or not the infringer was aware of its unfairness (*e.g.*, if it was aware that his advertisement contains false or misleading claims). The only important factors are if the practice was unfair and if the interests of another business or of clients were infringed or jeopardized by such unfair practice.

In the above-mentioned example of "Fair Trade" label, marketing of coffee with a Fair Trade label on it that was not sourced from Fair Trade coffee farmers may constitute an unfair competition conduct prohibited by the CUCA, specifically misleading designation and misleading advertising (Articles 10, 16 and 14 of the CUCA). It may also amount to an unfair commercial practice prohibited by the CUCPA. Therefore, in such case, injunctive relief may be granted by the court or by the President of OCCP.

Damage claims are not available against an entity that markets Fair Trade coffee that is purchased from farmers who fail to fulfill their Fair Trade CSR in case such entity is not aware of that failure and relies on false representations of the farmers.

Injunctive relief may be available against a business that has imported coffee using ships that emit excessive substances and do not comply with the business's green CSR policy, irrespective of whether such entity was or was not aware of excessive emissions. Such injunctive relief may be granted by the President of OCCP and/or by the courts. Damage claims, if any, may be possible if the business is aware of the above breach of green CSR policy.

In a situation in which coffee marketed by a business that advertises its CSR policy of providing 2 % of all sales revenue to educating children in the third world but upon audit is found not to have complied with that policy, the business will be found to promotes itself by means of a misleading advertisement, and therefore it commits an act of unfair competition (Article 16 of the CUCA). In such case, other businesses whose interests were infringed due to such misleading practice are entitled to seek injunctive relief in court. A more debatable issue is to what extent such misleading information affects the interests of consumers. If it appears that the promotion has an impact on the consumers' choice of products, it may also constitute an unfair commercial practice. Thus, injunctive relief may be granted by the President of OCCP. Such relief may also be sought by consumers or consumer organizations in court.

It seems less likely that such an unfair practice would lead to losses on the part of other businesses or consumers.

29.4 Obtaining Information Regarding Compliance of Businesses with Their Voluntary CSR Policies

In Poland, private actors do not have any power to obtain information from businesses with CSR policies to prove or disprove that they have complied with or are complying with such policies. In some cases, the plaintiff may, within existing proceedings, apply to the court to commit the defendant to submit some information and documents.

In court actions dealing with misleading promotion and labeling, the burden of proof is in some cases reversed: a person whose conduct is claimed to be a misleading commercial practice has to prove the veracity of the label or of the data on the product or its packaging or of the advertising claims (Article 18a of the CUCA, Article 13 of CUCPA).

As for public authorities, the President of the OCCP may require a business to submit necessary information and documents. This request, being an investigative measure, may be made even before the antimonopoly proceedings are commenced.

29.5 Effectiveness of the Polish Law Provisions in Regard to Commercial Practices Where a Business Commits a Breach of Its Own CSR Policy

There is no developed case law in Poland related to noncompliance with CSR policies, and the matter has not attracted much attention of the press. But it does feature in OCCP President's press releases and published decisions.

It seems that general laws such as CUCA or CUCPA provide sufficient remedies to the authorities, businesses and consumers to obtain injunctive reliefs and that appropriate information about incompliance be made public. However, there are no effective grounds for financial claims by businesses affected by unfair practices that involve CSR incompliance.

Furthermore, the authorities, in particular the President of OCCP, are entitled to impose fines in cases of such unfair practices and to demand information from businesses.

One issue to be considered is that the general legislation that, like CUCA, combats unfair competition in B2B relations should perhaps contain specific provisions that deal with CSR breaches. Such a regulation would probably release businesses from having to prove in each case that a CSR breach constitutes an unfair competition act.

29.6 Awareness of the CSR Policies Among Consumers and Businesses

The level of knowledge about CSR policies among the general public in Poland is still relatively low. A research "Coalition for Responsible Business" dated December 2010, prepared for an organization called "Employers of Poland," concludes that 93 % of the respondents have never heard of corporate social responsibility in any aspect.

Even though the concept of CSR policies attracts more and more attention on the part of the companies, government and NGOs, the issue of incompliance with one's own code of conduct is definitely not at the centre of public concern.

CSR policies are used by the businesses as a marketing tool. The companies often place information about its CSR policies on their websites, together with other communications addressed to the press and media.

Still, in legal practice, including administrative authorities' and courts' case law, the issues related to CSR policies, in particular those that are false and misleading, have not been considered and discussed.

29.7 Proposed Changes in Polish Law

In view of the above, it seems that the consumers are better protected in case of breach of a CSR policy than businesses. This is due to CUCPA regulation and the power and duties of the President of OCCP. Therefore, one might consider that the CUCA, namely the law pertaining to combating unfair competition in B2B relations, should be amended to include specific provisions that would deal with the breach of CSR policies. That would probably release businesses from having to prove in each case that a CSR breach constitutes an unfair competition act. It would also increase business and customer awareness of issues related to CSR incompliance.

A CSR breach may in many cases be very hard to identify. Perhaps a solution would be to require CSR policy adopters to publicly issue reports confirming CSR compliance. It is good to provide for a rule of reversed proof that requires CSR policy adopters to prove that they comply with CSR.

As regards the remedies, there are no effective grounds under the current legislation for financial claims by businesses affected by unfair practices that involve CSR incompliance precisely because, as stated above, in most of these cases it will be hard to identify loss incurred by a business as a result of a CSR breach.

29.8 Competition Law in Regard to CSR Policies

CSR policies, to which competitors may voluntarily accede and which are subsequently jointly applied by competitors, should be treated under competition law as horizontal standardization agreements. Generally, standardization is not a restriction of competition by object, and in case of any doubts as to its compliance with the ban on anticompetitive agreements, it should be assessed by its effect.

Under the CCP, the ban on agreements restricting or infringing competition covers a wide scope of activities, including horizontal as well as vertical coordination between independent entities. Article 6 of the CCP generally mirrors the regulations of Article 101 of the Treaty on the Functioning of the European Union (hereinafter "TFEU"). Bearing in mind that Polish competition law does not directly address standardization agreements,[17] the EU legislation and case law provides an important input for the President of the OCCP in his investigation of such agreements. In cases investigated under double jurisdiction (CCP and Article 101 TFEU), the EU approach towards standardization agreements should prevail due to the principle of convergence between national and EU competition laws, as established in Article 3.2 of Council Regulation (EC) No 1/2003 of 16 December 2002 on the implementation of the rules on competition laid down in Articles

[17] There are national Block Exemption Regulations for the insurance sector that partially regulate the conditions of standardization agreements in this sector.

81 and 82[18] of the Treaty. Therefore, in such cases, the application of the Polish and EU rules with respect to standardization agreements should be exactly the same. However, we believe that in "pure" national cases, the President of the OCCP should also follow the EU rules on standardization agreements[19] insofar as there are no separate or better Polish rules. According to the EU rules, a standardization agreement (*e.g.*, a CSR policy) does not constitute an agreement restricting competition on condition that

- participation in standard setting should be unrestricted, *i.e.* the rules of the standard-setting organization have to guarantee that all competitors in the market or markets affected by the standard can participate in the process leading to the selection of the standard;
- the procedure for adopting the standard in question is transparent, *i.e.*, the relevant standard-setting organization has procedures that allow stakeholders to effectively inform themselves of upcoming, ongoing and finalized standardization work in good time at each stage of the development of the standard;
- the standardization agreement does not contain an obligation to comply in order to maintain the freedom to develop alternative standards or products;
- the standard-setting organization's rules ensure effective access to the standard on fair, reasonable and nondiscriminatory terms;
- if there are intellectual property rights involved, they should be licensed to all third parties on fair, reasonable and nondiscriminatory terms ("FRAND commitment"); and
- the standard does not directly or indirectly cover any issues relating to prices.

Moreover, the standards should be objectively justified, as well as necessary and proportionate, to achieve the assumed objectives. In particular, the positive effect of the standard passed on to the final consumers should be significant enough to counterbalance any possible restriction of competition.

The risk of an anticompetitive object or effect of a standardization agreement may arise if the parties to such agreement hold significant market power and there is a small number of market players. In such a case, there is a risk that—as a result of the oligopolistic structure of the market—the standardization agreement will transform into a tacit or even explicit collusion. Therefore, in such situation, the standard-setting body and each party to the standardization agreement should act transparently and comply with the guidelines laid down by the European Commission.

[18] Currently Articles 101 and 102, respectively, of the Treaty on the Functioning of the European Union.

[19] These rules are established in the European Commission's Guidelines on the applicability of Article 101 of the Treaty on the Functioning of the European Union to horizontal co-operation agreements (OJ 2011/C 11/01 paras. 257–335).

Subject to one exception,[20] the concept of the collective dominant position has not yet been widely applied by the President of the OCCP.

As long as the *de facto* or *de jure* standard (private or government encouraged) for trade in goods or services complies with the rules on standardization agreements (in particular, it does not preclude market entry or market share expansion for any undertaking), there should be no risk of the President of the OCCP undertaking an antimonopoly intervention. Moreover, if a de jure standard (government encouraged) infringes the ban on anticompetitive agreements, the undertakings may try to apply the state action defense.

In Poland, there are no national regulations regarding FRAND-type commitments, and the President of the OCCP has not imposed such commitments in any of its decisions yet. A CSR policy may involve the use of a particular sign (logo/trademark) by participants to indicate compliance with that policy. If the policy maker owns [a European] trademark, the licensing of such trademark should comply with the FRAND requirements laid down in the European Commission's guidelines.

[20] There is ongoing antimonopoly investigation before the President of the OCCP regarding collective dominance of the mobile network operators.

Ukraine

30

Igor Svechkar

30.1 The Different Types of CSR Policies that Exist in Ukraine

CSR policies in Ukraine generally cover all aspects of activity under ISO 26000, including such issues as management, human rights, employment, environmental protection, fair business practices, consumer protection, etc., though only a limited number of these types became commonly used.

The results of a study covering the period 2005–2010 showed that labor and employment are the most common CSR practices for Ukrainian companies. The majority of CSR practices are mainly focused on remuneration, regulation of work hours, and nondiscrimination in employment.

Many companies, especially large corporations, also pay considerable attention to the policies dealing with responsibility towards customers and clients for the quality of their products and services.

Environmental and social projects, as well as many other types of policies, have not gained significant importance yet: only one-third of companies make social investments, half of the respondents do not have any environmental projects, only one-fourth has internal regulations (guidelines, rules, etc.) regarding CSR policies.[1]

The level of transparency in CSR issues is quite low. In Ukraine, in 2005–2010, only 38 companies published CSR reports (55 reports in total) prepared in COP, RI,

[1] Centre for CSR Development, *National strategy of social responsibility of business in Ukraine*, available at http://www.svb.org.ua/publications/kontseptsiya-natsionalnoi-strategii-sotsialnoi-vidpovidalnosti-biznesu.

I. Svechkar (✉)
Asters, Kyiv, Ukraine
e-mail: Igor.Svechkar@asterslaw.com

P. Kobel et al. (eds.), *Antitrust in the Groceries Sector & Liability Issues in Relation to Corporate Social Responsibility*, LIDC Contributions on Antitrust Law, Intellectual Property and Unfair Competition, DOI 10.1007/978-3-662-45753-5_30

and other formats.[2] There was an insignificant increase in the number of CSR reports from 15 in 2011 up to 35 in 2012.[3]

Main legal concerns predominantly owe to the lack of special legal framework for CSR policies. There are no mandatory rules or standards as regards the CSR practices, their implementation, and reporting. As a result, lack of regulation creates substantial constraint on CSR development limiting transparency, possibilities for efficient control over CSR compliance, and eventually the incentive to adopt and follow a CSR policy.

30.2 The Ukrainian Legislation Sanctioning Breaches of Self-Imposed CSR Policy

Generally, there is no legislation that prevents or sanctions breaches of voluntarily adopted CSR policy.

Ukrainian laws do not provide for a liability for a breach of self-imposed CSR policy unless such breach also qualifies as a violation of some legal provisions and requirements. Sometimes, CSR closely neighbors with legal requirements or is instrumental to assuming by companies of additional legal obligations or becoming subject to higher standard legal requirements. For example, driven by a CSR policy, an employer that enters into a collective bargaining agreement may want to set in there a relatively high standard of remuneration, social protection, insurance, and guarantees for employees. In this way, CSR policy is implemented into a binding legal obligation of the business and its breach entails a liability for both the company and its management, including fines that may be imposed by relevant public authorities.

Another example of a binding CSR policy (and a possibility to enforce against a noncompliant business) is a rule or a standard, which is undertaken as mandatory CSR commitment by a business association—members of such association may request compliance with the relevant policy by other members based on the contractual framework of the association. Refusal to comply may serve as a ground for expelling the CSR offender from the association or even amount to unfair competition where the relevant code of conduct or a similar set of rules gained the status of fair trade practices.

In addition, a breach of CSR policy may constitute violation of consumer protection[4] and competition laws.[5] In particular, it is prohibited to engage in unfair business practices or unfair competition in the form of dissemination of misleading

[2] *CSR reporting: instrument of socially responsible business*, Global Compact Network Ukraine. 2010.

[3] *Analytical report "CSR development in Ukraine in 2012. Forecasts for 2013,"* CSR Center, Ukraine.

[4] Art. 19 of the Law of Ukraine *On Protection of Consumer Rights* of 12 May 1991, available at http://www.consumerinfo.org.ua/en/must_know/legislation/LawOnConsumerRightsProtection_eng.pdf.

[5] Art. 15-1 of the Law of Ukraine *On Protection of Unfair Competition* of 7 June 1996, available at http://cis-legislation.com/document.fwx?rgn=9546.

information to consumers or clients (*e.g.*, false information about the manufacturer, production, and other applicable standards, as well as other information that may influence the choice of product or supplier by customers). It is not incompliance with the CSR policy itself that is actionable but rather a misleading reference to a certain CSR policy or standard that a company claims to follow, *e.g.*, while promoting or advertising its products or services. Thus, the availability of legal remedies is quite limited: it is not possible to require a business to follow a self-imposed CSR policy, but rather where such policy is not followed, an aggrieved party (be it a customer or a competitor) may compel the business to stop referring to the CSR policy for marketing purposes and also claim damages caused by the misleading information (*e.g.*, that contained in advertising or promotion materials that mention a CSR policy and associate the product or service with certain benefits that the compliance with such policy can bring). Public authorities may also sanction for relevant violations of consumer protection or competition laws.

There is no specific regulation on damages inflicted as a result of a CSR violation; thus, general civil law regulation applies.

30.2.1 Subjects Entitled to Enforcement of Breaches of Conduct Codes

30.2.1.1 Enforcement by the Antimonopoly Committee of Ukraine

As mentioned, CSR policies are enforceable by regulatory authorities to the extent they constitute a breach of relevant legal provisions. For example, noncompliance of an employer with a CSR obligation undertaken towards an employee (*e.g.*, a commitment to provide accommodation) entails administrative liability that may be imposed by the relevant regulatory authorities supervising compliance with labor laws.

Should the breach of CSR policy amount to unfair competition, the relevant laws may be enforced by the Antimonopoly Committee of Ukraine (the "AMC"). In particular, based on a complaint by a competitor or a consumer or on its own initiative, the AMC may wish to check whether the statements made by a business regarding its compliance with the CSR policy, such as environmental protection or production standards, are true. If these statements are untrue and are potentially misleading for customers in their choice of goods, the AMC may impose fines and compel the business to discontinue dissemination of misleading information. In order to ensure the enforcement of its decisions, the AMC may also resort to court. Such practice is not commonly used yet; however, there have already been some cases that confirm a possibility of its further development. For example, AMC viewed pharmacy's claim to be a "social pharmacy" in the advertisement materials as misleading toward consumers because it suggested more affordable prices or some social services that the pharmacy in fact did not offer. Having considered these actions as unfair competition, the AMC prohibited to use this motto and impose a fine on the relevant chain of pharmacies.

30.2.1.2 Enforcement by Consumers

The Law of Ukraine "On Protection of Consumer Rights" ensures to consumers the right to get true and complete information about the products and production technologies that should enable them to make conscious, competent, and free choice. The Law prohibits unfair business practice, including any activity (actions or inaction) that misleads the consumer. Therefore, should the company claim compliance with certain CSR standards and fail to do so, the consumers, which were misled by these statements and influenced in their choice of products, can seek enforcement and claim damages. As noted above, consumers cannot compel the CSR offender to comply with the CSR policy.

Damages are awarded by Ukrainian courts. In order to claim damages, the affected consumers should prove misconduct by the company and substantiate the amount of damages and the direct causation between the misconduct and the damages sustained. In practice, it may be uneasy to explicate the second and the third components in a way satisfactory for the court.

Consumers may also apply to the relevant regulatory authorities charged with supervision over compliance with consumer protection laws. While the enforcement powers of the authorities do not extend to damage claims, the fact that they have found a company to be in violation of the law is usually precedential for the courts and significantly contributes to the chances of the consumer to succeed in the damages suits.

30.2.1.3 Enforcement by Competing Businesses

A competitive business may bring an action under unfair competition laws. This would ideally involve filing a complaint with the AMC, which explains how the untrue CSR statement by the offender adversely affected the relevant competitor (increased customer churn rate, etc.) and lodging a follow-on damage suit. The first step is covered by the above discussion, while we are generally unaware of CSR-based lawsuits brought by competitors.

Alternatively, a competitive business may go directly to court and ask the court to both consider whether there was an offense and, if so, award damages.

30.2.1.4 Enforcement by Suppliers

Suppliers to and purchasers of the goods or services of the offending business may bring lawsuits against it based on general provisions of the Civil Code. To succeed, they will need to prove causation of damages resulting from the failure to follow the publicized CSR policy by the offender.

In application to purchasers, the central point of the relevant assessment by the court would again be the extent to which following by the offender of the CSR policy was decisive for the purchaser's choice to contract. Another relevant consideration would be the impact of a misleading CSR statement on the purchaser's own business and the "downstream" effects that may be inflicted by the untrue statement made by the offender in the first instance.

As it comes to suppliers, it appears that their claims against the CSR offender would not stand really good chances to be supported by the court, unless a supplier is able to prove that having been following the CSR policies the offender would certainly purchase from this particular supplier (*e.g.*, because of the unavailability of alternative sources of supply of the CSR-compliant products, considerable purchasing needs of the offender, etc.). Though even where the supplier would be capable of proving these facts, Ukrainian courts may still be unwilling to award damages, perhaps with the exception of cases where a competitive bidding process was involved.

Unlike competitors, suppliers and purchasers may not have a sufficient cause for complaint with the AMC. In practice, however, this should not prevent them from complaining, and the AMC, acting in public interest, is likely to bring the case forward on its own initiative.

30.2.2 Causes of Action and Range of Remedies Available to the AMC

Given that breach of company's own CSR policy is not actionable *per se*, the regulatory authorities may intervene only if such breach otherwise amounts to a violation of law.

The authorities may issue a cease and desist order and/or impose sanctions; further, they may also bring lawsuits to ensure enforcement of their decisions. For example, if a breach of the CSR policy amounts to unfair competition in the form of dissemination of misleading information, the AMC may impose fines and request termination of such practice. If the company fails to comply with the AMC decision, the AMC may bring a lawsuit, which, among others, may seek injunctive relief against the company.

If noncompliance with CSR policy amounts to a violation of law (e.g. labor, consumer protection, unfair competition, etc.), the regulatory authorities may impose fines for such violations.

Using the earlier example of the labor law violation: company's managers may be subject to administrative fines of up to UAH 1,700 (EUR 165) for the breach of their obligations under the collective bargaining agreement designed to meet the company's own CSR policy. Failure to pay salary is subject to fines of up to UAH 17,000 (EUR 1,650) or imprisonment of up to 2 years.

If the CSR statements are related (even indirectly) to marketing of products, noncompliance with CSR policy may be viewed as unfair competition. Unfair competition in the form of dissemination of misleading information is subject to fine of up to 5 % of the annual group-wide turnover of the undertaking in the previous financial year. Besides, the AMC would usually order to discontinue the violation and, if needed, may bring lawsuits to ensure enforcement.

Given that it is not mere incompliance with CSR policies that matters for finding a company to be in violation of unfair competition laws but rather the effects on competition that such incompliance (or, better to say, an untrue statement claiming compliance) has had, the type of breached CSR policy will always matter. For example, false claims about gender nondiscrimination in employment and equal career opportunities most likely will not amount to an unfair competition offense (unless one can prove that such claims misled the consumers or clients and decisively influenced their choice, which would normally be impossible to achieve). On the contrary, false claims about the use of 100 % environmental-friendly technologies is likely to amount to unfair competition because this issue is usually more important for customers in their choice of a product.

If a company violates consumer protection laws via dissemination of inaccurate, incomplete, or unreliable information, the consumer protection authority may impose fines in the amount of up to 30 % of the relevant sales revenue. Company's officers may be subject to fines in the amount of up to UAH 3,400 (approx. EUR 330). If there is a need, the authority may bring a lawsuit to enforce its decisions.

30.2.3 Causes of Action and Remedies Available to Private Undertakings (*e.g.*, Competing Businesses)

As mentioned under Sect. 30.2.2 above, depending on the type of violation, the aggrieved private undertakings (*e.g.*, competing businesses) may seek discontinuing by the CSR offender of referring to the CSR policy that it actually does not follow (whether in court or by complaining to the regulatory authority having powers to order termination of the misconduct) and recovery of damages. In practice, where the compensation claim bases exclusively on incompliance with a voluntary CSR policy, the competing business will need to prove that all of the following are in place:

- offender's conduct amounts to a violation under unfair competition laws or other laws that protect competitors and give cause for a damage claim;
- the violation indeed led to the competitor suffering damages (such as loss of business), *i.e.*, there is a direct causation between the offense and the damages sustained; and
- the amount of the damages is measurable.

In case of violation under unfair competition laws, it would be extremely helpful for the affected competitor if the AMC favorably decides on the first point because Ukrainian courts strongly prefer to refer this issue to the competition authority and are generally reluctant to make their own assessment in this regard (and are even more reluctant to conclude contrary to the findings of the authority). In practical terms, this means that getting the favorable AMC decision is almost indispensable for the success of the follow-on damage claim. If the competitor fails to obtain such decision, it will probably need to first challenge the (unhelpful) AMC decision in court so that the AMC reassesses the matter and arrives at a conclusion that will then lay basis for the damage claim.

In view of the current state of affairs with CSR issues in general, it appears that the AMC is unlikely to automatically view a self-imposed CSR policy incompliance as giving raise to unfair competition concerns (unless the effects of untrue CSR statements are particularly vivid, like something closer to the example with the "social pharmacy" given above). Thus, it is always essential to explicate to the authority the importance of actual CSR policy compliance as at least one of the key factors influencing consumer's or client's choice.

Once in court, the competitor may also face difficulties proving the amount of the damages sustained and the causation between the CSR incompliance and the damages. In theory, it is possible to justify the loss of business by customers switching to the CSR offender driven by its CSR compliance statements. However, in practice, the offender would most probably raise a number of defenses claiming that customer's preferences are explainable by various other factors. In a competitive environment, it is highly likely that the offender would be capable of providing a variety of evidence of its other marketing efforts that might have caused customers' switch. Thus, the court may be unwilling to award damages or award them *pro rata* to the weight that CSR policy compliance should have reasonably carried among the other factors influencing customer's choice. Such prorated award may result in the competitor being compensated for only a fraction of the original damage claimed.

It should be noted that competition laws provide the court with a possibility to award damages in the amount of double the amount of actual damages sustained for certain types of competition law violations. This provision was designed to create additional incentives for private competition litigation. It may make sense to introduce the same provision for unfair competition claims as in Ukraine, both competition and unfair competition laws share the same procedural platform, as well as liability principles. This may be particularly interesting for the AMC, which is almost always involved in unfair competition disputes for the reasons outlined above, and may improve its enforcement statistics trough the increased number of unfair competition complaints.

Another helpful tool for convincing courts to award damages would be a decision of consumer protection authorities finding the CSR offender to be in violation of consumer protection laws. While the affected competitor or supplier would not have cause for complaints with the consumer protection authorities, they often orchestrate individual or collective complaints by consumers. Such tactics have proved to be quite efficient—having seen the decisions of both the AMC and the consumer protection authority confirming the CSR offender to be in violation of relevant laws, the courts would usually be more willing to award damages as claimed.

It should be noted that there is virtually no court practice concerning damages stemming from untrue CSR compliance statements—such statements would usually be attacked by competitors in combination with other unfair practices by the CSR offenders.

30.2.4 The Nexus Between the Commercial Practice that Breaches the CSR Policy and the Goods Produced or Services Supplied by the Business with the CSR Policy

The nexus between the CSR statements and the products/services of the CSR offender is of paramount importance for the private business to be able to obtain both injunctive and financial relief.

For instance, in the case of coffee marketed by a business that has imported coffee using ships that emit excessive carbon dioxide and do not comply with the business's green CSR policy, the chance for success would be insignificant and almost nonexistent in the case of coffee marketed by a business that advertises its CSR policy of providing 2 % of all sales revenue to educating children in the third world but upon audit is found not to have complied with that policy.

30.2.5 Powers of Private or Public Entities to Obtain Information from Businesses Adopting CSR Policies for Controlling the Relevant Compliance with Such Policies

The possibilities of private concerns are quite limited as businesses are not legally required to publish CSR reports or respond to private inquiries in this regard. Thus, the only effective way to get information on CSR policy compliance would be placing a request through a regulatory authority, for which the relevant private entity would effectively need to express doubt regarding compliance by a given business and explicate in which way the entity placing such request may be adversely affected should the CSR policy compliance claim prove untrue.

Alternatively, the inquiry may be made by the court where there is an ongoing proceeding stemming from the alleged failure to comply with a CSR policy, which amounts to an unfair competition offense. In turn, the regulatory authorities and the courts so requested will only have powers to inquire into CSR policy compliance where there is a reasonable suspicion that possible incompliance may amount to an offense actionable by the relevant authority or the court.

30.3 Ukrainian Legal Treatment of Commercial Practices Where a Business Commits a Breach of Its Own CSR Policies

Ukrainian legal framework for CSR-related issues, including the treatment of breaches, is currently in an early stage of development. Though given that CSR policies and their following by businesses has not yet gained a critical importance for the society, it appears that possible underregulation of this area does not for now create any really significant issues. Vast majority of local companies do not consider it necessary or beneficial to implement CSR policy; many of them have very basic understanding of CSR issues in general. Lots of Ukrainian companies that do implement CSR policy view such implementation in the context of "civilizing" their business and becoming a more reliable partner to potential foreign investors and other transacting parties (for prospective IPOs, listings, debt/equity financing, etc.) rather than driven by the intention to make business more responsible before the society. It is primarily large international corporations present in Ukraine, mainly European and American, that implement CSR as a global policy pursuing the goals inherent to CSR globally.

A number of studies show that many companies describe their CSR policy in quite abstract manner and do not disclose any specific activities or involvements. Coupled with general lack of transparency (because there are no efficient ways for the interested private entities and individuals to obtain CSR-related information), it makes it difficult to assess CSR policy compliance since most companies do not publish any CSR reports or make other similar disclosures at all.[6] Nevertheless, the number of CSR reports grows year by year. Unlike in other Eastern European countries where the majority of companies that publish CSR reports are subdivisions of multinational corporations, in Ukraine these are mainly domestic companies or the companies having their major operations in the Ukrainian market.[7]

30.3.1 The View of Consumers/Businesses Environment on Noncompliance with CSR Policy

A number of surveys[8] show that many companies consider heavy tax burdens, insufficient funding, and the absence of legal incentives for CSR policy implementation as the main constrains for CSR development in Ukraine. Certain companies are potentially ready to implement CSR policy but are discouraged by low social demand for CSR and other relevant incentives. Against this background, it would probably be fair to think that failures of a business to adhere to its CSR policies are not taken seriously enough by consumers and other businesses—just because the importance of CSR in general and compliance with the self-imposed policies by the business in particular are not taken seriously either. This state of affairs owes to general lack of commitment to CSR values, as well as limited public awareness of the benefits that CSR policies bring. Over these reasons, society does not put enough pressure on business, which pressure would catalyze proliferation of CSR policies. In fact, Ukrainian business does not face a significant risk of losing customers and clients because of absence of or noncompliance with CSR policies. Thus, one might suggest that, currently, consumers neither feel that breaches of

[6] Available at http://jurliga.ligazakon.ua/news/2013/2/13/83639.htm; http://www.csr-ukraine.org/farmacy.html, http://www.csr-ukraine.org/banks.html.

[7] *CSR reporting: instrument of socially responsible business*, Global Compact Network Ukraine. 2010, available at http://www.globalcompact.org.ua/img/files/Nefinansova_zvitnist.pdf.

[8] "*CSR reporting: instrument of socially responsible business*." Global Compact Network Ukraine. 2010, available at http://www.globalcompact.org.ua/img/files/Nefinansova_zvitnist.pdf.

CSR policy should be a matter of legal sanction, nor do they subject the breaching business to an appreciable pressure through adverse public comment or commercial sanction.

30.3.2 Difficulties in Meeting Private and Public Concerns in Enhancing the Role of CSR Policy

To begin with, it is worth noting that private and public concerns in relation to CSR are not strong enough to call for immediate improvement of legal framework.

Thus, as the first step, it is probably more important to introduce legal instruments for encouragement of CSR policy implementation, *e.g.*, through affording the CSR-adopting business certain tax preferences or other benefits. Also it is necessary to increase awareness about the importance of CSR policy both for business and the society, as well as about the available positive experience and achievements in CSR implementation. Another concern is related to a lack of transparency in CSR policies. In order to increase public confidence in CSR policy, it would be helpful to introduce at least minimum requirements regarding CSR reporting and transparency in the implementation of CSR policies.

To encourage CSR adoption in Ukraine, the Centre for CSR Development elaborated the project "National Strategy of Social Responsibility of Business in Ukraine."[9] The project defines the priorities of CSR development in Ukraine, including the necessary legislative changes. In particular, it provides for the following measures:

- to adopt the National Strategy of CSR Development at the state level;
- to create a permanent body for study and assessment of CSR in Ukraine and its further development within the parliamentary committee;
- to improve the laws on implementation of environmental and social labeling and its enforcement;
- to introduce the system of preferences for the companies, which implement CSR policy and socially important programs;
- to encourage CSR reporting by the Ukrainian companies, *inter alia*, via Ukrainian and international specialized portals and databases;
- to introduce and conduct annual CSR competitions, including the annual Ukrainian National Quality Award;
- to promote CSR standards and systems of management;
- to support educational programs for professions such as "Manager of Social and Corporate Responsibility," "Expert of Social Responsibility of Business," "Social Auditor";

[9] Centre for CSR Development, *National strategy of social responsibility of business in Ukraine*, available at http://www.svb.org.ua/publications/kontseptsiya-natsionalnoi-strategii-sotsialnoi-vidpovidalnosti-biznesu.

- to organize public awareness campaigns, *e.g.*, for promotion of CSR-related media publications and TV programs;
- to increase CSR awareness among state officials, in particular by making CSR a part of the training programs for civil servants;
- to introduce “Social Responsibility of Business” as a course at higher education institutions and business schools, to support production of CSR textbooks and other educational materials.

30.3.3 Possible Amendments to Ukrainian Regulation of CSR Policies

Considering the peculiarities of the Ukrainian legal system and the existing law enforcement practice, introduction of binding CSR policy and sanctions for its breach may not be particularly efficient. Thus, it is mainly the incentivizing of implementation of CSR policies and the increased transparency in CSR-related issues that may call for legislative changes.

In particular, it would be helpful to introduce legal requirements regarding CSR reporting and transparency, such as

- to publish the CSR policies, reports, and evidence of compliance with CSR policies on the website;
- to implement a legal obligation to provide the customers and organizations with information on compliance with CSR policies.

Another helpful tool for efficient private enforcement would be introduction of provisions on awarding the double damages for unfair competition claims. This could create additional incentives for compliance with CSR policy and would encourage bringing CSR-based lawsuits against a noncompliant business.

30.4 Ability of Consumers and the AMC to Police the Compliance of Businesses with Their CSR Policy

The laws do not satisfactorily deal with the ability to monitor compliance of business with their CSR.

The possibilities of consumers are quite limited as businesses are not legally accountable before consumers as regards their CSR compliance. Thus, the only effective way to get information on CSR policy compliance would be placing a request through a regulatory authority. To do so, the consumer will need to express a grounded concern about the infringement upon his/her rights that possible CSR incompliance may entail. The regulatory authority in its turn will only have powers to inquire into CSR policy compliance where there is a reasonable suspicion that possible incompliance may amount to an offense actionable by such authority or the court.

30.5 Competition-Related Issues in Relation to Voluntary Adherence to CSR Policy by a Number of Undertakings in a Horizontal Relationship

Voluntary adherence to CSR policy by a number of the horizontally related undertakings may amount to potentially anticompetitive concerted practices and require individual authorization by the AMC. Such practices would usually be authorized where they contribute to improvement of production or distribution of goods, technological progress, or economic efficiency.

Both in legal provisions and in practice, the combined market share of the parties to concerted practices is considered to be the key indicator of potential negative impact of concerted practices on competition. Safe harbor for such type of horizontal agreements applies if the combined market share of the parties in the market concerned does not exceed 15 % and the parties do not exceed certain financial thresholds. A lower market share threshold—5 %—may apply if the parties exceed the said financial thresholds.

Should the combined market share of the parties exceed 15 %, there is no presumption of anticompetitive effects. However, agreements (including those by *de facto* conduct) on standards of behaviour or product quality are often considered as restrictive of competition, in particular, if they hinder market access for incompliant undertakings, especially where such agreement may result in setting unreasonably high standards limiting access to the market for those undertakings that do not have sufficient resources to comply with these standards.

As regards IPRs, if horizontal agreements in fact lead to establishment of standards protected by IPRs, such agreements should provide other competitors with a possibility to get the license to these IPRs so that they have equal opportunities to compete. Although the competition laws do not address these issues explicitly and Ukrainian law is unfamiliar with FRAND-type licenses, a similar concept will follow from the general provisions on nondiscrimination (equal opportunities) of undertakings and fair competition.

United Kingdom

31

Jonathan Moss

31.1 CSR Policies Adopted by UK Undertakings

There are numerous types of policies that fall under the umbrella term of 'corporate social responsibility'. The UK does not have any specific method of categorising CSR policies; however, they appear to fall into one of three distinct categories as set out below. These categories group CSR policies by looking at the aim of a given policy.

The first category of CSR policies comprises policies relating to any attributes that are intrinsic to the products/services offered by a company. Examples of this type of policy are:

- companies making commitments about the environment, *e.g.* that the carbon footprint for a certain product does not exceed a stated amount;
- companies making commitments over the working conditions of its staff or workers both domestically and overseas; this sort of policy would also include a commitment to providing foreign suppliers with a living wage (as in the case of Fair Trade products);
- companies making commitments about the quality of their products, *e.g.* that they only use locally sourced produce.

In addition to receiving the comments of the UK Competition Law Association, the author would like to thank Peter Malone of Clifford Chance (London) for his comments in relation to the discussion in Sect. 31.7. All errors and omissions remain those of the author.

J. Moss (✉)
Hogarth Chambers, London, UK
e-mail: jmoss@hogarthchambers.com

P. Kobel et al. (eds.), *Antitrust in the Groceries Sector & Liability Issues in Relation to Corporate Social Responsibility*, LIDC Contributions on Antitrust Law, Intellectual Property and Unfair Competition, DOI 10.1007/978-3-662-45753-5_31

The second category comprises policies where a company provides its own staff for work on projects that are outside the normal remit of the company in question. Examples of this type of policy include

- companies allowing staff to undertake local community projects on company time;
- companies sending staff into schools to educate children. This can be in relation to the market in which the company itself operates,[1] or it could be something completely outside the scope of the company, such as helping children to learn to read. Put simply, this would cover any form of work that is seen as objectively beneficial and for the public good.

The third category includes policies whereby a company donates money (or something else of value, *e.g.* old equipment such as computers) to a charitable institution or to other community projects.

CSR policies can originate from one of three places—government regulation, the company themselves or NGOs. Of these three, only the last two types of CSR policies are considered in this report.

31.2 Categorisation of NGO Policies

NGO policies can also be broken down into two further categories. First are those policies that emanate from NGOs that are in some way associated with the industry in question, for example trade bodies. Second are those policies that emanate from NGOs that are truly independent of the industry, for example Greenpeace campaigning on environmental issues.

The key difference between an internally set policy and an NGO set policy is that with the NGO policy, there is potentially more accountability as the NGO will be, to different extents, outside of the control of the company.

31.3 Legal Rights That May Apply to Breach of a CSR Policy

Whether or not any of the above gives rise to legal concerns depends on how the policy is implemented and presented to the outside world. It is important to note that the way these policies are conveyed to the public varies tremendously, and this impacts upon whether or not they give rise to legal concerns. The promotion of CSR policies in the UK can be achieved by actual marking on products, through corporate statements or news reports, in company literature or through traditional advertising.

There is a patchwork of legal rights that may, under certain circumstances, give rise to a cause of action. These include trademark infringement, breach of contract, passing off and various statutory torts relating to advertising and trading standards.

[1] For example, an alcohol manufacturer going into a school to teach drink awareness.

31.3.1 Sanctions Under UK Law for Breach of a Voluntarily Adopted CSR Policy

There is no law in the UK aimed specifically at preventing or sanctioning a business that has breached a voluntarily adopted CSR.

The UK has a range of general IP laws and associated consumer protection laws that may provide for legal recourse against a company that breaches its own voluntary CSR policy. However, the applicability of these laws is entirely dependent on the policy in question, how the company has marketed this policy to the public and the manner in which is has been breached.

The terms of any given CSR policy play a crucial role in determining whether or not breaching it will provide for a legal remedy. The difference between a company saying that they 'only use dolphin-friendly tuna' and that they 'endeavor to only use dolphin-friendly tuna' is significant from a legal point of view: one is an absolute statement; the other a strong intention or commitment. The latter of these is considerably more difficult to police. It is therefore relatively easy for companies to word their CSR policies in a manner that would allow them to almost completely avoid the possible legal remedies set out below.

31.3.2 Consumer Protection from Unfair Trading Regulations 2008

The most relevant legal scheme is that governed by the Consumer Protection from Unfair Trading Regulations 2008 (hereinafter 'CPUTR 2008').[2] This scheme applies where there is a misleading commercial practice that contravenes the requirements of professional diligence and materially distorts the economic behaviour of the average consumer.[3]

31.3.2.1 Legal Test for When a Commercial Practice Will Be Misleading

A commercial practice will be deemed misleading if it either:

- contains false information and is therefore untruthful in relation to any of the matters set out below or if it or its overall presentation in any way deceives or is likely to deceive the average consumer in relation to any of the matters set out below, even if the information is factually correct, and it causes or is likely to cause the average consumer to take a transactional decision he would not have taken otherwise[4]; or
- concerns any marketing of a product (including comparative advertising) that creates confusion with any products, trademarks, trade names or other distinguishing marks of a competitor,[5] or it concerns any failure by a trader to

[2] SI 2008/1277. This implements the EU Unfair Commercial Practices Directive (O.J. L 149/22).

[3] CPUTR 2008 reg 3(3).

[4] Reg 5(2).

[5] Reg 5(3)(a).

comply with a commitment contained in a code of conduct that the trader has undertaken to comply with,[6] if the trader indicates in a commercial practice that he is bound by that code of conduct[7] *and* the commitment is firm, capable of being verified and is not aspirational.[8]

31.3.2.2 Factors to Be Considered Under the CPUTR 2008

The factors that fall under this scheme and that are to be considered include, *inter alia*:

- the nature of the product,
- the extents of the trader's commitments,
- the motives for the commercial practice, and
- any statement or symbol relating to direct or indirect sponsorship or approval of the trader or the product.[9]

31.3.2.3 Enforcement Against Misleading Practices

The statutory scheme embodied by the CPUTR 2008 is relatively wide ranging in scope and is enforced by the Local Authority Trading Standards and the Office of Fair Trading. The remedies available are civil enforcement orders or, depending on the severity of the breach, potentially criminal proceedings. At present, these regulations cannot be used by consumers to bring a direct action for compensation. The directive on which the Consumer Protection from Unfair Trading Regulations 2008 is based on contains an optional set of provisions that allow for a consumer to have a direct course of action against a company. The UK opted not to include these provisions when implementing the directive.

31.3.2.4 Problems with Enforcement of the CPUTR 2008 in the UK

A potential problem with the Trading Standards regime in the UK is that because each local Trading Standards is autonomous, there is a lack of consistency in what they will investigate or prosecute. This is also impacted by the different budgets that each local Trading Standards has.

However, if a consumer could show that they had been induced to buy a product because of a misleading practice, then it is highly likely that the consumer would be able to bring a breach of contract action directly themselves against the company. The problem with doing this is that the consumer will generally only get their money back, and the cost of bringing a case is likely to be disproportionate to the amount in issue.

---

[6] Reg 5(3)(b).

[7] Reg 5(3)(b)(i).

[8] Reg 5(3)(b)(ii).

[9] Reg 5(4).

31.3.3 Role of the Advertising Standards Agency

For an overt breach of a voluntary CSR policy, the matter could also be dealt with by way of a complaint to the Advertising Standards Agency (ASA). The basis of such a complaint would be heavily fact dependent but could arise where a company has stated that, for example, its products conform to certain standards (*e.g.*, dolphin-friendly tuna) but it turns out these standards have not been met. For a successful complaint to the ASA, the statement would need to be in the form of an advertisement. A complaint can be made by a consumer or a competitor. There is no financial compensation available to competitors or consumers.

31.3.4 Breach of a Third Party Originated CSR Policy

If a company has adopted a CSR policy that is run or orchestrated by a third party (either a trade body or an independent NGO) and the company breaches that policy, then the body from whom the CSR policy originates may be able to bring one of two actions. The first would be a passing off action on the basis that the company in question is using the goodwill associated with the policy (*e.g.*, Fair Trade coffee) and has misrepresented to the public that it conforms to this standard or policy. So long as the body that orchestrates the policy can prove damage (either financial or reputational), then they will be able to sue in passing off and obtain injunctive relief to stop the company. This injunctive relief may potentially be obtained on an interim basis.

The second possible action would be for breach of a trademark or a collective mark, if such marks were owned by a third party. Whether or not an action could be brought for infringement would depend on the type of agreement in place to allow the company to use the mark in the first place. It may also be possible in such a case to bring a breach of contract action if there was a contract in force (*e.g.*, a licence) that allowed the company to use the mark.

31.3.5 Could Fair Trade Farmers Bring an Action?

Could Fair Trade farmers themselves bring an action against a company that misrepresents a relationship with them? In theory, they would have locus standi to bring a passing off action if they could prove that they are the owners of the goodwill (they would clearly have locus standi if they owned a trademark) and that the public regards them as the owners of the goodwill.

However, as discussed above at Sect. 31.3.1, if a CSR policy is worded in general terms, it would be very hard to enforce any of the above legal remedies. This is because there is a general view in English law that consumers are capable of distinguishing between clear statements of intention and other statements that are really only regarded as being commercial hype.[10] English law also does not have the notion of 'good faith' that is found in a number of civil law jurisdictions.

31.3.6 What Remedies Would Be Available?

As for the potential financial remedies available if a passing off or trademark action succeeds, there would need to be a clear nexus between the breach of the CSR and the goods/services over which lost sales/revenue is claimed. There would also be the possibility of an injunction restraining future infringing conduct. Three scenarios are now dealt with in turn.

Action taken by a coffee producer against a competing coffee producer marketing its coffee under a Fair Trade logo or label although the coffee is not sourced from Fair Trade coffee makers

In this scenario, if Fair Trade farmers (or some collective on their behalf) was able to sue for passing off or trademark infringement, then any products marked incorrectly would be held infringing and the farmers would be either entitled to the lost sales that they suffered or an account of profits made by the company from the products sold under the false Fair Trade sign.

Action taken by a coffee producer against a competing coffee producer which has imported coffee using ships which emit excessive carbon dioxide and not comply with the business's 'green' CSR policy

This second scenario would be too far removed from the products in question to lead to an award of damages. Unless a company could prove that consumers had shifted sales to a coffee company due to their green policy (and for no other reasons), then there would be no basis to claim damages.

Action taken by a coffee producer against a competing coffee producer advertising that 2 % of its sales and revenues are donated to charity, although an audit demonstrates non-compliance with said policy

This final scenario is even further removed from the product, as this is an action of the company that is completely distinct from the product in question.

31.4 Extent to Which Companies Must Reveal CSR Compliance

Companies have few legal obligations to reveal the extent to which they comply with their own CSR policies to other companies or consumers. For public companies, there are obligations to shareholders, but for private companies there is not the same ability to obtain information from a company. However, if there was enough evidence to bring a case for passing off or trademark infringement, then so

[10] This is sometimes referred to in the case law as 'mere puffery'.

long as the case had some prima facie merit, disclosure could be ordered by a court to determine whether or not the company had in fact complied with the policy.

31.5 Powers of Trading Standards to Investigate Complaints

Trading Standards have wide-ranging powers to investigate and the relevant enforcement officer may exercise the following powers:

- they may, for the purposes of ascertaining whether a breach of the regulations has been committed, inspect any goods and enter any premises other than the premises used only as a dwelling[11];
- if they have reasonable cause to suspect that a breach of the regulations has been committed, they may, for the purpose of ascertaining whether it has been committed, require any trader to produce any documents relating to his business and may take copies of, or of any entry in, any such document[12];
- if they have reasonable cause to believe that a breach of the regulations has been committed, they may seize and detain any goods for the purpose of ascertaining, by testing or otherwise, whether the breach has been committed[13]; and
- they may seize and detain goods or documents that they have reason to believe may be required as evidence in proceedings for a breach of the regulations.[14]

Therefore, the powers of public bodies investigating such practices are extensive. However, as set out above at Sect. 31.3.2, such powers are not necessarily uniformly applied.

31.6 Breaches of CSR Policies: The UK Approach in Practice

There have been no major studies in the UK showing that there is a significant issue with businesses not complying with their own CSR policies.

Businesses are concerned about non-compliance because they fear the negative publicity that accompanies this. Any instances of a failure to comply have generally been remedied by the company themselves reacting due to the potential negative publicity.

Consumers are concerned that businesses comply with their CSR policies because CSR is one factor of many that is weighed by consumers when making purchasing decisions. Furthermore, some consumers benefit directly from company

[11] Reg 21(1)(a).

[12] Reg 21(1)(b).

[13] Reg 21(1)(c).

[14] Reg 21(1)(d).

investment in local communities, and as such these consumers regard these types of policies as beneficial.

There is no evidence that indicates that consumers believe that breaches of CSR policies should be subject to legal sanction. It is likely therefore that the ability to move their purchasing decisions to other entities and adverse publicity are regarded as being more than enough to ensure companies comply with their CSR policies. Whilst there is no easy way for a consumer to obtain information about whether or not a given company is meeting its CSR goals, the consumer can request this from the company. Any response that is negative can be easily publicised (especially through social media), and as such the consumers themselves possess the ability to inflict negative publicity without the intervention of the standard media outlets who may not be interested in more minor infractions of a CSR policy.

Furthermore, the powers of trading standards are very broad, and this centralised mechanism for ensuring compliance with ethical business standards is more cost effective than granting consumers a direct right of action.

31.6.1 Comment on the UK Position

Therefore, the current law in the UK adequately meets the needs for consumers and other interested parties in obtaining the relevant information about CSR compliance.

Accordingly, no change in the law is necessary. There is also a genuine risk that if legal mechanisms were put in place to enforce compliance, or to allow consumers to seek disclosure to check compliance, those companies would be dissuaded from having CSR policies due to the fear of increased costs.[15] Furthermore, if companies still maintained CSR policies in light of such regulations, then the wording of these would likely be changed to make them more akin to stated goals as opposed to absolute standards that the company should meet. This would undermine the effectiveness of any such policies.

31.7 UK Position on Collectively Agreed Commitments to CSR Policies

The potential issues raised by a horizontal agreement of this sort are enormously complex. There are unfortunately very few guidelines on this type of agreement with Nestle recently calling for more information on the acceptable exchange of information regarding social or environmental issues.[16] Consider a scenario where

[15] This increase in costs would arise, firstly, in the increased cost of dealing with claims brought directly by consumers (which may be duplicative) and, secondly, due to the increased cost of any damages having to be paid out.

[16] Marceline Tournier senior competition counsel for Nestle speaking at the ABA Antitrust Law Spring Meeting, Washington DC, April 2013.

there are overly onerous requirements for the use of a collective mark. If market participants did feel that this was the case, then there is nothing to stop them from setting up their own competing collective mark to indicate that they also abide by certain standards.[17]

In general, industry standards on the environment, working conditions or other *bona fide* social objectives would likely be held acceptable if there was a genuine social benefit that arose from these policies. Whether or not such CSR policies were of genuine social benefit would have to be weighed against any corresponding change in the price of the product and also the size of the market in which the change occurs. In short, the social benefit would have to be seen as being socially beneficial by society as a whole and not merely by the industry or a subsection of the industry.

Other issues that would need to be addressed are whether or not the CSR policy raises rival costs, prejudices smaller undertakings or raises barriers to entry. There would also be issues on whether all industry stakeholders were invited to partake in any industry-wide CSR policy.

An industry-wide policy could be instigated by a trade body that has links with the market participants, or it could originate from a completely external body (*e.g.*, Greenpeace proposing that a certain industry abide by certain environmental standards). If the policy originates from outside the industry, then the competition concerns would be slightly reduced as the CSR policy would, in theory, be policed by a neutral and independent arbitrator.

31.7.1 Competition Law Framework

The basic competitive analysis would be under Article 101 of The Treaty on the Functioning of the European Union ('TFEU')[18] (and Chapter 1 of the Competition Act 1998 in the UK). Any agreement between competitors to harmonise their trading terms and activities needs to be justified. Thus, there would be a different analysis where a collective mark is being displayed on products compared to a scenario whereby a policy (stated only in their corporate literature) on carbon footprint is adopted. This difference in analysis arises from the different impact that positive actions (*i.e.*, placing a mark on a product) have in the mind of consumers, who expect signs on goods to mean something based on their knowledge of trademarks and other such collective marks.

Another factor to be considered is the potential foreclosure (normally considered under Article 102 TFEU) of entrants into the market. Any anti-competitive

[17] The creation of a rival standard would, of course, be subject to the strict requirements of Article 101 and Member State equivalents. Among other things, market participants would therefore be required to ensure that access to the standard was open to all and that consumers received a fair share of the resulting benefit of the standard.

[18] (O.J. C 326/47).

adoption of a standard that forecloses rivals from the market would be considered a collective boycott and likely to be anti-competitive.

31.7.2 Would FRAND-Type Licences Work?

It would, in theory, be possible to have access to *de jure* standard CSR policies by way of FRAND-type licences where a standard is covered by a registered trademark or collective mark. The question would then arise as to whom such licence fees would be payable. If the FRAND-type licence was merely that a company had to comply with certain obligations (*i.e.*, only fish in a certain manner) to allow it to use the mark, then this would likely be acceptable from a competition point of view if the above-mentioned issues are dealt with appropriately.

More difficult from a competition point of view would be if access to the trademark or collective mark was predicated on compliance and payment of a licence fee. This would raise more potential competition issues because it would depend on who this money was going towards and what it was being used for. For example, if the market leader owned the trademark and licensed it to others for a fee, then this may raise competition concerns.

Therefore, it is tolerably clear that access to FRAND-type terms would be possible, but the more difficult question is how a party could force access to them if, for example, an NGO didn't want to deal with a given company. At present, under UK law, the aggrieved company would not have any legal recourse to force the NGO to supply on these terms directly, though they could bring or threaten to bring a competition complaint on the basis that they are being precluded from the market.

Finally, as is the case in the area of FRAND licences for patents, the actual determination of what is fair and reasonable is exceptionally difficult and would be even more so in this case because there would be no absolute requirement to use the given collective mark. This is because in patent cases (such as mobile phones), a given patent must be infringed if it is in the standard. No such legal obligation exists in this case, even if the market itself pushes in that direction (i.e., you do not *have* to buy dolphin-friendly tuna).

MIX
Papier aus verantwortungsvollen Quellen
Paper from responsible sources
FSC® C105338

If you have any concerns about our products,
you can contact us on
ProductSafety@springernature.com

In case Publisher is established outside the EU,
the EU authorized representative is:
Springer Nature Customer Service Center GmbH
Europaplatz 3, 69115 Heidelberg, Germany

Printed by Libri Plureos GmbH
in Hamburg, Germany